DATE DUE

			PRINTED IN U.S.A.

SOMETHING ABOUT THE AUTHOR

ISSN 0276-816X

something ABOUT THE AUTHOR

Facts and Pictures about Authors
and Illustrators of Books for Young People

EDITED BY
ANNE COMMIRE

VOLUME 51

GALE RESEARCH COMPANY
BOOK TOWER
DETROIT, MICHIGAN
48226

Editor: Anne Commire

Associate Editors: Agnes Garrett, Helga P. McCue

Senior Assistant Editor: Dianne H. Anderson

Assistant Editors: Elisa Ann Ferraro, Eunice L. Petrini, Linda Shedd

Sketchwriters: Marguerite Feitlowitz, Rachel Koenig

Researcher: Catherine Ruello

Editorial Assistants: Catherine Coray, Joanne J. Ferraro, Dieter Miller, Karen Walker

Permissions Assistant: Susan Pfanner

In cooperation with the staff of *Something about the Author Autobiography Series*

Editor: Joyce Nakamura

Assistant Editor: Carolyn Chafetz

Research Assistants: Shelly Andrews, Carolyn Kline

Senior Editor, Something about the Author: Adele Sarkissian

Production Manager: Mary Beth Trimper

External Production Assistants: Linda Davis, Patty Farley

Internal Production Associate: Louise Gagné

Internal Senior Production Assistant: Sandy Rock

Layout Artist: Elizabeth Lewis Patryjak

Art Director: Arthur Chartow

Special acknowledgment is due to the members of the *Contemporary Authors* staff
who assisted in the preparation of this volume.

Library of Congress Catalog Card Number 72-27107

ISBN 0-8103-2261-7

ISSN 0276-816X

Computerized photocomposition by
Typographics, Incorporated
Kansas City, Missouri

Printed in the United States

Contents

Introduction ix   Acknowledgments xv

Illustrations Index 207   Author Index 227

A

Aaseng, Nate
  see Aaseng, Nathan 1

Aaseng, Nathan 1953- 1

Apfel, Necia H(alpern) 1930- 3

Austin, R. G.
  see Gelman, Rita Golden 70

Auth, Tony
  see Auth, William Anthony, Jr. 3

Auth, William Anthony, Jr. 1942- 3

B

Bacon, Joan Chase
  see Bowden, Joan Chase 16

Barbera, Joe
  see Barbera, Joseph Roland 6

Barbera, Joseph Roland 1911- 6

Beckman, Delores 1914- 15

Bellingham, Brenda 1931-
  Brief Entry 17

Blaine, John
  see Goodwin, Harold Leland 72

Bowden, Joan Chase 1925- 17

Brewster, Patience 1952- 19

Bromley, Dudley 1948-
  Brief Entry 21

Brook, Judith Penelope 1926-
  Brief Entry 21

Brook, Judy
  see Brook, Judith Penelope 21

Brown, Joseph E(dward) 1929-
  Brief Entry 21

Brown, Roy (Frederick) 1921-1982 22

C

Calder, Lyn
  see Calmenson, Stephanie 24

Calmenson, Stephanie 1952- 24

Campbell, Rod 1945- 26

Carew, Jan (Rynveld) 1925- 28

Carwell, L'Ann
  see McKissack, Patricia (L'Ann) C(arwell) 122

Chase, Emily
  see Sachs, Judith 152

Cole, Jennifer
  see Zach, Cheryl (Byrd) 200

Coombs, Patricia 1926- 31

Cross, Gilbert B. 1939-
  Brief Entry 44

D

de Angeli, Marguerite (Lofft) 1889-1987
  Obituary Notice 45

Deary, Terry 1946- 45

deGros, J. H.
  see Villiard, Paul 176

Demuth, Patricia Brennan 1948-
  Brief Entry 46

Desmond, Adrian J(ohn) 1947- 46

Diamond, Petra
  see Sachs, Judith 152

Diamond, Rebecca
  see Sachs, Judith 152

Dickmeyer, Lowell A. 1939-
  Brief Entry 47

Dillon, Diane 1933- 47

Dillon, Leo 1933- 49

E

Edelson, Edward   1932-   64

F

Fitz-Randolph, Jane (Currens)   1915-   65

Fox, Mem
  see Fox, Merrion Frances................................... 65

Fox, Merrion Frances   1946-   65

G

Gage, Wilson
  see Steele, Mary Q(uintard Govan).................. 159

Gelman, Rita Golden   1937-
  Brief Entry.. 70

Gerrard, Jean   1933-   70

Glenn, Mel   1943-   70

Godfrey, Jane
  see Bowden, Joan Chase................................... 17

Goodwin, Hal
  see Goodwin, Harold Leland............................. 72

Goodwin, Harold Leland   1914-   72

Gordon, Hal
  see Goodwin, Harold Leland............................. 72

Graham, Charlotte
  see Bowden, Joan Chase................................... 17

H

Hanna, Bill
  see Hanna, William 75

Hanna, William   1910-   75

Hayes, Sheila   1937-   88

Hearn, Emily
  see Valleau, Emily 174

Hines, Anna G(rossnickle)   1946-   89

Hoagland, Edward   1932-   91

Holl, Kristi D(iane)   1951-   92

Hough, Judy Taylor   1932-
  Brief Entry.. 93

Hull, Jesse Redding
  see Hull, Jessie Redding 94

Hull, Jessie Redding   1932-   94

Hutchins, Hazel J.   1952-
  Brief Entry.. 95

J

Jaquith, Priscilla   1908-   95

Jenkyns, Chris   1924-   96

Jones, Terry   1942-
  Brief Entry.. 99

K

Kassem, Lou
  Brief Entry.. 99

Kasuya, Masahiro   1937-   99

Kenny, Kathryn
  see Bowden, Joan Chase................................... 17

Kopper, Lisa (Esther)   1950-
  Brief Entry.. 100

L

Landon, Lucinda   1950-
  Brief Entry.. 101

Leder, Jane Mersky   1945-
  Brief Entry.. 101

Lerner, Marguerite Rush   1924-1987
  Obituary Notice... 101

Leroe, Ellen W(hitney)   1949-
  Brief Entry.. 101

Littke, Lael J.   1929-   101

Loring, Emilie (Baker)   1864(?)-1951 103

Luenn, Nancy   1954-   104

M

Mali, Jane Lawrence   1937-   107

Mannetti, Lisa   1953-
  Brief Entry.. 109

Marshall, Edward
  see Marshall, James (Edward) 109

Marshall, James (Edward)   1942-   109

Matthews, Jacklyn Meek
  see Meek, Jacklyn O'Hanlon 122

McKissack, Patricia (L'Ann) C(arwell)   1944-
  Brief Entry.. 122

Meek, Jacklyn O'Hanlon   1933-   122

Meyer, Kathleen Allan   1918-   122

Mirsky, Jeanette   1903-1987
  Obituary Notice... 124

Morey, Walt(er Nelson) 1907- 124

N

Nast, Thomas 1840-1902.................................. 131

O

O'Hanlon, Jacklyn
    see Meek, Jacklyn O'Hanlon 122

P

Paperny, Myra (Green) 1932- 142

Pascal, Francine 1938- 142

Pierce, Tamora 1954- 148

Powell, Ann 1951-
    Brief Entry.. 149

Provensen, Martin (Elias) 1916-1987
    Obituary Notice.. 149

Python, Monty
    see Jones, Terry.................................... 99

R

Rinaldi, Ann 1934- 149

Root, Shelton L., Jr. 1923-1986
    Obituary Notice.. 151

Ross, Wilda 1915- 152

Roy, Jessie Hailstalk 1895-1986
    Obituary Notice... 152

S

Saal, Jocelyn
    see Sachs, Judith 152

Sachs, Judith 1947-
    Brief Entry.. 152

Sandak, Cass R(obert) 1950- 152

Sarasin, Jennifer
    see Sachs, Judith 152

Savage, Blake
    see Goodwin, Harold Leland 152

Saxon, Antonia
    see Sachs, Judith 152

Schwark, Mary Beth 1954- 154

Schwartz, Joel L. 1940-
    Brief Entry.. 155

Slepian, Jan(ice B.) 1921- 155

Solomon, Joan.. 158

Stanovich, Betty Jo 1954-
    Brief Entry.. 159

Steele, Mary Q(uintard Govan) 1922- 159

Steele, William O(wen) 1917-1979 167

Story, Josephine
    see Loring, Emilie (Baker) 103

T

Taylor, Judy
    see Hough, Judy Taylor.................................... 93

Thomas, Patricia J. 1934- 173

U

Ulam, S(tanislaw) M(arcin) 1909-1984.............. 173

V

Valleau, Emily 1925- 174

Villiard, Paul 1910-1974 176

W

Wachter, Oralee Roberts 1935-
    Brief Entry.. 179

Waldman, Neil 1947- 179

Wallace-Brodeur, Ruth 1941- 181

Wallner, Alexandra 1946- 184

Wallner, John C. 1945- 184

Wellman, Alice 1900-1984 195

White, Martin 1943- 196

Wilson, Budge
    see Wilson, Marjorie.................................... 199

Wilson, Erica 197

Wilson, Marjorie 1927-
    Brief Entry.. 199

Winnick, Karen B(eth) B(inkoff) 1946- 200

Winters, Jon
    see Cross, Gilbert B. 44

Z

Zach, Cheryl (Byrd) 1947-
 Brief Entry.. 200

Zaid, Barry 1938- 200
Zaring, Jane (Thomas) 1936- 202

Introduction

As the only ongoing reference series that deals with the lives and works of authors and illustrators of children's books, *Something about the Author (SATA)* is a unique source of information. The *SATA* series includes not only well-known authors and illustrators whose books are most widely read, but also those less prominent people whose works are just coming to be recognized. *SATA* is often the only readily available information source for less well-known writers or artists. You'll find *SATA* informative and entertaining whether you are:

> —a student in junior high school (or perhaps one to two grades higher or lower) who needs information for a book report or some other assignment for an English class;

> —a children's librarian who is searching for the answer to yet another question from a young reader or collecting background material to use for a story hour;

> —an English teacher who is drawing up an assignment for your students or gathering information for a book talk;

> —a student in a college of education or library science who is studying children's literature and reference sources in the field;

> —a parent who is looking for a new way to interest your child in reading something more than the school curriculum prescribes;

> —an adult who enjoys children's literature for its own sake, knowing that a good children's book has no age limits.

Scope

In *SATA* you will find detailed information about authors and illustrators who span the full time range of children's literature, from early figures like John Newbery and L. Frank Baum to contemporary figures like Judy Blume and Richard Peck. Authors in the series represent primarily English-speaking countries, particularly the United States, Canada, and the United Kingdom. Also included, however, are authors from around the world whose works are available in English translation, for example: from France, Jean and Laurent De Brunhoff; from Italy, Emanuele Luzzati; from the Netherlands, Jaap ter Haar; from Germany, James Krüss; from Norway, Babbis Friis-Baastad; from Japan, Toshiko Kanzawa; from the Soviet Union, Kornei Chukovsky; from Switzerland, Alois Carigiet, to name only a few. Also appearing in *SATA* are Newbery medalists from Hendrik Van Loon (1922) to Sid Fleischman (1987). The writings represented in *SATA* include those created intentionally for children and young adults as well as those written for a general audience and known to interest younger readers. These writings cover the spectrum from picture books, humor, folk and fairy tales, animal stories, mystery and adventure, science fiction and fantasy, historical fiction, poetry and nonsense verse, to drama, biography, and nonfiction.

Information Features

In *SATA* you will find full-length entries that are being presented in the series for the first time. This volume, for example, marks the first full-length appearance of Nathan Aaseng, Joseph Barbera, Jan Carew, William Hanna, Chris Jenkyns, Thomas Nast, Francine Pascal, Tamora Pierce, Ann Rinaldi, and Jan Slepian.

Brief Entries, first introduced in Volume 27, are another regular feature of *SATA*. Brief Entries present essentially the same types of information found in a full entry but do so in a capsule form and without illustration. These entries are intended to give you useful and timely information while the more time-consuming process of compiling a full-length biography is in progress. In this volume you'll find Brief Entries for Terry Jones, Lisa Kopper, Jane Mersky Leder, Patricia C. McKissack, Ann Powell, and Judith Sachs, among others.

Obituaries have been included in *SATA* since Volume 20. An Obituary is intended not only as a death notice but also as a concise view of a person's life and work. Obituaries may appear for persons who have entries in earlier *SATA* volumes, as well as for people who have not yet appeared in the series. In this volume Obituaries mark the recent deaths of Marguerite de Angeli, Marguerite Rush Lerner, Jeanette Mirsky, Martin Provensen, and others.

Revised Entries

Since Volume 25, each *SATA* volume also includes newly revised and updated entries for a selection of *SATA* listees (usually four to six) who remain of interest to today's readers and who have been active enough to require extensive revision of their earlier biographies. For example, when Beverly Cleary first appeared in *SATA* Volume 2, she was the author of twenty-one books for children and young adults and the recipient of numerous awards. By the time her updated sketch appeared in Volume 43 (a span of fifteen years), this creator of the indefatigable Ramona Quimby and other memorable characters had produced a dozen new titles and garnered nearly fifty additional awards, including the 1984 Newbery Medal.

The entry for a given biographee may be revised as often as there is substantial new information to provide. In this volume, look for revised entries on Patricia Coombs, Diane Dillon, Leo Dillon, James Marshall, Walt Morey, Mary Q. Steele, and William O. Steele.

Illustrations

While the textual information in *SATA* is its primary reason for existing, photographs and illustrations not only enliven the text but are an integral part of the information that *SATA* provides. Illustrations and text are wedded in such a special way in children's literature that artists and their works naturally occupy a prominent place among *SATA*'s listees. The illustrators that you'll find in the series include such past masters of children's book illustration as Randolph Caldecott, Walter Crane, Arthur Rackham, and Ernest H. Shepard, as well as such noted contemporary artists as Maurice Sendak, Edward Gorey, Tomie de Paola, and Margot Zemach. There are Caldecott medalists from Dorothy Lathrop (the first recipient in 1938) to Richard Egielski (the latest winner in 1987); cartoonists like Charles Schulz, ("Peanuts"), Walt Kelly ("Pogo"), Hank Ketcham ("Dennis the Menace"), and Georges Rémi ("Tintin"); photographers like Jill Krementz, Tana Hoban, Bruce McMillan, and Bruce Curtis; and filmmakers like Walt Disney, Alfred Hitchcock, and Steven Spielberg.

In more than a dozen years of recording the metamorphosis of children's literature from the printed page to other media, *SATA* has become something of a repository of photographs that are unique in themselves and exist nowhere else as a group, particularly many of the classics of motion picture and stage history and photographs that have been specially loaned to us from private collections.

Indexes

Each *SATA* volume provides a cumulative index in two parts: first, the Illustrations Index, arranged by the name of the illustrator, gives the number of the volume and page where the illustrator's work appears in the current volume as well as all preceding volumes in the series; second, the Author Index gives the number of the volume in which a person's biographical sketch, Brief Entry, or Obituary appears in the current volume as well as all preceding volumes in the series. These indexes also include references to authors and illustrators who appear in *Yesterday's Authors of Books for Children* (described in detail below). Beginning with Volume 36, the *SATA* Author Index provides cross-references to authors who are included in *Children's Literature Review*.

Starting with Volume 42, you will also find cross-references to authors who are included in the *Something about the Author Autobiography Series* (described in detail below).

Character Index—New Feature

If you're like many readers, the names of fictional characters may pop more easily into your mind than the names of the authors or illustrators who created them: Snow White, Charlotte the Spider, the Cat in the Hat, Peter Pan, Mary Poppins, Winnie-the-Pooh, Brer Rabbit, Little Toot, Charlie Bucket, Lassie, Rip Van Winkle, Bartholomew Cubbins—the list could go on and on. But who invented them? Now these characters, and several thousand others, can lead you to the *SATA* and *YABC* entries on the lives and works of their creators.

First published in Volume 50, the Character Index provides a broad selection of characters from books and other media—movies, plays, comic strips, cartoons, etc.—created by listees who have appeared in all the published volumes of *SATA* and *YABC*. This index gives the character name, followed by a *"See"* reference indicating the name of the creator and the number of the *SATA* or *YABC* volume in which the creator's bio-bibliographical entry can be found. As new *SATA* volumes are prepared, additional characters will be included in the cumulative Character Index and published annually in *SATA*. (The cumulative Illustrations and Author Indexes will continue to appear in each *SATA* volume.)

It would be impossible for the Character Index to include every important character created by *SATA* and *YABC* listees. (Several hundred important characters might be taken from Dickens alone, for example.) Therefore, the *SATA* editors have selected those characters that are best known and thus most likely to interest *SATA* users. Realizing that some of your favorite characters may not appear in this index, the editors invite you to suggest additional names. With your help, the editors hope to make the Character Index a uniquely useful reference tool for you.

What a *SATA* Entry Provides

Whether you're already familiar with the *SATA* series or just getting acquainted, you will want to be aware of the kind of information that an entry provides. In every *SATA* entry the editors attempt to give as complete a picture of the person's life and work as possible. In some cases that full range of information may simply be unavailable, or a biographee may choose not to reveal complete personal details. The information that the editors attempt to provide in every entry is arranged in the following categories:

1. The "head" of the entry gives

    —the most complete form of the name,
    —any part of the name not commonly used, included in parentheses,
    —birth and death dates, if known; a (?) indicates a discrepancy in published sources,
    —pseudonyms or name variants under which the person has had books published or is publicly known, in parentheses in the second line.

2. "Personal" section gives

    —date and place of birth and death,
    —parents' names and occupations,
    —name of spouse, date of marriage, and names of children,
    —educational institutions attended, degrees received, and dates,
    —religious and political affiliations,
    —agent's name and address,
    —home and/or office address.

3. "Career" section gives

    —name of employer, position, and dates for each career post,
    —military service,
    —memberships,
    —awards and honors.

4. "Writings" section gives

> —title, first publisher and date of publication, and illustration information for each book written; revised editions and other significant editions for books with particularly long publishing histories; genre, when known.

5. "Adaptations" section gives

> —title, major performers, producer, and date of all known reworkings of an author's material in another medium, like movies, filmstrips, television, recordings, plays, etc.

6. "Sidelights" section gives

> —commentary on the life or work of the biographee either directly from the person (and often written specifically for the *SATA* entry), or gathered from biographies, diaries, letters, interviews, or other published sources.

7. "For More Information See" section gives

> —books, feature articles, films, plays, and reviews in which the biographee's life or work has been treated.

How a *SATA* Entry Is Compiled

A *SATA* entry progresses through a series of steps. If the biographee is living, the *SATA* editors try to secure information directly from him or her through a questionnaire. From the information that the biographee supplies, the editors prepare an entry, filling in any essential missing details with research. The author or illustrator is then sent a copy of the entry to check for accuracy and completeness.

If the biographee is deceased or cannot be reached by questionnaire, the *SATA* editors examine a wide variety of published sources to gather information for an entry. Biographical sources are searched with the aid of Gale's *Biography and Genealogy Master Index*. Bibliographic sources like the *National Union Catalog*, the *Cumulative Book Index*, *American Book Publishing Record*, and the *British Museum Catalogue* are consulted, as are book reviews, feature articles, published interviews, and material sometimes obtained from the biographee's family, publishers, agent, or other associates.

For each entry presented in *SATA*, the editors also attempt to locate a photograph of the biographee as well as representative illustrations from his or her books. After surveying the available books which the biographee has written and/or illustrated, and then making a selection of appropriate photographs and illustrations, the editors request permission of the current copyright holders to reprint the material. In the case of older books for which the copyright may have passed through several hands, even locating the current copyright holder is often a long and involved process.

We invite you to examine the entire *SATA* series, starting with this volume. Described below are some of the people in Volume 51 that you may find particularly interesting.

Highlights of This Volume

JOSEPH BARBERA......first used his artistic talent in parochial school to illustrate religious scenes on the classroom blackboard. Years later, while working as an animator at MGM studios, he met Bill Hanna, who collaborated with him on a cartoon of "a cat chasing a mouse." Their second story, "Tom and Jerry," launched their professional career as an animation team. Through the years, Hanna-Barbera has created such world-renowned cartoon characters as: "Tom and Jerry," "Huckleberry Hound," "Yogi Bear," "The Flintstones," and "The Jetsons." "The secret," says Barbera, "is creativity." Today, the Hanna-Barbera company has established animation studios in Spain, Australia, and the United States. "We've got a good team of people...with more animation being done now than ever before. It's a major industry."

PATRICIA COOMBS......didn't discover libraries for a long time because "my mother had a phobia about germs," and libraries were full of germs; but reading and drawing gave her "something...to hold onto" through many family relocations. Coombs discovered that she could write to entertain by composing letters to her older brother and sister in college, who found them humorous. When it was her time to attend college, she discovered "the reality of writing" and "the emotional power of words" from poet Theodore Roethke. Later on, she combined her writing and artistic talents with the stories she made up for her two young daughters into children's books about a blue witch. *Dorrie's Magic* became the forerunner of the "Dorrie" books, as well as other stories written and illustrated in the morning hours from her home in Connecticut or her flat in London. "Whether poetry or children's books, I have always written with chamber music, usually Bach, in the background."

DIANE and LEO DILLON......met as competitors in art school long before they became well-known illustrators. As fellow students at Parsons School of Design, they were first attracted to each other through their art, and felt "threatened" by the excellence of each other's work. Competition could not separate them for long, however, and after their marriage, they found that by pooling their styles and working together they could produce better results. They are the first—and thus far, only—artists to have won the Caldecott Medal for children's picture book illustration in two consecutive years (1976 and 1977). Winning the Caldecott forced them to "look at ourselves with a critical distance." From this objective viewpoint, the Dillons discovered that they have fused their creativity to "a point where our work is done by an agent we call 'the third artist.'"

WILLIAM HANNA......has won seven Academy Awards and seven Emmy Awards for animated cartoons with partner Joseph Barbera. "I have written most of the main titles and lyrics for the Hanna-Barbera cartoons and quite a bit of the music as well." Hanna credits an early interest in music for his success in the animation field. For twenty years he worked with Barbera on the "Tom and Jerry" cartoons at MGM until they started their own production company using their "vested interest in a [MGM] pension plan" as collateral. Their first series was "Ruff and Ready," with many other cartoon characters in the making. Hanna-Barbera productions currently total nearly 300 different series, specials, television movies, and films that have been seen in over eighty countries. Of his phenomenal success, Hanna commented with humility: "My work makes me feel needed and appreciated."

JAMES MARSHALL......quit drawing at the age of seven after his second-grade teacher ridiculed his creative efforts. "It wasn't until my late twenties that I passionately took up drawing again." Growing up on an eighty-five acre farm near San Antonio, Texas, Marshall remembers being alone a great deal, living in his imagination, and reading. "Books were the major force in my life." Eventually, he combined his love for drawing and his passion for books into a career as a writer/illustrator, creating for his first effort *George and Martha,* followed by six additional books in that series. Since then, Marshall has teamed up with writer Harry Allard to create "The Stupids" and "Miss Nelson" series. Asked why his books are so appealing, Marshall said, "I *loved* grade school. I'm sure my love of those years infuses the...books with a certain energy."

WALT MOREY......grew up "like Mark in *Gentle Ben,*...a sickly kid." He loathed school, which began in a one-room schoolhouse in Oregon. Three years later, Morey could neither read nor write. Until the age of fourteen, he couldn't read with ease; by nineteen he was "booted out, with a diploma" from high school. He subsequently held a wide variety of jobs—managing a theater, working in construction, in saw mills, and veneer plants—before selling his first story. Writing for magazines taught him how to use dialogue, weave plot, and be concise. His award-winning book for children, *Gentle Ben,* gave Morey the financial freedom he needed to write full time and "opened a whole new type of writing for me."

FRANCINE PASCAL......adored movies and reading comic books, high adventure series, fairy tales, and, since there was no "young adult" literature, the classics. Although she "began to write poetry when I was about eight," Pascal's professional career waited until she was married to newspaperman John Pascal. "He loved everything I wrote and encouraged me unceasingly." Her first professional assignment was a fictionalized account for *Modern Screen* of singer Connie Francis's wedding, followed by soap opera scripts, and a collaboration with her husband and brother on the Broadway musical, "George M." Inspired by her "two favorite words, 'what if,'" Pascal wrote her first teenage novel, *Hangin' Out with Cici,* which proved so popular that it was quickly followed by another. Her "Sweet Valley High" and "Sweet Valley Twins" series of romance novels for teenagers are written under her name by "a stable of authors," with Pascal maintaining artistic control. "I may not write every word, but they are very much mine."

These are only a few of the authors and illustrators that you'll find in this volume. We hope you find all the entries in *SATA* both interesting and useful.

Yesterday's Authors of Books for Children

In a two-volume companion set to *SATA, Yesterday's Authors of Books for Children (YABC)* focuses on early authors and illustrators, from the beginnings of children's literature through 1960, whose books are still being read by children today. Here you will find "old favorites" like Hans Christian Andersen, J. M. Barrie, Kenneth Grahame, Betty MacDonald, A. A. Milne, Beatrix Potter, Samuel Clemens, Kate Greenaway, Rudyard Kipling, Robert Louis Stevenson, and many more.

Similar in format to *SATA, YABC* features bio-bibliographical entries that are divided into information categories such as Personal, Career, Writings, and Sidelights. The entries are further enhanced by book illustrations, author photos, movie stills, and many rare old photographs.

In Volume 2 you will find cumulative indexes to the authors and to the illustrations that appear in *YABC*. These listings can also be located in the *SATA* cumulative indexes.

By exploring both volumes of *YABC*, you will discover a special group of more than seventy authors and illustrators who represent some of the best in children's literature—individuals whose timeless works continue to delight children and adults of all ages. Other authors and illustrators from early children's literature are listed in *SATA*, starting with Volume 15.

Something about the Author Autobiography Series

You can complement the information in *SATA* with the *Something about the Author Autobiography Series (SAAS)*, which provides autobiographical essays written by important current authors and illustrators of books for children and young adults. In every volume of *SAAS* you will find about twenty specially commissioned autobiographies, each accompanied by a selection of personal photographs supplied by the authors. The wide range of contemporary writers and artists who describe their lives and interests in the *Autobiography Series* includes Joan Aiken, Betsy Byars, Leonard Everett Fisher, Milton Meltzer, Maia Wojciechowska, and Jane Yolen, among others. Though the information presented in the autobiographies is as varied and unique as the authors, you can learn about the people and events that influenced these writers' early lives, how they began their careers, what problems they faced in becoming established in their professions, what prompted them to write or illustrate particular books, what they now find most challenging or rewarding in their lives, and what advice they may have for young people interested in following in their footsteps, among many other subjects.

Autobiographies included in the *SATA Autobiography Series* can be located through both the *SATA* cumulative index and the *SAAS* cumulative index, which lists not only the authors' names but also the subjects mentioned in their essays, such as titles of works and geographical and personal names.

The *SATA Autobiography Series* gives you the opportunity to view "close up" some of the fascinating people who are included in the *SATA* parent series. The combined *SATA* series makes available to you an unequaled range of comprehensive and in-depth information about the authors and illustrators of young people's literature.

Please write and tell us if we can make *SATA* even more helpful to you.

Acknowledgments

Grateful acknowledgment is made to the following publishers, authors, and artists for their kind permission to reproduce copyrighted material.

ABELARD-SCHUMAN LTD. Illustration by John Vernon Lord from *Reynard the Fox,* retold by Roy Brown. Copyright © 1969 by Abelard-Schuman Ltd. Reprinted by permission of Abelard-Schuman Ltd.

ABINGDON PRESS. Illustration by Julie Vivas from *Possum Magic* by Mem Fox. Text copyright © 1983 by Mem Fox. Illustrations copyright © 1983 by Julie Vivas. Reprinted by permission of Abingdon Press.

AMERICAN LIBRARY ASSOCIATION. Poster by Leo and Diane Dillon for American Library Association's Book Week. Reprinted by permission of American Library Association.

ANDERSEN PRESS LTD. Sidelight excerpts from an article "Roy Brown—A Personal Appreciation" by Bernard Ashley, December, 1982 in *Junior Bookshelf.* Reprinted by permission of Andersen Press Ltd.

ATHENEUM PUBLISHERS. Jacket illustration from *Perfect or Not, Here I Come* by Kristi D. Holl. Text copyright © 1986 by Kristi D. Holl. Jacket illustration copyright © 1986 by Eileen McKeating./ Jacket illustration by Deborah Chabrian from *Steps in Time* by Ruth Wallace-Brodeur. Text copyright © 1986 by Ruth Wallace-Brodeur. Jacket illustration copyright © 1986 by Deborah Chabrian. Both reprinted by permission of Atheneum Publishers.

BANTAM BOOKS, INC. Cover illustration by James Mathewuse from *Winter Carnival* by Kate William. Created by Francine Pascal. Text copyright © 1986 by Francine Pascal. Cover illustration copyright © 1986 by Cloverdale Press, Inc. Reprinted by permission of Bantam Books, Inc.

BLACKIE & SONS LTD. Illustration by Rod Campbell from *Buster's Morning* by Rod Campbell. Reprinted by permission of Blackie & Sons Ltd.

BRADBURY PRESS. Illustration by Patricia Mullins from *Hattie and the Fox* by Mem Fox. Text copyright © 1986 by Mem Fox. Illustrations copyright © 1986 by Patricia Mullins. Reprinted by permission of Bradbury Press.

CLARION BOOKS. Illustration from a poem by Stacey Fowler in *Class Dismissed II: More High School Poems* by Mel Glenn. Photographs by Michael J. Bernstein. Text copyright © 1986 by Mel Glenn. Photographs copyright © 1986 by Michael J. Bernstein. Reprinted by permission of Clarion Books.

CROWN PUBLISHERS, INC. Illustration by John Wallner from *The Night Stella Hid the Stars* by Gail Radley. Text copyright © 1978 by Gail Radley. Illustrations copyright © 1978 by John Wallner. Reprinted by permission of Crown Publishers, Inc.

DELL PUBLISHING CO., INC. Illustration by Patricia Coombs from *Dorrie and the Haunted House* by Patricia Coombs. Copyright © 1970 by Patricia Coombs. Reprinted by permission of Dell Publishing Co., Inc.

DIAL BOOKS FOR YOUNG READERS. Illustration by Leo and Diane Dillon from *Ashanti to Zulu: African Traditions* by Margaret Musgrove. Text copyright © 1976 by Margaret Musgrove. Illustrations copyright © 1976 by Leo and Diane Dillon./ Jacket illustration by Leo and Diane Dillon from *Why Mosquitoes Buzz in People's Ears* by Verna Aardema. Text copyright © 1975 by Verna Aardema. Illustrations copyright © 1975 by Leo and Diane Dillon./ Illustration by James Marshall from *Four on the Shore* by Edward Marshall. Text copyright © 1985 by Edward Marshall. Illustrations copyright © 1985 by James Marshall./ Illustration by James Marshall from *Fox at School* by Edward Marshall. Text copyright © 1983 by Edward Marshall. Illustrations copyright © 1983 by James Marshall. All reprinted by permission of Dial Books for Young Readers.

DOUBLEDAY & CO., INC. Frontispiece illustration by Marylin Hafner from *The Laugh Book: A New Treasury of Humor for Children,* compiled by Joanna Cole and Stephanie Calmenson. Copyright © 1986 by Joanna Cole and Stephanie Calmenson./ Photograph from *Visions of Tomorrow: Great Science Fiction from the Movies* by Edward Edelson. Copyright © 1975 by Edward Edelson. Photograph courtesy of Republic Pictures./ Photographs by Paul Villiard from *Birds as Pets* by Paul Villiard. Copyright © 1974 by Paul Villiard./ Jacket illustration by Clifford Geary from *The Real Book about Space Travel* by Hal Goodwin. All reprinted by permission of Doubleday & Co., Inc.

E. P. DUTTON, INC. Illustration by Tony Auth from *Mean Murgatroyd and the Ten Cats* by Nathan Zimelman. Text copyright © 1984 by Nathan Zimelman. Illustrations copyright © 1984 by Tony Auth./ Jacket illustration by Judith Cheng from *Who Loves Sam Grant?* by Delores Beckman. Copyright © 1983 by Delores Beckman./ Illustration by Leo and Diane Dillon from *Gassire's Lute: A West African Epic,* translated and adapted by Alta Jablow. Translation and adaptation copyright © 1971 by Alta Jablow. Illustrations copyright © 1971 by Leo and Diane Dillon./ Jacket illustration by Ellen Thompson from *You've Been Away All Summer* by Sheila Hayes. Copyright © 1986 by Sheila Hayes./ Illustration by John Schoenherr from *Gentle Ben* by Walt Morey. Copyright © 1965 by Walt Morey./ Jacket illustration by Konrad Hack from *Sandy and the Rock Star* by Walt Morey. Copyright © 1979 by Walt Morey./ Jacket illustration by Michael Hampshire from *Runaway Stallion* by Walt Morey. Copyright © 1973 by Walt Morey./ Illustration by Peter Parnall from *Kavik, the Wolf Dog* by Walt Morey. Copyright © 1968 by Walt Morey./ Illustration by Mary Beth Schwark from *The Kid with the Red Suspenders* by LouAnn Gaeddert. Text copyright © 1983 by LouAnn Gaeddert. Illustrations copyright © 1983 by Mary Beth Schwark. All reprinted by permission of E. P. Dutton, Inc.

GARRARD PUBLISHING CO. Illustration by Edward Malsberg from *Around Another Corner* by Emily Hearn. Copyright © 1971 by Emily Valleau. Reprinted by permission of Garrard Publishing Co.

GREENWILLOW BOOKS. Illustration by Anna Grossnickle Hines from *Taste the Raindrops* by Anna Grossnickle Hines. Copyright © 1983 by Anna Grossnickle Hines./ Illustration by Marylin Hafner from *The Crow and Mrs. Gaddy* by Wilson Gage. Text copyright © 1984 by Mary Q. Steele. Illustrations copyright © 1984 by Marylin Hafner./ Illustration by James Stevenson from *Cully Cully and the Bear* by Wilson Gage. Text copyright © 1983 by Mary Q. Steele. Illustrations copyright © 1983 by James Stevenson./ Illustration by Glen Rounds from *Down in the Boondocks* by Wilson Gage. Text copyright © 1977 by Wilson Gage. Illustrations copyright © 1977 by Glen Rounds./ Illustration by Glen Rounds from *Squash Pie* by Wilson Gage. Text copyright © 1976 by Wilson Gage. Illustrations copyright © 1976 by Glen Rounds./ Illustration by Marylin Hafner from *Miss Gaddy and the Fast-Growing Vine* by Wilson Gage. Text copyright © 1985 by Mary Q. Steele. Illustrations copyright © 1985 by Marylin Hafner. All reprinted by permission of Greenwillow Books.

GROSSET & DUNLAP, INC. Jacket illustration from *The Phantom Shark* by John Blaine. Reprinted by permission of Grosset & Dunlap, Inc.

HARCOURT BRACE JOVANOVICH, INC. Jacket illustration by Darrel Millsap from *Shanny on Her Own* by Lael Littke. Copyright © 1985 by Lael Littke./ Illustration by Michael Hague from *The Dragon Kite* by Nancy Luenn. Text copyright © 1982 by Nancy E. Jones. Illustrations copyright © 1982 by Michael Hague./ Illustration by Paul Galdone from *Tomahawks and Trouble* by William O. Steele. Copyright 1955 by William O. Steele./ Illustration by Charles Beck from *The Year of the Bloody Sevens* by William O. Steele. Copyright © 1963 by William O. Steele./ Illustration by Paul Coker from *The Spooky Thing* by William O. Steele. Copyright © 1960 by William O. Steele./ Illustration by Michael Ramus from *Andy Jackson's Water Well* by William O. Steele. Copyright © 1959 by William O. Steele. All reprinted by permission of Harcourt Brace Jovanovich, Inc.

HARPER & ROW PUBLISHERS, INC. Illustration by Thomas Nast from *Robinson Crusoe's Money; or, The Remarkable Financial Fortunes and Misfortunes of a Remote Island Community* by David A. Wells. Reprinted by permission of Harper & Row Publishers, Inc.

HASTINGS HOUSE PUBLISHERS, INC. Illustration by John Wallner from *The Sick Story* by Linda Hirsch. Text copyright © 1977 by Linda Hirsch. Illustrations copyright © 1977 by John Wallner. Reprinted by permission of Hastings House Publishers, Inc.

HOLIDAY HOUSE, INC. Jacket illustration by Ellen Thompson from *Time Enough for Drums* by Ann Rinaldi. Copyright © 1986 by Ann Rinaldi./ Illustration by John Wallner from "The Easter Parade" by William Jay Smith in *Easter Poems,* selected by Myra Cohn

Livingston. Text copyright © 1985 by Myra Cohn Livingston. Illustrations copyright © 1985 by John C. Wallner. Both reprinted by permission of Holiday House, Inc.

HOLT, RINEHART & WINSTON GENERAL BOOK. Illustration by Vernon Wooten from *Tomahawk Border* by William O. Steele. Copyright © 1966 by Colonial Williamsburg, Inc. Reprinted by permission of Holt, Rinehart & Winston General Book.

HOUGHTON MIFFLIN CO. Illustration by Marc Brown from *Why the Tides Ebb and Flow* by Joan Chase Bowden. Text copyright © 1979 by Joan Chase Bowden. Illustrations copyright © 1979 by Marc Brown./ Illustration by Leo and Diane Dillon from *Hakon of Rogen's Saga* by Erik Christian Haugaard. Copyright © 1963 by Erik Christian Haugaard./ Illustration by Leo and Diane Dillon from *Burning Star* by Eth Clifford. Copyright © 1974 by Ethel Clifford Rosenberg./ Illustration by James Marshall from *George and Martha Encore* by James Marshall. Copyright © 1973 by James Marshall./ Illustration by James Marshall from *The Stupids Die* by Harry Allard. Text copyright © 1981 by Harry Allard. Illustrations copyright © 1981 by James Marshall./ Illustration by James Marshall from *George and Martha* by James Marshall. Copyright © 1972 by James Marshall./ Illustration by James Marshall from *Miss Nelson Is Back* by Harry Allard. Text copyright © 1982 by Harry Allard. Illustrations copyright © 1982 by James Marshall./ Illustration by James Marshall from *The Stupids Have a Ball* by Harry Allard. Text copyright © 1978 by Harry Allard. Illustrations copyright © 1978 by James Marshall./ Illustration by James Marshall from *Miss Nelson Is Missing!* by Harry Allard. Text copyright © 1977 by Harry Allard. Illustrations copyright © 1977 by James Marshall. All reprinted by permission of Houghton Mifflin Co.

JUDSON PRESS. Illustration from *The Tiniest Christmas Star* by Masahiro Kasuya. Adapted by Mildred Schell. Copyright © 1977 by Shiko Sha Co. Ltd. Illustrations copyright © 1979 by Judson Press. Reprinted by permission of Judson Press.

KANE/MILLER BOOK PUBLISHERS. Illustration by Julie Vivas from *Wilfred Gordon McDonald Partridge* by Mem Fox. Text copyright © 1984 by Mem Fox. Illustrations copyright © 1984 by Julie Vivas. Reprinted by permission of Kane/Miller Book Publishers.

ALFRED A. KNOPF, INC. Illustration by Leo and Diane Dillon from "A Wolf and Little Daughter" in *The People Could Fly: American Black Folktales* by Virginia Hamilton. Text copyright © 1985 by Virginia Hamilton. Illustrations copyright © 1985 by Leo and Diane Dillon./ Illustration by Leo and Diane Dillon from "The Talking Cooter" in *The People Could Fly: American Black Folktales* by Virginia Hamilton. Text copyright © 1985 by Virginia Hamilton. Illustrations copyright © 1985 by Leo and Diane Dillon./ Text excerpts from *Emilie Loring: A Twentieth Century Romanticist* by Dorothea Laurance. All reprinted by permission of Alfred A. Knopf, Inc.

LITTLE, BROWN & CO. Illustrations by Leo and Diane Dillon from *The Third Gift* by Jan Carew. Text copyright © 1974 by Jan Carew. Illustrations copyright © 1974 by Leo and Diane Dillon./ Jacket illustration by Ted CoConis from *No Time for Love* by Emilie Loring. Copyright © 1970 by Robert M. Loring and Selden M. Loring./ Illustration by David Wiesner from *The Ugly Princess* by Nancy Luenn. Text copyright © 1981 by Nancy Luenn. Illustrations copyright © 1981 by David Wiesner./ Illustration by Martha Perske from *A Word to the Wise* by Alison Cragin Herzig and Jane Lawrence Mali. Copyright © 1978 by Alison Cragin Herzig and Jane Lawrence Mali./ Illustration by James Marshall from *Mary Alice, Operator Number 9* by Jeffrey Allen. Text copyright © 1975 by Jeffrey Allen. Illustrations copyright © 1975 by James Marshall./ Illustration by Ken Stampnick from *The Wooden People* by Myra Paperny. Copyright © 1976 by Myra Paperny. All reprinted by permission of Little, Brown & Co.

LOTHROP, LEE & SHEPARD BOOKS. Illustration by Patience Brewster from *I Met a Polar Bear* by Selma and Pauline Boyd. Text copyright © 1983 by Selma and Pauline Boyd. Illustrations copyright © 1983 by Patience Brewster./ Illustration by Patricia Coombs from *Dorrie and the Goblin* by Patricia Coombs. Copyright © 1972 by Patricia Coombs./ Illustration by Patricia Coombs from *Lisa and the Grompet* by Patricia Coombs. Copyright © 1970 by Patricia Coombs./ Illustration by Patricia Coombs from *Dorrie and the Museum Case* by Patricia Coombs. Copyright © 1986 by Patricia Coombs./ Illustration by Patricia Coombs from *Dorrie and the Halloween Plot* by Patricia Coombs. Copyright © 1976 by Patricia Coombs./ Illustration by Patricia Coombs from *The Magician and McTree* by Patricia Coombs. Copyright © 1984 by Patricia Coombs./ Illustration by Patricia Coombs from *The Lost Playground* by Patricia Coombs. Copyright © 1963 by Patricia Coombs./ Illustration by Patricia Coombs from *Dorrie and the Witchville Fair* by Patricia Coombs. Copyright © 1980 by Patricia Coombs./ Illustration by Patricia Coombs from *Molly Mullet* by Patricia Coombs. Copyright © 1975 by Patricia Coombs./ Illustration by Patricia Coombs from *Dorrie and the Fortune Teller* by Patricia Coombs. Copyright © 1973 by Patricia Coombs./ Illustration by Mordicai Gerstein from *"There Are Rocks in My Socks!" Said the Ox to the Fox* by Patricia

Thomas. Text copyright © 1979 by Patricia Thomas. Illustrations copyright © 1979 by Mordicai Gerstein./ Illustration by John Wallner from *Hello, My Name Is Scrambled Eggs* by Jamie Gilson. Text copyright © 1985 by Jamie Gilson. Illustrations copyright © 1985 by John C. Wallner. All reprinted by permission of Lothrop, Lee & Shepard Books.

MACMILLAN PUBLISHING CO. Jacket illustration by Kenneth Francis Dewey from *Flight of Sparrows* by Roy Brown. Copyright © 1972 by Roy Brown. Reprinted by permission of Macmillan Publishing Co.

McLAUGHLIN BROTHERS. Illustration by Thomas Nast from "Little Red Riding Hood" in *Thomas Nast's Illustrated Almanac* [1872], edited by Thomas Nast./ Illustration by Thomas Nast from *Thomas Nast's Illustrated Almanac* [1873], edited by Thomas Nast. Both reprinted by permission of McLaughlin Brothers.

WILLIAM MORROW & CO., INC. Illustration by John Wallner from *Aldo Ice Cream* by Johanna Hurwitz. Copyright © 1981 by Johanna Hurwitz. Reprinted by permission of William Morrow & Co., Inc.

N. C. PRESS LTD. Illustration by Barry Zaid from *The Chocolate Moose* by Gwendolyn MacEwen. Copyright © 1982 by Gwendolyn MacEwen. Illustrations copyright © 1982 by Barry Zaid. Reprinted by permission of N. C. Press Ltd.

PARENTS MAGAZINE PRESS. Illustration by John C. Wallner from *The Terrible Thing That Happened at Our House* by Marge Blaine. Text copyright © 1975 by Marge Blaine. Illustrations copyright © 1975 by John C. Wallner. Reprinted by permission of Parents Magazine Press.

PRENTICE-HALL INC. Illustration by Neil Waldman from *Tales of Terror: Ten Short Stories* by Edgar Allan Poe. Selected by Neil Waldman. Copyright © 1985 by Neil Waldman./ Illustration by John Wallner from *Rumpelstiltskin* by the Brothers Grimm. Copyright © 1984 by John Wallner. Both reprinted by permission of Prentice-Hall, Inc.

PUFFIN BOOKS. Illustration by James Marshall from *The Cut-Ups* by James Marshall. Copyright © 1984 by James Marshall. Reprinted by permission of Puffin Books.

THE PUTNAM PUBLISHING GROUP. Illustration by Glen Rounds from *Mike's Toads* by Wilson Gage. Text copyright © 1970 by Wilson Gage. Illustrations copyright © 1970 by Glen Rounds./ Jacket illustration by Harold James from *Time of Fearful Night* by Alice Wellman. Copyright © 1970 by Alice Wellman Harris. Both reprinted by permission of The Putnam Publishing Group.

SCHOLASTIC, INC. Illustration by Richard E. Martin from *The Cat Who Wore a Pot on Her Head* by Jan Slepian and Ann Seidler. Copyright © 1967 by Ann G. Seidler and Janice B. Slepian. Reprinted by permission of Scholastic, Inc.

THE SCRIBNER BOOK COMPANIES, INC. Illustration by Erica Wilson from *Erica Wilson's Embroidery Book* by Erica Wilson. Reprinted by permission of The Scribner Book Companies, Inc.

TRANSWORLD PUBLISHERS LTD. Illustration by James Marshall from *Portly McSwine* by James Marshall. Copyright © 1979 by James Marshall. Reprinted by permission of Transworld Publishers Ltd.

THE VANGUARD PRESS. Illustration by Chris Jenkyns from *Andy Says Bonjour!* by Pat Diska. Copyright 1954 by Pat Diska and Chris Jenkyns. Reprinted by permission of The Vanguard Press.

VIKING PENGUIN, INC. Detail of jacket illustration by Leo and Diane Dillon from *A Fair Wind for Troy* by Doris Gates./ Illustration by Leo and Diane Dillon from "Abu Kassem's Slippers" in *Two Pairs of Shoes*, retold by P. L. Travers. Text copyright © 1976 by P. L. Travers. Illustrations copyright © 1980 by Leo Dillon and Diane Dillon./ Illustration by Leo and Diane Dillon from *The Hundred Penny Box* by Sharon Bell Mathis. Text copyright © 1975 by Sharon Bell Mathis. Illustrations copyright © 1975 by Leo and Diane Dillon./ Jacket illustration by Martha Perske from *The Hand-Me-Down Kid* by Francine Pascal. Copyright © 1980 by Francine Pascal. All reprinted by permission of Viking Penguin, Inc.

WALKER & CO. Jacket illustration from *Term Paper* by Ann Rinaldi. Copyright © 1980 by Ann Rinaldi. Reprinted by permission of Walker & Co.

WHITMAN PUBLISHING CO. Jacket illustration from *Rip Foster Rides the Gray Planet* by Blake Savage. Reprinted by permission of Whitman Publishing Co.

Illustration by Mercedes Limona from *The Adventures of Strawberry Shortcake and Her Friends* by Alexandra Wallner. Copyright © 1980 by American Greetings Corp. Reprinted by permission of American Greetings Corp./ Sidelight excerpts from an article "Caldecott Acceptance Speech" by Leo and Diane Dillon, August, 1977 in *Horn Book.* Reprinted by permission of Leo Dillon./ Illustration by Thomas Nast from *Hans Brinker; or, The Silver Skates* by Mary Mapes Dodge. Reprinted by permission of James O'Kane./ Sidelight excerpts from an article "A Conversation with Bill Hanna" by Eugene Stafer from *The American Animated Cartoon,* edited by Danny and Gerald Peary. Copyright © 1980 by Eugene Stafer. Reprinted by permission of Danny Peary.

Appreciation also to Jennifer R. Raabe for acquiring stills of theme parks featuring Hanna-Barbera characters; and to the Performing Arts Research Center of the New York Public Library at Lincoln Center for permission to reprint the cover of *TV Guide* featuring the cast of "Gentle Ben."

PHOTOGRAPH CREDITS

William Anthony Auth, Jr.: Ed Reinke; Stephanie Calmenson: Tony Vanaria; Adrian J. Desmond: Peter Hujar; Leo and Diane Dillon: Lee Dillon; Mel Glenn: Howard Wallach; Harold Leland Goodwin: RoJay Photographers; Edward Hoagland: Nancy Crampton; Masahiro Kasuya: Yoko Watari; Nancy Luenn: Paul Fischburg; Francine Pascal: Lou Schwartz; Tamora Pierce: George Zarr; Ann Rinaldi: *Trentonian* photograph by Bill Phillips; Cass R. Sandak: F. R. Sloan; Mary Q. Steele: Susan Hirschman; Alice Wellman: Bruno of Hollywood; Barry Zaid: Hans of Boulder.

something ABOUT the AUthor

AASENG, Nathan   1953-
(Nate Aaseng)

PERSONAL: Born July 7, 1953, in Park Rapids, Minn.; son of Rolf E. (a minister) and Viola (a librarian; maiden name, Anderson) Aaseng; married Linda Jansen (a homemaker), December 20, 1975; children: Jay, Maury, Makhaila, Evan. *Education:* Luther College, B.A., 1975. *Home and office:* 109 West Grant Ave., Eau Claire, Wis. 54701.

CAREER: Bio-Tech Resources, Manitowoc, Wis., microbiologist-biochemist, 1975-79; writer, 1979—. *Awards, honors: Baseball: You Are the Manager* and *Football: You Are the Coach* were both selected a Children's Choice by the International Reading Association/Children's Book Council, 1984, *Baseball: It's Your Team* and *Football: It's Your Team,* 1986; *Carl Lewis: Legend Chaser* was selected one of Child Study Association of America's Children's Books of the Year, 1985; *More with Less: The Future World of Buckminster Fuller* was selected one of *Children and Science's* Outstanding Science Trade Books, 1986.

WRITINGS—For young people; all published by Lerner, except as noted: *Bruce Jenner: Decathlon Winner,* 1979; *Football's Fierce Defenses* (self-illustrated with photographs), 1980; *Basketball's High Flyers* (self-illustrated with photographs), 1980; *Little Giants of Pro Sports,* 1980; *Winners Never Quit: Athletes Who Beat the Odds,* 1980; *Baseball's Finest Pitchers,* 1980; *Football's Winning Quarterbacks,* 1980; *Football's Breakaway Backs,* 1980; *Football's Sure-Handed Receivers,* 1980; *Eric Heiden: Winner in Gold,* 1980; *Winning Men of Tennis,* 1981; *Winning Women of Tennis,* 1981; *Track's Magnificent Milers,* 1981; *Football's Cunning Coaches,* 1981; *Football's Steadiest Kickers,* 1981; *Football's Toughest Tight Ends,* 1981; *Pete Rose: Baseball's Charlie Hustle,* 1981; (under name Nate Aaseng) *I'm Learning, Lord, but I Still Need Help: Story Devotions for Boys,* Augsburg, 1981; *Football's Super Bowl Champions: I-VIII,* 1982; *Football's Super Bowl Champions: IX-XVI,* 1982; *Football's Crushing Blockers,* 1982; *World-Class Marathoners,* 1982; *Batting Ninth for the Braves,* Cook, 1982; *Memorable World Series Moments,* 1982; *Baseball's Brilliant Managers,* 1982; *Superstars Stopped Short,* 1982.

Baseball's Hottest Hitters, 1983; *Baseball's Playmakers,* 1983; *Basketball's Sharpshooters,* 1983; *Forty-Two Red on Four,* Cook, 1983; *Hockey: You Are the Coach,* 1983, published as *You Are the Coach: Hockey,* Dell, 1984; *Supersubs of Pro Sports,* 1983; *Football's Hardhitting Linebackers,* 1983; *Basketball: You Are the Coach,* 1983, published as *You Are the Coach: Basketball,* Dell, 1983; *Basketball's Sharpshooters,* 1983; *Baseball's Power Hitters,* 1983; *Basketball's Playmakers,* 1983; *I'm Searching, Lord, but I Need Your Light,* Augsburg, 1983; *Football: You Are the Coach,* 1983, published as *You Are the Coach: Football,* Dell, 1983; *Comeback Stars of Pro Sports,* 1983; *Baseball: You Are the Manager,* 1983, pub-

NATHAN AASENG

1

If it's possible to build domes over rooms, courtyards, and sports arenas, why not domes over entire cities? ■ (From *More with Less: The Future World of Buckminster* by Nathan Aaseng. Photograph courtesy of Buckminster Fuller Institute.)

lished as *You Are the Manager: Baseball,* Dell, 1984; *Hockey's Fearless Goalies,* 1984; *Hockey's Super Scorers,* 1984; *Baseball's Ace Relief Pitchers,* 1984; *Football's Daring Defensive Backs,* 1984; *Steve Carlton: Baseball's Silent Strongman,* 1984; *Which Way Are You Leading Me, Lord? Bible Devotions for Boys,* Augsburg, 1984; *Football's Punishing Pass Rushers,* 1984; *College Basketball: You Are the Coach,* 1984, published as *You Are the Coach: College Basketball,* Dell, 1986; *College Football: You Are the Coach,* 1984, published as *You Are the Coach: College Football,* Dell, 1985.

Basketball's Power Players, 1985; *Baseball: It's Your Team,* 1985; *Carl Lewis: Legend Chaser,* 1985; *Football: It's Your Team,* 1985; *Bob Geldof: The Man behind Live Aid,* 1986; *Baseball's Worst Teams,* 1986; *More with Less: The Future World of Buckminster Fuller,* 1986; *Baseball's Greatest Teams,* 1986; *Pro Sports' Greatest Rivalries,* 1986; *Football's Most Controversial Calls,* 1986; *Football's Most Shocking Upsets,* 1986; *Record Breakers of Pro Sports,* 1987; *Ultramarathons: The World's Most Punishing Races,* 1987; *College Football's Hottest Rivalries,* 1987; *Football's Incredible Bulks,* 1987; *The Disease Fighters: The Nobel Prize in Medicine,* 1987; *The Inventors: Nobel Prizes in Chemistry, Physics, and Medicine,* 1987; *The Peace Seekers: The Nobel Peace Prize,* 1987; *Playing for Life: Sports Stories for Teens,* Augsburg, 1987; *Prey Animals,* 1987; *Meat-Eating Animals,* 1987; *Bob Dylan: Spell-*

binding Songwriter, 1987; *Dwight Gooden: Strikeout King,* in press.

WORK IN PROGRESS: A fantasy series for the middle grades; *The Last Race of Jefferson Dark,* a futuristic thriller; a business origins series.

SIDELIGHTS: "I have been interested in being an author since at least third grade, and have enjoyed books for as long as I can remember. I was always considered a creative kid, actually 'clever' is the word I remember teachers writing on my papers. Yet I was never very successful in writing stories for school assignments.

"In high school I enjoyed writing humor. Even in things that started out seriously, something would strike me as funny and I would end up with something light and humorous.

"By college I had given up the idea that I could make it as an author and explored other career possibilities. I still received great satisfaction from writing, such as when I was recruited to be the sports editor of my college newspaper. But again, I could very rarely write anything completely serious. My submissions to the college literary magazine were not accepted, I am sure, because they were not serious enough.

"The most valuable course I have received in writing was actually a rhetoric course. That class was far more useful in teaching me what writing was all about than any creative writing class I had taken.

"I tried for a brief time to get some stories published and experienced the frustration of the publishing world. So I gave up and worked as a research microbiologist-biochemist. (My college majors were English and biology.) After three years, though, I came to believe that writing was my best talent.

"In making one last effort to break into writing, I accidentally discovered the key to getting published: instead of submitting your own ideas and stories, find out what the publishers want published. I had no intention of writing for children or of writing about sports, but that was where I found an opening in the market. Ever since then, I have been trying to persuade publishers to let me write about what really interests me. Sometimes I win, sometimes I lose, and since I need to make my living at this business, I try to be flexible.

"As far as writing for younger readers, I often find it frustrating. Words are my tools and the younger the reader, the fewer tools (words) I can use. I have to stay within their vocabulary. On the other hand, I have felt comfortable writing for young people because I do not believe in trying to impress people with huge words or intimidating style. I always thought the idea in writing was to communicate, not to show off."

APFEL, Necia H(alpern) 1930-

PERSONAL: Born July 31, 1930, in Mount Vernon, N.Y.; daughter of Simon A. and Sidonia (Frank) Halpern; married Donald A. Apfel (an orthodontist), September 7, 1952; children: Mimi, Steve. *Education:* Tufts University, B.A. (magna cum laude), 1952; graduate study at Harvard University, 1953-54, and Northwestern University, 1963-67. *Home and office:* 3461 University Ave., Highland Park, Ill. 60035. *Agent:* Ray Peekner Literary Agency, 3210 South Seventh St., Milwaukee, Wis. 53215.

CAREER: Worked at miscellaneous jobs in Boston, Mass., 1954-55; Standard Oil Company, Chicago, Ill., research analyst, 1955-57; Adler Planetarium, Chicago, Ill., associate director of Astro-Science Workshop, 1973-79; writer, 1979—. Lecturer in astronomy at elementary and junior high schools, 1973—; conducts classes in astronomy for children at Adler Planetarium. *Member:* American Association for the Advancement of Science, Astronomical Society of the Pacific, League of Women Voters (member of board of directors, 1960-62), Phi Beta Kappa. *Awards, honors: It's All Relative* was chosen one of New York Public Library's Books for the Teen Age, 1982.

WRITINGS: (With J. Allen Hynek) *Astronomy One* (college textbook), W. A. Benjamin, 1973, second edition published as *Architecture of the Universe*, W. A. Benjamin, Cummings, 1979; *It's All Relative: Einstein's Theory of Relativity* (juvenile), Lothrop, 1981; *Stars and Galaxies* (juvenile), F. Watts, 1982; *The Moon and Its Exploration* (juvenile), F. Watts, 1982; *Astronomy and Planetology: Projects for Young Scientists* (juvenile), F. Watts, 1983; *Astronomy Projects for Young Scientists*, Arco, 1984; *It's All Elementary: From Atoms to the Quantum World of Quarks, Lepton, and Gluons* (juvenile), Lothrop, 1985; *Calendars*, F. Watts, 1985; *Space Station*, F. Watts, 1987; *Nebulae: The Birth and Death of Stars*, Lothrop,

1988; *Space Law*, F. Watts, 1988. Author of "Ask Ulysses," a monthly column in *Odyssey*. Contributor to magazines.

SIDELIGHTS: "After I left Harvard University Graduate School in 1954, I held miscellaneous jobs while my husband completed dental school. In 1963 I went back to school, this time to Northwestern University Graduate School (astronomy department). This was a field I had always been interested in since childhood but was discouraged from pursuing. 'Women don't become astronomers,' I was told. My decision to return to school came after being given a telescope for my birthday by my husband. I then took an adult education class in astronomy and realized how very interested I was in this subject.

"In 1967 I was appointed a research assistant at Northwestern. The project that I worked on involved the study of spectroscopic binary stars. Dr. J. Allen Hynek was in charge of this project, and this association eventually led to our co-authorship of *Astronomy One*, which was published in 1973.

"From 1979 to 1982 I was busy writing three juvenile books. The first one was especially difficult because I wanted to be sure that my explanations of Einstein's theory could really be understood by a high school (and possibly a very bright junior high school) student. And, of course, by an adult! I feel it is important for young people to be exposed to these concepts as early as possible so that they will be more comfortable with them later on. And I was always fascinated with the subject, especially when I was told many years ago that only a handful of people could understand it, let alone write about it. The book contains no math but has lots of photos and diagrams. I'm quite proud of it. It is currently being translated into Japanese.

"The other two books are 'First Books' and are meant for elementary school children. They were fun to write because both subjects were very familiar to me from my work on the textbooks and also from my school lectures.

"*Astronomy and Planetology* is a book filled with ideas for science fair projects in the field of astronomy. It is for elementary, junior high and high school students and has information about other science competitions open to this age group.

"At the Adler Planetarium I give courses in astronomy for children. I particularly like to teach the eight- to eleven-year-old group because I find that they are by far the most exciting and imaginative. It is the same group that I write for in *Odyssey* magazine. My monthly column in that magazine answers readers' questions. Only children can think up the kind of questions I receive. They are marvelous. Several times a year I write an article for this same magazine. Some of my subjects have been black holes, stellar evolution, nebulae, sunspots, comets, sidereal time, galaxies, and relativity."

AUTH, William Anthony, Jr. 1942- (Tony Auth)

PERSONAL: Born May 7, 1942, in Akron, Ohio; son of William Anthony (an executive with Firestone Tire and Rubber Co.) and Julia Kathleen (a housewife; maiden name, Donnally) Auth; married Eliza Drake (an artist), August 28, 1982; children: Kathleen. *Education:* University of California, Los Angeles, B.A., 1965. *Home:* 1137 Rodman St., Philadelphia, Pa. 19147. *Agent:* Toni Mendez, 141 East 56th St., New York, N.Y. 10022. *Office:* 400 North Broad St., Philadelphia, Pa. 19101.

WILLIAM ANTHONY AUTH, JR.

CAREER: Rancho Los Amigos Hospital, Downey, Calif., chief medical illustrator, 1964-70; *Philadelphia Inquirer,* Philadelphia, Pa., editorial cartoonist, 1971—; illustrator of children's books, 1984—. *Awards, honors:* Overseas Press Club Award, 1975, 1976, and 1985, all for editorial cartoons; Pulitzer Prize, Society of Professional Journalists Award, Sigma Delta Chi Award, and Columbia University Trustees Award, all 1976, all for editorial cartooning.

WRITINGS: (Under name Tony Auth) *Behind the Lines: Cartoons,* Houghton, 1977.

Illustrator; under name Tony Auth: Stephen Manes, *That Game from Outer Space: The First Strange Thing That Happened to Oscar Noodleman,* Dutton, 1983; Nathan Zimelman, *Mean Murgatroyd and the Ten Cats* (Junior Literary Guild selection), Dutton, 1984.

WORK IN PROGRESS: Another collection of political cartoons, to be published by Andrews, McMeel, and Parker.

SIDELIGHTS: Auth studied biological illustration at UCLA, and worked as a medical illustrator before he became a political cartoonist, inspired by the Vietnam War. "In my youth I had always thought that I would probably be a cartoonist, but I was totally apolitical, so that throughout high school and college the cartoons I was drawing were not political in nature at all, but social commentary. It was very rewarding suddenly to find that the same talents I was using in medical illustration, where I was in fact doing a lot of cartooning, could be turned toward politics.

"Cartooning is an excellent medium for making one point at a time, and the point is usually one that I anticipate will provoke a reaction of sadness or joy or laughter or nostalgia or any number of things. . . . I tend to think of information as being a torrent of particles: some of it is public relations material; some of it is half-truths; some honest. Everybody's putting out information, and people get subjected to a torrent of it and then form an opinion of what's going on. I contribute one particle a day to the torrent.

"There's one thing that I'm particularly interested in, which is the relationship between the way a drawing is done and the content of the cartoon. I try to have a mesh there, so that the cartoon works better because of the way it's drawn. That means that stylistically I'm all over the place, depending on the subject matter and the emotional content of the particular drawing. If it's a very serious cartoon, I'll be more realistic and dignified in a drawing; I try to avoid using the same style I might use in a whimsical cartoon. I don't want to get tied into one particular way of doing my drawings. Many editorial cartoonists are so hung up on their style that it seems to me they back themselves into a corner.

"I became interested in political cartoons when I was in the sixth or seventh grade, and started noticing drawings by Bruce Russell and Karl Hubenthal who were in Los Angeles at the time. But I lost interest because I was only superficially interested in politics and had no real depth of knowledge. Later, I was influenced by people like Paul Conrad, Pat Oliphant, Ronald Searle, as well as the children's book illustrators Tomi Ungerer and Maurice Sendak. I find there's a lot of overlap; Ernest Shepard's work and Hans-Georg Rauch's work have been very significant to me."

Auth feels it is important to be emotionally involved in an issue to do a good cartoon. "If you don't feel strongly about what you're drawing, I think the work shows that lack of interest, and that's what we call hack work. You're not into it anymore; you're cranking out stuff because you have a job.

"There are five issues that are guaranteed to cause a storm of mail. We have an acronym here, IIGAD (pronounced e-gad!): Ireland, Israel, gun control, abortion, and the death penalty. Ten years ago the acronym would have been something else—Watergate would have been one of the issues; Vietnam would have been one. They change, but there's always a handful of issues that are driving people up the wall in one way or another. It doesn't matter what I say about them. Those topics tend to be the same subjects on which there really is no communication going on among people who hold various points of view. Any cartoon I do on them will excite some people to say 'Yes, that's right' and get others angry.

"I always answer serious criticism, but I get very little of that. Most of the mail is either fan mail or hate mail, and I tend not to answer it unless somebody is asking for a print of a cartoon or something."

Editorial cartooning has won Auth the Overseas Press Club Award, the Sigma Delta Chi Award, and the Pulitzer Prize. "It's very rewarding to be recognized by your peers. There are a lot of people I would like to see get the Pulitzer Prize who haven't received it yet. But I found it liberating to get [it].

Arabella owned ten cats. ■ (From *Mean Murgatroyd and the Ten Cats* by Nathan Zimelman. Illustrated by Tony Auth.)

"I find that I perform better under deadline pressure. I like to read and study and think about issues when I'm not feeling that pressure and then under pressure come up with the drawings."

Behind the Lines, Auth's first book, was published in 1977. "It grew out of my early lectures; it follows the lecture pattern closely. I've pretty much cut out lecturing for the time being because I've taken on some other activity, but I used to. I spoke at colleges, high schools, and to civic groups."

Auth became interested in doing illustrations for children's books. "I got my agent in New York to pick out some of my cartoons that are in the style I would like to use for children's books, and she approached various publishers. I'd nursed the desire for a while and done a lot of watercolors, trying to prepare myself for this kind of work.

"I have illustrated two children's books, and I would very much like to do some picture books at some point. I haven't had much time to put another anthology together, but I would like to do another one. It solidifies what you have done. Newsprint is fragile."

Auth encourages young people, who think they'd like to be cartoonists, if he feels they have talent. "I try to be as honest with them as I possibly can. A lot of kids, and some of them not such young kids either, are under the illusion that they're very talented because their parents or their friends have been saying, 'Boy, that's pretty good.' They haven't been subjected to any sort of professional criticism at all. So I try to disillusion them as kindly as I can. I'll often get a book of somebody's work that I think their work is distantly related to, and they usually see the vast gulf that separates them from a real professional. On the other hand, occasionally someone will come through who *is* very talented, and I encourage him or her to keep working on whatever I sense needs work. A lot of people like the idea of being a cartoonist but haven't really decided what kind of cartoonist. They don't realize that cartooning is very specialized. So I try to find out where their inclination is, find out what direction it might lead them, and give them appropriate advice."

HOBBIES AND OTHER INTERESTS: "I read fiction for enjoyment. I'm a big fan of children's books, and also science fiction and fantasy. I like Ursula Le Guin, among others. I swim, travel, watch movies, read books, and spend time with friends."

FOR MORE INFORMATION SEE: New York Times Book Review, October 9, 1977; *Washington Post Book World,* October 16, 1977; *Newsweek,* October 13, 1980.

BARBERA, Joseph Roland 1911-
(Joe Barbera)

PERSONAL: Born March 24, 1911, in New York City; son of Vincente and Frances Barbera; married Dorothy Earl (marriage ended); married Sheila Holden; children: (first marriage) Lynn Meredith, Jayne Earl, Neal Francis. *Education:* Attended American Institute of Banking, Pratt Institute, Art Students League. *Office:* Hanna-Barbera Productions, 3400 Cahuenga Blvd., Hollywood, Calif. 90068.

CAREER: Irving Trust Company, New York City, banking clerk, 1930-32; Van Beuren Studios, New York City, animator, 1932-34; Terrytoons, New Rochelle, N.Y., animator, 1934-37; Metro-Goldwyn-Mayer (MGM), Hollywood, Calif., story man, director and producer, 1937-57; Hanna-Barbera Productions, Hollywood, president, 1957—. President, Southern California Theatre Associations. On advisory board of St. Joseph's Medical Center, Greater Los Angeles Visitors and Convention Bureau and Children's Village. Co-chairman of Los Angeles Earthquake Preparedness Committee. *Member:* National Academy of Television Arts and Sciences, Academy of Motion Picture Arts and Sciences, Cousteau Society, Greek Theatre Association (former president), Wildlife Waystation (honorary board member), James A. Doolittle Theater (president).

AWARDS, HONORS—All with Bill Hanna: Seven Academy Awards for Animated Short Subjects from the Academy of

JOSEPH ROLAND BARBERA

Motion Picture Arts and Sciences, all for cartoons featuring the characters Tom and Jerry: "Yankee Doodle Mouse," 1943; "Mouse Trouble," 1944; "Quiet, Please," 1945; "The Cat Concerto," 1946; "The Little Orphan," 1948; "The Two Mouseketeers," 1951; "Johann Mouse," 1952.

Seven Emmy Awards from National Academy of Television Arts and Sciences, all for Outstanding Achievement in the Field of Children's Programming, except as noted; all animation, except as noted: "Huckleberry Hound," 1960; "Jack and the Beanstalk" (live-action and animation), 1966; "The Last of the Curlews," 1973; "The Runaways" (live-action), 1974; "The Gathering" (live-action), for Outstanding Special—Drama or Comedy, 1978; "The Smurfs," for Outstanding Children's Entertainment Series, 1982, and 1983.

Golden Globe Award from Hollywood Foreign Press Association for Outstanding Achievement in International Television Cartoons, for "The Flintstones," 1965; Annie Award, for "Charlotte's Web," 1977; Christopher Award, for "The Gathering," 1978; Golden Reel Award, for Animation Sound Editing, and Bronze Award from the International Film and Television Festival of New York for Best Children's Special, both for "The Smurfs' Springtime Special," both 1982; Bronze Award from the International Film and Television Festival of New York for Best Children's Special, for "The Smurfic Games," 1984; Man of the Year with co-recipient Bill Hanna from the National Center for Hyperactive Children, 1986; Religion in Media's Gold Angel Award for Excellence in Media, 1986, and the Distinguished Service Award from the National Religious Broadcasters, and Award of Excellence from the Film Advisory Board, both 1987, all for "The Greatest Adventure: Stories from the Bible"; Humanitas Prize for "The Lure of the Orb" (Smurf episode), 1987.

FILMS—Producer with Bill Hanna; all animated features, except as noted: "Hey There, It's Yogi Bear," 1964; "A Man Called Flintstone," 1966; "Charlotte's Web," 1973; "C.H.O.M.P.S." (live-action), 1978; "Heidi's Song," 1982; "GoBots: Battle of the Rock Lords," 1986. Also producer of "Forever Like a Rose."

TELEVISION—Producer with Bill Hanna; all live-action movies, except as noted: "Hardcase," ABC, 1972; 'Shootout in a One-Dog Town" (animated), ABC, 1974; "The Gathering," ABC, 1977; "The Beasts Are in the Streets," NBC, 1978; "KISS Meets the Phantom of the Park," NBC, 1978; "The Gathering, Part II," NBC, 1979; "Belle Starr," CBS, 1980; "Stone Fox," NBC, 1987. Also producer of "Rock Odyssey" (animation).

Animated movies; all syndicated in 1987, unless otherwise noted: "Lucky Luke," syndicated, 1985; "Ultraman! The Adventure Begins"; "Yogi and the Magical Flight of the Spruce Goose"; "Yogi's Great Escape"; "The Jetsons Meet the Flintstones"; "Yogi and the Invasion of the Space Bears"; "Scooby-Doo and the Ghoul School"; "The Good, the Bad and the Huckleberry Hound"; "Top Cat and the Beverly Hills Cats"; "Scooby and the Reluctant Werewolf"; 'Scooby-Doo Meets the Boo Brothers"; "Judy Jetson and the Rockers."

Live-action series: "Banana Splits," NBC, 1968-70; "Danger Island," NBC, 1968-70; "The New Adventures of Huck Finn," NBC, 1968-69; "Korg: 70,000 B.C.," ABC, 1974-75; "Skatebirds," CBS, 1977-78; "Mystery Island," CBS, 1977-78; "Benji," CBS, 1983-84; "Going Bananas," 1984-85.

Animated series: "Ruff and Reddy," NBC, 1957-60; "Huckleberry Hound," syndicated, 1958-62; "Pixie and Dixie"

Yogi Bear rides the wind in the 1983 Macy's Thanksgiving Day Parade. (Photograph courtesy of Macy's, New York, N.Y.)

syndicated, 1958-62; "Snooper and Blabber," syndicated, 1959-62; "Augie Doggie & Doggie Daddy," syndicated, 1959-62; "Quick Draw McGraw," syndicated, 1959-62; "Yakky Doodle," syndicated, 1960-62; "Yogi Bear," syndicated, 1960-62; "Hokey Wolf," syndicated, 1960-62; "The Flintstones," ABC, 1960-65; "Snagglepuss," syndicated, 1960-62; "Top Cat," ABC, 1961-62; "Lippy the Lion," syndicated, 1962; "Touche Turtle," syndicated, 1962; "Wally Gator," syndicated, 1962; "The Jetsons," ABC, 1962-63, syndicated, 1984-88; "Magilla Gorilla and Peter Potamus," syndicated, 1963-67; "Punkin' Puss," syndicated, 1963-67; "Breezly and Sneezly," syndicated, 1963-67; "Yippee, Yappee, and Yahooey," syndicated, 1963-67; "Ricochet Rabbit," syndicated, 1963-67.

"Jonny Quest," ABC, 1964-65, syndicated, 1986-88; "Secret Squirrel, NBC, 1965-67; "Precious Pupp," NBC, 1965-67; "Hillbilly Bears," NBC, 1965-67; "Atom Ant," NBC, 1965-67; "Winsome Witch," NBC, 1965-67; "Squiddly Diddly," NBC, 1965-67; "Sinbad, Jr." (distributed by AIP), 1965; "Laurel and Hardy" (distributed by Wolper), 1966-67; "Space Kidettes," syndicated, 1966-67; "Space Ghost," CBS, 1966-68, NBC, 1981-82; "Dino Boy," CBS, 1966-67; "Frankenstein, Jr.," CBS, 1966-67; "The Impossibles," CBS, 1966-67; "Abbott and Costello" (distributed by RKO and Jomar), 1967-68; "Herculoids," CBS, 1967-68, NBC, 1981-82; "Samson and Goliath," syndicated 1967-68; "The Fantastic Four," ABC, 1967-68; "Mightor," CBS, 1967-68;

"Shazzam," CBS, 1967-68; "Moby Dick," CBS, 1967-68; "Birdman," NBC, 1967-68; "Cattanooga Cats," ABC, 1967-70; "Three Musketeers," NBC, 1968-70; "Arabian Knights," NBC, 1968-70; "Micro Ventures," NBC, 1968-70; "Adventures of Gulliver," ABC, 1968-69; "Wacky Races," CBS, 1968-69; "Penelope Pitstop," CBS, 1969-70; "Motormouse and Autocat," ABC, 1969-70; "It's the Wolf," ABC, 1969-70; "Scooby-Doo," CBS, 1969-74, ABC, 1976-79; "Dastardly & Muttley," CBS, 1969-70; "Around the World in 79 Days," ABC, 1969-70.

"Josie and the Pussycats," CBS, 1970-71; "Where's Huddles?," CBS, 1970; "The Harlem Globetrotters," CBS, 1970-72; "Pebbles and Bamm Bamm," CBS, 1971-73; "Help! It's the Hair Bear Bunch," CBS, 1971-72; "The Funky Phantom," ABC, 1971-72; "Sealab 2020," NBC, 1972-73; "Roman Holidays," NBC, 1972-73; "The Amazing Chan and the Chan Clan," CBS, 1972-73; "The Flintstones Comedy Hour," CBS, 1972-73; "Josie and the Pussycats in Outer Space," CBS, 1972-73; "The New Scooby-Doo Movies," CBS, 1972-74; "Wait Till Your Father Gets Home," syndicated, 1972-74; "Jeannie," CBS, 1973-74; "Speed Buggy," CBS, 1973-74; "The Addams Family," NBC, 1973-74; "Inch High Private Eye," NBC, 1973-74; "Butch Cassidy," NBC, 1973-74; "Goober and the Ghost Chasers," ABC, 1973-74; "Superfriends," ABC, 1973-74, 1979-83; "Yogi's Gang," ABC, 1973-74; "Peter Puck," NBC, 1973-74; "Hong Kong Phooey," ABC, 1974-75; "These Are the Days," ABC, 1974-75;

Hanna-Barbera cartoon characters pose at "Carowinds" theme park (Charlotte, N.C.).

"Devlin," ABC, 1974-75; "Valley of the Dinosaurs," CBS, 1974-75; "Wheelie and the Chopper Bunch," NBC, 1974-75; "The Partridge Family: 2200 A.D.," CBS, 1974-75; "The Great Grape Ape," ABC, 1975-76; "Tom and Jerry," ABC, 1975-79.

"Dynomutt," ABC, 1976-78; "Jabberjaw," ABC, 1976-77; "Mumbly," ABC, 1976-77; "Clue Club," CBS, 1976-77; "CB Bears," NBC, 1977-78; "Shake, Rattle and Roll," NBC, 1977-78; "Undercover Elephant," NBC, 1977-78; "Robonic Stooges," CBS, 1977-78; "Woofer and Wimper Dog Detectives," CBS, 1977-78; "Blast-Off Buzzard," NBC, 1977-78; "Heyyy, It's the King," NBC, 1977-78; "Posse Impossible," NBC, 1977-78; "Wonder Wheels," CBS, 1977-78; "Captain Caveman and the Teen Angels," ABC, 1977-79; "The New Superfriends Show," ABC, 1977-79; "Scooby-Doo's All Star Laff-A-Lympics," ABC, 1977-79; "Yogi's Space Race," NBC, 1978-79; "Yogi's Galaxy Goof-Ups," NBC, 1978-79; "Challenge of the Superfriends," ABC, 1978-79; "Galloping Ghost," NBC, 1978-79; "Buford Files," NBC, 1978-79; "Jana of the Jungle," NBC, 1978-79; "Godzilla," NBC, 1978-80; "The All-New Popeye Show," CBS, 1978-82; "Dinky Dog," CBS, 1978-81; "The New Schmoo," NBC, 1979-80; "Super Globetrotters," NBC, 1979-80; "Casper and the Angels," NBC, 1979-80; "The Thing," NBC, 1979-80; "The Flintstones," NBC, 1979-80; "Scooby and Scrappy Doo," ABC, 1979-82, 1983-84; "The New Fred and Barney Show," NBC, 1979-80.

"Flintstone Family Adventures," NBC, 1980-82; "Pebbles, Dino and Bamm Bamm," NBC, 1980-82; "The Bedrock Cops," NBC, 1980-82; "Dino and the Cavemouse," NBC, 1980-82; "The Frankenstones," NBC, 1980-82; "Captain Caveman," NBC, 1980-82; "Drak Pak," CBS, 1980-81; "Fonz and the Happy Days Gang," ABC, 1980-82; "Richie Rich," ABC, 1980-83; "Space Stars," NBC, 1981-82; "Astro and the Space Mutts," NBC, 1981-82; "Teen Force," NBC, 1981-82; "Crazy Claws," CBS, 1981-82; "Kwicky Koala," CBS, 1981-82; "Dirty Dawg," CBS, 1981-82; "Bungle Brothers," CBS, 1981-82; 'The Smurfs," NBC, 1981-88; "Laverne and Shirley," ABC, 1981-82; "Private Olive Oyl," CBS, 1981-82; "The Trollkins," CBS, 1981-82; "Mork and Mindy," ABC, 1982-83; "Laverne and Shirley/Fonz," ABC, 1982-83; "The Little Rascals," ABC, 1982-83; "Scooby, Scrappy and Yabba Doo," ABC, 1982-83; "Pac-Man," ABC, 1982-84; "Shirt Tales," NBC, 1982-84; "The Gary Coleman Show," NBC, 1982-83; "The Dukes," CBS, 1983-84; "The Little Rascals/Richie Rich," ABC, 1983-84; "Monchhichis," ABC, 1983-84; "Baskitts," CBS, 1983-84; "The Snorks," NBC, 1984-85; "The Pink Panther and Sons," NBC, 1984-85; "The New Scooby-Doo Mysteries," ABC, 1984-85; "Superfriends: The Legendary Super Powers Show," ABC, 1984-85; "GoBots," syndicated, 1984-85; "The Funtastic World of Hanna-Barbera" (consisting of three segments: "Paw Paws," "Galtar and the Golden Lance," and "Yogi's Treasure Hunt"), syndicated, 1985-86; "The Super Powers Team: Galactic Guardians," ABC, 1985; "The Thirteen Ghosts of Scooby-Doo," ABC, 1985; "Challenge of the GoBots," syndicated, 1985.

'The Funtastic World of Hanna-Barbera (consisting of four segments: "Paw Paws," "Galtar and the Golden Lance," "Yogi's Treasure Hunt," and "Jonny Quest"), syndicated, 1986; "The Flintstone Kids," ABC, 1986-88; "The Greatest Adventure: Stories from the Bible," Home Video, 1986-88; "Pound Puppies," ABC, 1986; "Wildfire," CBS, 1986; "Foofur," NBC, 1986-88; "Popeye and Son," CBS, 1987; "The Funtastic World of Hanna-Barbera (consisting of four segments: "Yogi's Treasure Hunt," "Jonny Quest," "Sky Commanders," and "Snorks"), syndicated, 1987.

TELEVISION SPECIALS—Producer with Bill Hanna; all animated, except as noted: "Alice in Wonderland," ABC, 1966; "Jack and the Beanstalk" (live-action and animated), NBC, 1966; "The Thanksgiving That Almost Wasn't," syndicated, 1971; "Love American Style" (consisting of three segments: "Wait Till Your Father Gets Home" [pilot], "Love and the Private Eye," "Melvin Danger"); "A Christmas Story," syndicated, 1971; "The Last of the Curlews," ABC, 1972; "Yogi's Ark Lark," ABC, 1972; "Robin Hoodnik," ABC, 1972; "Oliver and the Artful Dodger," ABC, 1972; "Here Come the Clowns," ABC, 1972; "Gidget Makes the Wrong Connection," ABC, 1972; "The Banana Splits in Hocus Pocus Park," ABC, 1972; "20,000 Leagues under the Sea," syndicated, 1973; "The Three Musketeers," syndicated, 1973; "Lost in Space," ABC, 1973; "The Count of Monte Cristo," syndicated, 1973; "The Runaways" (live-action), ABC, 1974; "Cyrano de Bergerac," ABC, 1974; "Crazy Comedy Concert" (live and animated), ABC, 1974; "The Last of the Mohicans," syndicated, 1975; "Phantom Rebel" (live-action), NBC, 1976; "Davy Crockett on the Mississippi" (live-action), CBS, 1976.

"Taggart's Treasure" (live-action), ABC, 1976; "Five Weeks in a Balloon," CBS, 1977; "Yabba-Dabba-Doo!" (live and animated), CBS, 1977; "The Flintstones' Christmas," NBC, 1977; "Energy: A National Issue," syndicated, 1977; "Beach Girls" (live-action), syndicated, 1977; "It Isn't Easy Being a Teenage Millionnaire" (live-action), ABC, 1978; "Hanna-Barbera's Happy Hour" (animated mini-series), NBC, 1978; "Hanna-Barbera's All Star Comedy Ice Revue" (live and animated), CBS, 1978; "The Funny World of Fred and Bunni" (live and animated), CBS, 1978; "The Flintstones' Little Big League," NBC, 1978; "Black Beauty," CBS, 1978; "Yaba-Dabba-Doo II," CBS, 1978; "Superheroes Roast" (live-action), NBC, 1979; "Challenge of the Superheroes" (live-action), NBC, 1979; "America vs. the World" (live-action), NBC, 1979; "Scooby Goes Hollywood," ABC, 1979; "Casper's First Christmas," NBC, 1979; "Sgt. T.K. Yu" (live-action), NBC, 1979; "Popeye: Sweethearts at Sea," CBS, 1979; "Gulliver's Travels," CBS, 1979; "Casper's Halloween Special: He Ain't Scary, He's Our Brother," NBC, 1979.

"The Harlem Globetrotters Meet Snow White" (serialized in "Fred and Barney" series), NBC, 1980; "The Flintstones Meet Rockula and Frankenstone," NBC, 1980; "The Flintstones' New Neighbor," NBC, 1980; "Fred's Final Fling," NBC, 1980; "The Gymnast" (live-action), ABC, 1980; "B. B. Beagle," syndicated, 1980; "Hanna-Barbera Arena Show" (live-action), NBC, 1981; "Jogging Fever," NBC, 1981; "Wind-Up Wilma," NBC, 1981; "The Great Gilly Hopkins" (live-action), CBS, 1981; "Daniel Boone," CBS, 1981; "The Smurfs," NBC, 1981; "The Smurfs' Springtime Special," NBC, 1982; "The Jokebook," NBC, 1982; "The Smurfs' Christmas Special," NBC, 1982; "Christmas Comes to Pac-Land," ABC, 1982; "Yogi Bear's All-Star Christmas Caper," CBS, 1982; "My Smurfy Valentine," NBC, 1983; "The Secret World of Og," ABC, 1983; "The Amazing Bunjee Venture," CBS, 1984; "The Smurfic Games," NBC, 1984; "Smurfily-Ever-After," NBC, 1985; "Star Fairies," syndicated, 1985; "Pound Puppies," syndicated, 1985; "Flintstones 25th Anniversary Celebration" (animated and live-action), CBS, 1986. Also producer of "Johnny Yune Variety Special."

Also creator with Bill Hanna of cartoons featuring the characters Tom and Jerry; all produced by Metro-Goldwyn-Mayer including, "Yankee Doodle Mouse," 1943; 'Mouse Trouble," 1944; "Quiet, Please," 1945; "The Cat Concerto,"

Joseph Barbera and William Hanna with a few of their more prominent characters.

1946; "The Little Orphan," 1948; "The Two Mouseketeers," 1951; "Johann Mouse," 1952. Also creators of television special "Yogi's First Christmas," 1980. Many Hanna-Barbera cartoons are available in videocassette form.

WORK IN PROGRESS: Live-action feature film versions of "The Flintstones," "The Jetsons," "The Green Hornet," and

"Johnny Quest"; creation of Saturday morning cartoons; additional tapes in the homevideo series "Hanna-Barbera's The Greatest Adventure: Stories from the Bible."

SIDELIGHTS: "My parents were immigrants. My mother was eight years old when she came over from Sicily, the oldest of a line of six that went down to a babe in arms. On her journey, the boat lost its rudder, drifted for three weeks before it was finally found and brought to New York. They settled in the very depths of New York City. She was left with the job of raising her brothers who were out selling newspapers for pennies until one, two, three in the morning.

"My parents had an arranged marriage. My mother was sixteen when she had her first child. When I was born, she decided that Delancey Street was not the neighborhood in which to bring me up and moved us to Brooklyn."

Barbera's interest in drawing was manifested in early childhood. "I was sent to Holy Innocence, a Catholic school in Brooklyn where the nuns soon discovered my talent for drawing and sent me to the blackboard copying such religious scenes as Christ riding a donkey, entering Jerusalem on Easter Sunday carrying the palms. When visitors came, they pointed to the kid with the chalk dust all over him which reminded them of Michaelangelo covered with plaster, lying on his back, painting the ceiling.

"One day my mother asked me for the answer to 'two plus two.' When I was unable to come up with it, she pulled me out of Holy Innocence and enrolled me in Public School 139, where I finished my last two years of grammar school before going on to Erasmus Hall High School." As a student Barbera was involved in all of the school plays, served as editor of the school's paper "The Dutchman."

"I, along with other kids from high school were invited to a Broadway musical. I couldn't believe that there was such a great thing as musicals—great songs, marvelous music. I at-

tended every one after that, 'The Three Musketeers,' 'Mr. Roberts,' 'Oklahoma,' 'Carousel,' 'Annie Get Your Gun,' 'Red Hot and Blue.'''

After graduation Barbera went out to earn his livelihood at the Irving Trust Company on Wall Street. "I used to sit in the Trinity churchyard reading the classics by day and then went home to draw cartoons until four and five in the morning, delivering them to magazines during my lunch hour from the bank. They were the comic single-box cartoons you see in *New Yorker, Collier's,* and *Saturday Evening Post.*"

A letter addressed to Walt Disney was "the first and last fan letter" Barbera ever wrote. Disney responded with "I'm coming to New York and I will contact you," but never called or arranged a meeting. That turn of events was the best thing that ever happened to Barbera. "I would have disappeared. I would have just vanished into this great organization, which grew bigger and bigger.

"I thoroughly hated my bank job, especially since I couldn't add. I kept submitting cartoons and kept getting rejected. I attended Pratt Institute at night, attended the Art Students League for a couple of nights a week, and went to a dramatic school for a couple more nights. I was invited to attend the American School of Dramatic Arts. The five hundred dollar fee, however, eliminated me immediately.

"At Pratt I met a teacher whose nephew worked at Fleischer's Studio—the 'Popeye the Sailor' studio. I went to see him to plead for an opportunity to work at Fleischer's. They gave me a chance. I took vacation time from the bank, went to Fleisch-

Entrance to "Hanna Barbera Land" at "Australia's Wonderland" theme park in Sydney, Australia.

er's and hated it. It was tedious work brushing the color on by hand and inking all the drawing onto a piece of celluloid as well. I lasted for four days, went back to the bank from which I was promptly fired two weeks later. That was the happiest moment of my life.'' [From an interview by Rachel Koenig for *Something about the Author*.[1]]

Headed for Greenwich Village to ''starve to death'' in the company of his friends. Barbera was sidetracked, however, and found employment with the Van Beuren Studio. The studio closed a year and a half later and Barbera headed for Terrytoons in New Rochelle. ''I was now earning a lot of money—$50 a week. I used to take the hour-and-a-half trip from Brooklyn to New Rochelle every day. One day we were contacted by MGM people in California who were looking to hire seven people and I was one of them.

''I hated [California]—talk about getting homesick! I left the car and started to get on an Eastbound train, but my friends stopped me. . . .''

Met Bill Hanna at MGM. ''Hanna and I did a cartoon during a vacation. I drew it and he timed it and handled production. It was a cat chasing a mouse, 'Puss Gets the Boot.' The second story was called 'Tom and Jerry.' Although the effort was criticized at first, the cartoon had a twenty-year lifespan, won seven Oscars, and has recently made twenty-six million dollars in syndication. We had a whole different approach. We weren't doing the regular cat and mouse thing of chasing scenes. We had some brilliant story lines. The cartoons still run all over the world. I was told that there was a 'Tom and Jerry' festival in Rome and that it outdrew *Quo Vadis*.

''We did one episode called 'Johann Mouse.' One of the best concert pianists Jacob Gimpel played the music.'' 'Johann Mouse' was researched by Hanna and Barbera. ''Showing Johann Strauss' home in Vienna, the story related that every time Johann Strauss practised his piano, the mouse would come waltzing out of his little mouse hole completely carried away by the music. Now the cat knows this and waits for him. . . . Strauss goes on a trip and the cat can't stand this, so he rushes into the attic to a dusty old piano. He looks through sheets of music and finds 'How to Play the Piano in Six Easy Lessons' by Johann Strauss. He opens to the first lesson, which is one note, baamb, two notes, baamb, baamb, and so on. He then closes the music book and starts playing the 'Blue Danube.' He is brilliant. He goes downstairs and plays on Strauss' piano, and sure enough, out comes the waltzing mouse. He leaps for him, misses, and goes back to play some more. I think we won an Oscar for that one. Those were the kind of ideas we were doing . . . and they're still out there.''

Twenty years later, in 1957, the studio shut down for financial reasons and Barbera and Hanna found themselves unemployed. ''. . . We got this phone call saying, 'Close down production and fire everybody.' We had seven Oscars to our credit and getting fired was our reward. MGM found out they could make 90 percent of the same revenue just by re-releasing our old cartoons instead of making new ones. It didn't take courage for us to start our own company, it took sheer terror. Bill and I had been making $600 or $700 a week, and suddenly we weren't making anything. What were we supposed to do, sell real estate? We were cartoonists.'' [Digby Diehl, ''Joe Barbera: He's America's Busiest Baby-sitter—The Prolific Craftsman of TV Cartooning,'' *People*, March 16, 1987.[2]]

Fred Flintstone and Yogi Bear welcome visitors to "Canada's Wonderland" (Toronto, Ontario).

Peyo's "Smurfs," animated by Hanna-Barbera for NBC-TV, greet visitors at "Greet America" theme park (Santa Clara, Calif.).

They went to Screen-Gems T.V. and struck a deal. "To get into this business where nobody wanted to talk to you, we had to make a deal to do a five-minute cartoon which usually averages $40,000 to $45,000 for $2,700. Impossible, right? Well, we were able to do it by drawing less, a process called 'limited animation.'"[1]

"If a mouse was running, I would do two drawings, one with the left foot in front, one with the feet reversed. Bill exposed it on film so that the feet were blurring and we got the impression of running. Instead of 26,000 drawings, we were able to do it with 1,200. We did it out of desperation, but it looked sharp because it was so explosive with the kind of action we did. Disney's shorts had great technique and quality, but they were too expensive. They would show you some characters walking through a field of flowers, and as they walked the flowers would be swaying slightly in the breeze. Well, to show a character walking you don't *have* to animate 3,000 flowers."[2]

Hanna, the tireless coordinator with a meticulous eye for drawing, painting, inking, timing, filming and processing and Barbera, the compulsive inventor, established their own studio and went into production of their first TV short, "Ruff and Reddy." Their success was established in 1958 with the debut of "The Huckleberry Hound Show."

The team went on to create a stable of cartoon stars from "Tom and Jerry," to "Huckleberry Hound," to "Yogi Bear," "The Flintstones," "Quick Draw McGraw," "Topcat," and "The Jetsons." "'The Flintstones' was shown on prime time and nominated for an Emmy the first year, but Jack Benny beat us." "Huckleberry Hound" won an Emmy the first year. "The secret," said Barbera, "is creativity."[1]

"The Flintstones," a prime-time family cartoon show, which borrowed a little from "Ozzie and Harriet" and a lot from "The Honeymooners," is concerned with the domestic misadventures of a suburban cave family circa 10,000 B.C. "We tried all kinds of families. We drew them as Pilgrims, as Romans, everything imaginable. Nothing clicked until we made them cave people.... Selling 'The Flintstones' was tough. I had to pitch the show by acting out all the parts myself. I did all the voices and sound effects, and sometimes I would give five presentations in one day. Then I would go back to my hotel room and collapse."[2]

In 1967 Hanna-Barbera sold their studio to Taft Broadcasting Co. to establish a firm financial base while continuing to control production. "The business is bigger than ever. We're now discussing doing features for Home Box Office, home videos, and investigating computer animation." Hanna-Barbera has also established its own studios in the U.S., Europe, and in Australia. "Out of them have come some very good people. The trouble is that we don't like to train people to have them go to other studios. So we put key personnel under contract."

Hanna-Barbera also initiated classes that cover a curriculum which includes animation, writing, illustration, and storyboard. "We've got a great team of people all over the world with more animation being done now than ever before. It's a major industry. The only thing lacking, however, is enough good talent to support it."[1]

The classes, offered at no cost to the students, feature lectures by top craftsmen from every production department and lots of practice at drawing and animating. "What we are trying not to do is to train them in the television technique of limited animation. We're teaching them the feature technique (full animation) that we were trained on, which means teaching them motion, style and design.

"We're keeping the art going. No computer will ever replace it." [Lee Margulies, "An Art Alive," *Los Angeles Times*, n.d.[3]]

Barbera's function with the organization is to concentrate on new ideas, future productions, and new directions to keep one step ahead of the competition while Hanna concentrates on production. "It is very expensive. We have excellent musicians who handle the music ... we'll bring in the best people in a particular field: heavy metal, new wave, pop. We have artists who earn $1,500 and writers $2,500 a week.... And every season we start brand new again. There is no such thing as taking a day off. I haven't had a holiday in twenty years."[1]

They maintain creative control over their material. "I must be honest though, the final say will come from the networks."[1]

In 1978 Hanna-Barbera won an Emmy for their first live-action TV movie, "The Gathering," starring Ed Asner and Maureen Stapleton.

"Heidi's Song," a nine million dollar full-animation cartoon feature, premiered in 1982. The film's staff of over 200 people included twelve background painters, sixty assistant animators, eight layout people, and eighteen top character animators. "The thrust was to do one every year and to build a superb perennial library, which Disney had for years." [John Canemaker, "Hanna-Barbera: Will Heidi's Song Be Its Snow White," *Millimeter*, February, 1981.[4]]

"Heidi's Song" was based on Johanna Spyri's internationally known book, *Heidi*. Barbera explained why the film was in production for five years. "When we are in the slow season, which happens in television all the time, everybody has to be laid off. We were going to keep people busy on the feature. We found that doesn't work. The kind of people you use on a feature are the old super-pros of our industry, and there are few of them left.

"Secondly, we wanted to use 'Heidi's Song' as a training ground for new animators. The first three or four years the picture would go into production and stop, then go back into production and then stop. That was not good for the picture. We were losing momentum, the enthusiasm of the artists and the excitement we wanted to build up. So finally, about a year and a half ago, we marshalled the last remnants of what we think are the best people in the business. When we brought these people in we had to change directors. We had a fine guy, but he had forgotten how to go back and really work these old-timers—really get the good animation! We then hired a brilliant young director, Bob Taylor, who did a fabulous job."[4]

The thinking behind the choices for a feature film is carefully calculated toward box-office success. "If you are going to do a feature, you must have something people will identify with. You can't do 'Willie the Glowworm!' That's why 'Heidi' was such a logical choice. It's always a problem finding material. *Watership Down* is a marvelous book, but we would have hesitated to do it because it's just not that well known. It's a gamble. You have to put four to five million dollars into something like that."[4]

Barbera has also dabbled in playwriting. "I've written two plays, both optioned for Broadway, but I didn't have the time to pursue it. If I had to say what my first love is, it would be playwriting. 'The Maid and the Martian,' a play about an accidental visit to earth by a man from another planet who had never seen a woman before, was optioned for three years. Then optioned for a motion picture. All that we were waiting for was an okay initial from Howard Hughes which we were never able to get because we could never find him.''

Barbera is actively involved with many charitable organizations, flying to England as a guest of the Duke of Westminster for the Prevention of Cruelty to Children Fund drive, and building "Laffing Places" for children in hospitals, believing that "laughter is the best medicine."

Hanna-Barbera characters are featured in the company's amusement parks at home, in Canada, and in Australia.

For young people who are interested in becoming animators, Barbera believes that "one must first want to do it very much, and one must persevere with constant practice and art classes.''[1]

FOR MORE INFORMATION SEE: Roger Manvell, *The Animated Film,* Hastings House, 1955; Ruth Harbert, ''Mr. Tom and Mr. Jerry,'' *Good Housekeeping,* March, 1956; Ralph Stephenson, *Animation in the Cinema,* A. S. Barnes, 1967; Bruno Edera, *Full-Length Animated Feature Films,* Hastings House, 1977; *The World Encyclopedia of Cartoons,* Chelsea House, 1980; George Peary and Danny Peary, *The American Animated Cartoon,* Dutton, 1980; Leonard Maltin, *Of Mice and Magic: A History of American Animated Cartoons,* McGraw-Hill, 1980; John Canemaker, ''Hanna-Barbera: Will Heidi's Song Be It's Snow White,'' *Millimeter,* February, 1981; Joseph Barbera, ''Suspended Animation,'' *Continental,* July, 1984; Ken Speranza, ''Hanna-Barbera from Cavemen to Computers,'' *Video,* December, 1984; Ellen Farley, ''Saturday Morning Turf Now Being Invaded,'' *Los Angeles Times,* March 8, 1985; *Variety,* April 17, 1985, June 24, 1987; Maurice Horn, *Contemporary Graphic Artist,* Volume 1, Gale, 1986; Digby Diehl, ''Joe Barbera: He's America's Busiest Baby-sitter—The Prolific Craftsman of TV Cartooning,'' *People,* March 16, 1987.

BECKMAN, Delores 1914-

PERSONAL: Born August 12, 1914, in Grover Hill, Ohio; daughter of Earl L. (a teacher) and Minnie (a teacher; maiden name, Miller) Sheely; married Jack E. Beckman (retired from the California State Board of Equalization; a national park volunteer and artist), September 1, 1935; children: George E. *Education:* Attended secondary schools in Ohio and California. *Politics:* Republican. *Religion:* Protestant. *Home and office:* P. O. Box 98, Rimrock, Ariz. 86335. *Agent:* Dorothy Markinko, McIntosh & Otis, 475 Fifth Ave., New York, N.Y. 10017.

CAREER: Homemaker and writer. Has worked as a supermarket checker. Member of board of directors, Montezuma-Rimrock Fire and Rescue Fund. *Member:* Authors Guild, Authors League, Society of Children's Book Writers, Tennessee Literary Arts Society, California Scholarship Society (lifetime member), Chicago Reading Round Table. *Awards, honors:* International Reading Association Children's Book Award, 1981, for *My Own Private Sky.*

WRITINGS—Juvenile fiction: *My Own Private Sky,* Dutton, 1980; *Who Loves Sam Grant?,* Dutton, 1983. Also author of short stories for McFadden-Bartell, 1960-72, and Dell, 1960-72.

DELORES BECKMAN

WORK IN PROGRESS: Please Don't Let the Music Stop, for middle-graders, the story of a sixth-grade boy whose father looks like a famous movie star; research for a book set in Ohio during the 1920s for middle-graders, tentatively titled *Buckeye Girl; I Am Right and You Are Right,* for young adults.

SIDELIGHTS: ''I was born in a very small town in Ohio, with three sisters, one older than me. Because my father was a teacher and a town councilman as well as a Sunday school teacher and choir singer, I grew up with love, books, music and play. We loved roller-skating on the broad sidewalks leading to the consolidated school in the summer and ice-skating on the ponds in winter. In the fifth and sixth grades I was taught by my father's brother, John; and in the seventh and eighth grades by my father!

''I loved school, got all but perfect grades from first grade on, and was popular. I won an art contest sponsored by the Toledo Art Museum with a water-color of a Shakespearean garden (which I still have), was president of my junior class, and acted in plays. I went to Sunday school, Epworth League, Lyceum lectures, Chatagua; and sang in what are now known as glee clubs. I took piano lessons from the age of six to sixteen and played for both church and school affairs when older.

''My father died when I was fourteen, and we left for California in the summer of '31 where I entered my senior year of high school. It was a much larger school than the one I had left, and I suppose I suffered culture shock. Yet, I was soon

(Jacket illustration by Judith Cheng from *Who Loves Sam Grant?* by Delores Beckman.)

playing piano for all the Glee Clubs, soloists, and even the orchestra. Even though I was homesick for Ohio and my friends, I made friends in California, too. With my grade records from Ohio, I was accepted into the California Scholarship Society even before beginning my senior year, so I took only the two 'solids' required then and had a great time with drama, music and art! I am a lifetime member of the California Scholarship Society.

"I received a full scholarship to LaVerne College upon graduating, but could not accept it as we had no money and I was required to live in the dorms. The Depression affected both my life and, later, my writing. I try to instill in children a sense of values and responsibility. I feel this can only be done by telling a *good* story, with both humor and poignancy.

"I now live with my husband, Jack, on a hill in Rimrock, Arizona. He is a volunteer in parks, and works part time at Montezuma Well, a national monument near our home. He also is enamored of ancient Indian art, especially petroglyphs and pictographs. Jack does art work on stone, shells, and glasses, both etched and sand-blasted, which he sells once a year in the Art Gallery at the American Rock Art Research Association (ARARA) symposiums in different parts of the United States and Canada.

"I wrote my first short story while on our honeymoon at Yosemite Park, and, thankfully, have not been able to find it since.

"I believe a good book for children should have an irresistible beginning, VERY tight writing, and short chapters. I began writing in 1957 when my son was in school and my husband was at the office. I sold short stories for a long time and was turned on to children's books by my son, George, and his wife, Ruth, who are both teachers and reading specialists. I pulled the plug on my typewriter for over a year and did nothing but read children's books of all categories and for all age-groups. I have never regretted it. I believe the children's books printed today are the best books *anywhere.*

"I want to write books for children with an upbeat tone, hoping to show that one must consider the consequences of one's actions. In *My Own Private Sky,* an eleven-year-old boy and a sixty-year-old woman help each other to their feet. They, by restoring confidence in each other, and love, manage to overcome their individual fears. In *Who Loves Sam Grant?* a high school sophomore learns the difference between infatuation and friendship, and the limits and responsibilities in relationships with other people. The girl, Sam, short for Samantha, grows with the help of a handicapped next-door neighbor who she has all but ignored all her life.

"I consider any subject vital which addresses the doubts, fears and frailties of children today. I do not think any book for children should leave a child without hope, no matter how real and hard the situation, or the subject matter.

"I have been greatly influenced by other writers, most of whom I met at writers conferences across the country. Workshops taken under Scott O'Dell (who got me my agent), Madeleine L'Engle, Betsy Byars and others, helped me enormously. Also, writers of adult fiction: Guy Owen, Jack Matthews, Joe Hensley, Walter Tevis and Paul Darcy Boles, in particular. I admire a few writers of today's young adult fiction tremendously and have benefitted from their lectures and workshops: Norma Fox Mazer, Richard Peck and Robert Cormier.

"I have found other writers invariably kind, compassionate and eager to help any writer who shows evidence of discipline and talent. In all of my travels to workshops and conferences, only two writers have turned me off as cruel, vindictive and self-centered.

"If the children today wish to know more about authors, I suggest that they urge their teachers to read aloud to them in the classroom. Teachers should then allow children to write to the authors. Most will receive answers. I ALWAYS answer letters from children. I also urge children to READ READ READ. And write! I have found to my dismay that a large number of children today cannot express their thoughts on paper. I love to go to schools and libraries. The kids are such fun, and the questions they ask are a never-ending series of surprises and joys. They are honest, they tell the truth, and they WANT TO KNOW."

HOBBIES AND OTHER INTERESTS: "My family, my community, my church."

BELLINGHAM, Brenda 1931-

BRIEF ENTRY: Born August 14, 1931, in Liverpool, England. After receiving diplomas from Liverpool University and the University of Alberta, Bellingham worked as a social worker for the government of Canada, and then as a schoolteacher until 1977. Her first book, *Joanie's Magic Boots* (Tree Frog Press, 1979), centers around ten-year-old Joanie's struggle to come to terms with the reality of an unfulfilling childhood. "The youngest reader in the six-to-ten range for which the novel is recommended could hardly fail to understand Joanie Taylor's need for a little magic in her life," observed *Canadian Children's Literature.* The source of inspiration for Bellingham, however, stands firmly in reality. "I write about topics that grab my interest. Often, these arise directly from remarks made by children," she explains. Bellingham is also the author of *Two Parents Too Many* (Scholastic-TAB, 1985) and *Storm Child* (Lorimer, 1985), a tale about Isobel Macpherson, an eighteenth-century girl who trades domestic life in rural Canada for an Indian lifestyle among the people of her grandparents' tribe. "As Storm Child, she experiences a lifestyle full of love, hardship and intrigue . . . that she is 'country born' and must learn to live somewhere between teepee and trading post," wrote the *Toronto Globe and Mail.* Bellingham is currently working on more books for children, as well as researching western Canadian history. *Home and office:* 266-52249 Range Road 233, Sherwood Park, Alberta, Canada T8B 1C7.

BOWDEN, Joan Chase 1925-
(Joan Chase Bacon, Jane Godfrey, Charlotte Graham, Kathryn Kenny)

PERSONAL: Born May 1, 1925, in London, England; came to the United States in 1953, naturalized citizen, 1960; daughter of Charles William Chase (an accountant) and Adelaide M. F. (a housewife; maiden name, Godfrey) Bacon; married Archie N. Bowden, September 11, 1948; children: Frances, Andrew, Pamela. *Education:* Attended school in London, England. *Religion:* Episcopalian. *Home:* 4276 Santa Cruz Ave., San Diego, Calif. 92107.

CAREER: Stenographer in London, England, 1943-47, private secretary, 1947-49; London Films Association, London, executive secretary, 1949-50; Minneapolis-Honeywell Corp., Toronto, Ontario, Canada, executive secretary, 1951-53; writer for children, 1968—; Institute of Children's Literature, Redding Ridge, Conn., instructor, 1979—; University of California at San Diego, teacher of writing for young people, 1981—, lecturer, 1982; free-lance editor, 1982—. Guest lecturer at college writing conferences. *Member:* Authors League of America. *Awards, honors: The Bean Boy* was chosen a Children's Choice by the Children's Book Council and the International Reading Association Joint Committee, 1980, and *Strong John,* 1981; *Boston Globe-Horn Book* Honor Book for Illustration, 1980, for *Why the Tides Ebb and Flow.*

WRITINGS—All juvenile: *A New Home for Snowball* (illustrated by Jan Pyk), Golden Press, 1974; *Who Took the Top Hat Trick?* (illustrated by Jim Cummins), Golden Press, 1974; *Bear's Surprise Party* (illustrated by Jerry Scott), Golden Press, 1975; *The Waltons and the Birthday Present,* Golden Press, 1975; *The Ice Cream Parade,* Golden Press, 1976; *Ginghams and the Backward Picnic* (illustrated by Joanne Koenig), Golden Press, 1976; *The Island Adventure,* Golden Press, 1976; *The Bouncy Baby Bunny Finds His Bed* (illustrated by Christine Westerberg), Golden Press, 1976; *Something Wonderful Happened,* Concordia, 1977; *Little Gray Rabbit* (illustrated by Lorinda B. Cauley), Golden Press, 1979; *The Bean Boy* (illustrated by Sal Murdocca), Macmillan, 1979; *Why the Tides Ebb and Flow* (ALA Notable Book; *Horn Book* honor list; illustrated by Marc Brown), Houghton, 1979; *Strong John* (illustrated by S. Murdocca), Macmillan, 1980; *My Measuring Book* (illustrated by Dan Robison), Golden Press, 1980; (with Louis Corbo) *Candy Claus* (illustrated by Al Lowenheim), Oak Tree, 1986; *The World of Sandy Sandman* (illustrated by Pat Paris), Oak Tree, 1987.

"Dragonflies" series; editor; co-author with Jim Patton and Dee Patton; illustrated by Steve Pileggi; published by Oak Tree, 1986: *In Search of the Dragonflies; The Discovery of the Dragonflies; Rock with the Dragonflies; A Watcher's Guide to Dragonflies.*

Under name Joan Chase Bacon: *Thin Arnold,* Western, 1970; *The Pussycat Tiger* (illustrated by Lilian Obligado), Golden Press, 1972; *A Hat for the Queen* (illustrated by Olindo Giacomini), Golden Press, 1974; *Boo and the Flying Flews* (illustrated by Don Leake), Golden Press, 1974.

Under pseudonym Jane Godfrey: *The Dinosaur Adventure,* Golden Press, 1975.

Under pseudonym Charlotte Graham: *Elizabeth and the Magic Lamp,* Western, 1975.

Under pseudonym Kathryn Kenny: *The Mystery of the Headless Horseman,* Golden Press, 1979; *The Mystery of the Ghostly Galleon,* Golden Press, 1979; *Mystery of the Whispering Witch,* Golden Press, 1980; *Mystery of the Midnight Marauder,* Golden Press, 1980.

Contributor to adult and children's magazines, including *Humpty Dumpty, Happy Times, Wonder Time,* and *Friend.*

SIDELIGHTS: "I am a transplanted American citizen who was born in London on May 1, 1925. On this date in England, most schoolchildren dance around the maypole to celebrate May Day. Being more enchanted with maypole-dancing than

She knew exactly which rock she wanted. So she climbed into her stewpot and set sail on the great green ocean.

(From *Why the Tides Ebb and Flow* by Joan Chase Bowden. Illustrated by Marc Brown.)

JOAN CHASE BOWDEN

with writing of any kind, my progress through school was unremarkable—if you discount the fact that World War II broke out in Europe just as I was about to begin my senior years in high school.

"In spite of Hitler's shenanigans, I received a thorough grounding in the use of the English language.

"My children have, I think, inspired most of my writing. Their trials and tribulations, their triumphs and defeats, their likes and dislikes in reading, have always been watched closely.

"I began writing professionally in 1968 and sold the first children's book I ever wrote. It took me another two years to discover what I had done right! I learned, at last, by applying the old adage—seat of the pants to the seat of the chair.

"Some of my books were written for the beginning reader, a favorite audience of mine. If a child can't read, I feel he is handicapped for the rest of his life. My books are usually entertaining and have the appearance of having been rushed through my typewriter in two minutes flat, which, of course, they are not. Throughout my story, I'm trying to beckon and encourage the child to read on to discover for himself what happens next. For some children reading is difficult. These youngsters need the special encouragement which comes from reading a story entirely on their own.

"My interests revolve around children's books and the publishing world. These days, when I wear the three hats of writer, editor and teacher, it's hard to know which is the most enjoyable. I do know that it's a source of great pride when one of my students sells his or her work. It's as much fun for me as it is for the student."

BREWSTER, Patience 1952-

PERSONAL: Born October 26, 1952, in Plymouth, Mass.; daughter of Spencer Hatch (a retired executive; a trainer and exhibitor of horse and carriages) and Marietta (a trainer of riding dressage driving; maiden name, Withington) Brewster; married Holland Chauncey Gregg III (a television producer), June 18, 1977; children: Holland Chauncey IV, Marietta. *Education:* Philadelphia College of Art. B.F.A., 1974. *Home:* 643 W. Genesee, Skaneateles, N.Y. 13152. *Agent:* (Illustrations) Dilys Evans, 1123 Broadway, New York, N.Y. 10010.

CAREER: Harlow House, Plymouth, Mass., guide to Pilgrim living and crafts, 1964-73; free-lance artist in calligraphy and advertising, 1974—; part-time waitress and cook, 1974-77; author and illustrator of children's books, 1979—. Lecturer in illustration, writing, and creativity. Has executed posters for Opera Theater of Syracuse, Skaneateles Festival, "The Original Art" and "Every Page" exhibits at Master Eagle Gallery, New York City, 1985, and Houghton Mifflin Co. *Exhibitions:* Harriet Griffin Gallery, New York City, 1975-77; Renaissance Gallery, Ithaca, N.Y., 1977; Main Street Gallery, Nantucket, Mass., 1978-82; "The Original Art," Master Eagle Gallery, New York City, 1982-85; Chilmark Gallery, Martha's Vineyard, Mass., 1985. *Awards, honors:* California Reader's Choice Award, and *Booklist's* "Pick of the Lists" selection, both 1982, both for *Good as New* by Barbara Douglass; *Don't Touch My Room* was exhibited at the Bologna International Book Fair, 1985.

WRITINGS—For children; self-illustrated: (Reteller) *Dame Wiggins of Lee and Her Seven Wonderful Cats*, Crowell, 1980; *Ellsworth and the Cats from Mars* (Junior Literary Guild selection), Clarion Books, 1981; *Nobody* (Junior Literary Guild selection), Clarion Books, 1982. Also author and illustrator of "A Pampers Blue Ribbon Baby Goes through the Bunny Hole," an advertising vehicle.

Illustrator; for children: Barbara Douglass, *Good as New* (Junior Literary Guild selection), Lothrop, 1982; Morse Hamil-

PATIENCE BREWSTER

ton, *Who's Afraid of the Dark?*, Avon, 1983; M. Hamilton, *How Do You Do Mr. Birdsteps?*, Avon, 1983; Selma Boyd and Pauline Boyd, *I Met a Polar Bear*, Lothrop, 1983; Cathy Warren, *Victoria's ABC Adventure*, Lothrop, 1984; Nikki Yektai, *Sun Rain*, Four Winds, 1984; Patricia Lakin, *Don't Touch My Room*, Little, Brown, 1985. P. Laiken, *Oh, Brother*, Little, Brown, 1987; Myra C. Livingston, *Valentine Poems*, Holiday House, 1987; Sue Alexander, *"There's More, Much More," Said Squirrel*, Harcourt, 1987.

Also illustrator of textbooks for Houghton Mifflin, Co. and Harcourt Brace Jovanovich, and an anthology for Reader's Digest; contributor of illustrations to *Cricket*.

WORK IN PROGRESS: Illustrations for a book about a boy handing his bear over to a babysitter for the first time, by Elizabeth Winthrop, for Holiday House.

SIDELIGHTS: Brewster, one of six children, grew up in Plymouth, Massachusetts. "We lived adjacent to a working dairy farm. Our property housed not only a mass of energetic siblings but an ever-growing menagerie consisting of several horses and dogs and any combination of cows, sheep, goats, donkeys, chickens, peacocks, pigs, rabbits, and cats.

"I got great inspiration from the talents of my parents and grandparents. We were all encouraged in our varied interests. I never enrolled in art classes at school but preferred working at home, drawing and dabbling with an older sister's college art supplies. My high school teachers, therefore, were not too supportive of my idea of going to an art college. But my family and friends were, and I had chosen the Philadelphia College of Art. Once there, I had my first real exposure to city life and full-time concentration on art. I graduated as a printmaking major, but my four years included a lot of drawing and a thesis on bookmaking.

"After college I worked at advertising and calligraphy while showing in galleries in Massachusetts and New York and building up a portfolio. After several years of this, my husband, Holly, finally took action. I'd always been told I ought to get involved in children's books, but I never knew where to begin. Holly made appointments for me to show my work to several publishers in New York and forced me out the door. I prepared for painful rejection but we found a warm reception everywhere. That sent me into a state of elated shock.

"I had my first baby, Holland Chauncey Gregg IV, while working on my first book. Embarking on those two careers

I stopped at the corner for just a minute to look in the bakery window. ■ (From *I Met a Polar Bear* by Selma and Pauline Boyd. Illustrated by Patience Brewster.)

simultaneously taught me a lot about discipline. I learned how to work on command rather than pure inspiration. *Dame Wiggins of Lee and Her Seven Wonderful Cats* offered many opportunities to incorporate some of my growing son's expressions and positions into those of the cats in the old-fashioned nonsense verse. In *Ellsworth and the Cats from Mars,* I used his humor even more. He was beginning to talk and commented and laughed at the 'funny pictures' that occupied so much of my time.

"My daughter, Marietta, as well as my son are great sources of information as well as painfully honest critics of manuscripts and artwork going in and out of my studio.

"After years of juggling part-time illustrating with motherhood, I'm finally seeing the time approaching when, with both children in school, I will attend to writing more of my own stories to illustrate.

"I am dreaming of the day when my calendar will be empty, my house quiet, animals fed; and my studio clean so I can walk in and begin a work based totally on inspiration. I also want to do this in secret so that I will have no deadline to meet.

"Once illustrating for a living was only a dream, so there's a chance!"

As an artist, Brewster draws with "pencil and paint with inks or water colors. I use 100% rag paper, bristol smooth, or watercolor paper by Strathmore.

"My advice to newcomers or hopefuls: Use good materials. The best brushes, paints and paper. Work hard on a small portfolio that you feel proud of and then go after the best publishers first. Take advice and *don't give up.*"

Brewster has appeared on television, including "PM Magazine" and "Bud's Journal."

FOR MORE INFORMATION SEE: Junior Literary Guild, March, 1981.

BROMLEY, Dudley   1948-

BRIEF ENTRY: Born December 9, 1948, in Odessa, Tex. Author of science fiction, adventure, and mystery books for reluctant readers. Bromley's "Doomsday Journals" series (Pitman, 1981) chronicles, through the writings of fictional astronomer Dr. Carla Lancaster, scenarios of scientific catastrophies. The first book in the series, *Bedford Fever,* recounts a fever that killed thousands of people and may strike again at any time. *Comet!* is the story of the earth's last great disaster which has left few survivors. Other titles in the series are *Final Warning, Fireball, Lost Valley* and *The Seep.* Bromley is also the author of the detective book *Bad Moon* (Fearon Pitman, 1979), in which a private eye tries to unravel the mysterious death of a famous magician thirteen years earlier, and the adult basic education books *North to Oak Island* (Pitman, 1978) and *Balloon Spies* (Fearon Pitman, 1981). In addition, Bromley has contributed to the television series "Gunsmoke" and "The Rookies," and is the editor of *United States Government* (Bowmar). *Home:* P.O. Box 1207, Spokane, Wash. 99210.

FOR MORE INFORMATION SEE: Contemporary Authors, Volume 77, Gale, 1979; *International Authors and Writers Who's Who,* International Biographical Centre, 1982.

BROOK, Judith Penelope   1926-
(Judy Brook)

BRIEF ENTRY: Born December 22, 1926, in Weymouth, England. After graduating from the Chelsea School of Art, where she received two art scholarships, Brook was employed part time for ten years at the Hans Schleger and Associates studio, during which time she also illustrated children's books. Among the dozens of books she illustrated during the fifties and sixties is Margery Sharp's *The Rescuers,* commended by the Carnegie Award committee. The first books Brook wrote and illustrated were in the "Tim Mouse" series (World's Work), which featured Tim Mouse and Mr. Brown, a hedgehog, in assorted adventures. In *Tim Mouse Visits the Farm* (1968), Tim and Mr. Brown go to Barleybeans Farm for some milk. When Tim whistles at one of the cows, the whole barnyard is thrown into a panic. "The wild flight of the cows over fields and through a quiet English village provides gentle humor and enough action to hold the interest of young children," noted a reviewer for *School Library Journal.*

In *Tim Mouse Goes down the Stream* (1969), Tim and Mr. Brown rescue Willy Frog, who has been captured by the water rats. "Illustrations in black and white and pastel color wash portray the quiet loveliness of the English countryside," observed *School Library Journal,* "in a manner reminiscent of E. H. Shepard's illustrations for Kenneth Grahame's *Wind in the Willows.*" Other books in the series are *Tim Mouse and the Major* (1967), *Tim Mouse and Helen Mouse* (1970), and *Tim Mouse and Father Christmas* (1971). Brook has also written and illustrated *Noah's Ark* (1972), a modern-day version of the biblical story. "The delightful illustrations range from pastel to vivid and are full of the detailed, cheerful Peter Spier-like goings-on that pre-schoolers love," wrote *New York Times Book Review.* This World's Work series also includes *Mrs. Noah and the Animals* (1977) and *Mrs. Noah's ABC, 123* (1979). Among Brook's other books, also published by World's Work, are *Belinda* (1975), *Belinda and Father Christmas* (1978), *Around the Clock* (1980), and *Hector and Harriet, the Night Hamsters* (1984).

BROWN, Joseph E(dward)   1929-

BRIEF ENTRY: Born December 14, 1929, in San Francisco, Calif. Brown has written a number of young adult books about nature, published by Dodd. *The Sea's Harvest: The Story of Aquaculture* (1975), is an exploration of sea life and how it can be cultivated to offset food shortages. "... His use of statistics and clear, meaningful photographs, makes this a valuable contribution to materials on ocean study," noted *Booklist.* A comprehensive study of the seal is the focus of *Wonders of Seals and Sea Lions* (1976). "No other source has as much information for this age group, and since the seal is a favorite with many children, this is bound to be appealing," noted a reviewer in *School Library Journal.* Other nature books include *Wonders of a Kelp Forest* (1974) and *Rescue from Extinction* (1981).

The Return of the Brown Pelican (Louisiana State University Press, 1983), written for an older audience, was hailed in *Library Journal* as "an attractive, well-written book that should find a good audience in both public and undergraduate libraries." This book concerns the plight of the endangered pelican and the successful attempts to provide new homes for these displaced birds. *Publishers Weekly* wrote, "This is for everybody interested in birds or conservation." Brown has also written *Oil Spills* (Dodd, 1978), *The Mormon Trek West* (Doubleday, 1980), and *Yesterday's Wings* (Doubleday, 1982), about World War II military aircraft. In addition, he is the author of guidebooks on national parks of the Pacific Southwest and Hawaii. *Residence:* San Diego, Calif.

FOR MORE INFORMATION SEE: Contemporary Authors, New Revision Series, Volume 6, Gale, 1982.

BROWN, Roy (Frederick)   1921-1982

PERSONAL: Born December 10, 1921, in Vancouver, British Columbia, Canada; died September 14, 1982; married Wendy Landman; children: two sons, two daughters. *Residence:* Gravesend, Kent, England.

CAREER: Author. Primary school teacher, 1946-69; Helen Allison School for Autistic Children, Gravesend, Kent, England, deputy headmaster, 1969-75. Writer for British television program "Jackanory." *Military service:* Royal Air Force, four years. *Awards, honors: The Viaduct* was one of Child Study Association of America's Children's Books of the Year, 1968, *The Day of the Pigeons,* 1969, *Escape the River,* 1972, and *The White Sparrow,* 1975; *Find Debbie!* was named one of *School Library Journal's* Best Books, 1976; *The Cage* was selected one of New York Public Library's Books for the Teen Age, 1980 and 1981.

ROY BROWN

In due course, Bruin the Bear arrived at Reynard's chief fortress. . . . ■ (From *Reynard the Fox,* retold by Roy Brown. Illustrated by John Vernon Lord.)

WRITINGS—Juvenile: *A Book of Saints,* Cassell, 1959; *The Children's Book of Old Testament Stories* (illustrated by Hugh T. Marshall), Harrap, 1959.

(Editor) Carlo Collodi, *The Children's Pinocchio* (illustrated by Sheila Rose), Harrap, 1960; (editor) Johanna Spyri, *The Children's Heidi* (illustrated by Sheila Connelly), Harrap, 1963; *Port of Call* (illustrated by Jack Trodd), Abelard (New York), 1965; *The Legend of Ulysses* (illustrated by Mario Logli and Gabriele Santini), Hamlyn, 1965; (with William Stuart Thomson) *The Battle against Fire* (illustrated by James Hunt), Abelard, 1966; *A Saturday in Pudney* (illustrated by J. Hunt), Abelard, 1966, Macmillan, 1968, new edition, Hutchinson, 1968; *The Viaduct* (illustrated by J. Hunt), Abelard, 1967, Macmillan, 1968; *The House on the Green* (illustrated by Trevor Parkin), Oliver & Boyd, 1967; *Little Brown Mouse* (illustrated by Constance Marshall), University of London Press, 1967; *The Wonderful Weathercock* (illustrated by Ferelith Eccles Williams), University of London Press, 1967; *The Day of the Pigeons* (illustrated by J. Hunt), Abelard, 1968, Macmillan, 1969; *The Saturday Man: As Told on "Jackanory" by*

Joe Melia (illustrated by Trevor Ridley), British Broadcasting Corp., 1969; (reteller) Joseph Jacobs, *Reynard the Fox* (illustrated by John Vernon Lord), Abelard (New York), 1969; *The Wapping Warrior* (illustrated by J. Hunt), Chatto & Windus, 1969.

The River (illustrated by J. Hunt), Abelard, 1970, published as *Escape the River,* Seabury, 1972; *The Battle of Saint Street* (illustrated by J. Hunt), Macmillan, 1971; *The Thunder Pool* (illustrated by Gareth Floyd), Abelard, 1971; *Flight of Sparrows,* Abelard, 1972, Macmillan, 1973; *Bolt Hole,* Abelard, 1973, published as *No Through Road,* Seabury, 1974; *The White Sparrow,* Abelard, 1974, Seabury, 1975; *Shep the Second* (illustrated by Clifford Bayly), Abelard, 1975; *The Siblings,* Abelard, 1975, published as *Find Debbie!,* Seabury, 1976; *The Million Pound Mouse* (illustrated by Joanna Stubbs), Abelard, 1975; *The Cage,* Abelard, 1976, Seabury, 1977; *Chubb on the Trail* (illustrated by Margaret Belsky), Abelard, 1976; *The Big Test . . . and the Kidnapping That Failed* (illustrated by J. Hunt), Hutchinson, 1976; *A Nag Called Wednesday* (illustrated by Jeroo Roy), Hutchinson, 1977; *Chubb to the Rescue,* Abelard, 1977; *The Swing of the Gate,* Seabury, 1978; *Trojan Rides Again* (illustrated by Ivan Hissey), Abelard, 1978; *Undercover Boy* (illustrated by Pauline Carr), Andersen Press, 1978; *Cover Drive,* Abelard, 1979; *Chips and the Crossword Gang* (illustrated by P. Carr), Andersen Press, 1979; *Chubb Catches a Cold* (illustrated by M. Belsky), Abelard, 1979.

Collision Course, Andersen Press, 1980, published as *Suicide Course,* Clarion Books, 1980; *Octopus,* Andersen Press, 1981; *Chips and the River Rat* (illustrated by Victoria Cooper), Andersen Press, 1981; *Chips and the Black Moth* (illustrated by V. Cooper), Andersen Press, 1982.

Also author of numerous short stories and of a series of radio plays, ''News Extra!'' 1973.

SIDELIGHTS: Although Brown is best remembered as an English author of books for children, he began his professional career as a primary school teacher and later served as the deputy headmaster at the Helen Allison School for autistic children in Gravesend, Kent, England. Experience in this special handicap helped to produce his fourth novel, *Escape the River,* which featured a boy with autistic behavior.

The author of more than thirty books for young people, Brown wrote the first of his numerous mystery and suspense novels, *A Saturday in Pudney,* in 1966. Other books followed, all with settings in London, at almost yearly intervals. His detective series featured Chips Regan and included such titles as: *Undercover Boy, Chips and the Crossword Gang,* and *Chips and the Black Moth.* Brown was also a creator for the popular British television program, ''Jackanory.'' In addition, two of his books, *A Saturday in Pudney* and *The Day of the Pigeons* were adapted into movies and *The Viaduct* was aired twice on British television. Bernard Ashley, a friend, described Brown as an ''apologetic, unpretentious man who just happened to have found out a thing or two a step before you: the sort of man we give school assemblies about: a person of talent, using it well, and with all the humility in the world.'' [Bernard Ashley, ''Roy Brown—A Personal Appreciation,'' *Junior Bookshelf,* December, 1982.[1]]

Ashley also commented on the reaction that Brown had to the publication of his first novel. ''The school was King's Farm, Gravesend, and it was there, in the gents' lavatory while we washed our hands—typically removed from the public glare

Their damp clothing had a uniform grayness and shabbiness of rough travel. ■ (Jacket illustration by Kenneth Francis Dewey from *Flight of Sparrows* by Roy Brown.)

of the staffroom—that Roy told me of his success: a first novel accepted by Abelard Schuman, *A Saturday in Pudney*. His round face smiled like a gleeful schoolboy's, still red from his lunch-time walk home to see what the post had brought. It had brought him all he could have wished, that day—but he didn't want to bore me. . . .

''Roy had been writing for some time; real professional stuff to order—Rupert Bear scripts, Lives of the Saints re-told: and now he'd got a novel off the ground, could spread his wings. At home in his 1930's semi he had the front room looking like Fleet Street, at school he had one of the best-organized writing workshops for children I've seen. In both areas of his life he made big demands on himself—and yet he read what I gave him to look at as if he really wanted to; made constructive comments, compared notes, perhaps to add, in a typical Roy Brown way: 'Don't want to take any notice of me—could be wrong, of course—but it seems to me these publishers quite like their stuff sent in on *quarto*. And double-spaced: seem to go a lot on double-spaced. Black ribbon, perhaps? Just a thought. . . .' Not the successful author telling the novice, but the apologetic, unpretentious man who just happened to have found out a thing or two a step before you. . . .

''He wrote marvellous books. As Graham Greene created Greeneland, so Roy Brown had his Brownland: a place edged with foggy docks, stitched with railway sidings; dotted with warm tea-steamed interiors where the doors could never quite shut out the sound of the river. A place of troubled children, where plain-clothed policemen knew what kids were all about, their coat collars turned up against the chill of a failing society. A land of sensitivity, insight, atmosphere, humour, excitement; and its writing run through with a quiet, undemonstrative line in description that had you throwing down your pen in disappointment.''[1]

Brown died at the age of sixty-one, on September 14, 1982. Some of his books have been translated into German, Italian, Swedish, French, and Japanese.

FOR MORE INFORMATION SEE: Children's Literature in Education, November, 1971; Doris de Montreville and Elizabeth D. Crawford, editors, *Fourth Book of Junior Authors and Illustrators*, H. W. Wilson, 1978; D. L. Kirkpatrick, editor, *Twentieth-Century Children's Writers*, St. Martin's, 1978, 2nd edition, 1983; Bernard Ashley, ''Roy Brown—A Personal Appreciation,'' *Junior Bookshelf*, December, 1982.

CALMENSON, Stephanie 1952-
(Lyn Calder)

PERSONAL: Born November 28, 1952, in Brooklyn, N.Y.; daughter of Kermit (a podiatrist and educator) and Edith (a medical secretary; maiden name, Goldberg) Calmenson. *Education:* Brooklyn College of the City University of New York, B.A. (magna cum laude), 1973; New York University, M.A., 1976. *Home:* 150 East 18th St., Apt. 2P, New York, N.Y. 10003.

CAREER: Teacher of early childhood grades at public schools in Brooklyn, N.Y., 1974-75; Doubleday & Co., New York City, editor, 1976-80; Parents Magazine Press, New York City, editorial director, 1980-84; author of children's books. *Member:* Society of Children's Book Writers, Mystery Writers of America.

WRITINGS—Juvenile: (Editor) *Never Take a Pig to Lunch and Other Funny Poems about Animals* (illustrated by Hilary

STEPHANIE CALMENSON

Knight), Doubleday, 1982; *One Little Monkey* (illustrated by Ellen Appleby), Parents Magazine Press, 1982; *That's Not Fair!*, Grosset, 1983; *The Kindergarten Book* (illustrated by Beth L. Weiner), Grosset, 1983; *The Birthday Hat: A Grandma Potamus Story* (illustrated by Susan Gantner), Grosset, 1983; *Where is Grandma Potamus?* (illustrated by S. Gantner), Grosset, 1983; *Where Will the Animals Stay?* (illustrated by E. Appleby), Parents Magazine Press, 1983; *The Afterschool Book* (illustrated by B. L. Weiner), Grosset, 1984; *Ten Furry Monsters* (illustrated by Maxie Chambliss), Parents Magazine Press, 1984; *All Aboard the Goodnight Train* (illustrated by Normand Chartier), Putnam, 1984.

Waggleby of Fraggle Rock (illustrated by Barbara McClintock), Holt, 1985; *Rainy Day Walk*, Parachute Press, 1985; *The Shaggy Little Monster* (illustrated by M. Chambliss), Simon & Schuster, 1986; *The Little Bunny* (illustrated by M. Chambliss), Simon & Schuster, 1986; *The Little Chick* (illustrated by M. Chambliss), Simon & Schuster, 1986; (compiler with Joanna Cole) *The Laugh Book: A New Treasury of Humor for Children* (illustrated by Marilyn Hafner), Doubleday, 1986; (compiler with J. Cole) *The Read-Aloud Treasury for Young Children* (illustrated by Ann Schweninger), Doubleday, 1987; *Fido* (illustrated by M. Chambliss), Scholastic, 1987; *The Busy Garage*, Parachute Press, 1987; *Who Said Moo?*, Parachute Press, 1987; *A Visit to the Firehouse*, Parachute Press, 1987; *The Giggle Book*, Parents Magazine Press, 1987; *The Cabbage Patch Talking Kids' Diary*, Parachute Press, 1988; *Where's Rufus*, Parents Magazine Press, 1988; *Bathtime*, Parents Mag-

(From *The Laugh Book: A New Treasury of Humor for Children,* compiled by Joanna Cole and Stephanie Calmenson. Illustrated by Marylin Hafner.)

azine Press, 1988; *What Do the Animals Say?*, Parents Magazine Press, 1988, *All about Me*, Parents Magazine Press, 1988; *The Children's Aesop* (illustrated by Robert Byrd), Doubleday, 1988; *What Am I?* (illustrated by Karen Gundersheimer), Harper, 1988. Also author of *Beginning Sounds: A Little People Workbook*, published by Parachute Press.

All published by Western: *My Book of the Seasons*, 1982; *Barney's Sand Castle* (illustrated by Sheila Becker), 1983; *Bambi and the Butterfly*, 1983; *The Three Bears*, 1983; *Ten Items or Less*, 1985; *The Toy Book*, 1986; *Babies*, 1986; *The Sesame Street ABC Book*, 1986; *Little Duck's Moving Day*, 1986; *The Sesame Street Book of First Times*, 1986; *Tiger's Bedtime*, 1987; *The Bambi Book*, 1987; *One Red Shoe (The Other One's Blue!)*, 1987; *Spaghetti Manners*, 1987; *Little Duck and the New Baby*, 1988.

Under pseudonym, Lyn Calder: *Happy Birthday, Buddy Blue: A Rainbow Brite Story*, Western, 1985; *Blast Off, Barefoot Bear!*, Cloverdale Press, 1985; *Gobo and the Prize from Outer Space* (illustrated by Frederic Marvin), Holt, 1986; *The Gloworm Bedtime Book* (illustrated by Toni Scribner), Random House, 1986. Also author under pseudonym, Lyn Calder of *The Little Red Hen* and *Little Red Riding Hood*.

Contributor to textbooks, workbooks and teacher's guides for D. C. Heath and Macmillan Educational Publishing. Contributor of features and stories to *Parents, Humpty Dumpty* and *Children's Digest*.

WORK IN PROGRESS: Wanted: Warm, Furry Friend, illustrated by Amy Schwartz, to be published by Macmillan; several picture books and anthologies.

SIDELIGHTS: "I am often asked how I came to be a children's book writer. Some might imagine that I spent my childhood furiously filling up notebooks with wild and wonderful stories. I didn't. I never even considered the possibility that I might someday earn my living as a writer. For me, having found work I enjoy so much is a happy surprise.

"There are two things I remember that might have been clues. The first was that from the day I learned to read, I never missed reading a word on a copyright page. No matter how tiny the notice, or how long the roman numeral copyright date, I read it. It was not that I dreamed of seeing my name there someday. It was just that I wanted to know every inch of this amazing thing called a book.

"The second clue, which came somewhat later and has lasted to this day, was that as soon as I learned to write, I wrote letters. I wrote to a pen pal on the other side of the world; I wrote to friends and family when I went away to summer camp; I wrote to companies and to magazines, letting them know what I thought of their product or point of view. I see now that this was a good way to begin writing because letters are not scrutinized the way school compositions are. (And I would do anything to avoid writing school compositions!)

"The one thing I have always been sure of is that I wanted to work with children in some way. So I pursued a degree in elementary education. In the end, I taught only briefly, being a casualty of a city-wide budget crisis, but I turned to something related, finding a job as an editorial secretary (eventually becoming an editorial director) for a children's book publisher. In the evenings I went to graduate school and it was there that I took a course called, 'Writing for Children.' The first story I wrote was called 'Buffy's Wink.' It needed work, but everyone seemed to like it and the story was eventually published

in a children's magazine. Over the next few years several professors and editors, to whom I will always be grateful, encouraged me to keep on writing. And I have never stopped.

"I assume that many of the people reading this article have been flirting with the idea of writing professionally. To those people I would say, try looking for clues of your own. Do you write lots of letters, as I did? Do you leave more notes than necessary on the refrigerator door? When the bathroom gets steamy, do you find yourself writing poems on the mirror? Don't stop there. Take the next step. Give yourself a writing assignment with a specific market in mind. Or take a writing course to get some feedback on your work. You may be in for a happy surprise."

CAMPBELL, Rod 1945-

PERSONAL: Born May 4, 1945, in Scotland; son of Charles Edward (a carpenter) and Isabella (a housewife; maiden name, Munro) Campbell. *Education:* University College of Rhodesia and Nyasaland (now University of Zimbabwe), B.Sc., 1966, M. Phil., 1968; University College Cardiff, graduate study, 1968-69; University of Nottingham, Ph.D., 1971; University of Rhodesia (now University of Zimbabwe), postdoctoral study, 1971-72. *Home and office:* 19 Hazeldon Rd., London SE4, England.

CAREER: Full-time artist, London, England, 1972-81; illustrator and author of children's books, 1980—. Has also worked part-time as a picture-framer, in an art gallery, and as a decorator. *Awards, honors:* American Institute of Graphic Arts Certificate of Excellence, 1983, and Book Show, 1984, both for *Dear Zoo; Buster's Bedtime* was exhibited at Bologna International Children's Book Fair, 1985.

WRITINGS—Self-illustrated; published by Abelard-Schuman, except as noted: *Dressing Up*, 1980; *Great, Greater, Greatest*,

ROD CAMPBELL

Let's fill the laundry basket!

Look who's here!

(From *Buster's Morning* by Rod Campbell. Illustrated by the author.)

1980; *An A.B.C.*, 1980; *A Grand Parade Counting Book*, 1980; *Charlie Clown*, 1981; *Nigel Knight*, 1981; *Eddie Engine-Drive*, 1981; *Freddie Fireman*, 1981; *Gertie Gardener*, 1981; *Nancy Nurse*, 1981; *All Dressed Up*, 1981; *Rod Campbell's Book of Board Games*, 1982, Prentice-Hall, 1984; *Wheels*, 1982, Peter Bedrick, 1985; *Dear Zoo*, 1982, Four Winds, 1983, miniature edition, Blackie, 1987, Macmillan, 1988; *Pocket Wheels!* (4 books; includes *Big and Strong* and *Speed*), 1982, Price, Stern, 1985; *Look Inside! All Kinds of Places*, 1983, Peter Bedrick, 1984; *Look Inside! Land, Sea, Air*, 1983, Peter Bedrick, 1984; *Rod Campbell's Magic Circus*, 1983; *Rod Campbell's Magic Fairground*, 1983; *My Farm*, Blackie, 1983; *My Garden*, Blackie, 1983; *My Pets*, Blackie, 1983; *My Zoo*, Blackie, 1983; *Oh Dear!*, Blackie, 1983, Four Winds, 1984; *Rod Campbell's Noisy Book*, Blackie, 1983; *Pet Shop*, Scholastic, 1984; *Baby Animals*, Scholastic, 1984; *Circus Monkeys*, Scholastic, 1984; *Toy Soldiers*, Scholastic, 1984; *Buster's Morning*, Blackie, 1984; *Buster's Afternoon*, Blackie, 1984; *From Gran*, Blackie, 1984; *Take the Wheel*, Blackie, 1984; *Look Up at the Sky*, Blackie, 1984, Peter Bedrick, 1986; *Lots of Animals*, Blackie, 1984, Peter Bedrick, 1986; *What Colour Is That?*, Blackie, 1984, published as *What Color Is That?*, Peter Bedrick, 1986; *How Many Hats?*, Blackie, 1984, Peter Bedrick, 1986; *Henry's Busy Day*, Viking Kestrel, 1984.

Big and Strong, Blackie, 1985; *Cars and Trucks*, Blackie, 1985; *Road Builders*, Blackie, 1985; *Speed!*, Blackie, 1985; *Funwheels with Moving Parts!*, Simon & Schuster, 1985; *Playwheels with Moving Parts*, Simon & Schuster, 1985; *Buster's Bedtime*, Blackie, 1985; *Misty's Mischief*, Viking Kestrel, 1985; *I'm a Mechanic*, Barron, 1986; *I'm a Nurse*, Barron, 1986; *My Bath*, Blackie, 1986; *My Favourite Things*, Blackie, 1986; *My Teatime*, Blackie, 1986; *My Toys*, Blackie, 1986; *My Day*, Collins, 1986; *It's Mine*, Blackie, 1987, Macmillan, 1988; *Lift the Flap ABC*, Blackie, 1987; *Lift the Flap 123*, Blackie, 1987.

WORK IN PROGRESS: Two dressing books with split pages, *Buster Keeps Warm* and *Buster Gets Dressed;* a set of four basic concept books for the nursery—ABC, numbers, shapes, and colors.

SIDELIGHTS: "I have come to the world of children's books quite late. I was brought up in Rhodesia and from an early age had an interest in, and talent for drawing. There were no art schools, and the prevailing attitude regarded art as a hobby at best, so I went to university to train as a teacher. However, I stayed on after my degree and did research and eventually came to England on a scholarship to do a Ph.D. in organic chemistry. During this period I had continued to draw and paint, and I finally decided that this was what I really wanted to do, so I gave up a scientific career, to everyone's horror, and came to London where I have been ever since. I supported myself with various part-time jobs while continuing to paint.

"Toward the end of 1978 I had produced some simple drawings of toys for my own amusement and sent them off to a toy manufacturer who commissioned a mobile and one or two other pieces of artwork. At about the same time a friend took some work in to Blackie, the publisher, who was looking for an illustrator for some little books for very young children—a very happy coincidence. This was the beginning of a long association with them and my gradual absorption into the world of children's books.

"My area within this world is very much that of the under fives—indeed it has found me, rather than the other way around! After the initial books I did, I regarded *Dear Zoo* as my real starting point as I wrote the words and did the pictures, in fact conceived the idea and layout. This has been true for all subsequent books. I have done a number of flap books now, and feel they are an important type of book for young children, especially those who can't yet read. The flaps appeal to children's curiosity and afford an element of physical participation. These sorts of books have been labelled 'novelty' books and have generally become rather complicated and specialized, in fact more for adults than children. This is certainly true of 'pop-ups.' I feel that a novelty element will always be legitimate for certain books for the very young where one is bridging the toy/book gap, so long as the novelty element is simple and integral to the idea of the book.

"Apart from flap books I have done a book with plastic wheels which, on turning the board pages, becomes entirely different vehicles. On the last page of *Henry's Busy Day* where Henry the dog is asleep in his basket, one can stroke his furry coat because it is made of fake fur! *Magic Circus* and *Magic Fairground* were an attempt to use simple pop-up mechanisms in an appropriate way for the very young.

"The amount of writing I have done has been quite small, but it's very important to get it right. There are so many books for the very young that are too adult, in my view, presenting an adult's attitude and humor, often in a quirky way, too. I think any storyline should be quite simple, and for the very young repetitive elements are vital. Words which have a nice sound to them, or familiar words, will quickly be picked up by the child. To a small child repetition is not boring. On completing the idea for *Dear Zoo,* I tried the dummy out on a friend's three year old. On reaching the last page he said, 'again!' and this happened three times!! I was fascinated that to the child repetition did not mean boredom, but rather a re-experiencing of a pleasant experience. Also, knowing what is to come provides a wonderful sense of security which allows one to get excited, scared, etc. in complete safety.

"When people ask me what I do, I find it difficult to answer as I don't see myself as an illustrator or an author. I find playing around with an idea for a book a very exciting process—taking an idea and working out the means and format that suit it best, then developing the illustrations and story. I want to make books for the under fives that are fun, warm, and reassuring. Well, that's a rationalization I suppose! I actually make books that please me; they are done for me in the first instance, and the doing of them allows me free play with whatever childlike intuitions I may have, and personally I feel that the world of the young child should be warm, reassuring, and fun. Learning should be fun and completely unconscious at this age, and that's a great challenge—to convey simple ideas and concepts in an entertaining way, in a visual and written language that the child not only feels at home in, but positively delights in!

"My own childhood up to the age of six is an almost complete blank, so perhaps I have now been given the opportunity of discovering it, or at least participating in that very magical, innocent part of one's development. I go to schools and libraries from time to time, drawing for groups of children four to seven years old, which is very instructive. I think it important to keep in touch with children and, happily, I get on well with them. One does not get ideas directly from them, but it serves to remind one of what sort of things amuses them or they respond to. I find it a necessary part of my activity in children's books."

HOBBIES AND OTHER INTERESTS: "My work is my hobby. My interests extend to all aspects of art and design."

CAREW, Jan (Rynveld) 1925-

PERSONAL: Born September 24, 1925, in Agricola, Guyana, South America; son of Charles Alan (a planter) and Kathleen (a teacher; maiden name, Robertson) Carew; married Joy Gleason (a university lecturer), September 28, 1975; children: Lisa Gioconda, Christopher David. *Education:* Attended Howard University, 1945-46, and Western Reserve University (now Case Western Reserve University), 1946-48; Charles University, Prague, D.Sc., 1951; Sorbonne, University of Paris, post-doctoral studies. *Office:* Department of African-American Studies, Northwestern University, 2003 Sheridan Rd., Evanston, Ill. 60201.

CAREER: Customs officer in British Colonial Civil Service, Georgetown, Guyana, 1940-43; price control officer for government of Trinidad, Port-of-Spain, 1943-44; artist and writer in Paris, France, and Amsterdam, Holland, 1950-51; toured as an actor/director trainee with Laurence Olivier Productions, 1953-55; University of London, England, lecturer in race relations, 1953-59; director of culture, government of British Guyana, 1962; Latin American correspondent for *London Observer,* 1962; artist and writer under contract to Associated Television (London) on island of Ibiza, Spain, 1963-64; advisor to the publicity secretariat of the government of Ghana, 1965-66; artist and writer, commissioned by Canadian Broadcasting Co. (CBC) to do numerous programs in Toronto, Ontario, 1966-69; Princeton University, Princeton, N.J., lecturer in Third World literature and creative writing, 1969-1972; Northwestern University, Evanston, Ill., professor of African-American and Third World studies, 1973—, chairman of department of African-American studies, 1973-76.

Consultant for English language and literature programs at New York University, 1968-73; guest lecturer at Livingston College, Douglass College, and Rutgers University, 1969-72; guest lecturer at University of Surinam Teacher's Training College, 1975; visiting professor, Hampshire College, 1986-87. Exhibitions of paintings at Imperial Institute, London, 1948; Cleveland Public Library, Ohio, 1949; Commonwealth Institute, London, England, 1953. Broadcaster of regular weekly programs for British Broadcasting Corp. (BBC) in London, 1953-59. Toured Federal Republic of Germany as an official guest of the Ministry of Culture, 1963 and 1967, and the Soviet Union as a guest of the Soviet Writer's Union, 1963 and 1965. Consultant, National Council of Churches, Fifth Commission, 1975—, Pan African Skills Project, Inc., 1978—, Organization of American States, Cultural Division, 1980—, Field Museum of Natural History, Chicago, Ill., 1983—, Futures Conference Project, 1986—; director of Caribbean Foundation for Rural Development and Education, 1975—; advisor, Appropriate Technology, government of Jamaica, 1976-78, Illinois

JAN CAREW

He was clenching his fist and holding his hand high above his head. ■ (From *The Third Gift* by Jan Carew. Illustrated by Leo and Diane Dillon.)

Senate Committee on Higher Education, 1984—; co-founder and co-director of Third World Energy Institute International, 1977—, Caribbean Society for Culture and Science, 1978—, Jamaica Support Committee, 1980; member of board of directors, Linear Alpha, Inc., 1978—; president of Association of Caribbean Studies, 1982—; chairman of executive board, Black Press Institute, 1982—; advisor and member of board of directors, Kindred Spirits Project, 1982—.

MEMBER: American Union of Writers, American Association of University Professors. *Awards, honors:* "The Big Pride" (television play) was selected as best play of the year by the *London Daily Mirror*, 1964; Canada Council grant, 1969, for significant contributions to the arts; Burton International Fellowship from Harvard University Graduate School of Education, 1973 and 1974; Illinois Arts Council Award for fiction,

1974, for short story "Ti-Zek"; American Institute of Graphic Arts Certificate of Excellence, 1974, for *The Third Gift;* Pushcart Prize, 1979-80, for essay "The Caribbean Writer and Exile"; Walter Rodney Award from the Association of Caribbean Studies, 1985; National Film Institute Award for screen play "Black Midas," 1985.

WRITINGS—Juvenile: *The Third Gift* (illustrated by Leo Dillon and Diane Dillon), Little, Brown, 1974; *Children of the Sun* (illustrated by L. Dillon and D. Dillon), Little, Brown, 1978. Also author of seven books in the "Knockouts" series, published by Longmans.

Other: *Streets of Eternity* (poetry), privately printed, 1950; *Black Midas* (novel), Secker & Warburg, 1958, published as *A Touch of Midas*, Coward, 1959; *The Wild Coast* (novel),

Secker & Warburg, 1958; *The Last Barbarian* (novel), Secker & Warburg, 1960; *Moscow Is Not My Mecca* (novel), Secker & Warburg, 1964, published as *Green Winter*, Stein & Day, 1965; (contributor) Andrew Salkey, editor, *Breaklight* (poetry), Hamish Hamilton, 1971; (contributor) Cecil Gray, editor, *Bite In* (poetry), T. Nelson, 1971; *Sea Drums in My Blood* (poetry), New Voices (Trinidad), 1981; *Grenada: The Hour Will Strike Again* (history), International Organization of Journalists Press, 1985; *Fulcrums of Change: Origins of Racism in the Americas and Other Essays*, Africa World, 1987; *The Riverman* (novella), Africa World Press, 1987; *The Sisters* (novella), Africa World Press, 1987.

Plays: "Miracle in Lime Lane" (adaptation of a play by Coventry Taylor), produced in Spanish Town, Jamaica, 1962; "The University of Hunger" (three-act), produced in Georgetown, Guyana, at Georgetown Theatre, 1966; "Gentlemen Be Seated," produced in Belgrade, Yugoslavia, 1967; *Black Horse, Pale Rider* (two-act), University of the West Indies Extramural Department, 1970; *Behind God's Back*, Carifesta, Volume II, 1975; "The Peace Play," 1987.

Television plays; all written for Associated Television, London, 1963-64, except as indicated: "The Big Pride," "The Day of the Fox," "Exile from the Sun," "The Baron of South Boulevard," "No Gown for Peter," "The Raiders," "The Smugglers," "A Roof of Stars," "The Conversion of Tiho," "Behind God's Back," Canadian Broadcasting Co., 1969.

Radio plays; broadcast by British Broadcasting Corp., 1960-69: "Song of the Riverman," "The Riverman," "The University of Hunger," "The Legend of Nameless Mountain," "Ata," "Anancy and Tiger."

Work represented in several anthologies, including *Stories from the Caribbean*, edited by A. Salkey, Elek, 1965; *Island Voices*, edited by A. Salkey, Liveright, 1970; *West Indian Stories*, edited by A. Salkey, (London), 1971; *New Writing in the Caribbean*, edited by A. J. Seymour, Guyana Lithographic, 1972; *Carifesta Anthology*, edited by A. J. Seymour, Guyana Lithographic, 1972; *The Sun's Eye*, edited by Anna Walmsley, (London), 1973; *Anthology of Writing in English*, T. Nelson, 1977.

Contributor of articles, short stories and essays to *New England Review and Bread Loaf Quarterly*, *New York Times*, *Saturday Review*, *New Statesman*, *African Review*, *Listener*, *Journal of African Civilizations*, *Black Press Review*, *New Deliberations*, *Journal of the Association of Caribbean Studies*, *Black American Literature Forum*, *Pacific Quarterly*, *Race and Class*, and other periodicals. Editor of *De Kim* (multilingual poetry magazine in Amsterdam), 1951; *Kensington Post* (London newspaper), 1953, and *African Review*, 1965-66; reviewer for *John O'London's Weekly*, *Art News and Review* and British Broadcasting Company, 1963-64; publisher of *Cotopaxi* (a third-world literary magazine), 1969; member of editorial board, *Obsidian, Journal of the Association of Caribbean Studies*, and *Journal of African Civilizations*, 1976—.

WORK IN PROGRESS: A biography of Maurice Bishop, to be published by the International Organization of Journalists Press; *Green Mansions of the Sun*, a novel; *An Anthology of Latin American Writing in Transition*; *The Destruction of Caribbean Civilization*, an historical account of the first forty years of the Columbia era; *A Study of Three Maroon Wars*, about the Black-Seminole wars in Florida, Palmares, and the Maroon wars in Surinam; "Pageant of the Gods," a play for the stage; *Cry Black Power*, completed novel.

SIDELIGHTS: When asked to comment on the aspirations of Third World peoples and on how he expressed his philosophy of life through his writing, Carew shared the following passages from his novel in progress, *Green Mansions of the Sun:* "... His Carib hero, Kai, said that everyone has a place, a piece of terrain, a spot on earth that was his very own, like the black leopard ... if a hunter tried to kill him, that leopard would find his spot in the forest, and once he found it—look out hunter—for on his turf, he was invincible!

"This was something that Atlassa understood, not just the trappings, but the power to make the lowliest believe in themselves. Atlassa succeeded where no one else had, he began with the most despised, he made us all see ourselves as we really were. After his return, he started out by listening to us. No one had ever listened since Christobal and his cutthroat sailors had been discovered by the Amer-indians on their beaches.... After that, it was a long history of colonizers shouting orders, and the colonized never talking back. After long years of listening, Atlassa showed us new images of ourselves without the distortions."

In his essay, "The Caribbean Writer and Exile," Carew elaborated on his philosophy, "The Carribean writer today is a creature balanced between limbo and nothingness, exile abroad and homelessness at home, between the people on the one hand and the creole and the colonizer on the other.... The writer is, therefore, islanded in the midst of marginal tides of sorrow, despair, hope, whirlpools of anxiety, cataracts of rage. He is the most articulate member of the marginal class, articulate, that is, with the written word. There are others of his class who speak to the mind's ear with music—the calypso, raggae, the folksong—and who speak with immediacy and a sensuous ease to a much vaster audience.... At a time when independence, that is, an anthem, a flag and a color on the map, brings into sharper focus questions of national identity and liberation, the Caribbean writer is faced with harsh choices. The end of his marginal status is now in sight. As an honorary member of the marginal class he has both consciously and unconsciously internalized the mounting chaos that is pushing this class inexorably, not into revolution but revolutionary situations....

"They are often unsure of what they are for, but are absolutely certain of what they're against: the corrupt, bullying, pompous, dishonest, cruel, incompetent and often mindless regimes under which they live.... 'All people have a right to share the waters of the River of Life and to drink with their own cups, but our cups have been broken' laments the Carib poem-hymn. The writer, artist, musician, is directly involved in the creative process of reshaping the broken cups.... Therefore, while we shape exquisite new cups, we must side by side with the disinherited millions of the Third World, confront those who would deny us our fair share of the waters of the River of Life...."

Carew's works have been published in foreign languages including, Japanese, Spanish, Russian, and German.

FOR MORE INFORMATION SEE: James Vinson and D. L. Kirkpatrick, editors, *Contemporary Novelists*, 2nd edition, St. Martin's, 1972; Jan Carew, "Walking with Caesar," *New Writing in the Caribbean*, 1972; *Journal of Black Studies*, 1977.

It is impossible to read properly without using all one's engine-power. If we are not tired after reading, common-sense is not in us.

—Arnold Bennett

COOMBS, Patricia 1926-

PERSONAL: Born July 23, 1926, in Los Angeles, Calif.; daughter of Donald Gladstone (an engineer) and Katherine (Goodro) Coombs; married C. James Fox (a technical writer and editor), July 13, 1951; children: Ann Fox Austin, Patricia Taylor. *Education:* Attended DePauw University, 1944, and Michigan State University of Agriculture and Applied Science (now Michigan State University), 1945-46; University of Washington, B.A., 1947, M.A., 1950; further study at New York University and New School for Social Research. *Politics:* Independent. *Religion:* Episcopalian. *Home:* 178 Oswegatchie Rd., Waterford, Conn. 06385 and London, England. *Agent:* Dorothy Markinko, McIntosh & Otis, Inc., 475 Fifth Ave., New York, N.Y. 10017.

CAREER: Writer. *Awards, honors: Dorrie's Magic* was named one of *New York Times* Ten Best Books of the Year, 1962; *Dorrie and the Haunted House* was chosen one of Child Study Association of America's Children's Books of the Year, 1970, *Dorrie and the Birthday Eggs,* 1971, *Dorrie and the Goblin,* 1972, *Dorrie and the Fortune Teller,* 1973, *Dorrie and the Witch's Imp,* 1975, *Dorrie and the Halloween Plot,* 1976, and *Dorrie and the Museum Case,* 1986; *Mouse Café* was named one of *New York Times* Ten Best Illustrated Books of the Year, 1972.

WRITINGS: "Dorrie" series; all self-illustrated; all published by Lothrop: *Dorrie's Magic,* 1962; *Dorrie and the Blue Witch* (Junior Literary Guild selection), 1964; *Dorrie's Play,* 1965; *Dorrie and the Weather-Box* (Junior Literary Guild selection), 1966; *. . . and the Witch Doctor* (Weekly Reader Book Club selection), 1967; *. . . and the Wizard's Spell,* 1968; *. . . and the Haunted House,* 1970; *. . . and the Birthday Eggs,* 1971; *. . . and the Goblin,* 1972; *. . . and the Fortune Teller,* 1973; *. . . and the Amazing Magic Elixir,* 1974; *. . . and the Witch's Imp,* 1975; *. . . and the Halloween Plot,* 1976; *. . . and the Dreamyard Monsters,* 1978; *. . . and the Screebit Ghost,* 1979; *. . . and the Witchville Fair,* 1980; *. . . and the Witches' Camp,* 1983; *. . . and the Museum Case,* 1986.

Other juveniles; all self-illustrated; all published by Lothrop: *The Lost Playground,* 1963; *Waddy and His Brother,* 1963; *Lisa and the Grompet,* 1970; *Mouse Café,* 1972; *Molly Mullett,* 1975; *The Magic Pot* (Weekly Reader Book Club selection), 1977; *Tilabel,* 1978; *The Magician and McTree* (Junior Literary Guild selection), Lothrop, 1984.

Illustrator: Shelagh Williamson, *Pepi's Bell,* Singer, 1961; Noel B. Gerson, *P. J., My Friend,* Doubleday, 1969; Gladys Yessayan Cretan, *Lobo,* Lothrop, 1969; G. Y. Cretan, *Lobo and Brewster,* Lothrop, 1971; Alice Schertle, *Bill and the Google-Eyed Goblins,* Lothrop, 1987.

Contributor of poetry to *Partisan Review, Poetry, Western Review,* and other magazines.

ADAPTATIONS—Read-along cassettes; all produced by Listening Library: "Dorrie and the Haunted House," 1982; "Dorrie and the Halloween Plot"; "Dorrie and the Goblin"; "Dorrie and the Blue Witch," 1983.

SIDELIGHTS: Patricia Coombs was born in Los Angeles, had her first birthday in Hawaii, her second in San Francisco, her third in Boston, and her fourth in New York. "My father was operations manager for Shell Oil. Corporation life is a very definite world; you live and breathe it. And if the corporation wants you to move, you either move or lose out on your promotion. My father was devoted, so we just kept moving.

PATRICIA COOMBS

"I don't remember Hawaii, San Francisco or Boston; my first memories are of New York. It's odd what one remembers from childhood. I recall that my brother and the kid next door had BB guns, and that the house we rented had a deep, beautiful garden full of tulips, which my brother and his friend used for target practice. We had an entire garden full of tulips with holes shot in them.

"My mother read to us, mostly when we were sick with chicken pox and tonsilitis. I nursed my own daughters through childhood illnesses by spinning stories for them and these tales became the 'Dorrie' books."

From New York the family moved to St. Louis and stayed put for the next nine years. "I attended an interesting 'progressive' school. We learned French grammar beginning in third grade, kept animals, made gardens, built Aztec temples and took turns being the human sacrifice. It was called creative learning. All of this was in the heart of the Depression, well before St. Louis had been 'cleaned up.' They burned soft coal at the time, and the city was often so black from smoke that you had to use your headlights at high noon on a clear day.

"It was here I discovered reading. I read absolutely everything, but my mother had a phobia about germs, so I didn't discover libraries for a long time. Library books had germs, and other kids had germs, so I entertained myself with the 'Oz' books and the complete works of W. Somerset Maugham. I had a passion for books; eventually scoring junior college level on a seventh-grade vocabulary test. I read so much my mother worried that I'd ruin my eyesight, so she'd chase me outside, but I'd hide books under my clothes, and go out behind the garage and read. As I was the youngest—my brother was eight years older, my sister, ten—I had a lot of time to myself. I was in some ways an only child with the disadvantages of being an only child as well as the disadvantages of being the youngest—the 'low man on the totem pole.'

"I loved Albert Payson Terhune's *Lad, a Dog* books and *Dr. Dolittle,* which my brother had loved and passed on. I also enjoyed the series books by Lucy Fitch Perkins (*The Irish Twins, The Scotch Twins,* etc.), illustrated with wonderful line drawings. I fell in love with line drawings through those books.

They seemed miraculous—the details in a woven laundry basket were endlessly fascinating. And still are. Reading series books gave me a sense of security, even if we did move again and again. No matter where we went there was a continuity with books and with the characters in the books. Books can give kids something outside themselves to hang on to.

"I adored my older brother. He had a very peaceable disposition. Rarely did I see him angry. He took everything with

Once upon a time, about a week, or maybe a year ago, a little girl named Lisa got tired of being told what to do. ■ (From *Lisa and the Grompet* by Patricia Coombs. Illustrated by the author.)

"Here," said Dorrie. "We'll toss the ball back and forth for awhile. That's quiet." ■ (From *Dorrie and the Goblin* by Patricia Coombs. Illustrated by the author.)

humor; it was marvelous to be around someone so quiet-natured and funny.

"I also drew all the time, but I didn't write until my sister and brother went off to college. I wrote long letters to cheer them up, and these letters were the beginning of my writing career. I discovered I could be *funny*. That things I wrote could entertain people. It gave me a sense of power to be able to make people much older than me laugh. I was hooked on writing from then on.

"I don't remember having any heroes or role models to look up to. I certainly did not want to live the kind of life my mother or sister had opted for—getting married and having children quite young seemed so pointless. When I was ten, my sister was twenty. Her make-up, clothes and dating seemed very absurd and unimportant to me. What mattered was being able to roller skate better than anybody else—that was a valid goal and getting married really paled by comparison.

"We moved to Chicago shortly before America entered the war. It was an awful shock; St. Louis was all I'd known, and suddenly I was transplanted into a totally different environment. With my brother off at school and my sister married, I felt very isolated, living at home alone with my mother and father. My airedale was all I had in the way of company from our previous life."

Attended Roycemore School for Girls in Chicago. "We wore uniforms—itchy blue serge skirts, white middies and colored ties—and played hockey in itchy blue serge bloomers. Roycemore was structured after the English form school. It was a wonderful education. I learned more in that year, than the following three years in a Florida public school. I learned how to study, how to focus, how to get things done. All of which came in very handy once I went to college. At Roycemore, discipline was strict and there was no nonsense. Their standards were so much higher than at my former school. There were gaps to be filled. I knew French grammar but not English, so for nine months I diagrammed sentences after school.

"My parents were not inclined toward art, and I doubt I even knew what an art museum was. I'd have gone mad with joy if I had known they existed. Nor did I have any notion of how books were made; I just assumed they came into the world fully realized—a nice notion and a very natural one. I recall one little boy who wrote me and said he didn't know *how* I could print so neatly. In his mind, we were back to the monks

This is Dorrie. She is a witch. A little witch. Her hat is always on crooked and her socks don't match. She lives with her mother, the Big Witch, and Cook. Wherever Dorrie goes, her black cat, Gink, goes with her.

One Friday Dorrie jumped out of bed. She did a somersault. "Gink," said Dorrie, "it's Halloween! Last Halloween Mother said she'd give me a flying lesson *this* Halloween!"

(From *Dorrie and the Halloween Plot* by Patricia Coombs. Illustrated by the author.)

and illuminated manuscripts. I can just see him pouring over books, thinking that some person had written them out by hand just the way he writes out his stories in school, all the while wondering why he could never print a story that neatly!''

Moved to Daytona Beach, Florida. ''The war broke out after we left Chicago. My father had decided we should retire to Florida, so he went down and bought a house—a seven bedroom mansion for the three of us—without even consulting my mother. It was a good buy, he thought; he was not what you would call practical. He was very focused in his work, but once he stepped out of the office, he was really very spacey. So here we were, rattling around a very beautiful, very large house, which was situated on the Halifax River. The yard went right down to the water, we had a little island, and a bridge. The ocean was just a few blocks away. Now that was an adventure.

''It was my sophomore year in high school. We had been in Daytona six months when the Japanese bombed Pearl Harbor. I had an awareness of the war, but it was not much of a reality until we were suddenly called out of class to hear the announcement around the flagpole. There was a great deal of worry about German submarines in our area. We were required to carry identification, and were not allowed to cross the bridge to the mainland. There was a complete blackout every night and the Coast Guard patrolled the beaches with police dogs. The Naval Air Force camp was nearby, as was the WAAC [Women's Army Auxiliary Corp] containment. My father, a real patriot, signed up for civilian service and was given an engineer post at the women's camp. Daytona Beach became an army base. Many of the young personnel at the base had come from the Ozarks. They had never seen indoor plumbing, and suddenly here they were, put up in luxury hotels along the beach. The plumbers were on constant duty because people would flush grapefruit and orange peels down the johns.

''My mother hated Florida, the house, the whole situation. As a result of her unhappiness and preoccupation I had more freedom than I had ever had in my life.

''The public high school was small. There were only fifty kids in my graduating class, and I made good friends. I was always going steady with someone. Because it was such a small school, there were a half dozen of us constantly exchanging ID bracelets in a sort of round robin. I was happy, ever the joker in our crowd, and even loved geometry, but the school was a far cry from Roycemore. The teachers had a hard time being strict when young men were about to be drafted. They knew some of their young students might not be alive in six months. I didn't write during that time and I don't recall an art department at our school, where everything was rather minimal because of wartime, but reading was a constant in my life, always.

Attended DePauw University in Indiana. ''I didn't *choose* DePauw. Females didn't choose anything in those days, at least in my part of the world. One was sent to college in order to meet someone of more or less the same economic class, to marry, and to settle down. I was sort of backing through life. I wasn't sure what I would *do*, but I knew *exactly* what I wouldn't do. I wouldn't marry and disappear into a kitchen. So I attended classes, and blundered about for a while. There was a very good art teacher at DePauw. He taught life drawing, we worked with models and I learned a great deal.''

Attended Michigan State University, where she declared an art major. ''After the war, Michigan State grew into an enormous campus, but at the time I attended, it was a little cow college. We would literally have to close the windows when

the cows outside were making too much noise. I continued to study life drawing, but always had trouble with legs. Whenever we were given a coffee break, I would return to find that my art teacher had drawn great galoshes around my nude drawing. That has remained a constant source of inspiration to me, and there are galoshes in many of my stories. I still have trouble with legs, which perhaps accounts for the fact that I tend to cover them up. Dorrie, for instance, is always wearing stockings.

''I studied at Michigan State with a gifted woman artist, a fabulous teacher. We worked on experimental pieces and one of my projects was to illustrate a storybook. I worked in an abstract vein, playing with shapes and, for the first time, color.

''I lived in a sorority house, but sororities were much different then, and hadn't anything to do with snobbery or elitism. They sprang up because there wasn't much in the way of dorms; things were very casual, and practically anyone who wanted to live in a sorority could. Our house was a complete shambles but I loved it. The fire marshall was forever showing up at our door, and we'd race around swiftly removing violation electrical cords from under the carpets.

''I was happy, I had good friends. Whenever I went home to visit, all I heard was, 'Have you met anyone yet?'

''A depressingly large number of girls in my sorority had bought those ideals, but I looked up to a wonderful, gorgeous girl—our campus queen—who was studying to be a veterinarian. She was the first person on my horizon who seemed to offer the possibility of escape from the doom of marriage closing in on us.''

When her family moved west to Washington State, Coombs enrolled at the University of Washington where she completed her final year of college. ''My parents were not happy in Michigan, and wanted to go back to Washington State to be near family. My mother was born in Olympia, and my father grew up in Tacoma. They were not in good health, so I offered to drive them to Seattle. I liked the look and the feel of the University of Washington, and so decided to finish my undergraduate work there.

Awful, my dear fellow, simply awful! ■ (From *The Lost Playground* by Patricia Coombs. Illustrated by the author.)

Dorrie got dressed. She looked at Gink and sighed. "I'll be glad when Cook gets back from her holiday," she said. She went into the hall and Gink went with her.

"How was it that time?" the Big Witch called out.

"A little better," said Dorrie. "I had time to get out of bed before the sheets took off."

Someone was knocking at the front door. Dorrie ran down the stairs and opened it. It was the Post-Witch. "Special Delivery," she said. "It's from your Uncle Flagstone."

Dorrie took the letter up, up, up the stairs to the Big Witch's secret room. The cauldron was bubbling and steaming and smelled like soap.

"A letter came, Mother. It's from Uncle Flagstone."

Dorrie stirred while the Big Witch read the letter. The Big Witch groaned.

(From *Dorrie and the Museum Case* by Patricia Coombs. Illustrated by the author.)

He saw the old woman, a pig, and a basket that howled and jerked. ■(From *The Magician and McTree* by Patricia Coombs. Illustrated by the author.)

"The campus was woodsy and free and very lively. There were many wonderful professors of literature, but the art department was a disaster, so I switched my major to English. Poet Theodore Roethke was there, as well as the eminent Milton scholar, Arnold Stein, who became my mentor in 17th-century English literature. The whole English Department was vibrant and alive; they sponsored visiting poets and writers from all over the country—it was a very creative environment.

"I attended poetry workshops with Roethke, who would come roaring down the hall, his coattails flying, his whole brain full of poetry. He could quote any poet of any century at the drop of a hat. His mood decided who he would recite as he came in the classroom and sprawled his great piles of books across the table. He was a big bear of a man, with great and genuine enthusiasm. The English language meant so much to him. He had us writing constantly and through his example I finally understood the reality of writing. One simply had to sit down at the typewriter and *write,* an important discovery for me. I fell in love with words, with words *as* words, capable of endless association and imagery. It was a tremendous period. I would get so excited I would have migraines, literally blowing all the circuits in my brain. My gratitude to Roethke is boundless. I'm sure that anybody who came in contact with him during those years came away with a completely different awareness and perception of language, and of the emotional power of words.''

Coombs enrolled in graduate school at the University of Washington. "The metaphysical poets prompted another migraine-producing love affair. I began to write a thesis on the extended similies in the first five books of Milton's *Paradise Lost.* My plan had been to complete a doctorate; I suppose it was Arnold Stein's influence, because he felt I had the makings of a scholar.

The fact that I wanted to be a poet was not something I was very assertive about, so Stein more or less directed me toward various possibilities. It would have been very unacceptable to me at the time to declare myself a poet; I was not accomplished enough, I was just beginning.

"I finished my masters degree and decided to stay at the University for the summer. I signed up for a course in Anglo-Saxon English and took a job on the swing shift at Boeing Aircraft. I worked in the purchasing department, the last place anyone with any brains would have placed me. I lost twenty-four toilets for a B-26 Bomber. They disappeared in the paperwork, never to be found again.

"It was during this interlude that I met and married my husband, Jim Fox. We had been in classes together at the University, but we never got to know each other until that summer at Boeing. We were in the same car pool, started dating, and two weeks later, got married.

"With Jim I felt no ambivalence about marriage. All of our interests were the same—poetry, novels, writers—he wasn't the enemy, he was the companion. He was facing the same direction, and our shared passions have kept us together all these years. He could even cook better than I could; we were off to a good start. He could scramble eggs and I could make grilled cheese sandwiches.

"Jim had a year of the G.I. bill left. Although, a native of Washington state, from a little town in the heart of apple country, he had fallen in love with New York on his way overseas. So we drove across the country with some friends from graduate school and rented a living room in an apartment on Manhattan's lower East Side. One friend rented the maid's room,

The shapes banged heads, and they landed in a heap on the hall floor. ■ (From *Dorrie and the Haunted House* by Patricia Coombs. Illustrated by the author.)

"Pig Wizard," said Dorrie, "the Big Witch doesn't want the pigs near the pies this year. . . ." ■
(From *Dorrie and the Witchville Fair* by Patricia Coombs. Illustrated by the author.)

another a room down the hall, and we shared a kitchen and a bathroom. Some of us were students, others had regular nine-to-five jobs, so we were all on different schedules. It was wonderful—we used to scrounge around the streets for things to burn in our glamorous fireplace. Jim and I slept together on a studio couch. We had strange electricity, and every time we sat down on our couch, the lights in the apartment would flash on and off.

"I took courses at New York University toward my doctorate, but eventually grew dissatisfied with graduate school. Then I became pregnant, stopped my course work toward the doctorate, and went over to the New School [for Social Research] to study poetry with Stanley Kunitz. We were living on nothing and our rent took what little was left of Jim's G.I. Bill, so I worked part-time at a second-hand bookstore. It was Kunitz who said one day, 'Have you considered publishing your work?' and thereby changed my life.

"When the G.I. Bill was up, we bought a car for seventy-five dollars, packed up our typewriters and books, pressure cooker and coffee pot and headed to Minneapolis. We'd heard that the University of Minnesota had a wonderful librarian's program and we felt that as librarians, we could find jobs in Europe. A great idea. But we had *no* notion of what having a child involved. We had so little money that I didn't even see a doctor until I was seven months pregnant. I felt fine, except that I had an insatiable desire to sleep, quite an inconvenience. Jim got a job as a technical writer at Honeywell, I continued to write poetry, and Ann was born in September.

"A friend from graduate school, Ralph Ross, was hired as head of the humanities department at the University of Minnesota. He offered me a part-time teaching job, which I gratefully accepted. I probably would have continued to teach there, had it not been for the unbearable climate in Minneapolis. Most of the year it's thirty below, with forty-mile-an-hour winds whipping across the plains. When midsummer comes at last, it becomes too hot to sleep. We wanted to move back to the New York area. New York was *life*. Every Sunday we sat together with the *New York Times* want ads and a map, measuring the distance between job offerings and New York City. When Jim was offered a job at Electric Boat in Connecticut, which was equidistant from both Boston and New York, he decided to take it.

"We bought a house. Soon after, my father, who was recovering from a heart attack came to stay with us. He was a semi-invalid and needed comfort and care. It was not an easy time, but our lives were very full. I had to give up writing during that period. Once the kids were down for their nap, there was my father to fix meals for and take to the doctor—there were not enough hours in the day. Finally, my father was able to live on his own, and took a place downtown.

"We became very close friends with novelist Noel Gerson, who lived right up the road. It was Noel who got me started, in a practical way, with the idea of doing children's books. He told me there was a market opening up and that agents were becoming more interested in representing authors of children's books. I'd already been making up stories to entertain my daughters during their bouts of illness. So when my youngest girl, Trish, started first grade, I gave myself a year. Either I would write something marketable or go back to school to get my teaching certificate. I began to write stories and draw pictures about a blue witch. One morning I was inking in the witches' hats and cutting out balloons for the collage illustrating a witches' party, when the children went off to school. I was still cutting out balloons when they came home. They

didn't say much about it, but every once in a while they would tell me what other mothers did.

"Very shortly after the first manuscript [*Dorrie's Magic*] was finished, before I had even sent it out, my husband Jim interviewed a writer, Roswell G. Ham, Jr., for a job with his company. Rod was a novelist. He hadn't written much, but was a good writer whose books were well received. There was a blizzard that night, so Jim brought Rod home to spend the night. I showed him *Dorrie's Magic,* and he suggested I send it to his agent.

"I sent the manuscript, along with pencil drawings I'd done to convey what the pictures should be like. One publisher wanted the story, but was not interested in the 'illustrations.' Without consulting me, my agent refused to sell the manuscript without my drawings. She sent it Lothrop, a tiny house at the time, and they loved it. I met their production manager, Stu Benick, who showed me how to do illustrations. He literally said, 'Well, you need to use pen and ink instead of pencil, and you'll have to do some color overlays and so forth.' I went home to work, and with many mishaps, finished the illustrations. The book was published in the fall of 1962.

"One Saturday morning, a special delivery arrived at the door. It was the children's book section of the *New York Times Book Review,* featuring a great big reproduction of a drawing from *Dorrie's Magic* and a marvelous review. It was an incredible encouragement for someone up over her ears in family situations. I could hardly believe it. I nailed it to the kitchen wall, so I would at least pass it as I hurried to and fro to let cats and kids in and out.

"I had one idea in mind when I began [writing]. I wanted to do something about witches, because I felt it would never be dated. It had always bothered me when the kids brought home books which were trendy. Fashion—for instance the length of a skirt—would never be a problem with witches. And it solved the problem of legs. I set [the witches] in a more or less 1930s decor of my childhood, but I'm not sure why. Maybe that's where we first get our mental imagery.

"The writing doesn't come from a conscious level. When I first write a story, I don't know how it will end. It's just as much a surprise to me as it is to the reader. I am very visual, so I tend to draw as I write. I wanted young children who already knew the story by heart to be able to reread the book by following the illustrations. As a result, my drawings followed the pattern of the action very closely.

"Another challenge I set for myself was to use simple, but imagistic language. You are limited by number of pages in a children's book. My experience with poetry was invaluable—every word counts.

"I had always loved witches, especially those in Grimm's fairy tales. I can still remember a story wherein a witch read the future from entrails. 'Entrails' was a word I didn't know at the time, and I was too young to look it up, so I asked my mother, who refused to tell me. My own girls loved witches, too. They wanted to read by themselves, but were too young to read Grimm's alone. So it seemed to me it would be great to invent a witch like my own little girls who were very no-nonsense about things, and had the same kinds of problems: messy rooms, adults who were *always* busy.

"Children have a way of seeing right through adults. We are always harried and busy busy busy, but children understand how hypocritical we can be. I tried to capture children's very

The Ogre's snores were deafening. And they smelled terrible. ∎ (From *Molly Mullet* by Patricia Coombs. Illustrated by the author.)

real and accurate perceptions of adults in the 'Dorrie' books. I remember one day, after yelling at the kids to clean their rooms, they came in and stood in front of me, looking very indignantly at my messy desk, the spilt coffee, the papers in chaotic disarray. It struck me as funny, the fact that we're always giving children directions, always telling them to do things that we don't do. We push them toward an abstract ideal. Even as we fall into chaos, we continue to urge them on towards hygiene, tidiness, order and perfection.

"What appealed to me, as I went along, was taking the kind of life I was living with my own two children and making it come alive. I have boxes and boxes of letters from children. Only one child ever asked me where Dorrie's father is. The letter brought home the fact that women's lives are very isolated from the male world. Children, for the most part, grow up in a world of women. The 'Dorrie' books capture the domestic reality of children's lives; although some of the scenes are magical, the situations and feelings are basically naturalistic.

"It was a great comfort to read Carol Klein's book on the myth of the 'happy child.' Klein demonstrates how all children share common fears: from a simple fear of the dark to the fear of being eaten alive by wild lions and tigers. I was full of fears as a child, and my books address the fears all children share. *Dorrie and the Blue Witch* is about the fear of being left alone. But Dorrie is funny, and she is *coping*. She is not an exaggerated heroine, she simply deals with her fears, and that is what makes her so appealing to children.

"It was my editor at Lothrop who realized *Dorrie's Magic* was possibly the forerunner of other books; she encouraged me to carry the Dorrie character on. Her support, in combination with the encouragement from the *New York Times,* made it difficult for anyone to stop me. As long as someone pats me on the head, as long as someone is there to share a joke with, I'll go on, indefinitely.

"Kids frequently write to me and ask, 'Where do you get your ideas?' It's hard to say. Sometimes I read and read until my

"Come on, Gink," Dorrie said. "Let's go see what's over there." ■ (From *Dorrie and the Fortune Teller* by Patricia Coombs. Illustrated by the author.)

brain gets overloaded, then I suddenly wake up and write something without any conscious preplanning. This happened with *Molly Mullet*. I had been looking for a story to adapt and illustrate and so was steeped in English folktales. Then one night I woke up and wrote *Molly Mullet;* it went from the typewriter into print, and not a word was changed. The same happened with *Mouse Café* and *Lisa and the Grumpet*. There are mysterious facets of creativity. One's head is like a cauldron sometimes, you just stir everything up, add a few things, and wait to see what happens.

"*Molly Mullet* works on a deeper level than folktales usually do because the emotions are more complex. The book grew out of my own experience. I adored my father, but there was never any question that my brother, his *son,* was more important to him than my sister or I could ever be. Of course we were loved; he was simply a chauvinist. The book also grows out of my sense of injustice at being told all my life, 'You can't do that, you're a girl. You can't climb trees, you can't run the boat' . . . the list of can'ts was endless, and of course, I frequently violated it. Thank heaven for my brother, who could always get around my mother. For the small price of being a 'good sport,' of never crying no matter what, he let me tag along and do all sorts of exciting things with him like ride the aquaplane (early water skis) on his shoulders. Whenever there was a really wild storm on Lake Michigan, he would tell my mother we were going somewhere 'safe sounding,' then we'd go out to the lighthouse, hang on the railing for dear life and let the huge waves wash over us. I am grateful to my brother. I didn't have the strength, the means or the courage to stand up to my mother, but he did, and he made it possible for me."

Coombs also illustrates books for other authors. "It's great fun. The only disadvantage is that I often have an overwhelming desire to change an author's text when it's not working visually. I'm so used to working and reworking my own books that it's frustrating to be limited to a text I can't fool around with. When I illustrate a 'Dorrie' book and come across a place which doesn't work visually, I take it as a clue that there is a flaw in my story. I go back to the text and try to figure out where I've gone awry. But when I illustrate someone else's text, I'm not at liberty to work in a 'back and forth' manner."

Coombs often works with reference. "Often I use what's around the house. A chair in my living room turned up in *Mouse Café* and I used chicken bones as my model for the dinosaur bones in *Dorrie and the Museum Case*. Our pet goat, Vincent, inspired *Dorrie and the Goblin*. Vincent was impossible; he loved to be yelled at and got into the weirdest kinds of trouble, but we adored him. He made a splendid goblin."

To develop a character, Coombs sketches extensively. "The text usually comes first, though sometimes a character begins as an image. For instance, the dream witch came from an actual dream. It was seven years before I was able to write a story around her; all that time she was floating around the hodgepodge of my mind. I should add that all of my creatures—goblins, witches, ogres—have human gestures, and human feeling.

"The letters I get from kids are so moving and funny. One little girl, who was writing a book of her own about time travel, said that so far, her characters had met God and Columbus. She wanted to know what I thought might happen next."

About work and discipline Coombs commented, "I'm a maniac. I have to work every morning. If I can't get a dental

appointment in the afternoon, I'm panic stricken. My strict schedule began when the kids were in school; I had precious few hours to work and learned to take full advantage of them. Back when I didn't have to worry about getting up in the morning, I was more relaxed and often wrote poetry late at night. I work straight through the weekends. It's nice when I don't have interruptions, I simply get more done. And, whether poetry or children's books, I have always written with chamber music, usually Bach, in the background."

Since 1986, Coombs has spent most of the year in London, with summers in Connecticut. "I love our flat in London because there is so little to look after, it's like I'm back in my student days in New York. There is a municipal pool four blocks away, so I swim laps every morning, along with all the British ladies who do the breast stroke and the side stroke and who emerge from the water with their hair perfectly dry. I haven't seen that since the thirties!

"I *live* at the National Gallery; all the help in the tearoom know who I am, because I'm there every day. I especially like the Dutch landscapes. The Dutch painted cows the way Renoir painted nudes: there is such passion and appreciation in the way they portray the velvetiness of light on flanks, or the edge of a horn—it's marvelous, and I have learned a great deal from them."

—Based on an interview by Rachel Koenig

Coombs works are included in the Kerlan Collection at the University of Minnesota.

HOBBIES AND OTHER INTERESTS: Organic gardening, beach combing, jogging, sailing, animal and bird life, bicycling.

FOR MORE INFORMATION SEE: New York Times Book Review, September 16, 1962, October 25, 1964, October 29, 1972, June 19, 1977; *Horn Book,* October 1962; *Saturday Review,* October 17, 1964; *Christian Science Monitor,* October 22, 1964; *Book World,* October 20, 1968; Lee Kingman and others, compilers, *Illustrators of Children's Books: 1957-1966,* Horn Book, 1968; *Library Journal,* May 15, 1970; Martha E. Ward and Dorothy A. Marquardt, *Illustrators of Books for Young People,* Scarecrow, 1975; *Kirkus Reviews,* March 15, 1978; L. Kingman and others, compilers, *Illustrators of Children's Books: 1967-1976,* Horn Book, 1978; Sally Holmes Holtze, editor, *Fifth Book of Junior Authors and Illustrators,* H. W. Wilson, 1983.

CROSS, Gilbert B. 1939-
(Jon Winters)

BRIEF ENTRY: Born in Walkden, near Manchester, England. University professor and author of books for children and adults. "I can say that all my writing, whether it be academic or of children's books or adult thrillers, has been satisfying to me," Cross said in a *Detroit Free Press* interview. He is the author of almost a dozen books, including an espionage trilogy, written under the pseudonym Jon Winters, and an award-winning work on British theater history entitled *Next Week-East Lynne: Domestic Dramas in Performance, 1820-1874* (Bucknell University Press, 1977). He is also co-editor, with Atelia Clarkson, of the folktale collection *World Folktales: A Scribner Resource Collection* (Scribner, 1980).

Cross's first novel for children, *A Hanging at Tyburn* (Atheneum, 1983), concerns fourteen-year-old George Found, an orphan. ''As in the novels of Leon Garfield, the perilous possibilities of eighteenth-century life and the element of coincidence make the narrative a lively adventure story,'' observed *Horn Book*. *Mystery at Loon Lake* (Atheneum, 1986), a children's mystery tale, is set in a fictional town in New Hampshire and centers around two brothers, a neighbor girl, and a band of dangerous smugglers. ''The mystery is easy to figure out, but there are many genuine chills—exploring an abandoned house and a subterranean escape are real nail-biters,'' wrote *School Library Journal*. Its sequel is entitled *Terror Train*. *Home:* 1244 Ferdon, Ann Arbor, Mich. 48104.

FOR MORE INFORMATION SEE: Contemporary Authors, Volume 105, Gale, 1982; *Detroit Free Press*, April 23, 1987.

de ANGELI, Marguerite (Lofft) 1889-1987

OBITUARY NOTICE—See sketch in *SATA* Volume 27: Born March 14, 1889, in Lapeer, Mich.; died June 16, 1987, in Philadelphia, Pa. Singer, illustrator, and author. One of America's most popular writers and illustrators of children's books during the 1940s and 1950s, de Angeli was particularly admired for her pioneering stories about minorities as well as historical fiction about the Middle Ages. She began her career as a concert singer and soloist; however, following her marriage in 1910 and the births of her children, she turned instead to illustrating. By 1934 she was illustrating her own stories. De Angeli received several Newbery Honor Book and Caldecott Honor Book awards and won the Newbery Medal in 1950 for her book *The Door in the Wall*, a historical novel set in medieval England. She was also awarded the Lewis Carroll Shelf Award in 1961. De Angeli's other books include *Henner's Lydia; Thee, Hannah!; Copper-Toed Boots; Bright April; Book of Nursery and Mother Goose Rhymes*, a Caldecott Honor book; and *Black Fox of Lorne*, a Newbery Honor book and her last major work for children. De Angeli also wrote an autobiography *Butter at the Old Price*, published in 1971.

FOR MORE INFORMATION SEE: Children's Literature Review, Volume 1, Gale, 1976; *Contemporary Authors, New Revision Series*, Volume 3, Gale, 1981; *Dictionary of Literary Biography*, Volume 22: *American Writers for Children, 1900-1960*, Gale, 1983; *The Writer's Directory: 1984-1986*, St. James Press, 1983. Obituaries: *Chicago Tribune*, June 20, 1987; *Los Angeles Times*, June 20, 1987.

DEARY, Terry 1946-

PERSONAL: Born January 3, 1946, in Sunderland, England; son of William (a butcher) and Freda (a store manager; maiden name, Hanson) Deary; married Jennifer Trick (a teacher), January 3, 1975; children: Sara. *Education:* Sunderland College of Education, Teacher's Certificate, 1968. *Politics:* ''Anarchist.'' *Religion:* ''Existentialist.'' *Home.* Board Inn, Burnhope, Durham DH7 ODP, England. *Office:* Grindon Broadway Teachers' Centre, Sunderland, England.

CAREER: Red House School, Sunderland, England, teacher, 1968-72; Breconshire Theatre Company, Powys (formerly Breconshire), Wales, actor, 1972-75; Lowestoft Theatre Centre, Suffolk, England, director, 1975-77; author, 1976—; Kirkley High School, Suffolk, teacher, 1977-79; Tynewear Theatre Company, Newcastle, England, theatre education officer, 1979-80; Hetton School, Hetton, England, drama teacher and department head, 1983-87; Sunderland Schools, Sunderland, educational advisor, 1987—. Writer and presenter of children's

educational magazine programs for British Broadcasting Corp. (BBC-Radio), Durham, England, 1970-71. *Member:* British Actors Equity Association.

WRITINGS: Teaching through Theatre, Samuel French, 1977; *The Custard Kid* (juvenile novel; illustrated by Charlotte Firmin), A. & C. Black, 1978, Carolrhoda, 1981; *The Real Maria Marten* (adult documentary novel), East Anglian Publishers, 1979; *Calamity Kate* (juvenile; illustrated by C. Firmin), A. & C. Black, 1980, Carolrhoda, 1981; *Hope Street* (young adult novel), Cassell, 1980; *The Lambton Worm* (juvenile novel; illustrated by C. Firmin), Carolrhoda, 1981; *Twist of the Knife* (young adult novel), Longman, 1981; *Walking Shadows* (young adult), Longman, 1983; *The Wishing Well Ghost* (juvenile; illustrated by C. Firmin), A. & C. Black, 1983; *The Silent Scream* (young adult), Hutchinson, 1984; *The Windmill of Nowhere* (juvenile; illustrated by C. Firmin), A. & C. Black, 1984; *I Met Her on a Rainy Day* (young adult), Longman, 1985; *Don't Dig Up Your Granny When She's Dead* (young adult), Longman, 1985; *A Witch in Time* (juvenile; science-fiction; illustrated by P. Lynch), A. & C. Black, 1986; *The Ice House of Nightmare Avenue* (young adult), Longman, 1986; *The Treasure of Skull Island* (young adult), Longman, 1986.

Contributor of stories to anthologies, including *Thrilling Stories of Mystery and Adventure*, Hamlyn, 1982, and *Spine Chilling Stories*, Longman, 1987.

SIDELIGHTS: ''The printed word is revered more highly than the truth. A reader will accept almost anything simply because it is printed in black and white. That is sad, but it is sadder when the writer himself begins to believe his own infallibility. The first lesson a writer must learn is the lesson of humility—he must remember the force his words will carry once they appear in print and the responsibility that this entails.''

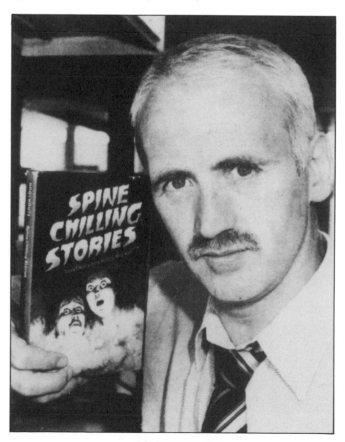

TERRY DEARY

"Those who have the talent for writing must exercise that skill with self-awareness and self-criticism, constantly reappraising their work for signs of pretentiousness. Writers and readers must remember that a 'book' is not an article of paper, ink, and leather that stands on a bookshelf gathering dust—a book is only a 'book' at the moment it is being read, at the moment the writer and his reader are actually communicating.

"I first began writing plays and novels for children when I discovered a dearth of material to suit my needs—many stories fulfilled some of my criteria but few fulfilled all. As a teacher, I wanted a story with pace and humor written in accessible language. But I also wanted sufficient depth of characterization for readers to *care* about what happened to the protagonist; I wanted to see the conflicts resolved through the exercise of resourcefulness, not through the exercise of violence. Having exhausted my store of suitable material, I had to set about writing my own. To my delight publishers backed my approach to fiction for young people, and I sell well over fifty percent of what I now write.

"I enjoy talking to school and community groups about writing but find it difficult to explain *how* to write. To me writing is automatic—I just sit at a typewriter and do it. At the end of the day I scarcely recognize the words on the typescript as my own. The urge to create is so strong that I would probably go on writing even if I'd never succeeded in being published. The 'next' book bubbling in my head will always be more important to me than my 'last' book sitting there on the shelf."

HOBBIES AND OTHER INTERESTS: Playing cricket, road-running up to half-marathon distance, restoring and driving Mini-Cooper sports cars, playing folk-guitar and listening to contemporary country music.

DEMUTH, Patricia Brennan 1948-

BRIEF ENTRY: Born March 16, 1948, in Sioux City, Iowa. Free-lance educational writer and author of books for children. Demuth received two awards for her book *Joel: Growing Up a Farm Man* (Dodd, 1982), a true account of thirteen-year-old Joel Holland, who lives and works on his family's 245-acre farm in northwestern Illinois. The accompanying photographs were taken by Demuth's husband, Jack. Demuth is also the author of *City Horse* (Dodd, 1979), co-written by her husband, and *Max, the Bad-Talking Parrot* (Dodd, 1986). In the latter, Max gets into trouble when he misunderstands neighbor Mrs. Goosebump and thinks she calls him "ugly." "The brief text flows along smoothly for reading aloud or for independent reading," observed *School Library Journal. Home:* 1412 Ashland, Evanston, Ill. 60201.

FOR MORE INFORMATION SEE: Contemporary Authors, Volume 118, Gale, 1986.

DESMOND, Adrian J(ohn) 1947-

PERSONAL: Born October 6, 1947, in Guildford, Surrey, England; son of William John and Barbara (Dew) Desmond. *Education:* University of London, Chelsea College of Science and Technology, B.Sc., 1969, M.Sc. (history and philosophy of science), 1971, University College, M.Sc. (vertebrate palaeontology), 1973; graduate study, Harvard University, 1973-76; University of London, Ph.D. (history of science), 1984. *Home:* 8 Albert Terrace Mews, London NW1, England.

CAREER: Writer, science historian, and palaeontologist; Honorary Research Fellow in the Department of Zoology, University College, London, England. *Member:* British Society for the History of Science, Society of Vertebrate Palaeontology, Zoological Society of London (fellow). *Awards, honors:* South East Arts Literature Prize (United Kingdom), 1977, for *The Hot-Blooded Dinosaurs: A Revolution in Palaeontology* which was also selected one of New York Public Library's Books for the Teen Age, 1980, 1981, and 1982.

WRITINGS: The Hot-Blooded Dinosaurs: A Revolution in Palaeontology, Blond & Briggs, 1975, Dial, 1976; *The Ape's Reflexion,* Dial, 1979; *Archetypes and Ancestors: Palaeontology in Victorian London, 1850-1875,* Blond & Briggs, 1982, University of Chicago Press, 1984. Contributor to scientific journals and to newspapers.

ADAPTATIONS: "Hot-Blooded Dinosaurs" (television documentary), BBC-TV, 1977, PBS-TV, January 12, 1977.

WORK IN PROGRESS: A study of the political uses of evolutionary science in the radical 1830s, to be called *Politics of Evolution: Morphology, Medicine, and Reform in Radical London.*

SIDELIGHTS: "*The Hot-Blooded Dinosaurs* was born out of a desire to show that ideas as much as animals fossilize. The archaic dinosaur image bedevilled palaeontology for more than a century. By presenting a radical alternative I hoped to shift the onus onto supporters to substantiate the Victorian myth, or bury it.

"I move freely between academic and more popular work; indeed, one generally sends me scurrying towards the other. But I wouldn't have it any other way. Unlike institutionalised academics, however, I do have to resort to the publishing marketplace for funding. The upshot of this is that I have tended to look more deeply into the financial predicaments of my Victorian subjects, producing as a result more materialistic interpretations of their scientific work."

ADRIAN J. DESMOND

Desmond's work has been translated into German, Japanese, Italian, Spanish, Swedish, and Dutch.

FOR MORE INFORMATION SEE: Financial Times, December 11, 1975; *Observer Review*, December 28, 1975; *New Scientist*, August 23, 1979; *Washington Post Book World*, October 28, 1979; *Contemporary Psychology*, November, 1980; *Social Studies of Science*, Volume 15, 1985.

DICKMEYER, Lowell A. 1939-

BRIEF ENTRY: Born May 14, 1939, in Fort Wayne, Ind. Dickmeyer received his bachelor's degree from Concordia Teacher's College in 1962 and his master's from Ball State University three years later. He then worked as a classroom teacher and a learning disabilities specialist at schools in California before becoming involved in sports education for children. He is the author of many of the books in the "Sports for Me" series (Lerner), including *Soccer Is for Me* (1978); *Baseball Is for Me* (1978); and *Tennis Is for Me*, with Annette Jo Chappell (1980). Of these, *Booklist* wrote, "The books' plots follow the narrators' realistic efforts to gain expertise and to learn good sportsmanship." About his book *Basketball Is for Me*, photographed by Alan Oddie (1979), the same journal commented, "Lots of appealing black-and-white photographs and a large-print format will interest the young reader and serve as introductory material for the budding athlete."

Dickmeyer co-authored the six volume "Soccer Adventure Series" (Dillon), which follows school-aged American soccer players on travels through different parts of the world. In *A. J. Goes to Germany* (1983), a young boy having difficulty adjusting to his parents' divorce learns a lot from his German hosts. In *Hana Discovers Japan* (1984), a girl is rude to her hosts until she becomes aware of the different customs of the country. ". . . These are competently written, low-key stories," noted *School Library Journal*. Dickmeyer has also written books for children on teamwork and sportsmanship, *Winning and Losing* (F. Watts, 1983) and *Teamwork* (F. Watts, 1983), as well as articles for magazines, including *Young Athlete* and *Soccer America*. *Home and office:* 4611 Alta Canyada, La Canada, Calif. 91011.

FOR MORE INFORMATION SEE: Contemporary Authors, Volume 109, Gale, 1983.

DILLON, Diane 1933-

PERSONAL: Born March 13, 1933, in Glendale, Calif; daughter of Adelbert Paul (a teacher) and Phyllis (a pianist and homemaker; maiden name, Worsley) Sorber; married Leo J. Dillon (an artist), March 17, 1957; children: Lee. *Education:* Attended Los Angeles City College, 1951-52, Skidmore College, 1952-53, Parsons School of Design, 1954-56, and School of Visual Arts, 1958. *Home:* 221 Kane St., Brooklyn, N.Y. 11231.

CAREER: Artist, illustrator. Dave Fris Advertising Agency, Albany, N.Y., staff artist, 1956-57. *Exhibitions:* Has had several exhibitions, including: Gallery on the Green, Boston, Mass.; Metropolitan Museum, N.Y.; Boulder Center for the Visual Arts, Boulder, Colo.; Butler Institute of American Art, Youngstown, Ohio; Delaware Art Museum, Wilmington, Del.; Bratislava Book Show; American Institute of Graphic Arts, N.Y.; Art Directors Club of New York; Brooklyn Public Li-

brary, N.Y.; New York Historical Society; Earthlight Gallery, Boston, Mass.; The Pentagon, Washington, D.C. *Member:* Society of Illustrators, Graphic Artists Guild.

AWARDS, HONORS: New York Herald Tribune's Children's Spring Book Festival Award honor book, 1963, for *Hakon of Rogen's Saga; Dark Venture* was chosen one of Child Study Association of America's Children's Books of the Year, 1968, *The Untold Tale*, 1971, *Behind the Back of the Mountain*, 1973, *Burning Star* and *Songs and Stories from Uganda*, 1974, *The Hundred Penny Box*, *Why Mosquitoes Buzz in People's Ears* and *Song of the Boat*, 1975, *Ashanti to Zulu*, 1976, and *The People Could Fly*, and *Brother to the Wind*, 1986; Hugo Award from the International Science Fiction Association, 1971, for illustration of a series of science-fiction book jackets; *The Untold Tale* was chosen one of *School Library Journal's* Best Books, 1971; *Behind the Back of the Mountain* and *The Third Gift* were both included in the American Institute of Graphic Arts Children's Books Show, 1973-74, and *Ashanti to Zulu*, 1976; *Behind the Back of the Mountain* was included in the Children's Book Showcase of the Children's Book Council, 1974, *Whirlwind Is a Ghost Dancing*, 1975, and *Song of the Boat*, 1976; *Why Mosquitoes Buzz in People's Ears* was selected one of *New York Times* Outstanding Books of the Year, and one of *School Library Journal's* Best Books, both 1975, and received Art Books for Children Citation from the Brooklyn Museum and Brooklyn Public Library, 1977 and 1978; *The Hundred Penny Box* was chosen one of *New York Times* Outstanding Books of the Year, 1975.

Illustrator of Newbery honor book, *The Hundred Penny Box*, 1976; Caldecott Medal from the American Library Association, 1976, for *Why Mosquitoes Buzz in People's Ears* and 1977, for *Ashanti to Zulu; Ashanti to Zulu* was chosen one of *New York Times* Best Illustrated Children's Books, 1976, and *The People Could Fly*, 1985; *Boston Globe-Horn Book* Award honor book for illustration, 1976, for *Song of the Boat*, and 1977, for *Ashanti to Zulu;* Hamilton King Award for excellence in illustration from the Society of Illustrators, 1977, for *Ashanti to Zulu;* Hans Christian Andersen Medal "Highly Commended" citation for illustration, 1978; Lewis Carroll Shelf Award, 1978, for *Who's in Rabbit's House? A Masai Tale;* Balrog Award for "Lifetime Contribution to Sci-Fi/Fantasy Art," 1982; *Brother to the Wind* and *The People Could Fly* were each chosen a Notable Children's Trade Book in the Field of Social Studies by the joint committee of the National Council for Social Studies and the Children's Book Council, 1985; International Board on Books for Young People honor list for illustration, and Other Award from *Children's Book Bulletin*, both 1986, both for *The People Could Fly*.

ILLUSTRATOR—All with husband, Leo Dillon: Erik C. Haugaard, *Hakon of Rogen's Saga* (ALA Notable Book; *Horn Book* honor list), Houghton, 1963; E. C. Haugaard, *A Slave's Tale* (ALA Notable Book; *Horn Book* honor list), Houghton, 1965; Basil Davidson and the editors of Time-Life, *African Kingdoms*, Time-Life, 1966; Sorche Nic Leodhas (pseudonym of Leclair G. Alger), *Claymore and Kilt: Tales of Scottish Kings and Castles*, Holt, 1967; F. M. Pilkington, *Shamrock and Spear: Tales and Legends from Ireland*, Holt, 1968; E. C. Haugaard, *The Rider and His Horse* (*Horn Book* honor list), Houghton, 1968; Audrey W. Beyer, *Dark Venture*, Knopf, 1968; Frederick Laing, *Why Heimdall Blew His Horn: Tale of the Norse Gods*, Silver, 1969.

John Bierhorst and Henry R. Schoolcraft, editors, *The Ring in the Prairie: A Shawnee Legend*, Dial, 1970; Alta Jablow, *Gassire's Lute: A West African Epic*, Dutton, 1971; Alma Murray and Robert Thomas, editors, *The Search*, Scholastic,

"Sing that sweetest, goodest song again," says the big, bad wolf. ■ (From "A Wolf and Little Daughter" in *The People Could Fly: American Black Folktales* by Virginia Hamilton. Illustrated by Leo and Diane Dillon.)

1971; E. C. Haugaard, *The Untold Tale* (ALA Notable Book), Houghton, 1971; Verna Aardema, *Behind the Back of the Mountain: Black Folktales from Southern Africa* (ALA Notable Book), Dial, 1973; Eth Clifford (pseudonym of Ethel C. Rosenberg), *Burning Star,* Houghton, 1974; W. Moses Serwadda, *Songs and Stories from Uganda* (ALA Notable Book), Crowell, 1974; Jan Carew, *The Third Gift,* Little, Brown, 1974; Natalie Belting, *Whirlwind Is a Ghost Dancing,* Dutton, 1974; Lorenz Graham, *Song of the Boat* (ALA Notable Book), Crowell, 1975; Harlan Ellison, editor, *Dangerous Visions,* New American Library, 1975; Sharon Bell Mathis, *The Hundred Penny Box* (ALA Notable Book; *Horn Book* honor list), Viking, 1975; V. Aardema, reteller, *Why Mosquitoes Buzz in People's Ears: A West African Tale* (ALA Notable Book), Dial, 1975; Margaret W. Musgrove, *Ashanti to Zulu: African Traditions* (ALA Notable Book; *Horn Book* honor list), Dial, 1976; V. Aardema, reteller, *Who's in Rabbit's House? A Masai Tale* (*Horn Book* honor list), Dial, 1977; Eloise Greenfield, *Honey, I Love, and Other Love Poems* (Reading Rainbow selection), Crowell, 1978; F. Laing, *Tales from Scandinavia,* Silver, 1979.

P. L. Travers, *Two Pairs of Shoes,* Viking, 1980; J. Carew, *Children of the Sun,* Little, Brown, 1980; Dorothy S. Strickland, editor, *Listen Children: An Anthology of Black Literature,* Bantam, 1982; Mildred P. Walter, *Brother to the Wind,* Lothrop, 1985; Virginia Hamilton, reteller, *The People Could Fly: American Black Folktales,* Knopf, 1985; (contributor) *Once Upon a Time: Celebrating the Magic of Children's Books in Honor of the Twentieth Anniversary of Reading Is Fundamental,* Putnam, 1986. Also illustrator of *All in a Day,* [Japan], 1986.

Contributor of illustrations to periodicals, including *Ladies' Home Journal, Saturday Evening Post,* and *Washington Post.*

ADAPTATIONS: "Why Mosquitoes Buzz in People's Ears" (filmstrip with cassette; motion picture), Weston Woods, 1976; "Ashanti to Zulu" (filmstrip with cassette), Weston Woods, 1977.

WORK IN PROGRESS: See Dillon, Leo.

SIDELIGHTS: See Dillon, Leo for joint interview.

Dillon's works are included in the Kerlan Collection at the University of Minnesota.

HOBBIES AND OTHER INTERESTS: Sculpture, "building on our house."

FOR MORE INFORMATION SEE: "Winners! Honors! Prizes!," *American Libraries,* March, 1976; *Top of the News,* April, 1976, summer, 1977; *Horn Book,* August, 1976, August, 1977; *School Library Journal,* March, 1977; Lee Kingman and others, compilers, *Illustrators of Children's Books: 1967-1976,* Horn Book, 1978; Byron Preiss, editor, *The Art of Leo and Diane Dillon,* Ballantine, 1981; Jim Roginski, compiler, *Newbery and Caldecott Medalists and Honor Book Winners,* Libraries Unlimited, 1982; Sally Holmes Holtze, editor, *Fifth Book of Junior Authors and Illustrators,* H. W. Wilson, 1983.

Wynken, Blynken and Nod one night
   Sailed off in a wooden shoe—
Sailed on a river of crystal light
   Into a sea of dew.

               —Eugene Field
         (From *Wynken, Blynken and Nod*)

DILLON, Leo   1933-

PERSONAL: Born March 2, 1933, in Brooklyn, N.Y.; son of Lionel J. (an owner of a truck business) and Marie (a dressmaker; maiden name, Rodriques) Dillon; married Diane Sorber (an artist), March 17, 1957; children: Lee. *Education:* Parsons School of Design, 1953, 1956; also attended School of Visual Arts, 1958. *Home:* 221 Kane St., Brooklyn, N.Y. 11231.

CAREER: West Park Publishers, New York, N.Y., art editor, 1956-67; free-lance artist and illustrator, 1958—; School of Visual Arts, New York, N.Y., instructor, 1969-77. Lecturer. *Exhibitions:* Has had several exhibitions, including: Gallery on the Green, Boston, Mass.; Metropolitan Museum, N.Y.; Boulder Center for the Visual Arts, Boulder, Colo.; Butler Institute of American Art, Youngstown, Ohio; Delaware Art Museum, Wilmington, Del.; Bratislava Book Show; American Institute of Graphic Art, N.Y.; Art Directors Club of New York; Brooklyn Public Library, N.Y.; New York Historical Society; Earthlight Gallery, Boston, Mass.; The Pentagon, Washington, D.C. *Military service:* U. S. Navy, 1950-53. *Member:* Society of Illustrators, Graphic Artists Guild.

AWARDS, HONORS: New York Herald Tribune's Children's Spring Book Festival Award honor book, 1963, for *Hakon of Rogen's Saga; Dark Venture* was chosen one of Child Study Association of America's Children's Books of the Year, 1968, *The Untold Tale,* 1971, *Behind the Back of the Mountain, 1973, Burning Star* and *Songs and Stories from Uganda,* 1974, *The Hundred Penny Box, Why Mosquitoes Buzz in People's Ears* and *Song of the Boat,* 1975, *Ashanti to Zulu,* 1976, and *The People Could Fly,* and *Brother to the Wind,* 1986; Hugo Award from the International Science Fiction Association, 1971, for illustration of a series of science-fiction book jackets; *The Untold Tale* was chosen one of *School Library Journal's* Best Books, 1971; *Behind the Back of the Mountain* and *The Third Gift* were both included in the American Institute of Graphic Arts Children's Books Show, 1973-74, and *Ashanti to Zulu,* 1976; *Behind the Back of the Mountain* was included in the Children's Book Showcase of the Children's Book Council, 1974, *Whirlwind Is a Ghost Dancing,* 1975, and *Song of the Boat,* 1976; *Why Mosquitoes Buzz in People's Ears* was selected one of *New York Times* Outstanding Books of the Year, and one of *School Library Journal's* Best Books, both 1975, and received Art Books for Children Citation from the Brooklyn Museum and Brooklyn Public Library, 1977 and 1978; *The Hundred Penny Box* was selected one of *New York Times* Outstanding Books of the Year, 1975.

Illustrator of the Newbery honor book, *The Hundred Penny Box,* 1976; Caldecott Medal from the American Library Association, 1976, for *Why Mosquitoes Buzz in People's Ears* and 1977, for *Ashanti to Zulu; Boston Globe-Horn Book* Award honor book for illustration, 1976, for *Song of the Boat,* and 1977, for *Ashanti to Zulu; Ashanti to Zulu* was chosen one of *New York Times* Best Illustrated Children's Books, 1976, and *The People Could Fly,* 1985; Hamilton King Award for excellence in illustration from the Society of Illustrators, 1977, for *Ashanti to Zulu;* Hans Christian Andersen Medal, "Highly Commended" citation for illustration, 1978; Lewis Carroll Shelf Award, 1978, for *Who's in Rabbit's House? A Masai Tale;* Balrog Award for "Lifetime Contribution to Sci-Fi/Fantasy Art," 1982; *Brother to the Wind* and *The People Could Fly* were each chosen a Notable Children's Trade Book in the Field of Social Studies by the joint committee of the National Council for Social Studies and the Children's Book Council, 1985; International Board on Books for Young People honor list for

DIANE and LEO DILLON

illustration, and Other Award from *Children's Book Bulletin,* both 1986, both for *The People Could Fly.*

ILLUSTRATOR—All with wife, Diane Dillon: Erik C. Haugaard, *Hakon of Rogen's Saga* (ALA Notable Book; *Horn Book* honor list), Houghton, 1963; E. C. Haugaard, *A Slave's Tale* (ALA Notable Book; *Horn Book* honor list), Houghton, 1965; Basil Davidson and the editors of Time-Life, *African Kingdoms,* Time-Life, 1966; Sorche Nic Leodhas (pseudonym of Leclair G. Alger), *Claymore and Kilt: Tales of Scottish Kings and Castles,* Holt, 1967; F. M. Pilkington, *Shamrock and Spear: Tales and Legends from Ireland,* Holt, 1968; E. C. Haugaard, *The Rider and His Horse* (*Horn Book* honor list), Houghton, 1968; Audrey W. Beyer, *Dark Venture,* Knopf, 1968; Frederick Laing, *Why Heimdall Blew His Horn: Tale of the Norse Gods,* Silver, 1969.

John Bierhorst and Henry R. Schoolcraft, editors, *The Ring in the Prairie: A Shawnee Legend,* Dial, 1970; Alta Jablow, *Gassire's Lute: A West African Epic,* Dutton, 1971; Alma Murray and Robert Thomas, editors, *The Search,* Scholastic, 1971; E. C. Haugaard, The Untold Tale (ALA Notable Book), Houghton, 1971; Verna Aardema, *Behind the Back of the Mountain: Black Folktales from Southern Africa* (ALA Notable Book), Dial, 1973; Eth Clifford (pseudonym of Ethel C. Rosenberg), *Burning Star,* Houghton, 1974; W. Moses Serwadda, *Songs and Stories from Uganda* (ALA Notable Book), Crowell, 1974; Jan Carew, *The Third Gift,* Little, Brown, 1974; Natalie Belting, *Whirlwind Is a Ghost Dancing,* Dutton,

1974; Lorenz Graham, *Song of the Boat* (ALA Notable Book), Crowell, 1975; Harlan Ellison, editor, *Dangerous Visions,* New American Library, 1975; Sharon Bell Mathis, *The Hundred Penny Box* (ALA Notable Book; *Horn Book* honor list), Viking, 1975; V. Aardema, reteller, *Why Mosquitoes Buzz in People's Ears: A West African Tale* (ALA Notable Book), Dial, 1975; Margaret W. Musgrove, *Ashanti to Zulu: African Traditions* (ALA Notable Book; *Horn Book* honor list), Dial, 1976; V. Aardema, reteller, *Who's in Rabbit's House? A Masai Tale* (*Horn Book* honor list), Dial, 1977; Eloise Greenfield, *Honey, I Love, and Other Love Poems* (Reading Rainbow selection), Crowell, 1978; F. Laing, *Tales from Scandinavia,* Silver, 1979.

P. L. Travers, *Two Pairs of Shoes,* Viking, 1980; J. Carew, *Children of the Sun,* Little, Brown, 1980; Dorothy S. Strickland, editor, *Listen Children: An Anthology of Black Literature,* Bantam, 1982; Virginia Hamilton, reteller, *The People Could Fly: American Black Folktales,* Knopf, 1985; Mildred Pitts Walter, *Brother to the Wind,* Lothrop, 1985; (contributor) *Once Upon a Time: Celebrating the Magic of Children's Books in Honor of the Twentieth Anniversary of Reading Is Fundamental,* Putnam, 1986. Also illustrator of *All in a Day,* [Japan], 1986.

Contributor of illustrations to periodicals, including *Ladies' Home Journal, Washington Post,* and *Saturday Evening Post.*

ADAPTATIONS: "Why Mosquitoes Buzz in People's Ears" (filmstrip with cassette; motion picture), Weston Woods, 1976;

Jim sat there listenin and thought he just was dreamin. ■ (From "The Talking Cooter" in *The People Could Fly: American Black Folktales* by Virginia Hamilton. Illustrated by Leo and Diane Dillon.)

(Poster by Leo and Diane Dillon for American Library Association's Book Week.)

"Ashanti to Zulu" (filmstrip with cassette), Weston Woods, 1977.

WORK IN PROGRESS: "We're currently illustrating *The Porcelain Cat* by Michael Patrick Hearn about a sorcerer's apprentice whose master sends him out for Baselisk's blood. All kinds of fantastical things happen. The writing is miraculous—we believe this work is destined to become a classic. We're having a marvellous time with it."

SIDELIGHTS: "We have been working together our entire career," explained Leo and Diane Dillon during a joint interview. "In terms of our art, it is virtually impossible to consider us separately. On every project we undertake, we hash out ideas together, jointly decide on style and technique, and both work on every illustration, passing the piece back and forth several times. This doesn't always go smoothly. Particularly in the past, we would argue about colors and approach. But after years of collaboration—in spite of competition between us—we have reached a point where our work is done by an agent we call 'the third artist.' We each have our distinct styles and particular strengths, but to look at our work, you could never say, 'That's Diane's line, or Leo's palette.' After a work is finished, not even we can be certain who did what. The third artist is a combination of the two of us and is different than either of us individually. We prefer 'it' is separate from our personal lives, and often as we work, seems to go off on its own. It comes up with things neither of us would have done.

"In terms of where we come from and how we grew up, we are very different, and we believe that those differences have lent breadth to the third artist."

Diane Dillon grew up in Los Angeles "which really is like coming from a small town. I felt very much a small-town girl. In many ways, my life was sheltered. There were no art high schools, for example. Art class in my high school was just as it was in grammar school. At the back of the classroom were jars of tempera; you went back and helped yourself to pigment and then painted a still life while the teacher read the newspaper. I had to wait until college to get any kind of real training. Still, as a child I drew all the time, and my parents encouraged me, particularly my father, who had artistic talent. He would look carefully at what I'd done and then offer corrections, telling me which side the shadow should fall on, for example. He was away for a year during the war from 1943 to 1944, and he sent me a big box of pastels, which meant a lot. It was not only permission to do what I wanted to do, but the *tools* I needed to do it with. My father was a school teacher and an inventor and had a knowledge of drafting. He, perhaps more than anyone else, was my mentor, although my mother also encouraged me.

"My mother was a pianist and performed engagements locally. She had been offered a world concert tour as a young woman, but turned it down to get married. In those days, women were brought up to become homemakers, my generation, too. Marrying an artist, enabled me to have a family and keep working as well—the best of both worlds: home and career.

"As a girl, the first woman artist I was inspired by was Dorothy Hood, the famous fashion illustrator. I was introduced to her work by my aunt, who was head fitter at RKO Studios. I remember waiting every Sunday for the New York and Los Angeles newspapers and then poring over the Hood drawings published there. Hood was way ahead of her time. Her drawing style was very modern. I loved the look of her line, so

different from anything else being done then. That those wonderful figures were drawn by a woman was an inspiration for me.

"I went to Los Angeles City College for two years, where I majored in art and advertising. Then I contracted tuberculosis and spent about a year in a sanitarium in California, passing most of my time reading, drawing, and knitting, because the treatment was *no* physical activity. After that, I went to live with an aunt and uncle to attend Skidmore College. I felt alien there, as though I had dropped in from another solar system. I had never seen bermuda shorts or camel hair coats, played bridge, and didn't speak their language. I was an outsider. After a year, the head of the art department told me that there was little more I could take in art there, unless I was interested in weaving or jewelry making, which at the time I was not. Now I feel it would have been good to have experienced that, since all forms of art are related and overlap in some way. My passions were life drawing and graphics. So I transferred to Parsons, where I met Leo.

"I started Parsons in the summer session, after classes had begun. I walked into a classroom and saw a student painting

(From *Gassire's Lute: A West African Epic*, translated and adapted by Alta Jablow. Illustrated by Leo and Diane Dillon.)

What was to be done? How could he free himself from his slippers and all their devil's tricks? ■
(From "Abu Kassem's Slippers" in *Two Pairs of Shoes*, retold by P. L. Travers. Illustrated by Leo and Diane Dillon.)

of various pieces of fabric and a sewing machine. It was very realistic—the subtle shadows of the pins in the cloth and the way the folds were done gave it an extraordinary three-dimensional quality. I was immediately overcome by two feelings: 'I'm in over my head,' and 'Here is a challenge I *must* meet.' The painting was Leo's, and to this day, his work sets a standard for me.''

Leo Dillon grew up in the East New York section of Brooklyn. ''My parents emigrated to this country from Trinidad. My father had a small trucking business; my mother was a dressmaker. They both encouraged my drawing. From the time I was eight or so, I worked afternoons, Saturdays and vacations with my father on the truck. He was always happy to pay for art classes. His best friend, Volman, was my mentor—a painter, a draftsman, a writer, a world traveler. It was Volman who took me to Greenwich Village for the first time to see the annual sidewalk art show. Just as Diane's father gave her pastels, Volman gave me a drawing board. He came to our house every Sunday and would show me his pen and ink drawings, a very tight 'English style.' He also spent a good deal of time with my drawings, giving me criticism and encouragement. He died in Liberia—he was always following world events. Although I never questioned the fact of his death, I don't really feel he's dead. I talk about Volman as if he'll stop by for dinner on Sunday.

''Books were also important to me. One of my father's trucking clients was a paper company who were always giving him books. I still have the one that changed my life—*The Arabian Nights*. I'd never before seen drawings of that quality, and still strive to equal that excellence. In our local library was a section of illustrated French classics, and although I couldn't read French, I was captivated by the drawings. Old Masters, I couldn't get enough of the Old Masters.

''Drawing was a way for me to learn about things I hadn't yet been exposed to. I remember one summer I went to camp. The kids there were really into jazz, which I knew nothing about. For a while I drew nothing but groups of musicians. Only *after* that phase did I get to see my first jazz concert.

''At the High School of Industrial Design, teacher Benjamin Clements was crucial to my development. The training prepared us for a commercial career, but Clements realized that I could do more than illustrate Coke bottles, and pushed me to expand my mind. After graduation, I enlisted in the Navy, partly because I wasn't sure what I wanted to do next, and partly because I wanted to attend college on the GI Bill. For the three years I spent in the service, I drew lots of portraits on 'commission' from guys who wanted pictures of their girlfriends. I painted in the ship's hold, and mixed my pigments from nautical paint. When I completed my stint, I went back to see Clements who pretty much insisted that I go to Parsons. I had a scholarship to Pratt, a more commercial school, but I turned it down. I was intimidated at the prospect of being with 'artsy types,' but I so respected Clements that I swallowed my fear. He went over my portfolio with me, told me what to include, what to leave out. I worked like a demon at Parsons, and kept mostly to myself.''

(Illustration by Leo and Diane Dillon for the album cover of L. Frank Baum's "The Wogglebug." Caedmon Records, 1982.)

"... One day I noticed a painting hanging on the wall at a student exhibition. It was a painting of a chair—an Eames chair—and I knew it had to be by a new student because nobody in our class at the time could paint like that. I looked at the painting, and thought, 'I'm in trouble now!'.... This artist knew perspective, which is one of the most difficult things a beginner has to learn. And most important—this artist had the ability to *render*! This artist was a whole lot better than I. I figured I'd better find out who he was. *He* was Diane.

"I hadn't spoken to her yet—in fact, I wasn't sure I was going to—when she came over to me and said, 'You are very good.' 'Hah!' I thought. 'Miss Talent is now going to condescend to tell one of the menials he's good. I know better.' I said, 'I see that one of your pieces is very nice too.' And that pretty much set the tone of our relationship for the next several years." [Leo Dillon, "Diane Dillon," *Horn Book,* August, 1977.¹ Amended by Leo Dillon.]

"This wasn't merely competition,' said Leo, 'it was *war*. We spent a lot of time and energy trying to prove ourselves to each other. In the midst of all this, born of the mutual recognition of our respective strengths, we fell in love. We tried to keep our relationship a secret not only because we were in the rather ingrown world of Parsons, but because in those days inter-racial couples were not easily accepted. We knew of couples like us who had been beaten up walking down the street.

"Our competitiveness reached a crisis point in 1956, and at graduation we separated. Diane went to Albany to work in the

art department of an advertising firm, I freelanced in New York, mostly for men's and science magazines. But we weren't meant to be separated, and we married in March of 1957.''

Leo went to work full-time as art director at West Park Publications, which specialized in men's magazines. ''The good thing about the job,'' said Diane ''was that Leo had quite a lot of autonomy and was in a position to go in late and bring work home. I worked with him at home. But we still felt confined and decided to go totally freelance. We set up as Studio 2. The competition between us was still so strong that we knew we would never survive separate careers. Working as a team, we felt, would not only enhance our professional lives, but probably keep our marriage from going under. Because we wanted to work in a variety of styles, we thought it

better not to use our names. We figured, rightly, that we would have more variety if clients thought we were a studio full of artists. We were more likely to be pigeon-holed into a particular medium or approach by clients who wanted to categorize artists into a particular style.

''We had Studio 2 from the late fifties until the early sixties. Times were different then,'' said Leo, ''and I wanted to make sure that potential clients knew that a black man was part of the operation. I made a habit of showing up at virtually all important meetings. I didn't want anyone to think I was hiding. Perhaps there were a few people who didn't call us again because of the race issue, but there was never any overt hostility. Perhaps our anxiety made us overcompensate and force the issue. We learned that what really counts is what an artist

(Illustration by Leo and Diane Dillon for cover of *Ashanti to Zulu: African Traditions* by Margaret Musgrove.)

has on paper. If you do beautiful work, people don't care who or what you are.

"Together we encompass so much. We have done a vast range of work from African folk tales to Scandinavian epics to science fiction and fantasy. In the sixties, during the 'hot years'

for Civil Rights, we were thought of as black artists. We did a lot of illustrations for articles and books on jazz musicians and what was then referred to as 'the black experience.' A big break for us was meeting Harlan Ellison, a Chicago magazine editor, who had us illustrate work by Nat Hentoff, Ben Hecht and other 'hip' writers. We also did the cover for *Gentleman*

"Just sit there," she said. "And don't move until I tell you!" ■ (From *The Hundred Penny Box* by Sharon Bell Mathis. Illustrated by Leo and Diane Dillon.)

(Detail of jacket illustration by Leo and Diane Dillon from *A Fair Wind for Troy* by Doris Gates.)

Junkie and Other Stories of the Hung-Up Generation. This cover was very important in terms of our development. We had the freedom to experiment with mixed media, hand-lettering and type. We used a strong black graphic style with vivid color which was very bold for the times.

"Because we both work on every piece of art, we favor techniques that give us a lot of control. We don't leave ourselves open to 'accident.' We need a technique so sure that a line begun by one of us can be completed by the other with no visual hint of interruption. We are constantly experimenting.

(Jacket illustration from *Why Mosquitoes Buzz in People's Ears* by Verna Aardema. Illustrated by Leo and Diane Dillon.)

This is exhilarating, but there are times when it's extremely frustrating, trying to overcome the unknown. That period of not knowing what is wrong can be excruciating. But over the years we've come to accept that trial and error is part of the process. Technique is to the graphic artist what words are to the writer.

"In the mid-sixties, we did a number of books for Time-Life, whose art director, Ed Hamilton, essentially gave us carte blanche. For Carson McCullers' *The Member of the Wedding* we did the cover in crewel. Why, we really can't say, except that we hadn't done it before and wanted to give it a try. I had embroidered dish towels as a young girl and sewn for years, Leo had some experience basting and sewing, helping his mother. We designed and built a special frame to work

on, in lieu of a traditional embroidery hoop, that would both stretch the fabric and keep it from puckering. It could be swiveled so that we could tie off threads in the back. We were trying to paint with thread. In the process, we 'invented' a number of stitches, and unknowingly came up with some classic stitches. We were so pleased with the textural nuances and light play of the various threads, and then learned how difficult it was to reproduce those subtleties photographically. We remember that job very vividly. Our son, Lee, had just been born. For hours on end, he lay in his crib watching our arms go up and down, up and down, up and down. . . .

"Another innovative Time-Life cover was for C. S. Lewis' *Till We Have Faces.* We did that one with plastic and leading made with liquid steel, which gave a stained-glass effect. To give the leading a patina, we burnished the liquid steel with silver and copper. For photographic reproduction, the piece was lit from behind, which gave it new reproduction problems since it got hot spots with the lighting.

"Erik Haugaard's books, most of which are retellings of Scandinavian tales and legends, have also presented us with some great subject matter. For *The Untold Tale,* we were obsessed with getting a linen-like texture. We sandpapered the surface of the illustration board both horizontally and vertically then applied a coat of walnut floor wax. We weren't sure if after it dried the wax would be stable, but it was. We also weren't sure if the paint we planned to use (a water-soluble paint called cassein) would adhere. But it did. We drew right on the wax with pen and ink and then applied paint. The lighter colors we did in linear-type brush strokes or else scratched in with a knife. The whole point was to achieve a linen-like surface. Of course, we could have bought linen board to begin with, but we preferred experimenting and the challenge of solving all the problems we put in our path!

"Much of our work appears to be woodblock prints, but that is an illusion. We wanted to do woodcuts but because of the time element of deadline, we developed a two-dimensional

"Say you so?" a voice inquired from behind us. ■ (From *Burning Star* by Eth Clifford. Illustrated by Leo and Diane Dillon.)

I stood up, and at that moment, I realized that I was not the only hunter on the Mountain of the Sun that day. ■ (From *Hakon of Rogen's Saga* by Erik Christian Haugaard. Illustrated by Leo and Diane Dillon.)

technique, one of which is the frisket, a sort of stencil. When we were at Parsons, they introduced us to the technique of rubber cementing vellum tracing paper to the illustration board and then cutting out the working area to keep the borders protected. We thought, 'Why not cut out shapes, too?' We cut areas with an X-Acto knife and used ink. If we were working in color, we applied pastel in thin layers which gave an interesting texture. The frisket enabled us to have the cut edges that you get in a woodcut. We were able to work on a single sheet, using separate friskets for the various images.

"Our innovation in the frisket technique is the use of shaved pastel dust. We scrape the pastel with an X-Acto blade to get the dust which we apply with a brush or cotton. At the frisket edge you get a little build-up which looks like an etched line. Frisket with pastel may be our main technique; we go back to it again and again. Many people think that they're looking at watercolor applied with an air brush. The similarity between the two is an 'airiness' in the pigment, which gives a light, bright look. The air brush tends to be too smooth with no texture. The pastel has a grainy texture, as opposed to the smoothness of air brush.

"During the sixties, for Washington Square Press, we did a number of covers for classic works of literature. The range was extraordinary—medieval literature, Shakespeare, Kafka. We used an 'art historical' approach, doing woodcuts in keeping with the period and style of the subject matter. We have done actual woodcuts also. It's a combination of sculpture, in a way, and graphics.

"Another example of experimentation was *The Hundred Penny Box*. This was a very difficult story. The text was basically dialogue with no action to speak of. We wanted to keep that intimacy, to give the reader the feeling he was looking through an old family photo album. We used the frisket to protect the outside edge and laid a ground of Brown water color. We then applied a solution of Chlorox and water to etch out the light tones which gave us brown, beiges, tans, and we worked from dark to light, each new application making lighter tones."

Leo and Diane Dillon are the first, and, thus far, the only artists to have won the Caldecott Medal for the most distinguished American picture book for children in two consecutive years—1976 and 1977. "*Why Mosquitoes Buzz in People's Ears* [a retelling of a West African folk tale by Verna Aardema, published in 1975] was the first time we illustrated a book intended for young children. We were delighted that this book was perfect for reading aloud. It is an illustrators job to

He stood in the center of the village square holding this marvelous Flower. . . . ■ (From *The Third Gift* by Jan Carew. Illustrated by Leo and Diane Dillon.)

go beyond the text, to illustrate what is between the lines, not just to repeat the words. *Mosquitoes* is a repetitive tale in which the events are interpreted by different animals, each with a distinct point of view. We found ourselves concentrating on the play between the animals.''

''The antelope has a very minor part in the story—he is simply sent to bring Mother Owl and later the iguana before the council. We decided he really wanted a more important part—he wanted to be a star. So he began trying to get attention, peering out and grinning, hamming it up, until finally on one spread he is seen up front in the center, with a great toothy smile. . . . The little red bird never appears in the text at all. We put her in one spread and became rather fond of her. We began to think of her as the observer or reader and added her to the other spreads. Thus on each page you will find her watching, witnessing the events as they unfold. On the last page, when the story is over, she flies away. For us she is like the storyteller, gathering information, then passing it on to the next generation.'' [Leo and Diane Dillon, ''Caldecott Award Acceptance,'' *Horn Book,* August, 1976.[2]]

''The style of the illustrations for *Mosquitoes* was inspired by African batik. For this book, we used an air brush to apply pigment. Because at a certain point in the story, the sun refuses to rise, half the backgrounds are white, half are black. With air brush we were able to slowly build up light layers on paint to go from a nearly transparent hue to opaque.''

''Someone asked us recently who was the perfectionist,'' said Diane ''and I'd say it was Leo, but sometimes it's hard to tell when you work so closely together. I do know, though, that our real feeling about aiming for perfection began with *Why Mosquitoes Buzz in People's Ears.* Suddenly it seemed that neither of us could tolerate even a tiny flaw, a minute speck on the black night sky, and we strove for artistic perfection on that book more than on any other except *Ashanti to Zulu.*'' [Diane Dillon, ''Leo Dillon,'' *Horn Book,* August, 1977.[3]]

''[After the 1976 Caldecott Award was announced and we won for *Mosquitoes,*] we returned home from Chicago to work on *Ashanti to Zulu: African Traditions.* Our primary concern was to do a book that would show our gratitude for such an honor. We wanted our next book to be the best we had ever done. It would not only be a way of saying thank you, but a way of proving to *ourselves* that we deserved the award. . . .

''The text for the most part deals with people in everyday pursuits. We began to appreciate the grandeur in ordinary living, in what actually exists. It is the intelligence in a person's eyes or the nuances of body language—things shared by all people—that make for real beauty. We strove to be accurate with the factual details but especially wanted to stress the things we all have in common—a smile, a touch, our humanity. We took artistic license with particular situations so that they reflected the tenderness that exists among all peoples. It didn't matter if the Ga man would ever be around when his wife was making foufou; the tenderness of his touch, the warmth passing between them is a universal truth. Or with the Quimbande it was irrelevant whether the husband, wife, and children would sit down to play a game in the middle of the compound; the love and family closeness were true. . . . The more we read and learned about each group, the more we realized that each was unique. The customs were as varied as the types of peoples. The dwellings were far more varied than we had been aware of. Some were made of mud and wattle, some of stone or mud bricks, some of woven mats. Some were square, others were round. Some roofs were flat, others conical. The clothing and patterns were specific, from the special blankets of the Sotho with their hats that repeat the shape of the mountains in that area to the ornate, embroidered clothing of the Hausa. Even the style of hair had meaning, as did the jewelry. The peoples themselves ranged from warm red tones through yellow ochres to ebony. There was no way of faking it. Like Europe, Africa is comprised of many peoples and customs, even more varied than our own continent.'' [Leo and Diane Dillon, ''Caldecott Acceptance Speech,'' *Horn Book,* August, 1977.[4]]

''We felt very ambitious on this book. We wanted our illustrations for *Ashanti to Zulu* to be something other artists could look to as source material. We strove to combine realism, for we wanted to be absolutely accurate with the elegance one normally associates with fairy tales. We used pastels, water color, acrylic, black ink. The corners of every page are adorned with an interwoven design based on the Kano Knot, a design originally used in the city of Kano which flourished in northern Nigeria in the sixteenth and seventeenth centuries, and symbolizes endless searching.

''People often ask us if we have spent time in Africa. We have not, although we would love to. People have said that we have 'captured African light,' for example. But you know, if you look up at the sky anywhere in the world, you see the same sunsets, the same clouds. You get the same feeling of wonder. This really hit us when we were in Brazil, one of the few trips we have taken. The sky was marvellous, the shadows beguiling, but really, it was the same sky and the same shadows we see at home in Brooklyn.

''There have been times in our career during which we felt invisible. Sometimes this was frustrating, and the isolation sometimes dulled our motivation. The Caldecott Awards were something we were unprepared for. We hadn't realized that people had really been looking at our work over the years. Suddenly, we had opportunities to travel, to do interviews. The attention, and the fact that we were called upon to give a meaningful acceptance speech, forced us to clarify certain things to ourselves, among them the third artist. This was tremendously important to us. We hadn't before stepped back to examine our ways of working, we'd just worked. We were made to look at ourselves with a critical distance, and this was healthy.

''We were unaccustomed to having attention focused on us. At first, it was fun and forced us to grow—to travel more readily and talk to people, for example. But we also realized that what we really prefer is to be working out of the spotlight.

''Our lives have turned out to be even richer and happier than we had dreamed. Not only have we given birth to our third artist, but to a fourth, our son, Lee, who makes exquisite jewelry. We have learned so much from him, and this has affected the way we do children's books. We don't believe that there is a characteristic called 'childlike.' A child is a whole, not a partial person. And a child is more honest, more demanding than an adult. A child does not easily tolerate error, inconsistency or illogicalness. That children are our audience is at once a responsibility, an honor, and a profound joy.''

Dillon's works are included in the Kerlan Collection of the University of Minnesota.

—Based on an interview by Marguerite Feitlowitz

FOR MORE INFORMATION SEE: ''Winners! Honors! Prizes!,'' *American Libraries,* March, 1976; *Top of the News,* April, 1976, summer, 1977; *Horn Book,* August, 1976, August, 1977; *School Library Journal,* March, 1977; Lee Kingman and others, compilers, *Illustrators of Children's Books, 1967-1976,* Horn Book, 1978; Byron Preiss, editor, *The Art of Leo and Diane Dillon,* Ballantine, 1981; Jim Roginski, compiler, *Newbery and Caldecott Medalists and Honor Book Winners,* Libraries Unlimited, 1982; Sally Holmes Holtze, *Fifth Book of Junior Authors and Illustrators,* H. W. Wilson, 1983.

EDELSON, Edward 1932-

PERSONAL: Born September 10, 1932, in New York, N.Y.; son of Saul (a restaurateur) and Sarah (Sunshine) Edelson; married Phyllis Kaplan, October 26, 1957; children: Noah, Daniel, Anne. *Education:* New York University, B.S., 1953; Columbia University, student in advanced science writing program, 1963-64.

CAREER: Times-Herald Record, Middletown, N.Y., telegraph editor and city editor, 1959-62; reporter and science editor for *New York World Telegram,* 1962-66; science editor for *New York World Journal Tribune,* 1966-67, and WNDT-TV, New York City, 1968-70; *Family Health,* New York City, senior staff writer, 1968-71, contributing editor, 1971—; *New York Daily News,* New York City, science writer, 1971—. *Military service:* U. S. Army, 1954-55. *Member:* National Association of Science Writers. *Awards, honors:* New York Citizens for Clean Air Award, 1965; Writing Award Certificate of Merit, American Medical Association, 1970; Science Writing Award, American Dental Association, 1970; Science Writing Award in physics and astronomy, American Institute of Physics, 1973; *Great Animals of the Movies* was selected one of New York Public Library's Books for the Teen Age, 1981, 1982.

WRITINGS: Parents' Guide to Science, Crowell, 1966; (with Fred Warshofsky) *Poisons in the Air,* Pocket Books, 1966; *Healers in Uniform,* Doubleday, 1971; *Help for Your Headache,* Grosset, 1971; *Great Monsters of the Movies,* Doubleday, 1973; *The Book of Prophecy,* Doubleday, 1974; *Visions of Tomorrow: Great Science Fiction from the Movies,* Doubleday, 1975; *Funny Men of the Movies,* Doubleday, 1976; *Great Movie Spectaculars,* Doubleday, 1976; (with William Leo Nyham) *The Heredity Factor: Genes, Chromosomes, and You,* Grosset, 1976; *Tough Guys and Gals of the Movies,* Doubleday, 1978; (with Robert Boikess) *Chemical Principles,* Harper, 1978, 2nd edition, 1981; *Great Kids of the Movies,* Doubleday, 1979; *Great Animals of the Movies,* Doubleday, 1980; *Who Goes There? The Search for Intelligent Life in the*

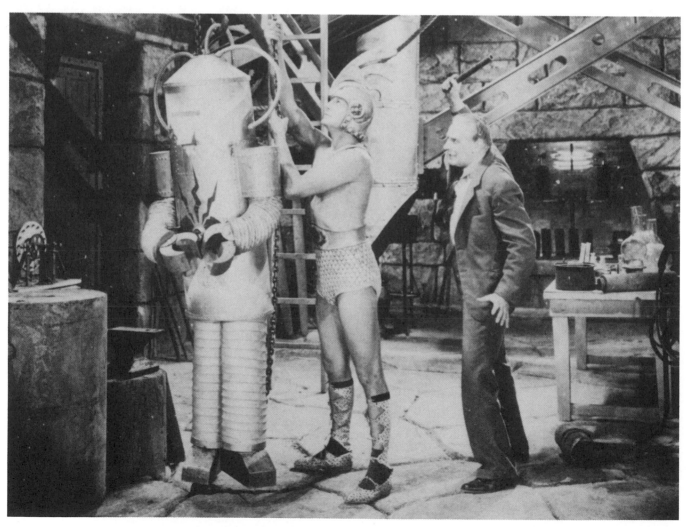

"Undersea Kingdom." That's Crash Corrigan doing the repair work on the robot, unaware of what awaits him. ■ (From *Visions of Tomorrow: Great Science Fiction from the Movies* by Edward Edelson. Photograph courtesy of Republic Pictures.)

Universe, McGraw, 1980; *ABC's of Prescription Drugs,* Doubleday, 1987.

Interviewer for "Speaking of Science" cassette series, American Association for the Advancement of Science, 1972-73. Contributor of articles to periodicals, including *Smithsonian, Saturday Review,* and *Popular Science.*

FITZ-RANDOLPH, Jane (Currens) 1915-

PERSONAL: Name legally changed in 1951; born June 23, 1915, in Boulder, Colo.; daughter of Jesse Wilson (a Presbyterian minister) and Gertrude (a teacher; maiden name, Fitz-Randolph) Currens; married Frederick Charles Porter (an engineer), June 19, 1935 (divorced, 1950); children: Frederick Charles, Jr., Philip Edward, Priscilla Jane. *Education:* University of Colorado, B.A., 1937; graduate study at Tulane University of Louisiana, George Washington University, and University of California, Los Angeles. *Politics:* Independent. *Religion:* Christian Science. *Home:* 1845 Bluebell Ave., Boulder, Colo. 80302.

CAREER: National Writers Club, Denver, Colo., critic and teacher, 1950-62, member of board of directors, 1972—, vice-president, 1979—; University of Colorado, Denver and Boulder, instructor in writing, 1950-79. *Member:* Society of Children's Book Writers, Colorado Authors League. *Awards, honors:* Golden Eagle Award from Council on International Nontheatrical Events (CINE), 1978, for "What's So Great about Books?"; Award of Excellence from the Society for Technical Communication, 1979, for *From Sundials to Atomic Clocks;* honorable mention from the New York Academy of Sciences, 1980, for *Time and Clocks for the Space Age,* and 1982, for *Mercury's Web: The Story of Telecommunications.*

WRITINGS: Writing for the Juvenile and Teenage Market, Funk, 1969, revised edition published as *How to Write for Children and Young Adults,* Barnes & Noble, 1980, new edition, Johnson Publishing, 1987; (with James Jespersen) *From Sundials to Atomic Clocks,* U.S. Government Printing Office, 1978; (with J. Jespersen) *Time and Clocks for the Space Age,* Atheneum, 1980; (with J. Jespersen) *Mercury's Web: The Story of Telecommunications,* Atheneum, 1981; (with J. Jespersen) *RAMs, ROMs, and Robots: The Inside Story of Computers,* Atheneum, 1984; (with J. Jespersen) *From Quarks to Quasars: A Tour of the Universe,* Atheneum, 1987.

Author of scripts for more than forty educational films and filmstrips, including "If You're for Colorado," 1966, "Pacific Neighbors States," 1968, "The Search for the Hidden Sugar," 1973, "Sharing Literature with Children," 1976, "What's So Great about Books?," 1978, "America's Railroads: How the Iron Horse Shaped Our Nation," 1980, and "You Too Can Make a Map," 1983.

SIDELIGHTS: "I began writing part time for magazines in my college days, but I was first and foremost a career mother. When supporting my family became necessary, I began writing scripts for nontheatrical films and filmstrips. At one time I wrote for the national radio program of the Christian Science Church. My church and religion are my central interest and activity; whatever I've done in writing or as a person would have been impossible without a foundation in spiritual values. My greatest joys are the achievements of my children and grandchildren, and, also, the achievements of my students and former students. I love to teach—it is the most exciting and rewarding profession in the world.

JANE FITZ-RANDOLPH

"I am admittedly a perfectionist and have no patience with 'good enough' or 'it will get by.' If I'm going to do something at all, I expect to do it to the very best of my ability, and I want to work with others whose aims are the same."

HOBBIES AND OTHER INTERESTS: The outdoors, gardening, hiking, swimming, birds, horses, reading, classical music.

FOX, Merrion Frances 1946-
(Mem Fox)

PERSONAL: Born March 5, 1946, in Melbourne, Australia; daughter of Wilfrid Gordon McDonald (a missionary) and Nancy Walkden (a writer; maiden name, Brown) Partridge; married Malcolm Fox (a teacher), January 2, 1969; children: Chloë Catienne. *Education:* Rose Bruford Drama School, London, diploma, 1968; Finders University, South Australia, B.A., 1978; South Australian College of Advanced Education, B.Ed., 1979, graduate diploma, 1981. *Politics:* Labour. *Religion:* Christian. *Home:* 40 Melton St., Blackwood, South Australia 5051. *Agent:* Caroline Lurie, 2A Armstrong St., Middle Park, Australia 3206. *Office:* South Australian College of Advanced Education, Sturt Rd., Bedford Park, South Australia 5042.

CAREER: Teacher and professor. Cabra Dominican School, Adelaide, South Australia, drama teacher, 1970-72; South Australian College of Advanced Education—Sturt, Adelaide, South Australia, lecturer, 1973-86, senior lecturer, 1987—. *Member:* South Australian Story Telling Guild (president, 1981), Actors Equity, Australian Society of Authors, National Council for Teachers of English, Primary English Teachers Association (Australia), Children's Book Council (Australia), Association for Study of Australian Literature. *Awards, honors:* High commendation from the Australian Children's Book Council Picture Book of the Year Award, and New South Wales Premier's Literary Award for Best Children's Book, both 1984, both for *Possum Magic;* short-listed for Picture Book of the Year, Australia, and chosen one of Child Study Association of America's Children's Books of the Year, both 1985, and selected one of *New York Times* Notable Books, 1986, all for *Wilfrid Gordon McDonald Partridge.*

WRITINGS—All under name Mem Fox: *Possum Magic,* Omnibus, 1983; *Wilfrid Gordon McDonald Partridge* (ALA Notable Book; illustrated by Julie Vivas), Omnibus, 1984, Kane Miller, 1985; *How to Teach Drama to Infants without Really Crying,* Ashton Scholastic, 1984, published in America as *Teaching Drama to Young Children,* Heinemann, 1986; *A Cat Called Kite,* Ashton Scholastic (New Zealand), 1985; *Hattie and the Fox* (illustrated by Patricia Mullins), Ashton Scholastic, 1986, Bradbury, 1987; *Sail Away,* Ashton Scholastic, 1986; *Arabella,* Ashton Scholastic, 1986; *Just Like That,* Hodder & Stoughton, 1986; *Zoo Looking,* Martin Educational, 1986; *Koala Lou,* Dent, 1987; *A Bedtime Story,* Martin Educational, 1987; *The Straight Line Wonder,* Martin Educational, 1987; *Shoes from Grandpa,* Ashton Scholastic, 1988; *Night Noises,* Omnibus, 1988; *Guess What,* Omnibus, 1988; *Sophie,* Dent, 1988; *Feathers and Fools,* Roehring (Melbourne), 1988.

WORK IN PROGRESS: Beach Dog, about a boy who finds a lost dog by the sea.

SIDELIGHTS: Born March 5, 1946, in Melbourne, Australia. "At the age of six months, I was taken by my parents to live in Zimbabwe, which was then called Rhodesia. My parents were missionaries, which sounds very old-fashioned and calls up troubling images of religious fanaticism and cultural im-

MERRION FRANCES FOX

perialism. My parents were not of this mold: they were left-wing and supportive of African movements for independence, essentially educators who taught in public and mission schools.

"In our mission home, I grew up among black people, and until I was five or so, I believed I was black. I was the only white child at the mission school, blind to my own whiteness and absolutely astonished when the local authorities told my parents I would be required to attend a school for white children. I clearly remember thinking, 'Gee, I must be *special* if I have to go to a white school.' It really didn't occur to me that I was white. All of my friends were black. This decision by the local authorities was made mid-way through the school year, and my parents simply kept me out of school for the rest of the term. It was an odd time. I spent hours swinging on our gate feeling alone, bewildered and posh all at once.

"I was quite the tomboy and loved to climb trees, ride bikes and play football. But I also loved to read. I still read voraciously. From a literary standpoint, the nineteenth is 'my' century. I love those big fat books with lots of characters and subplots. My parents had many, many books, mostly classics. I tore through them all. But the world of books—*those* books at any rate—was a fantasy world completely removed from my way of life. For example, a house with an 'upstairs' was as exotic to me as the planet Mars. Common English expressions, like 'Go up to bed now, dear,' completely mystified me. I remember reading only two books about Africa as a child—*Rhodesian Adventures* and *A House on the Kopje.* Both of these were quite good, but neither dealt with life on a mission. In fact, writers then simply did not write about relations between blacks and whites. The two races were separate. The only way the vast majority of whites met blacks was to hire them as maids, servants and workers.

"My mother, who has just published her second novel, wrote while I was growing up. But during those years, she never attempted to publish, which to this day I cannot understand. Why write, if not to publish and get reactions? I wrote my first book at the age of ten on the subject of soil erosion. I remember reading it in its entirety to my mother, who obviously was trying not to fall asleep—that's how dull it was! My next book, written at age fourteen, was about a friendship between a black and white girl—very personal for me.

"High school was a particularly difficult time. Of course, I was still made to attend an all-white school. The bigotry of genteel whites made me sick. I was living a sort of double life—I had friends and boyfriends, but on some level I knew that, for me, it was make-believe. It was probably not noticeable from the outside, but I was carrying a tremendous amount of rage.

"I could no longer tolerate the political and social repression in Rhodesia, and decided to go to England to attend drama school. I got the idea to become an actress from one of my uncles with whom we spoke frequently on our ham radio. 'Mem's the only one I can hear clearly,' he'd always say. 'She's got a beautiful voice, Mem has.' That was it, I wanted to be a radio actress. We were, in many ways, extremely isolated in Rhodesia. That the human voice, with the aid of a box and some wire, could pierce that isolation was to me a life-changing realization.

"I arrived in London in the heyday of Carnaby Street, the Beatles, miniskirts, pantyhose, and words like psychedelic. I was a real hick, and in more ways than one. Never exposed to television, I had no clue about what to expect on a daily basis on the street. I also had no idea about the social class

She smiled at the puppet on strings and remembered the one she had shown to her sister, and how she had laughed with a mouth full of porridge. ■ (From *Wilfrid Gordon McDonald Partridge* by Mem Fox. Illustrated by Julie Vivas.)

system. Because my parents were missionaries and we were poor, I assumed we were working class. But no, because we were educated and knew which fork to use and when, we were considered well within the scope of the genteel set. The whole system, and the attitudes that went with it, disgusted me. I played with it as though it were a diabolical toy. Because I can do accents well, I experimented: I'd go into a posh store and talk posh or Cockney depending on what reaction I was trying to elicit—dark fun, that.

"In drama school, I particularly liked acting in Shakespearean and restoration plays. Comedy, too. I didn't like doing Noel Coward, had no patience or sympathy for his characters who seem to me quite useless.

"In school I met Malcolm Fox who later became my husband. We traveled to Australia as an adventure. At the time the Australian government was seeking migrants and through their lavish incentives we were able to travel from England to Australia for a mere ten pounds, or about forty dollars. That was in 1970, and we thought we'd stay two years. We're still there!

"I thought that the last thing I would want to do is teach, but I am endlessly fascinated with the science of teaching—how people learn, what keeps them motivated, what spurs their creativity. I teach drama and language arts—the love of language and literature. Increasingly, I have been driven to expose my students to Australian books. In the 1950s, even within Australia, the intellectuals were saying, 'There is no Australian literature.' In the schools, British literature was the order of the day—Jane Austen, Thomas Hardy, Virginia Woolf. I don't deny that these are great writers, but they are not the *only* ones. Australians have had a cultural inferiority complex, and it's been part of my mission as a writer and educator to combat that.

"My first book, which I wrote in 1978, was rejected nine times over five years. 'Too Australian,' they said. The whole point of the book was its Australian-ness! I got so discouraged that I buried the manuscript in my desk drawer. Finally, it was my husband who said, 'If you don't send that thing around, I will!' He shamed me into sending it off. And lo and behold, it was finally accepted. The irony—a crowning irony if I might say so—is that *Possum Magic* is the best-selling children's

"Well, well!" said the pig. ■ (From *Hattie and the Fox* by Mem Fox. Illustrated by Patricia Mullins.)

And they both danced
"Here We Go Round the Lamington Plate"
Till early in the morning.

■ (From *Possum Magic* by Mem Fox. Illustrated by Julie Vivas.)

book in the history of Australia, has won a number of awards, and been published internationally.

"The process of writing *Possum Magic* was excruciating. A novel is like an oak tree with all its branches. A picture book, however, is more like a polished plank of wood. With it, you cannot exceed the bare minimum. Because you haven't many words to play with, rhythm is extremely important. In fact, I believe that rhythm is the most important element in the text of a picture book. There must be no evidence of strain, the story must fall into place apparently effortlessly. *Apparently!* The first paragraph of *Possum Magic* took me twenty-three drafts. I can't remember who originally said it, but it's true:

'It's not how well you write, but how well you *rewrite* that matters.'

"*Wilfrid Gordon McDonald Partridge,* the first of my books to be published in the United States, came to me while I was threatening to 'lose my temper' with my daughter. Afterward, I got to thinking, 'What does it mean, to *lose* one's temper? Can one *find* one's temper?' I made a mental list of expressions we have for losing intangibles—memory, for instance. We quite routinely say, 'I'm losing my memory,' but never, 'I'm finding my memory.' My book is about a small boy with a very long name who helps an elderly friend 'find' her memory.

"I write 'up' to children, never 'down.' I write to move children. All of my ideas for books come from my life. I frequently tell my students, 'I've no imagination at all.' *Possum Magic* came about because I was enraged that my daughter had no books to help her identify herself as an Australian, to help her feel proud of her country and heritage. *Wilfrid* came out of my very close relationship with my grandfather who, like Miss Nancy in the book, lived to be ninety-six. *Sail Away* was inspired by the America's Cup Sailing Regatta, which Australia won in 1983. (You don't need to care a wit about the America's Cup to read the book!) A funny little dog I saw on the beach one day inspired a forthcoming book.

"My book *Feathers and Fools* was deliberately written in a style which recalls Hans Christian Andersen. It is about a community of swans and a community of peacocks. Owing to an innocuous difference between them—swans swim, while peacocks do not—the peacocks conceive a mortal fear of the swans and begin sharpening feathers to use as weapons in the event of an attack. The swans respond by also sharpening and stockpiling feathers. One day, a swan flies overhead with a twig for nestmaking in its mouth. Mistaking the twig for a sharpened feather, the peacocks declare war, and the two communities wipe each other out. Or so it would seem. Hidden near the water's edge is a swan's egg, and in the brush is a peacock's egg. The eggs hatch, the newborns are struck by the degree to which they *resemble* each other and swear everlasting friendship.

"This book, obviously, has political overtones, and makes a comment on the nuclear stalemate and impending disaster between the superpowers. None of the publishers who had done my books previously would touch this story. 'Too macabre,' they said, 'too depressing.' Instead, it is being published by a relatively small, and I guess I must say *brave* house.

"But that publisher isn't the only brave cultural force around, I am happy to say. There is an extremely popular radio program in Australia called 'The Science Show.' I sent them this story with a note which read, 'Here is what the artists do while the scientists screw things up.' To my surprise and delight, they sent someone to record me reading the piece and played it at the end of one of their programs, followed only by music.

"In 1982 I joined a women's writing group, something I never thought I would do. I came of age before Women's Liberation and tended to avoid the company of women. I assumed that men were more clever and amusing. The women's movement of the late sixties and seventies did a lot to change my attitudes and change the way I have raised my daughter. My writing group is one of the best things to have happened to me.

"I like to keep a journal, though I do so rather sporadically. I think that for me having a journal is a bit like having a shrink. I also like to write letters, particularly when I'm traveling. I prefer my writing to be directed outward to others. I write to *converse.*

"Don't be easily discouraged." Fox tells aspiring writers. "To write well is very difficult. Draft and redraft. And if publishers knock you back, just remember, it's all part of it. After nine rejections over five years, *Possum Magic* became a runaway bestseller. The same can happen to you!"

Fox has had shows on television as a storyteller of Bible stories, Greek legends, African folktales, and traditional stories.

—*Based on an interview by Marguerite Feitlowitz*

HOBBIES AND OTHER INTERESTS: Films, travel, spring cleaning.

GELMAN, Rita Golden   1937-
(R. G. Austin)

BRIEF ENTRY: Born July 2, 1937, in Bridgeport, Conn. After receiving her bachelor's degree from Brandeis University in 1958, Gelman was a staff writer for *Young American* magazine and an editor for various New York-based publishing companies before she became a full-time, free-lance writer in 1974. Her first book, *Dumb Joey* (Holt, 1973), was followed by more than forty titles covering a wide range of topics of interest to juvenile readers, including riddle books, how-to's, and fiction. Among her titles are *The Me I Am* (Macmillan, 1975); *Comits: A Book of Comic Skits* (Macmillan, 1975); *Great Quarterbacks of Pro Football* (Scholastic Book Services, 1975), written with husband, Steve; *Professor Coconut and the Thief* (Holt, 1977), written with Joan Richter; and *The Biggest Sandwich Ever* (Scholastic Book Services, 1979). Since 1982 Gelman has collaborated with author Nancy Austin on Archway's "Which Way" series, including *Castle of No Return* (1982), *The Spell of the Black Raven* (1982), and *The Visitors from Outer Space* (1983). These are only a few choices in this collection which puts the reader in the driver's seat, making him the hero or victim of his exploits. While free-lancing, Gelman returned to school and, in 1984, received her master's degree from the University of California, Los Angeles. She is presently a Ph.D. candidate at that same university. *Agent:* Marilyn Marlow, Curtis Brown Ltd., 575 Madison Ave., New York, N.Y. 10022.

FOR MORE INFORMATION SEE: Contemporary Authors, New Revision Series, Volume 16, Gale, 1986.

GERRARD, Jean   1933-

PERSONAL: Born July 23, 1933, in Blackpool, Lancashire, England; daughter of John (an electrical contractor) and Dorothy (a teacher) Thatcher; married Roy Gerrard (an artist and author), March 28, 1958; children: Sally Gerrard Turpie, Paul. *Education:* Avery Hill College, Teaching Diploma, 1953. *Home:* 10 Maynestone Rd., Chinley, Derbyshire SK12 6AQ, England.

CAREER: Secondary school art teacher, 1953-60; secondary school remedial education teacher, 1966-68; Marple Ridge High School, Stockport, Cheshire, England, head of remedial department, 1968-81, head of lower school, 1981—. *Awards, honors:* Mother Goose Award runner-up from Books for Your Children Bookshop, 1982, for *Matilda Jane.*

WRITINGS: Matilda Jane (illustrated by husband, Roy Gerrard; juvenile), Gollancz, 1981, Farrar, Straus, 1983.

GLENN, Mel   1943-

PERSONAL: Born May 10, 1943, in Zurich, Switzerland; son of Jacob B. (a doctor) and Elizabeth (Hampel) Glenn; married Elyse Friedman (a teacher), September 20, 1970; children: Jonathan, Andrew. *Education:* New York University, A.B., 1964; Yeshiva University, M.S., 1967. *Religion:* Jewish. *Home:* 4288 Bedford Ave., Brooklyn, N.Y. 11229. *Office:* Abraham Lincoln High School, Brooklyn, N.Y. 11235.

CAREER: Served with the Peace Corps, Sierra Leone, West Africa, 1964-66; Junior High School 240, Brooklyn, N.Y.,

MEL GLENN

teacher, 1967-70; Abraham Lincoln High School, Brooklyn, N.Y., English teacher, 1970—; author, 1980—. *Member:* Society of Children's Book Writers. *Awards, honors: Class Dismissed! High School Poems* was selected one of the Best Books for Young Adults, 1982, by the American Library Association, and a Golden Kite Honor Book, 1982, by the Society of Children's Book Writers; Christopher Award, 1987, for *Class Dismissed II.*

WRITINGS—All published by Clarion Books: *Class Dismissed! High School Poems* (illustrated with photographs by Michael J. Bernstein), 1982; *One Order to Go* (young adult novel), 1984; *Play-by-Play* (juvenile), 1986; *Class Dismissed II: More High School Poems* (illustrated with photographs by M. J. Bernstein), 1986.

WORK IN PROGRESS: Back to Class and *Room 104,* both high school poetry; a baseball novel for elementary school children.

SIDELIGHTS: "I came to the United States in 1945 from Switzerland, but was born an American citizen since my father had American citizenship. If I have one picture of my father it is one of him sitting at the dining room table writing in English (and sometimes Yiddish) on yellow legal pads. If there is a gene on my chromosomes that shouts 'writer,' it is one that he passed to me.

"My growing up in Brooklyn was fairly conventional. I adored the Brooklyn Dodgers and afternoons spent in the local park shooting baskets till it was too dark to see the hoop.

"At New York University, I fit my classes around my schedule at the undergraduate newspaper. I covered games at the old Garden, wrote feature stories and columns. I thought at the time I would become a journalist. That was the year before President Kennedy was assassinated.

"Following his death, I joined the Peace Corps. Whether that desire came out of a desire to escape Brooklyn or to do something 'noble,' I don't know, but I became an English teacher in a small town in Sierra Leone, West Africa. I found out between bouts of dysentery and rains that lasted for days that I really loved teaching. I loved it all—the class discussions, marking reports in fractured English. But most of all I loved the students I taught.

"When I came back to the States I started teaching junior high and, three years later (1970), I came to Lincoln High and have been here ever since. (Actually, I returned to Lincoln, since I had graduated from this school in 1960.)"

Glenn believes that writing was "a natural outgrowth of my interest in teaching. The idea for *Class Dismissed* sprang, philosophically, from Master's *Spoon River Anthology* and a New Year's resolution made in 1980. Another teacher had shown me his unpublished manuscript, and I said to myself that if he could write a book, so could I. I put myself on a strict schedule

**My mother told me that boys are supposed
to make the first move.
But what does she know, anyway, about hunks?**

■ (From a poem by Stacey Fowler in *Class Dismissed II: More High School Poems* by Mel Glenn. Photograph by Michael J. Bernstein.)

and wrote the book in six months. The source for the book came easily: I have always prided myself on the fact that I am a good listener, and surrounding me were hundreds of stories—some sad, some happy, some tragic—but all terribly real and poignant. Though styles and fashions may change, there are certain common denominators in being a teenager that connect all generations—the feelings of being alone, different, in love, in conflict with parents. No matter how old we grow there will always be a part of us that will be sixteen years old.

"I write about what I know. My second book [*One Order to Go*], a novel, is set in a Brooklyn candy store, the old kind where you can get a real malted and an egg cream. The story concerns a young boy who is not sure about his future. I am sure that a large part of it is autobiographical but, in the larger sense, what writing isn't? You bring to your characters a sense of your own personal values and memories.

"In each of my books I have tried to do something different. First poetry, then a novel. My third book [*Play-by-Play*] is a fictional account of a fourth grader learning about soccer. Again, the material was all around me. My son, Jonathan, was actively involved in a local soccer league, and between practices and games on cold Saturday mornings I learned about this 'foreign' sport. As a writer, I tried to pay close attention to the language, characteristics, and social mores of nine year olds.

"I consider myself very lucky to be a writer. Most people are shocked when I tell them that *Class Dismissed* was my very first submission to a publishing house. I'm also lucky to have a wonderful editor at Clarion—Ann Troy.

"Teaching is hectic; heck, living is hectic, but I hope I'll always make the time to write about the people I care about very much."

GOODWIN, Harold Leland 1914-
(John Blaine, Hal Goodwin, Hal Gordon, Blake Savage)

PERSONAL: Born November 20, 1914, in Ellenburg, N.Y.; son of Frank Elmer (a salesman) and Imogene (Van Arman) Goodwin; married Elizabeth Swensk, April 12, 1947; children: Alan, Christopher, Derek. *Education:* Attended Elliot Radio Institute, 1934-35. *Home and office:* 6212 Verne St., Bethesda, Md. 20034. *Agent:* McIntosh and Otis, Inc., 475 Fifth Ave., New York, N.Y. 10017.

CAREER: WNBC-Radio, New Britain, Conn., announcer, writer, program director, 1934-37; WHAI-Radio, Greenfield, Mass., announcer, continuity director, writer, commentator, 1937-40; Blackett-Sample-Hummert (advertising agency), New York, N.Y., copywriter, 1940; TransRadio News Service, New York and Washington, reporter and writer, 1941-53; freelance writer, 1945—; U.S. Foreign Service, Philippines, member of staff, 1947-50; Federal Civil Defense Administration, Washington, D.C., director of atomic test operations, 1951-58; U.S. Information Agency, Washington, D.C., science advisor, 1958-61; National Aeronautics and Space Administration, Washington, D.C., member of staff, 1961-67; National Science Foundation, Washington, D.C., planning officer and deputy director of National Sea Grant Program, 1967-70; National Oceanic and Atmospheric Administration, U.S. Department of Commerce, Washington, D.C., deputy director of National Sea Grant Program, 1970-74; self-employed with wife, Elizabeth

HAROLD LELAND GOODWIN

S. Goodwin, in marine services and education, Bethesda, Md., 1974—. *Military service:* U.S. Marine Corps, 1942-45; became first lieutenant; received Air Medal.

MEMBER: World Aquaculture Society (vice-president, 1977; honorary life member), National Marine Education Association (honorary life member), Professional Association of Diving Instructors (member of international board). *Awards, honors:* Flemming Award from the U.S. Junior Chamber of Commerce, 1953, for outstanding young man in federal service; Federal Civil Defense Administration Meritorious Service Award, 1958, U.S. Information Agency Meritorious Service Award, 1959, U.S. Department of Commerce Silver Medal, 1971, and James Dugan Award from the American Littoral Society, 1973, all for contributions to aquatic science.

WRITINGS—Juvenile: "Rick Brant Science Adventure" series; under pseudonym John Blaine; all published by Grosset: (With Peter Harkins) *Rocket's Shadow*, 1947; (with P. Harkins) *Lost City*, 1947; (with P. Harkins) *Sea Gold*, 1947; *100 Fathoms Under*, 1947; *Whispering Box Mystery*, 1948; *Phantom Shark*, 1949; *Smuggler's Reef*, 1950; *Caves of Fear*, 1951; *Stairway to Danger*, 1952; *Golden Skull*, 1954; *Wailing Octopus*, 1956; *Electronic Mind Reader*, 1957; *Scarlet Lake Mystery*, 1958; *Pirates of Shan*, 1958; *Rick Brant's Science and Adventure Projects*, 1960; *Blue Ghost Mystery*, 1960; *Egyptian Cat Mystery*, 1961; *Flaming Mountain*, 1962; *Flying Stingaree*, 1963; *Ruby Ray Mystery*, 1964; *Veiled Raiders*, 1965; *Rocket Jumper*, 1966; *Deadly Dutchman*, 1967; *Danger Below*, 1968.

Other: (Under pseudonym Hal Goodwin) *A Microphone for David*, William Penn, 1939; *Aerial Warfare*, Garden City,

1943; (under pseudonym Hal Goodwin) *The Feathered Cape,* Westminster, 1947; (under pseudonym Hal Goodwin) *Real Book about Stars,* Garden City, 1951; (under pseudonym Hal Goodwin) *Real Book about Space,* Garden City, 1952; (under pseudonym Blake Savage) *Adventure in Outer Space,* A. Whitman, 1952; (under pseudonym Blake Savage) *Rip Foster Rides the Gray Planet,* A. Whitman, 1952, also published as *Assignment in Space,* 1958; *Science Book of Space Travel,* F. Watts, 1955; *Space: Frontier Unlimited,* Van Nostrand, 1962; *The Images of Space,* Holt, 1965; *All about Rockets and Space Flight,* Random House, 1966; (with Claiborne Pell) *Challenge of the Seven Seas,* Morrow, 1966; (under pseudonym Hal Gordon) *Divers Down,* A. Whitman, 1971; (with Joe A. Hanson) *The Aquaculture of Freshwater Prawns,* Oceanic Institute (Wainalo, Hawaii), 1975; (with J. A. Hanson) *Shrimp and Prawn Farming in the Western Hemisphere,* Dowden, Hutchinson & Ross, 1977; *Americans and the World of Water,* Delaware University Sea Grant Press, 1978; (under pseudonym Hal Goodwin) *Seafaring with Hal Goodwin,* Review Press, 1984.

Contributor to *World Book Encyclopedia* and *Book of Knowledge,* and to periodicals and journals.

WORK IN PROGRESS: "*The Young Captains* is a true tale of youths in their teens who captained Yankee windships in the great days of American sail from 1790 to 1890, like John Boit of Boston who was fifth mate on the *Columbia* when Captain Gray discovered the Columbia River, and later at age nineteen commanded the sloop *Union* which traded for furs and fought Indians in the Northwest, sailed to China to trade and thence around the world; or Nathaniel Silsbee, later a U. S. Senator, who took the brig *Benjamin* at age seventeen to Mautitius for

trade and had many close calls." Also working on technical papers concerning problems of environment and aquaculture to be issued as reports by the New Jersey Marine Sciences Consortium.

SIDELIGHTS: Born November 20, 1914, in Ellenburg, New York; grew up in Springfield, Massachusetts. "I wrote my first novel, all of ten pages, at the age of eight—not a much-lauded debut. My first literary effort to attract attention was a junior high school essay about the rehabilitation of an old car. I didn't have a license, but I owned a car, circa 1925. Some friends and I put the differential gear in backwards giving us three speeds in reverse and one in forward. Great sport! My English teacher so loved the way I wrote about our feats of engineering that she reproduced my essay into a model for future classes.

"Overall, school didn't interest me very much, so my grades were just average. But I did love to read. In high school my study periods were taken in the school library, roughly the size of a large closet with only a small collection of books. I can't recall whether I was assigned to study in the library because I was very good or very bad, but it had to be one or the other. Anyway, I found a few things to read because I certainly wasn't going to waste time on homework. I quickly became an authority on mythologies by Bulfinch and Hamilton. Then I picked up a book by a Frenchman who had been dead for nearly 400 years. His name was Michel de Montaigne, and I read and loved his essays, and perhaps grew a little wiser. I also read poetry, especially the poets who wrote about heroic or comic subjects. To this day, I can recite Kipling's poetry by the yard. After school, I read Leo Edwards' *Jerry Todd* series—*Jerry Todd and the Mummy,* and so on. *American Boy*

(Jacket illustration from *Rip Foster Rides the Gray Planet* by Blake Savage.)

(Jacket illustration from *The Phantom Shark* by John Blaine.)

Magazine, to which I most enthusiastically subscribed, featured some mind-stretching, marvelous writers.''

Attended the Elliot Radio Institute in Springfield, Massachusetts, and later taught there. ''I wrote continuity, commercials, little dramas—the best training I could have received. The rhythms had to be right, and you had to be precise. You had five minutes in which to report in the news, and there was plenty of it. Your copy had to be clean, sparse, tasteful and loaded with information. Really, I can't imagine a better apprenticeship.

''I moved to New York in 1938 to take a job with an advertising agency to write copy for products like Dr. Lang's Tooth Powder. I also did some work for the New York Bureau of TransRadio, and wrote pulp, mostly adventure stories and romances. Many writers of my generation 'cut their teeth' on pulps. They taught you how to write fast and tight. 'If you have to describe a sunset in an adventure story, do it in a footnote,' I once had an editor tell me.

''When the war broke out, TransRadio transferred me to the Washington Bureau. One day a hand-out from the Marine Corps with a byline that read 'Jeremy J. O'Leary, Company Correspondent' came across my desk. Now *that* sounded like an exciting job! So I went over to Marine headquarters and learned that company correspondents were professional radio and print journalists who were taken into the Corps as sergeants of combat units. I signed up and was immediately sent

to the South Pacific. On the train to California, where I was to ship out, I finished my first nonfiction *Aerial Warfare,* mailing it chapter by chapter to a friend at TransRadio who as editor was having it retyped. After some firsthand war experience, I was very embarrassed about *Aerial Warfare.* When I wrote it I was very young and green, and had accepted as fact a lot of what I'd read in U. S. military public relations materials, which were designed to impress, rather than to inform, and which routinely exaggerated capability.

'''I had a good war,' as the saying goes. My first posting was aboard the aircraft carrier *Saratoga.* But she left before I reached California and I ended up chasing her around most of the South Pacific. I got to see just about all of Australia and a lot of India. I finally caught up with her in Ceylon, now Sri Lanka. I did a story on every man in the air group for home town papers plus a lot of features for such publications as *Liberty, Post, The New York Times Magazine* and *Blue Book.* After having seen a lot of action, the *Saratoga* drydocked in Bellingham, Washington, which left me at liberty. I was informed that the Marine Corps intended to commission me, something I didn't particularly want. By then I was a five-stripe sergeant, aiming to become a six-stripe sergeant. To me, that had more class than being an officer. But you don't turn down a commission.

''So, off I was again as a first lieutenant, this time on the *Essex,* from which I covered the first Navy air strikes over Tokyo and the battle at Okinawa. I went back to Hawaii to get ready for Operation Olympia—a 'beach party' in military

(Jacket illustration by Clifford Geary from *The Real Book about Space Travel* by Hal Goodwin.)

parlance—an attack from the sea, with men rushing the shores of Japan backed up by heavy artillery from ships close to shore. The atomic bombs caused the operation's cancellation, and I was glad, because the attacks would have caused far more American casualties than Japanese casualties from the atomic explosions.

"At the end of the war, I returned to the States and became a full-time freelance writer. At first, all my good TransRadio training worked to my detriment. As we were paid by the word, I was going hungry with my lean prose. So I quickly learned to 'pad' in order to up my income. 'How would you like to write a series?' my agent asked one day. 'What's a series?' I inquired. I came up with the outline that eventually became my 'Rick Brant' adventure series, written under pseudonym John Blaine. I started collaborating with Peter Harkins, a childhood friend who was also freelancing. He and his wife, and my wife and I rented a cottage on a lake in Connecticut and got down to work. Unfortunately, by the time we had finished our third book, Peter's wife became homesick for her native Arkansas, and so our collaboration, not our friendship, ended.

"I was invited to Washington to attend a farewell party for a couple of marine buddies—one was going to Calcutta, and the other to Shanghai—both were traveling under the auspices of the United States Information Program. I still had the wanderlust, and went right over to talk to someone at the State Department. I ended up with a three-year job in Manila, where our first son was born. My official responsibilities included serving as press attaché for the embassy, writing and editing articles, pamphlets and magazines about what scientists call the 'cutting edge' of developments in nuclear energy, space and oceanic studies.

"After a hard day of working for the government, I would come home to relax and write. All of my jobs required a great deal of travel, both at home and abroad. Being a kind of human sponge, as all writers must be, I soaked up background, language, geography and ideas that went far beyond my scientific and technical missions.

"All of my experience gave me material for writing both fact and fiction, as well as large numbers of scientific and technical papers for scholarly journals. Most of all, I enjoyed writing teen fiction because I could combine the science background with mystery and adventure, often in a setting I had experienced personally in Egypt, Nigeria, Europe, China, the Philippines, Hawaii and the Western Pacific.

"Because I believe that learning should be fun, my teen fiction mixes science and engineering with exciting stories and authentic backgrounds. In foreign locales I followed my heroes on street maps, used photographs I'd taken as visual notes for accurate descriptions. If a reader happened to visit Cairo, for instance, and wanted to follow the exact route taken by the heroes in the *Egyptian Cat Mystery*, the story could be used as a guide book.

"Apart from social and cultural backgrounds, an historian could also find technical clues in book series. For instance, reading Sam Epstein's 'Ken Holt' series would give a picture of newspaper publication in the days of hot lead typesetting by linotype, writing for the publication with manual typewriters, and using a camera that needed flash bulbs inserted. My 'Rick Brant' series gives some indication of the various scientific and technical developments looming on the horizon so that a writer could extrapolate to the actual developments ten or fifteen years ahead with some accuracy.

"I can't speak for other series, but literary or poetic references in mine certainly showed a macho young male that there was nothing sissy in appreciating or even quoting literature. Such references might even lead a few readers to the original, as in *The Electronic Mind Reader* when Scotty responds to a situation by muttering 'A dagger of the mind' and Rick recalls that the phrase is in *MacBeth,* Act II, which, because of the horror of the situation, brings to mind another quotation from the same work, 'MacBeth has murdered sleep.' Or, when Rick is on the edge of drowning at the hands of the Deadly Dutchman and finds new energy to fight by recalling Dylan Thomas' 'Do not go gentle into that good night.'

"In a series the reader can identify with the protagonist, especially in the Post World War II series. But, I think, of greater importance is pace. Things happen fast, and the reader is caught up in the story line and must read on to see what happens. Series book readers enjoy reading, and continue to read long after they've outgrown teen books.

"My greatest satisfaction has been with the letters I receive from people who read my books while in junior high school, and reread them after reaching college age to find them just as exciting and authentic and informative as when first read. A few readers were steered into scientific or technical careers because of my books, and a few have even decided to become writers themselves. To me, that's what writing is all about—opening new horizons and possibilities for the reader."

—*Based on an interview by Marguerite Feitlowitz*

HOBBIES AND OTHER INTERESTS: Boating, archery, scuba diving.

HANNA, William 1910-
(Bill Hanna)

PERSONAL: July 14, 1910, in Melrose, New Mexico; son of William John and Avice Joyce (Denby) Hanna; married Violet Blanch, August, 1936; children: David William, Bonnie Jean. *Education:* Attended Compton Junior College, 1929-30. *Residence:* San Fernando Valley, California. *Office:* Hanna-Barbera Productions, 3400 Cahuenga Blvd., Hollywood, Calif. 90068.

CAREER: Harmon-Izing Animation Studios, Hollywood, Calif., directed, wrote and timed cartoons to his own music, 1931-38; Metro-Goldwyn-Mayer (MGM), Hollywood, Calif., director of cartoons, 1938-57; Hanna-Barbera Productions, Hollywood, senior vice president, 1957—. Established cartoon studios all over the world, including Australia, Spain, Argentina, and the Philippines.

AWARDS, HONORS—All with Joe Barbera: Seven Academy Awards for Animated Short Subjects from the Academy of Motion Picture Arts and Sciences, all for cartoons featuring the characters Tom and Jerry: "Yankee Doodle Mouse," 1943; "Mouse Trouble," 1944; "Quiet, Please," 1945; "The Cat Concerto," 1946; "The Little Orphan," 1948; "The Two Mouseketeers," 1951; "Johann Mouse," 1952.

Seven Emmy Awards from National Academy of Television Arts and Sciences, all for Outstanding Achievement in the Field of Children's Programming, except as noted; all animation, except as noted: "Huckleberry Hound," 1960; "Jack and the Beanstalk" (live-action and animation), 1966; "The Last of the Curlews," 1973; "The Runaways" (live-action),

1974; "The Gathering" (live-action), for Outstanding Special—Drama or Comedy, 1978; "The Smurfs," for Outstanding Children's Entertainment Series, 1982, and 1983.

Golden Globe Award from Hollywood Foreign Press Association for Outstanding Achievement in International Television Cartoons, for "The Flintstones," 1965; Annie Award, for "Charlotte's Web," 1977; Christopher Award, for "The Gathering," 1978; Golden Reel Award, for Animation Sound Editing, and Bronze Award from the International Film and Television Festival of New York for Best Children's Special, both for "The Smurfs' Springtime Special," both 1982; Bronze Award from the International Film and Television Festival of New York for Best Children's Special, for "The Smurfic Games," 1984; Man of the Year with co-recipient Joseph Barbera from the National Center for Hyperactive Children, 1986; Religion in Media's Gold Angel Award for Excellence in Media, 1986, and the Distinguished Service Award from the National Religious Broadcasters, and Award of Excellence from the Film Advisory Board, both 1987, all for "The Greatest Adventure: Stories from the Bible"; Humanitas Prize for "The Lure of the Orb" (Smurf episode), 1987.

FILMS—Producer with Joe Barbera; all animated features, except as noted: "Hey There, It's Yogi Bear," 1964; "A Man Called Flintstone," 1966; "Charlotte's Web," 1973; "C.H.O.M.P.S." (live-action), 1978; "Heidi's Song," 1982; "GoBots: Battle of the Rock Lords," 1986. Also producer of "Forever Like a Rose."

TELEVISION—Producer with Joe Barbera; all live-action movies, except as noted: "Hardcase," ABC, 1972; "Shootout in a One-Dog Town" (animated), ABC, 1974; "The Gathering," ABC, 1977; "The Beasts Are in the Streets," NBC, 1978; "KISS Meets the Phantom of the Park," NBC, 1978;

"The Gathering, Part II," NBC, 1979; "Belle Starr," CBS, 1980; "Stone Fox," NBC, 1987. Also producer of "Rock Odyssey" (animation).

Animated movies; all syndicated in 1987, unless otherwise noted: "Lucky Luke," syndicated, 1985; "Ultraman! The Adventure Begins"; "Yogi and the Magical Flight of the Spruce Goose"; "Yogi's Great Escape"; "The Jetsons Meet the Flintstones"; "Yogi and the Invasion of the Space Bears"; "Scooby-Doo and the Ghoul School"; "The Good, the Bad and the Huckleberry Hound"; "Top Cat and the Beverly Hills Cats"; "Scooby and the Reluctant Werewolf"; "Scooby-Doo Meets the Boo Brothers"; "Judy Jetson and the Rockers."

Live-action series: "Banana Splits," NBC, 1968-70; "Danger Island," NBC, 1968-70; "The New Adventures of Huck Finn," NBC, 1968-69; "Korg: 70,000 B.C.," ABC, 1974-75; "Skatebirds," CBS, 1977-78; "Mystery Island," CBS, 1977-78; "Benji," CBS, 1983-84; "Going Bananas," 1984-85.

Animated series: "Ruff and Reddy," NBC, 1957-60; "Huckleberry Hound," syndicated, 1958-62; "Pixie and Dixie," syndicated, 1958-62; "Snooper and Blabber," syndicated, 1959-62; "Augie Doggie & Doggie Daddy," syndicated, 1959-62; "Quick Draw McGraw," syndicated, 1959-62; "Yakky Doodle," syndicated, 1960-62; "Yogi Bear," syndicated, 1960-62; "Hokey Wolf," syndicated, 1960-62; "The Flintstones," ABC, 1960-65; "Snagglepuss," syndicated, 1960-62; "Top Cat," ABC, 1961-62; "Lippy the Lion," syndicated, 1962; "Touche Turtle," syndicated, 1962; "Wally Gator," syndicated, 1962; "The Jetsons," ABC, 1962-63, syndicated, 1984-88; "Magilla Gorilla and Peter Potamus," syndicated, 1963-67; "Punkin' Puss," syndicated, 1963-67; "Breezly and Sneezly," syndicated, 1963-67; "Yippee, Yappee and Yahooey," syndicated, 1963-67; "Ricochet Rabbit," syndicated, 1963-67.

"Jonny Quest," ABC, 1964-65, syndicated, 1986-88; "Secret Squirrel," NBC, 1965-67; "Precious Pupp," NBC, 1965-67; "Hillbilly Bears," NBC, 1965-67; "Atom Ant," NBC, 1965-67; "Winsome Witch," NBC, 1965-67; "Squiddly Diddly," NBC, 1965-67; "Sinbad, Jr." (distributed by AIP), 1965; "Laurel and Hardy" (distributed by Wolper), 1966-67; "Space Kidettes," syndicated, 1966-67; "Space Ghost," CBS, 1966-68, NBC, 1981-82; "Dino Boy," CBS, 1966-67; "Frankenstein, Jr.," CBS, 1966-67; "The Impossibles," CBS, 1966-67; "Abbott and Costello" (distributed by RKO and Jomar), 1967-68; "Herculoids," CBS, 1967-68, NBC, 1981-82; "Samson and Goliath," syndicated, 1967-68; "The Fantastic Four," ABC, 1967-68; "Mightor," CBS, 1967-68; "Shazam," CBS, 1967-68; "Moby Dick," CBS, 1967-68; "Birdman," NBC, 1967-68; "Cattanooga Cats," ABC, 1967-70; "Three Musketeers," NBC, 1968-70; "Arabian Knights," NBC, 1968-70; "Micro Ventures," NBC, 1968-70; "Adventures of Gulliver," ABC, 1968-69; "Wacky Races," CBS, 1968-69; "Penelope Pitstop," CBS, 1969-70; "Motormouse and Autocat," ABC, 1969-70; "It's the Wolf," ABC, 1969-70; "Scooby-Doo," CBS, 1969-74, ABC, 1976-79; "Dastardly & Muttley," CBS, 1969-70; "Around the World in 79 Days," ABC, 1969-70.

"Josie and the Pussycats," CBS, 1970-71; "Where's Huddles?," CBS, 1970; "The Harlem Globetrotters," CBS, 1970-72; "Pebbles and Bamm Bamm," CBS, 1971-73; "Help! It's the Hair Bear Bunch," CBS, 1971-72; "The Funky Phantom," ABC, 1971-72; "Sealab 2020," NBC, 1972-73; "Roman Holidays," NBC, 1972-73; "The Amazing Chan and the Chan Clan," CBS, 1972-73; "The Flintstones Comedy Hour," CBS, 1972-73; "Josie and the Pussycats in Outer Space,"

WILLIAM HANNA

Peyo's "Smurfs," animated by Hanna-Barbera for NBC-TV, come alive at "Carowinds," the Charlotte, N.C. theme park.

CBS, 1972-73; "The New Scooby-Doo Movies," CBS, 1972-74; "Wait Till Your Father Gets Home," syndicated, 1972-74; "Jeannie," CBS, 1973-74; "Speed Buggy," CBS, 1973-74; "The Addams Family," NBC, 1973-74; "Inch High Private Eye," NBC, 1973-74; "Butch Cassidy," NBC, 1973-74; "Goober and the Ghost Chasers," ABC, 1973-74; "Superfriends," ABC, 1973-74, 1979-83; "Yogi's Gang," ABC, 1973-74; "Peter Puck," NBC, 1973-74; "Hong Kong Phooey," ABC, 1974-75; "These Are the Days," ABC, 1974-75; "Devlin," ABC, 1974-75; "Valley of the Dinosaurs," CBS, 1974-75; "Wheelie and the Chopper Bunch," NBC, 1974-75; "The Partridge Family: 2200 A.D.," CBS, 1974-75; "The Great Grape Ape," ABC, 1975-76; "Tom and Jerry," ABC, 1975-79.

"Dynomutt," ABC, 1976-78; "Jabberjaw," ABC, 1976-77; "Mumbly," ABC, 1976-77; "Clue Club," CBS, 1976-77; "CB Bears," NBC, 1977-78; "Shake, Rattle and Roll," NBC, 1977-78; "Undercover Elephant," NBC, 1977-78; "Robonic Stooges," CBS, 1977-78; "Woofer and Wimper Dog Detectives," CBS, 1977-78; "Blast-Off Buzzard," NBC, 1977-78; "Heyyy, It's the King," NBC, 1977-78; "Posse Impossible," NBC, 1977-78; "Wonder Wheels," CBS, 1977-78; "Captain Caveman and the Teen Angels," ABC, 1977-79; "The New Superfriends Show," ABC, 1977-79; "Scooby-Doo's All Star Laff-A-Lympics," ABC, 1977-79; "Yogi's Space Race," NBC, 1978-79; "Yogi's Galaxy Goof-Ups," NBC, 1978-79; "Chal-

lenge of the Superfriends," ABC, 1978-79; "Galloping Ghost," NBC, 1978-79; "Buford Files," NBC, 1978-79; "Jana of the Jungle," NBC, 1978-79; "Godzilla," NBC, 1978-80; "The All-New Popeye Show," CBS, 1978-82; "Dinky Dog," CBS, 1978-81; "The New Schmoo," NBC, 1979-80; "Super Globetrotters," NBC, 1979-80; "Casper and the Angels," NBC, 1979-80; "The Thing," NBC, 1979-80; "The Flintstones," NBC, 1979-80; "Scooby and Scrappy Doo," ABC, 1979-82, 1983-84; "The New Fred and Barney Show," NBC, 1979-80.

"Flintstone Family Adventures," NBC, 1980-82; "Pebbles, Dino and Bamm Bamm," NBC, 1980-82; "The Bedrock Cops," NBC, 1980-82; "Dino and the Cavemouse," NBC, 1980-82; "The Frankenstones," NBC, 1980-82; "Captain Caveman," NBC, 1980-82; "Drak Pak," CBS, 1980-81; "Fonz and the Happy Days Gang," ABC, 1980-82; "Richie Rich," ABC, 1980-83; "Space Stars," NBC, 1981-82; "Astro and the Space Mutts," NBC, 1981-82; "Teen Force," NBC, 1981-82; "Crazy Claws," CBS, 1981-82; "Kwicky Koala," CBS, 1981-82; "Dirty Dawg," CBS, 1981-82; "Bungle Brothers," CBS, 1981-82; "The Smurfs," NBC, 1981-88; "Laverne and Shirley," ABC, 1981-82; "Private Olive Oyl," CBS, 1981-82; "The Trollkins," CBS, 1981-82; "Mork and Mindy," ABC, 1982-83; "Laverne and Shirley/Fonz," ABC, 1982-83; "The Little Rascals," ABC, 1982-83; "Scooby, Scrappy and Yabba Doo," ABC, 1982-83; "Pac-Man," ABC, 1982-84;

"Smarter than the av-er-age bear." (Copyright © 1987 by Hanna-Barbera Productions, Inc.)

"Shirt Tales," NBC, 1982-84; "The Gary Coleman Show," NBC, 1982-83; "The Dukes," CBS, 1983-84; "The Little Rascals/Richie Rich," ABC, 1983-84; "Monchhichis," ABC, 1983-84; "Baskitts," CBS, 1983-84; "The Snorks," NBC, 1984-85; "The Pink Panther and Sons," NBC, 1984-85; "The New Scooby-Doo Mysteries," ABC, 1984-85; "Superfriends: The Legendary Super Powers Show," ABC, 1984-85; "GoBots," syndicated, 1984-85; "The Funtastic World of Hanna-Barbera" (consisting of three segments: "Paw Paws," "Galtar and the Golden Lance," and "Yogi's Treasure Hunt"), syndicated, 1985-86; "The Super Powers Team: Galactic Guardians," ABC, 1985; "The Thirteen Ghosts of Scooby-Doo," ABC, 1985; "Challenge of the GoBots," syndicated, 1985.

"The Funtastic World of Hanna-Barbera (consisting of four segments: "Paw Paws," "Galtar and the Golden Lance," "Yogi's Treasure Hunt," and "Jonny Quest"), syndicated, 1986; "The Flintstone Kids," ABC, 1986-88; "The Greatest Adventure: Stories from the Bible," Home Video, 1986-88; "Pound Puppies," ABC, 1986; "Wildfire," CBS, 1986; "Foofur," NBC, 1986-88; "Popeye and Son," CBS, 1987; "The Funtastic World of Hanna-Barbera (consisting of four segments: "Yogi's Treasure Hunt," "Jonny Quest," "Sky Commanders," and "Snorks"), syndicated, 1987.

TELEVISION SPECIALS—Producer with Joe Barbera; all animated, except as noted: "Alice in Wonderland," ABC, 1966;

"Jack and the Beanstalk" (live-action and animated), NBC, 1966; "The Thanksgiving That Almost Wasn't," syndicated, 1971; "Love American Style" (consisting of three segments: "Wait Till Your Father Gets Home" [pilot], "Love and the Private Eye," "Melvin Danger"); "A Christmas Story," syndicated, 1971; "The Last of the Curlews," ABC, 1972; "Yogi's Ark Lark," ABC, 1972; "Robin Hoodnik," ABC, 1972; "Oliver and the Artful Dodger," ABC, 1972; "Here Come the Clowns," ABC, 1972; "Gidget Makes the Wrong Connection," ABC, 1972; "The Banana Splits in Hocus Pocus Park," ABC, 1972; "20,000 Leagues under the Sea," syndicated, 1973; "The Three Musketeers," syndicated, 1973; "Lost in Space," ABC, 1973; "The Count of Monte Cristo," syndicated, 1973; "The Runaways" (live-action), ABC, 1974; "Cyrano de Bergerac," ABC, 1974; "Crazy Comedy Concert" (live and animated), ABC, 1974; "The Last of the Mohicans," syndicated, 1975; "Phantom Rebel" (live-action), NBC, 1976; "Davy Crockett on the Mississippi" (live-action), CBS, 1976.

"Taggart's Treasure" (live-action), ABC, 1976; "Five Weeks in a Balloon," CBS, 1977; "Yabba-Dabba-Doo!" (live and animated), CBS, 1977; "The Flintstones' Christmas," NBC, 1977; "Energy: A National Issue," syndicated, 1977; "Beach Girls" (live-action), syndicated, 1977; "It Isn't Easy Being a Teenage Millionaire" (live-action), ABC, 1978; "Hanna-Barbera's Happy Hour" (animated mini-series), NBC, 1978; "Hanna-Barbera's All Star Comedy Ice Revue" (live and an-

Hanna-Barbera characters pose at "Great America" theme park in Santa Clara, Calif.

Yogi Bear joins a guest for a ride on "Boo Boo's Balloon Race" at "Carowinds" theme park (Charlotte, N.C.).

imated), CBS, 1978; "The Funny World of Fred and Bunni" (live and animated), CBS, 1978; "The Flintstones' Little Big League," NBC, 1978; "Black Beauty," CBS, 1978; "Yabba-Dabba-Doo II," CBS, 1978; "Superheroes Roast" (live-action), NBC, 1979; "Challenge of the Superheroes" (live-action), NBC, 1979; "America vs. the World" (live-action), NBC, 1979; "Scooby Goes Hollywood," ABC, 1979; "Casper's First Christmas," NBC, 1979; "Sgt. T. K. Yu" (live-action), NBC, 1979; "Popeye: Sweethearts at Sea," CBS, 1979; "Gulliver's Travels," CBS, 1979; "Casper's Halloween Special: He Ain't Scary, He's Our Brother," NBC, 1979.

"The Harlem Globetrotters Meet Snow White" (serialized in "Fred and Barney" series), NBC, 1980; "The Flintstones Meet Rockula and Frankenstone," NBC, 1980; "The Flintstones' New Neighbor," NBC, 1980; "Fred's Final Fling," NBC, 1980; "The Gymnast" (live-action), ABC, 1980; "B. B. Beagle," syndicated, 1980; "Hanna-Barbera Arena Show" (live-action), NBC, 1981; "Jogging Fever," NBC, 1981; "Wind-Up Wilma," NBC, 1981; "The Great Gilly Hopkins" (live-action), CBS, 1981; "Daniel Boone," CBS, 1981; "The Smurfs," NBC, 1981; "The Smurfs' Springtime Special," NBC, 1982; "The Jokebook," NBC, 1982; "The Smurfs' Christmas Special," NBC, 1982; "Christmas Comes to Pac-Land," ABC, 1982; "Yogi Bear's All-Star Christmas Caper," CBS, 1982; "My Smurfy Valentine," NBC, 1983; "The Secret World of Og," ABC, 1983; "The Amazing Bunjee Venture," CBS, 1984; "The Smurfic Games," NBC, 1984; "Smurfily-Ever-After," NBC, 1985; "Star Fairies," syndicated, 1985; "Pound Puppies," syndicated, 1985; "Flint-

stones 25th Anniversary Celebration" (animated and live-action), CBS, 1986. Also producer of "Johnny Yune Variety Special."

Also creator with Joe Barbera of cartoons featuring the characters Tom and Jerry; all produced by Metro-Goldwyn-Mayer including, "Yankee Doodle Mouse," 1943; "Mouse Trouble," 1944; "Quiet, Please," 1945; "The Cat Concerto," 1946; "The Little Orphan," 1948; "The Two Mouseketeers," 1951; "Johann Mouse," 1952. Also creators of television special "Yogi's First Christmas," 1980. Many Hanna-Barbera cartoons are available in videocassette form.

WORK IN PROGRESS: Live-action feature film versions of "The Flintstones," "The Jetsons," "The Green Hornet," and "Jonny Quest"; creation of Saturday morning cartoons; additional tapes in the home video series "Hanna Barbera's The Greatest Adventure: Stories from the Bible."

SIDELIGHTS: **July 14, 1910.** Born in Melrose, New Mexico. The family moved to San Pedro, California when Hanna was seven years old. He has lived in California ever since.

"During the war we lived up on a hill near the military establishment, home of General MacArthur. I used to hear the soldiers' target practice, and watch them mark the targets.

"We moved to the San Fernando Valley, full of orchards and fairgrounds, where heavy rains flooded and washed out new rivers. I've seen houses fall into rivers. I still live in the area, and have been a resident of San Fernando Valley for 56 years."

Joseph Barbera and William Hanna "Meet the Flintstones...." (Photograph copyright © 1987 by Hanna-Barbera Productions, Inc.)

An interest in music flourished at an early age. "One of my sisters played violin and another, the piano. I fooled around with wind instruments and studied piano, voice and harmony. I have been interested in music all of my life. I've always written lyrics and poetry. I have written most of the main titles and lyrics for the Hanna-Barbera cartoons and quite a bit of the music as well." Writing was also a preoccupation in the household. Hanna wrote poems at the age of twelve, his mother published two books in that genre, his aunt wrote a comedy show for radio, his sister writes.

1929-30. Attended Compton Junior College. The Depression forced him to drop his studies. "I was the only boy in a family of seven children. My father wasn't well and we children worked to keep the family going. You didn't have many job choices; you took whatever work you could get. When I was twenty-one, an opportunity came up in a cartoon department at Harmon-Izing animation studios and I went to work as a gag writer for the early 'Looney Tunes.' For five cents on pay day I would take the red Hollywood Boulevard streetcar into Hollywood and have a thirty-five-cent lunch at Musso-Franks."

"In the early days at Harmon Izing, I directed, wrote cartoons, and became involved in timing and composing of music for animated cartoons. My early musical training came in handy. The first song I wrote for an animated cartoon was about three little monkeys. I developed a timing technique based on musical notation and have been using it ever since. I wrote the melody, broke it down into quarter notes, eight notes, sixteenth notes, and so forth, and discovered that by using a metronome and tempo I could figure out how many frames of animation move through the camera per second. Working this way enabled me to estimate precisely how much time it would take to say each word. All the timing of our Hanna-Barbera cartoons has its roots in music." [From an interview by Rachel Koenig, for *Something about the Author*, 1986.[1]]

1938. Hanna became one of MGM animation unit's first staff members, directing, together with William Allen, many of the "Captain and the Kid" cartoons. It was at MGM that Hanna first met his future partner, Joe Barbera. They formed a partnership. Their first collaborative effort was directing a "short" entitled "Gallopin' Gals," followed by the first "Tom and Jerry" cartoon. Over the years "Tom and Jerry" has become world-renowed, receiving seven Academy Awards. "We had a large desk. I sat on one side, and Joe on the other and we'd develop material. Joe did all of the drawing, sketching and storyboards, and I did the animation, direction, and timing. I also wrote many of the lyrics and the music."[1]

"Joe and I worked on 'Tom and Jerry' for twenty years and I got to think of them as people. I was deeply involved with the writing and I directed the animation, and when you do that you feel you are inside the character's head. Jerry would come off very much the way I was feeling on that particular day. It's very therapeutic—I was able to lose myself totally in what I was doing.

"Tom? He's not an evil cat, he's not a mean cat, but he's very mischievous and while I don't think he's cruel, he does delight in tormenting Jerry. Now Jerry usually triumphs over Tom, even though he's frightened of him. I think he has enough spunk and courage that when he's had enough he still manages to triumph against all odds.... You get to know what [your characters] will do and not do and you come to know how they will behave under certain conditions. For instance, you would know what Yogi would say if he was caught stealing a picnic basket. I'd end up feeling I was Yogi and that I had stolen the picnic basket." [Janise Beaumont, "Meet Tom and Jerry's 'Dad' ...," *Sun-Herald*, December 8, 1985.[2]]

1957. Hanna and Barbera left MGM with a view toward producing cartoons for television and theatrical release. "When Joe and I left MGM we each had a vested interest in a pension plan. We used this money, about twenty-seven thousand dollars altogether, to start our own cartoon production company for television. The first thing we bought was a camera for five thousand dollars."[1]

Hanna's precise understanding of comic tempo and his ability to marshal top talent into an efficient unit were perfect complements for Barbera's draftsmanship, strong storytelling sense, and comic inventiveness. At the infant studio, this long-standing division of labor led to Barbera's acting as the pitch man to network executives while Hanna supervised all production.

In addition to their own perfectly complementary skills, Hanna and Barbera were able to draw upon an outstanding creative team. Much of the best talent in the business was available, thanks to the disbanding of the animation departments at most of the major studios. Among those who joined Hanna and Barbera's new studio were such top writers as Mike Maltese and Warren Foster, as well as voice actors Don Messick and Daws Butler.

"Ruff and Reddy" was the first Hanna-Barbera cartoon series. The team drew fifty dollars a week expense money from their savings, no salaries and worked at desks Hanna had built in his garage. "We didn't borrow a penny.

"Sustaining a weekly television series was an economic problem more than anything else. The innovation in going to TV was to devise ways to do fewer drawings, but give the illusion of more animation. Our early productions, such as 'Ruff and Reddy' and 'Huckleberry Hound' use more dialogue than the early cartoons like 'Tom and Jerry.' We had to use less animation to meet our budget, so heads and arms moved while bodies remained still. Drawings were manipulated so that fewer drawings were required to animate a scene. These shortcuts created the illusion of more animation than was actually there. The result was an ability to meet the production and budget demands of a weekly animated series."[2]

The success of their early television series, "Huckleberry Hound" and "Yogi Bear," the phenomenal success of "The Flintstones," and the first nighttime television cartoon series, put Hanna-Barbera Studios at the top of the cartoon field. "Screen Gems wanted us to do a nighttime show. At the time, Jackie Gleason's 'The Honeymooners' was very popular. I watched it regularly and laughed so much that tears would come. I talked to Joe and said we should somehow do a show like 'The Honeymooners.' We never admitted to ripping off the idea, but if you study 'The Flintstones' you can see that Fred and Barney, Wilma and Betty are modeled on the couples in 'The Honeymooners.' Fred is Jackie Gleason, Barney, Art Carney. We had artist Dan Gordon work up some sketches for us. We tried the characters out as modern couples, as pilgrims, as Romans and Indians. Then Dan made a sketch of a guy in animal skins near a bird with a long beak playing phonograph records. Dan, Joe, and I felt immediately that this Neanderthal was *it*. We named them 'The Flagstones,' then discoverd there was a comic strip by that name and so settled on 'Flintstones.'

The premise of "The Jetsons" was the same as that of "The Flintstones," namely that people don't change, only their surroundings do. Instead of being Stone Age suburbanites, the Jetsons were Space Age apartment dwellers. "The Jetsons" premiered in prime time in 1962.

Other cartoon characters were in the making. "Animator Tex Avery had done a cartoon about a bear in a park at MGM.

"The greatest show in town/Is Huckleberry Hound." (Copyright © 1987 by Hanna-Barbera Productions, Inc.)

Our bear was completely different in character, but we liked the idea of putting the bear in a park. And so we came up with Yogi.

"Huckleberry Hound was developed around one of our voice actors who did a terrific Southern accent, which gave us the image of a little blue hound. In that case, the voice came first, and then the character.

"We always try to come up with a cartoon character that we can work off another character. When Joe and I work on stories, we always try to set up a situation that we can develop material around. If the characters go well together, then the story is easier to develop."[1]

"The evolution of a character is a gradual process. When you first think up a character, almost anything new adds to it. When a character is given a voice, for instance, a whole new dimension has been added that has a lot to do with whether the character is accepted or not. Next comes the writing end. A writer can help the cartoon by writing material that goes with the particular voice being used. Then . . . we have to find a second character to work with the first. It takes many elements before a character really starts to build. From then on, it is just a question of getting a writer who understands the basic characteristics that your characters have. All the ingredients have to be right to make a success. Also a lot depends on luck." [Danny Peary and Gerald Peary, *The American Animated Cartoon,* Dutton, 1980.[3]]

"As the studio grew and developed, I had to devise different ways of working with voice tracks. We had to produce much more quickly than we had before. Our pace was ten-fold what it had been back at MGM. I devised more economical ways of timing the cartoon. My system is still in use and other cartoon studios continue to use the method I devised thirty years ago in producing cartoons for television. At one point, I was timing and directing two one-half hour shows per week single-handedly—more than I had timed in a whole year's work at MGM. In my opinion, it isn't the *amount* of animation which makes a cartoon work—it's the way in which it is planned and executed. Limited animation that is well thought out and produced reads just as well as full animation with all the trimmings.

In 1967 Hanna-Barbera Productions was acquired by Taft Broadcasting. Their relationship with the parent company became symbiotic in nature—the studio received support and stability from its backing by one of the nation's most successful broadcasting companies, while Cincinnati-based Taft gained a solid cornerstone for its expansion into the entertainment industry. Direction of the studio's operations remained in the hands of Barbera and Hanna, as president and vice president, respectively of Hanna-Barbera Productions. "I've never regretted selling, and we sold to some of the finest men I've ever met. Why we sold, I don't know. There was no reason. We were successful, clearing several millions more appealed to us.

The decade of the 70s was one of new directions for Hanna-Barbera Productions. The studio continued to dominate the Saturday morning network schedule. "Superfriends," an action-adventure, featuring Superman, Batman and Robin, Wonder Woman, Aquaman, and other superheroes began a twelve year reign. Live-action production was also a new arena for the studio with such films as "The Runaways" and "The Gathering."

The Smurfs, a creation of the Belgian artist Peyo, were little blue people only three apples high. Hanna-Barbera's animated version of their adventures became a television phenomenon. When "Smurfs" debuted, NBC was so deep in third place on Saturday morning that it was considering dropping children's programming in favor of a Saturday "Today Show." "Smurfs," however, rocketed NBC to such an enormous ratings lead over the other networks that they expanded the show to ninety minutes, a block of time never before set aside, or since, for any single animated series.

"As our company grew I spent less and less time writing and working on stories. Joe was more involved in the creative areas, working on the development of material and characters and its presentation to the networks. My talent, I believe, has been in organization, of expanding our production facilities. I went to Sydney, Australia and developed a studio which now employs over two hundred fifty people. The studio carries the name, Hanna-Barbera, but when we sold our company to Taft, we sold the studio in Australia as well. We also started up a production facility in Spain and had part ownership in a studio in Taipan which, under the direction of James Wong, today has over eight hundred employees—the largest producing cartoon studio in the world. They produce cartoons for Hanna-Barbera as well as Lucasfilms, Disney, Rank and Bass. This year we have nine new network shows and the bulk of the work is being done by James Wong. We have also set up a studio in Buenos Aires, which is directed by an Argentinian fellow who worked with us here in California for many, many years. And we've just started another facility in the Philippines. I'm still directing cartoons, and I also spend a lot of time with the writers. But I travel quite a bit, visiting our various studios and overseeing projects.

"It is difficult to get scripts for as many hours of animation as we produce each year. Not enough people are trained as scriptwriters. And, many times networks cannot make up their minds as to what they want to buy. By the time they decide to buy a series, it is a big hassle to develop the concepts. We have a lot of writers under contract. I assign a few writers as editors and they work with the network to come up with a format that is acceptable to them. Many times, when you see a program that looks rough, it is because there was not enough time to rework it, refine it, improve or polish before the deadline because the networks were unable to decide. It's hard to come out with a quality finished product given the exigencies of the networks. You get stuck with something that is not one hundred per cent.

To honor over 100 television series since 1957 and seven Emmy awards, a Hanna-Barbera star was placed in front of 6753 Hollywood Boulevard on the Walk of Fame in 1976.

During the 80s, Hanna-Barbera has continued to produce theatrical motion pictures. "Heidi's Song," an animated musical adaptation of Spyri's classic tale *Heidi* was released in 1982. Their most recent live-action television show "Stone Fox" tells the story of a Wyoming boy who is forced to become a man during the harsh winter of 1905. The 1987-88 season begins Hanna-Barbera's fourth decade. In production is a package of ten original two-hour movies, made especially for syndication and featuring some of the studio's classic characters in new adventures.

With the objective of finding a faster, more practical way to turn out their cartoons, Hanna traveled to Cornell University to review the work researchers had done on a new computer process for 'flooding' color into drawings. The Hanna-Barbera Studios now use a computer system which can control xerography, opaquing and camera work. "Computer animation has helped us tremendously. Ten years ago the chairman of

"Meet George Jetson.... His boy, Elroy.... Daughter, Judy.... Jane, his wife." (Copyright ©
1987 by Hanna-Barbera Productions, Inc.)

the board of Taft Broadcasting, Charlie Mechem, asked me to stay abreast of any new animation technology. Well, I had seen many types of computer work, but nothing which seemed to fit what we needed at Hanna-Barbera. Then I heard of a computer that had been developed at MIT. I went to see it, but the process of computer animation was slower and not as refined as doing it by hand. A year later, some people from Cornell University came out to the Studio to show me some backgrounds which had been painted by a computer. They also demonstrated a computer painting process, which appealed to me because I knew how tedious and time consuming the painting process was when done by hand.

"In my early years at Harmon-Izing studios I had been the head of the ink and paint department. The work was very expensive—sometimes it actually cost us more to ink and paint a picture than to animate it. I gave the people from Cornell my feedback, they went back to work on their computer, and we met many times to confer over what needed to be refined and shaped. Some of my ideas called for new software, which they developed. When they finally came up with a system, we invested in its development, and a year later, we set up the computer painting system at Hanna-Barbera. It's embarrassing, but five people computer painting can produce as much work in one week as a hundred would have produced by hand painting in the old days. A good painter can produce fifty

frames a day of complicated character; a computer operator can color the same character in 30 seconds, or 120 frames per hour. What used to cost $60,000 to $70,000, can now be done on the computer for about $10,000. Although this method could be converted for use in big screen feature animation, we keep busy enough with television. We still can't do *all* of our animation work on the computer. But as the computer expands and technology changes I think we will be able to produce what we do now, and more.

About his present role at Hanna-Barbera Studios, Hanna explained, "Joe is now responsible for development, and I have the administrative role. But I still do the creative timing, and enjoy it. I'm often at the studio seven days a week. I get there at 8:30 in the morning and never leave before 7:00 p.m. I work many Saturdays and often Sundays and holidays. I have been involved in animation for so long that my only friends are in the business. I go to lunch with them, and at night, if my wife is out with friends, I see them for dinner. My social life and my work life are totally entwined.

"When you do something and do it well and see it up on the screen, you are given a tremendous feeling of accomplishment. And my work makes me feel needed and appreciated. I would dearly like to have more time off, but I could not endure not having this studio.

(From the television movie "The Gathering, Part II," starring Maureen Stapleton and Efrem Zimbalist, Jr. Presented on NBC-TV, 1979.)

"I have five producers who work under me and deal with the networks and the program practices personnel. Our agent negotiates business deals. I deal with outside production."[1]

The anti-violence movements forced Hanna-Barbera to come up with cartoons that met strict network and program planning guidelines. "For the most part, the networks control what you see on the screen. You have to submit premises to them, and they must approve a premise. You write an outline, they read it, and determine whether or not its okay to go to script. They may approve something that program practices will not allow. So aside from the network, we must deal with programming control. They look at the storyboard and critique it. They are very much in control of what you see on the screen."[1]

"'Miami Vice,' 'Starsky and Hutch,' and so on, with their shooting, murder, rape and reckless driving—that's violence and that violence is imitated. But when, let's say, Jerry holds up a flat iron and Tom crashes into it and his face is momentarily in the shape of a flat iron, that's slapstick and not imitative.... The area that does disturb me is the porno cartoons made for the adult market; they are invariably seen by children. I am not a prude but I do not wish to see our industry prostituted with something that does not provide wholesome entertainment."[2]

"My argument against our critics is that there are two kinds of violence. There is violence just for violence's sake, presented in a realistic form; and there is fantasy violence, done in comedy form. I agree with critics who say that imitative violence is bad. Now the psychologists and program practices people are easing up on us because they have come to realize that our type of fantasy violence is just for fun and is not imitative.

"I always say that the ones setting the standards for our cartoons were raised on 'Tom and Jerrys' and I don't think they were hurt by them. I think we have a pretty good grade of adults in our country, and I would like to think that the young people of today will grow up to have the same values as the older people who watched 'Tom and Jerrys' and 'Bugs Bunnys' and all the other 'rough' cartoons.

"It is interesting to note that the early Warner Bros. cartoons are still run on Saturday mornings. They may be edited a bit, but they are nevertheless the 'roughest' cartoons on the air and contain things that we could never get away with if we were making cartoons fresh for television."[3]

When asked how he felt about the animation of today, Hanna responded, "There are simply not enough good animators to go around. There is a reason for the sad current situation. For the last fifteen or twenty years there has been almost no work done on animated features, so all the old animators have been involved in Saturday morning cartoons, which is a different kettle of fish altogether. Now most of the veterans are dead or retired; and most of the new animators have been trained solely in Saturday morning techniques. So it's hard to find a really good animator. Dick Williams gathered animators from all over the world for 'Raggedy Ann and Andy' [1977], but couldn't even find twenty.

"In the last couple of years several animated features have gotten underway; and there seems to be a resurgence toward full animation. There's a mad scramble to snatch up all the good animators for these features, and Saturday morning cartoons suffer because TV producers can't afford to pay animators as much as feature filmmakers can pay.

"... We have started an animation school. We have interviewed literally thousands of young artists, and from that group have trained between sixty and seventy-five new people. Unfortunately, we have trained them in Saturday-morning-type animation. At least when we made the feature... 'Heidi's Song' [1982], we placed our trainees with our veteran animators so they'd be exposed to full-animation techniques. In this way, we hope to develop some more 'old-type' animators.

"The pressures of television are much greater than the pressures of producing films for theatres. Back when we made MGM cartoons, we worked at a more leisurely, almost relaxed pace. There was infinitely more care put into the drawing, timing, sound effects, and the recording of the music. Much more time was taken to discuss the stories and to design the characters; pictures were reviewed in pencil-test form, and changes were made before they were inked and painted. It was an elaborate process. Every phase of production was handled much more carefully than it is today. We just don't have the time today to put in all that effort.... [Now] one person works on more footage per day than all of us combined used to. Back in the 'Tom and Jerry' days, I personally did a minute and a half of film a week; now I do as much as thirty-five minutes a week. So you can see the quantity produced is much greater today. The economics has a lot to do with it, of course. The economics of TV dictates the quality. I think we do a fair job on character design and we do a good job in voice casting and in backgrounds, but we fall short in actual animation. The cost per foot of 'Tom and Jerry'-type animation would be prohibitive, even for theatrical shorts. I think that to achieve the same standards today, a six-minute 'Tom and Jerry' would cost in the area of $100,000. They only cost $30,000 to make in the forties."[3]

Over the years, some of Hollywood's most famous acting talents have provided voices for Hanna-Barbera cartoons, including Tony Curtis, Sammy Davis, Jr., Jose Ferrer, Zsa Zsa Gabor, Gene Kelly, Debbie Reynolds, Ann-Margret, James Earl Jones, Mariette Hartley, Ed Asner, Lorne Greene, Charlotte Rae, Sandy Duncan, Gavin McLeod, Jodie Foster, Cheryl Ladd, Penny Marshall, Cindy Williams, Henry Winkler, Sally Struthers, Perry King, and Linda Purl, among many others.

All in all, Hanna-Barbera Productions has produced nearly 300 different series, specials, television movies, and theatrical films. These shows have been seen in more than eighty countries, and have been heard in twenty-two different languages. Every hour of every day, somewhere in the world, people are watching a Hanna-Barbera production. Hanna is the father of a son and a daughter, now in their forties. "[My wife] devoted her life very much to me and the children and she made the family the most dominant thing in her life. I would feel perfectly safe, even though I was expected home for dinner at eight, ringing and saying 'Honey, I'm sorry but so-and-so's in town and I should take him to dinner.... [My own children did not watch much television because] there wasn't all that much in those days. Today, though, I feel kids should be disciplined—television should be worked in with seeing friends, reading and exercise."[2]

"My advice to young people [who wish to get into the industry] is to develop their natural talents. We have many people working here who were first visual artists and have now become writers as well. Writing and being a good artist are two essentials in this industry. There is also room now for computer specialists and administrators. But the bulk of the work is based on writing and on the artistic talents of the people that are involved in the creative side of animation. If you have some ability, develop it and pursue it."[1]

FOR MORE INFORMATION SEE: Danny Peary and Gerald Peary, *The American Animated Cartoon,* Dutton, 1980; "TV Channels and Cable TV," *News* (Port Arthur, Texas), April 15-21, 1984; Virginia Hahn, "Hanna's Proud of Early Efforts," *Southeast Apartment Weekly* (Pasadena, Texas), Volume 2, number 17, April 26, 1984; Adrian Swift, "Bill Hanna: Yogi's Father," *Sydney Morning Herald,* (Australia), April 22, 1985; Janise Beaumont, "Meet Tom and Jerry's 'Dad' . . . ," *Sun-Herald,* December 8, 1985; Maurice Horn, editor, *Contemporary Graphic Artists,* Volume 1, Gale, 1986; Digby Diehl, "Joe Barbera: He's America's Busiest Baby-sitter—The Prolific Craftsman of TV Cartooning," *People,* March 16, 1987; "Hanna-Barbera Having Talks toward Producing Animated 'Cats' Feature," *Variety,* June 24, 1987.

HAYES, Sheila 1937-

PERSONAL: Born June 16, 1937, in New York, N.Y.; daughter of Michael (a carpenter) and Mary (Flaherty) Hagan; married Michael Hayes (an attorney), May 26, 1962; children: Laura, Allison, Susannah. *Education:* Attended Marymount College (now Marymount Manhattan College), 1955-57, and Columbia University, 1957-58. *Politics:* Independent. *Religion:* Roman Catholic. *Home:* Deer Hill Lane, Briarcliff Manor, N.Y. 10510.

CAREER: Ted Deglin & Associates (public relations firm), New York City, receptionist and public relations assistant, 1957-59; *Simplicity Pattern Book,* New York City, beauty editor, 1959; Peck & Peck (retail store chain), New York City,

SHEILA HAYES

(Jacket illustration by Ellen Thompson from *You've Been Away All Summer* by Sheila Hayes.)

assistant to director of public relations, 1960-62; writer, 1969—. *Member:* Authors Guild.

WRITINGS—Juvenile: *Where Did the Baby Go?,* Golden Press, 1974; *The Carousel Horse,* T. Nelson, 1978; *Me and My Mona Lisa Smile,* Elsevier / Nelson, 1981; *Speaking of Snapdragons* (Junior Literary Guild selection), Lodestar Books, 1982; *No Autographs, Please,* Lodestar Books, 1984; *You've Been Away All Summer* (sequel to *The Carousel Horse;* Junior Literary Guild selection), Lodestar Books, 1986. Contributor to periodicals, including *Friend.*

ADAPTATIONS: "The Carousel Horse" (After-school Special), ABC-TV, 1982-83.

SIDELIGHTS: Hayes studied writing and public relations at Marymount College and Columbia University. "I was determined to starve in a garret and write the great American novel. Looking back on it, it was all very convenient: not only was it a short walk to the campus, but since I still lived at home, while my *soul* may have been starving, my body was getting three square meals a day."

Hayes rediscovered her childhood love of libraries when she became a mother. "I had always loved to read, and I think every writer feels at home among the rows and rows of books. Coming back to the children's room after twenty-five years was the time when the mother in me and the writer in me melted into one person. There's never been any conflict. I knew then that, if I was going to be a writer, this was the room I wanted my books to be in."

You've Been Away All Summer is a sequel to *The Carousel Horse*. ''As I imagine most sequels do, it grew out of that perennial question asked by readers, 'What happened next?' In this case: What happened to Fran Davies when she returned home to New York City after spending the summer in a home where her mother worked as a cook? Did she continue her friendship with wealthy Andrea Fairchild? And did Fran finally admit the truth about the summer to her best friend, Sarah McAuliffe?

''Having grown up in New York City, I was excited at the prospect of setting a story on the West Side of Manhattan, very near the neighborhood where I had lived as a child. But I wasn't prepared for some of the changes. More than once, I was shocked to discover that a sturdy old landmark I had been sure would last forever was long gone. Some of the changes were more subtle. I used to walk to the corner and buy an ice cream cone; when Fran goes to the corner, she buys Tofutti. But girls, and friendship, and most of all, best friends? I discovered it all over again: that part hasn't changed at all.''

''I feel very fortunate that, for me, creativity is fueled in a very direct way by my personal life. To write for children you must *be* a child, remembering how it feels to be low man on the totem pole in this adult world. Keeping these feelings fresh adds an extra dimension to parenthood. Parent and writer don't just co-exist; they give essential nourishment to each other.''

HOBBIES AND OTHER INTERESTS: Gardening, paddle tennis, tennis, theatre, books.

HINES, Anna G(rossnickle) 1946-

PERSONAL: Born July 13, 1946, in Cincinnati, Ohio; daughter of Earl S. (a mathematical analyst) and Ruth (a personnel service representative; maiden name, Putnam) Grossnickle; married Steve Carlson, August 12, 1965 (divorced, 1973); married Gary Roger Hines (a forest ranger, writer and musician), June 19, 1976; children: (first marriage) Bethany, Sarah; (second marriage) Lassen. *Education:* Attended San Fernando Valley State College (now California State University, Northridge), 1964-67; Pacific Oaks College, B.A., 1974, M.A., 1979. *Home:* P.O. Box 923, Twain Harte, Calif. 95383.

CAREER: Los Angeles City Children's Centers, Los Angeles, Calif., preschool teacher, 1967-68, 1969-70; Columbia Elementary School, Columbia, Calif., third grade teacher, 1975-78; full-time writer and illustrator, 1978—. *Member:* Society of Children's Book Writers, California Reading Association (Tuolumne Reading Council). *Awards, honors: All by Myself* was selected one of Child Study Association of America's Children's Books of the Year, 1985.

WRITINGS—Self-illustrated children's books, except as noted: *Taste the Raindrops,* Greenwillow, 1983, large print edition, 1983; *Come to the Meadow* (Junior Literary Guild selection), Clarion Books, 1984; *Maybe a Band-Aid Will Help,* Dutton, 1984; *All by Myself,* Clarion Books, 1985; *Bethany for Real,* Greenwillow, 1985; *Cassie Bowen Takes Witch Lessons* (juvenile novel; illustrated by Gail Owens), Dutton, 1985; *Daddy Makes the Best Spaghetti* (Junior Literary Guild selection), Clarion Books, 1986; *Don't Worry, I'll Find You,* Dutton, 1986; *I'll Tell You What They Say,* Greenwillow, 1987; *It's Just Me, Emily,* Clarion, 1987; *Keep Your Old Hat,* Dutton, 1987; *Grandma Gets Grumpy,* Clarion, 1988. Contributor to magazines including *Society of Children's Book Writer's Bulletin.*

WORK IN PROGRESS: ''A sequel to *Cassie Bowen Takes Witch Lessons,* to be published by Dutton, a story about Cassie, now in fifth grade, who is disturbed by the fact that her friends are showing interest in boys, and upset that her father is not keeping his promise to write and be there for her in spite of her parents' divorce; *They Really Like Me,* to be published by Greenwillow, a story of the teasing back and forth between Josh and his two older sisters who are left to look after him while mother does her marketing. This story was inspired by my own children's recent reminiscing about some of the things that went on in our house when I left the two older girls in charge of the younger one. Mothers should probably never know the truth!; *Sky All Around,* a gentle story about a little girl and her father watching the sun go down and the stars come out, to be published by Clarion Books.''

SIDELIGHTS: ''In early college I was discouraged from pursuing my interest in picture books. I was told it was not a worthy interest because a picture book was not truly 'fine art' on the one hand or 'commercial' on the other. To me, the art of the picture book, which can be held in the hands, carried about, taken to bed, is much more personal and intimate than the art which hangs in galleries or museums. I persisted and happily so, for I love what I now do.

''My stories come mostly from my experiences and feelings as a child and with my own children. The stories are mostly about the discovery, imagination, playfulness, and wonder in young children's everyday lives, so often missed by busy adults.

''It was a few months after the birth of my third child that I decided I should either pursue my goal of doing children's

ANNA G. HINES

books more seriously or give it up. I had been submitting work and receiving encouragement from editors over the years but kept letting myself get sidetracked by other demands. It wasn't easy at first, but I made writing and illustration a priority. Twenty months later I sold my first book—*Taste the Raindrops*. I'm thrilled to finally be doing exactly what I've always wanted to do.

''*Come to the Meadow* started with an idea for a story about a child playing and discovering things in a meadow. For several months the idea was nothing more than a seed in my mind. Then one night just as I was falling asleep the whole story played itself through. I often have insights as I'm falling asleep, but not word for word stories like this one.

''*Maybe a Band-Aid Will Help* was inspired by an incident with my daughter Sarah and her beloved cloth doll, Abigail. In the book, Abigail's leg comes off and Mama is too busy to fix her right away. *Don't Worry, I'll Find You* has Sarah and Abigail lost in a big shopping mall. *All by Myself* is about a child taking a big step toward independence by giving up night diapers and getting up in the middle of the night to go to the

bathroom all by herself. It also started from an incident with Sarah.

''*Bethany for Real* was inspired by my older daughter, who always loved pretending and is a talented young actress. It is a fun story of the mix-up that results when Bethany pretends to be somebody else.

''*Cassie Bowen Takes Witch Lessons* is a story of one friendship ending and a new one beginning as a fourth-grade girl's values mature. It is also about the cruel teasing that goes on when a child dares to be a little bit different. I wrote it as a result of a dream I had about writing a book. The basic plot and characters were all in that dream.

''*Daddy Makes the Best Spaghetti* is a simple story of family warmth. I wanted to do a story about a nurturing father. He ended up being a rather fun-loving fellow, too.''

''I thought the idea a good one, and since my husband shares domestic duties in our household, I watched him, waiting for a story to come. The title came first, which is unusual for me

I want to go walking in the rain, but it's always the same. . . . ■ (From *Taste the Raindrops* by Anna Grossnickle Hines. Illustrated by the author.)

because titles are almost always a struggle. Spaghetti is one of my husband's favorite things to cook, second only to popcorn. His spaghetti is very good, but it got to be kind of a family joke that if he were cooking it would be spaghetti for dinner . . . again. At our house, Daddy makes the spaghetti. Add 'Best' in there and it sounded like a fun title and the beginning of a fun book.

"I must say, though he is a very nice daddy and looks great in a shower cap, Gary is not nearly as silly as the fellow in the book. In fact, I'm known as the 'Silly Goose' in our family, a title lovingly bestowed upon me by our youngest.

"The drawings for this book were a family affair. Lassen posed as the boy in the story, Sarah the mother, and my husband the father. I took snapshots of them and referred to the photos while doing the illustrations. Lassen, especially, thought this was great fun and feels this book is partly hers since she made such an important contribution."

"In *I'll Tell You What They Say* Andy takes his teddy bear, Oliver, for a ride to see the animals, giving Sam, the dog, orders to stay home. Andy is busy telling Oliver what the animals are saying, and doesn't see that Sam has followed along. But it's Sam to the rescue when Oliver gets snatched by a goose. The seed for this story was planted years ago when we lived next door to an old man who spent hours talking to his geese. Beth and Sarah, quite young then, would stand by the fence and watch, occasionally joining in the conversation.

"My latest published works include *It's Just Me, Emily, Keep Your Old Hat* and *Grandma Gets Grumpy*. The first is a game between a toddler and her mother with the child hiding and the mother guessing what could be growling behind the door, thumping under the table, splashing in the tub and so on. *Keep Your Old Hat* is a third Sarah and Abigail story in which Sarah has a fight with her friend Mandy over who is to be the mother when they play house. *Grandma Gets Grumpy* is a picture book about five little cousins who spend the night with Grandma. They think anything goes at Grandma's house but learn that Grandma has rules, too."

HOBBIES AND OTHER INTERESTS: Needlework, crocheting.

HOAGLAND, Edward 1932-

PERSONAL: Born December 21, 1932, in New York, N.Y.; son of Warren Eugene and Helen (Morley) Hoagland; married Amy J. Ferrara, 1960 (divorced); married Marion Magid, March 28, 1968; children: Molly. *Education:* Harvard University, A.B., 1954. *Home:* 463 West St., New York, N.Y. 10014. *Agent:* Robert Lescher, 155 East 71st St., New York, N.Y. 10021.

CAREER: Novelist and essayist. Instructor at New School for Social Research, 1963-64, Rutgers University, 1966, Sarah Lawrence College, 1967, 1971, City College of the City University of New York, 1967-68, University of Iowa, 1978, 1982, Columbia University, 1980, 1981, and Bennington College, 1987. *Military service:* U.S. Army, 1955-57. *Member:* American Academy and Institute of Arts and Letters. *Awards, honors:* Houghton Mifflin literary fellowship, 1956, for *Cat Man;* Longview Foundation award, 1961; American Academy of Arts and Letters travelling fellow, 1964; Guggenheim fellow, 1964, 1975; O. Henry Award, 1971; New York State Council on the Arts award, 1972; Brandeis University Creative Arts Awards Commission citation in literature, 1972; National Book Award nominee for *Walking the Dead Diamond River,*

EDWARD HOAGLAND

1974; National Book Critics Circle award nomination in nonfiction, 1979, selected one of New York Public Library's Books for the Teen Age, 1980, 1981, and 1982, and American Book Award nominee (for paperback edition), 1981, for *African Calliope: A Journey to the Sudan;* Harold D. Vursell award of the American Academy of Arts and Letters, 1981; National Endowment for the Arts award, 1982.

WRITINGS—Published by Random House, except as indicated: *Cat Man,* Houghton, 1956; *The Circle Home,* Crowell, 1960; *The Peacock's Tail,* McGraw, 1965; *Notes from the Century Before: A Journal from British Columbia,* 1969; *The Courage of Turtles,* 1971; *Walking the Dead Diamond River,* 1973; *The Moose on the Wall: Field Notes from the Vermont Wilderness,* Barrie & Jenkins, 1974; *Red Wolves and Black Bears,* 1976; *African Calliope: A Journey to the Sudan* (ALA Notable Book), 1979; *The Edward Hoagland Reader,* edited by Geoffrey Wollf, 1979; *The Tugman's Passage,* 1982; *City Tales,* Capra Press, 1986; *Seven Rivers West,* Summit Books, 1986. Contributor of short stories to *Esquire, New Yorker, New American Review, Transatlantic Review,* and other publications.

SIDELIGHTS: Hoagland, an American essayist, travel writer, and novelist, instills much of his own personality into his writing, particularly his essays. He is a man who delights in the small details and peculiarities of life and vividly portrays these details along with his own reminiscences in his work. Because of a childhood stutter, he was naturally drawn to writing. "I could easily talk to dogs, goats, and pet alligators—though not to people—and so to the extent that stuttering directed my course as a writer, the choice for me all along may have been whether to become an essayist or to write about animals.'' [Beaufort Cranford, ''Edward Hoagland,'' *Detroit News,* June 5, 1983.¹]

''Since 1979 I have been writing unsigned nature or cityscape editorials for the *New York Times* editorial page, and I frequently write longer essays for magazines such as *Harper's, Vanity Fair, The Nation, Antaeus* and others.

''[I have also written] two travel books, which particularly in the case of the African book [*African Calliope*] are not so joyous, optimistic, boyish. There are few American writers nowadays who write travel books at all. (Part of our trouble is that there are so few.) My most ambitious and perhaps successful book to date is my recent novel, *Seven Rivers West.*''

FOR MORE INFORMATION SEE: Newsweek, June 2, 1969, January 18, 1971; *Commentary,* September, 1969; *Book World,* September 7, 1969; *New York Review of Books,* September 11, 1969; *Village Voice,* October 23, 1969; *Washington Post,* January 14, 1971, September 21, 1986; *New York Times,* January 15, 1971, September 11, 1979, March 17, 1982; *New York Times Book Review,* March 25, 1973, September 16, 1979, April 19, 1981, June 12, 1983, September 21, 1986; *Washington Post Book World,* September 23, 1979; *Chicago Tribune Book World,* September 23, 1979, April 4, 1982; *Chicago Tribune,* November 12, 1979, September 21, 1986; *Detroit News,* March 28, 1982, June 5, 1983; *The Boston Globe Magazine,* October 5, 1986.

HOLL, Kristi D(iane) 1951-

PERSONAL: Surname is pronounced Hall; born December 8, 1951, in Guthrie Center, Iowa; daughter of Delbert Richard (a salesman) and Melva (a realtor; maiden name, Hanysh) Couchman; married Randy Holl (a landscape nursery owner), June 17, 1973; children: Matthew (adopted), Jennifer, Laurel, Jacqueline. *Education:* University of Northern Iowa, B.A., 1974. *Religion:* Baptist. *Home and Office:* Route 2, Box 26, Conrad, Iowa 50621.

CAREER: Hawthorne Elementary School, Waterloo, Iowa, reading teacher, 1972; writer, 1980—; Institute of Children's Literature, Redding Ridge, Conn., correspondence instructor, 1983—. *Member:* Society of Children's Book Writers, Mystery Writers of America. *Awards, honors: The Rose beyond the Wall* was named a Notable Children's Trade Book in the field of Social Studies by the joint committee of the National Council of Social Studies and the Children's Book Council, 1985, and nominated for the Mark Twain Award, 1988; *Just Like a Real Family* was nominated for the Mark Twain Award, the Iowa Children's Choice Award, and the Sequoya Children's Book Award, all 1986, and the Golden Sower Award, 1987.

*WRITINGS—*Children's books: *Just Like a Real Family,* Atheneum, 1983; *Mystery by Mail,* Atheneum, 1983; *Footprints Up My Back* (Junior Literary Guild selection), Atheneum, 1984; *The Rose beyond the Wall,* Atheneum, 1985; *First Things First,* Macmillan, 1986; *Cast a Single Shadow,* Atheneum, 1986; *Perfect or Not, Here I Come* (Junior Literary Guild selection), Macmillan, 1986; *The Haunting of Cabin Thirteen,* Atheneum, 1987; *Patchwork Summer,* Macmillan, 1987; *No Strings Attached,* Macmillan, 1988.

Contributor of articles and short stories to magazines, including *Child Life, Jack and Jill, Health Explorer, Hi-Call, Chil-*

KRISTI D. HOLL

dren's Playmate, Family Life Today, Touch, Vibrant Life, Your Life and Health, Children's Digest, Living with Children, Writer, and *Society of Children's Book Writers Bulletin.*

WORK IN PROGRESS: ''I am now working on a sequel to *Just Like a Real Family,* my first book.''

SIDELIGHTS: ''My first experience with writing was in fifth grade. I wrote a story called 'Four Sisters,' a thinly disguised remake of *Little Women.* I wrote the story, not because I dreamed of becoming a writer, but because I didn't want the book to end.

''After putting the 'four sisters' away in a box, I forgot about writing for more than fifteen years. Then one morning I sat in the doctor's waiting room thumbing through magazines. My third child was overdue, so when I read the ad for the Institute of Children's Literature, I merely sighed. With the advent of a newborn, it didn't seem the ideal time to start a new career. But when I was back in the doctor's office the next week, still awaiting the stork, I noticed the ad again. On impulse I ripped it out and sent for the aptitude test. That day I went into labor (I'm not sure there was a connection) and forgot about the test. When the test arrived, the baby was ten days old. I filled it out during her naptime.

''I didn't really believe that I could become a writer, but I enjoyed doing each lesson. It was gratifying to see that, after years of full-time mothering, I remembered a few words longer than two syllables. My instructor's encouragement was the single most important factor in my success. She helped me stretch beyond what I considered to be my capabilities.

''Before the course was over, I had sold three stories, two of them class assignments. (However, the sales were preceded by months of rejection slips while my husband looked askance at my postage bill.)

"After selling twenty-five stories and articles, it seemed like the optimal time to give books a try. I had a serious case of morning sickness and was already spending hours lying on the couch. To put the time to use, and to take my mind off my queasy stomach, I dreamed up some characters and began outlining a book.

"When I finished the first book I jumped into another 8-12 novel, a mystery this time. Since child number four was three weeks overdue, I had time to finish the mystery before going to the hospital. I was back to work on another book when our baby girl was a month old. I guarded my writing time jealously. It was never more than an hour or two each day, often accumulated in ten-minute segments, but I made sure I took that time for myself every day. The three books sold within a short time.

"*Perfect or Not, Here I Come* is for all of us with perfectionist tendencies who need to learn to relax and enjoy life. As a child I always felt driven to do things perfectly. And since I never could, I was rarely satisfied with myself or life. Even as an adult, I could seldom enjoy my accomplishments. Somehow my efforts were never quite good enough. It wasn't until I realized I was passing that attitude along to my kids that I made a conscious effort to change. Things don't have to be perfect to be good and enjoyable.

At the end of the hall, Tara took the stairs three at a time. . . . ■ (Jacket illustration from *Perfect or Not, Here I Come* by Kristi D. Holl.)

"Writing is one of my greatest enjoyments, second only to my husband and children. Things finally came full circle when I joined the Institute of Children's Literature as an instructor.

"When people ask me if I hope someday to write for adults, they're often surprised when I say no. I much prefer to write for children. Kids have the ability to believe in 'impractical' ideas, in fantastic places and people. Children are fun to write for because they still believe all things are possible. When I write, I enjoy becoming a child again, letting down all the barriers adults build up. When I was a child, I thought writers, who actually got paid to stay home and make up stories, must be the luckiest people in the world. I still think so.

"I am very family-oriented. I believe every child deserves a home (which is why we adopted Matt from Korea at the age of five) and a child needs to feel loved for himself, not just when he 'measures up' to someone's standards. I try to convey this in my books.

"One of my children is still at home, and my home life is busy. I truly dread the day when all four kids will catch the school bus and be gone. I've never written without a baby on my lap or under my feet.

"My advice to aspiring writers: The one factor I think you must have in order to succeed in writing is this—a strong belief in your ability. You must believe in the value of your work. You must believe that you have something to say to readers. Each writer has a unique perspective and unique experiences to bring to his writing. I think you get this belief in yourself by writing about what you *care* about. If you write about something you care deeply about you will write with enthusiasm. This enthusiasm will be transmitted to your readers. So I advise a student not to write science-fiction if he hates to read it, and not to write romances if a swooning heroine turns his stomach. Don't jump on bandwagons, writing something just because you think it will sell. Your 'lukewarm-ness' will show in your writing—your readers will feel it as you do."

HOBBIES AND OTHER INTERESTS: Civil War era, *Gone with the Wind* memorabilia, camping, hiking, reading, museums, steamboating on the Mississippi.

FOR MORE INFORMATION SEE: Times-Republican (Marshalltown, Iowa), March 17, 1984; Kristi D. Holl, "The Emotional Touch in Juvenile Fiction," *Writer,* August, 1986.

HOUGH, Judy Taylor   1932- (Judy Taylor)

BRIEF ENTRY: Born August 12, 1932, in South Wales. Hough, who writes under the name Judy Taylor, was named a Member of the British Empire in 1971 for her services to children's publishing in Great Britain, a career that began as a Girl Friday in 1951 and ended when she stepped down as director of The Bodley Head publishing company in 1984. Since her retirement, Hough has written two picture books series as well as books on Beatrix Potter, including *Beatrix Potter: Countrywoman, Artist and Storyteller* (Warne, 1987) and *That Naughty Rabbit: Beatrix Potter and Peter Rabbit* (Warne, 1987). Hough's interest in Potter extends past her role as a biographer to her position, since 1981, as Penguin's consultant on the licensing and commercial use of Potter's creations.

Sophie and Jack (Bodley Head, 1982), Hough's first book, concerns the exploits of two young hippopotamus friends on a picnic. "The humor inherent in the dead-pan text is perfectly visualized in the double-paged paintings," wrote *Horn Book.* The other books in the series are *Sophie and Jack Help Out* (1983) and *Sophie and Jack in the Snow* (1984). The "Dudley" series, published in America by Putnam, is about a mouse whose humor holds him in good stead amidst his muddled incompetence in the face of danger. Titles include *Dudley Goes Flying* (1986), *Dudley and the Monster* (1985), and *Dudley in a Jam* (1987). Taylor is completing *Dudley Bakes a Cake* as well as *The Selected Letters of Beatrix Potter. Home and office:* 31 Meadowbank, Primrose Hill, London NW3 1AY, England.

FOR MORE INFORMATION SEE: Publishers Weekly, July 22, 1983; *Who's Who,* St. Martin's, 1985.

HULL, Jessie Redding   1932-
(Jesse Redding Hull)

PERSONAL: Born July 27, 1932, in Urbana, Ohio; daughter of William (an accountant) and Ethel (a florist; maiden name, Botkin) Redding; married Robert C. Hull (a writer), June 27, 1959; children: Robert W., Lisa K. *Education:* Ohio Wesleyan University, B.A., 1954; University of Missouri, A.M., 1956; also attended Cleveland State University, 1975-76. *Home and office:* 606 Crestview Dr., Bay Village, Ohio 44140.

CAREER: Montevallo College, Montevallo, Ala., speech clinic supervisor, summer, 1956; Affton, Missouri Public Schools, speech therapist, 1956-59; Bob Hull Books, Bay Village, Ohio, business manager, 1980—. Volunteer language development teacher, 1967-73. Hostess at Rose Hill Museum, 1976—. Demonstrator of Early American crafts, weaver. *Member:* Bay Village Historical Society.

WRITINGS—Juvenile, except as indicated: *Take Care of Millie* (adult novel), New Readers Press, 1980; *The Other Side of Yellow* (adult novel), New Readers Press, 1980; *Marathon Madness,* Bowmar/Noble, 1980; *Operation Airdrop,* Bowmar/Noble, 1980; *The Ghost Car of Apple Valley,* Bowmar/Noble, 1980; *The Bicycle Rip-Off,* Bowmar/Noble, 1980; *Danger at the Racetrack,* Bowmar/Noble, 1980; (under name Jesse Redding Hull) *Stanley's Secret Trip* (illustrated by Paul Furan), Crestwood House, 1981. Contributor of poems, articles, and stories to magazines, including *Pets and People of the World, Ohio Motorist,* and *The Christian.*

WORK IN PROGRESS: A Season of Doubts, a suspense novel for young people; two juvenile animal books, *Trouble with Four Legs* and *The Dog Nobody Wanted; The Return of Sandy*

Jessie Redding Hull with her cat, C.C.

Allen; researching and writing a fictional family saga for adults entitled *The Well Witch;* research for fictional and non-fictional stories for children of the revolutionary period and for craft books covering skills of Early America.

SIDELIGHTS: "Possibly, I am the only author who grew up in a florist shop. My father died when I was an infant, and my mother took me to work with her everyday. Flowers and bits of ribbon were my earliest toys. My early vacations were spent on my uncle's farm where I learned the discipline of 'chores' and developed a love of nature while wading in the creek and watching wild ducks nest in tall marsh grass.

"For as long as I can remember, writing has been as important to me as breathing. My transition from writing for pleasure to writing as a career had an almost miraculous beginning. It started in 1979, and eight books were in print by the end of 1981. Since 1981, I have not been as fortunate. Perhaps time is needed for 'paying my dues'—that is, I am polishing my skills and improving my marketing techniques.

"The books for New Readers Press were the most difficult to write, not because they were marketed for adults with low reading skills, but because they were problem situations. I suffered with my characters as I role-played my way through the stories. The problems of my characters became my problems, and I was emotionally drained at the conclusion of each book. Critics were kind, and I am proud of the books; however, I have much to learn about creating problem situation fiction. I tend to wrap up situations with neat little endings that aren't likely in real life.

"My other published books were easy to write, because they involved escapism in the form of unlikely escapades that allow our imaginations to deliver us from the real world for a brief adventure—usually fast-paced and humorous. These books were pure joy to write.

"My juvenile writing is moving in the direction of stories with historical background. Young people are often turned off by history because their exposure involves dry descriptions of events, without thorough characterizations of the exciting people involved in history. With my present research on Mary Katherine Goddard, I hope to convince a publisher that I can enliven history for children as John Jakes did for adults.

"In the future I hope to share my love of Early America with young people. A funny thing happened on the way to the series about Early American crafts. My research led to a demand for my services as a festival demonstrator, and I presently make more money with my woven specialties than I do with my writing. However, I still write.

"When I write, I loosely structure my storyline. I role-play my characters and try to give them enough freedom that they make changes in my story according to their feelings and values instead of mine. I hope that people enjoy my stories and are inspired to write stories of their own."

HOBBIES AND OTHER INTERESTS: "Camping, weaving, old time typesetting, playing with my two dogs and three cats, hostessing at Rose Hill Museum, researching Early America."

Books are the quietest and most constant of friends; they are the most accessible and wisest of counsellors, and the most patient of teachers.

—Charles W. Eliot

HUTCHINS, Hazel J. 1952-

BRIEF ENTRY: Born August 9, 1952, in Calgary, Alberta, Canada. Author of books for children. According to Hutchins, she "likes to write . . . stories that play with imaginative possibilities." This is evident in her first book, *The Three and Many Wishes of Jason Reid* (Annick, 1983), which takes its plot from the fairy tale of the genie who grants someone three wishes; in this case, Jason knows how to capitalize on the third wish. "The book is very fast moving, exciting, and should appeal to young readers," observed *Carleton Miscellany.* Hutchins followed this book with *Anastasia Morningstar and the Crystal Butterfly* (Annick, 1984) and *Leanna Builds a Genie Trap* (Annick, 1986). The latter is about a sofa that seems to be harboring a thieving genie. "Anyone who has found lost objects down the side of a sofa will understand this humorous story," wrote *Canadian Children's Literature.* Hutchins is currently working on *Ben's Ski Song,* a preschool picture book. *Home:* Box 185, Canmore, Alberta, Canada T01 0M0.

FOR MORE INFORMATION SEE: Toronto Globe and Mail, May 17, 1986.

JAQUITH, Priscilla 1908-

PERSONAL: Born August 21, 1908, in Brooklyn, N.Y.; daughter of Frank H. (a civil engineer) and Isidora (a teacher; maiden name, Morehouse) Hicks; married Stephen M. Jaquith, July, 1929 (divorced, July, 1949); children: Carol Jaquith Patton. *Education:* Cornell University, B.A., 1930. *Home:* 6A Wildflower Dr., Ithaca, N.Y. 14850. *Agent:* Dorothy Markinko, McIntosh & Otis, Inc., 475 Fifth Ave., New York, N.Y. 10017.

CAREER: Cornell University, Ithaca, N.Y., woman's editor of *Cornell Daily Sun,* 1929-31; newspaper reporter, 1929-31; Rockefeller Center, New York, N.Y., member of public relations department, 1932-41, editor of *Rockefeller Center Magazine,* 1938-41; free-lance writer for national magazines, including *Reader's Digest, Today's Woman, Everywoman's,* 1939-60. Worked as library volunteer and publicist for Has-

PRISCILLA JAQUITH

tings Gallery, New York, and Westchester Group of Artists. *Member:* National League of American Pen Women, Jean Fritz Juvenile Writers Group (chairman 1983-84), Cornell Mortarboard, Cornell Raven and Serpent. *Awards, honors: Bo Rabbit, Smart for True: Folktales from the Gullah* was chosen a *Booklist* Reviewer's Choice, and one of *School Library Journal's* Notable Children's Books, both 1981, a Notable Children's Trade Book in the Field of Social Studies, one of Library of Congress' Children's Books of the Year, one of New York Public Library's Outstanding Books of the Year, and an American Institute of Graphic Arts Book Show selection, all 1982.

WRITINGS: (Reteller) *Bo Rabbit, Smart for True: Folktales from the Gullah* (ALA Notable Book; *Horn Book* honor list; illustrated by Ed Young), Philomel, 1981. Contributor of articles and columns to magazines.

WORK IN PROGRESS: Historical novel about the War of 1812; short novel about a girl in the 1860s.

SIDELIGHTS: "If it weren't for my grandchildren, I probably would never have started writing for children. But when my oldest grandchild began to read, I became interested in children's books. And since folktales had always beguiled me (I once did a magazine piece on tall tales), it was natural for me to research and rewrite the Gullah folktales. Also, these stories about the animals reminded me of the many hours I spent as a child roaming the meadows and fields near my house with fieldglasses and nature books and the years spent raising the big June moths, the Saturniidae. They have wings as beautiful as Persian rugs and four to six inches wide. Someday, I hope to do a book about them.

"For anyone interested in writing for children, I'd like to say, although I've written all my life, I find this the most exacting task of all. Not only do you have to write simply and interest children, you have to interest adults, too, as they are the ones who buy the books. Yet for some strange reason, most people think they could toss off a children's book any time they want to—nothing to it!"

Jaquith's works are included in the Kerlan Collection at the University of Minnesota.

JENKYNS, Chris 1924-

PERSONAL: Born July 3, 1924, in North Hollywood; Calif.; son of Mignon and Cams Jenkyns; children: two. *Education:* Attended Los Angeles City College, 1945, Art Center School, Los Angeles, Calif., 1946, Chouinard Art Institute, 1946, Art Students League, 1949, and Académie Julian, Paris, France, 1950. *Home:* 2929 Waverly Drive, 218, Los Angeles, Calif. 90039.

CAREER: Producer, writer, director, and designer of films, and illustrator of books for children. Writer and design artist for Storyboard, Inc., 1954; free-lance writer for "The Bullwinkle Show," produced by Jay Ward Productions, 1960-64; president of Jenkyns, Shean, and Elliot, Inc., 1964-70; president and founder of Jenkyns & Associates, Inc., 1970-73. Professor of animation at Ministere de la Culture Francaise, Chambre de Commerce et D'Industrie de Paris, France, and Centre de Formations Technologique, 1985-86. *Military service:* U. S. Navy, circa 1942-45. *Member:* Screen Cartoonists Guild, Academy of Television Arts and Sciences, Société des Auteurs et Compositeurs Dramatiques.

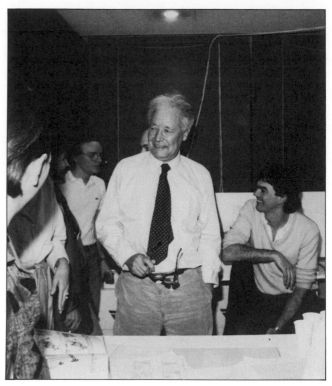

CHRIS JENKYNS

AWARDS, HONORS—Books: *Andy Says Bonjour!* was selected one of *New York Times* Best Illustrated Books of the Year, 1954.

Films: Jenkyns has received over 150 major awards for writing and design from the New York, Los Angeles, Chicago, San Francisco, Detroit, and Atlanta Art Director's Clubs, plus foreign honors at Tours, Annecy, Cork, London, Edinburgh, and Venice Film Festivals, including: New York Art Director's Club Medal for "John and Marsha," 1956, "Fairy Godmother," 1958, "Rope," 1959, "Subliminal," 1960, "Just a Commercial," 1960; Los Angeles Art Director's Club Medal for "Subliminal," 1960; "Oscar" Award nomination from the Academy of Motion Picture Arts and Sciences, 1964, for animated film, "Self-Defense for Cowards"; Bronze Medal from the International Film and Television Festival, 1973, Golden Eagle award from CINE (Council on Internationl Nontheatrical Events), 1973, both for animated film series, "The Most Important Person"; "Emmy" Award from the National Academy of Television Arts and Sciences for best title design, 1984, for "The Duck Factory." "Muppet Babies," an animated series for which Jenkyns did the storyboard, won an "Emmy" Award from the National Academy of Arts and Sciences, 1984; "Les Triples," an animated series that Jenkyns directed, won a Bronze Medal from the International Film and Television Festival, 1986.

ILLUSTRATOR: Pat Diska, *Andy Says Bonjour!,* Vanguard, 1954; Thomas McGrath, *About Clouds,* Melmont, 1959; T. McGrath, *Beautiful Things,* Vanguard, 1960; Florence M. White, *How to Lose Your Lunch Money,* Ward Richie Press, 1970; F. M. White, *How to Lose Your Best Friend,* Ward Richie Press, 1972; Marylinn Huse, *Eddie's Absolutely Incredible Birthday (and Treasure Hunt),* Ward Richie Press, 1973. Has also illustrated *Self-Defense for Cowards* by A. McGrath, Price, Stern & Sloan; *The What to Do While You're Holding the Phone Book,* Tarcher/Hawthorne; and *Backyard Treasure Hunting,* Ward Richie Press.

FILMS: (Writer) "Judo Jerry" ("Tom and Jerry" series), M.G.M., 1963; (writer) "Clyde Crashcup" sequences in "The Alvin Show," Format Films, 1963; (director and designer), "Panic on Wall Street," (ten-minute graphic film), Charles Eames & Associates, 1963; (story and design) "Self-Defense for Cowards" (animated film), Rembrandt Films, 1964; (producer and director) "The Story of Navigation" (thirty-minute film with graphics and live action), Litton Industries, 1968; (producer and director) "My Mother Is the Most Beautiful Woman in the World" (ten-minute animated film), Bailey Film Associates, 1968; (producer, director, and designer) "How to Lose Your Lunch Money" (ten-minute animated film), Bailey Film Associates, 1972; (story) "The Rescuers" (feature length animation film), Walt Disney Productions, 1973; (storyboard)

The man with the long pole was still standing and catching fish after fish. ■ (From *Andy Says Bonjour!* by Pat Diska. Illustrated by Chris Jenkyns.)

"The Dispatcher" (a Doctor Seuss CBS-TV thirty-minute special), De-Patie/Freleng, 1974; (director) "A Storm of Strangers / Irish" (thirty-minute film with graphics and live-action), PBS-TV, 1975.

(Storyboard and title design) "Grease," starring John Travolta, Paramount, 1980; (storyboard) "Stanley" (animated), ABC-TV, 1982; (storyboard) "He-Man and the Masters of the Universe," (sixty-five half-hour animated films), Cable TV, 1983; (writer of animation segments and storyboard) 'The Duck Factory'' (live-action situation comedy series for NBC-TV), Mary Tyler Moore Enterprises, 1983; (storyboard) "Heathcliff" (animated series), DIC Enterprises, 1984-85; (storyboard) "Muppet Babies" (animated half-hour series), Marvel Productions, 1984-85; (title design and direction) "Detective in the House" (live-action television series), starring Judd Hirsch, Playhouse Pictures, 1985; (storyboard and character design) "Harry, the Fat Bear Spy" (half-hour children's program), 1985; (consultant) "Les Monde engloutis" (series), France Animation, 1985; (director) "Les Triples" (animated series), Télé Hachette (Paris), 1986. Has also been engaged in the production of over 1000 animated and live-action films for television advertising and promotional films for television. Also writer for "The Smurfs" (animated series for television), Hanna-Barbera Productions.

SIDELIGHTS: "During the Depression, my mother and father both worked, so I spent my early childhood with my grandmother and my three aunts who lived next door. From the time I can remember I always drew. When I was seven years old, I had an experience that had a profound effect on my drawing. While I was making yet another drawing, my aunt Connie praised my artwork, asking if she could have it. The next day, when she returned home from work, she told me that she had sold my drawing to a national publication to be used for their cover. She didn't tell me what publication, but I was so thrilled with the news, that I didn't ask her anyway. It wasn't until years later that I realized that she had been teasing me—that incident, however, kept me drawing.

"Through high school and later in the Navy, I never stopped drawing—illustrating letters with drawings, making drawings of service men, and drawing satirical cartoons of some of the ridiculous situations that happened in the service. After the Navy, I attended Los Angeles City College, The Art Center School of Design, and went to Chouinard Institute at night. During this time, I did the gardening on Saturdays for a painter and art instructor, Harold Kramer, in exchange for drawing and painting lessons from him. What I primarily learned from his classes was how to correctly pronounce the names of the French impressionists.

"I left the Art Center after two years determined to see if I could 'make it' in New York. What I hadn't realized was that there was a mini-depression in advertising art and animation at the time. With a portfolio that was really dreadful, I looked for a job for three-and-a-half months and lived at the YMCA on 34th Street. I can remember answering an ad for a lettering artist to do match book covers. When I arrived, there was a line of artists that extended around the block. After waiting in the line for a half an hour, I asked myself what I was doing there. I couldn't even letter! So I left.

"I was finally hired when someone I knew called the owner of a studio, Graphics Institute, who hired me as an apprentice. I did paste-up and mechanicals for them, but the most interesting aspect of the job was doing the drawings, although there weren't many because their specialty was charts, maps and graphs. During the time that I worked for the Graphics Institute (1948), I came to realize that in New York advertising all humorous illustration had to be drawn in a certain manner. They called it 'decorative illustration.' The word 'cartoonist' was considered a dirty word in advertising. One was called a 'decorative illustrator' or a 'graphic designer,' but never (unless you worked for the *New Yorker* magazine) a cartoonist.

"The art director at the Graphics Institute was Bill Dove whose father was the American pioneer of abstract painting, Arthur Dove. Bill Dove, who was also a 'decorative illustrator' of some fame, and I frequently would have lunch together and would discuss painting, the work of his father, and Paris. Bill convinced me to finish my art school training in Paris using the two years that I had left on my GI Bill of Rights for tuition."

Jenkyns studied at the Académie Julian, where he became interested in filmic expression. "While I was in Paris, I met Andre Francois, the French cartoonist and painter. He was also a great influence on my art career. I met him through his cousin who was a student at the Sorbonne. Together we would visit Andre at his home in Grisy les Platre and would watch him work on children's books."

In Paris, Jenkyns met Pat Diska and illustrated her book, *Andy Says Bonjour!* "Children's books excite me—here was an opportunity to work with a story that had a beginning, middle, and an end. You could draw characters who were human, and the editors were not concerned with your style of drawing as long as you illustrated the story in an interesting and convincing manner. There was also the continuity of visually illustrating the story when you are working on a children's book that excited me. It made my transition into film, when I returned to Hollywood, very easy. All the elements were there plus the added element of movement."

Since 1954, Jenkyns has worked continuously in film production, working briefly for John Sutherland Productions, Ray Patin Productions, and Playhouse Pictures. He freelanced as a writer for Jay Ward Productions' series, "The Bullwinkle Show." Later, he formed his own companies, Jenkyns, Shean & Elliot, Inc. and then Jenkyns & Associates, Inc. and produced commercial films for television. "Doing a storyboard for a film gives you control of the film. You are actually directing the film since all the other artists work from your storyboard. I have been fortunate to have worked in many mediums and in various capacities—writer, director, designer, and producer."

Andy Says Bonjour!, which was illustrated over thirty years ago by Jenkyns, is still in print today. "Currently, I am involved in consultant work on films. It is also quite possible that Pat Diska and myself, after all these years, may collaborate on another 'Bonjour' book, using perhaps the granddaughter of Andy as a character and depicting how Paris has changed over the years."

Jenkyns' works are included in the Kerlan Collection at the University of Minnesota.

FOR MORE INFORMATION SEE: Bertha E. Miller, and others, compilers, *Illustrators of Children's Books: 1946-1956,* Horn Book, 1958; Donnarae MacCann and Olga Richard, *The Child's First Books,* H. W. Wilson, 1973; Martha E. Ward and Dorothy A. Marquardt, *Illustrators of Books for Young People,* 2nd edition, Scarecrow, 1975.

'Tis the good reader that makes the book.
—Ralph Waldo Emerson

JONES, Terry 1942-
(Monty Python)

BRIEF ENTRY: Born February 1, 1942, in Colwyn Bay, North Wales. After leaving Oxford University in 1964, Jones embarked on a comedy writing career which included scripts for television personality David Frost and for the series "Do Not Adjust Your Set," in which Jones also performed. In 1969 Jones and co-writer Michael Palin teamed up with comedy writers Eric Idle and Terry Gilliam to form a group collectively known as Monty Python. Together they produced "Monty Python's Flying Circus," an offbeat BBC show featuring a collection of skits written and performed by the troupe. From Monty Python came such classic satirical sketches as "Upper Class Twit of the Year," "The Ministry of Silly Walks," and "Hell's Grannies," as well as a number of feature-length movies, including "Monty Python and the Holy Grail" and "Monty Python's Life of Brian."

Jones published his first book for children, *Fairy Tales* (Schocken), in 1981. The collection of thirty original tales, illustrated by Michael Foreman, features the tongue-in-cheek wit associated with Monty Python and introduces such creatures as the rainbow cat, monster trees, and sea tigers. "Monty Python's Terry Jones—a medieval scholar as well as an accomplished lunatic—springs from the tradition of Andersen and the brothers Grimm like a slightly inebriated chameleon," observed the *New York Times Book Review*, "adding new color and his own whacky humor to the classic style and form of the fairy tale."

In 1984 both Jones and illustrator Foreman received a children's book award for *The Saga of Erik the Viking* (Schocken, 1983). "As in *Fairy Tales,* Mr. Jones and Mr. Foreman fashion from traditional materials a tale of high deeds and adventure that is startlingly fresh," declared the *New York Times Book Review*. Jones' other juvenile books include *Bert Fegg's Nasty Book for Boys and Girls* (Eyre Methuen, 1974), co-written with Palin, which was later revised and published as *Dr. Fegg's Encyclopaedia of All World Knowledge* (Methuen, 1984); and *Nicobobinus* (Pavilion, 1985), a story about the adventures of two children in search of a dragon. Jones has also co-written, with Palin, *Ripping Yarns* (Eyre Methuen, 1978) and *More Ripping Yarns* (Eyre Methuen, 1980), collections of stories based on the television series, and has contributed to five Monty Python books. *Office:* c/o Python Pictures, Ltd., 6/7 Cambridge Gate, London N.W. 1, England.

FOR MORE INFORMATION SEE: Rolling Stone, November 13, 1980; *Contemporary Literary Criticism,* Volume 21, Gale, 1982; *Newsweek,* July 12, 1982; *People,* August 2, 1982, February 6, 1984; *Washington Post,* April 4, 1983; *New Republic,* April 18, 1983; *Contemporary Authors,* Volume 116, Gale, 1986.

KASSEM, Lou

BRIEF ENTRY: Born in the mountains of eastern Tennessee. Author of books for young adults. Kassem's first book, *Dance of Death* (Dell, 1984), is a suspense thriller about a girl who recovers from a broken leg at haunted Ferncrest Manor, the home of her aunt and uncle. "There's enough tension and romance to please most readers," noted *Voice of Youth Advocates.* Kassem followed that book with *Middle School Blues* (Houghton, 1986), a chronicle of the first year of middle school as seen through the eyes and experiences of protagonist Cindy. "All of this is lightweight, palatable, and encouraging to read-

ers approaching the middle school years," wrote *Bulletin of the Center for Children's Books.* Kassem's most recent book is *Listen for Rachel* (Margaret K. McElderry Books, 1986), described by *Publisher's Weekly* as "an absorbing, old-fashioned romance." After fourteen-year-old Rachel's parents die in a fire, she is sent to live with her mother's family in the Appalachian Mountains. She eventually begins to adjust to her new life, learns mountain medicine healing, and finds love with an injured soldier. "Kassem's sprawling narrative beautifully captures Rachel's move toward maturity while encompassing events such as the Civil War and its divisive effect on families," observed *Booklist. Residence:* Southwestern Virginia.

KASUYA, Masahiro 1937-

PERSONAL: Born July 18, 1937, in Hyogo, Japan; son of Kichisuke and Toshie (Arai) Kasuya; married Yoko Watari (a poet), January 28, 1966; children: Kimiko, Nami (daughters). *Education:* Attended public schools in Japan. *Politics:* "Let it be." *Religion:* Roman Catholic. *Home:* 577 Hayama-cho Ishiki Miura-gun, Kanagawa Prefecture, Japan 240-01.

CAREER: Illustrator, artist, and author of books for children. Has worked for a printing company, a papermaker, an advertising agency, and as a producer of plays, movies and television programs for children. *Awards, honors:* Winner of West Japan Cross-Country Motorcycle Event.

WRITINGS—For children; all self-illustrated; all originally published in Japanese by Shiko-Sha: *Little Mole and His World,* 1970; *White Blossom,* 1972; *Kurisumasu,* 1972, translation by Chieko Funakoshi published as *The Way Christmas Came,* edited by Mildred Schell, Judson, 1973 (translation by Peggy Blakeley published in England as *Long Ago in Bethlehem,* A. & C. Blake, 1973); *A Tower Too Tall,* 1975, retold by M. Schell, Judson, 1979 (translation by Shona McKellar published in England as *The Tower of Babel,* Evans Brothers, 1978); *The Beginning of the Rainbow,* 1976, translation by S. McKellar published by Evans Brothers, 1977; *The Tiniest Christmas Star,* 1977, adapted for English by M. Schell, Jud-

MASAHIRO KASUYA

One star seemed to shine more brightly than the others. It sang the beautiful song of the Good News to a gentle donkey. ■ (From *The Tiniest Christmas Star* by Masahiro Kasuya. Illustrated by the author.)

son, 1979; *Swim and Swim Like a Fish,* 1978; *Creation,* 1979; *The Smallest Christmas Tree,* 1979, Judson, 1981; *David Sings,* 1980; *Martin the Cobbler,* 1980.

Also author of *The Beginning of the World* (self-illustrated), Abingdon, 1982; *The Shoemaker's Dream* (self-illustrated), Judson, 1982.

SIDELIGHTS: "Works that 'show' the artist's feelings are the best. When my illustrations are printed and take the form of a book, it is an exhibition in itself. The customary exhibition, with framed pictures expressing only one theme and no continuing story, does not appeal to me. I am most happy when my own song is expressed through my works. For me, illustration should be as such. I hope to someday realize the 'communion of the inner and the outer.'"

HOBBIES AND OTHER INTERESTS: Motorcycling.

KOPPER, Lisa (Esther) 1950-

BRIEF ENTRY: Born August 8, 1950, in Chicago, Ill. Illustrator. Kopper moved to England in 1970, but remembers her childhood in Chicago during the years of the civil rights movement. Due to her parents' involvement, she was made aware of social issues, poverty, and discrimination at an early age.

In 1978 her first published illustrations appeared in "Children of Soweto," a pamphlet of the anti-apartheid movement in England. She recalls the arduous process of unlearning the stereotypes of black people while drawing the characters as individuals. Since then, Kopper has become an advocate in assisting the Third World in creating their own cache of illustrations. She has illustrated more than thirty children's books, many portraying minorities. Among her most celebrated books are "The Jafta Family" series (Evans Bros., 1981), written by former South African Hugh Lewin. In these books about Lewin's childhood, Kopper achieves "a remarkable visual impact by the copper-tinted images of the boy," according to *Language Arts.* The titles in the series include *Jafta, My Mother, My Father, The Wedding,* and *The Town;* Carolrhoda published the series in America under a slight variance of titles, such as *Jafta's Mother* (1983) and *Jafta and the Wedding* (1983).

Among Kopper's other works are illustrations for Leila Berg's "Small World" series, published by Methuen in 1983, including *Bees, Dogs,* and *Worms;* Mollie Clarke's *The Chief's Sons* and *The Wonderful Wigwam* (both Collins Educational, 1984), about American Indians; Kate Petty's "What's That" series (F. Watts, 1986), and Tony Bradman's "Baby Shape Books" (Methuen, 1987). Kopper won the Wilfred Radio Memorial Award in 1970 for best studio work, the Premio per la Poesia in 1980, and the Best of British Illustrations in 1982. She is also a contributor to *Women and Creativity,* published by Women's Press. *Home:* 1 Peary Place, London, England.

LANDON, Lucinda 1950-

BRIEF ENTRY: Born August 15, 1950, in Galesburg, Ill. Illustrator and author of mystery books for children. After attending art schools in England and the United States, Landon worked at the Boston Center for the Arts and later as a special education teacher in Cambridge, Mass. Since 1978 she has been an artist at Visualizations in Providence, R.I. In 1986 her first book in the "Meg Mackintosh" mystery series was published, *Meg Mackintosh and the Case of the Missing Babe Ruth Baseball* (Atlantic Monthly Press), in which the reader must solve the mystery based on clues in the illustrations as well as in the text. "The clues are simple enough that youngest Sherlocks will be able to keep up with Meg,"noted *School Library Journal*. Its sequel is titled *Meg Mackintosh and the Case of the Curious Whale Watch*. Landon is currently working on more titles for the series. She is also the illustrator of *The Young Detective's Handbook* (Atlantic Monthly Press, 1981), by William V. Butler. *Home:* Tucker Hollow RFD 2, Box 798, North Scituate, R.I. 02857.

LEDER, Jane Mersky 1945-

BRIEF ENTRY: Born July 25, 1945, in Detroit, Mich. After receiving degrees from the University of Michigan and Roosevelt University, Leder taught English in junior and senior high schools until 1972. In 1977 she became a writer and producer for the Singer Society for Visual Education and then a producer at WLS-TV in Chicago. Since 1981 Leder has been a free-lance writer and independent documentary filmmaker. Her independent films include "Mama Florence and Papa Cock," and "Orwell's 1984: The Prophecy and the Reality" for which she received the Gold Award from the International Film and Television Festival in 1983.

Leder's books for children, all published by Crestwood, include *Cassettes and Records* (1983), *Champ Cars* (1983), and *Video Games* (1983). *Stunt Dogs* (1985) is one of a series of books describing dogs that work and the different jobs they hold. "No other books list in such detail (and yet so concisely) the types of 'careers' that dogs can have," wrote *School Library Journal*. Leder has also contributed to Crestwood's "Sports Close-Ups" series, with *Martina Navratilova; Marcus Allen; Moses Malone; Wayne Gretzky* (all published in 1985); and *Walter Payton* (1986). *Booklist* hailed the series as ". . . narratives with exciting play-by-play actions that will capture readers' interest." Leder is presently working on a book about teenage suicides, "an emotional and creative challenge" impelled by the suicide of her brother. *Home and office:* 3531 North Bosworth, Chicago, Ill. 60657.

FOR MORE INFORMATION SEE: Contemporary Authors, Volume 117, Gale, 1986.

LERNER, Marguerite Rush 1924-1987

OBITUARY NOTICE—See sketch in *SATA* Volume 11: Born May 17, 1924, in Minneapolis, Minn.; died after a long illness, March 3, 1987, in Woodbridge, Conn. Physician, educator, and author. Lerner, a dermatologist, taught clinical dermatology for more than thirty years at the Yale University School of Medicine and directed the dermatology clinic at the University Health Service for several years. Lerner also wrote fifteen books for children, including a series on childhood illnesses: *Dear Little Mumps Child, Michael Gets the Measles*, and *Peter Gets the Chickenpox*. She was the recipient of the Brotherhood Award in 1965 for *Red Man, White Man, African Chief*, a book about differences in skin color.

FOR MORE INFORMATION SEE: Authors of Books for Young People, Scarecrow, 1971; *Contemporary Authors,* Volume 13R, Gale, 1975; *American Men and Women of Science: The Physical and Biological Sciences,* 15th edition, 1982. Obituaries: *Minneapolis Star and Tribune,* March 14, 1987.

LEROE, Ellen W(hitney) 1949-

BRIEF ENTRY: Born April 26, 1949, in Newark, N.J. After receiving her bachelor's degree from Elmira College in 1971, Leroe worked at a series of jobs before settling down to full-time, free-lance writing in 1979. Of her novels for young adults, Leroe says: "Because I put so much of myself and my own experiences into my novels I tend to focus on main characters confronting, and eventually successfully altering, their insecure and vulnerable self-images." Popular themes in her books are romance and popularity. In *Have a Heart, Cupid Delaney* (Lodestar, 1986), a real cupid in the guise of a teenage girl is sent from the Love Bureau to match up two unlikely couples in time for the high school prom. Unfortunately, Cupid herself falls in love with one of the candidates. "A delightful, offbeat romance/fantasy for younger teens. . . . Funny scenes, witty dialogue and wonderful absurdity of plot add up to an unusual and lighthearted teen romance," wrote a reviewer for *School Library Journal*.

Robot Romance (Harper & Row, 1985) describes the antics of human and robot students at Silicon Valley High School. "The combination of farcical situations, offbeat humor, outrageous puns, and kaleidoscopic shifts in perspective is engaging, original, and fast-moving and offers a pleasant escape from the ordinary," observed *Horn Book*. Leroe is also the author of *Confessions of a Teenage TV Addict* (Lodestar, 1982); *Enter Laughing* (Silhouette, 1983); *Give and Take* (Silhouette, 1984); *The Plot against the Pom-Pom Queen* (Lodestar, 1985); and *Single Bed Blues* (Tandem, 1982), a book of poetry. *Home and office:* 2200 Leavenworth St., No. 504, San Francisco, Calif. 94133.

FOR MORE INFORMATION SEE: Contemporary Authors, Volume 116, Gale, 1986.

LITTKE, Lael J. 1929-

PERSONAL: Born December 2, 1929, in Mink Creek, Idaho; daughter of Frank George and Ada Geneva (Petersen) Jensen; married George C. Littke (a college professor), June 29, 1954; children: Lori S. *Education:* Utah State University, B.S., 1952; graduate study at City College (now of the City University of New York), 1955-59, and University of California, Los Angeles, 1968. *Politics:* Democrat. *Religion:* Church of Jesus Christ of Latter-Day Saints (Mormons). *Home:* 1345 Daveric Dr., Pasadena, Calif. 91107. *Agent:* Larry Sternig, 742 Robertson, Milwaukee, Wis. 53213. *Office:* Department of Community Services, Pasadena City College, Pasadena, Calif. 91106.

CAREER: Gates Rubber Co., Denver, Colo., secretary, 1952-54; Life Insurance Association of America, New York City, secretary, 1954-60; employed as a medical secretary by a physician in New York City, 1960-63; writer, 1963—; Pasadena City College, Community Services Department, Pasadena,

LAEL J. LITTKE

Calif., teacher of writing classes, 1979—. *Member:* PEN International, Mystery Writers of America, Society of Children's Book Writers, California Writer's Guild, Southern California Council on Literature for Children and Young People. *Awards, honors:* Special Achievement Award from PEN International, 1986, and one of International Reading Association's Children's Choices, 1987, both for *Shanny on Her Own.*

WRITINGS: Wilmer the Watchdog, Western, 1970; *Tell Me When I Can Go,* Scholastic Book Services, 1978; *Cave In!,* Childrens Press, 1981; *Trish for President* (young adult novel), Harcourt, 1984; *Shanny on Her Own* (young adult novel; Junior Literary Guild selection), Harcourt, 1985; *Loydene in Love* (young adult novel), Harcourt, 1986; *Where the Creeks Meet* (young adult novel), Deseret, 1987.

Stories represented in numerous anthologies, including *Best Short Stories of 1973,* edited by Martha Foley, Houghton, 1973. Contributor of short stories to *Ellery Queen's Mystery Magazine, Seventeen, Ladies' Home Journal, Boys' Life, McCall's, Young Miss,* and *Co-ed.*

WORK IN PROGRESS: The Boycott at Cedarville High.

SIDELIGHTS: "I was born and grew up in Mink Creek, Idaho, a tiny farming community in the mountains of southeastern Idaho. People in other parts of the county used to say that the way to get to Mink Creek was to go as far back in the hills as you can—then go a little farther. We didn't even have a paved highway when I was growing up, and a trip to Preston, the county seat twenty miles away (population 4,000), was like a journey to another planet. What I liked most of all there was the Carnegie Public Library.

"I loved books from the time my mother bought a copy of *Three Little Pigs* for me when I was about four. I read all the books that my mother owned plus all of those in our little country school. My idea of heaven was when big crates of books would arrive from the State Circulating Library in Boise. I read every one of them and still have vivid memories of one about elephants going to a special place to die, and another one about Eskimos. I think the one I loved most of all was *The Box Car Children.*

"Growing up on a ranch as I did, I always had horses and other animals around. It was my job each morning to get my horse and take our cows to a distant pasture. Then each evening I rode over to bring them home for milking. This was my favorite time to dream and I thought of the time when I would become a writer and write about the valley which spread before me and the people who lived there. Many of my short stories have been set there in Mink Creek, and it is also the setting for my four young adult novels—*Trish for President, Shanny on Her Own, Loydene in Love,* and *Where the Creeks Meet.*

"For more than twenty years I sold short stories for all ages, then found myself concentrating on stories for teenagers. I decided to try a novel for that age, so I wrote *Trish for President,* about a girl living in Mink Creek (which I renamed Wolf Creek).

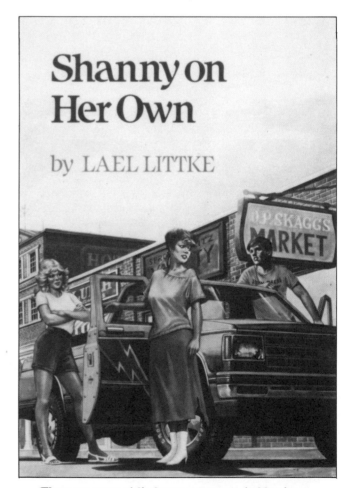

Thor was every girl's dream come true, in blue jeans, cowboy boots, and a yellow T-shirt that advertised John Deere Farm Machinery. ■(Jacket illustration by Darrel Millsap from *Shanny on Her Own* by Lael Littke.)

"Then I decided to write one about a girl from somewhere else who comes to live in Wolf Creek, because I wanted to look at the town and its people through the eyes of someone who hadn't grown up there. That's when Shanny came into being. It's a totally different world for Shanny, especially since her companions are an elderly aunt, a nine-year-old boy, and a sagging, cranky old rodeo horse. And of course there is a young man for her to fall in love with. She learns a lot from each of them, and the summer changes her life.

"Next I wrote *Loydene in Love,* which takes a character who was introduced in *Shanny on Her Own* and sends her from her home in Wolf Creek to visit Shanny in Los Angeles, where she meets a guy who sort of takes her mind off the young man she'd planned to marry back in Wolf Creek. For *Where the Creeks Meet,* I renamed the town Blue Creek since it was for a different publisher, and I told about a girl from California who reluctantly moves with her family to this little Idaho town where she meets a young man who tells her he is a ghost.

"After teaching writing classes for several years, I have decided that the difference between a successful author and one who gets only rejections is often a matter of discipline: the discipline to stick with a project to completion, to revise it endlessly if necessary, and to send it out again and again if it keeps coming back. It takes a hard disciplinarian to sit down to a cold typewriter each morning and go at it again, but that's what it takes. I had a friend who kept her ironing board set up next to her typewriter, and each morning she told herself that if she didn't write, she would have to iron, a task she hated more than scrubbing bathrooms. Even so, she often spent the day ironing. That's how hard it is to become a successful writer. But most of us agree that it's worth every effort we've made."

HOBBIES AND OTHER INTERESTS: Travel (has seen most of the United States, eastern Canada, and parts of Mexico and Europe).

FOR MORE INFORMATION SEE: Pasadena Star-News, September 2, 1976; *Preston Citizen* (Preston, Idaho), March 23, 1978.

LORING, Emilie (Baker) 1864(?)-1951 (Josephine Story)

PERSONAL: Born about 1864, in Boston, Mass.; died March 14, 1951, in Wellesley, Mass.; daughter of George M. (a playwright and publisher) and Emily Frances (Boles) Baker; married Victor J. Loring (a lawyer); children: Robert Melville, Selden Melville. *Education:* Attended private schools.

CAREER: Novelist; began as a writer for magazines.

*WRITINGS—*Novels; all originally published by Penn and republished by Grosset in 1961: *The Trail of Conflict,* 1922; *Here Comes the Sun!* (illustrated by Paul Gill), 1924; *A Certain Crossroad* (illustrated by R. Pallen Coleman), 1925; *The Solitary Horseman,* 1927; *Gay Courage,* 1928; *Swift Water,* 1929; *Lighted Windows,* 1930; *Fair Tomorrow,* 1931; *Uncharted Seas,* 1932; *Hilltops Clear,* 1933; *With Banners,* 1934; *We Ride the Gale!,* 1934; *It's a Great World!,* 1935; *Give Me One Summer,* 1936; *As Long as I Live,* 1937.

Novels; all originally published by Little, Brown and republished by Grosset in 1961: *High of Heart,* 1938; *Today Is Yours,* 1938; *Across the Years,* 1939; *There Is Always Love,*

EMILIE LORING

1940; *Where Beauty Dwells,* 1941; *Stars in Your Eyes,* 1941; *Rainbow at Dusk,* 1942; *When Hearts Are Light Again,* 1943; *Keepers of the Faith,* 1944; *Beyond the Sound of Guns,* 1945; *Bright Skies,* 1946; *Beckoning Trails,* 1947; *I Hear Adventure Calling,* 1948; *Love Came Laughing By,* 1949; *To Love and to Honor,* 1950; *For All Your Life,* 1952; *I Take This Man,* 1954; *My Dearest Love,* 1954; *The Shadow of Suspicion,* 1955; *What Then Is Love,* 1956; *Look to the Stars,* 1957; *Behind the Cloud,* 1958; *With This Ring,* 1959.

Novels; all published by Little, Brown: *How Can the Heart Forget?,* 1960; *Throw Wide the Door,* 1961; *Follow Your Heart,* 1963; *A Candle in Her Heart,* 1964; *Forever and a Day,* 1965; *Spring Always Comes,* 1966; *A Key to Many Doors,* 1967; *In Times Like These,* 1968; *Love with Honor,* 1969; *No Time for Love,* 1970; *Forsaking All Others,* 1971; *The Shining Years,* 1972.

Other: (Under pseudonym Josephine Story) *For the Comfort of the Family: A Vacation Experiment* (essays on homemaking), G. H. Doran, 1914; (under pseudonym Josephine Story) *The Mother in the Home* (essays on homemaking), Pilgrim, 1917; *Where's Peter?* (three-act play), Penn, 1928. Contributor of short stories, serials, and articles to periodicals.

SIDELIGHTS: Loring was born in Boston, Massachusetts into a family of writers, publishers and playwrights. Her grandfather Alfred Baker was one of the founders of *The American Eagle,* the forerunner of the *Boston Herald,* and her father, George M. Baker, a noted playwright of his day, was associated with the Boston publishing company of Lee and She-

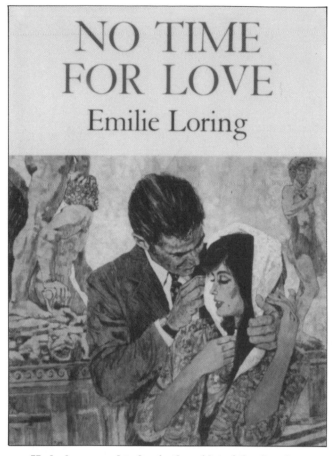

He had proposed to her in the midst of the thunderstorm.... ■ (Jacket illustration by Ted CoConis from *No Time for Love* by Emilie Loring.)

phard. "We always had books and books. My father might have refused us a toy we asked for but he would never have thought of denying us a book we wanted." [Dorothea Laurance Mann, *Emilie Loring: A Twentieth-Century Romanticist,* Penn, 1928.[1]]

Reading was only one of the many activities that the family shared. Since her father was both a publisher and a playwright, Loring grew up spending hours in publishers' offices and acting in some of her father's plays that were staged at home. It was not just the parlor that was taken over for production, but the upstairs sitting room was also used for painting scenery. "I recall particularly a forest backdrop. A huge cloth was stretched across one wall, for we couldn't afford canvas. An honest-to-goodness artist had painted in the trunks of the trees but the foilage had been left to the family to finish. Whenever one of us had a minute he or she would dash into the room and scatter green paint in varying shades, till finally a forest stood there in all its glory. It was a huge success on the stage in spite of the fact that on close inspection it resembled nothing so much as an explosion of green-worms."[1]

"Our house was a theatrical workshop, it is small wonder that I developed a dramatic sense that will burst forth in my novels." [Harry R. Warfel, editor, "Emilie Loring," *American Novelists of Today,* American Book Company, 1951.[2]]

Loring waited many years, however, before taking up writing professionally. She married a Boston lawyer, Victor J. Loring, and assumed the responsibilities of raising their two sons. It was not until her sons went away to prep school that she began

to write stories, first under the pseudonym of "Josephine Story," coined from her husband's two middle names. Initially she wrote stories and articles for magazines, eventually turning to novels. When asked who her favorite writer was, she replied: "Dickens! . . . I never forget the way in which, if he introduces a character even for a few moments, Dickens gives you some bit of description which makes the character vivid to you."[1]

Some of Loring's popular romantic novels were translated into other languages and reproduced in Braille. During her thirty-year writing career her books sold over 3,360,000 copies in the United States alone. The author claimed that the secret to her success was "a wholesome love story." ["Emilie Baker Loring: Author of 30 Novels," *New York Times,* March 15, 1951.[3]]

Shortly after her death in 1951, Loring's two sons discovered a large amount of unfinished materials—short stories, unfinished novels, and outlines for books—that were developed into romantic novels. The books were published by Little, Brown, at the rate of one a year over a twelve-year period from 1960 to 1972.

FOR MORE INFORMATION SEE: Dorothea L. Mann, *Emilie Loring: A Twentieth-Century Romanticist,* Penn, 1928; Harry R. Warfel, *American Novelists of Today,* American Book, 1951. Obituaries: *New York Times,* March 15, 1951; *Publishers Weekly,* March 24, 1951; *Time,* March 26, 1951; *Wilson Library Bulletin,* May, 1951.

LUENN, Nancy   1954-

PERSONAL: Name legally changed; surname is pronounced *Loo*-in; born December 28, 1954, in Pasadena, Calif.; daughter of Gilbert Frederick (a professor) and Elizabeth (a professor; maiden name, Jensen) Jones. *Education:* Evergreen State College, B.A., 1978. *Religion:* Society of Friends (Quakers). *Home:* 8033 Sunnyside N., Seattle, Wash. 98103.

NANCY LUENN

Ishikawa watched while the old man painted a curling wave onto the strong kite paper. ■ (From
The Dragon Kite by Nancy Luenn. Illustrated by Michael Hague.)

CAREER: The Little School, Bellevue, Wash., teaching aide, 1978-79; White Water Sports, Seattle, Wash., bookkeeper and assistant manager, 1979-82; The Mountaineers, Seattle, administrative assistant, 1982—. Member of recreation and fire prevention staff of U.S. Forest Service at Rogue River National Forest, summers, 1977-78; volunteer coordinator of the Nature Conservancy's Speakers Bureau, 1984-85. *Member:* Society of Children's Book Writers, Pacific Northwest Writers Conference. *Awards, honors:* Pacific Northwest Writers Conference, first prize for juvenile short story, 1980, for "The Dragon Kite," first prize for juvenile novel, and grand prize, both 1982, both for the manuscript of *Arctic Unicorn; The Ugly Princess* was chosen one of International Reading Association's Children's Choices, 1982; *The Dragon Kite* was included in the American Institute of Graphic Arts Book Show, 1983.

WRITINGS—Juvenile: *The Ugly Princess* (illustrated by David Wiesner), Little, Brown, 1981; *The Dragon Kite* (illustrated by Michael Hague), Harcourt, 1982; *Arctic Unicorn*, Atheneum, 1986; *Unicorn Crossing*, Atheneum, 1987.

WORK IN PROGRESS: Goldclimber, a young adult novel about a goldsmith's apprentice; "British Fantasy Settings," a slide

show documenting the settings of children's fantasy books by such authors as A. A. Milne, Kenneth Grahame, and Alan Garner.

SIDELIGHTS: Luenn is the oldest of six children and grew up in Los Angeles, California. "Our house was full of cats, puzzles and books. We made frequent trips to the local library and often checked out sixty books at a time. I remember walking down the library steps with a huge stack of books tucked under my chin. We made a game of carrying as many as we could. Dropping them was unthinkable. Instead of watching TV (we didn't have one), my mother read aloud to us every evening.

"My first memory is of a new litter of kittens. When I was quite young, we had a pet king snake which I used to carry coiled around my arm. At various times, we also kept chinchillas, white rats, guinea pigs, and ducks. There were always lots of cats. They sometimes had their kittens in the linen closet, and once or twice we watched the kittens being born.

"I had other types of animals as well. My mother tells me I kept invisible coots under my highchair. I had a huge collection of stuffed animals, and we played elaborate games in the

"Tell me, Lord Owen," she said shyly, "how can you be a dragon, but wear the shape of a man?"
■ (From *The Ugly Princess* by Nancy Luenn. Illustrated by David Wiesner.)

backyard with plastic horses, dogs, wildlife, and farm animals. The Museum of Natural History had a lending library of animals for teachers to borrow, and my parents once brought home a stuffed wombat.

"We also visited the zoo and museums on a regular basis. My father, a marine biologist, took us exploring in the tidepools of southern California. He introduced me to fascinating creatures with names like mollusk and nudibranch. During the summer we went camping in the deserts and mountains.

"We had a big, untidy backyard where children could play and dig holes without parental censure. My brothers and several friends and I once dug an underground fort five feet deep. When we outgrew the backyard, we began exploring the college across the street. Above the college was 'The Hill.'

"'The Hill' was a wonderful place. From the top of it you could see the whole city, and on clear days you could see the ocean. Most of the year it was covered with dry grass. Clumps of eucalyptus trees and poison oak grew on the slopes. We pretended that hobbits lived under the hill, and played in a little valley which sometimes had a stream. Partway down the hill was a Greek theatre where we went to watch play rehearsals, and later in the summer, the plays themselves."

Somewhere in the process of growing up, Luenn fell in love with fantasy. "My mother read me *The Hobbit* when I was five. Later she read me *The Lord of the Rings,* and she read them again to each of my brothers and my sister. We used to discuss Middle Earth at the dinner table. She also read us C. S. Lewis, E. B. White, Marjory Sharp, A. A. Milne, Kenneth Grahame, and so on. I went through stages of reading horse books, historical fiction, etc., but fantasy remained my favorite form of literature. In 1977, while working for the U.S. Forest Service in southern Oregon, I discovered that I had read all of the fantasy in the Medford library. I decided I would write some."

Luenn remembers growing up in the 60s with pleasure. "In 1965, I saw the Beatles in concert in Dodger Stadium. My father took us to see Pete Seeger and Joan Baez at the Hollywood Bowl. As a teenager, I discovered Donovan, who strengthened my fascination with images and fantasy. When I was fifteen, I began working on a large embroidered tapestry of a unicorn in the woods. I attended Quaker meetings and silent vigils protesting the Vietnam War. In high school I left public school for several alternative schools where I had time to explore creative paths and learn about group process. When I was sixteen, my aunt and uncle invited me to stay with them in England, which for someone in love with fantasy, the Beatles, Donovan, English history, and castles, was a dream come true."

Luenn attended college at Evergreen State in Olympia, Washington. While she was at Evergreen, she lived in a tipi for a year, traveled in Israel, and went whitewater kayaking. She and a group of students designed a program in outdoor education, which was taught by Barry Williams and Willi Unsoeld. She also studied art, and spent a lot of time trying to decide whether to become an artist or a teacher. In her last year at Evergreen, she started writing children's books.

"Writing is hard work. When I began writing, I discovered how difficult it was to shape an idea into a story. People often ask me how I learned to write. Mostly it was trial and error, and lots of practice. It was also very helpful to get feedback from people who knew about books. I expect that the journal I had kept throughout high school and college helped, as did

my own familiarity with books. I wrote stories, sent them out, and received rejection letters for three years before Little, Brown and Company accepted *The Ugly Princess.*

"I write because I enjoy creating worlds. One begins with an idea of a plot or a character. For example, *The Dragon Kite* began as a single sentence from the *Encyclopedia Britannica:* 'A Japanese bandit was said to have suspended himself from a large kite in an effort to steal some golden ornamental fish from a castle tower.' From that idea, with a great deal of research, coaxing, writing and rewriting, something comes into existence which didn't exist before. If I as the writer do the job well enough, the imaginary world which is created will seem just as real as our daily one. I don't expect to meet unicorns, or hobbits, or Winnie-the-Pooh in my neighborhood, but on some level, I believe they are real.

"The ideas for my stories come from three basic sources, an interest in animals (especially peculiar ones); an unlimited fascination with the stuff of fantasy and legends; and a love for the natural environment. I have also been intrigued by unusual foreign places, but the amount of research involved in *Arctic Unicorn,* and a recent trip to Great Britain have convinced me to explore the possibilities closer to home.

"In May of 1984, my mother and I traveled to Great Britain and visited the settings of our favorite British fantasies. I realized to my astonishment that Tolkien, Cooper, Grahame, Milne and Garner were writing about the places where they lived or went on holiday. It should have been obvious, but to me England was such a magical faraway place that I never thought of it as being everyday and ordinary. That experience inspired me to seek out the potential for fantasy in Washington State. Washington is not as thoroughly soaked in legend as Great Britain, but it has plenty of natural environment to work with, and in the tensions between nature and humans I believe there is potential for fantasy."

Luenn lives in Seattle, Washington with several friends, two cats, and a large garden. She is active in the environmental movement and is especially concerned about the worldwide effects of deforestation, and the destruction of the rain forests. She works for the Conservation Division of the Mountaineers, and has volunteered for the Nature Conservancy and Friends of the Earth. She has also volunteered for Physicians for Social Responsibility, an organization concerned about the threat of nuclear war. On weekdays, she writes everyday from eight a.m. until noon, and is currently working on another book.

HOBBIES AND OTHER INTERESTS: Travel (including Great Britain and Israel), skiing, reading, exploring the rivers and mountains of Washington, gardening.

FOR MORE INFORMATION SEE: New York Times Book Review, January 24, 1982, March 28, 1982.

MALI, Jane Lawrence 1937-

PERSONAL: Born June 2, 1937, in New York, N.Y.; daughter of James Freeman (an investment counselor) and Barbara (a homemaker and volunteer; maiden name, Childs) Lawrence; married Henry Allen Mali (in textiles), December 31, 1960; children: Adair and Kate (twins), Taylor, Peter. *Education:* Columbia University, B.S., 1961. *Home and office:* 147 West 15th St., New York, N.Y. 10011.

CAREER: Homemaker, 1960—; writer, 1974—. *Awards, honors:* American Book Award for children's nonfiction from

JANE LAWRENCE MALI

Association of American Publishers, 1981, for *Oh, Boy! Babies!*; *Oh, Boy! Babies!* was selected a Notable Book in the Field of Social Studies by the joint committee of the National Council for Social Studies and the Children's Book Council, 1981, and *A Season of Secrets,* 1983; *Thaddeus* was chosen one of *Booklist*'s Children's Editor's Choice, 1985.

WRITINGS—Juvenile; with Alison Cragin Herzig; published by Little, Brown: *A Word to the Wise* (illustrated by Martha Perske), 1978; *Oh, Boy! Babies!* (Junior Literary Guild selection; illustrated with photographs by Katrina Thomas), 1980; *A Season of Secrets,* 1982; *Thaddeus* (Junior Literary Guild selection; illustrated by Stephen Gammell), 1984; *The Ten-Speed Babysitter,* Dutton, 1987.

WORK IN PROGRESS: A novel for the nine- to twelve-year-old reader that deals with the homeless.

SIDELIGHTS: "I would guess that one of the most interesting aspects of my writing is that I collaborate with Alison Herzig. We met through our children at nursery school, and when one of the school's most beloved young teachers was killed in a car accident, Alison came to me with the suggestion that we try to make some kind of sense out of that tragedy. The resulting manuscript still lies in the bottom of a drawer, but after composing it we were hooked on writing.

"The idea for *A Word to the Wise* came when we were searching through a thesaurus and found that many of the entries made us weak with laughter. Our nonfiction book, *Oh, Boy! Babies!,* arose out of an afternoon elective course I proposed, in which fifth and sixth grade boys learned how to take care of infants. The course took off like a rocket, attracting media attention and convincing us that we had a good book idea. In *A Season of Secrets,* the parallel themes of epilepsy and bats and the irrational fear they engender were subjects we knew of first hand. *Thaddeus* is a wild, rollicking tale with two protagonists: an elderly man and his great-great nephew. The idea of different generations making a connection appeals to us.

"Many people ask us how and why we write together. The 'why' is easy: we enjoy it; we find that we strike sparks off each other; the arrangement provides a built-in discipline; we are rarely both in a slump at the same time; we find that collaboration combats the inherent loneliness of writing; and our different skills seem to balance. But the 'how' is almost impossible to explain. I can say that we sit side by side at Alison's apartment and opposite each other at my apartment and that we forge each sentence together, word by word. I can say that everything we write is read out loud and that it must sound right to our ears before we go on to the next part. I can say that occasionally we separate to write a section alone; but none of these details really explain how the collaboration works. I do know that Alison is particularly strong on the overall shape and direction of a story and that I am strong on dialogue and small, telling details.

"I cannot say that I always wanted to be a writer, but I have always been a letter writer and I can see now that the desire to spin tales and to entertain has always been with me. I grew up in a large, extended family where reading aloud and dressing up for plays and making up stories were common practices. When I got married I wanted to be a full-time mother to my four children. I found that job fascinating, exhausting, constantly changing, and rich (even now I consider myself a writer only until my children come home, at which time I rather happily lapse back into being a homemaker). I kept a file on each of my children into which I put drawings, notes, valentines, school work, stories, and letters—in fact, everything flat

The handle on his locker door pressed into his back. ∎
(From *A Word to the Wise* by Alison Cragin Herzig and Jane Lawrence Mali. Illustrated by Martha Perske.)

enough to file. Now I use that material. It can give me the feeling of a certain-aged child, furnish background details, or else actually provide me with a way of expressing something. My children like to have their past used in my work and enjoy recognizing character traits based on them.

"I like to write for children. People who ask me when I'm going to move on (and by that they mean 'move up') to adults don't understand that good literature knows no age group and that children, in my opinion, are the more demanding readers. To be able to tap in to their sense of wonder is exhilarating."

HOBBIES AND OTHER INTERESTS: Gardening, skiing, tennis, being in the western part of the U.S., reading.

FOR MORE INFORMATION SEE: Los Angeles Times Book Review, December 7, 1980; *New York Times Book Review,* December 14, 1980; *Christian Science Monitor,* December 22, 1980; *New York Times,* May 5, 1981; *Washington Post Book World,* May 10, 1981; *Changing Times,* June, 1982.

MANNETTI, Lisa   1953-

BRIEF ENTRY: Born January 9, 1953, in White Plains, N.Y. Author of nonfiction books for children. After receiving her B.A. from Fairfield University in 1971, Mannetti worked as an editorial assistant for two years at magazines in New York. She then worked as a substitute teacher while pursuing her master's degree, which she received from Fordham University in 1981. Her first book for children, *Equality* (F. Watts, 1985), is one in a series about the American value system. It provides an outline of the struggle for equality in America, from the colonization of this country through the present. In a review of her next book, *Iran and Iraq: Nations at War* (F. Watts, 1986), aimed at young adult readers, *School Library Journal* noted that "Mannetti details the many, varied, and controversial causes of the Irani-Iraqi War . . . [and] distills this complex subject into clear, readable prose." Mannetti, who is enrolled in the Ph.D. program at Fordham, is currently writing fiction. *Residence:* Wappingers Falls, N.Y. 12590.

MARSHALL, James (Edward)   1942-
(Edward Marshall)

PERSONAL: Born October 10, 1942, in San Antonio, Tex.; son of George E. (an insurance salesman) and Cecille (Harrison) Marshall. *Education:* Attended New England Conservatory of Music (Boston), 1960-61, and Trinity College, 1967-68; Southern Connecticut State College, B.A., 1967. "No art school (self-taught)." *Home:* 93 Mansfield Hollow Rd., Mansfield Center, Conn. 06250. *Agent:* Sheldon Fogelman, 10 East 40th St., New York, N.Y. 10016.

CAREER: Cathedral High School, Boston, Mass., French and Spanish teacher, 1968-70; free-lance writer and illustrator, 1970—.

AWARDS, HONORS: George and Martha was selected one of *New York Times* Outstanding Books of the Year, 1972, and *Miss Nelson Is Missing!* and *A Summer in the South,* both 1977; *George and Martha* was selected one of *New York Times* Ten Best Illustrated Books of the Year, 1972, *George and Martha Encore,* 1973, and *The Tutti-Frutti Case: Starring the Four Doctors of Goodge,* 1975; *George and Martha* was selected as a Children's Book Showcase title of the Children's Book Council, 1973, *All the Way Home,* 1974, *The Stupids*

Step Out, 1975, and *Bonzini! The Tattooed Man,* 1977; *All the Way Home* and *The Piggy in the Puddle* were included in American Institute of Graphic Arts Children's Book Show, 1973-74, and *I Will Not Go to Market Today,* 1980; Academy Award nomination for best animated film from the Academy of Motion Picture Arts and Sciences, 1978, for movie adaptation of *It's So Nice to Have a Wolf around the House;* Edgar Allan Poe Award runner-up from the Mystery Writers of America, 1978, Georgia Children's Picture Storybook Award from the University of Georgia College of Education, 1980, Young Reader Medal from the California Reading Association, and Buckeye Children's Book Award honor book from the State Library of Ohio, both 1982, all for *Miss Nelson Is Missing!;* Children's Choice Award from the International Reading Association, 1979, for *The Stupids Have a Ball* and *George and Martha One Fine Day,* and 1982, for *The Stupids Die* and *There's a Party at Mona's Tonight; The Stupids Step Out* was included on *School Library Journal*'s "Best of the Best 1966-1978" list, 1979.

The Stupids Die was chosen one of *School Library Journal*'s Best Books, 1981, and was runner-up for the Kentucky Bluegrass Award from Northern Kentucky University, 1983; Arizona Young Readers Award, 1981, for *Miss Nelson Is Missing!,* and 1985, for *The Stupids Die;* California Young Reader Medal, 1982, for *Miss Nelson Is Missing!;* Parents' Choice Award for literature from the Parents' Choice Foundation, 1983, for *Rapscallion Jones;* Colorado Children's Book Award from the University of Colorado, and Washington Children's Choice Picture Book Award from the Washington Library Media Association, both 1983, both for *Space Case;* Nebraska Golden Sower Award, 1984, and Colorado Children's Book Award, 1985, both for *Miss Nelson Is Back;* California Young Readers Medal, 1986, for *Space Case;* Kentucky Bluegrass Award, second-place winner, for *Miss Nelson Has a Field Day,* 1987.

WRITINGS—All self-illustrated juveniles; all published by Houghton, except as indicated: *George and Martha* (ALA Notable Book; *Horn Book* honor list), 1972; *What's the Matter with Carruthers?,* 1972; *Yummers!,* 1973; *George and Martha Encore,* 1973; *Miss Dog's Christmas Treat,* 1973; (with Harry Allard) *The Stupids Step Out,* 1974; *Willis,* 1974; *The Guest,* 1975; *Four Little Troubles,* 1975, Volume I: *Eugene,* Volume II: *Someone Is Talking about Hortense,* Volume III: *Sing Out Irene,* Volume IV: *Snake—His Story; Speedboat,* 1976; *George and Martha Rise and Shine,* 1976; *A Summer in the South,* 1977; *George and Martha One Fine Day,* 1978; (with H. Allard) *The Stupids Have a Ball,* 1978; (selector) *James Marshall's Mother Goose,* Farrar, Straus, 1979; *Portly McSwine,* 1979; *George and Martha Tons of Fun,* 1980; (with H. Allard) *The Stupids Die,* 1981; *Taking Care of Carruthers,* 1981; *Rapscallion Jones,* Viking, 1983; *George and Martha Back in Town,* 1984; *The Cut-Ups,* Viking, 1984; *Wings: A Tale of Two Chickens,* Viking, 1986; *Yummers Two: The Second Course,* 1986; *Three Up a Tree,* Dial, 1986; *Merry Christmas, Space Case,* Dial, 1986; *Red Riding Hood,* Dial, 1987; *The Cut-Ups Cut Loose,* Viking, 1987.

All under pseudonym Edward Marshall; all self-illustrated; all published by Dial: *Troll Country* (Junior Literary Guild selection), 1980; *Space Case* (Junior Literary Guild selection), 1980; *Three by the Sea,* 1981; *Fox and His Friends,* 1982; *Fox in Love,* Dial, 1982; *Fox on Wheels,* 1983; *Fox at School,* 1983; *Fox All Week,* 1984; *Four on the Shore,* 1985.

Illustrator: Byrd Baylor, *Plink, Plink, Plink,* Houghton, 1971; Lore Segal, *All the Way Home,* Farrar, Straus, 1973; Norma Klein, *Dinosaur's Housewarming Party* (Junior Literary Guild selection), Crown, 1974; Charlotte Pomerantz, *The Piggy in* the Puddle, Macmillan, 1974; Jakob Grimm and Wilhelm Grimm, *The Frog Prince,* retold by Edith H. Tarcov, Four Winds Press, 1974.

Harry Allard, *The Tutti-Frutti Case: Starring the Four Doctors of Goodge,* Prentice-Hall, 1975; Russell Hoban, *Dinner at Alberta's* (ALA Notable Book; Junior Literary Guild selection), Crowell, 1975; Cynthia Jameson, *A Day with Whisker Wickles,* Coward, 1975; Jeffrey Allen, *Mary Alice, Operator Number 9,* Little, Brown, 1975; J. Allen, *Bonzini! The Tattooed Man,* Little, Brown, 1976; Diane Wolkstein, reteller, *Lazy Stories,* Seabury, 1976; H. Allard, *It's So Nice to Have a Wolf around the House* (Junior Literary Guild selection), Doubleday, 1977; H. Allard, *Miss Nelson Is Missing!,* Houghton, 1977; Frank Asch, *MacGoose's Grocery,* Dial, 1978; Jan Wahl, *Carrot Nose,* Farrar, Straus, 1978; H. Allard, *I Will Not Go to Market Today* (Junior Literary Guild selection), Dial, 1979; H. Allard, *Bumps in the Night,* Doubleday, 1979.

Jane Yolen, *How Beastly! A Menagerie of Nonsense Poems,* Philomel, 1980; John McFarland, reteller, *The Exploding Frog: And Other Fables from Aesop,* Little, Brown, 1981; H. Allard, *There's a Party at Mona's Tonight* (Junior Literary Guild selection), Doubleday, 1981; H. Allard, *Miss Nelson Is Back,* Houghton, 1982; Daniel Pinkwater, *Roger's Umbrella,* Dutton, 1982.

H. Allard, *Miss Nelson Has a Field Day,* Houghton, 1985; Clement C. Moore, *The Night before Christmas,* Scholastic, 1985; J. Allen, *Nosey Mrs. Rat* (*Horn Book* honor list), Viking, 1985; J. Allen, *Mary Alice Returns,* Little, Brown, 1986;

(contributor) *Once Upon a Time . . . : Celebrating the Magic of Children's Books in Honor of the Twentieth Anniversary of Reading Is Fundamental,* Putnam, 1986.

ADAPTATIONS: "It's So Nice to Have a Wolf around the House" (full-length television cartoon feature), Learning Corporation of America, 1978; "Miss Nelson Is Missing" (motion picture), Learning Corporation of America, 1979 (filmstrip), Weston Woods, 1984; "Miss Nelson Is Back" (TV segment; introduced by LaVar Burton and narrated by Ruth Buzzi), Reading Rainbow, PBS-TV, 1983; "Three by Sea," Reading Rainbow, PBS-TV, 1983 (follow the reader series; cassette with paperback book and teacher's guide), Listening Library, 1985; "The Night before Christmas" (filmstrip with cassette), Listening Library, 1986.

All produced by Random House: "George and Martha" (filmstrip with cassette); "George and Martha Encore" (filmstrip with cassette); "George and Martha Rise and Shine" (filmstrip with cassette); "George and Martha One Fine Day" (filmstrip with cassette); "The Stupids Step Out" (read-along cassette; filmstrip with cassette); "The Stupids Have a Ball" (read-along cassette; filmstrip with cassette); "The Stupids Die" (read-along cassette; filmstrip with cassette); "I Will Not Go to Market Today," (filmstrip with cassette), 1984; "James Marshall's Mother Goose" (cassette); "Fox and His Friends" (cassette), 1986; "Fox at School" (cassette), 1986; "Fox in Love" (cassette), 1986; "Fox on Wheels" (cassette), 1986.

WORK IN PROGRESS: George and Martha All Year Round; Goldilocks.

JAMES MARSHALL

National Snout Day was only a day away, and Portly was giving a huge party. ■ (From *Portly McSwine* by James Marshall. Illustrated by the author.)

SIDELIGHTS: ''In retrospect I can say that my character, Viola Swamp, is partly based on my second grade teacher—a horrible woman who laughed at my early creative efforts. 'You'll *never* be an artist,' she pronounced. The result being that at seven years old, I quit drawing. Viola also bears a slight resemblance to a librarian in San Antonio, as well as to a friend of my mother's, who was not very amused by the likeness—in fact, she may never forgive me.

''It wasn't until my late twenties that I passionately took up drawing again. I am self-taught, much to the chagrin of my former students at Parsons, who had a hard time imagining anyone becoming an artist without 'real training,' by which they meant art school. Not realizing I was talking myself out of a job, I quickly pointed out to them that even if every art school in America were to close down tomorrow, people would still continue to make art.''

Marshall grew up in Texas, where his family has lived since the turn of the century. ''I love Texas, and have great feeling for the arid landscape of the Southwest. My family is from west Texas, a little town called Marathon. They moved there in the 1880's when life was very very hard. The land was infertile, the earth full of limestone. I have photographs that look like something out of a Georgia O'Keefe painting. Legend has it that Pancho Villa raided my grandmother's ranch. She has photographs of the raid, taken from a high mesa, which show Pancho crossing the Mexican border when the river was low, galloping into her ranch in a cloud of dust and stealing her cattle. I recently tried to find out more about what her life was like back then. 'What did you do all day, grandmother?' I asked. And she replied, 'All we did was take pictures.' This was the 1890's when the Brownie camera was first invented. She has boxes and boxes of wonderful pictures of tumbleweed and daily life out on the old ranch. Now the town of Marathon has shrunk to a tenth its size; with less than 300 residents, it is a real ghost town.

''I grew up on a big, eighty-five acre farm just outside of San Antonio, Texas. My great uncle built the house we lived in—a big, expanded log cabin with immense rooms and surrounding porch. I was an only child until I was twelve, and spent most of my after-school hours and the hot, Texan summers alone, daydreaming.

''Our house was sixteen miles from town; my mother would drive me to school each day in her 1925 Pierce Arrow hearse. I didn't realize that being chauffeured in a hearse was a strange

Martha was so discouraged. Her garden was an ugly mess of weeds. ■ (From *George and Martha Encore* by James Marshall. Illustrated by the author.)

way to go to school until many years later, and it has only occurred to me recently that mine was an unusual childhood. Like many children who are alone a great deal, I had to fall back on my own resources. I lived in my imagination.

"I didn't have many children's books, but I read all the time. My mother was a real lover of literature and great Anglophile. She brought me Dickens. I read above my age level, not quite understanding what I was reading half the time, and spent much time between the covers of one of the twenty-four volume leather-bound books on the history of England.

"We moved from San Antonio to Beaumont, Texas, when my father was offered a job on the railroad. Beaumont is deep south and swampy and I hated it. I knew I would die if I

stayed there, so I diligently studied the viola, and eventually won a scholarship to the New England Conservatory in Boston.''

Marshall once said that he feels grateful to have been born in the forties, rather than the fifties. "Because I wasn't really influenced by television. Books were the major force in my life. I find the television generation much less imaginative. Books give the reader a chance to recreate the story in his or her own imagination. My sister, who was born a decade after me, never really got hooked on reading."

After a minor accident, Marshall stopped playing the viola. "I flew out of my seat on a plane and injured my hand, but ignored the injury and continued to play. As a result I developed a condition which forbad me to play more than twenty minutes a day. That prohibited me from becoming a profes-

"How do you expect to walk home with your loafers full of split pea soup?" she asked George. ∎
(From *George and Martha* by James Marshall. Illustrated by the author.)

sional musician, but looking back, I think this turn of events was all for the good. It helped me realize something that had before been only subconscious. That is, I did not want to be a professional musician, and having the injury made it easier for me to stop. I had worked hard to develop a technique and style, but I started late as a musician—did not even begin playing until I was thirteen. By the time I got to the conservatory, I flip-flopped between feeling like a 'wunderkind' and a fraud. I think I was a little bit of both. I had neither a base in musical theory nor a trained ear. But I played well and can

even remember Joseph Szigeti, a famous Hungarian violinist, telling me after a scholarship audition, 'Kid, you've got a great career ahead of you.' But even when I felt exhilarated, as if I would really be somebody special someday, a little voice told me that something was 'not quite right.' After I left the conservatory, I realized everything I'd been missing—I hadn't seen a movie in years, I hadn't really traveled. The hard part was being without a career. I had nowhere to go. Except Texas. And what was there? I was terrified. If you go back to Beaumont, Texas, chances are you won't get out a second time.''

Eric was not right for the time service. He had such a sinister little voice. ■ (From *Mary Alice, Operator Number 9* by Jeffrey Allen. Illustrated by James Marshall.)

Marshall moved back to Texas to attend college. "I shifted around between six different undergraduate schools before I finally took my bachelors in French and history. I went on working toward my masters at Trinity College, the only good school I ever attended. There I suddenly realized I did not want to be an academician. I did not want to wind up writing 'The History of Beauty Marks.' There was no future for me at the academy.

"I went back to Boston and taught French and Spanish for two years. I desperately needed a job but didn't have any teaching credentials. I called the Mother Superior of a Catholic school in Boston, told her I had a degree in French, and she promptly asked if I knew any Spanish. 'Sister,' I said, 'I was once in Mexico City for two weeks.' 'Come right over,' she said. I taught three Spanish classes and two French. The first course I taught was third year Spanish and half the kids were Puerto Rican. I kept them all after class and said, 'If any of you Spanish-speaking kids give me away, I have the power of the Catholic Church behind me. You will never get into another school.' This was already the lowest ranking high school in Boston. 'However,' I continued, 'If you teach *me* Spanish, you'll get a B in the class.' My salary was $4,800 a year, which even *then* was impossible to live on. But I learned Spanish, and began to spend my weekends drawing.

"A friend of mine had a neighbor who worked in publishing at Houghton-Mifflin. She saw my stuff, called up [vice president and director of children's books] Walter Lorraine, and said, 'I have a young man here and I think you should see his work.' I brought my drawings in to Walter, and he called me the next day. 'We have a book for you to illustrate,' he said, and I asked, 'How much do I have to pay?' He told me 'Come right over, sign your name to a contract, and we'll pay *you* two thousand dollars.' I was in shock. That was Byrd Baylor's *Plink, Plink, Plink* (1971), which was a commercial flop, but after working on this first assignment, I knew that books and illustration were for me.

"I quit teaching and gave myself six months off. I didn't know what would come of it, I often felt I would wind up driving a cab. You could say I went about things in a very backward way. I knew I wanted to live the life of an artist. But you can't do that unless you produce art. So I began to draw. Of course, I did love to draw and was gifted."

Marshall's first effort as a writer/illustrator resulted in the classic *George and Martha*, whose well-loved characters have since been featured in six books. Marshall recalled the creation of the characters: "I was in a hammock. It was a hot, hundred and ten degree, San Antonio, Texas day. My mother was watching Albee's 'Who's Afraid of Virginia Woolf?' on television while I was working on some drawings, and had some trouble coming up with names. Half-listening to Burton and Taylor, I named them George and Martha. When the book took off, I knew I had found my life's work."

Asked about his creative process, Marshall commented, "When I was young and looked at a picture book, I fell into the whole world of the story without ever thinking about an author actually writing the book, or an illustrator actually drawing the pictures. Kids are savvy these days, with questions like 'Where do your ideas come from?' and I really can't answer.

"Robert Graves said that one must be in a trance to create, that one must give over to this other way of being while working. Everything I've ever done well came from spontaneous, subconscious impulses which I cannot explain. When I try to

force things, to sit down and really work at a specific idea or plan, the work suffers; it just dies.

"The trick is to find your own personal working rhythms, your own *way* of working. I know that the kind of books I do grow directly out of my very short attention span; it stems from my ability to work quickly, in a sort of white heat. I used to keep that quiet, and not let on how little time it took me to do a book. 'You mean you didn't work for three years like Maurice Sendak worked on his last book?' librarians would ask. I have tried to slow myself down, but the results have been disasterous. Three weeks of writing, three weeks of illustrating is about all I can handle. Anything longer and I'm in trouble. Of course, the short format of children's books is perfect for my particular rhythm and style.

"Everyone has his own way of scheduling himself. My friend Arnold Lobel puts in shopkeeper's hours, working from nine till four, five days a week and produces wonderful imaginative stuff. If I worked that way, it would be deadly. I work better at night—whereas Arnold says, 'Only students do that.' He wouldn't put pen to paper after five o'clock in the afternoon if he was paid a million dollars. I do 'cleanup' work in the morning—busy work—then take a long Texas afternoon to relax and work at night. The later, the better—I figured that out after fifteen years; it took me that long to discover what

"Spider," said Lolly, "your little brother is getting on my nerves." ■ (From *Four on the Shore* by Edward Marshall. Illustrated by James Marshall.)

works for _me_. I do think that in order to do good work you have to build up a momentum, so I try to clear up blocks of time for myself—to let things happen without interruption, without breaking my stride.

''Perhaps the spare quality of the 'George and Martha' tales derives from the same part of me that is attracted to Japanese prints, and Japanese novelists as Kawabata. All of his writings are very concise. Not a word is wasted in any of his short novels and they are all exquisite. Marcel Proust, Kawabata's polar opposite is also one of my favorite writers. I love the richness of his worlds, his meticulously detailed writing. I could never write that way, but this doesn't bother me—I feel it is fruitful to know the limitations of one's talents.

''I feel more comfortable working with animal characters, but they're always human-like. I can recognize gestures and expressions in them that are similar to those of my friends. People ask me why I draw so many pigs, and all I can come up with is that when I was five, on my mother's farm, a great big pig named Dotty bit me, and this is my revenge. Pigs are fun to draw, as are balloons, which are also in my books. Visual

themes are not always repeated because of deep, psychological reasons. Sometimes they appear and reappear simply because they are beautiful to look at or fun to draw.''

Marshall and Harry Allard teamed up to create some of the best-loved characters in children's books, including 'The Stupids' and 'Miss Nelson.' ''We met in San Antonio. Harry taught French, and on every Monday, Wednesday and Friday we would get together to speak French. He has a doctorate from Yale, had high academic honors and has spent a lot of time in Paris. He amused me with his wonderful stories about Jean Cocteau and Simore Signoret . . . of life in the early fifties bohemian Paris.

''Sometimes we work on the text together. Harry often comes up with titles. He will call me at three in the morning and whisper, _'Miss Nelson Is Missing,'_ and hang up the phone. At one early point he had envisioned the students as alligators, but I disagreed—I wanted to use real kids. Sometimes I think an idea was mine, then I see from our notes that it was really Harry's and vice versa. In that sense, it is a real collaboration.

''This time Buster and Petunia flunked _everything_!''

''And _that's_ hard to do,'' said his wife.

■ (From _The Stupids Have a Ball_ by Harry Allard. Illustrated by James Marshall.)

"Collaborating on comedy can be nerve wracking. Harry and I have known each other since 1963, and we are pretty much on the same wave length. But if one of us thinks something is very funny, and becomes very excited about it and the other looks up and says after a pause, 'That is *not* funny. You're hysterical,' you can get very hurt, mad, crushed. You can stop speaking for three or four days. But we always work things through.

"It's difficult for the up-and-coming young artists because of the present economics of publishing and the conservative climate of the nation. There are many watchdog committees and all sorts of similar associations influencing publishers who are scaring editors to death with threats of what they should and what they should not publish. I've been fairly lucky, but every so often some real hate mail comes in, concerning the 'Stupids' in particular. Some of our critics say Harry and I are making fun of mentally deficient people—which is pure nonsense. I find that the people who vehemently hate the books have never read them—and this is usually true of censorship on all levels. If these people would take the trouble to open up the books, they would see that the 'Stupids' are very innocent indeed."

Asked what he feels makes his character, Miss Nelson, so popular, Marshall responded, "I'm sure it's the strong character [of her alter ego] Viola Swamp. I hated high school and junior high, but I *loved* grade school, I still love going back when I give talks to kids. I'm sure my love of those years infuses the *Miss Nelson* books with a certain energy. My affection for that time must come across in the way I convey the classroom, the students, their antics, and Miss Nelson herself."

Marshall often visits local schools. "You never know what kids will say or do. I remember fondly the time I was in a Connecticut school library, drawing George and Martha as sixty kids sat quietly and attentively on the floor. Suddenly a little girl stood up and faced me, 'Yes?' I inquired. 'Well,' she said, 'You are scarcely going to believe this . . . ' After a pregnant pause, I said, 'Try me.' 'My mother,' she continued in a most serious tone, 'actually likes *sardines.*'

Marshall has written some books under the pseudonym, Edward Marshall. "I wanted to do an easy-to-read book, but I was under an exclusive contract at a publishing house so I made up Edward, supposedly a cousin of mine from San An-

And Petunia watered all the houseplants. ■ (From *The Stupids Die* by Harry Allard. Illustrated by James Marshall.)

tonio. One day an editor called me and said, 'We're having so much trouble reaching your cousin to get publicity material, could *you* tell me something about him?' 'Well,' I said, 'It's very difficult for him living way out there near the crematorium with his eighteen children, Bubba, Jimmy Ray, Alice. . . .' I just spun a whole yarn about this so-called cousin, and before I knew it, it was printed in a publication. Now people know Edward is really James and I have a new book,

Merry Christmas, Space Case coming out under my name using the Space Case character originally invented under my pseudonym, 'Edward.'

Marshall prefers to work in four colors. ''I used to have a lot of trouble with color overlays. I couldn't visualize how the finished piece would look. I would make the color so heavy that the only thing I had going for me—my *line quality*—

"My name is Viola Swamp," said the lady in a scratchy voice. ■ (From *Miss Nelson Is Back* by Harry Allard. Illustrated by James Marshall.)

One afternoon the cut-ups were relaxing between activities. ■ (From *The Cut-Ups* by James Marshall. Illustrated by the author.)

would disappear. Finally, after thirty-five books I've figured out how to work with separations. While many illustrators prefer full-color illustration, I prefer the limitations of four color separation.''

Asked whom he admires in the field of children's books, Marshall replied, ''I love Ludwig Bemelmans' 'Madeline' books. He also worked in a sort of frenzied, almost sloppy way and his illustrations are very energetic. Sendak's books have often inspired me. I look at that very special quality of placing figures on a page which is so much a part of his style. I didn't imitate him, though. Why bother? God knows people have made careers of faking Sendak without ever coming close. I also love Edward Gorey's work, which makes everything on the page count, every moment of the illustration matters with Gorey, and yet, what he 'leaves out' is also essential. I deeply admire the work of Arnold Lobel. His freshness, his wit, and the singularity of his vision. We shouldn't scoff at the notion of individuality. It's not a boring nineteenth century idea that's going to die. People love a Sendak or a Lobel because of the special, very individual, subjective vision they bring to their work—that they dare to expose it, rings a subconscious bell in the child. This is why the artists I love are not the cool technicians, but those who have a vision to share.''

Marshall designs all of his books. ''I like my books to flow. I want each page to be something new. That way, you are forced to look. I want the books to look as if they were done in a very short period, and I get annoyed when art directors step in and try to make them look more 'finished.' The books I like the most were done in a short period—*George and Martha, Miss Nelson . . .*—and were illustrated quickly. Because of that, the immediacy of the line comes through and I want

That night Fox could not sleep. ■ (From *Fox at School* by Edward Marshall. Illustrated by James Marshall.)

to preserve that energy—which means I must be careful not to overdesign my books.

''With the exception of my collaborative work with Harry, I have virtually stopped illustrating other authors' work. I prefer to work on my own texts. It's usually very difficult for me to illustrate someone else's manuscript, partly because I have a good editorial sense and tend to overstep my domain as illustrator. I'm not a prima donna, but I know what works. I feel uncomfortable when I haven't the liberty to fix something I know is wrong.

''During the last few years, the books that made me most happy were hell to do. I had to redo them again and again in the planning stage. It is hard to maintain one's style while producing fresh material. Even though the books themselves are light and silly, the process is not always fun.

''I carry a sketchbook around with me. I try to develop character, and once I know the character is really living, I write dialogue, put the character in situations. It is a very simple process in which everything grows out of character. I like to put my characters into unusual situations. I like to shock, to surprise my readers. That's what comedy is about—the unexpected, the element of surprise. But I don't believe in pure surrealism. Too many people over the past fifty years have been exposed to the surrealist spirit to be truly surprised by a mink covered spoon, or whatever. These kinds of images and now familiar juxtapositions are not shocking twice. Working with humor, one must keep pushing toward new frontiers and yet remain rooted in reality. I have never liked the Marx Brothers silly slapstick brand humor. I prefer the wit and irony of W. C. Fields or the satiric twist of Molière.

''Chekhov has also been a good teacher. He makes you aware of how you should never fake or puff things up. Everything has a place in his stories and plays. He doesn't ever hedge or fatten things out.''

To his students at Parsons, Marshall emphasized, ''A book must have a good beginning and a strong middle, but without a knockout ending, you're shot. I've done books which featured wonderful characters, and some of the funniest lines I've ever written, but I blew the endings and they just don't work. You have to make a full circle because ending is emotionally satisfying. If not, everything valuable which preceeds your bad ending will go out the window, no matter how hard you worked on it. I also teach that pacing is essential. You don't kill a story from page to page, you kill it by stalling. You have to make a book *move*, there always has to be a reason to turn the next page.''

Marshall's advice to young people is ''work every day and set reasonable and attainable daily goals for yourself.''

Marshall divides his time between New York City and Connecticut. ''I live in a little village, Mansfield Hollow, Connecticut, which consists of twelve houses built around an old mill. The surrounding area is state forest. My house was built in the 1840s and was the old village store. It's got charm, but it's not 'cutesy.' After ten years of working at a kitchen table, I finally have a real studio. I was terrified to work in it at first, it seemed all-too-serious. It was like being a real artist.

''The creators of children's books are often regarded as second-rate professionals in our culture. David Hockney has said, 'The imagination is *everything*.' I would add that the *teaching* of imagination is everything. My imagination makes books, which may perhaps inspire others to develop their own imagination. If there is any message in my books, it is that books can be fun to make, and that imagination plus a certain subject

The kids in Room 207 were misbehaving again. ■ (From *Miss Nelson Is Missing!* by Harry Allard. Illustrated by James Marshall.)

can result in something tangible which may in turn inspire others to endeavor to create something of their own. I'm not a very political person, but I really believe in the power of human imagination. If we could only figure out how to spark everyone's imagination, we could change the world. That is why education, and by extension, children's books are so vitally important. Some of the most creative people in the art world are doing children's books—major artists are doing major art in this format. Painting is at an ebb. We aren't seeing terribly exciting exhibitions these days. But the creators of children's books, which function to excite the imagination of young people and adults alike *are* doing wonderful and important work. Their efforts should not be devalued.''

—*Based on an interview by Rachel Koenig*

Marshall's works are included in the Kerlan Collection at the University of Minnesota, University of Connecticut at Storrs, and in the de Grummond Collection at the University of Southern Mississippi.

FOR MORE INFORMATION SEE: Horn Book, February, 1970, August, 1972, February, 1973, June, 1973; *New York Times Book Review,* April 30, 1972, November 18, 1973, May 5, 1974; Doris de Montreville and Elizabeth D. Crawford, *Fourth Book of Junior Authors and Illustrators,* H. W. Wilson, 1978.

A boy's will is the wind's will,
And the thoughts of youth are long, long thoughts.
—Henry Wadsworth Longfellow

McKISSACK, Patricia (L'Ann) C(arwell) 1944-
(L'Ann Carwell)

BRIEF ENTRY: Born August 9, 1944, in Nashville, Tenn. After receiving her bachelor's degree from Tennessee Agricultural and Industrial State University (now Tennessee State University) in 1964, McKissack taught English at a junior high school in Kirkwood, Missouri. She later began teaching English at Forest Park College in St. Louis, where she continues to teach part time. Since completing her master's degree in 1975, McKissack has held a variety of jobs, including children's book editor, college instructor, and consultant on minority literature. In addition, she is co-owner of All-Writing Services. McKissack's books for children cover a range of topics, including religious stories, biographies of black historical figures, and a series on American Indians. *Flossie and the Fox* (Dial, 1966) is based on a folktale McKissack's grandfather told her as a child. The action surrounds little Flossie Finley as she delivers a basket of eggs to a neighbor and outsmarts the fox who wants the eggs for himself. "This tale of wit triumphant from the black tradition of the rural South . . . fairly sings on the page," wrote *Horn Book. School Library Journal* noted that the "spirited little girl will capture readers from the beginning, and they'll adore her by the end of this delightful story."

McKissack's series of books on the American Indian—*Aztec Indians, The Maya, The Inca* (Children's Press, 1985)—delivers a brief overview of the daily lives, religions, and government of these tribes. "It is a credit to these three titles that one can read them . . . and finish with a sense of the distinctive characteristics of three separate civilizations," observed *School Library Journal.* Her other books include *Martin Luther King, Jr.: A Man to Remember* (Children's Press, 1983); *Paul Laurence Dunbar* (1984); and *Mary McLeod Bethune* (1985). *Abram, Abram, Where Are We Going?* (David Cook, 1984), is a retelling of the biblical stories about Abraham as father to many nations. McKissack also contributes articles and short stories to magazines, including *Friend, Happy Times,* and *Evangelizing Today's Child. Home:* 5900 Pershing Ave., St. Louis, Mo. 63112.

FOR MORE INFORMATION SEE: Contemporary Authors, Volume 118, Gale, 1986.

MEEK, Jacklyn O'Hanlon 1933-
(Jacklyn Meek Matthews, Jacklyn O'Hanlon)

PERSONAL: Born December 5, 1933, in California; children: Margaret, Stephen, Clifford, Anne, Catherine, John. *Education:* Attended private high school in San Francisco, Calif. *Politics:* Democrat. *Religion:* Christian Scientist. *Residence:* Santa Barbara, Calif.

CAREER: Writer. Operator of a boarding house in Santa Barbara, Calif. *Awards, honors: The Door* was chosen as a Children's Choice by the International Reading Association, 1979.

WRITINGS—For children: (Under name Jacklyn Meek Matthews) *Edward and the Night Horses,* Golden Gate, 1970; (under name Jacklyn O'Hanlon) *Fair Game,* Dial, 1977; (under name J. O'Hanlon) *The Other Michael,* Dial, 1977; (under name J. O'Hanlon) *The Door,* Dial, 1978.

WORK IN PROGRESS: Always Be Green, a fantasy, under name Jacklyn O'Hanlon.

SIDELIGHTS: "It's simple—I write for children. They have always been my focus and concern. They are very discriminating, so I must be careful and as *truthful* as I can be—for young people will not be deceived or fooled. I *love* writing. It is a privilege to work at it."

MEYER, Kathleen Allan 1918-

PERSONAL: Born February 25, 1918, in Dunellan, N.J.; daugher of Andrew A. (a bank accountant) and Ethel (a nurse; maiden name, Creen) Allan; married Joseph V. Meyer, February 12, 1941 (an insurance underwriter; died, 1982); children: Jane S., Leslie A. (daughter). *Education:* New York University, B.S. (summa cum laude),1940; Hofstra University, elementary education certificate, 1955; San Jose State College, nursery school certificate, 1971. *Religion:* First Christian Church. *Address:* P.O. Box 1005, San Mateo, Calif. 94403. *Office:* St. Ambrose Episcopal Day School, Edgewater Blvd., Foster City, Calif. 94404.

CAREER: Blackett-Sample-Hummert (radio advertising), Park Ave., New York, N.Y., secretary to script editors, 1940-43; Grace Church, Massapequa, N.Y., preschool director, 1956-63; St. Matthew's Episcopal Day School, San Mateo, Calif., preschool director, 1963-86, third-grade creative writing teacher, 1981-83; author, 1969—; St. Ambrose Episcopal Day School, Foster City, Calif., preschool teacher, 1986—. *Member:* Society of Children's Book Writers, California Writer's Club, Burlingame Writer's Club.

KATHLEEN ALLAN MEYER

On Christmas Eve the Christmas candle is placed in the window. . . . ■ (Photograph from *Ireland: Land of Mist and Magic* by Kathleen Allan Meyer.)

WRITINGS—For children, except as noted: *Kindergarten Guide* (teacher's manual), Hayes School Publishing, 1977; *The Time-to-Sleep Book,* Western, 1978; *Ishi: The Story of an American Indian,* Dillon, 1980; *God Sends the Seasons* (illustrated by James McIlrath), Our Sunday Visitor, 1981; *Gerrie, the Giraffe,* Ideals, 1981; *Ireland: Land of Mist and Magic,* Dillon, 1983; *Bear, Your Manners Are Showing!* (with cassette), Standard, 1987.

"God's Gifts" series; all illustrated by Robert H. Cassell; published by Abingdon, 1985: *Hearing, Seeing, Smelling, Tasting, Touching.* Has also contributed poetry and fiction to children's periodicals such as *Ranger Rick, Accent on Youth, Wee Wisdom,* and *Jack and Jill* and teaching materials to *First Teacher* and *Instructor.*

WORK IN PROGRESS: A biography of Beatrix Potter for first to third graders; two historical books (one a biography) on California history; two series books to go with *Bear, Your Manners Are Showing!*; scriptwriting for a talking toy product.

SIDELIGHTS: "I was born in Dunellan, New Jersey, the youngest of five children of English-born parents. As far back as the sixth or seventh grade I was very interested in writing

for publication. I wrote for the school newspaper in both junior and senior high school, my aim being to eventually study journalism at New York University. Being one of five, there was never any money to send the children to college, but I applied for a scholarship at NYU and received one. I also got a job on a small hometown newspaper during the summer after graduation from high school. I was given special feature articles to write as well as the gossip column. I was given free reign over the contents and title of the column. I called it 'Over the Bridge Table' (bridge was very popular in those days), and my by-line was Pearl Button. How clever I thought I was!

"The scholarship and summer work continued for the next three years. I was in seventh heaven! Besides taking journalism and advertising courses with some of the finest professors of the day, I joined the college newspaper staff and the yearbook staff. I felt very proud when I was chosen to be the one to go down to deserted Bleeker Street in New York City on a Sunday and 'put the paper to bed.' I knew 'I had arrived.' And I was the first girl ever allowed to do that!

"I was also chosen to be the first woman literary editor of the yearbook, another big event for me as woman's lib was not even whispered about in those days. Several other exciting highlights of my college years were being elected president of the NYU chapter of Theta Sigma Phi, the national honorary journalism society, and being included in the 1940 edition of the collegiate *Who's Who Hall of Fame.* Keeping on top of my studies, I graduated summa cum laude.

"A wonderful four years ended for me with graduation. For lack of money—my mother had died and my father was moving—I could not fulfill the dream under my picture in the high school yearbook—attend Columbia University's graduate school of journalism and win the Pulitzer Prize Traveling Scholarship. Instead, I found a job in Blackett-Sample-Hummert's radio advertising company working for the script editor of 'Stella Dallas,' 'John's Other Wife,' and 'Young Widder Brown.' And the following year, I married the young man I met at New York University.

"The war years loomed ominously, and then came Pearl Harbor, and my husband enlisted. In 1943 our first daughter, Jane, was born, and he did not see her for the first time until she was two years old, as he was on a Navy ship in the Pacific Theatre. After the war ended, we had our second daughter, Leslie, and she was about two when I began to write stories to amuse her and her sister. But I never thought to send them out to a publisher.

"When both girls were out of college, I began writing in earnest and sold my first piece in 1969 to *Jack and Jill.* I was overjoyed, and I haven't stopped writing since. Shortly after the first sale I was dusting one day when a robin came by to say 'hello.' In five minutes I had written a poem about him, sent it in to *Ranger Rick,* and it was accepted. I was hooked on writing! And I bought *Writer's Market* to find out who the publishers were and their needs.

"And then I started to write books. In writing them, I find the most difficult step for me is getting the first sentence and the first paragraph down. Once I have gotten past these, and I am completely satisfied with them, I can forge ahead.

"As for advice to a young writer, I would suggest two things: first, write only about those things or persons you have a genuine interest in. You will have a much better chance of selling. I found this to be true with my two best sellers, *Ishi: The Story of an American Indian* and *Ireland: Land of Mist and Magic.* If your subject captures you, you will be able to capture your readers and have a very successful book. *Ishi* was so successful and received such excellent reviews from *Kirkus, Book List* and *School Library Journal,* that it has been adapted by the California State Department of Education as approved supplementary reading material for a period of six years with renewal privileges.

"Second, if you really believe in your book and the message it imparts, never give up on it. As fast as it comes back to your desk from a publisher, send it right out again to the next on the list. Perhaps it was my Irish persistence, but I sold a book on the thirtieth attempt and seven years after it was first written. Never give up on what you believe in!"

MIRSKY, Jeanette   1903-1987

OBITUARY NOTICE—See sketch in *SATA* Volume 8: Married name Jeanette Mirsky Ginsburg; born September 3, 1903, in Bradley Beach, N.J.; died March 10, 1987, in Princeton, N.J. Editor and author. Mirsky was the author of highly regarded books on explorers, travelers, and inventors. Among her writ-

ings are *To the North!: The Story of Arctic Times to the Present; Crossings: Balboa, Mackenzie, Lewis and Clark; Elisha Kent Kane and the Seafaring Frontier;* and *The Gentle Conquistadors: The Ten Year Odyssey across the American Southwest of Three Spanish Captains and Esteban, a Black Slave.* She also edited the anthology *The Great Chinese Travelers.*

FOR MORE INFORMATION SEE: Contemporary Authors, Permanent Series, Volume 2, 1978; *Who's Who in America,* 43rd edition, Marquis, 1982. Obituaries: *New York Times,* March 20, 1987; *Ocala Star-Banner* (Fla.), March 21, 1987.

MOREY, Walt(er Nelson)   1907-

PERSONAL: Born February 3, 1907, in Hoquiam, Wash.; son of Arthur Nelson (a carpenter) and Gertrude (Stover) Morey; married Rosalind Ogden (a teacher and secretary), July 8, 1934 (died February, 1977); married Peggy Kilburn, June 26, 1978. *Education:* Attended Benkhe Walker Business College, 1927-28. *Home:* 10830 S.W. Morey Lane, Wilsonville, Ore. 97070. *Agent:* Lenniger Literary Agency, 437 Fifth Ave., New York, N.Y. 10016.

CAREER: Writer, 1928—; mill worker, construction worker, and theater manager in Oregon and Washington during the 1930s and 1940s; filbert farmer, 1938—; shipbuilder and supervisor of burners at Kaiser Shipyards in Vancouver, Wash., 1940-45; deep sea diver and fish trap inspector in Alaska, 1951. Director of Oregon Nut Growers Cooperative, 1960-61. *Member:* Oregon Freelance Club. *Awards, honors:* Dutton Junior Animal Book Award, 1965, for *Gentle Ben,* and 1968, for *Kavik, the Wolf Dog;* Sequoyah Children's Book Award, 1968, and Yippee Award, 1970, both for *Gentle Ben;* Northwest Bookseller's Award, 1968, Tonawanda (N.Y.) School Children's Award, 1968, Dorothy Canfield Fisher Award, 1970, and William Allen White Children's Book Award, 1971, all for *Kavik, the Wolf Dog; Kavik, the Wolf Dog* was chosen one of the Children's Books of the Year by the Children's Book Committee of the Child Study Association, 1968, *Canyon Winter* and *Runaway Stallion* were chosen, 1973, *Run Far, Run Fast,* 1974, and *The Year of the Black Pony,* 1976; Evelyn Sibley Lampman Award from the Oregon Library Association, 1982, for his significant contribution to children's literature.

WRITINGS—All juvenile, except as indicated; all published by Dutton, except as noted: (With Virgil Burford) *North to Danger* (adult), John Day, 1954, revised edition, Caxton, 1969; *Gentle Ben* (ALA Notable Book; illustrated by John Schoenherr), 1965; *Home Is the North* (illustrated by Robert Shore), 1967; *Kavik, the Wolf Dog* (illustrated by Peter Parnall), 1968; *Angry Waters* (illustrated by Richard Cuffari), 1969; *Gloomy Gus,* 1970; *Deep Trouble,* 1971; *Scrub Dog of Alaska,* 1971; *Canyon Winter,* 1972; *Runaway Stallion,* 1973; *Run Far, Run Fast,* 1974; *Operation Blue Bear: A True Story* (young adult), 1975; *The Year of the Black Pony,* 1976; *Sandy and the Rock Star,* 1979; *The Lemon Meringue Dog,* 1980. Also author of *No Cheers, No Glory* (adult), 1945. Contributor to men's magazines, 1930-1950, including *Saga, True,* and *Argosy.*

ADAPTATIONS: "Gentle Giant" (motion picture; based on book *Gentle Ben*), Paramount, 1966; "Gentle Ben" (television series), starring Dennis Weaver, first broadcast on CBS-TV, 1967; "The Courage of Kavik, the Wolf Dog" (television movie), Pantheon/Stanley Chase/Jon Slan Productions, 1980, presented on NBC-TV, 1980; "Sultan and the Rock Star" (television movie), based on *Sandy and the Rock Star,* Walt Disney Studio, first broadcast on NBC-TV, 1980.

WORK IN PROGRESS: "I am finishing *Death Wall,* about three hundred people who, after having committed capital crimes, fled to Alaska before the police could catch up with them. It would be too expensive and time-consuming to attempt to comb the half-million square miles of frozen land up there, so the authorities simply let them live their lives. These men are essentially divorced from civilization as we know it. My story centers on three such men who have been in Alaska a long time, and an eighteen-year-old who has just arrived there. As with just about all of my books, my main characters are based on people I have known." Books on pre-statehood Alaska, the fishing industry and associated activities; a juvenile book on the Snake River area of Oregon and Utah.

SIDELIGHTS: **February 3, 1907.** Born in Hoquiam, Washington. "Like Mark in *Gentle Ben,* I was a sickly kid. We moved around a lot with my father's construction work. We went not only where he found jobs, but homesteaded in northern Canada, as well. We built our home and hunted and farmed so we could eat. Our nearest neighbors were about five miles away. This was very hard for my father; my mother, the model for Mark's mother in *Gentle Ben,* had grown up on a farm in Michigan and took the life much better. In any case, after about two years we were completely broke and moved down to the Portland area, where I've lived ever since.

"I can honestly say that I never enjoyed a single second of school in my life. I first attended a one-room school in Jasper, Oregon. All told, I guess we were about fourteen students. The teacher didn't have but an eighth-grade education. The first day, the assignment was to copy the first page from a particular book—well, until that moment, I had never seen a book. After three years, I could neither read nor do the simplest arithmetic. When I was eight, the family moved to Oakland, Washington, and for the third year in a row, I was placed in the first grade.

"By the time I was fourteen, reading was still a torture for me. I could make out individual words, but it took so long that by the time I got to the end of a sentence, I couldn't remember what it was all about. If it hadn't been for a miraculous coincidence, I might never have learned to read. We had moved, again, this time to Great Falls, Montana and next door to us lived Charles Russell, the great western painter. Russell was probably Montana's most famous character and it was a thrill to see him sitting outside his cabin on the lake, painting. My mother got me a fictionalized account of his life, and with the help of my family I struggled through it. The story so gripped me, I learned to read. Through reading I discovered my imagination and from then on, I read everything I could get my hands on. Edgar Rice Burroughs had just published *Tarzan of the Apes,* which I read two or three times in a row. Then I tore into Zane Grey, went to the *Knights of the Round Table* and then to early American adventure books like *The Riflemen of Ohio.* Mark Twain and Stephen Crane were other favorite writers. I began getting glimmers that I, too, wanted to write.

"I was now nineteen—far too old for high school—so they booted me out, with a diploma. I knew that no college would

WALT MOREY

accept me, so I went to work. Over the next few years, I held jobs in saw mills, veneer plants and construction sites. I was also a prize fighter, a career I came to quite by accident. I played football in high school. One day I missed a tackle and dislocated my left arm causing the muscle to become so weak and loose that it couldn't hold the arm in the socket. My chiropractor suggested that I learn boxing in order to strengthen and tighten the injured muscle. I found that I had an aptitude for it and was managed by a man who had fought the light heavyweight champion of the world. I won all of my twenty-three professional bouts, and beat the light heavyweight champion of Idaho. One day I walked into the gym and saw a fellow I knew well but hadn't seen in a year and a half. His face was all mashed in. 'This could be you,' I said to myself, picked up my gloves, my jump rope and walked out, never to fight again.

"While I was fighting, I also worked as a projectionist/manager in a movie theater, a job I kept for seven years. I'd watch those films over and over, taking them apart in my mind to see how the stories were put together. Finally, I got up the courage to try writing a story of my own. I rewrote that story—an adult tale—thirteen times, for a grand total of two million words. But eventually I had to face it: the story was no damn good.''

For help with his writing, he joined a freelance writers club where he met John Hawkins, a writer who proved instrumental to Morey's development. "Hawkins was born to write. He started out writing for magazines and then with the advent of television went to Hollywood where he was story editor for 'Bonanza,' 'Wagon Train,' and a number of other shows. His first suggestion to me was to write about a subject I knew like the back of my hand. So I wrote a boxing yarn and made my first sale to *Knockout Magazine,* a pulp.

"The pulps were the training ground for countless writers, among them Hemingway and Steinbeck. The craftsmanship I learned writing for the pulps has stayed with me. Techniques picked up then I use to this day. One of the first rules was, 'Get your hero in trouble on page one and keep him in trouble until the very end.' You've also got to set the scene, tell the reader what type of story he's about to read and throw in a narrative hook to get him curious. I try to do all this in one hundred and fifty words. I generally rewrite the first page a dozen or more times. Until the first page is right, I can't go on to anything else. But once I've got page one, I've got all the pieces and the story is poised to take off, almost on its own.

"But plot and setting are not the only important elements in a story. Character is crucial. How does your protagonist think? What are his hopes, his dreams, and his ambitions? And then, of course, how does he—and all your characters—talk? Until I can hear the dialogue in my head, I can't begin to write. Dialogue is where conflict generally comes out, and without

(From the movie "Gentle Giant," starring Dennis Weaver and Clint Howard, based on the novel *Gentle Ben* by Walt Morey. Copyright © 1966 by Ivan Tors Films, Inc.)

Mark leaned back against Ben's solid side. ■ (From *Gentle Ben* by Walt Morey. Illustrated by John Schoenherr.)

conflict you don't have much of a story. Dialogue should be as crisp as a stalk of celery breaking, as sharp as people fencing.

"Another thing the pulps taught was conciseness. Because they would assign stories to conform to a specific—and inviolable—word count, you'd learn the weight of each individual word without a syllable to spare. To me, a story is good not because of the number of words you've used, but because of the number of words you didn't use and still were able to tell your yarn. To write a really good yarn takes a lot of work. By the time I've finished a book, I have usually rewritten it about five times.

"No matter where my story is set, I go there. I want the reader to see the country exactly as I saw it, to see the people exactly as I saw them, to feel the heat and cold, and to smell the countryside. Also, the world is changing so fast. Readers of my books can get to know an Alaska (among other places) that no longer exists. They will become acquainted with animals—like the Kodiak bear—that are now exceedingly rare, or endangered species."

Morey made his first trip to Alaska in 1950, nine years before statehood. At this time he was freelancing for a variety of magazines. "I met Virgil Burford, a pretty famous deep-sea diver whose business consisted mainly of fishing for salmon with enormous underwater traps. He invited me to come north, do some diving and see the country. My job was to inspect

and repair the sections. You see, these traps were basically huge corrals (covering an acre or more of ocean) divided into four parts, or sections, hung with chicken wire from the ocean bottom to the surface. This was hard-hat diving in a forty-pound suit. We once had a whale go through the trap—he did more damage in three minutes than a bulldozer could do in two hours. He ripped that trap completely to pieces, and we had to rewire the whole thing. I made over a hundred dives in Alaska, which provided me with material for many magazine stories.

"Alaska in 1950 was nothing short of amazing. I remember coming upon my first ghost town, an old copper mining spot whose vein had petered out. Three people lived in the town, and occasionally others would drop in from wherever they were diving or trapping. The center of this town was the Copper Lady Saloon. For six days out of seven, you could drink and carouse to your heart's content. But on Sunday, they would let down an altar from the ceiling and hold a church service. The beer mugs you'd been drinking from all week were used for the contributions. A bar in a million, the Copper Lady.

"I was doing pretty well until television hit. That wiped out most of the pulps and in order to survive many writers went over to TV. That never interested me. I had been writing part-time while running a 60-acre filbert farm in Oregon and for the first twelve years after TV, I barely wrote a word. I'd sit

The stubby ears came forward. . . . He began to move through the gloom like a wraith. ■ (Jacket illustration by Konrad Hack from *Sandy and the Rock Star* by Walt Morey.)

The cast of the television series "Gentle Ben," as featured on the cover of *TV Guide,* August, 1968.

down at the typewriter and start in on a story, but the realization that I'd probably never sell it was so discouraging I'd just tear the paper out of the machine. My wife, who was teaching school at the time, sometimes read my old published stories to her students, who loved them. She kept encouraging me to write some stories for kids. There was nothing I wanted to do less. I felt discouraged enough about the writing business and the idea of resorting to kids for an audience made me feel even more like a wash-out. Besides, I was active in local farming associations and didn't have a lot of free time. But she hectored me for the better part of ten years and to get her off my back—to prove that I couldn't do it—I began the story that became *Gentle Ben*.

"I had met Ben during one of the summers I'd spent diving in Alaska. Ben was the world's biggest bear, an Alaska Kodiak bear. Standing on his hind legs, he was over thirteen and a half feet tall. He weighed over twenty-two hundred pounds.

"*Gentle Ben* was a very hard book to write. I found out that it is harder to write a story for young people than for adults. It opened a whole new type of writing for me. With adults, you have certain gimmicks that just won't wash with kids. For one thing, if the action slows down a little, you can add a sexy scene or two. Not so, if you're writing for kids. You are forced to become a better storyteller, to have a tighter plot, and to make your characters absolutely believable. *Gentle Ben* hooked me on writing for kids. This book—which I had originally begun in order to prove to my wife that I couldn't do it—turned out to be my breakthrough. Not until *Gentle Ben*, which sold millions of copies and was made into a movie, was I able to earn my living as a writer.

"Naturally enough, I continued to mine my Alaskan adventures, and to add new ones. *Kavik, the Wolf Dog* is based on another animal I knew. I had spent a good deal of time in Kotsabu, which I believe is still the largest Eskimo settlement in the world. When I was there, there were thirteen hundred people and over three thousand dogs. In order to get a tougher, fiercer animal, the Eskimos bred their dogs with wolves. One day I was out walking and came upon the most beautiful animal with big golden eyes. I squatted down and started petting him, and the next moment he was all over me licking my face. Suddenly, a voice behind me yelled, 'Mister, are you crazy? You want to get your throat ripped out? Didn't you see that sign?' Well, who looks for signs north of the Arctic circle? But sure enough, there was one and in big block letters, it said BEWARE, VICIOUS DOGS. I still wasn't convinced and sought out the dog's owner, because I wanted to buy this animal and bring him home to my farm. The owner was an Eskimo woman who lived in a cabin with her baby. When I visited the cabin during the day, the dog was very friendly; but at night, just the smell of a stranger nearby turned him into a lethal guard dog. I understood that the wolf dog could live nowhere but in Alaska. I could never own that dog, but I could write about him."

Most of Morey's books are based on people—not just animals—he has known. "One of the most extraordinary characters I have ever met became Ten Day Watson (a goldminer) in *Gloomy Gus*. Ten Day, in the book, is just as I knew him. He lived alone in a small cabin and sluiced enough gold from the river in ten days to last him most of the year. The rest of the time he just enjoyed living in the wilderness. He could easily go six months without seeing a single person. One day

Fly-by galloped across the spongy earth.... ■ (Jacket illustration by Michael Hampshire from *Runaway Stallion* by Walt Morey.)

There he stood, ears pricked forward, and looked across the water. ■ (From *Kavik, the Wolf Dog* by Walt Morey. Illustrated by Peter Parnall.)

I said, 'Ten Day, don't you get lonesome out here?' And he said, 'No. I feel fine. I can walk to the top of the hill in the back of the cabin and yell at the top of my lungs: "Ten Day, you're the greatest man in the world!" and nobody argues with me.' He was a legendary figure—scary in his way, but kind deep down. He just wanted to be left alone to live as he chose.

"I also knew the circus people in *Gloomy Gus*. The book is dedicated to Charlie Allen and Jim Bear. I traveled with their circus for about a week. Jim, the bear in the book, is taken from his natural home to be in a circus act. He stood about eight feet on his hind legs and weighed about 750 pounds. He was one of the very few of his kind in captivity who never even scratched anyone. He was not only in the circus, but in movies and on television—he had all his claws and all his teeth. I used to get down in front of him and put sugar cubes in my mouth. He would walk right up and lick them out of my mouth. Those were sloppy kisses, let me tell you!

"You know, as private citizens it's easy to become frustrated with situations that seem beyond our power to change. But being a writer can be a way around that. *Sandy and the Rock Star* is a book in which I took on the enemy, so to speak. It is set on Spiegen Island, a small island off the coast of Washington. It was owned by a rich businessman who used to stock his island with exotic animals from all over the world, and he and his friends would hunt them. I objected to this and wrote about it in pretty strong terms. Disney eventually made a movie based on my story and the island got such bad press that the owner stopped hunting there."

The importance of nature is an abiding theme in Morey's work. "It's true that a number of my protagonists 'find themselves' in the country. Dan Edwards, for example, a juvenile delinquent in *Angry Waters*, is sent to a farm instead of prison. The boy's guardian, an alcoholic, couldn't really care for him, and town life didn't test his mettle. On the farm, Dan is made to grow physically, mentally and emotionally. On all these levels, growth is painful. But at book's end, his hard work is rewarded. I do believe it is important for us to try to stay close to nature. The more divorced we become from the country, the more likely I think we are to become unhappy."

When asked if he had a typical day, Morey responded, "If I am working on a story, I like to be at my desk by nine in the morning. If I get away by seven or eight in the evening, I'm doing pretty well. Sometimes the next morning—particularly if I've worked late the previous day—it can be hard getting started. So, I use a trick I learned years ago. I force myself to stop just at the spot I'm *itching* to say something, at the brink of a climactic scene, for example. The next morning, I can't wait to get to my desk. I also do a lot of speaking engagements at schools, universities and international library associations. I estimate I do about 300 appearances a year. That means several week-long trips during which I'll do four or five talks a day. It's tiring, but I love doing it. Knowing that people read your books is one thing, but meeting your readers is a whole different ball game."

When asked if he had any advice for aspiring writers, Morey said, "The most important thing is to read. Figure out the kind of story you want to write, and then read everything and anything in the same vein. Learn to analyze a story. When you're trying to learn, you do not read for fun. I haven't read for fun in fifty years. By now it's automatic: the minute I start to read something, I'm taking it apart. Characterization, dialogue, plot. When I started out and would find a story I really admired, I would copy it word for word on my typewriter. You know,

you look at a story in a magazine a certain way—it seems very final in published form. But on your own machine it looks different. You have to look at each word when you're copying it. You can't skip so much as a comma. Copying, you're looking at the story from the inside out.

"Of course you learn by doing. Nobody can really teach you to write. Not even God can teach you that. But if you're determined to write, not even God can stop you."

—*Based on an interview by Marguerite Feitlowitz*

Gentle Ben has been translated into French, Japanese, German, Swedish, Norwegian, and Spanish.

FOR MORE INFORMATION SEE: Books and Bookmen, November, 1968; *Children's Book World,* November 3, 1968; *Times Literary Supplement,* June 26, 1969; *Horn Book,* December, 1969, June, 1971; Doris de Montreville and Donna Hill, editors, *Third Book of Junior Authors,* H. W. Wilson, 1972; Larry Leonard, "The Fighter, the Writer," *Writer's Digest,* September, 1984.

NAST, Thomas 1840-1902

PERSONAL: Born September 27, 1840, in Landau, Germany (now West Germany); came to the United States in 1846; died of yellow fever, December 7, 1902, in Guayaquil, Ecuador; son of Thomas (a musician) and Apollonia (Apres) Nast; married Sallie Edwards, September 26, 1861; children: five. *Education:* Attended public schools in New York, N.Y.; studied art at the National Academy of Design and with Theodore Kaufmann and Alfred Fredericks. *Residence:* Morristown, N.J.

CAREER: Political cartoonist, artist, and illustrator. *Frank Leslie's Illustrated Newspaper,* staff artist, 1855-59; traveled through Italy covering Garibaldi's successful campaign for *New York Illustrated News, Illustrated London News,* and *Le Monde Illustré,* 1859-62; *Harper's Weekly,* staff artist, 1862-84; *Nast's Weekly,* publisher, 1892-93; U.S. consul general of Guayaquil, Ecuador, 1902. Lecturer. *Member:* Regiment Veteran Club, Union League, The Players. *Awards, honors:* Honored by the Union League Club of New York City in recognition of his services to the Federal cause.

*ILLUSTRATOR—*For children; selected works: Clement C. Moore, *A Visit from St. Nicholas,* L. Prang, 1864, reprinted, Library of Congress, 1976; (with F.O.C. Darley) Mary Mapes Dodge, *Hans Brinker; or, The Silver Skates,* James O'Kane, 1866; Sophie May (pseudonym of Rebecca S. Clarke), *Dottie Dimple at Home,* Lee & Shepard, 1868; George P. Webster, *Rip Van Winkle,* McLaughlin Brothers, circa 1869; G. P. Webster, *Santa Claus and His Works,* McLaughlin Brothers, circa 1869, reissued, Evergreen, 1972; *The Wonderful Adventures of Humpty Dumpty,* two volumes, McLaughlin Brothers, circa 1869; S. May, *Dottie Dimple Out West,* Lee & Shepard, 1869; Betty Chancellor, *A Child's Christmas Cookbook,* Denver Art Museum, 1964.

Other selected works: (With others) Frank B. Goodrich, *The Tribute Book,* Derby & Miller, 1865; George F. Harrington (pseudonym of William Mumford Baker), *Inside: A Chronicle of Secession,* Harper, 1866; Orville J. Victor, editor, *Incidents and Anecdotes of the War,* James D. Torrey, 1866; Warren L. Gross, *The Soldier's Story of His Captivity at Andersonville, Belle Isle and Other Rebel Prisons,* Harper, 1866; Albert D. Richardson, *Beyond the Mississippi,* American Publishing, 1867; William D. O'Connor, *The Ghost,* [New York], 1867; Petro-

THOMAS NAST

leum V. Nasby (pseudonym of David R. Locke), *"Swingin Round the Cirkle"*, Lee & Shepard, 1867; May Mannering, *The Cruise of the Dashaway; or, Katie Putnam's Voyage,* Lee & Shepard, 1868; P. V. Nasby, *Ekkoes from Kentucky,* Lee & Shepard, 1868; Oliver Optic (pseudonym of W. T. Adams), *Our Standard-Bearer; or, The Life of General Ulysses S. Grant,* Lee & Shepard, 1868; O. Optic, *Young America Abroad: Dykes and Ditches,* Lee & Shepard, 1868; O. Optic, *Down the River,* Lee & Shepard, 1869; *Our Admiral's Flag Abroad,* [New York], 1869.

William Swinton, *History of the Seventh Regiment, National Guard, State of New York, During the War of the Rebellion,* Fields, Osgood, 1870; Henry William Pullen, *The Fight at Dame Europa's School,* Francis B. Felt, 1871; William J. Linton, *The House That Tweed Built,* privately printed, 1871; A. Cosmopolitan (pseudonym of Charles Henry Pullen), *Miss Columbia's Public School; or, Will It Blow Over?,* Francis B. Felt, 1871; *The Sunnyside Book,* [New York], 1871; David R. Locke, *The Struggles (Social, Financial, and Political) of Petroleum V. Nasby,* Richardson, 1872; (with F.O.C. Darley), Vieux Mustache (pseudonym of Clarence Gordon), *Boarding School Days,* Hurd & Houghton, 1873; (with Phiz [pseudonym of Hablot Knight Browne]), Charles Dickens, *The Posthumous Papers of the Pickwick Club,* Harper, 1873, later edition abridged by Joshua G.M. Karton, Hart, 1976; David A. Wells, *Robinson Crusoe's Money; or, The Remarkable Financial Fortunes and Misfortunes of a Remote Island Community,* Harper, 1876; C. Dickens, *"Pictures from Italy," "Sketches by Boz"* and *"American Notes",* Harper, 1877; Rufus E. Shapley, *Solid for Mulhooly,* Gebbie & Co., 1889; *Thomas Nast's*

Christmas Drawings for the Human Race, Harper, 1890, reissued, Dover, 1978; (with others) Edgar Fawcett, *A New York Family,* Cassell, 1891.

Also editor of *Thomas Nast's Illustrated Almanac,* McLaughlin Brothers, 1870-74; contributor of illustrations to periodicals, including *Vanity Fair, Mrs. Grundy,* and *The Riverside Magazine for Young People.*

SIDELIGHTS: **September 27, 1840.** Born in the military barracks of Landau, Bavaria, a small fortified German town near Alsace. Nast's father was a German musician who played the trombone in the Ninth Regiment Bavarian Band. Surrounded by soldiers, young Nast spent hours drawing their pictures, or carving their figures from beeswax and pressing them against windows.

1846. The liberal political opinions of Nast's father led to his emigration to New York and to the relocation of his family soon afterwards. The family settled in New York City and Nast, who could not speak any English, attended a neighborhood school.

His father became a member of the Philharmonic Society and played in an orchestra at a local theater house. Although young Nast enjoyed the theater, efforts by his father to encourage his son to study music or a trade were futile. Nast was also not interested in school, but preferred to spend his time and attention pursuing his artwork.

1855. Left public school to attend a drawing class taught by Theodore Kaufman, a German historical painter. Later, Nast

(From "Little Red Riding Hood" in *Thomas Nast's Illustrated Almanac* [1872], edited and illustrated by Thomas Nast.)

studied at the National Academy of Design in New York City. "I believe that I am the first person who ever accepted caricaturing in this country as a profession. I say accepted, because it was my youthful dream to become a great historical painter. But I saw Burton in the old Chambers Street theater in 'Toodles' and was impressed with the power of his humor and caricature to such an extent that I would go away from the show and from the impressions of broad humor which Burton left upon my mind to draw him in all his ridiculous and laughable posturing. This is the 'Toodles' of my youth and the 'Toodles' that first inspired me." ["Thomas Nast," *The Daily Journal* (Lincoln, Nebraska), November 17, 1887.[1]]

Applied to Frank Leslie, the publisher who owned the popular *Frank Leslie's Illustrated Newspaper* for a position as staff artist. "I have often been asked how a young draughtsman gets into a profitable practice of his vocation. I will tell you how I proceeded myself. When I was fourteen years old and about half grown I went to the proprietor of an illustrated paper in New York and told him that I wanted work at drawing pictures for his paper.

"He said to me, 'My little man'—he called me a little man even then—'you want to draw for my paper? Go down to Hoboken ferry and draw a picture of a boat leaving the dock.' It was a hard task to give a boy, but I drew the picture and got the job, and he started me off at the munificent salary of $5 a week."[1] Nast remained on Leslie's staff for three years.

1858. Joined the staff of the *New York Illustrated News*.

1860. At the request of the *New York Illustrated News*, went to England to cover the Heenan-Sayres heavyweight prize-fight. "It came about in a rather curious manner, somewhat

(From *Hans Brinker; or, The Silver Skates* by Mary Mapes Dodge. Illustrated by Thomas Nast.)

Thomas Nast, 1862. (Photograph by Mathew Brady.)

in this wise: When I was but 19, after the manner of young men, I fell in love. The young lady, being somewhat doubtful of my steadfastness of purpose, advised that I should absent myself for a year and see how I felt then. After considerable demur I accepted the proposition.

"After some rustling round town I secured a position as European artist for the *New York News*, then the leading illustrated paper. I sailed from New York in February . . . detailed to send a drawing of the celebrated Heenan-Sayres fight. I did my work, spent what money I had with me, and, some time after the fight, found myself stranded. The *News* somehow failed to remit. Several applications to friends and acquaintances failed of the desired result and I was really in a serious position.

"About this time I learned that Garibaldi was in a seaport town of Sicily. I wanted to get to him, but lacked the wherewithal. Heenan was about the last man from whom I cared to borrow money, but I finally went to him and explained matters. He immediately handed me £20, saying that he would collect it from the paper. He did so subsequently, and I may say that that 20 was all I ever got from the *News*.

"By dint of economy I managed to reach Sicily just in time for Garibaldi's great expedition, in which he reduced Naples and made his triumphant march through Central and Northern

I smiled at myself at the sight of all this money. ■ (From *Robinson Crusoe's Money; or, The Remarkable Financial Fortunes and Misfortunes of a Remote Island Community* by David A. Wells. Illustrated by Thomas Nast.)

Italy. Ours was the third detachment of vessels to sail, although it was the second to arrive at Castello di Mari. The ships, by the way, had nearly all been purchased by a wealthy American, who represented that they were to be employed in American trade, and sail under the American flag. Some little distance out from shore we were intercepted by a large man-of-war, whose nationality we were unable to determine; she eventually proved to be Sardinian and our friend. Just outside of her, however, was a fleet of three of the enemy's vessels, who would gladly have pounced down upon us had it not been for her intervention. Several Americans were captured in this manner at other times and experienced severe treatment. We escaped under cover of darkness that night.

"After our arrival upon the main land I accompanied Garibaldi through the whole of that eventful campaign. I was not engaged in active military service, as being a neutral, I was more useful in carrying dispatches, and gaining information. I, at this time, was sending drawings to the *New York Illustrated News,* the *London News,* the leading Parisian illustrated paper and several others. In Palermo, where I was immediately after its capture, I made the acquaintance of the famous Gen. Medici, who, at that time but a colonel, subsequently rose to the rank of aide-de-campe of King Victor Emanuel. I also met Col. John Peard, known as 'Garibaldi's Englishmen,' who bore so marked a resemblance to Garibaldi himself that he was frequently welcomed by rapturous thousands, who mistook him for the chieftain himself.

"I remained in Italy till the expiration of my year of probation, seeing much of active service and a great deal that was interesting and exciting." ["Campaigning with Garibaldi," *The Omaha Herald,* November 29, 1887.[2]]

September 26, 1861. Married Sarah Edwards. After their marriage, she frequently read historical and dramatic works to Nast, and often suggested the Shakespearean quotations that accompanied so many of his cartoons.

1862. Began work as a staff artist for *Harper's Weekly.* "I was in Washington a few days prior to the inauguration of Lincoln . . . having been sent by *Harper's* to take sketches when that event should come off. I did nothing but walk around the city and feel the public pulse, so to speak. There was no necessity of saying anything to anybody.

"You intuitively recognized that trouble was brewing. Southerners had sworn that Lincoln should not be inaugurated. Their utterances had fired the Northern heart, and the people loyal to the old flag were just as determined that the lawfully elected president should be inaugurated, though blood should flow in the attempt. It was an awful time. People looked different then than they do now. Little knots of men could be seen conversing together in whispers on street corners, and even the whispers ceased when a person unknown to them approached. Everybody seemed to suspect every one else. Every woman looked askance at each other, and children obliged to be out would

The Tammany Tiger Loose.   —"What Are You Going To Do About It?"   November 11, 1871

One of Nast's famous Tammany cartoons, responsible for the downfall of "Boss" Tweed's political machine.

NAPOLÉON

"DEAD MEN'S CLOTHES SOON WEAR OUT."

Nast's September 10, 1870 cartoon for *Harper's Weekly*.

skurry home as if frightened, probably having been given warning by their parents. The streets at night, for several nights prior to the inaugural ceremonies, were practically deserted. There was a hush over everything. It seemed to me that the shadow of death was hovering near. I had constantly floating before my eyes sable plumes and trappings of woe. I could hear dirges constantly, and thought for awhile that I would have to leave the place or go crazy. I knew all these sombre thoughts were but imagination, but I also knew that the something which had influenced my imagination was tangible, really excited. The 4th of March came and Mr. Lincoln was inaugurated. . . .

The September 30, 1871 cartoon by Thomas Nast for *Harper's Weekly*.

("Santa Claus Can't Say That I've Forgotten Anything," by Thomas Nast. *Harper's Weekly,* December 25, 1886.)

Nast's prototypical image of the rotund, bearded Santa Claus. *Harper's Weekly,* **January 1, 1881.**

"I went to my room in the Willard and sat down to do some work. I couldn't work. The stillness was oppressive. At least a dozen times I picked up my pencils only to throw them down again. I got up and paced the floor nervously. I heard men on either side of me doing the same thing. Walking didn't relieve the severe mental strain. I sat down in my chair and pressed my head in my hands. Suddenly I heard a window go up and some one step out on the balcony of the Ebbitt House, directly opposite. Everybody in the hotels had heard him.

"What is he going to do? I asked myself, and I suppose everyone else propounded the same mental interrogation. We hadn't to wait long. He began to sing the 'Star Spangled Banner' in a clear, strong voice. The effect was magical, electrical. One window went up, and another, and then another, and heads popped out all over the neighgborhood. People began to stir on the streets. A crowd soon gathered. The grand old song was taken up and sung by thousands. The spell was broken, and when the song was finished tongues were loosened, and cheer after cheer rent the air. The man rooming next to me rapped on my door and insisted that I should take a drink with him. As we passed along the corridors we were joined by others, men wild with joy, some of them weeping and throwing their arms around each other's neck. Others were singing and all were happy, as Washington was itself again. . . ." ["A Song Saved It," *The World,* November 6, 1887.[3]]

1863. Worked as a war artist, Nast drew his cartoons on the phases of the Civil War, gaining support from the union's cause. So successful was his propaganda, that Abraham Lincoln commented: "Thomas Nast has been our best recruiting sergeant. His emblematic cartoons have never failed to arouse enthusiasm and patriotism, and have always seemed to come just when these articles were getting scarce." [J. Henry Harper, *The House of Harper: A Century of Publishing in Franklin Square,* Harper, 1912.[4]]

By war's end, Nast had gained a national reputation and a secure place on *Harper's Weekly.* He also found time to devote to painting and book illustration.

1868. The nomination of Ulysses S. Grant for President was hailed by Nast in his cartoons. A staunch Grant supporter, Nast used his pen to get the general elected. When the results of Grant's election for a second term became known, Samuel L. Clemens (Mark Twain) wrote enthusiastically to Nast: "Nast, you more than any other man have won a prodigious victory for Grant—I mean for Civilization and Progress. These pictures were simply marvelous, and if any man in the land has a right to hold his head up and be honestly proud of his share in this year's vast events, that man is unquestionably yourself. We all do sincerely honor you and are proud of you."[4]

1871. Nast's cartoons in *Harper's* and editorials in the *New York Times* demanded the ousting of the Tammany Ring group and their leader, "Boss" Tweed. They insisted that these corrupt politicians, who had stolen millions of dollars of public money, be arrested, prosecuted, and sentenced to jail terms. To represent the Tammany Hall organization Nast invented an emblem, the tiger. ". . . I thought it was time to show the press of the country what they could do if they wanted to. So . . . I made a cartoon of the [Tammany] ring, all looking innocent and called it 'That's Too Thin.' Every one of ordinary intelligence knows the result of the . . . cartoons." ["The Man Who Draws," *The Independent* (Helena, Montana), December 28, 1887.[5]]

1874. During the presidential campaign, Nast used an elephant to represent the Republican party in his cartoons. Besides pop-

ularizing the elephant as a symbol for the Republican party, the Democratic donkey, Uncle Sam, and the Tammany tiger, he also made famous our present-day image of a white-bearded, rotund Santa Claus in a red suit.

Thirty-one-year-old Nast became a national hero. The circulation of *Harper's Weekly* rose from one to three hundred thousand readers during the Tammany Ring battle, and the Tammany Ring was swept out of power. "Boss" Tweed, was reported to have said about Nast's cartoons, "I don't care what they print about me, most of my constituents can't read anyway—but them damn pictures!" [*The American Scholar,* Volume III, United Chapters of Phi Beta Kappa, 1934.[6]]

Speaking about his cartoons, Nast remarked: "No man can become a successful cartoonist unless he believes in what he portrays. It is utterly impossible for a man to make a strong cartoon unless he believes strongly.

"I am a strong Republican. I take a great deal of interest in the party, I could not make a cartoon from a Democratic standpoint because I don't believe in Democracy.

"Just what influence cartoons have on politics is a matter hard to estimate. Their influence does not show plainly on the surface, but I think that they have a great influence nevertheless, and the politicians seem to be of the same opinion. I have never used an idea that was not my own. That is one reason why I have been so successful. If a man comes to me with an idea and I know that it is good, I will not use it because I have a pride in the matter. Then I know that a man can carry out his own ideas better than he can those of another.

"I know that it is the custom of a great many of the artists to take ideas that are furnished them. They carry their ideas out from an artistic standpoint. They make a pretty, well rounded picture. It may be thoroughly artistic, but the point is liable to suffer.

"There again is where I am successful. Ideas come to me easily. I am never at loss for one. The great trouble with the artists is that they do not study enough. I read a vast quantity of stuff that is of no value to me for I fear that I might miss something I ought to know. Then I study men most carefully. I watch how they talk. I am constantly on the lookout for their peculiarities. I know what their ideas are on great questions. I get so sometimes that I know pretty clearly what their conclusions will be on certain important matters.

"I make a great many of my cartoons before any expected event happens. That is why some of them are so timely. When Grant vetoed the silver bill, my cartoon was ready almost a week before the veto was known." ["The Pencil's Power: Thomas Nast Talks of His Art," *Evening Journal* (Minneapolis), November 30, 1887.[7]]

1893. Realized a life-long dream with the publication of his own paper, *Nast's Weekly.* Unfortunately, however, the paper never flourished as he had intended it to, and its circulation was short-lived.

1894. Travelled to London at the request of the *Pall Mall Gazette* to draw cartoons.

Although he never completely gave up drawing, the last ten years of Nast's life were mainly devoted to the lecture circuit, where he illustrated his talk with sketches. ". . . I was suffering by nervous prostration brought on by overwork, and my physicians cautioned me to stop. I was occupied in the prep-

22   *NAST'S ALMANAC FOR 1873.*

THE STORY OF THE GOOD LITTLE BOY WHO DID NOT PROSPER.

BY MARK TWAIN.

ONCE there was a good little boy by the name of Jacob Blivens. He always obeyed his parents, no matter how absurd and unreasonable their demands were; and he always learned his book, and never was late at Sabbath-school. He would not play hookey, even when his sober judgment told him it was the most profitable thing he could do. None of the other boys could ever make that boy out, he acted so strangely. He wouldn't lie, no matter how convenient it was. He just said it was wrong to lie, and that was sufficient for him. And he was so honest that he was simply ridiculous. The curious ways that Jacob had surpassed every thing. He wouldn't play at marbles on Sunday, he wouldn't rob birds' nests, he wouldn't give hot pennies to organ-grinders' monkeys; he didn't seem to take any interest in any kind of rational amusement. So the other boys used to try to reason it out, and come to an understanding that Jacob had surpassed every understanding of him, but they couldn't arrive at any satisfactory conc. ion; as I said

(From *Thomas Nast's Illustrated Almanac* [1873], edited and illustrated by Thomas Nast.)

aration of a book and had intended it for publication during the holidays but it will have to go over a year. On my way out [West] several people asked me to lecture at the different places I stopped. Now it has been two years since I have been on the lecture platform, and I had intended to do no work out here, but the requests were so numerous that I began to think about the matter. I went to San Francisco and then came to Denver to see my son, who is engagd in mining at Silverton and to rest, permitting the lecture proposition to take flight. You can imagine my surprise when a friend here suggested that I lecture. 'People would like to see you,' said he, 'and know something about your profession.' I assured him that I did not come to lecture, but there was persistency somewhere, and Manager McCourt followed up with the request that I lecture in the opera house. I consulted with him, and Mr. John McGuire, who manages the North Pacific theatrical circuit, appeared, and the result has been that he and Manager Mc-Court are to manage me during a tour I shall make, extending to the coast...." ["He Makes Pictures," *Omaha Daily World,* November 25, 1887.[8]]

About his lectures, Nast said: "... I shall deliver a dissertation on the things that make people laugh and why they do it. I may devote some attention to English critics who accuse us of being too serious, when the fact is that most of their wit and humor is copied from us. You know there are chestnuts,

and I shouldn't be surprised but what our friends, the paragraphers, might come in for a share of attention. As for caricature, the history may be of interest, and I shall attempt to demonstrate its distinctive features, with probably a little descriptive matter relating to my work. There is a difference between a flattering likeness and caricature, and people always enjoy the latter, if it is not personal. I shall describe some of the Tweed pictures and explain the source of some ideas that come to me in that line and their effects. I will execute a historical subject in oil and show how oil painting is done. Then I may give three or four others...."[9]

1902. Deep in debt from the financial undertaking of his own paper, Nast accepted an appointment from President Theodore Roosevelt as U.S. consul in Guayaquil, Ecuador, serving under trying conditions for six months. The climate was hot and humid, the living conditions miserable, and an epidemic of yellow fever threatened the city. On **December 7,** he succumbed to the fever. "While some call man a laughing animal, others choose to consider him a tool-making animal. Ordinary artists consider him as the delightful creature who buys pictures, but I like best to consider him as the only animal who laughs." ["Thomas Nast," *The Morning Call,* February 28, 1888.[9]]

Nast has often been referred to by historians as the "Father of American Caricature." To honor him, one of the highest summits in Colorado was named Mount Nast. In 1947, Michael Todd and Sigmund Romberg romanticized him in the Broadway operetta, "Up in Central Park." In 1971, Nast's work was resurrected by German journalist Hermann Glessgen. His cartoons began to appear in leading German newspapers and were collected into two touring exhibitions. A German foundation established biennial Thomas Nast prizes to the "Best American" and "Best German" political cartoonists.

FOR MORE INFORMATION SEE: The National Cyclopaedia of American Biography, Volume 7, James T. White, 1892; Albert B. Paine, *Thomas Nast: His Period and His Pictures,* Peter Smith, 1904, reprinted, Chelsea House, 1981; A. B. Paine, *Life and Letters of Thomas Nast,* Harper, 1910; J. Henry Harper, *The House of Harper: A Century of Publishing in Franklin Square,* Harper, 1912; Walter Gutman, "An American Phenomenon," *Creative Art,* September, 1929; *Arts Weekly,* March 18, 1932; William A. Murrel, *A History of American Graphic Humor,* Macmillan, Volume 1, 1933, Volume 2, 1938; Frank Weitenkampf, "Thomas Nast—Artist in Caricature," *Bulletin of the New York Public Library,* Volume 37, 1933; *The American Scholar,* Volume III, United Chapters of Phi Beta Kappa, 1934; Nancy Veglahn, *The Tiger's Tail: A Story of America's Great Political Cartoonist, Thomas Nast* (juvenile), Harper, 1964; Dieter Cunz, *They Came from Germany* (juvenile), Dodd, 1966; John C. Vinson, *Thomas Nast, Political Cartoonist,* University of Georgia Press, 1967; Morton Keller, *The Art and Politics of Thomas Nast,* Oxford University Press, 1968; R. A. Sokolov, "Nast's World," *Newsweek,* May 6, 1968; Albert Boime, "Thomas Nast and French Art," *American Art Journal,* spring, 1972; *McGraw-Hill Encyclopedia of World Biography,* McGraw, 1973; Larry Freeman, "Nast, Prang and St. Nicholas," *Hobbies,* December, 1973; Thomas Nast St. Hill, editor, *Thomas Nast: Cartoons and Illustrations,* Dover, 1974; J. Culhane, "Cartoon Killers Thrive Again," *New York Times Magazine,* November 9, 1975; M. Evans, "Thomas Nast, Ringmaster," *American Opinion,* February, 1977; S. Hoff, *Boss Tweed and the Man Who Drew Him* (juvenile), Coward, 1978; A. Levy, "Thomas Nast's Triumphant Return to German," *Art News,* March, 1979; *The World Encyclopedia of Cartoons,* Chelsea House, 1980.

PAPERNY, Myra (Green) 1932-

PERSONAL: Born September 19, 1932, in Edmonton, Alberta, Canada; daughter of Michael (a businessman) and Jessie (Cohen) Green; married Maurice Paperny (a businessman), July 5, 1954; children: Marina, David, Cathy, Lorne. *Education:* University of British Columbia, B.A., 1953; Columbia University, M.Sc., 1954. *Religion:* Jewish. *Home and office:* 1224 Riverdale Ave. S.W., Calgary, Alberta, Canada T2S 0Y8.

CAREER: Vancouver Province, Vancouver, British Columbia, Canada, reporter, 1952; *Vancouver News Herald,* Vancouver, reporter, 1953; Mount Royal College, Calgary, Alberta, Canada, instructor of creative writing, 1965-66; University of Calgary, Alberta, lecturer in creative writing, 1966-75. Has worked in public relations. Member of board of Calgary Region Arts Foundation, 1977—. National vice-president of National Council of Jewish Women, 1971-73. *Member:* Alberta Authors Association. *Awards, honors:* Little, Brown Canadian Children's Book Award, and achievement award from Province of Alberta, both 1975, and Canada Council Award for children's literature, 1976, all for *The Wooden People.*

WRITINGS: The Wooden People (juvenile; illustrated by Ken Sampnick), Little, Brown, 1976. Editor of *Councilwoman,* 1970-73.

"Suzanne, I told you not to stick your tongue on things like frozen pumps...." ■ (From *The Wooden People* by Myra Paperny. Illustrated by Ken Stampnick.)

WORK IN PROGRESS: Take One Giant Step, a juvenile novel; *Second Go-Around,* an adult novel; stories.

SIDELIGHTS: Paperny believes that "children are the most sensitive and critical of readers," and tries "to communicate with them honestly and in depth."

FOR MORE INFORMATION SEE: Quill and Quire, January, 1977; Jacqueline Hunt, "*The Wooden People* as Introduction to Literary Study," *Canadian Children's Literature,* number 10, 1978; Susan Anderson, "Myra Paperny," *Profiles 2,* Canadian Library Association, 1982.

PASCAL, Francine 1938-

PERSONAL: Born May 13, 1938, in New York, N.Y.; married John Robert Pascal (a journalist and author; died, 1981); children: Laurie, Susan, Jamie (daughter). *Education:* Attended New York University. *Residence:* New York, N.Y. and France.

CAREER: Writer and lecturer. *Member:* PEN, Dramatist's Guild. *Awards, honors: Hangin' Out with Cici* was listed in the New York Public Library's Books for the Teenage, 1978-85; *My First Love and Other Disasters* was named a Best Book for Young Adults by the American Library Association, 1979; Dorothy Canfield Fisher Children's Book Award from the Vermont Congress of Parents and Teachers, and *Publishers Weekly*'s Literary Prize list, both 1982, both for *The Hand-Me-Down Kid.*

WRITINGS—Young adult novels, except as noted: (With husband, John Pascal) *The Strange Case of Patty Hearst* (adult nonfiction), New American Library, 1974; *Hangin' Out with Cici,* Viking, 1977, paperback edition published as *Hangin' Out with Cici; or, My Mother Was Never a Kid,* Dell, 1985; *My First Love and Other Disasters,* Viking, 1979; *The Hand-Me-Down Kid,* Viking, 1980; *Save Johanna!* (adult novel), Morrow, 1981; *Love and Betrayal and Hold the Mayo!* (sequel to *My First Love and Other Disasters*), Viking, 1985.

"Sweet Valley High" series; creator; novels for young adults; published by Bantam: *Double Love,* 1984; *Secrets,* 1984; *Playing with Fire,* 1984; *Power Play,* 1984; *All Night Long,* 1984; *Dangerous Love,* 1984; *Dear Sister,* 1984; *Heartbreaker,* 1984; *Racing Hearts,* 1984; *Wrong Kind of Girl,* 1984; *Too Good to Be True,* 1984; *When Love Dies,* 1984; *Kidnapped!,* 1984; *Deceptions,* 1984; *Promises,* 1985; *Rags to Riches,* 1985; *Love Letters,* 1985; *Head over Heels,* 1985; *Showdown,* 1985; *Crash Landing,* 1985; *Runaway,* 1985; *Too Much in Love,* 1986; *Say Goodbye,* 1986; *Memories,* 1986; *Nowhere to Run,* 1986; *Hostage!,* 1986; *Lovestruck,* 1986; *Alone in the Crowd,* 1986; *Bitter Rivals,* 1986; *Jealous Lies,* 1986; *Taking Sides,* 1986; *The New Jessica,* 1986; *Starting Over,* 1987; *Forbidden Love,* 1987; *Out of Control,* 1987; *Last Chance,* 1987; *Rumors,* 1987; *Leaving Home,* 1987; *Secret Admirer,* 1987.

"Sweet Valley High Super Editions"; creator; all published by Bantam: *Perfect Summer,* 1985; *Malibu Summer,* 1986; *Special Christmas,* 1986; *Spring Break,* 1986; *Spring Fever,* 1987; *Winter Carnival,* 1987.

"Sweet Valley Twins" series; creator; all published by Bantam: *Best Friends,* 1986; *Teacher's Pet,* 1986; *The Haunted House,* 1986; *Choosing Sides,* 1986; *Sneaking Out,* 1987; *The New Girl,* 1987; *Three's a Crowd,* 1987; *First Place,* 1987; *Against the Rules,* 1987; *One of the Gang,* 1987; *Buried Trea-*

sure, 1987; *Keeping Secrets,* 1987; *Stretching the Truth,* 1987; *Tug of War,* 1987.

"Caitlin" series; creator; novels for young adults; all published by Bantam: "The Love Trilogy," Volume 1: *Loving,* 1986; Volume 2: *Love Lost,* 1986; Volume 3: *True Love,* 1986; "The Promise Trilogy," Volume 1: *Tender Promises,* 1986; Volume 2: *Promises Broken,* 1986; Volume 3: *A New Promise,* 1987; "The Forever Trilogy," Volume 1: *Dreams of Forever,* 1987; Volume 2: *Forever and Always,* 1987; Volume 3: *Together Forever,* 1987.

Co-author with J. Pascal and Michael Stewart of script for musical "George M!," first produced on Broadway, April 10, 1968, adapted for television with J. Pascal, ninety-minute special, NBC-TV, September 12, 1970. Creator for television of "The See-Through-Kids,"a live-action family series. Also adapter of television scripts; co-writer with J. Pascal of television scripts for soap opera serial "The Young Marrieds," ABC-TV; past contributor of humor, nonfiction, and travel articles to *True Confessions, Modern Screen, Ladies' Home Journal* and *Cosmopolitan.*

ADAPTATIONS—Television: "My Mother Was Never a Kid" (Afterschool Special; based on *Hangin' Out with Cici*), ABC-TV; "The Hand-Me-Down Kid," ABC-TV, October 5, 1983.

WORK IN PROGRESS: "As usual, I have a number of projects going. Each month, I do two plot outlines—one for my *Sweet Valley High* series, the other for *Sweet Valley Twins.* I'm also working on a novel and have an idea for a screenplay."

SIDELIGHTS: "When I was about five, my parents moved from Manhattan, where I was born, to Jamaica, Queens. The neighborhood we lived in was essentially the one in which Cici of *Hangin' Out with Cici* grew up. The houses had yards, and it was safe enough for kids to play unattended in the street. If it wasn't for the subway station on the corner, it would almost have been like living in a small town. In fact, back then, when people moved to Jamaica, they said they were 'going to the country.'

FRANCINE PASCAL

(Cover illustration by James Mathewuse from *Winter Carnival* by Kate William. Created by Francine Pascal.)

"Like Cici, I adored movies and went to the cinema every Saturday for the afternoon double feature with my friends. It was always exciting, because it was the one place kids could go to on their own. I also loved reading comic books—*Sheena of the Jungle,* and other high adventure series. Fairy tales were another passion. There was virtually no 'young adult' literature, so I read the classics—Stendhal's *The Red and the Black,* a favorite, along with Jane Austen, the Brontës, and other nineteenth-century masterpieces.

"I began to write poetry when I was about eight. My oldest brother, Michael Stewart, grew up to be a very successful playwright with such theater pieces as *Hello, Dolly!, Forty-Second Street, Bye-Bye Birdie* to his credit. He began writing at an early age and was the first in our family to do so. Writing in general, and my brother's in particular, was taken very seriously. Mine was not, at least not within the family. In school, however, and among my friends, I was recognized as a poet, and this was extremely important to me. One of my earliest efforts was a long lyric poem on Ulysses. I remember reading it aloud—it seemed to go on for pages and pages—and feeling so proud that my teacher and classmates were impressed and pleased. I also liked writing plays, casting and directing my friends for everyone in the neighborhood.

"I was not at all pleased to be a girl, for I realized early on that it was a man's world (the Women's Movement in the 1960s greatly improved my attitude toward being a woman).

(From the movie "My Mother Was Never a Kid," presented as an Afterschool Special on
ABC-TV, 1981. Photograph courtesy of Learning Corporation of America.)

I feel like I'm all alone and Elizabeth is an army. ■ (From *The Hand-Me-Down Kid* by Francine Pascal. Photograph from the movie adaptation. Produced by Learning Corporation of America, 1983.)

Growing up, most of my friends were boys. I felt demeaned when I was counted in with the girls. My mother, a traditional homemaker, is a wonderful woman, but I identified almost entirely with my father. I admired his intelligence, his sense of humor, his being out in the world. I, too, wanted to be 'out in the world.'

"In fact, I wanted to save the world. By the time I was fifteen, I was a passionate communist, a position I would later rethink, believing at the time that that form of government would solve all our problems. I had gotten hold of a book by the 'Red Dean' of Canterbury, which became a Bible for me. This made me something of a curiosity, and I can remember my parents, who were liberal Jews, inviting me down to their get-togethers to explain my ideas to their friends. They probably thought I was 'quaint' or something, but I think my parents were a little proud that I was so idealistic.

"I absolutely hated high school. Learning by rote made the whole system repressive. I couldn't wait to go to college. I went to NYU [New York University] during the days when Washington Square Park was filled with poets and musicians. Greenwich Village then was very 'beat,' and there was lots of activity in the coffeehouses. It was wonderful, everything I had dreamed it would be. I was writing poetry and felt very much a part of it all.

"I married a newspaperman, John Pascal, who wrote for the *Herald Tribune,* the *New York Times,* and *Newsday,* among other publications. He was an excellent writer, and in many ways my mentor. He loved everything I wrote and encouraged me unceasingly.

"I began my writing career with articles for *True Confessions* and *Modern Screen.* My first assignment for *Modern Screen* was a fictionalized story about Connie Francis' wedding and a touching, tear-jerking scene between her and her father in the chapel before the ceremony. The article was very flattering, so there was no danger of being sued, and besides, no one really *believes* anything they read in those magazines. From there, I graduated to such magazines as *Ladies' Home Journal* and *Cosmopolitan.* This was okay, but not really what I wanted. I've never really enjoyed writing nonfiction, and was beginning to feel locked into that genre.

"In 1965, my husband and I became second writers on a soap opera 'The Young Marrieds.' As second writers, we'd be given a situation by the head writer—today Amelia tells George she is pregnant and is leaving him for his best friend. Something like that. My husband would write the male dialogue, I the female. It was easy work. The only difficult part was having to watch the show every day. This was the 'old days' of the soaps when you weren't allowed to say the word *pregnancy* more than once in a single episode, and where the heroine couldn't smoke or drink. Nineteen sixty-eight was the year of dramatic change, including soaps. We stayed with the show until it moved to California, a move we were unwilling to make.

"My husband and I had always been attracted to the theatre and wrote a number of plays together. With my brother, we wrote the book for *George M!,* which turned out to be a hit on Broadway. But theatre is very scary. You can work on a play for two years, maybe more, during which time you're not being paid a dime, knowing that a show can open and close on the same night. At least with a book, even if it gets panned, it still exists. No one marches into the bookstores and removes it from the shelves.

"In 1974, my husband was sent to San Francisco to cover the Patty Hearst trial. Hungry writers that we were, we thought, 'Gee, maybe we can get a book out of this.' And indeed we did. *The Strange Case of Patty Hearst* was the first book to come out on the trial. The publisher gave us only thirty days to write it. We submitted the completed manuscript in twenty-nine. We had newspaper clippings all over the dining room. We set up one table for source material and another for writing. The editor stopped by every five days and collected a chapter or two. I think if we hadn't had pages ready, he would have taken one of our children for ransom! We worked around the clock, smoked a billion cigarettes, and lived on adrenalin. It was great fun, although I don't think I'd want to do that kind of book again.

"I was lying in bed early one morning, musing over my two favorite words, 'what if.' And it came to me. What if a thirteen-year-old girl who didn't like her mother went back in time and became her mother's best friend? I woke my husband, who immediately thought I was on to something. He encouraged me to sit right down and begin writing. I had no idea at that point what 'young adult' novels or books for the 'middle-aged child' [eight to twelve] were. I had also never written a novel. But I plunged in and 144 pages later, I knew it was time to send the book to an agent. I had been told there were three agents I should approach. Naively, I sent them each a copy of the manuscript, never occurring to me that all three wanted to take it on, which proved to be extremely awkward. *Hangin' Out with Cici* was sold within two weeks and did extremely well. It was made into a TV movie called 'My Mother Was Never a Kid' and was named on the New York Public Library's Books for the Teenage honor list, which made me very proud." Critics praised the novel for its handling of mother/daughter conflict and reconciliation and for its innovative time-travel structure.

Pascal's next novel, *My First Love and Other Disasters,* named a Best Book for Young Adults by the American Library Association, centers on fifteen-year-old Vicky, who convinces her parents to let her take a job on Fire Island so she can spend the summer near her boyfriends. "It was gratifying that the novel was praised for the way it deals with teenage sex. I didn't try to be coy or sensational, but rather tried to express the delicacy, the awkwardness, the fear and exhilaration that make falling in love so complicated—at once happy and painful."

In *The Hand-Me-Down Kid,* Pascal takes on the difficulties of surviving childhood and adolescence in New York City. Ari Jacobs, the eleven-year-old protagonist who without a second's hesitation can defend a homeless person from abuse by neighborhood punks, has trouble sticking up for herself. Her older brother and sister always seem able to bend her to their will, and she is prey to bullies and manipulators at school. "It's a book about learning to be independent and about recognizing that true strength is not expressed violently.

"My books have generally been well received, not only by critics and library associations, but by kids. The awards that mean the most to me are those voted by kids themselves. That said, I should mention that a couple of my books have been censored in a few places. *Hangin' Out with Cici* was removed from the shelves in a number of libraries, I guess, because there is pot-smoking at the beginning of the book and candor throughout about sex and general open-mindedness. *The Hand-Me-Down Kid* was banned from a classroom by a teacher in Georgia, who had all of her students write me obviously dictated letters of harsh criticism. That a teacher could impose a point of view on her students and force them to act on it

THE HAND-ME-DOWN KID

Francine Pascal

I would like to look like Elizabeth when I grow up but I don't think I ever will. . . . I look more like my brother Neddy. . . . ■ (Jacket illustration by Martha Perske from *The Hand-Me-Down Kid* by Francine Pascal.)

horrified me beyond words. I wrote back to each child, but as I had to send the letters in care of the teacher, I don't know if they were passed on. I suspect not, since I received no responses. The fact that Ari's older sister has a boyfriend who is Puerto Rican is what I believe riled that narrow-minded teacher. Fortunately, each time one of my books has been removed from libraries or schools, a community group has intervened. I belong to PEN, the international writers organization, which keeps a close eye on censorship, but still masterpieces like *Huckleberry Finn* are banned in some places, which is maddening.''

Pascal's ''Sweet Valley High'' and ''Sweet Valley Twins'' series have sold almost twenty million copies, have been translated into twelve languages and were the first young adult novels to make *New York Times* bestseller list. ''These books are romances in the classic sense. They deal with the ideals of love, honor, friendship, sacrifice, which account for their popularity. Adolescents are at a unique stage in their lives. They're terribly idealistic and on the brink of the adult world where they will be confronted with the trendiness, consumerism and other pressures that impinge on idealism. Because these books sell in the millions, I feel a tremendous responsibility. Teenagers are always asking themselves the difficult questions that adults often shuffle past. 'Am I doing the right thing?' preoccupies them. To a much higher degree than adults, teenagers consciously strive to be ethical. They deserve novels that recognize and applaud this. I tend to reward characters who make and act on idealistic, rather than opportunistic, choices.

''I've gotten many, many letters from kids who say that they had never been readers before the 'Sweet Valley' series. If my books have 'hooked' them on reading, that's important. It means they'll go on and read other things and become readers for the rest of their lives. I was pleased when I learned that these series were being used in literacy programs in various parts around the country.

''Every month a book is published in each series. I do all the plot outlines, descriptions of characters, time, setting, and so forth. We have a stable of authors who generally do one title every three months. I maintain artistic control over every aspect of these novels. I may not write every word, but they are very much mine.

''When I'm working on my own novels, I write four pages a day—not three, not five. I do not copyedit my pages until the next morning. After copyediting, I start in on my four pages for that day. At the end, of course, I copyedit again and usually do rewrites. I also revise as I write, knowing that I may well re-do them later. I try each day to make those four pages perfect. I recently bought a computer, an innovation I had resisted for several years. It may well be the biggest advance in writing since writing began. It makes revisions a snap, and the whole process of writing more fluid. You can move whole sections just by pressing a key; you never feel uncomfortably 'locked in.'''

When she is not writing, Pascal likes to read. ''Anne Tyler and Alice Munro are among my favorites on the contemporary scene. I like Elmore Leonard, as well. I also like going to plays and films. And for years, now, I've played in a weekly poker game with a group of writer friends, most of whom are journalists.''

When asked if she had any advice for aspiring writers, Pascal added, ''Yes. One word, repeated three times: *Write, Write,*

Write. It's the only way to learn your craft. If you've got talent but are undisciplined, you may as well not have talent.''

—*Based on an interview by Marguerite Feitlowitz*

PIERCE, Tamora 1954-

PERSONAL: Given name is pronounced *Tam*-a-ra; born December 13, 1954, in Connellsville, Pa.; daughter of Wayne Franklin and Jacqueline S. Pierce. *Education:* University of Pennsylvania, B.A., 1976. *Home and office:* 212 West 91st St., #720, New York, N.Y. 10024. *Agent:* Claire M. Smith, Harold Ober Associates, Inc., 40 East 49th St., New York, N.Y. 10017.

CAREER: City of Kingston, N.Y., tax data collector, 1977-78; Towns of Hardenburgh and Denning, N.Y., tax clerk, 1978; McAuley Home for Girls, Buhl, Idaho, social worker and housemother, 1978-79; Harold Ober Associates, Inc., New York, N.Y., assistant to literary agent, 1979-82; creative director of ZPPR Productions, Inc. (radio producers), 1982-86; Chase Investment Bank, New York, N.Y., secretary, 1985—.

WRITINGS: Alanna: The First Adventure (fantasy novel), Atheneum, 1983; *In the Hand of the Goddess* (fantasy novel), Atheneum, 1984; (contributor) Steve Ditlea, editor, *Digital Deli,* Workman Publishing, 1984; (contributor) Douglas Hill, editor, *Planetfall,* Oxford University Press, 1985; *The Woman Who Rides Like a Man* (fantasy novel), Atheneum, 1986; *Li-*

TAMORA PIERCE

oness Rampant, Atheneum, 1988. Also author of radio scripts aired on National Public Radio, 1987—. Contributor to periodicals, including *Christian Century.* Editor of *OpenSpace,* 1978-79.

WORK IN PROGRESS: Home Is Where the Runt Is, a young adult fantasy novel; *Architect of Rage,* an adult novel about "the radicals of the 1960s, Vietnam, the fugitive underground, and an unusual woman in an unusual time," completion expected in 1988; radio plays for National Public Radio on such subjects as the occult, child abuse, and science fiction satire.

SIDELIGHTS: "I owe my career as a writer and my approach to writing to people like my writing mentor, David Bradley, who taught me that writing is not an arcane and mystical process, administered by the initiate and fraught with obstacles, but an enjoyable pastime that gives other people as much pleasure as it does me. I enjoy telling stories, and, although some of my topics are grim, people get caught up in the stories.

"I have a number of research topics that I use in ongoing work or that I plan to deal with in the future. I am interested in medieval customs and chivalry. I am a former instructor in the history of witchcraft at the University of Pennsylvania's Free Woman's University, and I write about the occult. I study Japanese history and culture; martial arts cinema; film (writing, production, and popular film); history of the sixties and seventies; terrorism; and the history of Hungary, Wallachia, and the Ottoman Empire in the 1400s and 1500s. I worked as a psychiatric research assistant at the University of Pennsylvania Hospital and as a student social worker with the public defender of the Philadelphia Juvenile Court, and I am interested in social work, psychiatry, and psychology. I also write about radio history and production, management, and folklore.

"Like all writers, I hate to be misunderstood. Why go to the trouble of putting something down in black and white, revising repeatedly, unless you want to avoid all misunderstanding? I like talking to people who want to write and giving them as much help as possible. I remember what it was like to begin, and I had no one at that time to give me a hand.

"I have traveled all over the continental United States, but I have never been outside its mainland borders, and I would give my eyeteeth to go abroad. As soon as it is humanly possible, I plan to make a grand tour of Europe and Japan, seeing the places I've read about for so many years.

"As a social worker I burned out, but my interest in social work—particularly in the problems faced by teenagers—continues. I enjoy writing for teenagers, because I feel I help to make life easier for kids who are like I was."

POWELL, Ann   1951-

BRIEF ENTRY: Born May 25, 1951. Powell lives in Toronto, Ontario, Canada. Illustrator and puppeteer. Powell's parents met at art school; her mother is a painter and her father is a sometime cartoonist. His professional career was the British Army, and he took the family on assignments all over the world. Powell spent many years in English boarding schools before her family settled in Canada in 1968. Afer graduating from the Ontario College of Art in 1974, she spent the following year as a visiting artist in Canada's public schools. Her illustrations first appeared in *The Travels of Ms. Beaver* (Women's Press, 1973), by Rosemary Allison, the first in a trilogy about Ms. Beaver, "obviously a mover and shaker by

nature," observed *Canadian Children's Literature.* The other titles in the series are *Ms. Beaver Travels East* (1978) and *Ms. Beaver Goes West* (1982). Since the first book, Powell has continued her association with Women's Press, and has published, among other books, *Overnight Adventure* (1977) and *The Recyclers* (1979), both written by Frances Kilbourne, and *My Grandma the Monster* (1985), by Ascher Davis.

Jennie Greenteeth (Rhino Books, 1981), by Mary Alice Downie, is a clever tale about a witch who eats candy and never brushes her teeth, and whose favorite activity is pushing children into the river. "The illustrations and text are skillfully intertwined," wrote *Canadian Children's Literature.* "The modest sketches leave enough to the imagination, but provide adequate detail." Powell received a Citation of Excellence with her puppeteering brother at the 1978 Union Internationale de la Marionnette, and the Marguerite Bagshaw Award from the Toronto Public Library, also for puppeteering. She demonstrated puppetry at the Science Centre in Toronto for the "In Praise of Hands" exhibition in 1974, made a puppet film in 1973, "Cardinal Knowledge," and has commissioned puppets for various agencies in Canada. In addition, she and her brother present puppet shows throughout Toronto as the Puppetmongers Powell. *Residence:* Toronto, Ontario, Canada.

FOR MORE INFORMATION SEE: Profiles 2, Canadian Library Association, 1982.

PROVENSEN, Martin (Elias)   1916-1987

OBITUARY NOTICE—See sketch in *SATA* Volume 9: Born July 10, 1916, in Chicago, Ill.; died of a heart attack, March 27, 1987, in Clinton Corners, N.Y. Illustrator and author. Provensen and his wife, Alice, spent more than forty years creating scores of books for children. Noted for its originality and excellence in design, the Provensens' critically acclaimed work won numerous awards, including a 1984 Caldecott Medal for *The Glorious Flight: Across the Channel with Louis Bleriot.* Among the diverse range of titles also published by the Provensens are *Karen's Curiosity; The Year at Maple Hill Farm; A Peaceable Kingdom; Iliad and Odyssey,* adapted by Jane Werner Watson; *Shakespeare: Ten Great Plays,* edited by George Wolfson; the classic *Fireside Book of Folksongs;* and a child's version of the Bible. Prior to teaming up with his wife in 1946, Provensen worked in the story department at Walt Disney Studios from 1938 to 1942.

FOR MORE INFORMATION SEE: Contemporary Authors, New Revisions Series, Volume 5, Gale, 1982; *Children's Literature Review,* Volume 11, Gale, 1986; *Who's Who in America,* 44th edition, Marquis, 1986. Obituaries: *New York Times,* March 30, 1987; *Publishers Weekly,* April 10, 1987; *School Library Journal,* May, 1987.

RINALDI, Ann   1934-

PERSONAL: Born August 27, 1934, in New York, N.Y.; daughter of Michael (a newspaperman) and Marcella (Dumarest) Feis; married Ronald P. Rinaldi (a lineman), July, 1960; children: Ronald P., Jr., Marcella. *Education:* Attended high school in New Brunswick, N.J. *Home:* 302 Miller Ave., Somerville, N.J. 08876. *Office: Trentonian,* 600 Perry St., Trenton, N.J. 08602.

CAREER: Writer. *Somerset Messenger Gazette,* Somerset, N.J., author of column, 1969-70; *Trentonian,* Trenton, N.J., feature

ANN RINALDI

writer and author of column, 1970—. Member of Brigade of the American Revolution. *Awards, honors:* New Jersey Press Awards from the New Jersey Press Association, first place, 1978, and several second place awards in subsequent years, all for newspaper columns; *But in the Fall I'm Leaving* was selected a Notable Children's Trade Book in the Field of Social Studies by the joint committee of the National Council for Social Studies and the Children's Book Council, 1985; *Time Enough for Drums* was selected one of American Library Association's Best Books for Young Adults, 1986.

WRITINGS—Young adult novels: *Term Paper*, Walker & Co., 1980; *Promises Are for Keeping* (sequel to *Term Paper*), Walker & Co., 1982; *But in the Fall I'm Leaving*, Holiday House, 1985; *Time Enough for Drums* (Junior Literary Guild selection), Holiday House, 1986; *The Good Side of My Heart*, Holiday House, 1987; *The Last Silk Dress*, Holiday House, 1988. Contributor of columns and editorials to the *Trentonian*.

SIDELIGHTS: "I was my mother's fifth child, and she died right after I was born. For two years I lived in Brooklyn with an aunt and uncle who wanted to adopt me. In the household were a lot of older teenage cousins who pampered and spoiled me, but my father came one day and took me home abruptly. The only happy part of my childhood ended.

"I was taken to New Jersey to live with my real siblings and a stepmother. My father—a newspaperman in the golden age of newspapers—did everything he could to prevent me from becoming a writer. At school they attempted to take out of me what spirit had eluded my stepmother. My father did not believe in college for his daughters, so I was sent into the business world to become a secretary. I kicked around in the typing pool until marriage to my husband, Ron, in 1960.

"Ron was middle-class and sane. I wanted sanity after my crazy upbringing. After marriage and two wonderful children,

I started to write. Previously I'd only written poetry, but now I wanted to be a novelist. I wrote four full-length novels which were terrible. Then, in 1969, I approached my weekly newspaper, the Somerset *Messenger Gazette,* for a weekly column. The editor gave it to me. I earned seven dollars a week, but I was writing! I proceeded to syndicate my column to various weekly newspapers in New Jersey. The children were now six and eight. Then, one day in 1970, I called the *Trentonian* newspaper, a daily, and got an editor on the phone who said, 'Come in and talk to me.'"

"... I was hired ... to write two columns a week. Within a couple of years I was writing features and soft news as well as columns, and learning the newspaper business. In 1978 my column won first place in the New Jersey Press Awards. In 1979, with two teen-agers in high school and a full-time job as a newspaperwoman, I reworked at night the ten-thousand-word short story I'd worked on so painstakingly for years. My experience in the newspaper business and as a parent gave me so much more to bring to my fiction. The first publisher to read it, bought it.

"I wrote [*Term Paper*] because the characters had been part of me for years. Most of the motivation came from my own life. Family relationships, especially the tremendous influence older siblings have over younger ones, have always intrigued me. The overall theme of the novel is love and forgiveness. I

Let's face it; having your own brother for a teacher... does not give you very much room to move around. ■
(Jacket illustration from *Term Paper* by Ann Rinaldi.)

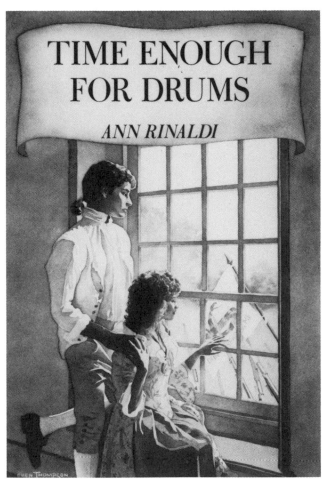

It was as if our quarrel had never happened. ■ (Jacket illustration by Ellen Thompson from *Time Enough for Drums* by Ann Rinaldi.)

think I have answered, for young Nicki in my book, some of the questions I have not been able to answer yet for myself in my own life.'' [*Library Journal*, October, 1980.]

''My good friend was writing for young adults and succeeding very well, and I realized that what I had was a young adult novel. I hadn't written it for young people. It was a story with a fourteen-year-old protagonist. But I never knew how to market it. So I turned it into a novel, it sold, then I wrote the second one. *Promises Are for Keeping* is a sequel.''

Family involvement in American Revolution re-enactment groups led to the novel *Time Enough for Dreams*. ''My son was always interested in American history and the bicentennial was going on. Through my newspaper coverage of bicentennial events in Trenton and Princeton, he became involved in the American Revolution. He joined a local re-enactment group and crossed the river on Christmas Day with 'Washington.' Then my daughter joined and we started following them all over the East to living history re-enactments of the Revolutionary War. My son dragged us to every battlefield, monument, fort, and battleground, north and south, from Saratoga to Yorktown. I began to see the history of my country as it was, from the bottom up, hands on, instead of out of a history book. When we returned, in 1981, from the re-enactment of the British surrender at Yorktown, where we'd met four thousand other re-enactment troops like ourselves from all over the country, I couldn't forget it. Over the years we'd made the food of the era, learned the crafts and lifestyle, the dances and

songs. Yorktown was very much with me that day in October, 1981, when I went to cover the story of the re-enactment of the day Trenton received word of the victory there. And it was then that I realized I was going to write a young adult novel on the American Revolution. A good one. Not one utilizing all the myths and the famous figures. I would do it on Trenton, because I knew the town, I went there every day.

''I did it, the research and all, in a year. I stole off to the library at noon or before work. I used my historical re-enactments as constant research and stimulation for my work. I found out there was a thriving community in Trenton at the time. Using fictional characters, I created a story about a family that came through the war and the Hessian occupation of the town, but all the people I researched from the era I also used in my book. I finished the book in little over a year. Before it was published it was rejected by ten publishers who wouldn't touch it because it was history. And it is a known fact in the young adult world that you don't give children history.

''*Time Enough for Drums* is close to my heart, my favorite—the one everyone told me not to write! I went against the grain of what everybody told me, but then, that's what I did in my lifetime, too, and thankfully, I succeeded.

''I write young adult novels because I like writing them. But, as with my first book, I don't write for young people. I just write. Real life, as I know it, as I've learned it to be from my newspaper experience and own past, goes into my books. I draw all my characters fully, give my adults as many problems and as much dimension as the young protagonist. I give my readers good writing, literary writing. My books have been praised for the strength of my characters and my dialogue. I believe there are only about four good writers of young adult novels on the market. I am the fifth.''

HOBBIES AND OTHER INTERESTS: Historical re-enactments, reading, writing, and studying American history.

FOR MORE INFORMATION SEE: Library Journal, October, 1980.

ROOT, Shelton L., Jr. 1923-1986

OBITUARY NOTICE: Born August 1, 1923, in Berea, Ohio; died November 12, 1986. Educator, writer, and editor. A leader in educational reading for children, Root compiled a number of juvenile anthologies, including *The Arbuthnot Anthology of Children's Literature* and *Adventuring with Books*. He was also the author of *Doing Choral Speaking* and co-author of both *Time for Poetry* and *Ideas in Literature,* as well as a contributor to the *Encyclopedia of Education* and *Using Literature with Young Children.* Root's teaching career spanned more than two decades, during which time he was an instructor in education and a professor of children's literature. He also founded the Children's Literature Conference and the Georgia Book Award Program at the University of Georgia where he taught.

FOR MORE INFORMATION SEE: Leaders in Education, 5th edition, R. R. Bowker, 1974. Obituaries: *School Library Journal,* February, 1987.

I read forever and am determined to sacrifice my eyes like John Milton rather than give up the amusement without which I should despair.

—John Adams

ROSS, Wilda   1915-

PERSONAL: Born October 23, 1915, in Santa Barbara, Calif.; married Edward S. Ross, 1942 (divorced, 1971); children: Martha Ross Gauthier, Clark. *Education:* University of California, Berkeley, A.B., 1941. *Home:* 328 Las Casitas Court, Sonoma, Calif. 95476.

CAREER: Technician for Bureau of Insect Identification, Washington, D.C. Developed natural history programs for schools and junior museums. *Member:* Sierra Club, Audubon Society, California Native Plant Society (local co-founder). *Awards, honors:* Golden Junior Literary Guild award, for *Can You Find the Animal?*

WRITINGS—All for children: *Who Lives in This Log?*, Coward, 1971; *What Did Dinosaurs Eat?*, Coward, 1972; *Can You Find the Animal?*, Coward, 1974; *Cracks and Crannies: What Lives There?*, Coward, 1975; *The Rain Forest: What Lives There?*, Coward, 1977. Editor of local newsletter of California Native Plant Society.

WORK IN PROGRESS: A children's book about tigers born in an animal park.

SIDELIGHTS: "Since children have more to learn now, why not get them started as they learn to read? My experience with young children interested in insects and plants convinces me that they can understand scientific ideas if this information is stated in simple terms. That is what I try to do.

"A childhood need to be involved in a natural environment is still with me and this feeling is what I want to share with my readers. I grew up in Santa Barbara, California. There we had sort of compression of life zones, from rugged mountains and hills, to plains and seashore, all in a relatively short distance. At age seven I invaded the ocean and taught myself to swim. A new enchanting world was now open to me. Beachcombing and snorkeling are still favorite pastimes.

"I am presently establishing a garden of native plants used by California Indians and *padres* at Sonoma Mission. I have traveled on all the continents, collecting insects for a museum, with self-contained research expeditions."

FOR MORE INFORMATION SEE: Martha E. Ward and Dorothy A. Marquardt, *Authors of Books for Young People*, supplement to the 2nd edition, Scarecrow, 1979.

ROY, Jessie Hailstalk   1895-1986

OBITUARY NOTICE: Born October 29, 1895, in Warrenton, Va.; died of pneumonia and congestive heart failure, December 29, 1986, in Washington, D.C. Educator and author. Roy was a teacher in the Washington, D.C., public schools for twenty-five years before retiring in 1961. She was a member of the American Association of University Women and a founding member of an Alpha Kappa Alpha sorority chapter. Roy co-wrote *Word Pictures of the Great*, 2nd edition, profiles of twenty-eight famous black Americans, and *Pioneers of Long Ago* with Geneva Turner, and was co-editor with G. Turner of *The Negro in Print*, a bibliographical survey. Roy and Turner also wrote books for black elementary school children.

FOR MORE INFORMATION SEE: In Black and White, 3rd edition, Gale, 1980; *Who's Who Among Black Americans*, 4th edition, Who's Who Among Black Americans, 1985. Obituaries: *Washington Post*, December 31, 1986.

SACHS, Judith   1947-
(Emily Chase, Petra Diamond, Rebecca Diamond, Jocelyn Saal, Jennifer Sarasin, Antonia Saxon)

BRIEF ENTRY: Born February 13, 1947, in New York, N.Y. After graduating from Brandeis University in 1968, Sachs became an associate editor for the *Saturday Review Press* in New York and held successive editorial positions at other publishing houses until 1979, when she began free-lance writing full-time. She has published more than twenty juvenile and adult romance novels under various pseudonyms, and said that the inspiration for her young adult works come from her own teenage struggles. "My teenage years, I think, were the most formative—the adolescents I write about are often parts of me, struggling to find out how to become an adult," she said. Sachs' other writing includes two screenplays, co-written with Anthony Bruno for the American Automobile Association's teenage driver education program, articles for magazines, and ghost-writing.

Sachs' romance novels for young adults include *Dance of Love* and *Trusting Hearts* for Bantam's "Sweet Dreams" series under the pseudonym Jocelyn Saal; *Splitting, Cheating,* and *Taking Over* for Scholastic's "Cheerleader" series under Jennifer Sarasin; *The Big Crush* and *With Friends Like That* for Scholastic's "Canby Hall" series under Emily Chase; and *Summer Romance* for Silhouette's "First Love" series under Rebecca Diamond. Her adult romance novels are written under Antonia Saxon and Petra Diamond. Sachs is presently working on *Rites of Spring*, about a family of doctors in Romania and New York from 1906 to 1952. *Home:* 404 Burd St., Pennington, N.J. 08534.

SANDAK, Cass R(obert)   1950-

PERSONAL: Born May 4, 1950, in Johnstown, Pa.; son of Casimer (an engineering designer) and Pauline (a retailer and buyer; maiden name, Skvarna) Sandak. *Education:* Union College, Schenectady, N.Y., B.A. (summa cum laude), 1972; University of Pennsylvania, graduate study, 1972-73. *Religion:* Episcopalian. *Home:* 145 Seeley St., Scotia, N.Y. 12302.

CAREER: U.S. Department of the Army, Fort Hamilton, Brooklyn, N.Y., civilian management analyst, 1974-76; Letitia Baldrige Enterprises, New York City, public relations consultant, 1977; Medcom, Inc., New York City, medical editor, 1977-78; General Electric Co., Schenectady, N.Y., technical writer, 1978—; author of children's books, 1980—. Co-chairman of Schenectady County Christmas Bureau, 1979-82. Loan executive for National Alliance of Business, 1982. *Member:* Society of Children's Book Writers (upstate New York regional advisor, 1986—), Academy of American Poets, Phi Beta Kappa, U.S. Jaycees. *Awards, honors:* Prize from Academy of American Poets, 1971, for poem, "The Garden of the Mint Green Unicorn"; community service awards for outstanding human improvement from the New York State Jaycees, 1981, 1982; named outstanding young man of America by U.S. Jaycees, 1982.

WRITINGS—For children; published by F. Watts: *Christmas* (illustrated by Cynthia Pickard), 1980; *Easter* (illustrated by Diana Uehlinger), 1980; *Halloween* (illustrated by Frank Bozzo), 1980; *Thanksgiving* (illustrated by Carla Bauer), 1980; *Valentine's Day* (illustrated by Michael Deas), 1980; *The White House*, 1981; *Museums: What They Are and How They Work,*

1981; *Football,* 1982; *Baseball and Softball,* 1982; (with Susan Purdy) *Ancient Egypt* (illustrated by Beverly Pardee), 1982; (with S. Purdy) *Ancient Greece* (illustrated by Bert Dodson), 1982; (with S. Purdy) *Ancient Rome* (illustrated by Francis Livingston and B. Dodson; diagrams by David Wenzel), 1982; (with S. Purdy) *Aztecs* (illustrated by Pamela Ford-Johnson), 1982; (with S. Purdy) *Eskimos* (illustrated by James Watling; diagrams by Jane F. Kendall), 1982; (with S. Purdy) *North American Indians* (illustrated by Hal Frenck; diagrams by George Guzzi), 1982; *Explorers and Discovery,* 1983; *Bridges,* 1983; *Canals,* 1983; *Dams,* 1983; *Roads,* 1984; *Skyscrapers,* 1984; *Tunnels,* 1984; *Poland,* 1986; *Benjamin Franklin,* 1986; *The Arctic and Antarctic,* 1987; *The World's Oceans,* 1987; *Remote Places,* 1988; *The World of Space,* 1988.

WORK IN PROGRESS: Fiction for children and adults; book illustration. "My true ambition is to write fiction. At the present time, I have several manuscripts in various stages of completion: a couple of children's stories that would make nice picture books; outlines for several young adult novels; plans for some biographies; some slowly evolving tales of adventure and horror; a semi-autobiographical novel in the *Bildungsroman* tradition."

SIDELIGHTS: "Books have always been an important part of my life. Ever since I found out that there were people who wrote books, I knew that I wanted to be one of them.

"I was fortunate to grow up in a family that valued language and liked books. Reading aloud is an important family tradition. We still celebrate holidays with candlelight readings of ghost stories, poems, and well-told tales. And as in many families, the storytelling art was much practiced and honored.

"One of the master storytellers in the family is my aunt, whose accounts of her frequent travels were highlights of family gatherings—details of characters she met along the way complete with their dialects and idiosyncrasies, tales of hotels where every towel bred contagion, and restaurants where every sauce held the promise of certain disease. Stories in which fact became entangled with the fictive garments of a natural story-teller became a way of life for me as a youngster. Ordinary happenings take on extraordinary properties when the power of the imagination is unleashed.

"When I was six or seven I started to make my own story books out of paper and cardboard fastened together with glue and yarn. I was both writer and illustrator for these early works. Thus far, as an adult, I have only *written* books, but I would also like to illustrate them. In 1984 I created a series of illustrations for a software packager, and some of my photographs have been used in several of my books as well as in books by other writers.

"I began my professional writing career in 1980. I was doing free-lance work for a number of New York publishers, editing the words of other writers and meeting with other editors responsible for acquiring manuscripts, when I recognized the opportunity to write that had been present all along. I was drawn to children's nonfiction because I still find the world a vast, incomprehensible, and exciting place to live. And it is both fun and helpful to know how and why people do the things they do, and say things the way they say them. Sharing knowledge is part of the joy of learning and living. Few pleasures can be greater than helping others to make sense of the bewildering labyrinth of images and phrases that confront us every day.

"For me the continual wonder of writing is this: it is an art form that you can practice almost entirely in your head. You

CASS R. SANDAK

don't need sophisticated and expensive equipment, and you don't have to train your body to perform skilled muscular feats. Musicians have to master an instrument to practice the art that is inside them, dancers must train their bodies, singers their voices, graphic artists and sculptors their hand and eye coordination. But a storyteller or writer needs only his mind and a tongue or pen to bring to life the beauty that is within. There is a fierce economy of effort here—nothing is wasted.

"All of experience sharpens the instrument of the mind, and the accidents of the body cannot betray the integrity of the art. The art of writing is life itself. We all live our lives inside our heads (at least in a certain sense), but the writer is someone who transforms the essentially cerebral quality of life into the shorthand of language that can be vivified in the mind of the reader. Writing and reading are the supreme forms of participation.

"I view literature as a vehicle for social improvement and change. Writers and artists have a mission to keep alive and pass along the values that have informed civilization throughout the ages, especially as we stumble toward a new age of barbarism. The past is worth preserving not because of what it tells about the way things were, but because it helps explain the way things are. My book *Museums: What They Are and How They Work* evolved from this idea.

"In my work I want to express my personal vision of the joy and love of living and learning. Writing a book is a chance to share a unique pattern of experience, a perspective, a point of view—to touch readers who may live in other places and maybe even in other times.

The entrance to a mile-long tunnel in Zion National Park, Utah. The tunnel was cut through solid rock. ■ (From *Tunnels* by Cass R. Sandak. Photograph courtesy of Ewing Galloway.)

"Literature is like a philosopher's stone. A book is a magic prism that can be held up to the world to reveal its most brilliant colors. It is a camera that can freeze a segment of time—real or imagined—in the eternal present of art, where it remains unaltered from generation to generation. A book is a bridge that links 'now' with 'forever'—both the 'once upon a time' and the 'happily ever after.'

"My reading tastes have always been catholic—ranging from Marcel Proust to the *National Enquirer*—and Catholic, including *Lives of the Saints,* G. K. Chesterton, C. S. Lewis, and Flannery O'Connor. Both Proust and the *Enquirer* have this in common—they give deep insight into the ways that people feel and think and act. Readings in religion and philosophy provide moorings for the fundamental search for beauty and goodness that is the underpinning of personal growth and social order. Jane Austen, Elizabeth Bowen, and Isak Dinesen are esteemed because they seem to reflect an ordered fictional universe in their writings. And Vita Sackville-West is beloved, because of her rich humanity and personal style.

"I have always had a taste for the gothic and bizarre in literature. At college I wrote my senior honors thesis on characterization in the novels of Ann Radcliffe. Among the Americans, I have always loved Hawthorne, Poe, and H. P. Lovecraft. Franz Kafka is another favorite.

"Among contemporary writers I have enormous respect for Lawrence Durrell and John Fowles. And I admire the serious craftsmanship and wisdom evident in the works that Zilpha Keatley Snyder, Madeleine L'Engle, and Robert Cormier have written for young people."

HOBBIES AND OTHER INTERESTS: "Because I divide my time between Manhattan and upstate New York, I am able to enjoy the best that town and country have to offer in the way of cultural events and in opportunities for fresh-air activities such as gardening and collecting natural history specimens.

"I have studied eight ancient and modern languages and there is hardly a subject in which I do not take an active interest. Architecture, drawing and painting, collecting British antiques, and engaging in sports—especially swimming, polo, and snowshoeing—absorb some of my energies. In my free moments I enjoy traveling and taking part in community affairs."

SCHWARK, Mary Beth 1954-

PERSONAL: Born January 2, 1954, in Mt. Clemens, Mich.; daughter of Martin Francis (a recreational administrator and piano teacher) and Adelaide (a school and piano teacher; maiden name, Schulte) Schwark; married Robert Joseph Kuester (a commercial artist and portrait painter), October 7, 1978; children: Aimee Nicole. *Education:* Macomb Community College, Associate in Graphic Commercial Art, 1976.

CAREER: Free-lance illustrator, 1977—. *Member:* Graphic Artists Guild. *Awards, honors: Your Former Friend, Matthew* was selected one of Child Study Association's Children's Books of the Year, 1984.

ILLUSTRATOR: LouAnn Gaeddert, *The Kid with the Red Suspenders,* Dutton, 1983; L. Gaeddert, *Your Former Friend, Matthew* (Junior Literary Guild selection), Dutton, 1984; Mary Blount Christian, *Mystery at Camp Triumph,* A. Whitman, 1986.

SIDELIGHTS: "I've always drawn since I was little. My mother saved drawings of unclothed figures (belly buttons included) from kindergarten. I did not have the opportunity to take art courses in high school. By the age of twenty I finally became serious about being an artist and studied two years at a local community college. Upon graduation I was hired by the largest advertising/illustration studio in Detroit. First hand experience there was the best schooling possible. After fifteen months at the studio, I married my husband, Bob, who is an illustrator also. Both of us freelanced out of our home studio for four years. Bob recently went back to another large studio, but I am still freelancing out of my home studio.

But, all in all, he thought that the day had been very satisfactory. ■ (From *The Kid with the Red Suspenders* by LouAnn Gaeddert. Illustrated by Mary Beth Schwark.)

"We love to travel in the West. A recent trip to New Mexico has inspired landscape and portrait paintings of the state and people. We are going back this summer for a painting trip. We have hopes and plans to move to New Mexico.

"We have lots of music in our household. Bob played trumpet with a big band in Detroit for seven years, but gave it up to pursue painting full time. In the last two years I began playing drums—and love it. I also play a little keyboard which I learned from my piano teaching parents. My daughter, Aimee, loves to dance when Mom and Dad play swing. Every day is art filled!"

SCHWARTZ, Joel L.   1940-

BRIEF ENTRY: Born April 23, 1940, in Philadelphia, Pa. Psychiatrist and author of books for young adults. Schwartz has worked in private practice since 1972 and in 1980 became the director of the Child/Adolescent Fellowship at Hahnemann University. His interest in presenting psychiatry to youth in a positive light is apparent from his most recent novel, *Shrink* (Dell, 1986). Because of problems at home, Mike Brooks is sent to a psychiatrist and subsequently finds that the experience isn't all that bad. "... This book ... gives young people some notions about how to solve problems," noted *Kliatt.*

Upchuck Summer (Delacorte, 1982), Schwartz's first novel, introduces Richie, a bossy and self-centered summer camper. He is very disagreeable until he learns a valuable lesson about respect. "Schwartz has created a funny, easy-reading story that deals with a host of adolescent concerns in a convincing manner," observed *School Library Journal.* Its sequel, *Best Friends Don't Come in Threes* (Dell, 1985), concerns Richie's plight when he returns from camp to find that his best friend has found a new pal. "The story is full of action and laughs as the boys race from one predicament to the next," wrote *School Library Journal.* "While several books have addressed the 'third-friend syndrome' among girls," added *Booklist,* "Schwartz' offering ably fields the problem for the male gender." Schwartz received his B.A. from Franklin and Marshall College in 1962, his M.D. from Hahnemann University in 1965, and completed his residency in adult psychiatry at the Institute of Living. *Home:* 1333 Dillon Rd., Fort Washington, Pa. 19034.

SLEPIAN, Jan(ice B.)   1921-

PERSONAL: Born January 2, 1921, in New York, N.Y.; daughter of Louis (an engineer) and Florence (a housewife; maiden name, Ellinger) Berek; married Urey Krasnopolsky, October, 1945 (divorced, 1948); married David Slepian (a mathematician), April 18, 1950; children: Steven, Don, Anne. *Education:* Brooklyn College, B.A., 1942; University of Washington, M.A., 1947; New York University, M.A., 1964; attended University of California—Berkeley. *Home and office:* 212 Summit Ave., Summit, N.J. 07901. *Agent:* Sheldon Fogelman, 10 East 40th St., New York, N.Y. 10016.

CAREER: Massachusetts General Hospital, Boston, Mass., language therapist, 1947-49; private speech therapist, 1952-58; Red Seal Clinic, Newton, N.J., speech therapist, 1953-55; Matheny School for Cerebral Palsy, Farhills, N.J., speech therapist, 1955-57; author of books for children and young adults. *Member:* Society of Children's Book Writers, Authors Guild. *Awards, honors: The Alfred Summer* was selected one of *School Library Journal*'s Best Books of the Year, 1980;

JAN SLEPIAN

American Book Award finalist in children's fiction category, *Boston Globe-Horn Book* Award Honor Book for fiction, and New Jersey Institute of Technology Author's Award, all 1981, all for *The Alfred Summer; Lester's Turn* was selected one of *New York Times* Best Books for Children, and one of *School Library Journal*'s Notable Children's Books for Older Readers, both 1981, one of *Social Education*'s Notable Children's Trade Books in Social Studies, and one of New York Public Library's Books for the Teen Age, both 1982; *The Night of the Bozos* was selected one of American Library Association's Best Books for Young Adults, one of Child Study Association of America's Children's Books of the Year, one of Library of Congress' Books of the Year, and received the New Jersey Institute of Technology Author's Award, all 1983.

WRITINGS—Juvenile: (With Ann Seidler) *The Best Invention of All* (picture book; illustrated by Joseph Veno), Crowell-Collier, 1967.

Novels for young adults: *The Alfred Summer* (ALA Notable Book), Macmillan, 1980; *Lester's Turn* (sequel to *The Alfred Summer;* ALA Notable Book), Macmillan, 1981; *The Night of the Bozos* (ALA Notable Book), Dutton, 1983; *Getting On with It* (Junior Literary Guild selection), Four Winds, 1985; *Something beyond Paradise* (Junior Literary Guild selection), Philomel, 1987.

"Listen-Hear" picture book series; all with A. Seidler; all illustrated by Richard E. Martin; all published by Follett, 1964:

Lester and the Sea Monster; Cock Who Couldn't Crow; Alfie and the Dream Machine; Magic Arthur and the Giant; Mister Sipple and the Naughty Princess; Roaring Dragon of Redrose.

"Junior Listen-Hear" picture book series; all with A. Seidler; all illustrated by R. E. Martin; all published by Follett, 1967: *Bendemolena,* published as *The Cat Who Wore a Pot on Her Head,* Scholastic, 1981; *Ding-Dong, Bing-Bong; An Ear Is to Hear; The Hungry Thing; The Silly Listening Book.*

SIDELIGHTS: "It seems to me that what has shaped my life is largely chance, happenstance, sheer accident all the way, and I've been lucky all my life. For example, I'm a writer by chance. I didn't go from the cradle to the typewriter. I set out to be a clinical psychologist, turned to speech therapy and because of that work began writing picture books when my own children were young.

"I'm a New Yorker, born in Manhattan in 1921, and moved to Brooklyn when my engineer father lost his money in the stock market crash. Five of us shared a tiny bedroom in a tenement near the beach at Brighton. When I left graduate school at the University of Washington in Seattle, I couldn't get a job as a psychologist, so when I was offered one as a language therapist at the Mass. General Hospital in Boston I grabbed it. That's maybe the luckiest thing that ever happened to me because it was there that I met my husband David when he crawled through my bedroom window by accident. We were married in Paris and settled in New Jersey where David

(From *The Cat Who Wore a Pot on Her Head* by Jan Slepian and Ann Seidler. Illustrated by
Richard E. Martin.)

worked as a mathematician at Bell Labs and I as mother of three children full-time and speech therapist part-time.

"The writer part happened when a colleague of mine, Dr. Ann Seidler, suggested we collaborate on writing a series of newspaper articles about everyday speech problems for worried parents. To our surprise this worked out well, and so we became braver and wrote a series of picture books called the 'Listen-Hear' series. Perhaps I would still be writing books for young children if I hadn't happened to take a class in children's literature at the University of California in Berkeley.

"At that time we had the great good fortune to live alternately in Hawaii and New Jersey. We were on our way to the Islands when we stopped for a semester at that campus where my husband was guest professor. I thought the course was about picture books, but instead I was introduced by Mae Durham Rogers to a marvellous new (to me) genre that just didn't exist when I was growing up and reading everything in sight: books for older readers, teen-age novels, books published as children's books for pragmatic reasons, but which are really for readers between puberty and senescence.

"By chance, I was at loose ends professionally, emptied of ideas for more picture books and all fired up by the reading I had been doing for the course. I was ready to tackle a subject that had been in the back of my mind for ages but had never really had the nerve to write about. And now, because of the course, I knew the form. I had no intention in the world to write about handicaps, or what it was like to grow up with a handicapped person, or anything as high-minded as that. I just wanted to write as true a made-up story as I could about my brother Alfred, what he was like in his hey-day when he was young.

"To do this I had to go back in time, back to my childhood in Brooklyn when my passions were handball and books, and my hates were Brooklyn and my brother Alfred. I didn't know that those two parts of my early life that I wanted so earnestly to shake at the time were so tenaciously lodged within me, waiting to get their side said.

"*The Alfred Summer* was written as if dictated, so ready was it to be heard. That's a rare experience for a writer I have since learned from my subsequent struggles with other books. *Lester's Turn* was needed because I wanted to find out more about some characters I had met in the first novel.

"Now that those two are written, I marvel at the mystery and the irony of their existence. The books were grounded in an old family sorrow, and now all that has been turned around. Instead of a wasted life, I see that my brother Alfred has reached and touched more people than most because of the books. I can only echo Alfie's friend Lester and say, 'Sometimes life just knocks me out!'

"I've since gone on to write other books, and since writing is a process of self discovery, I can now see that my main concern seems to be with people who are out of the mainstream in some way. I have Alfred to thank for that too."

Slepian's works are included in the Kerlan Collection at the University of Minnesota.

HOBBIES AND OTHER INTERESTS: Mycology, reading, music, swimming.

FOR MORE INFORMATION SEE: Sally Holmes Holtze, editor, *Fifth Book of Junior Authors and Illustrators*, H. W. Wilson, 1983.

JOAN SOLOMON

SOLOMON, Joan

PERSONAL: Born in Johannesburg, South Africa; daughter of Philip (a printer) and Rose (a costume and dress designer; maiden name, Isaacs) Mendelsohn; married Louis Solomon (a surgeon), July 1, 1951; children: Caryn, Ryan, Joyce. *Education:* University of Witwatersrand, South Africa, B.A. (with honors), 1949; University of Cape Town, B.Ed., 1950; attended London College of Printing. *Home:* The Bungalow, 221 Willesden La., London NW6, England.

CAREER: English teacher in Johannesburg, South Africa, 1951-52; Johannesburg High School for Girls, Cape Town, South Africa, child welfare social worker, 1952-53; Baragwanath Hospital, Johannesburg, social worker, 1953-54; owner of an advertising studio, Upington, Cape Province, South Africa, 1954-57; free-lance tutor in London, England, 1958-62; University of Witwatersrand, Johannesburg, lecturer in English, 1963-76; taught English as a foreign language in London, 1978-81; Open University, London, lecturer in English, 1981-85. Taught creative writing to groups of black students in Soweto, South Africa.

WRITINGS—All published by Hamish Hamilton, except as noted: *Kate's Party*, 1978; *Spud Comes to Play*, 1978; *Berron's Tooth* (illustrated with photographs by Richard Harvey), 1978; *A Day by the Sea* (illustrated with photographs by R. Harvey), 1978; *Shabnam's Day Out*, 1980; *Gifts and Almonds*, 1980; *Bobbi's New Year*, 1980; *News for Dad*, 1980; *Wedding Day* (self-illustrated with photographs), 1981; *A Present for Mum* (illustrated with photographs with R. Solomon), 1981; *Sweet Tooth Sunil*, 1984; *Spiky Sunday*, 1987; *Chopsticks and Chips*, 1987; *Everybody's Hair*, A. & C. Black, 1988.

Also author of *Joyce's Day, Joyce Visits Granny, Joyce at the Circus, Sipho's Trumpet,* and *Joyce's ABC,* all published by Tswiri Books, 1974-76. Contributor of articles and photographs to academic journals.

WORK IN PROGRESS: Children's books; research on minority communities; research on racism, sexism, and classism in children's literature.

SIDELIGHTS: "In our back yard was a fig tree. We did not have a big yard, but the fig tree was enormous and it was the center of my world. When you walked beneath the branches, you were totally hidden by the big hairy leaves, and the cool, secret space inside was totally private. The figs it yielded were sweet and marvellous and you could eat them till you burst. Most wonderful of all was the ease with which you could climb and the wide hospitality of the branches. There aloft, amid the leaves you could snuggle with a book and read all afternoon. That is exactly what I did all through my childhood—scrambled through homework as fast as I could and made for a branch in the fig tree to while away the rest of the day with a book in my lap.

"For as long as I can remember I have always loved listening to stories, reading them and writing them. When I wasn't involved with books I was drawing. When I got my first camera, I swapped drawing for photographing and have been a writer and photographer ever since.

"My love for the fig tree developed into a passion for the country and one of the sharpest joys I know is to cycle for miles and miles in the countryside. I ride whenever I can, and camp quite often as well. My other great loves are music, dancing and the sea."

STANOVICH, Betty Jo 1954-

BRIEF ENTRY: Born July 13, 1954, in San Pedro, Calif. Author of books for children. Stanovich received her bachelor's degree from the University of California in 1977 and also attended classes at the Institute of Children's Literature. She says that all of her books revolve around three factors: "Theme, visualization, rhythm—all touch us somehow in a way that makes us put down a book after reading it and say, 'Yes, this is a good book.'" Stanovich has written a half dozen children's books, all published by Lothrop. Her first book, *Hedgehog Adventures* (1983), follows the antics of Hedgehog and his friend Woodchuck. In *Hedgehog Surprises* (1984), Hedgehog plans for Black Bear's birthday party. "The sequel to *Hedgehog Adventures* is more delicious nonsense brightly narrated by Stanovich . . . ," commented *Publishers Weekly.* Stanovich is also the author of *Silly Chester* (1986); the novels *The Mystery of the Phantom Ship* (1986) and *Kip and Cody* (1986); and *Big Boy, Little Boy* (1984), described by *School Library Journal* as "the restful, pensive mood and soothing story of a small boy who can enjoy grownup activities and then slip back easily into toddlerhood, secure in his grandmother's love." *Home:* P.O. Box 802, Mammoth Lakes, Calif. 93546.

FOR MORE INFORMATION SEE: Contemporary Authors, Volume 118, Gale, 1986.

Not that the story need be long, but it will take a long while to make it short.
　　　　　　　　　　　　—Henry David Thoreau
　　　　　　　　　　　　(From *Letter*)

STEELE, Mary Q(uintard Govan) 1922- (Wilson Gage)

PERSONAL: Born May 8, 1922, in Chattanooga, Tenn.; daughter of Gilbert Eaton (a librarian) and Christine (a writer; maiden name, Noble) Govan; married William O. Steele (a writer), June 1, 1943 (died, 1979); children: Mary Quintard, Jenifer Susan, Allerton William. *Education:* University of Chattanooga, B.S., 1943. *Politics:* Democrat. *Religion:* "Nominal" Episcopalian. *Home:* 329 Crestway Dr., Chattanooga, Tenn. 37411.

CAREER: Writer of children's books. Tennessee Valley Authority, Chattanooga, Tenn., map editor, 1943-44. *Awards, honors: New York Herald Tribune*'s Children's Spring Book Festival Honor Book, 1960, for *The Secret of Fiery Gorge;* Aurianne Award of the American Library Association, 1966, for *Big Blue Island;* Newbery Honor Book, 1970, and Lewis Carroll Shelf Award, 1971, both for *Journey Outside; The Eye in the Forest* was named a Notable Children's Trade Book in the Field of Social Studies, 1976, by the joint committee of the National Council for Social Studies and the Children's Book Council; Garden State Children's Book Award for easy-to-read books from the New Jersey State Library Association, 1982, for *Mrs. Gaddy and the Ghost.*

WRITINGS—Published by Greenwillow, except as noted: *Journey Outside* (ALA Notable Book; illustrated by Rocco Negri), Viking, 1969; *The Living Year: An Almanac for My Survivors* (adult essays), Viking, 1972; *The First of the Penguins* (illustrated by Susan Jeffers), Macmillan, 1973, reissued, Greenwillow, 1985; (with husband, William O. Steele) *The Eye in the Forest,* Dutton, 1975; *Because of the Sand Witches There* (illustrated by Paul Galdone), 1975; *The True Men,* 1976; (editor) *The Fifth Day* (poetry anthology; illustrated by Janina Domanska), 1978; *The Owl's Kiss: Three Stories,* 1978; *Wish, Come True* (illustrated by Muriel Batherman), 1979; *The Life (and Death) of Sarah Elizabeth Harwood,* 1980; *Anna's Summer Friends* (verse), Greenwillow, 1987.

Under pseudonym Wilson Gage; published by World Publishing, except as noted: *The Secret of the Indian Mound* (illus-

MARY Q. STEELE

Mrs. Gaddy was a farmer. ■ (From *Mrs. Gaddy and the Fast-Growing Vine* by Wilson Gage. Illustrated by Marylin Hafner.)

trated by Mary Stevens), 1958; *The Secret of Crossbone Hill* (illustrated by M. Stevens), 1959; *The Secret of Fiery Gorge* (illustrated by M. Stevens), 1960; *A Wild Goose Tale* (illustrated by Glen Rounds), 1961; *Dan and the Miranda* (*Horn Book* honor list; illustrated by G. Rounds), 1962; *Miss Osborne-the-Mop* (illustrated by P. Galdone), 1963; *Big Blue Island* (ALA Notable Book; illustrated by G. Rounds), 1964; *The Ghost of Five Owl Farm* (illustrated by P. Galdone), 1966; *Mike's Toads* (illustrated by G. Rounds), 1970; *Squash Pie* (ALA Notable Book; Junior Literary Guild selection; illustrated by G. Rounds), Greenwillow, 1976; *Down in the Boon Docks* (ALA Notable Book; illustrated by G. Rounds), Greenwillow, 1977, large print edition, 1977; *Mrs. Gaddy and the Ghost* (Junior Literary Guild selection; illustrated by Marylin Hafner), Greenwillow, 1979, large print edition, 1979; *Cully Cully and the Bear* (illustrated by James Stevenson), Greenwillow, 1983, large print edition, 1983; *The Crow and Mrs. Gaddy* (illustrated by M. Hafner), Greenwillow, 1984, large print edition, 1984; *Mrs. Gaddy and the Fast Growing Vine* (illustrated by M. Harris), Greenwillow, 1985.

Contributor of articles to *Horn Book* and of book reviews to *Chattanooga Times.*

WORK IN PROGRESS: "I am currently working on a book of fiction for eight- to eleven-year-olds, based on my own childhood."

ADAPTATIONS: "Journey Outside" (filmstrip with record), Random House; "Living Year" (cassette); "Ghost of Five Owl Farm" (talking book); "Mike's Toads" (talking book).

Braille Books: *Big Blue Island; Dan and Miranda; The Ghost of Five Owl Farm; Miss Osborne-the-Mop; The Secret of Crossbone Hill; The Secret of Fiery Gorge; A Wild Goose Tale.*

SIDELIGHTS: Steele was born in Chattanooga, Tennessee on May 8, 1922. "I was born under entirely the wrong sign. I am not awfully imaginative; I am easily discouraged, lazy and never have the courage of my convictions. Besides, Tauruses have short, thick necks, stubby hands and feet. I have often wanted to thrust one of my size 7 AAAA's down the throat of whoever had that idea, especially after a day of scouring the town for such a thing." [Pat Timberlake, "Profile: Mary Steele, Why She's a Taurus!" *Language Arts,* January, 1978.[1]]

Steele was born into a family of gifted and successful writers. Her father was a librarian and an author, and her mother, Christine Govan, was the author of several popular books for young people. "When I was young and lived in a house overflowing with books, I wasted many hours looking for something to read. There were the shelves of my parents' library and also stacks of new books, for my father was editor of the book review page of a local newspaper, and almost every book published lingered on our desks and tables for a few days. An embarrassment of riches, in the midst of which I could elect to be choosy—and I was. Not this, not that, to while away a rainy afternoon, to beguile me out of a somber adolescent mood, to soothe me to sleep, to help satisfy an insatiable curiosity about things and places and times and people, for someone must know, must tell me, what it is all about and how to cope with it. Not this, not that; what I was searching for was excellence in one form or another, and sometimes I found it, as often as not in books for which I would not care today.

"I can recall the feeling of these discoveries; I can remember closing Virginia Woolf's *To the Lighthouse* with the smug

The farmer's wife tasted the biggest pie. ■ (From *Squash Pie* by Wilson Gage. Illustrated by Glen Rounds.)

feeling that I was glad to be me, since my own particular enjoyment of this book must have been unique. To this day I can recite the sloppy lines which tell of Beth's demise in *Little Women.* And *The Bridge of San Luis Rey* always conjures up the feeling of my fingers in my ears—for that was how I read it, to shut out the screams and giggles of my fellow eighth-graders as I sat on a bench in the gym." [Mary Q. Steele, "As Far as You Can Bear to See: Excellence in Children's Literature," *Horn Book,* June, 1975.[2]]

Although Steele loved reading, she was not very fond of formal education. "I was a kindergarten drop-out. I attended school as seldom as possible and when I attended I spent most of my time planning how to get away. I went to both public and private schools at various points in my academic noncareer. Somewhere along the line I shed the things I hated, like arithmetic and geography, and began to see the light in the things I liked—algebra and languages—and graduated from the University of Chattanooga with an inexplicable degree in physics. Along the way also I trained myself to be a naturalist of better than average skills, but only slightly better. I have no hobbies. Birdwatching is An Important Duty. Who would see the water thrushes and wood thrushes safely back to streams and trees if I did not?"

While Steele was in college, she met a young serviceman named William O. Steele, whom she married in 1943. Their first daughter was born during World War II, and, when the war was over, another daughter and a son completed the family. "I scarcely found time to watch a bird. After my children, who were very close in age, all started school, I was able to devote more time to woods-walking and snake-studying and other really serious occupations. I also read a lot of books. I like books."

Steele liked writing as well, and it was inevitable that she would write books as her father, mother, sister and husband did. In 1958 her first book, *The Secret of the Indian Mound,* was published. "I did not become a writer, but was born one, waking up in the morning to sort the day into scenes and characters and descriptions, as presumably an artist sorts the world into lights and shadows and patterns whenever he looks at it.

"I write for whomever will listen. What I am talking about always is the world around us, about stars and mushrooms and foxes and birds and ants and trees. How can I convey to anyone else the magic and the marvel of it, the vast astonishment of being alive? I'm not sure I can but I intend to go on trying."

Since that first book, Steele and her husband developed reputations as prolific authors of books for children. From their rural home in Signal Mountain, Tennessee, the Steeles shared the same huge work desk as well as their ideas for many of their books. "I live in a mildly rural suburb of a manufacturing town in the southeastern corner of Tennessee. . . .

"When we moved to Signal Mountain, . . . this was still a fairly woodsy area. Vacant lots were grown up to weeds and sassafras. Possums trundled in the ditches, at night little foxes crossed the road in the headlights of cars, and toads trilled from every direction on summer evenings. In . . . [a] short time the trees have gone, the vacant lots have been cleared and built upon, the wet-weather springs dug up and blasted out and rechanneled. Foxes and possums come no more, the toads no longer sing; I must travel miles to hear a whippoorwill. . . ." [Mary Q. Steele, "Introduction," *The Living Year: An Almanac for My Survivors,* Viking, 1972.[3]]

Steele's books reflect her life-long interest in and vast knowledge of natural history, especially birds. Even part of her pen name, Wilson Gage, was chosen as a tribute to Alexander Wilson, an American ornithologist. "Among my earliest recollections is of myself standing transfixed by the song of a

And snoring and snoring.
If his wife didn't shake him
He would sleep for a year.

■ (From *Down in the Boondocks* by Wilson Gage. Illustrated by Glen Rounds.)

Once there was a hunter named Cully Cully. ■ (From *Cully Cully and the Bear* by Wilson Gage. Illustrated by James Stevenson.)

Bewick's wren. What it was, I did not at age four know or care. I recognized it simply as the essence of an April morning.

"From the wren I went on to more momentous occasions. I marked my days by Events, by the sight of wild turkeys rising above a little dark copse of pines; by the seldom-heard calls of chuck-will's-widows; by my first clear close look at ibises; by the spine-chilling sensation of a snake moving unexpectedly under my unwary hand.

"As I grow older I find myself returning to the less sophisticated attitudes of four years old. More and homelier things, the stems of grasses and the songs of crickets, seem to me miraculous.

"Life, in order to continue, must be at least endurable to its participants. But that it is possible in spite of implicit horrors, to find it beautiful fills me with astonishment, with gratitude. What I have hoped to convey . . . is my own sense of how valuable and how fragile it is, this tiny spark in an eternity of darkness, and how greatly to be treasured in whatever manifestation.''[3]

Several of Steele's books received literary honors and accolades from librarians and children's literary associations. For instance, her book *Journey Outside* was selected as a Newbery Honor Book in 1970 and awarded the Lewis Carroll Shelf Award the following year. About the book, Steele commented: "I told the story (*Journey Outside* [Viking]) of a boy who found his own life smothering and pointless and so found a way to leave it behind and come out into the open day. To come out and discover other ways of living and that each had its uniquely pleasant advantages and yet each was as flawed as what he had left behind; and to travel the world until he eventually came upon a man with sufficient objectivity to tell him his choices: to point out that having left the straight world behind he could either retire to Vermont and raise rhubarb and rhetoric or return whence he came to try to convince his family and friends that their way was not the only way and perhaps a less happy way than some others. The decision must be his alone, based not on experience or logic, for neither will tell him what to do. Something else must identify for him his own thing and that is what he will do, conscious of the fact that what he does is neither 'right' nor 'wrong,' but simply what he must do if he is not going to think of himself as having failed.

"I tried to be honest as I wrote, though I was not what is in general termed realistic. If I was dishonest in putting something over on my readers, I certainly did not stack the cards;

It was Monday.... ■ (From *The Crow and Mrs. Gaddy* by Wilson Gage. Illustrated by Marylin Hafner.)

I simply did a little finessing. I am used to doing it, for I have been doing it right along in all of my books, however mundane and however frivolous they may have been. For I have my own bit of truth to leave room for and to speak of sotto voce. I have had to walk around it a bit warily, for I have an idea it is not exactly a popular bit of truth. But what I have tried to say in all my books I do most honestly believe: that it is our differences, not our likenesses that matter. It is our dissimilarities that give life its astonishing richness and wonder and make life rewarding. Concede a spider its inalienable right to eight legs as it has never for a moment doubted your right to two, and you have gone a long way toward being truly human. A universe which has produced a quarter of a million species of beetles must have great respect for and put great value on differentiation. I think it is arrogance for us not to do the same.'' [Mary Q. Steele, ''Realism, Truth, and Honesty,'' *Horn Book,* February, 1971.[4]]

In reviews of her books, Steele has been praised for depicting people realistically and respectfully. ''I like to think that though I write for children, I am as free to write about anything I please as the next writer. I like to think that we respect our children's intelligence enough to suppose that the world need be presented to them in no rosy light, but as it is—as most of us know it is—a hard road strewn with stones and bordered with thorns, ending where, it is claimed, the paths of glory do but lead. The world has not spared children hunger, cold, sorrow, pain, fear, loneliness, disease, death, war, famine, or madness. Why should we hesitate to make use of this knowledge when writing for them?

''Truth is a great and slippery beast. Few people are capable of cramming it between the pages of a book. The writer can only hope that he has at best left some room to accommodate a particular piece, left some space in which the reader may walk around and perceive the general outline of some part of some vastness, seen stereoscopically through his own and the writer's eyes. Realism, contrariwise, is a small creature, almost moribund and suffering from partial paralysis, depending on how it was captured and in what net. It is never going to be a unicorn, a wild and graceful beast of the forest. But it can be a serviceable and sturdy beast of burden, provided you can drench it with sufficient honesty to save its life.

''I am not suggesting a new school of naturalism for the kiddies. I do not propose Zola in the third grade and Céline in the fifth; aside from other considerations I think children would be bored out of their minds. But what I would hope for is that books for children were more often written by people who wanted to write a book—not people who importuned an audience. What I would hope for is books written out of the heart, out of that strange generosity of the heart of the writer who is determined to speak and let who wishes hear.

''At the time I am writing, the country is in a state of turmoil and unrest. The aching frustration and agony of some of us, the heartchilling fear and distrust of many of us, the anger, the despair, the ever-widening chasms are possibly unique in the world's history. For one thing, the dangers have never been so great; and for another, the means of conveying the news of our disease are so efficient. The world has trembled on the brink of disaster before, but only recently has it balanced on the ledge and listened to the siren invitation to jump.

''I think perhaps teachers, librarians, writers, and editors might take some moments to ponder the fact that it is today's young people, and quite often the best of today's young people, who are most anguished, most disaffected, most despairing. I cannot suppress the persistent notion that we of an older generation are somehow and to some extent to blame.''[4]

Rather sad circumstances brought about the writing of Steele's book, *Mrs. Gaddy and the Ghost,* a book written for young six- to eight-year-olds. ''My mother had to leave her funny little old house, which she had lived in and loved for many years, and go into a nursing home. I knew how she hated leaving and I thought she would in all likelihood haunt it for the rest of its days. But my mother is a brave person and full of jokes and laughter. I knew she would make a funny ghost— and what's more, if the house had truly been haunted while she lived in it she would have treated the ghost with humor and even sympathy. And suddenly I found in my head the story of Mrs. Gaddy, who really had a ghost to contend with. Mrs. Gaddy, like my mother, was brave and resilient—but she wasn't too bright. The ways in which she strove to rid herself of the sleep-wrecking tenant were unconventional, to say the least, and not at all effective. The ploy which finally does work is one that country people have used for years to keep their houses and barns free of rats. How this scheme backfires and how Mrs. Gaddy solves her dilemma came as rather a surprise to me—but I think my mother approves of it!''

Mrs. Gaddy and the Ghost was the first in a ''Mrs. Gaddy'' series of books. Following its 1979 publication by Greenwillow, two more ''Mrs. Gaddy'' books were published in 1984 and 1985. In her books, Steele attempts to impart to her readers her own views of the world around her. ''. . . When it comes to the point where I sit down to work on a book, you cannot tell me what is an excellent book for me to write. But I can tell you, for when I write, I intend to write as good a book as possible. I have something I want to say and a particular way to say it. I write slowly and work hard. I try to avoid those things which I dislike in other books, because if my book does not please me I cannot believe it will please other people.

''I look at my characters often and carefully, for I want to know them well and I want to be prepared for the surprises they will inevitably spring on me. I look at what they have said, and I worry about whether this is what they would really say and the way they would say it. I try to bear in mind that the children I am writing about are different from me, that they do not always know what I know, feel what I feel, or think what I think. For surely the writer's foremost aim is to make up out of his experience, observations, compassion, and imagination a new person, as totally new and as complete as he can manage.

''And yet my characters must somehow convey to the reader what I am trying to say, my own view of the world, in the language, thoughts, and feelings of a ten-year-old. It isn't the easiest task, but I work at it conscientiously. How far I succeed, of course, depends on my puny talent.

''As a writer I am interested in language and in people and in how the two things go together, for they do bear considerably upon each other. I have been particularly concerned with the language of children and of people less glib and articulate than I am. I listen to their lean and flashy songs, for what is intrinsically interesting in the ways they express themselves, and because what they say may come in very handy one day. When I write about Dilar of the Raft People, it is perfectly permissible that he speak in rather fanciful and even poetic terms and that he find himself at a loss for words only when he is confronted with something he has never before seen or experienced. But when I am using for my protagonist a semiliterate ten- or twelve-year-old, I do not think that he should reveal the world in my voice and in my terms, or that he should speak fluently in my vocabulary. I think he should have to struggle with language and find himself ill at ease with it and occasionally get it wrong. I think sometimes even familiar things should be outside his powers of exact description, as I know him to be blessed occasionally with a word or a phrase of piercing insight. But I think the battle to make himself understood to others as well as to himself is very much an innate part of what I am attempting to get across in many of my books. When my characters speak, I hope they speak naturally and in words that come naturally to them."[2]

Besides writing and an avid interest in nature, Steele is also interested in politics and poetry. She describes herself as, ". . . a middle-aged amateur natural historian, author of a number of light-hearted entertainments for eight- to eleven-year-olds. . . . I am a most thoroughgoing old-fashioned square, who still reads Beatrix Potter. My motto has ever been, 'Live pure, speak true, right wrong, and follow the king.' . . ."[4]

Steele's works are included in the Kerlan Collection at the University of Minnesota, and in the de Grummond Collection at the University of Southern Mississippi.

HOBBIES AND OTHER INTERESTS: Family, politics, and poetry.

FOR MORE INFORMATION SEE: New York Times Book Review, October 12, 1969; *Horn Book,* August, 1970, February, 1971, June, 1975; *Times Literary Supplement,* October 30, 1970; Martha E. Ward and Dorothy A. Marquardt, *Authors of*

In his right hand he held something firm and wiggling. ■ (From *Mike's Toads* by Wilson Gage. Illustrated by Glen Rounds.)

Books for Young People, 2nd edition, Scarecrow, 1971; Mary Q. Steele, *The Living Year: An Almanac for My Survivors,* Viking, 1972; Doris de Montreville and Donna Hill, editors, *Third Book of Junior Authors,* H. W. Wilson, 1972; Virginia Haviland, *Children and Literature: Views and Reviews,* Lothrop, 1974; D. L. Kirkpatrick, *Twentieth-Century Children's Writers,* St. Martin's, 1978, 2nd edition, 1983; Pat Timberlake, "Profile: Mary Steele, Why She's a Taurus!," *Language Arts,* January, 1978; Jim Roginski, compiler, *Newbery and Caldecott Medalists and Honor Book Winners,* Libraries Unlimited, 1983.

STEELE, William O(wen)   1917-1979

PERSONAL: Born December 22, 1917, in Franklin, Tenn.; died June 25, 1979, in Chattanooga, Tenn.; son of Core (a purchasing agent) and Sue (a homemaker; maiden name, Johnston) Steele; married Mary Quintard Govan (a writer), June 1, 1943; children: Mary Quintard, Jenifer Susan, Allerton William. *Education:* Cumberland University, B.A., 1940; University of Chattanooga, graduate study, 1950. *Politics:* Democrat. *Religion:* Protestant. *Residence:* Signal Mountain, Tenn.

CAREER: Author. *Military service:* Army Air Corps, World War II, 1940-45. *Member:* Authors Guild, Lambda Chi Alpha, Blue Key National Honor Fraternity. *Awards, honors:* New York Herald Tribune's Children's Spring Book Festival Award, 1954, for *Winter Danger;* New York Herald Tribune's Children's Spring Book Festival Honor Book, 1956, for *Davy Crockett's Earthquake,* 1957, for *Flaming Arrows,* and 1958, for *Perilous Road;* special citation, Child Study Association of America, 1957, for *The Lone Hunt;* Jane Addams Children's Book Award, 1958, and Newbery Honor Book, 1959, both for *The Perilous Road;* William Allen White Children's Book Award, 1960, for *Flaming Arrows;* Lewis Carroll Shelf Award, 1962, for *Winter Danger;* Thomas Alva Edison Mass Media Award for "special excellence in portraying America's past," 1963, for *Westward Adventure; The Eye in the Forest* was selected as a Notable Children's Book in the Field of Social Studies by the joint committee of the National Council for Social Studies and the Children's Book Council, 1976.

WRITINGS: The Golden Root (illustrated by Fritz Kredel), Aladdin Books, 1951; *The Buffalo Knife* (illustrated by Paul Galdone), Harcourt, 1952; *Over-Mountain Boy* (illustrated by F. Kredel), Aladdin Books, 1952; *The Story of Daniel Boone* (illustrated by Warren Baumgartner), Grosset, 1953, another edition illustrated by Gerald Facey, Muller, 1957; *Wilderness Journey* (illustrated by P. Galdone), Harcourt, 1953; *John Sevier, Pioneer Boy* (illustrated by Sandra James), Bobbs-Merrill, 1953; *The Story of Leif Ericson* (illustrated by Pranas Lapé), Grosset, 1954; *Winter Danger* (ALA Notable Book; illustrated by P. Galdone), Harcourt, 1954; *Francis Marion, Young Swamp Fox* (illustrated by Dirk Gringhuis), Bobbs-Merrill, 1954, another edition illustrated by Frank Nicholas, 1962; *Tomahawks and Trouble* (illustrated by P. Galdone), Harcourt, 1955; *We Were There on the Oregon Trail* (illustrated by Jo Polseno), Grosset, 1955; *Story of . . . Reflection Riding (with Addenda): A Scenic, Historic, Botanic Drive-Thru,* [Chattanooga, Tenn.], 1955.

We Were There with the Pony Express (illustrated by Frank Vaughn), Grosset, 1956; *DeSoto: Child of the Sun; The Search for Gold* (illustrated by Lorence Bjorklund), Aladdin Books, 1956; *The Lone Hunt* (illustrated by P. Galdone), Harcourt, 1956; *Davy Crockett's Earthquake* (illustrated by Nicolas Mordvinoff), Harcourt, 1956; *Daniel Boone's Echo* (illus-

WILLIAM O. STEELE

trated by N. Mordvinoff), Harcourt, 1957; *Flaming Arrows* (ALA Notable Book; illustrated by P. Galdone), Harcourt, 1957; *The Perilous Road* (ALA Notable Book; illustrated by P. Galdone), Harcourt, 1958; *The Far Frontier* (illustrated by P. Galdone), Harcourt, 1959; *Andy Jackson's Water Well* (illustrated by Michael Ramus), Harcourt, 1959.

The Spooky Thing (illustrated by Paul Coker), Harcourt, 1960; *Westward Adventure: The True Stories of Six Pioneers* (illustrated with maps by Kathleen Voute), Harcourt, 1962; *The Year of the Bloody Sevens* (ALA Notable Book; illustrated by Charles Beck), Harcourt, 1963; *The No-Name Man of the Mountain* (illustrated by Jack Davis), Harcourt, 1964; *Wayah of the Real People* (illustrated by Isa Barnett), Colonial Williamsburg, 1964; *Trail through Danger* (illustrated by C. Beck), Harcourt, 1965; *Tomahawk Border* (illustrated by Vernon Wooten), Colonial Williamsburg, 1966; *The Old Wilderness Road: An American Journey,* Harcourt, 1968.

Hound Dog Zip to the Rescue (illustrated by Mimi Korach), Garrard, 1970; *The Wilderness Tattoo: A Narrative of Juan Ortiz,* Harcourt, 1972; *Surgeon, Trader, Indian Chief: Henry Woodward of Carolina* (illustrated by Hoyt Simmons), Sandlapper Store, 1972; *Triple Trouble for Hound Dog Zip* (illustrated by M. Korach), Garrard, 1972; (with wife, Mary Q. Steele) *The Eye in the Forest,* Dutton, 1975; *John's Secret Treasure* (illustrated by R. Dennis), Macmillan, 1975; *The Man with the Silver Eyes,* Harcourt, 1976; *The Cherokee Crown of Tannassy,* Blair, 1977; *The War Party* (illustrated by Lorinda B. Cauley), Harcourt, 1978; *Talking Bones: Secrets of Indian Burial Mounds* (illustrated by Carlos Llerena-Aguirre), Harper, 1978; *The Magic Amulet,* Harcourt, 1979.

Book reviewer for the *Chattanooga Times.* Contributor to *World Book Encyclopedia* and *Encyclopedia Americana,* and to magazines.

ADAPTATIONS: "The Perilous Road" (listening cassette; filmstrip with record or cassette), Random House, 1976.

Braille Books: *The Far Frontier; Francis Marion; The Lone Hunt; The Old Wilderness Road; Tomahawk Border; Tomahawks and Trouble; Westward Adventure.*

Talking Books: "Daniel Boone's Echo"; "The Far Frontier"; "Flaming Arrows"; "The Lone Hunt"; "The Wilderness Tatoo"; "Winter Danger"; "The Year of the Bloody Sevens."

SIDELIGHTS: William O. Steele was born in Franklin, Tennessee, where, as a boy, he hunted the fields for Indian arrowheads and explored old log cabins scattered throughout the area. He developed an early interest in the pioneers and the history of Tennessee and wanted to use this material in books and stories. He attended Cumberland University where he worked on the college newspaper and a weekly paper in Franklin. He graduated from college in 1940, and spent five years in the army during World War II.

In 1943, Steele married a fellow writer, Mary Quintard Govan, who encouraged him to pursue his writing career. He took a clerical job instead to help support his family—two daughters and a son. Steele developed an interest in children's books from reading stories about his favorite subject—the Old Southwest and the brave pioneers who inhabited it—to his oldest daughter. So he wrote his first book, *The Buffalo Knife,* which was followed by *The Golden Root.* Shortly thereafter, he gave up his job to devote his full time to writing stories and tales of his native Tennessee. His avid interest in pioneer history and Tennessee folklore was further developed after reading Donald Davidson's *The Tennessee: The Old River,* noting that, "The clash of cultures—red men against white—made for all sorts of situations just begging to be used. . . ."

Steele wrote his stories from his home on Signal Mountain in Tennessee, among the same kind of hills that Davy Crockett and Daniel Boone saw. Throughout his long writing career, he won many awards for his fictional books. "After . . . years as a published author I don't find it one bit easier to write a new book than when I first began. Shed no tears for me please, I couldn't or wouldn't be anything else but an author."

Since Steele concerned himself primarily with historical fiction, he found it necessary to devote long hours to researching for his background material. Since the mid-sixties, Steele shifted the viewpoint in some of his stories from the frontiersmen in conflict with the Indians to the conflict of Indian-white en-

(From the filmstrip "The Perilous Road." Produced by Random House, Inc., 1976.)

counters as told from the Indian's point of view. "My fiction for the 8- to 12-year-old reader has mostly been concerned with pioneer and Indian struggles in the southeastern U.S. during the 18th century when the red and white cultures clashed at the cutting edge of the frontier. I try always to see the past as it was, to put into my books, not 20th-century characters with a fake pioneer dress of split cow hide, but 18th-century boys and men with buckskin shirts rubbing against their shoulder blades, and the smell of sweat and woodsmoke around them, and their bellies only half-full of dried deer meat and gritty ashcake. What I am trying to get over to my readers is not events but people who make the events. History textbooks can give a reader the high spots—but it takes more than textbooks to give you the heart-squeezed hopelessness and fear that the sound of Indian warwhoops can cause.

"In my books I try to give a true picture of what the unspoiled frontier country was like when it began to be settled, of the dangers and hardships and rewards of settling it. Above all I try to convey something of the real essence of the times, something of the restless, tough-bodied, forward-looking pioneer who pushed further and further into the wilderness. And I try to accomplish this in as entertaining a fashion as I can.

"In the 1950s and 60s I could write historical fiction from the white pioneer's viewpoint and not be criticised as slighting the Indian's side. . . . In the 1970s I would not want to write that kind of book and probably would find no publisher if I did on account of . . . ethnic sensitivity. In the future, so as to not waste a quarter of a century of research on the frontier period, I may switch to the Indian viewpoint in his struggles against the whites on the frontier. I would prefer however to go back in time to the fascinating prehistoric Indian groups of Eastern America. It will be a challenge, but it seems to be a wide open field." [D. L. Kirkpatrick, *Twentieth-Century Children's Writers*, St. Martin's Press, 1978.[1]]

Besides writing adventure novels of the frontier, Steele also wrote several books of Tennessee folk tales, biographies of famous people, and nonfictional works such as *Westward Adventure: The True Stories of Six Pioneers*. Very frequently the research for one book became the impetus for another. "Children—and adults—constantly ask where I get ideas for books. Would I could answer as directly as Edward Gibbon: 'It was at Rome on the 15th of October 1764, as I was musing amidst the ruins of the Capitol while the bare-footed friars were singing vespers in the Temple of Jupiter, that the idea of writing the decline and fall of the city first started to my mind.'

"I do not get my ideas—ideas get me. My books start out as a sort of poltergeist, a disembodied creature racketing around, throwing cups and saucers and typewriters hither and yon. Let us say I am reading an old history for information about a trail I need to use in a partially completed book, but I cannot find a thing about it. However, I do find the mention of a couple of blockhouses which were on the trail, though the historian does not locate them for me. If I could pinpoint these forts, I would have a good idea where the trail went.

"I get out all my early travel journals. Michaux, the naturalist, used the trail but does not give its route nor mention the blockhouses. Nor do any of the other journals either. I am desperate, I need that trail, I need those blockhouses. I begin to look at old maps and find nothing. I believe I must have made the trail up, perhaps it never existed except in my head and in my unfinished book. And one day on a map illustrating the gradual depletion of the buffalo herds in the United States, I find the date 1810 in East Tennessee. The map says that the last buffalo killed in Tennessee was killed there and at that time.

He was hungry and cold and the ropes cut cruelly into his wrists. . . . ■ (From *Tomahawks and Trouble* by William O. Steele. Illustrated by Paul Galdone.)

"This is not what I am looking for at all, but it is a fact that cannot be ignored. I work on the assumption that an author who writes about the past can never have too many facts at hand. Who knows just what will prove useful? So I make a note of this on a card and file it carefully away in a little green box. Then I go back to running down that trail and those blockhouses.

"And lo! what crops up again but that buffalo? In a diary an old hunter tells of killing buffalo and how good the tongue is to eat when smoked. I am curious whether buffalo tongue looks like beef tongue. But the hunter does not mention what color the tongue is and I begin to wonder where I might find out. But I cannot. I just have to find that trail or else I am going to have to rewrite my book and leave it out. I read on and on through all sorts of diaries and local histories and old gazetteers.

"But I am getting nowhere, for the house is full of buffaloes. I reach for a pencil and a buffalo knocks over my file box. I close my eyes and see the shaggy beasts with, as one early explorer wrote, 'great bunches on their backs.' They trample across my desk and get underfoot at every move I make. . . . Here are poltergeists—buffalo poltergeists. They are not really there; and yet, they are so much there, so vivid and so real, I begin to stuff a few of them into my books. One here, one

Jamie was up in the tree, but he was not alone. ■ (From *Tomahawk Border* by William O. Steele. Illustrated by Vernon Wooten.)

there—an Indian kills one, a white man sees a herd moving single file across a grassy savannah.

"And always, way off, standing apart, yet seeing everything going on at my house and in my mind, is one great lone beast. He does not trot along the bookcase the way the others do; no, he is distinctive, something special. He is the last buffalo killed in Tennessee and there he stands; there, but not there at all, and still he bellows for attention while nobody hears him but me. . . . Weeks go by, and I am haunted by the buffalo poltergeist.

"Eventually, I find the location of the blockhouse and a piece of the trail. And I find too that stockings can be woven from buffalo hair, that Indians make large spoons out of buffalo horns, and that these spoons split and fall into pieces if poison is put in them. Facts and superstitions, random mentionings, buffaloes jump up at me from every printed page. . . . I file these things away for the future.

"I begin to wonder who in creation killed the last buffalo in Tennessee. Why 1810? Wasn't that too late a date? Was there one lone bull who wandered up the coves and down the valleys in the East Tennessee Mountains and was lucky enough to

escape detection till suddenly in 1810—? And there stands my poltergeist buffalo snorting softly to himself and to me. I am going to have to write a book about the last buffalo killed in Tennessee, I cannot get away from it. I shall just have to do it to have peace and quiet around my house; I shall have to write it to drive the poltergeist away. I see it in my mind as a nonfiction book. . . .

"It sounds fine to me. But search as I might, I cannot find out who actually killed that last buffalo. I write to the Tennessee Archives, and their reference department can run down no facts for me on this event. There goes my nonfiction book. Now the buffalo is drifting off slowly over the mountains; and, thank goodness, I have seen the last of him and can get down to some writing.

"Life goes on. I write, I correct proofs, I answer fan mail, and just for curiosity's sake I do some research on the 'moon-eyed people' of aboriginal times in Tennessee. Then one morning the buffalo is back, tracking through the heavy dew, crossing the yard toward the house. He is not alone. Something shadowy is sneaking along behind him. I strain to try to make out what it is. An Indian? A panther? No, it is a boy with a rifle. I can see that the boy is bound and determined to get close enough to shoot the buffalo.

He made sure the horses would be able to finish the journey in good style. ■ (From *Andy Jackson's Water Well* by William O. Steele. Illustrated by Michael Ramus.)

"Why not let him? Since I have no facts to write a nonfiction book, I can use the last buffalo killed in Tennessee for an adventure story. The buffalo has been around so long I see him clearly, but the boy stands back among the great tree butts and I have no idea what kind of boy he is. Is he alone or is that his older brother in the shadows? I do not know, but it is obvious he is here to keep the buffalo and me company.

"I read books about buffaloes, while the boy and the great beast stand nearby. I thumb through my notes. They wait patiently. I find an incident of a pack of dogs and a buffalo on a frozen river and their weight breaking through the ice. My poltergeist creature now stands in the middle of a frozen stream, one lone hound dog at his heels, my boy with a rifle tense on the riverbank, scared to follow lest he fall through the ice and drown. But he calls encouragement to his dog.

"Suddenly the poltergeist beast does break through; the dog also. The buffalo manages to flounder to the bank where the boy shoots it. The hound, alas, is swept away to its death under the ice. To gain the honor of killing the last buffalo in Tennessee, the boy had to lose his only hound, his best friend. A great truth is impressed upon my boy, for now he sees what his mother has told him: that a person cannot always get what he wants in life without paying some price for it. So, about three years after I found the 1810 date on the map, I begin to write the story which will eventually be published as *The Lone Hunt* (Harcourt).

"Ah, children, where indeed does a book come from? A head full of poltergeists and a shelf full of boxes? Does that sound strange, perhaps even disillusioning? But then isn't an author strange anyway because a tale grows out of his head?" [William O. Steele, "The Last Buffalo Killed in Tennessee," *Horn Book,* April, 1969.²]

Steele's last book, his thirty-ninth, was published in 1979 and entitled *The Magic Amulet.* The prolific author had been writing for twenty-seven years before his death at the age of sixty-one on June 25, 1979. Steele's works are included in the Kerlan Collection at the University of Minnesota and in a special collection at the John Brister Library at Memphis State University.

HOBBIES AND OTHER INTERESTS: Pioneers of the old Southwest (pre-Revolutionary times), Indians of the Southeast (particularly the Cherokees in historic times), anthropology, American folklore, walking, camping in the mountains, birdwatching, nature study, and reading.

FOR MORE INFORMATION SEE: Horn Book, February, 1958, April, 1969; *Elementary English,* December, 1960, December, 1961; *Chattanooga Times,* December 19, 1960, April 15, 1962; Muriel Fuller, editor, *More Junior Authors,* H. W. Wilson, 1963; Martha E. Ward and Dorothy A. Marquardt, *Authors of Books for Young People,* Scarecrow, 1971; *American Authors and Books, 1640 to the Present Day,* 3rd revised edition, Crown, 1972; D. L. Kirkpatrick, *Twentieth-Century Children's Writers,* St. Martin's Press, 1978, 2nd edition, 1983; Jim Roginski, compiler, *Newbery and Caldecott Medalists and Honor Book Winners,* Libraries Unlimited, 1982. *Obituaries: Publishers Weekly,* August 13, 1979; *Horn Book,* October, 1979; *School Library Journal,* November 1979.

They stopped when the rabbit told them he had troubles. ■ (From *The Spooky Thing* by William O. Steele. Illustrated by Paul Coker.)

His pa always said that nothing greased a body's joints like being good and scared. ■ (From *The Year of the Bloody Sevens* by William O. Steele. Illustrated by Charles Beck.)

THOMAS, Patricia J. 1934-

PERSONAL: Born January 26, 1934, in Sandy Lake, Pa.; daughter of Raeman Carl (a teacher) and Irene (Lee-Griffin) Jack; married Edward W. Thomas (a comptroller), June 28, 1955; children: Terri Lee, Suzanne Gail, William Raeman, Robert Stuart. *Education:* Attended Westminster College, New Wilmington, Pa., 1952; Pennsylvania State University, B.S., 1956. *Politics:* Republican. *Religion:* Church of Jesus Christ of Latter-Day Saints (Mormon). *Home address:* Box 213, East Butler, Pa. 16029.

CAREER: Spencer Gifts, Inc., Atlantic City, N.J., advertising copywriter, beginning 1969. Publicity director, Power Squadron Auxiliary.

WRITINGS: *"Stand Back," Said the Elephant, "I'm Going to Sneeze"* (juvenile; illustrated by Wallace Tripp), Lothrop, 1971; *"There Are Rocks in My Socks!" Said the Ox to the Fox* (illustrated by Mordicai Gerstein), Lothrop, 1979.

WORK IN PROGRESS: Children's books.

HOBBIES AND OTHER INTERESTS: Camping, water sports, volunteer work with the Girl Scouts.

(From *"There Are Rocks in My Socks!" Said the Ox to the Fox* by Patricia Thomas. Illustrated by Mordicai Gerstein.)

ULAM, S(tanislaw) M(arcin) 1909-1984

PERSONAL: Born April 13, 1909, in Lwów, Poland; became United States citizen; died of a heart attack, May 13, 1984, in Santa Fe, N.M.; son of Jozef (a lawyer) and Anna (Auerbach) Ulam; married Francoise Aron (a free-lance writer), August 19, 1941; children: Claire Anne (Mrs. Steven Weiner). *Education:* Polytechnic Institute, Lwów, Poland, Dr.Sci., 1933. *Residence:* Santa Fe, N.M.

CAREER: Mathematician, educator, and author. Princeton University, Princeton, N.J., visiting scientist at Institute for Advanced Study, 1936; Harvard University, Cambridge, Mass., junior fellow, 1936-40; University of Wisconsin, assistant professor, 1940-41, professor of mathematics, 1941-43; Los Alamos Scientific Laboratory, Los Alamos, N.M., member of scientific staff, 1944-57, research adviser, 1957-67; University of Colorado, Boulder, professor of mathematics, 1965-75. Graduate research professor at University of Florida, 1973-84; visiting professor at Harvard University, 1952, Massachusetts Institute of Technology, 1956, and University of California at San Diego, 1962. *Member:* American Academy of Arts and Sciences, National Academy of Sciences, American Philosophical Society, American Mathematical Society, American Physical Society. *Awards, honors: Adventures of a Mathematician* was selected one of New York Public Library's Books for the Teen Age, 1980, 1981, 1982.

WRITINGS: Collection of Mathematical Problems, Interscience, 1960; *Problems of Modern Mathematics,* Wiley, 1964; (with Mark Kac) *Mathematics and Logic,* Praeger, 1967; *Sets, Numbers, and Universes: Selected Works,* M.I.T. Press, 1974;

S. M. ULAM

Adventures of a Mathematician, Scribner, 1976; *Science, Computers, and People*, Birkhauser, 1985. Contributor to mathematics and physics journals, including *Advances in Applied Mathematics*.

WORK IN PROGRESS: Books to be published posthumously: *Conversations with Gian-Carlo Rota*, and *Collection of Los Alamos Reports: 1944-1984*.

SIDELIGHTS: Ulam was a brilliant mathematical theorist who played an essential role in the development of the H-bomb. His wife, Francoise Ulam, supplied the following biographical information: "Stanislaw Ulam was born in the city of Lwów, Poland in a well-to-do family. In his earliest years he was mostly educated privately, developing an early and precocious interest in science. He liked to recall how, around the age of ten, he signed one of his school notebooks: St. Ulam, astronomer, physicist and mathematician!

"At fifteen he came upon some calculus texts in high school which fascinated him. In 1927 he entered the Lwów Polytechnic Institute to study engineering, where he promptly solved an open problem posed by one of his professors who published it in *Fundamenta Mathematicae*, a leading mathematics journal. Several more papers followed, his self-confidence bloomed, and mathematics became his passion. Engineering was abandoned, and soon Ulam was one of the youngest members of the Lwów section of the Polish Mathematical Society, assiduously frequenting the cafés where the mathematicians met and worked.

"He first visited America in 1935 when John von Neumann invited him to the Institute for Advanced Study in Princeton. This was followed by a visit to Harvard University as a member of the Society of Fellows, then as a lecturer. Every summer he returned to Poland.

"After the outbreak of World War II, and the invasion of his homeland by Hitler, Ulam, cut off from his home base, be-

came a citizen of the United States. He taught at the University of Wisconsin until late 1943 when von Neumann recruited him for the secret Manhattan Project at Los Alamos, New Mexico, where the atom bomb was developed. He liked the frontiers of science and the unexplored, which Los Alamos provided in abundance. 'I am the type that likes to start new things, rather than improve and elaborate,' Ulam wrote in his memoirs, *Adventures of a Mathematician*.

"After the war and with occasional years at universities (Harvard, MIT and the University of California), Los Alamos remained the base from which he conducted most of his work. He retired in 1967 to join the University of Colorado. When he retired from Colorado in 1975, he became a part-time, graduate research professor at the University of Florida, and established residence in Santa Fe.

"Renowned in his youth for his contributions to set theory, topology, ergodic theory, probability theory and number theory, Ulam knew a great deal about the technical side of mathematics. He proposed 'cellular automata' to von Neumann, and invented the 'Monte Carlo' method, a method that grew in application with the development of modern computers. It is now a valuable tool in such diverse fields as the evaluation of multiple integrals, the study of Laplace and Shrödinger equations, neutron transport for nuclear reactors as well as such everyday matters as insurance and traffic control. He became an authority on computational methods and techniques, proposing ingenious schemes for computerized investigations of mathematical problems. As a result of his insights, the computer was brought to the service of the investigation of problems involving combinatorics and nonlinear transformations that anticipated today's interest in solitons and chaos.

"In his later years Ulam opened yet another area for investigation of combinatorial and analytic problems in biology. His insightful contributions to pattern recognition led him to propose new theories concerning actions of the human brain. In short, he became a sort of universal thinker who could bridge all sorts of relations through the use of mathematics. He led the way into what is now known as 'interdisciplinary science.'"

HOBBIES AND OTHER INTERESTS: Chess and tennis.

FOR MORE INFORMATION SEE: S. M. Ulam, *Adventures of a Mathematician*, Scribner, 1976; *American Men and Women of Science: The Physical and Biological Sciences*, 15th edition, Bowker, 1982. Obituaries: *New York Times,* May 15, 1984; *Washington Post,* May 16, 1984; *Newsweek,* May 28, 1984; *Los Alamos Science,* fall, 1987.

VALLEAU, Emily   1925-
(Emily Hearn)

PERSONAL: Born January 17, 1925, in Markham, Ontario, Canada; daughter of Edgar (a car and real estate salesman) and Ida Jane (a musician and teacher; maiden name, Martin) Wadley; married Ernest Reid (a film director), March 26, 1945 (divorced, 1957); married Charles Leslie Hayter (an actor; divorced, 1967); married Douglas John Valleau (a teacher, writer and musician); children: (first marriage) Susan Jane, Timothy David, Norman Douglas; (second marriage) Sam; (third marriage; stepchildren) Danuta, Jennet, Gailon, Karen. *Education:* Attended Trinity College, University of Toronto, 1941-44. *Home:* 980 Broadview Ave., #905, Toronto, Ontario M4K 3YI, Canada.

EMILY VALLEAU

CAREER: National Film Board, Ottawa, Ontario, Canada, library and production assistant, 1944-46; Howard Park United Church Nursery School, Toronto, Ontario, preschool teacher, 1958-61; Bloor Street Young Men's Hebrew Association, Toronto, preschool teacher, 1961-64; Canadian Broadcasting Company, Toronto, children's radio song and script writer, 1962-72; Thomas Nelson & Sons (now Nelson/Canada), Scarborough, Ontario, acquisitions editor, 1969—; writer, 1970—. Teacher trainer, workshop leader and conference speaker in children's literature, creative music, dance and language in early childhood, 1960—; visiting writer in elementary and high schools, 1970—; TV-Ontario, television script and song writer for preschool show "Polka Dot Door," 1972-82. *Member:* Canadian Society of Authors, Illustrators, and Performers; Writers' Union of Canada; Children's Broadcast Institute; Alliance of Canadian Cinema, Television and Radio Artists; Composers, Authors and Publishers Association of Canada.

WRITINGS—All under pseudonym Emily Hearn: (With John McInnes) *Around Another Corner* (illustrated by Edward Malsberg), Garrard, 1971; *Stop! It's a Birthday* (illustrated by William Hutchinson), Garrard, 1972; *Ring around Duffy* (illustrated by Paul Frame), Garrard, 1974; (with Maxine Hemrend and Jennifer Hardacre) *Learning through Play* (handbook), University of Toronto Press, circa 1975; *TV Kangaroo*, Garrard, 1975; (with Marnie Patrick Roberts and Ted Coneybeare) *Polka Dot Door* (handbook), TV Ontario, 1975; *Mighty Mites in Dinosaurland* (illustrated by Mark Thurman), Greey de Pencier, 1981; *Woosh! I Hear a Sound!* (illustrated by Heather Collins), Annick Press, 1983; *Good Morning Franny, Good Night Franny* (illustrated by M. Thurman), Women's Press, 1984; *Race You Franny* (illustrated by M. Thurman), Women's Press, 1986.

Plays: (With Anna Palo-Heimo), *The Pillow Machine,* Creative Drama, 1977; "How Much Wood Would a Woodchuck Chuck?" first produced at Frog Print Theatre, 1977.

Also author of stories and poems in Thomas Nelson's "Venture" and "Language" series; poetry is included in anthologies in Canada, the United States and England; author of limericks and comic features column "Starship," in *Toronto Star* (with illustrator Mark Thurman), 1978-79; originator and developer with artist Mark Thurman of comic strip "Mighty Mites" in *Owl: The Canadian Magazine for Children,* 1976—. Contributor to *Ms.*

WORK IN PROGRESS: A new "Franny" book; *Morningside Bus,* a poetry with children book; "Mighty Mites" episodes for *Owl* magazine; *Storyboarding with Kids* (tentative title), a book about "draw first-write after, a project Mark Thurman and I do in schools."

SIDELIGHTS: "I married young, I was just out of college and it was wartime. I was living in Ottawa and when I went to the National Film Board, it was in a ferment, it was a most creative time. I learned something about compression, every word has to be vital, and this is what children respond to. [Lorna Inness, "Author Showing Children How to Make Books," *Halifax Chronicle-Herald* (Nova Scotia), September 21, 1985.¹]

A nursery school teacher in the late 50s and early 60s, Valleau began writing for young children when "the CBC [Canadian Broadcasting Company] wanted to make its Kindergarten of the Air programs appealing to preschool children. At that point, writing radio broadcasts was a new challenge for me.

Peppino thought that it would be fun to help. ■ (From *Around Another Corner* by Emily Hearn. Illustrated by Edward Malsberg.)

"I wanted to get the children moving. I'd take a theme and turn it into a kind of creative dance-drama. I've found that if you give children a powerful stimulus, they will respond. For the next eight or ten years I was doing all my own research and writing scripts for different grade levels. I did thousands of school broadcasts."[1]

Valleau travelled extensively in Canada while working on a textbook series. "Then, in 1968, I was asked to adapt some of these scripts to print for a reading textbook series which was to be used across Canada. I met incredible people and there was all this wonderful material coming out of Canada. It impressed on me that a Canadian living in Nova Scotia is living in a totally different environment than a Canadian living in Winnipeg, or the Okanagan Valley or in Toronto, and the understanding of environmental differences shaping a child has always fascinated me. A Canadian is a Canadian wherever he or she is, and our broadcasts, whether dealing with St. John's or Vancouver, were heard nationally. I don't think you try to climinate the details that are different."[1]

Her radio work led to writing a series "Polka Dot Door" for television. "Everything was sound—words and music—and we added the visual aspect. For me, it was a totally different way to make an impact. Everything was paced differently."[1]

Valleau wrote early-reading books for Garrard in the 70s, collaborated with illustrator Mark Thurman on a comic feature "Mighty Mites" for *Owl* magazine, and wrote books for children, including her "Franny" books. "When you're surrounded by many wheelchair children you make friendships, same as anywhere, with people you're drawn to. If you like a quiet person, she's there. If you like a quick chatterer, she's there too. We're all individuals, running or sitting.

"In my life I've tended to be noisy and impulsive, not unlike Franny [in *Good Morning Franny, Good Night Franny*], and I've often thought that if I couldn't have chased about and danced, and had to steel myself in the face of curious glances whenever I moved, would I be as outgoing now?

"The urge to write feelings like this, to try to eliminate wheelchairs, has been with me for a long time but the approach eluded me. Until recently, when my work on 'Mighty Mites' for *Owl* magazine, has caused me to adapt camera techniques I learned in television and film writing, to print. When Mark Thurman (Franny's illustrator) and I plot 'Mighty Mite' episodes we vary closeup and wide 'shots' for the dramatic effects we want. It came to me that a book beginning with a closeup of a girl's lively face would pull you into her adventure. By the time our 'camera' has moved back enough to show her scooting in her chair all you care about is what's going to happen to her next.

"Both Mark and I live in the colourful locale of this Toronto story. Families move in and away from the area in their search for jobs and housing. Children's friendships can't always endure but surely some of the joy remains. Once in a while someone asks me to write about Ting and Franny meeting again but I'm not one to smooth out all the rough edges. There *is* another *Franny*. She's up to mischief again. And there's a dog. . . .

"Why did I write *Race You Franny*? Because she was already there and running, so to speak. I can't keep up with adventures for her that flash in my mind when I walk the lively, varied neighborhood streets that are hers, mine, and Mark's, her illustrator.

"*Race You* was triggered first by my seeing a frolicking dog scare little kids in a park pool and, on another occasion,

watching two children absorbed in manoeuvering a remote control boat. It became a car, Danny with the orange-est hair was created and Franny rolled herself into the scene, causing her usual fun and confusion.

"Her zest and curiosity are contagious. I can't let go of her. Children's response to the original Franny book, *Good Morning Franny, Goodnight Franny* gratifies my one wish, she is seen as a girl, not an invalid. A preschooler's drawing came my way from Newfoundland. There is Franny, tearing along, standing upright on her wheelchair!

"She loves people-happenings. A mystery and a colourful parade involve her next time around."

HOBBIES AND OTHER INTERESTS: "I make music as much as I write, favoring the harpsichord currently, and the recorder and fortepiano. I enjoy colour photography, an excuse for much walking and what travel I can manage in a lively schedule."

FOR MORE INFORMATION SEE: D. Melanie Zola, "On a Fantasy Flight with Emily and Mark," *Vancouver Sun*, April, 1984; *LDR Networks* (Canada), February, 1984; Lorna Inness, "Author Showing Children How to Make Books," *Halifax Chronicle-Herald* (Nova Scotia), September 21, 1985.

VILLIARD, Paul   1910-1974
(J. H. deGros)

PERSONAL: Surname pronounced Vee-yarh; born January 16, 1910, in Spokane, Wash.; died August 18, 1974, in Saxton, N.Y.; married Gertrude vanden Bergen, October 27, 1941; children: Paul, Jr., William John, Frederick. *Residence:* Saugerties, N.Y.

CAREER: Writer and photographer; in addition to illustrating his own work, supplied technical and scientific photographs to publishers and agents for use in books and magazines. *Awards, honors: Exotic Fishes as Pets* was selected one of Child Study Association of America's Children's Books of the Year, 1971, *Insects as Pets*, 1973, and *Collecting Stamps*, 1974; *Collecting Stamps* was selected one of New York Public Library's Books for the Teenage, 1980, 1981, and 1982, and *Birds as Pets*, 1980 and 1981.

WRITINGS—All self-illustrated: (Under pseudonym J. H. deGros) *Today's Woman Candy Cook Book*, Fawcett, 1953; (under pseudonym J. H. deGros) *Holiday Candy and Cookie Cook Book*, Fawcett, 1954.

Handy Man's Plumbing and Heating Guide, Fawcett, 1967; *A Manual of Veneering*, Van Nostrand, 1968; *A First Book of Ceramics*, Funk, 1969; *A First Book of Jewelrymaking*, Funk, 1969; *Reptiles as Pets* (juvenile), Doubleday, 1969; *Moths, and How to Rear Them*, Funk, 1969, 2nd revised edition, Dover, 1975.

Through the Seasons with a Camera, Doubleday, 1970; *Growing Pains: The Autobiography of a Young Boy*, Funk, 1970; *Exotic Fishes as Pets* (juvenile), Natural History Press, 1971; *Shells: Homes in the Sea*, Addison-Wesley, 1972; *Wild Mammals as Pets* (juvenile), Doubleday, 1972; *Insects as Pets* (juvenile), Doubleday, 1972; *Jewelrymaking* (juvenile), Doubleday, 1973; *Raising Small Animals for Fun and Profit*, Winchester Press, 1973; *Birds as Pets* (juvenile), Doubleday, 1974; *Gemstones and Minerals: A Guide for the Amateur Collector*, Winchester Press, 1974; *Collecting Stamps*, Double-

Paul Villiard with a pet great horned owl.

day, 1974; *The Hidden World: The Story of Microscopic Life* (juvenile), Four Winds Press, 1975; *Collecting Things* (juvenile), Doubleday, 1975; *The Art and Craft of Sandcasting,* Funk, 1975; *Wild Animals around Your Home* (juvenile), Winchester Press, 1975.

(With George Zappler) *A Pet of Your Own* (juvenile), Doubleday, 1981. Contributor to *Reader's Digest, Natural History, Audubon Magazine, Popular Homecraft,* and other magazines.

WORK IN PROGRESS: A First Book of Leatherwork, A First Book of Fly-Tying, A First Book of Enamelling, Candy Cook Book, all for Abelard; *Shells Built by Mollusks, Shells: Homes on Land, Shells: The Poisonous Ones,* all elementary grade texts with teachers' manuals, for Addison-Wesley; *Contemporary Furniture Design,* for Funk; *Flowers by the Way; A Manual of Marquetry; After the Camera; Nature Photography: A Manual.*

SIDELIGHTS: "I was born in Spokane, Washington, but my family moved to Seattle when I was only a few months old, and it was in this northwestern city that I did most of my growing up, except for periodic trips to Philadelphia, Pennsylvania, to visit my Aunt Marion and Uncle Harry with their six children, or an infrequent trip to Kansas City, Missouri, to visit my Uncle Dan and Aunt Daisy. All these relatives were my mother's. Father's relatives were all in Europe, and we never met any of them, nor did any of them ever write us that I can remember.

"My father was very strict. He was Alsatian, and, although he lived in the United States, obtaining his citizenship papers and raising his family here, he never quite relaxed from his rigid European way of life. A child was required to be instantly and unquestioningly obedient. To say 'no' to my father was equivalent to baiting a grizzly bear. Retribution was swift and severe.

"He did have a sense of justice, but was almost devoid of a sense of humor. Rather, his sense of humor was slow, ponderous, and not up to his children's rapid native wit. He found it easier to ignore me than to attempt to rear me, which, I

suppose, was one of the reasons I was always into something or other.

"Father spent much of his time in Europe. He was, by the time I was born, an importer and exporter, exchanging goods from America for those of Europe. Both exchanges found a ready market on both sides of the Atlantic, and father amassed not a small fortune several times, losing it each time to iniquitous dealers in bogus stocks, a commodity completely irresistible to father.

"Mother was a very gentle, rather harrassed soul, immersed in church work and living in a somewhat unreal world, unaware most of the time of what was going on around her. Hers was the task of rearing a family of two boys and a girl, with very little help from my father. Indeed, on more than one occasion father was in Europe for such an extended time that I, at least, did not recognize him when he finally did pay his family a visit. My sister, being four years older than I, and my brother, four years older still, probably did not have that difficulty, but I remember a couple of times living for days with a total stranger in the house, until I again became used to the idea that this was my father, finally accepting him as such.

"He was generous to his family when in funds, indifferent to its needs when his money was scarce. His trips to Europe were lavish affairs. . . . It is a matter of family record that at least once he did in fact take nine persons on a princely three-month tour of European cities, finally landing them again on the very dock from which they left New York, equipped with trunks of new clothing and personal belongings purchased to see them through the impromptu voyage.

"He died in Philadelphia in his mid-seventies, many years after my mother had passed away. My sister and I together paid the expenses of his interment, afterward sadly sorting through several million dollars' worth of phony stock certificates that were our sole legacy.

"And yet, I feel that I owe my father a debt of gratitude. When he finally threw me out of the family at the age of fourteen I was forced to go out into the world on my own.

Willy-nilly, I became self-reliant and able to earn my living. My curiosity about things around me continued undiminished. Rather, it increased, if possible, and I early learned that the more one knew about everything, the more easily one could find work and make a living.

"I suppose I was what could be termed 'incident-prone'; in any event, I lived my early years with intensity and relish. I was instantly ready to undertake anything just a little out of the ordinary.

"I never returned home to live. After arriving in New York, I went to see [brother] Fred, who let me stay with him for about a month. I found work in a hardware store, and as soon as my pay was coming in regularly, moved to a furnished room by myself.

"I wrote to mother, telling her where I was, and every once in a while, after receiving a letter from her in which she would casually state that father would be away the next weekend, I'd go to Philadelphia at her unspoken invitation, to see her. Usually I slept with Bert Bierman on the next street, going home to talk with mother.

"We . . . made plans to open a candy shop together, but mother died when I was about eighteen. I was in the far West at the time, and couldn't get home in time for the funeral. I had no word from father. . . .

"Some time later, I was living in West Philadelphia, doing some research work in veterinary medicine with Bert Bierman, at the University of Pennsylvania. Boarding a street car one afternoon, I saw father reading a newspaper. He looked up and saw me, so I went to sit beside him. He looked old and worn. He was at the time in his mid-seventies, I think. I took him home with me, and we talked for a time. This was really the first time I had ever talked at any length to father. He was pretty badly off, both physically and mentally, having lost all his money in the recent stock crash. He looked and acted ill, but claimed he was feeling all right, except that he was tired all the time and got out of breath at the slightest exertion. I offered to let him stay with me." [Paul Villiard, *Growing Pains: The Autobiography of a Young Boy,* Funk & Wagnalls, 1970.]

Villard eventually succeeded in becoming a research engineer, biophotographer, naturalist, and writer. He was the author of

A tame Budgie makes a wonderful pet for children. ■ (From *Birds as Pets* by Paul Villiard. Photograph by the author.)

many books for children and adults, including many "how-to" books and books on nature. He died on August 18, 1974.

FOR MORE INFORMATION SEE: Paul Villiard, *Growing Pains: The Autobiography of a Young Boy,* Funk & Wagnalls, 1970; Martha E. Ward and Dorothy A. Marquardt, *Authors of Books for Young People,* 2nd edition supplement, Scarecrow, 1979. *Obituaries: New York Times,* August 24, 1974; *Publishers Weekly,* September 30, 1974.

WACHTER, Oralee Roberts 1935-

BRIEF ENTRY: Born April 16, 1935, in Los Angeles, Calif. Wachter graduated from the University of California in 1958 and received her master's from San Francisco State University in 1978. She is also a certified teacher in California. Wachter was a university instructor and an education program director until 1975, when she became president and director of O.D.N. Productions, Inc., a media company. Wachter's first book for children, *No More Secrets for Me* (Little, Brown, 1983), is based on her award-winning movie, "No More Secrets," about child sexual abuse. "In forty-eight short pages this book goes a long way toward teaching kids to empower and protect themselves," wrote a reviewer for the *Los Angeles Times.* The book presents four scenarios, each with one child and a potentially harmful adult. In the resulting satisfying conclusions, each child finds a trusting adult with whom to share "the secret." *Publisher's Weekly* wrote, "Aaron's colored sketches animate the realistic, readily understood text.... The information is long overdue, and everyone should read this book." *Close to Home* (Scholastic, 1986), is written in the same format, and advises children how to avoid being abducted. "The stories are smoothly written and placed in a cleanly designed format; this is a worthy companion to the author's well-received first book," noted *Booklist.* Wachter has also written *Sex, Drugs and AIDS* (Bantam, 1987), for young readers. *Office:* 74 Varick St., New York, N.Y. 10013.

FOR MORE INFORMATION SEE: Who's Who of American Women, Marquis Who's Who, 1984.

WALDMAN, Neil 1947-

PERSONAL: Born October 22, 1947, in Bronx, N.Y.; son of Abraham (a businessman) and Jessie (a homemaker; maiden name, Herstein) Waldman; married Jeri Socol (an elementary school teacher), December 20, 1972; children: Sarah, Jonathan. *Education:* Rochester Institute of Technology, B.F.A., 1969, M.A., 1970. *Politics:* Liberal. *Religion:* Jewish—Reformed. *Home:* 47 Woodlands Ave., White Plains, N.Y. 10607.

CAREER: Kibbutz Neve Ur, Israel, olive farmer, 1970-73, 1975-76; Linbry Products, Yonkers, N.Y., art director, 1971; free-lance illustrator, 1973—; William Patterson College, Patterson, N.J., teacher, 1980-81. Designer of postage stamps, record album covers, book dust covers and theater posters. *Exhibitions:* Market Fair Gallery, Nyack, N.Y., 1971; Inland Sea Gallery, Pearl River, N.Y., 1982; Society of Illustrators, New York, N.Y., 1982, 1984, 1985; Studio 43, New Rochelle, N.Y., 1984. *Member:* Graphic Artists Guild. *Awards, honors:* Desi Award, 1980, for a poster for Sylvania; nominated for Grammy Award 1982, and 1983, both for record cover design; United Nations Poster Award, 1986.

WRITINGS—Self-illustrated: *Pitcher in Left Field,* Prentice-Hall, 1981.

NEIL WALDMAN

Illustrator: W. Harter, *Osceola's Head and Other Ghost Stories,* Prentice-Hall, 1974; David C. Knight, *The Moving Coffins: Ghosts and Hauntings around the World,* Prentice-Hall, 1983; Patricia T. Lowe, *The Runt,* Caedmon, 1984; Michael Mark, *Toba,* Bradbury, 1984; D. C. Knight, reteller, *Best True Ghost Stories of the Twentieth Century,* Prentice-Hall, 1984; Lee P. Huntington, *Maybe a Miracle,* Coward, 1984; (and selector) Edgar Allan Poe, *Tales of Terror: Ten Short Stories,* Prentice-Hall, 1985; William Warren, *The Headless Ghost: True Tales of the Unexplained,* Prentice-Hall, 1986; W. Warren, *The Screaming Skull,* Prentice-Hall, 1987.

WORK IN PROGRESS: Illustrations for Jeffrey Prusski's *Bring Back the Deer,* a mystical story of a young Indian boy, going through the rites of manhood.

SIDELIGHTS: "I was raised in a house where all the arts were encouraged. I sensed, as a small child, that finger paints and coloring books were more than just fun. They were important tools that lead to a road of joy, discovery and fulfillment.

"When I entered first grade, I learned very quickly that, within the classroom walls, the arts were 'secondary subjects,' not nearly as important as reading, math, and science. I resented this deeply, and unconsciously began to rebel. Through twelve years of school I was considered an 'underachiever.' In fact, I was doing the minimum possible to get by, while working on my art at home.

"When I graduated from high school (near the bottom of my class), I felt as though I had been liberated. I entered an art college, where I spent most of my time drawing and painting. Here, surrounded by other artists for the first time, I began to blossom. Though I'd always known that art was important too, now it was reenforced in my environment. Instead of strug-

Myself and my two brothers once owned a schooner-rigged smack . . . with which we were in the habit of fishing among the islands beyond Moskoe. . . . ■ (From *Tales of Terror: Ten Short Stories* by Edgar Allan Poe. Selected and illustrated by Neil Waldman.)

gling against the current, I was gliding freely, ever faster and deeper, to places I had never imagined.''

Waldman studied illustration and painting at Rochester Institute of Technology. ''During and after college there was never a plan for my life. I wanted to travel since I was a kid and I always wanted to draw and paint. It just never occurred to me I would end up doing what I like for a living.'' [John Dalmas, ''Neil Waldman: He Has Designs on Postage Stamps,'' *Sunday Journal-News* (Rockland County, N.Y.), December 30, 1984.[1]]

''When I graduated I did many things: I travelled to many countries; working as an olive farmer, businessman, package designer, art teacher, border guard, and a few other things. Two years later, in the summer of 1972, I travelled to Japan where I fell in love. Her name was Jeri Socol, and she was an elementary school teacher from New York. We returned together in September and were married three months later. She has allowed me to be an artist. It took many years to get to a point where I was able to make a living with illustrating. I was only able to do this because she had a job and we lived on her salary. She has a very positive attitude towards art, and at one point, she said to me that if I just wanted to be a painter, she would be willing to support us. I really don't know if I would be an illustrator today, had it not been for her.'' [Elsa B. Endrst, ''Westchester Spotlight on Neil Waldman,'' *Spotlight*, October, 1986.[2]]

''I began to look for work as an illustrator. This seemed a natural decision, because it would allow me to do what I love most, while earning a living. It was difficult at first, almost like learning a new language. But it was worth it.''

Waldman has designed numerous postage stamps for Sierra Leone, Grenada, Antigua and many other countries. ''A friend of mine had designed a stamp through the IPC and told me they were looking for another artist who might be interested. The company is located in New York because the city has the single largest concentration of illustrators in the world.

''I can come up with a concept and carry it through to the finish. I really like doing them and it's been a lot of fun.''[1]

Illustrating ''*Tales of Terror* is the realization of a dream I've had for many years: to illustrate a volume of my favorite Edgar Allan Poe stories. The many hours of intense work on this book have been a great satisfaction to me. The experience has been deeply rewarding.

''Now, fifteen years later, I'm still at it, and I love it. I love working for myself at home. I love not having to wear a tie. I love the growth and freedom I have experienced. I love being able to spend mornings and afternoons with my children. And I love the joy I feel as magical colors leap from my brush onto a blank sheet of paper.''

In 1986 Waldman won the competition for the U.N. poster representing the International Year of Peace. It was a picture depicting the universal child and, within the child's face, all the people of the world portrayed the universality of mankind. ''This is a wonderful example of the joy of being an artist. . . . An idea came to me. Now, because of that idea, not only did exciting things happen, but there is something tangible that exists which is the culmination of that idea. That's the most gratifying thing about being an illustrator: It's one of the few careers left in the world where the same person is directly involved from the first creative thought to the finished piece; in addition, the artist is in on the entire process, from beginning to end.''[2]

HOBBIES AND OTHER INTERESTS: Chess, guitar, classical music, travel, softball.

FOR MORE INFORMATION SEE: John Dalmas, ''Neil Waldman: He Has Designs on Postage Stamps,'' *Sunday Journal-News* (Rockland County, N.Y.), December 30, 1984; ''Ardsley Village Parade,'' *Enterprise* (N.Y.), September 19, 1986; Elsa B. Endrst, ''Westchester Spotlight on Neil Waldman,'' *Spotlight* (N.Y.), October, 1986.

WALLACE-BRODEUR, Ruth 1941-

PERSONAL: Born August 25, 1941, in Springfield, Mass.; daughter of Emery L. (a minister) and Dorothy (a teacher; maiden name, Blume) Wallace; married Paul Brodeur (a social worker), September 1, 1962; children: Jennifer, Jeremy, Rachel, Sarah. *Education:* University of Massachusetts, B.A., 1962. *Home and office:* Montpelier, Vt.

CAREER: Pineland Hospital and Training Center, Pownal, Maine, member of psychology staff, 1962-63; writer, 1975—. *Member:* Amnesty International, Fellowship of Reconciliation, American Civil Liberties Union, League of Vermont Writers, Green Mountain Club.

WRITINGS: The Kenton Year (juvenile novel), Atheneum, 1980; *One April Vacation* (juvenile novel), Atheneum, 1981; *Callie's Way*, Atheneum, 1984; *Steps in Time*, Atheneum, 1986. Contributor to magazines and newspapers, including *Cricket, Highlights, Boys' Life, Pennywhistle Press, Child Life, Backpacker, Family Journal, Vermont Life, Christian Science Monitor*, and *Vermont Woman*.

WORK IN PROGRESS: A novel for children, ages 8-12; two short stories for adults. ''The Vermont Migrant Education Program received a grant to publish three books written especially for the children of dairy farm workers reflecting their experiences and environment, and asked me to write a novel for children ages 8-12. This will be distributed to migrant programs throughout the United States and to the general public.''

SIDELIGHTS: ''I like writing for children because I cherish the directness of their experiences and expressions and of my own as a child: an affinity for primary colors. I want to achieve some of that immediacy, that distillation, in adult experience and writing.'' *Steps in Time* is currently being issued in paperback and in hardcover by Field Publications for their ''Especially for Girls Club.''

HOBBIES AND OTHER INTERESTS: Running, gardening, making quilts out of scraps (''a complementary physical, visual process to my writing, bringing bits and pieces from here and there into relationship'').

FOR MORE INFORMATION SEE: Rutland Herald and Times Argus, July 13, 1980; *Burlington Free Press*, January 28, 1981, March 27, 1985.

Come away, O human child!
To the waters and the wild
With a faery, hand in hand,
For the world's more full of weeping than you can understand.
—William Butler Yeats

I am always making resolutions one day and forgetting them the next.... ■ (Jacket illustration by Deborah Chabrian from *Steps in Time* by Ruth Wallace-Brodeur.)

The kids worked all night. ■ (From *The Adventures of Strawberry Shortcake and Her Friends* by Alexandra Wallner. Illustrated by Mercedes Limona.)

WALLNER, Alexandra 1946-

PERSONAL: Born February 28, 1946, in Germany; came to the United States in 1952, naturalized citizen, 1964; daughter of Severin (a physician) and Hildegard (an artist; maiden name, Waltch) Czesnykowski; married John C. Wallner (an illustrator), July 16, 1971. *Education:* Pratt Institute, B.F.A., 1968, M.F.A., 1970. *Home and office:* 82 Broadview Rd., Woodstock, N.Y. 12498. *Agent:* Kirchoff/Wohlberg, Inc., 866 United Nations Plaza, New York, N.Y. 10017. *Office:* Greywood, 82 Broadview Rd., Woodstock, N.Y. 12498.

CAREER: American Home, New York City, assistant art director, 1972-73; *New Ingenue,* New York City, associate art director, 1973-75; free-lance illustrator and writer, 1975—. Co-owner of "Greywood" studio, Woodstock, N.Y.

WRITINGS—Juvenile: *Munch* (poems; self-illustrated), Crown, 1976; *The Adventures of Strawberry Shortcake and Her Friends* (illustrated by Mercedes Llimona), Random House, 1980; *Strawberry Shortcake and the Winter That Would Not End* (illustrated by M. Llimona), Random House, 1982; *Ghoulish Giggles and Monster Riddles* (self-illustrated), A. Whitman, 1982; *Kerby on Safari* (self-illustrated with husband, John C. Wallner), Avon, 1984.

Illustrator: Martha Gamerman, *Trudy's Straw Hat,* Crown, 1977; Malcolm Hall, *The Friends of Charlie Ant Bear,* Coward, 1980; Joanne E. Bernstein and Paul Cohen, *Un-Frog-gettable Riddles,* A. Whitman, 1981.

WORK IN PROGRESS: ABC Book.

ALEXANDRA WALLNER

SIDELIGHTS: "I have always enjoyed writing and drawing. I had a lonely childhood, no brothers or sisters, and we always lived where there were no children my age. To entertain myself I made up stories and fantasies and wrote short books and comic strips."

At the age of six, Wallner emigrated from her native Germany to the U.S. with her parents. "I spoke no English until the first grade and learned [my new language] by reading comic books: *Donald Duck, Uncle Scrooge, Little Lulu, Katy Keene, Archie*—not a bad way for a person to learn a language; pictures and words right there together. I loved the bright colors and clever stories.

"My mother was an artist, greatly influenced by the 'Trash Can School' of art. She painted town scenes, bar scenes, portraits and wrote humorous stories. I was very much influenced by her, and, I suppose, subconsciously I was imitating her.

"After high school I studied art at Pratt Institute and received my BFA and MFA degrees. I started my career at *American Home* because I wanted to start somewhere in commercial art. It was in my position with *New Ingenue* that I really learned about typography, layout, illustration, graphic design.

"When my husband, who is also an illustrator, started his studio, he looked like he was having so much fun with illustration, that I decided I would do it too. I'm glad I made this decision. Although I have done much more illustration than writing, I am always thinking up projects and trying to get people interested in publishing them. Illustration is much easier for me than writing. In the last few years, I have felt a need to write more educational stories, because I feel I have certain things that I want to say. I've been illustrating a lot of textbook work lately, and although satisfying, there is very little feedback from my audience. It is always very gratifying when a child writes to me about one of the 'Strawberry Shortcake' books and tells me how much he enjoyed it. It makes me feel like I've touched someone's life.

"I like to capture the best of the good things in the world to retell in my own way. I like all of my books to have a sense of humor, so that people can have a sense of humor about themselves."

HOBBIES AND OTHER INTERESTS: Gardening, needlepoint.

WALLNER, John C. 1945-

PERSONAL: Born February 3, 1945, in St. Louis, Mo.; son of John C. (an insurance agent) and Rita (Ziegler; a beautician) Wallner; married Alexandra Czesnykowski (an illustrator and writer), July 16, 1971. *Education:* Washington University, B.F.A., 1968; Pratt Institute, M.F.A., 1970. *Home:* 82 Broadview Rd., Woodstock, N.Y. 12498. *Agent:* Kirchoff/Wohlberg, 866 United Nations Plaza, New York, N.Y. 10017. *Office:* Greywood, 82 Broadview Rd., Woodstock, N.. 12498.

CAREER: Free-lance illustrator, 1972—. Owner of "Greywood" studio, Woodstock, N.Y. *Exhibitions:* Has exhibited his works in New York, including Albany Small Print Show, Pratt Traveling Miniature Print Show, and Audubon Society. *Awards, honors:* Society of Illustrators, certificates of merit, 1972-75; *Follow Me Cried Bee* and *Little Fox Goes to the End of the World* were each selected one of Child Study Association of America's Children's Books of the Year, 1976, and *Easter Poems* and *Hello, My Name Is Scrambled Eggs,* 1985;

Little Fox Goes to the End of the World was included in the American Institute of Graphic Arts Book Show, 1976, and received the Friends of American Writers Award for illustration, 1977; *Good-Night to Annie* was included in the American Institute of Graphic Arts Book Show, 1980; Woodward Park School Annual Book Award, 1980, for *Charlotte and Charles; Aldo Ice Cream* was selected a Children's Choice by the International Reading Association, 1982; *Snow White and Rose Red* was exhibited as the Bologna International Children's Book Fair, 1985.

WRITINGS: (Reteller) *Rumpelstiltskin,* Prentice-Hall, 1984; (reteller) *Sleeping Beauty,* Viking, 1987; (reteller) *The Three Little Pigs,* Viking, 1987.

Illustrator: James McCrea and Ruth McCrea, *Marvelous Machines,* Holt, 1971; Georgess McHargue, *Mummies,* Lippincott, 1972; Morris Kirchoff, *Encyclopedia of Economics,* Doskin, 1972; Simone Beck, *Simca's Cuisine,* Knopf, 1972; Cecil Vye and Elizabeth Canar, editors, *Different Drummers,* Random House, 1972; Morris Kirchoff, *Scenes from American Life,* Random House, 1972; M. Kirchoff, *American Language Today,* McGraw, 1973; Sharyla Gold, *Amelia Quackenbush* (jacket and frontispiece), Seabury, 1973; Pat Ross, *Hi Fly,* Crown, 1974.

Marge Blaine, *The Terrible Thing That Happened at Our House,* Parents Magazine Press, 1975; Hila Coleman, *Ethan's Favorite Teacher* (Junior Literary Guild selection), Crown, 1975;

Ann Tompert, *Little Fox Goes to the End of the World* (ALA Notable Book), Crown, 1976; Elizabeth Levy, *Lizzie Lies a Lot,* Delacorte, 1976; John R. Townsend, *Top of the World,* Lippincott, 1976; J. Wahl, *Follow Me Cried Bee,* Crown, 1976; Linda Hirsch, *The Sick Story,* Hastings House, 1976; A. Tompert, *Little Otter Remembers and Other Stories,* Crown, 1977; Hubert David, editor, *A January Fog Will Freeze a Hog and Other Weather Folklore,* Crown, 1977; Johanna Hurwitz, *Much Ado about Aldo,* Morrow, 1978; Jamie Gilson, *Harvey, the Beer Can King,* Lothrop, 1978; Gail Radley, *The Night Stella Hid the Stars,* Crown, 1978; Eve Merriam, *Good-Night to Annie,* Four Winds, 1979; J. Hurwitz, *Aldo Applesauce,* Morrow, 1979; Dorothy Corey, *Pepe's Private Christmas,* Parents Magazine Press, 1979; A. Tompert, *Charlotte and Charles,* Crown, 1979; J. Gilson, *Dial Leroi Rupert, DJ,* Lothrop, 1979.

Jane B. Zalben, *A Perfect Nose for Ralph,* Philomel, 1980; Phyllis Green, *Gloomy Louie,* A. Whitman, 1980; Patricia Elmore, *Susannah and the Blue House Mystery,* Dutton, 1980; Carla Stevens, *Sara and the Pinch,* Houghton, 1980; J. Wahl, *Grandpa Gus's Birthday Cake,* Prentice-Hall, 1981; J. Hurwitz, *Aldo Ice Cream,* Morrow, 1981; Jim Aylesworth, *Tonight's the Night,* A. Whitman, 1981; Richard L. Allington and Kathleen Krull, *Winter,* Raintree, 1981; Steven Kroll, *One Tough Turkey: A Thanksgiving Story,* Holiday House, 1982; Susan Sussman, *Hippo Thunder,* A. Whitman, 1982; L. Hirsch, *You're Going Out There a Kid, but You're Coming Back a Star!,* Hastings House, 1982; Keith Brandt, *The Case of the*

JOHN C. WALLNER

(From *The Terrible Thing That Happened at Our House* by Marge Blaine. Illustrated by John C. Wallner.)

Missing Dinosaur, Troll Associates, 1982; Kathleen N. Daly, *The Macmillan Picture Wordbook,* Macmillan, 1982; J. Wahl, *The Pipkins Go Camping,* Prentice-Hall, 1982; Pat Fortunato, *A Colonial Williamsburg Activities Book: Fun Activities for Children Seven and Up,* Colonial Williamsburg Foundation, 1982; Maggie S. Davis, *Grandma's Secret Letter,* Holiday House, 1982; Susan Sussman, *Hippo Thunder,* A. Whitman, 1982; Nancy Larrick, compiler, *When the Dark Comes Dancing: A Bedtime Poetry Book* (ALA Notable Book), Philomel, 1983; Joan L. Nixon, *Days of Fear,* Dutton, 1983; J. Wahl, *More Room for the Pipkins,* Prentice-Hall, 1983; Marjorie W. Sharmat, *Frizzy the Fearful,* Holiday House, 1983; Jacob Grimm and Wilhelm Grimm, *Snow White and Rose Red,* Prentice-Hall, 1984; (with wife, Alexandra Wallner) Alexandra Wallner, *Kerby on Safari,* Avon, 1984.

Myra C. Livingston, editor, *Easter Poems,* Holiday House, 1985; Tom Sinclair, *Tales of a Wandering Warthog,* A. Whitman, 1985; S. Kroll, *Mrs. Claus's Crazy Christmas,* Holiday House, 1985; J. Gilson, *Hello, My Name Is Scrambled Eggs,* Lothrop, 1985; J. Grimm and W. Grimm, *Hansel and Gretel,* Prentice-Hall, 1985; Marjorie W. Sharmat, *Hooray for Mother's Day!,* Holiday House, 1986; Jane Yolen, *Ring of Earth: A Child's Book of Seasons,* Harcourt, 1986; Jim Diaz, *Old MacDonald Had a Farm: A Musical Pop-Up Book,* Dutton, 1986; M. W. Sharmat, *Hooray for Father's Day!,* Holiday House, 1987.

Also illustrator of text books for Harper & Row, Ginn & Company and American Book Company, and of book jackets. A cartoon story "Rolls and Jellylord" appeared in *Yo Yo* Magazine, 1972. Contributor of illustrations to *Children's Digest, Hi Fi and Stereo* and *Good Housekeeping.*

WORK IN PROGRESS: "I'm working on *The Boy Who Ate the Moon,* a book about a boy who climbs a tree in order to get close to the moon. He was warned against this because it was dangerous, but the moon is irresistible to him. He climbs the tree anyway, gets close enough to the moon to take a little nibble of it, then another, and another, until he has eaten the entire moon, for which he is rewarded with a fabulous journey. To me, this is a story about overcoming fear, learning to disobey if the rules mean you can't have your dream, and being rewarded for having the courage to follow your imagination."

SIDELIGHTS: "I was a coloring book fanatic as a kid—drawing all the time. And I would build theater stages and forts out of boxes that my mother would provide for me; especially good were the ones that dishwashers and other large appliances came in. I'd cut windows, make figures and separate areas and levels—pretty ambitious projects. My father was killed during World War II, so my authority figures were my mother and aunt, both of whom encouraged my drawing and praised me lavishly. I had absolute confidence in my drawing, absolute faith in my imagination. As much as I spent most of my childhood alone, I was not lonely.

"I remember one day in kindergarten we were told to draw the outline of a house and color it in. Well, that wasn't enough to keep *me* busy, so I added a chimney with lots of smoke pouring out. The teacher came to my desk and said, 'John, we don't scribble in kindergarten.' 'I'm not scribbling,' I told her, 'I'm making smoke.' I was outraged, appalled, and thought to myself, 'I must teach this woman about smoke and chimneys.'

"I hated school until I reached college. I attended very strict and regimented Roman Catholic elementary and high schools, where the most important attribute seemed to be sitting properly at one's desk—back straight, feet flat on the floor, hands

on the tabletop. Two things made it bearable for me: Friday afternoon art classes and the nuns' habits. Had the nuns not worn habits, I think I'd have lost my mind. But the fact that they wore wonderful costumes, complete with swinging rosary beads and fluttering veils made them a visual treat. That theatricality made it all worthwhile.

"I was never very good in sports, perhaps it was because I didn't have a father to explain the rules of the games and play catch with me. I didn't want the other kids to know how bad I really was, and so stayed out of the games. I'd be on the periphery, doing humorous commentary, amusing myself and the others. I was lucky as a kid, as different as I was from most of the children I grew up with, I was never ostracized. My drawing was important here—I'd do funny pictures and portraits for my admiring peers.

"In high school, I was part of the drama club. My specialty was comic monologues—monologue versions of epic movies like *Ben Hur* in which I'd tell the stories and 'review' the film. It was a tradition in my high school for the senior class to take a trip to New York City. As soon as I caught sight of Manhattan, I felt like I was 'home.' I loved everything—the elegance of Fifth Avenue, the grunge of Times Square, the museums, the galleries, the amazing energy of the people. It clicked—someday, I knew, I would come here to live."

Torrieney, a sculptor on the faculty at Webster College in St. Louis and teacher at Wallner's high school was an important influence. "As he talked about art, I suddenly recognized his voice as coming from one of my tribesmen. For years I'd felt I had been living in the Tower of Babel, and finally, I'd found someone who spoke my language. I showed him my drawings of nymphs in flowing robes executed in ballpoint pen. I was very nervous, and half expected him to say, 'John, in high

Aldo and Mrs. Nardo shared the peaches while Peabody ate the meat. ■ (From *Aldo Ice Cream* by Johanna Hurwitz. Illustrated by John Wallner.)

school we don't scribble.' But he was very kind and suggested I apply to Washington University. I did, and lo and behold, they accepted me.

"I attended college wearing a blazer, white shirt and tie—it was all I knew after years of Catholic schooling. But whole new worlds opened up to me. There were people from all over—Brooklynites with these incredible accents, Bostonians, hippies, feminists with paint all over their hands and feet. No fading violets at this school! For the first time, I found the right people for my spirit. I continued to live with my mother and aunt and came home every evening with pages of drawings and all sorts of three-dimensional constructions. My classmates turned me on to wonderful Medieval music, blues, jazz,

THE EASTER PARADE

What shall I wear for the Easter Parade?
A dress that's the color of marmalade
With a border embroidered in light blue cornflowers
Like the edge of a meadow after spring showers
And a matching hat round as a top you can spin
And elastic to hold it on under my chin
And brand-new shoes whiter than newly-poured cream
With heart-shaped, golden buckles that gleam;
And I'll carry a small purse of butterfly blue
With a penny for me and a penny for you
To buy us both glasses of cold lemonade
When we walk, hand in hand, in the Easter Parade.

WILLIAM JAY SMITH

films and art. My fellow students, in terms of my education, were at least as important as the classes I took.

"Washington University offered a solid foundation in anatomy, life drawing, composition, perspective, design. Their big emphasis was on technique. Little, if anything, was left to accident. I was a painting major, although I'm not a very good painter. I'm a linear artist and prefer to draw. I need to find the edges of the objects I draw; I'm unable to just let a table bleed into space, for example. I became very interested in printmaking, particularly etching, which is all about lines.

"The logical place for me to go then was to Pratt, in Brooklyn, New York. I didn't have a clue where Pratt was located and

(From "The Easter Parade" by William Jay Smith in *Easter Poems,* selected by Myra Cohn Livingston. Illustrated by John Wallner.)

just got off the subway at the first stop in Brooklyn Heights. I had typical beginner's luck. Walking around in the lovely, nineteenth-century neighborhood, I asked people if they knew of available apartments and ended up with one, just like that. During that first year I spent more time finding my way around the city than studying. I visited galleries, museums, the park. My favorite place in Central Park was near the reflecting pond where the statue of Alice in Wonderland is located. I'd sit there for hours and sketch. Perhaps all this was self-indulgent on my part, but when you're faced with so much new stimulation, you have to at least *try* to take it at your own pace. I needed my dream time.

"Still, I managed to learn a lot about printmaking at Pratt. I not only did etchings, but lithography, and mezzotints, which give a very soft smudgy line. I had no idea what I would do after graduation. I knew I didn't want to teach. A friend suggested I take up illustration, something I hadn't even consid-

ered. He got me an appointment with someone in the art department at Holt, Rinehart & Winston and helped me put together a portfolio, including a number of my drawings based on horror films with lots of odd machinery and contraptions. Those contraptions got me my first illustrating job—a children's book about a man who lives way up high in a tall house and spends his time inventing curious machines. Another case of beginner's luck. I was so green that after weeks went by and I hadn't been paid, I was bewildered. I hadn't realized that I was supposed to send a bill!

"I was hooked on children's books. To me, there is no valid distinction between illustration and fine art. It is a question of quality. I feel that my illustrations should support the writer's world as well as my own. I am not merely drawing the world the writer has created. I enter that world, to be sure, but I exist there and work from there as *myself*. Doing a picture book is like making a theater piece. You create the characters, the set, costumes, establish the pacing and rhythm. It's also

like directing a movie, because the illustrator selects the angles of vision, the 'close ups,' the 'distance shots,' almost as if he is moving a camera.

"I want balance in my work, I want all the elements, even the smallest, fully executed. I also like to experiment. On one book, I applied color with a toothbrush, which gave a wonderful earthy texture. My work is very much about the act of drawing. I am fascinated with line, color, materials, effects. As long as I have something to draw, I am happy. Drawing is my reality. I get up in the morning, have a cup of tea and go right to my studio. I work so intently my surroundings disappear. Except for music, I like to work to music. It helps to create a peaceful atmosphere. Working in the wee hours of the night is a special pleasure. I can put out all the lights except the one right on my drawing table, and just float in my imagination. Night is magical—you get the feeling that if a vase were to fall from a table and shatter, it wouldn't make a sound. Time feels suspended.

"I start every book with many pencil drawings. I use lots of tracing paper at this stage, transferring images and parts of images, that work. My dummies are generally pretty sketchy. I refine as I go along, and make changes even in the finishes. Often the drawings surprise me, as though the art work goes off on its own journey, and we catch up with each other down the road. I do most of my illustrations in pencil and water color or colored pencils. I'm extremely particular about my materials. I use Schwan pencils from Germany. They are rather thick with a waxy lead, but nowhere near as waxy as crayon, so they give a real nice surface with no build-up. Line density is one of the main ways I create rhythm in my books. A thicker line slows the pace, a thinner one accelerates rhythm.

"I recently got a set of oil paints and would love to use them for a children's book. Oil would be perfect for night scenes and for getting that magical opacity that seems to glow from within. It can capture twilight tones and the softened light of campfires, smoke, fog and the like. Another advantage is that

She sent her to bed with an aspirin and a glass of orange juice. ■ (From *The Sick Story* by Linda Hirsch. Illustrated by John Wallner.)

With a mighty heave, she threw the star onto the sky. It landed right next to the moon. She worked quickly now, and by the time Nero had dropped the darkest curtain, Stella had thrown trillions of shining stars all over the sky.

(From *The Night Stella Hid the Stars* by Gail Radley. Illustrated by John Wallner.)

oil paints reproduce better than water colors, which tend to get muddy when photographed. There is a relatively new reproduction technique which makes oil illustrations quite painless for the art department. Illustrations must be executed on heavy, flexible paper, rather than on canvas and are then wrapped around steel canisters. A laser beam travels back and forth across the painting picking up the different colors, which are fed into a computer. The computer translates the color intensity for the printer.''

Wallner admires Henri Rousseau's jungle scenes which have both primal power and hold incredible beauty.''Pink snakes slithering through the flora, for example. I also love the mystery captured in the work of Balthus. Among illustrators, I admire Nicole Bailey, Michael Hague (his work is so lush!) and Richard Egielski.

''I spend the lion's share of my time drawing and painting, but I do have other interests. My wife and I live in an old, restored house in Woodstock which we have furnished with antiques. I like to work out in the yard and have made a number of stone walls. It's therapeutic, and very satisfying. You don't need any mortar, you just stack the stones and they stay together. Because our soil is quite rocky, I also like to make raised beds for flowers. Woodstock is a beautiful area for walking around. There's always something to see. Our next

I'll give you three days to guess my name. . . . ■ (From *Rumpelstiltskin* by the Brothers Grimm. Illustrated by John Wallner.)

door neighbor keeps English longhorn cows that look like prehistoric bison, black chickens with beautiful light feet, peacocks and other exotic birds.

''I am pretty much a homebody. I don't like to leave my studio for very long, and, in fact, have trouble even imagining it. My wife likes to travel and so do our friends. So far, I have resisted their prodding, but I have a feeling that one day they will drug my tea and I'll wake up in Florence!''

As encouragement to aspiring artists Wallner quoted Maurice Sendak from *Where the Wild Things Are* in which he says, '''If something strange comes into your room, don't be afraid.' I would say the same thing—Don't be afraid of the 'wild things' in your imagination. If you watch, and listen to them, chances are they will delight, enchant, and teach you.''

—*Based on an interview by Marguerite Feitlowitz*

HOBBIES AND OTHER INTERESTS: Collecting antiques, crafts and collecting and reading books.

FOR MORE INFORMATION SEE: Lee Kingman and others, compilers, *Illustrators of Children's Books: 1967-1976*, Horn Book, 1978.

His grandmother sat by herself at the end of the table . . . . A white shawl Mom had found for her was tucked tightly around her like a cocoon. ■ (From *Hello, My Name Is Scrambled Eggs* by Jamie Gilson. Illustrated by John Wallner.)

The hills are dearest which our childish feet
Have climbed the earliest; and the streams most sweet
Are those at which our young lips drank.
—John Greenleaf Whittier

WELLMAN, Alice   1900-1984

PERSONAL: Born May 11, 1900, in Salt Lake City, Utah; died March 12, 1984; daughter of Frederick Creighton (a physician) and Lydia (a teacher; maiden name, Isely) Wellman; married Carl S. Flanders, March 15, 1932 (died November, 1936); married I. Harry Harris, April 12, 1939 (died August, 1974); children: (first marriage) Alison Elise Flanders Webster; (second marriage) Jeffrey Dewey Harris. *Education:* Pomona College, B.A., 1922; Wichita State University, B.S., 1923. *Politics:* Independent. *Religion:* Protestant. *Home and office:* Newport Beach, Calif. *Agent:* Larry Sternig Literary Agency, 742 Robertson St., Milwaukee, Wis. 53210.

CAREER: Actress and singer in Warner Bros. films and on stage in New York, N.Y., and Boston, Mass., including performances in light operas and John Murray Anderson's "Revues," 1926-49; performed in European concerts, on Broadway, and on tour; manager and director of summer sessions at Yardley Theater, Bucks County, Pa., and Berwyn Theater, Philadelphia, Pa.; casting director for Howard Film Productions; writer, 1965—. Lecturer at San Diego State College, Long Beach City College, University of California, Los Angeles, University of California, Irvine, and University of North Carolina; private writing teacher, adviser, and editor. *Member:* International P.E.N., California Writers Guild, Southern California Authors League, Southern California Council on Literature for Children and Young People, Quill-Pen Club, Newport Writers Group (founding member; chairperson), Fine Arts Club of Pasadena (president and honorary member), Friends of Newport Library, Friends of University of California, Irvine Library. *Awards, honors: Small-Boy Chuku* was selected one of Child Study Association of America's Children's Books of the Year, 1973, *Africa's Animals: Creatures of a Struggling Land,* 1974, and *The Wilderness Has Ears,* 1975.

WRITINGS—Juvenile: Tammy: Adventure in Hollywood, A. Whitman, 1964; *Time of Fearful Night* (Junior Literary Guild

ALICE WELLMAN

Pride filled him to overflowing. It held his head high and made his back straight. ■ (Jacket illustration by Harold James from *Time of Fearful Night* by Alice Wellman.)

selection), Putnam, 1970; *Tatu and the Honey Bird* (illustrated by Dale Payson), Putnam, 1972; *Small-Boy Chuku* (illustrated by Richard Cuffari), Houghton, 1973; *The Baby Elephant's Day,* Putnam, 1973; *The Wilderness Has Ears,* Harcourt, 1973; *White Sorceress,* Putnam, 1976.

Other: (Contributor) *A Treasury of Success Unlimited,* Hawthorn Books, 1966; (editor) *Rawhide and Orange Blossoms,* Pioneer Press, 1967; *Spirit Magic,* Berkly Medallion, 1973; *Africa's Animals: Creatures of a Struggling Land,* Putnam, 1974.

Ghost writer of portions of Michael Evlanoff's and Marjorie Fluor's *Alfred Nobel, the Loneliest Millionaire,* Ward Ritchie, 1969. Contributor of articles and stories to various adult and children's magazines. Writer and script editor for Hollywood television stations; contributing writer for Loretta Young's television series.

SIDELIGHTS: "I grew up in Angola, Portuguese West Africa, where my parents worked as missionaries. During my tenth to twelfth years I would accompany my father on his professional visits to London, Lisbon, Funchal and the West African cities of Bailundu and Chiyaka. Becoming thirteen was a memorable time—my first return to the States and Washington, D.C., and my father's visit to Teddy Roosevelt at Oyster Bay to confer on the planning of TR's coming safari in Africa. The ex-president didn't neglect me. He declared me to be a lovely little girl (John Murray Anderson was later to bill me in his

Broadway 'Revues' as the 'Toy Soprano'), presented me with a fatherly kiss and held me on his knee while we talked about what I liked about America.

"Of course, my writing career started late because of my musical involvement; but I watched with admiration and sisterly pride the rise of my three writing brothers: author-historian Paul I., science-fiction author Manly Wade, and the scientific plant researcher and professor emeritus, Frederick L., an honorary member of the American Phytopathological Society.

"My career as an actress-prima donna singer took me to Paris and London, and on tour to all major cities of the United States, Canada and the islands of the Caribbean. My books, from the vivid impressions on an active mind and later meticulous research and reading, have been written with the thought that my early associations and growing up among the highland natives should be visualized in words as I remembered them—the native huts we lived in, my pet savannah monkey, my playmates, the sick and the lame whom my father nursed, especially Wandenjoi my constant guard on medical research safaris, the honeybirds, my mother's ministrations, and the Chiyakan villagers who gifted me with love and taught me the way of the wild things. All in all, the essence of a life that is fast disappearing in Africa.

"I believe I have left some of me in my books."

Wellman's works are included in the Kerlan Collection at the University of Minnesota.

MARTIN WHITE

WHITE, Martin 1943-

PERSONAL: Born February 22, 1943, in Woolland, Dorset, England; son of Ralph Gordon (a teacher) and Freda Mary (a teacher and homemaker; maiden name, Beal) White; married Carole Irene Bond (a secretary and writer), April 20, 1964; children: Sharon Mary Julian, Rebecca Jane, Rachel Louise Newman, Matthew. *Education:* Farnham School of Art, national diploma in design and painting, 1966; University of London Institute of Education, art teacher's certificate, 1967. *Politics:* Nonaggressive anarchist. *Religion:* Pantheist. *Home and studio:* 21/23 Coxwell St., Faringdon, Oxfordshire SN7 7EA, England. *Agent:* Artists Inc., 15 Stokeley St., Covent Garden, London WC2B 5LT, United Kingdom.

CAREER: Postman in Farnham, Surrey, England, 1964-66; night watchman in Farnham, Surrey, 1966; school teacher in Abingdon, Oxfordshire, England,1967-79; free-lance artist and illustrator, 1979—. *Exhibitions*—One man shows: Studio 9, Dorking, Surrey, England, 1969; Theatre Foyer, Folkestone, Kent, England, 1971; Old Gaol Arts Centre, Abingdon, Oxfordshire, 1978; Thames Gallery, Henley-on-Thames, 1978; Borlase Gallery, Blewbury, Oxfordshire, 1979; Bio-Chemistry Department Library, Oxford University, Oxfordshire, England, 1984; Broad Canvas Gallery, Oxford, 1985; Halifax House, Oxford, 1986; Stables Gallery, Green College, Oxford, 1986; Playhouse Gallery, Oxford, 1987. Group shows: I.C.A. Gallery, London, 1978; Les Illustrateurs sont dans le Metro, Paris, France, 1978; "Paradise" Exhibition, Seven Dials Gallery, London, 1982; Watership Down Decade Exhibition, Henry Sotheran Ltd., London, 1982; Cross Tree Gallery, Filkins, Oxfordshire, 1984; Ardington Gallery, Oxfordshire, 1984.

ILLUSTRATOR: Encyclopedia, Mitchell Beazley, 1974; Bernard Stonehouse, *The Way Your Body Works,* Mitchell Beazley, 1974; Frank Walker, *Jack,* M. Joseph, 1975; Patrick Moore, *Legends of the Planets,* William Luscombe, 1975; Terry O'Neill and Peter Snow, *Crescent English Course,* Oxford University Press, 1977; Joy Chant, *The Grey Mane of Morning,* Bantam, 1978; Oliver Gregory, *Oxford Junior English Course,* Oxford University Press, 1978; (with Chris Orr and Joseph Wright) John L. Foster, editor, *A First Poetry Book,* Oxford University Press, 1978, Merrimack, 1982; Roderick Hunt, *Oxford Junior Readers,* Oxford University Press, Book 2, 1978, Book 4, 1979; Daniel Defoe, *Robinson Crusoe,* Oxford University Press, 1979; *A World of Folk Tales,* Hamlyn, 1979.

(With others) J. L. Foster, compiler, *A Second Poetry Book,* Oxford University Press, 1980; R. Hunt, *Oxford Junior Red Readers,* Books 2, 3, 4, Oxford University Press, 1980; Geoffrey Summerfield, *Short Tales,* Ward Lock, 1980; Carolyn Lloyd, editor, *Animal Ghosts,* Fontana, 1980; Haydn Richards, *Haydn Richards Junior English* Books 1, 3, 4, Ginn, 1981; R. Hunt, *An Oxford Christmas Book,* Oxford University Press, 1981; David Woolger, editor, *The Magic Tree: Poems of Fantasy and Mystery,* Oxford University Press, 1981; Haydn Richards, *Haydn Richards English Course,* Books 2, 3, Ginn, 1981; Eileen Dunlop, *The Maze Stone,* Oxford University Press, 1981; (with Peter Benton, Noel Connor, Allan Curless and Arthur Robins) J. L. Foster, compiler, *A Fourth Poetry Book,* Oxford University Press, 1981; W. Haydn Richards, *Caribbean Junior English 4,* Ginn, 1982; Dennis Pepper, *The Elephant Book,* Oxford University Press, 1982; Giles Bird and Jay Norris, *Worlds of English and Drama,* Oxford University Press, 1982; Jackson, *Animal Poems,* Oxford University Press, 1982; W. H. Richards, *Caribbean Junior English 3,* Ginn, 1983; Harrison and Stuart-Clarke, *The Oxford Book of Christmas Poems,* Oxford University Press, 1983; Jean Ure, *Hi There, Supermouse,* Hutchinson, 1983, Penguin (U.S.), 1985; Ronald

The Frail/are pressed/to the rail. ■ (Poster by Martin White.)

Deadman, *Our Post Office*, Hamlyn, 1983; Veronica Charnley, *He Made Their Glowing Colours,* Mowbray, 1983; *Caribbean English,* I and II, Ginn, 1983; *Traditional Tales from Around the World: The British Isles,* Ginn, 1983; J. Ure, *The You-Two,* Hutchinson, 1983; Beulah Candappa, *Tales of South Asia,* Ginn, 1983; *Tales of the Caribbean,* Ginn, 1984; J. Ure, *Nicola Mimosa,* Hutchinson, 1984; *At the Hospital,* Balberry Publishing, 1985; *Tales from the Mediterranean,* Ginn, 1985; D. Pepper, *An Oxford Book of Christmas Stories,* Oxford University Press, 1986; (with A. Curless, Peter Elson, Alastair Graham, and Tom Stimson) J. L. Foster, *Spaceways,* Oxford University Press, 1986; Rita Winstanley, *Happy Christmas,* Oxford University Press, 1986. Illustrator of over eighty book jackets and covers.

WORK IN PROGRESS: A continuing series of book jackets for crime novels for Macmillan; several personal projects, including a series of pictures illustrating "The Four Horsemen of the Apocolypse"; various private commissions, including portraits.

SIDELIGHTS: "I always reckoned that what I had to say was likely to be at least as relevant, valid, and interesting as what anyone else had to say. It was just a matter of how I was going to say it and how I was going to get anyone to listen or look.

"Like nearly everyone else I know, I wanted first to be a rock star, but I can't sing (some would say, 'So what?') and I couldn't see how to get into that without working with others and without making a pre-meditated exhibition of myself. Later, I was forever oscillating between writing and painting. After suffering inevitable rejections as a result of attempts in one area, I would bounce to the other with usually an equal lack of success, and so the cycle went.

"I wanted to study film and television, but my family intervened and I had to become a teacher to support them. I never wanted to be a teacher. At first I gave it eighteen months which stretched to five years which extended to ten years and then final extrication from the quicksand of mediocrity after twelve years. I enjoyed being with the students but rejected institutional politics and ingratiation.

"My attempts to show serious works of fine art were laughed at and withered in such conditions (I must conclude that they were laughable). The actual works were ceremonially incinerated in 1978.

"I wrote a children's story, illustrated it and took it to various publishers who nearly all said, 'The story is awful, but the pictures are quite nice.' I think they were just being kind, but it caused me to make up a portfolio of illustrations to little verses I had written. Again I trudged round the publishers until eventually some work was featured in *Image* magazine in 1973, and I did my first book jacket in 1974. This happened to be quite a prestigious book and I went home and sat by the telephone. I couldn't understand why nothing happened. Nowadays it does ring from time to time.

"I had some of the samples from the original portfolio printed with their verses as posters. That was the easy part. I am a terrible salesman. I end up agreeing with clients when they say, 'Well, it's not quite our thing, you see.' I'd say, 'Yes, you're right, I don't know what I'm doing here,' and go home. Or else I'd sell them way below cost price just because someone actually wanted them. I've still got piles of them in my bedroom, gathering dust.

"I used to say I would be happy if people would come to me and ask me to do a picture of this or that, and I'd do it. That is more or less what happens these days and so I am reasonably content. I'd be happier if it would happen just a bit more often, though. When I'm not doing commercial commissions, I pursue my own ideas—paintings in various styles on various subjects. I'm doing a series of drawings on the 'Seven Deadly Sins,' for example. When the weather's good I go and sit in a field and paint what's in front of me. I have begun to show and sell these landscapes recently.

"I have no difficulty responding visually to literature. I have done it since I was very small and was read to by my mother, which she did nightly and at length. I used to say to her, 'Is there a picture?' But I didn't much mind if there wasn't. They were often disappointing to me and didn't match my own inner vision. In Latin classes at school I drew pictures to illustrate *The Aeneid*—'O, you fortunate people whose city walls even now rise up!' Subsequently I had to learn the mechanics of drawing and some of the secrets of composition and much later various illustration techniques. I hope I'm still learning.

"I'm really only interested in art. I can't stop doing it. I like looking at it more and more. I can talk about it all day. I like walking but I have to have the means with me to stop and do some work when I need to. The only things I really enjoy apart from art are eating and drinking when I've finished work for the day; either out or at home where I like to cook sometimes. I make my own bread and beer."

FOR MORE INFORMATION SEE: The Image, number 18, 1973.

WILSON, Erica

PERSONAL: Born in England; came to United States, 1952; married Vladimir Kagan (a furniture designer); children: Vanessa, Jessica, and one son, Ulya. *Education:* Attended Royal School of Needlework. *Residence:* New York and Nantucket. *Office:* Erica Wilson Needle Works, 717 Madison Ave., New York, N.Y. 10022.

CAREER: Teacher of needlework at home and at Cooper Union Museum, New York City; owner of Erica Wilson Needle Works, retail stores in New York City, and Nantucket, Mass.; author and lecturer on needlework; syndicated crafts columnist for Tribune Syndicate, 1976-86. Organizer of needlework seminars, 1974—; has appeared on her own Public Broadcasting System television series, "Erica." *Exhibitions:* Wilson's needlepoint collection has been exhibited at the Metropolitan Museum, New York, N.Y. since 1981.

WRITINGS—Published by Scribner, except as indicated: *Crewel Embroidery,* 1962, abridged edition published as *Craft of Crewel Embroidery,* 1971; *Fun with Crewel Embroidery* (ALA Notable Book), 1965; *Erica Wilson's Embroidery Book,* 1973; *Needleplay,* 1975; *Ask Erica,* 1977; *The Animal Kingdom,* 1978; *New World of Plastic Canvas,* 1978; *Say It with Stitches,* 1978; *More Needleplay,* 1979; *Erica Wilson's Quilts of America,* Oxmoor, 1979; *Erica Wilson's Christmas World,* 1980; *Erica Wilson's Needlework to Wear,* Oxmoor, 1982; *Erica Wilson's Children's World: Needlework Ideas from Childhood Classics,* Scribner, 1982; *Erica Wilson's Smocking,* Children's Press, 1983; *Erica Wilson's Knitting Book,* Scribner, 1987; *Erica Wilson's Book for Brides,* Little, Brown, 1988. Has also produced four videos, "Quilting," "Cross Stitch," "Knitting," and "Needlepoint," for 3M Corporation.

Contributor to periodicals including *Family Circle, Good Housekeeping,* and *Ladies' Home Journal.* Designer of "Erica Wilson's Needleplay" for GTR Wallpaper Company, 1985.

SIDELIGHTS: To thousands of needleworkers, Wilson is America's first lady of stitchery; a master needleworker and creator of designs in every form of needlework from crewel to cross-stitch to quilting, from silk embroidery to needlepoint to knitting—which she sells through her own shops in New York and Nantucket as well as through packaged kits distributed nationwide. Her first book, *Crewel Embroidery,* has sold close to a million copies and has been continuously in print since 1962. Fourteen other books written subsequently have sold over a million copies between them, including *Children's World,* published in 1984, full of light-hearted needlework ideas from children's book illustrations, and *Erica Wilson's Quilts of America.*

Wilson was born in Scotland and her first needlework was inspired by nature walks through the English and Scottish countryside. "I'll tell you the moment—the exact moment—when I fell in love with crafts. I was twenty years old—oh, not twenty, nineteen—and I was on a holiday in Italy. I lived in England then and I could travel to Europe very cheaply, but I had absolutely no money to spend while I was there. Anyway, I was walking on a side street in Rome, and I saw a pocketbook woven like a basket and shaped like a ship's lantern in a window in a little shop. It was probably ugly, but I thought, when I saw it, that it was the loveliest thing I had ever seen, and I wanted it. It probably did not cost a great deal, but whatever it cost was too much for me. I looked at it, studied the shape and thought to myself, 'Why, I could make one.' I had studied basket weaving at school and I knew that I could do it. I would change it slightly—it would be original and it would be all *mine.*

"All at once I didn't feel poor any more and, in a sense, I never have since. I had the ability to create something that was unique, that was without price and that belonged only to me. I imagine that anyone who has ever been involved with any craft at all has had a moment like that—it's a coming together of past, present, and future and it's irreplaceable.

"I may have had a head start in the field of crafts because at a very early age I was lucky enough to go to a school where I was taught so many of them. I worked with clay; I learned to make leather sandals and fur-lined gloves; I first did basket weaving there. And I knitted. I remember knitting a tiny sweater for a very small doll—I had to use straight pins as knitting needles! Later, I loved fine white work. My eyes were young and I had no difficulty threading a number 12 needle with lace thread as fine as a hair." [Based on an article in *Woman's Day,* fall, 1987.[1]]

Wilson studied at London's Royal School of Needlework, where she later taught. Shortly after she came to the States in 1952, she founded a needlework guild in New York State and initiated her first correspondence courses in different areas of stitchery. Today her students number in the thousands upon thousands in both the U.S. and abroad. "I was trained in England where crafts were staid. It wasn't until I came to America that I was caught up in the wonderful irreverence, the feeling of color exploding all around, the young feeling, the whole lifestyle, the humor of the crafts movement here. (I still cherish a medal I was given in Birmingham, Alabama, inscribed, 'It's a crewel, crewel world.')

"No matter what area people were involved in, whether needlework or decoupage, furniture making or stenciling, there was the sense that each person had an empty canvas before her and she could create *anything.* Of course, there is a secret fascination to working with your hands that not everyone may be aware of and it appeals to two kinds of people: those who would fill the empty canvas with their own exuberant creations and those with mathematical minds who like to work with the precision they would devote to solving an intricate crossword puzzle. There is something here for everyone.

ERICA WILSON

Wilson's crewel interpretation of Beatrix Potter's "Hunca Munca."

"And in America, with its youth, we are always making traditions to hand down from one generation to the next, and making memories while we do. I no longer have a great deal of time to do as much as I would like, but not long ago I knitted for my grandson, Sandy, a simple sleeveless sweater for a teddy bear. This led to a whole array of sleeveless sweaters, in colors like crayons, for an array of bears. . . . Each year at Christmas we do something that is a tradition handed down to me—we make a 'kissenbaum.' This is a ring of evergreens studded with candles, ribbons, mistletoe, and apples that hangs above the holiday table during the season."[1]

Wilson has also designed the first wallcovering collection inspired by needlework. Titled "Erica Wilson's Needleplay," the collection has been introduced by General Tire's GTR Wallcovering Company, specialists in fabric-backed vinyl wallcoverings, and is available at paint and wallcovering stores and at home furnishings centers across the country. Because of an overwhelming response to the first collection, Wilson is now working on a fourth group of designs for the Metropolitan Museum. She has pioneered and produced "Stencil Stitch" kits for the Illinois Bronze Paint Company, as well as a special group for the Stacy Corporation, and she was for ten years the spokesperson and designer for "Creative Expressions," the party plan division of Needlecraft of America. She frequently produces special editorial features for magazines such as *Fam-*

ily Circle, Good Housekeeping, and *Ladies' Home Journal,* and designs clothing and craft patterns for *Vogue.*

Between all other activities, Wilson and her husband organize needlework tours internationally. Wilson's tour of China visited Hangchow to view the famous Chinese double-sided embroidery center in that city. "No one who falls in love with crafts falls out of love. I was asked recently if I were stranded on a desert island, what equipment would I like to have with me. I said that I would like to be able to stencil because the quick and easy satisfaction stenciling provides is so rewarding. I had to add, though, for old time's sake, don't ever leave me stranded anywhere without a needle!"[1]

FOR MORE INFORMATION SEE: Woman's Day, fall, 1987.

WILSON, Marjorie 1927-
(Budge Wilson)

BRIEF ENTRY: Born May 2, 1927, in Halifax, Nova Scotia, Canada. After receiving her bachelor's degree and a teaching diploma in physical education from Dalhousie University in Halifax, Wilson worked a variety of jobs which included teaching, illustrating, and writing a weekly column on child care for the *Globe and Mail* in Toronto. She has been a fitness instructor for the past seventeen years. Since the 1970s, Wilson has written short stories and novels for children and adults and is the recipient of three writing awards for short adult fiction. *Mr. John Bertrand Nijinsky and Charlie* (Nimbus, 1986), Wilson's first picture book, is the story of an old grumpy man and the cat who becomes his salvation. "Budge Wilson writes a good story. The prose is clean and thoughtful; Nijinsky's transformation from a grump to good neighbor is not overly sentimental nor is it unbelievable," wrote *Globe and Mail*. Wilson has also written a series of novels for children, all published by Scholastic-TAB, including *The Best Worst Christmas Present Ever* (1984); *A House Far from Home* (1986); and most recently, *Mystery Lights at Blue Harbour*. She also contributes short stories to magazines and periodicals in Canada. *Home:* North West Cove, RR #1, Hubbards, Nova Scotia, Canada B0J IT0 (summer); 672 Stannor Drive, Peterborough, Ontario, Canada K9J 4S7 (winter).

WINNICK, Karen B(eth) B(inkoff) 1946-

PERSONAL: Born June 28, 1946, in New York; daughter of Sanford (a certified public accountant) and Miriam (Sclar) Binkoff; married Gary Winnick (a bond broker), December 24, 1972; children: Adam Scott. *Education:* Syracuse University, B.F.A., 1968; graduate study at New York University and School of Visual Arts. *Religion:* Jewish.

CAREER: Grey Advertising, New York City, art director, 1970; Lois Holland Calloway, New York City, graphics designer, 1972-75; free-lance artist and writer, 1975—. *Member:* Art Directors Club.

WRITINGS—Juvenile; self-illustrated: *Patch and the Strings,* Lippincott, 1977; *Sandro's Dolphin,* Lothrop, 1980.

WORK IN PROGRESS: Several self-illustrated books for children.

ZACH, Cheryl (Byrd) 1947-
(Jennifer Cole)

BRIEF ENTRY: Born June 9, 1947, in Clarksville, Tenn. Author of romance novels for young adults. Zach received her bachelor's degree from Austin Peay State University in 1968, and her master's in 1977. She has been a teacher of English at high schools in Mississippi and Tennessee, as well as a free-lance journalist. Presently a full-time, free-lance writer, Zach believes that "young readers deserve the best, and writers for young people have even more responsibility as far as truth and excellence in their work than writers in general." *The Frog Princess* (1984), from Silhouette's "First Love" series, was a Romance Writers of America Golden Medallion winner for best young adult novel in 1984. "Fast and formulaic, this nevertheless does offer a nice glimpse of Kelly's relationship with her mother," wrote *Booklist*. Other books by Zach in this series are *Waiting for Amanda* (1985), another Golden Medallion winner, and *Fortune's Child* (1985). Zach is also the author, under the pseudonym Jennifer Cole, of novels in Fawcett's "Sisters" romance series, including *Three's a Crowd* (1986), *Star Quality* (1987), *Too Many Cooks* (1987), and *Mollie in Love* (1987). She is currently working on an adult mystery novel. *Home:* 9157 Belmont St., Bellflower, Calif. 90706.

BARRY ZAID

ZAID, Barry 1938-

PERSONAL: Born June 8, 1938, in Toronto, Canada; son of Irving (a gentleman's clothier) and Ruth (Rother) Zaid. *Education:* University of Toronto, B.A., 1961. *Home:* Boulder, Colo., and New York City. *Office:* 15 West 20th St., 9th floor, New York, N.Y. 10011.

CAREER: Rapier Arts Ltd., London, England, graphic designer and illustrator, 1961-62; Robert Colopy Associates, Toronto, Canada, studio art director, 1964-66; free-lance illustrator and designer, London, 1966-69; Push Pin Studios, New York, N.Y., illustrator and designer, 1969-74; School of Visual Arts, New York, N.Y., teacher, 1970-74; Virginia Commonwealth University, Richmond, assistant professor, 1976-78; Celestial Seasonings, Boulder, Colo., creative director, 1979; free-lance designer and illustrator, 1980—. Boulder Center for the Visual Arts, Board of Directors, 1985.

EXHIBITIONS: Work has been exhibited in numerous group shows, including Pollock Gallery, Toronto, 1961; "The Push Pin Style," Paris, Milan, Amsterdam, London, Tokyo and Sao Paulo, 1970-73; Society of Illustrators, New York; Art Directors Club, New York; American Institute of Graphic Arts; Art Directors Club of Denver; American Corporate Identity; Highland Gallery (retrospective), Boulder, Colo., 1983. *Member:* Graphic Artists Guild of Colorado (president, 1984-85). *Awards, honors: Rimes de la Mere Oie: Mother Goose Rendered into French* was included in the Children's Book Showcase, 1972, and was selected by the American Institute of Graphic Arts to be included in the Biennial of Illustrations Bratislava, 1973; Gold Medal from the New York Society of Illustrators, 1973, for *Chicken Little*.

ILLUSTRATOR: (With Milton Glaser and Seymour Chwast) Ormonde de Kaye, translator, *Rimes de la Mere Oie: Mother Goose Rendered into French*, Little, Brown, 1971; *Chicken*

Little, Random House, 1973; Gwendolyn MacEwen, *The Chocolate Moose,* N. C. Press, 1981.

Contributor of illustrations to numerous magazines and newspapers, including *Macleans* (Canada), *Chatelaine, Canadian Homes, Globe and Mail* (Canada), *Idea* (Japan), *Graphis, Esquire, Seventeen, New York, McCall's, Look, Ladies' Home Journal, Cosmopolitan, Children's Digest, Sesame Street, Art Direction, TV Guide, Ms., Horizon, Audience, New York Times Sunday Magazine, New York Times, Time, Mlle Age Tendre* (France), *London Times, Monthly Design* (Korea), and *Advertising Techniques.*

WORK IN PROGRESS: A variety of graphic design, product design and illustration projects.

SIDELIGHTS: ''I have played at art as long as I can remember. When I was in second grade, the school principal asked me to do a drawing for the showcase outside his office. I did a pastel drawing of bright yellow daffodils on a black background. I loved drawing and making things with my hands and had little interest in mathematics or sports. I decided when I was young to spend my time and energy on those things I enjoyed and could do well and not bother with the things I did poorly. (To this day I have never balanced my own checkbook.) I did beautiful maps and made booklets for social studies and a working miniature theater with pipecleaner dolls representing opera singers for music class.

''When I was fourteen, I had a summer job demonstrating art supplies in a toy store and made hand-painted greeting cards,

He loved to eat maple syrup on toast for breakfast. ■ (From *The Chocolate Moose* by Gwendolyn MacEwen. Illustrated by Barry Zaid.)

stationery and signs for neighborhood shops. I learned calligraphy and was kept busy filling in certificates for various institutions. I became art editor of the school yearbooks and director of prom decorations in high school.

"My college career was checkered: I studied, among other things, architecture, psychology, French, Latin, music, archaeology and art history. When my sign-painting and art abilities were discovered, I was hired to design silk screen posters for the University theater and various musical events. On graduation, I showed my posters in London (England) and got a job in a design studio (Rapier Arts). Traveling in Europe allowed me to see firsthand the great art and architecture of the past. This was my real art education, and strongly influenced the work that was to follow. I especially loved the late Gothic Italian masters (Fra Angelico, the Lorenzetti Brothers, and Simone Martini) for their planar perspectives and brilliant coloring.

"I subsequently worked in Canada doing backgrounds for children's television films (lots of castles), then freelanced in London once again before moving to New York to work at the exciting Push Pin Studios where I did two children's books. One, a French version of *Mother Goose,* in which I first experienced small silhouette drawings with which I was later to become strongly identified; and the second, a version of *Chicken Little,* with pages that increase in size as more characters join Chicken Little's band. The latter won the Gold Medal of the New York Society of Illustrators.

"When I left Push Pin I spent a year traveling and working in Switzerland and Holland, lived for several months in a commune in Northern Scotland (Findhorn) and several months traveling and studying eastern philosophy in India, before returning to the U.S. to join the design faculty at Virginia Commonwealth University in Richmond, Virginia. Two years later I moved to Boulder, Colorado when I worked as creative director for Celestial Seasonings Herb Teas, then freelanced for several years, living in a charming little white house with a magical garden. In 1987 I returned to New York City.

"I feel that my mission on earth is to create beauty and spread cheer through my work."

HOBBIES AND OTHER INTERESTS: Small space gardening, vegetarian cookery, ancient history and sociology.

ZARING, Jane (Thomas)   1936-

PERSONAL: Born December 26, 1936, in Nelson, Glamorgan, Wales; came to the United States in 1968; daughter of Edward (a farmer) and Gwyneth J.M. (a teacher; maiden name, Lewis) Thomas; married Philip B. Zaring (a professor of history), August 6, 1966; children: David Thomas, Noah Samuel. *Education:* University of London, B.A., 1959; Cambridge University, Diploma in Education, 1960; Indiana University, M.A., 1968. *Politics:* Democrat. *Religion:* Episcopalian. *Home and office:* R.R. 5, Ames, Iowa 50010.

CAREER: Putney High School, London, England, geography teacher, 1960-63; Howell's School, Llandaff, Wales, geography teacher, 1965; College of Education, Cardiff, Wales, lecturer in education, 1966; Iowa State University, Ames, in-

JANE ZARING

structor in earth sciences, 1968-78; writer, 1978—. *Member:* Society of Children's Book Writers.

*WRITINGS—*For children: *The Return of the Dragon* (illustrated by Polly Broman), Houghton, 1981; *Sharkes in the North Woods; or, Nish Na Bosh Na Is Nicer Now,* Houghton, 1982. Contributor to *Annals of the Association of American Geographers.*

WORK IN PROGRESS: A children's book about Latin-speaking snails; a history adventure set in Iowa.

SIDELIGHTS: "I started writing for children recently, when I turned forty, because it seemed high time to write down some of the stories I had told my own children. Until then, I had taught geography in Britain and the United States. My books try to give pleasure rather than improve, probably a result of happy memories as a child bookworm. I grew up in Wales, and return there as often as possible.

"My stories about Caradoc the dragon are animal fantasy, loosely historical, and set in Wales. They are based partly on local tales my father—a great storyteller—used to recount, partly on inventions to make long American car journeys more endurable, and partly on ideas from Welsh literature, notably *The Mabinogion,* a collection of medieval Welsh legends. The country I write about is a pre-industrial Wales, geographically true but historically leaning towards what ought to have happened, rather than what actually did occur.

"*Sharkes in the North Woods* is a farce set in a summer camp and the surrounding woods of northern Minnesota. I am writing another farcical adventure for twelve to fourteen-year-olds, this time set in Iowa."

FOR MORE INFORMATION SEE: Columbus Republic, October 12, 1981; *Ames Tribune,* October 31, 1981; *Ninnau,* February 1, 1982.

Illustrations Index

(In the following index, the number of the volume in which an illustrator's work appears is given *before* the colon, and the page on which it appears is given *after* the colon. For example, a drawing by Adams, Adrienne appears in Volume 2 on page 6, another drawing by her appears in Volume 3 on page 80, another drawing in Volume 8 on page 1, and another drawing in Volume 15 on page 107.)

YABC

Index citations including this abbreviation refer to listings appearing in *Yesterday's Authors of Books for Children,* also published by the Gale Research Company, which covers authors who died prior to 1960.

Aas, Ulf, *5:* 174
Abbé, S. van. *See* van Abbé, S.
Abel, Raymond, *6:* 122; *7:* 195; *12:* 3; *21:* 86; *25:* 119
Abrahams, Hilary, *26:* 205; *29:* 24-25
Abrams, Kathie, *36:* 170
Abrams, Lester, *49:* 26
Accorsi, William, *11:* 198
Acs, Laszlo, *14:* 156; *42:* 22
Adams, Adrienne, *2:* 6; *3:* 80; *8:* 1; *15:* 107; *16:* 180; *20:* 65; *22:* 134-135; *33:* 75; *36:* 103, 112; *39:* 74
Adams, John Wolcott, *17:* 162
Adamson, George, *30:* 23, 24
Adkins, Alta, *22:* 250
Adkins, Jan, *8:* 3
Adler, Peggy, *22:* 6; *29:* 31
Adler, Ruth, *29:* 29
Adragna, Robert, *47:* 145
Agard, Nadema, *18:* 1
Agre, Patricia, *47:* 195
Ahl, Anna Maria, *32:* 24
Aichinger, Helga, *4:* 5, 45
Aitken, Amy, *31:* 34
Akaba, Suekichi, *46:* 23
Akasaka, Miyoshi, *YABC 2:* 261
Akino, Fuku, *6:* 144
Alain, *40:* 41
Alajalov, *2:* 226
Albrecht, Jan, *37:* 176
Albright, Donn, *1:* 91
Alcorn, John, *3:* 159; *7:* 165; *31:* 22; *44:* 127; *46:* 23, 170
Alda, Arlene, *44:* 24
Alden, Albert, *11:* 103
Aldridge, Andy, *27:* 131
Alex, Ben, *45:* 25, 26
Alexander, Lloyd, *49:* 34
Alexander, Martha, *3:* 206; *11:* 103; *13:* 109; *25:* 100; *36:* 131
Alexeieff, Alexander, *14:* 6; *26:* 199
Aliki. *See* Brandenberg, Aliki
Allamand, Pascale, *12:* 9
Allan, Judith, *38:* 166
Alland, Alexander, *16:* 255
Alland, Alexandra, *16:* 255
Allen, Gertrude, *9:* 6
Allen, Graham, *31:* 145
Allen, Pamela, *50:* 25, 26-27, 28
Allen, Rowena, *47:* 75
Allison, Linda, *43:* 27

Almquist, Don, *11:* 8; *12:* 128; *17:* 46; *22:* 110
Aloise, Frank, *5:* 38; *10:* 133; *30:* 92
Althea. *See* Braithwaite, Althea
Altschuler, Franz, *11:* 185; *23:* 141; *40:* 48; *45:* 29
Ambrus, Victor G., *1:* 6-7, 194; *3:* 69; *5:* 15; *6:* 44; *7:* 36; *8:* 210; *12:* 227; *14:* 213; *15:* 213; *22:* 209; *24:* 36; *28:* 179; *30:* 178; *32:* 44, 46; *38:* 143; *41:* 25, 26, 27, 28, 29, 30, 31, 32; *42:* 87; *44:* 190
Ames, Lee J., *3:* 12; *9:* 130; *10:* 69; *17:* 214; *22:* 124
Amon, Aline, *9:* 9
Amoss, Berthe, *5:* 5
Amundsen, Dick, *7:* 77
Amundsen, Richard E., *5:* 10; *24:* 122
Ancona, George, *12:* 11
Anderson, Alasdair, *18:* 122
Anderson, Brad, *33:* 28
Anderson, C. W., *11:* 10
Anderson, Carl, *7:* 4
Anderson, Doug, *40:* 111
Anderson, Erica, *23:* 65
Anderson, Laurie, *12:* 153, 155
Anderson, Wayne, *23:* 119; *41:* 239
Andrew, John, *22:* 4
Andrews, Benny, *14:* 251; *31:* 24
Angel, Marie, *47:* 22
Angelo, Valenti, *14:* 8; *18:* 100; *20:* 232; *32:* 70
Anglund, Joan Walsh, *2:* 7, 250-251; *37:* 198, 199, 200
Anno, Mitsumasa, *5:* 7; *38:* 25, 26-27, 28, 29, 30, 31, 32
Antal, Andrew, *1:* 124; *30:* 145
Apple, Margot, *33:* 25; *35:* 206; *46:* 81
Appleyard, Dev, *2:* 192
Aragonés, Sergio, *48:* 23, 24, 25, 26, 27
Araneus, *40:* 29
Archer, Janet, *16:* 69
Ardizzone, Edward, *1:* 11, 12; *2:* 105; *3:* 258; *4:* 78; *7:* 79; *10:* 100; *15:* 232; *20:* 69, 178; *23:* 223; *24:* 125; *28:* 25, 26, 27, 28, 29, 30, 31, 33, 34, 35, 36, 37; *31:* 192, 193; *34:* 215, 217; *YABC 2:* 25

Arenella, Roy, *14:* 9
Armer, Austin, *13:* 3
Armer, Laura Adams, *13:* 3
Armer, Sidney, *13:* 3
Armitage, David, *47:* 23
Armitage, Eileen, *4:* 16
Armstrong, George, *10:* 6; *21:* 72
Arno, Enrico, *1:* 217; *2:* 22, 210; *4:* 9; *5:* 43; *6:* 52; *29:* 217, 219; *33:* 152; *35:* 99; *43:* 31, 32, 33; *45:* 212, 213, 214
Arnosky, Jim, *22:* 20
Arrowood, Clinton, *12:* 193; *19:* 11
Arting, Fred J., *41:* 63
Artzybasheff, Boris, *13:* 143; *14:* 15; *40:* 152, 155
Aruego, Ariane, *6:* 4
   See also Dewey, Ariane
Aruego, Jose, *4:* 140; *6:* 4; *7:* 64; *33:* 195; *35:* 208
Asch, Frank, *5:* 9
Ashby, Gail, *11:* 135
Ashby, Gwynneth, *44:* 26
Ashley, C. W., *19:* 197
Ashmead, Hal, *8:* 70
Assel, Steven, *44:* 153
Astrop, John, *32:* 56
Atene, Ann, *12:* 18
Atherton, Lisa, *38:* 198
Atkinson, J. Priestman, *17:* 275
Atkinson, Wayne, *40:* 46
Attebery, Charles, *38:* 170
Atwood, Ann, *7:* 9
Augarde, Steve, *25:* 22
Austerman, Miriam, *23:* 107
Austin, Margot, *11:* 16
Austin, Robert, *3:* 44
Auth, Tony, *51:* 5
Averill, Esther, *1:* 17; *28:* 39, 40, 41
Axeman, Lois, *2:* 32; *11:* 84; *13:* 165; *22:* 8; *23:* 49
Ayer, Jacqueline, *13:* 7
Ayer, Margaret, *15:* 12; *50:* 120

B.T.B. *See* Blackwell, Basil T.
Babbitt, Bradford, *33:* 158
Babbitt, Natalie, *6:* 6; *8:* 220
Bachem, Paul, *48:* 180
Back, George, *31:* 161
Bacon, Bruce, *4:* 74

Bacon, Paul, *7:* 155; *8:* 121; *31:* 55; *50:* 42
Bacon, Peggy, *2:* 11, 228; *46:* 44
Baker, Alan, *22:* 22
Baker, Charlotte, *2:* 12
Baker, Jeannie, *23:* 4
Baker, Jim, *22:* 24
Baldridge, Cyrus LeRoy, *19:* 69; *44:* 50
Balet, Jan, *11:* 22
Balian, Lorna, *9:* 16
Ballantyne, R. M., *24:* 34
Ballis, George, *14:* 199
Baltzer, Hans, *40:* 30
Bang, Molly Garrett, *24:* 37, 38
Banik, Yvette Santiago, *21:* 136
Banner, Angela. *See* Maddison, Angela Mary
Bannerman, Helen, *19:* 13, 14
Bannon, Laura, *6:* 10; *23:* 8
Baptist, Michael, *37:* 208
Bare, Arnold Edwin, *16:* 31
Bare, Colleen Stanley, *32:* 33
Bargery, Geoffrey, *14:* 258
Barker, Carol, *31:* 27
Barker, Cicely Mary, *49:* 50, 51
Barkley, James, *4:* 13; *6:* 11; *13:* 112
Barks, Carl, *37:* 27, 28, 29, 30-31, 32, 33, 34
Barling, Tom, *9:* 23
Barlow, Perry, *35:* 28
Barlowe, Dot, *30:* 223
Barlowe, Wayne, *37:* 72
Barner, Bob, *29:* 37
Barnes, Hiram P., *20:* 28
Barnett, Moneta, *16:* 89; *19:* 142; *31:* 102; *33:* 30, 31, 32; *41:* 153
Barney, Maginel Wright, *39:* 32, 33, 34; *YABC 2:* 306
Barnum, Jay Hyde, *11:* 224; *20:* 5; *37:* 189, 190
Barrauds, *33:* 114
Barrer-Russell, Gertrude, *9:* 65; *27:* 31
Barrett, Angela, *40:* 136, 137
Barrett, John E., *43:* 119
Barrett, Ron, *14:* 24; *26:* 35
Barron, John N., *3:* 261; *5:* 101; *14:* 220
Barrows, Walter, *14:* 268
Barry, Ethelred B., *37:* 79; *YABC 1:* 229
Barry, James, *14:* 25
Barry, Katharina, *2:* 159; *4:* 22
Barry, Robert E., *6:* 12
Barry, Scott, *32:* 35
Bartenbach, Jean, *40:* 31
Barth, Ernest Kurt, *2:* 172; *3:* 160; *8:* 26; *10:* 31
Barton, Byron, *8:* 207; *9:* 18; *23:* 66
Barton, Harriett, *30:* 71
Bartram, Robert, *10:* 42
Bartsch, Jochen, *8:* 105; *39:* 38
Bascove, Barbara, *45:* 73
Baskin, Leonard, *30:* 42, 43, 46, 47; *49:* 125, 126, 128, 129, 133
Bass, Saul, *49:* 192
Bassett, Jeni, *40:* 99
Batchelor, Joy, *29:* 41, 47, 48
Bate, Norman, *5:* 16

Bates, Leo, *24:* 35
Batet, Carmen, *39:* 134
Batherman, Muriel, *31:* 79; *45:* 185
Battaglia, Aurelius, *50:* 44
Batten, John D., *25:* 161, 162
Battles, Asa, *32:* 94, 95
Bauernschmidt, Marjorie, *15:* 15
Baum, Allyn, *20:* 10
Baum, Willi, *4:* 24-25; *7:* 173
Baumann, Jill, *34:* 170
Baumhauer, Hans, *11:* 218; *15:* 163, 165, 167
Bayley, Dorothy, *37:* 195
Bayley, Nicola, *40:* 104; *41:* 34, 35
Baynes, Pauline, *2:* 244; *3:* 149; *13:* 133, 135, 137-141; *19:* 18, 19, 20; *32:* 208, 213, 214; *36:* 105, 108
Beame, Rona, *12:* 40
Beard, Dan, *22:* 31, 32
Beard, J. H., *YABC 1:* 158
Bearden, Romare, *9:* 7; *22:* 35
Beardsley, Aubrey, *17:* 14; *23:* 181
Bearman, Jane, *29:* 38
Beaton, Cecil, *24:* 208
Beaucé, J. A., *18:* 103
Beck, Charles, *11:* 169; *51:* 173
Beck, Ruth, *13:* 11
Becker, Harriet, *12:* 211
Beckett, Sheilah, *25:* 5; *33:* 37, 38
Beckhoff, Harry, *1:* 78; *5:* 163
Beckman, Kaj, *45:* 38, 39, 40, 41
Beckman, Per, *45:* 42, 43
Bedford, F. D., *20:* 118, 122; *33:* 170; *41:* 220, 221, 230, 233
Bee, Joyce, *19:* 62
Beeby, Betty, *25:* 36
Beech, Carol, *9:* 149
Beek, *25:* 51, 55, 59
Beerbohm, Max, *24:* 208
Behr, Joyce, *15:* 15; *21:* 132; *23:* 161
Behrens, Hans, *5:* 97
Beisner, Monika, *46:* 128, 131
Belden, Charles J., *12:* 182
Belina, Renate, *39:* 132
Bell, Corydon, *3:* 20
Beltran, Alberto, *43:* 37
Bemelmans, Ludwig, *15:* 19, 21
Benda, Wladyslaw T., *15:* 256; *30:* 76, 77; *44:* 182
Bendick, Jeanne, *2:* 24
Bennett, F. I., *YABC 1:* 134
Bennett, Jill, *26:* 61; *41:* 38, 39; *45:* 54
Bennett, Rainey, *15:* 26; *23:* 53
Bennett, Richard, *15:* 45; *21:* 11, 12, 13; *25:* 175
Bennett, Susan, *5:* 55
Bentley, Carolyn, *46:* 153
Bentley, Roy, *30:* 162
Benton, Thomas Hart, *2:* 99
Berelson, Howard, *5:* 20; *16:* 58; *31:* 50
Berenstain, Jan, *12:* 47
Berenstain, Stan, *12:* 47
Berg, Joan, *1:* 115; *3:* 156; *6:* 26, 58
Berg, Ron, *36:* 48, 49; *48:* 37, 38
Berger, William M., *14:* 143; *YABC 1:* 204

Bering, Claus, *13:* 14
Berkowitz, Jeanette, *3:* 249
Bernadette. *See* Watts, Bernadette
Bernath, Stefen, *32:* 76
Bernstein, Michel J., *51:* 71
Bernstein, Ted, *38:* 183; *50:* 131
Bernstein, Zena, *23:* 46
Berrill, Jacquelyn, *12:* 50
Berry, Erick. *See* Best, Allena.
Berry, William A., *6:* 219
Berry, William D., *14:* 29; *19:* 48
Berson, Harold, *2:* 17-18; *4:* 28-29, 220; *9:* 10; *12:* 19; *17:* 45; *18:* 193; *22:* 85; *34:* 172; *44:* 120; *46:* 42
Bertschmann, Harry, *16:* 1
Beskow, Elsa, *20:* 13, 14, 15
Best, Allena, *2:* 26; *34:* 76
Bethers, Ray, *6:* 22
Bettina. *See* Ehrlich, Bettina
Betts, Ethel Franklin, *17:* 161, 164-165; *YABC 2:* 47
Bewick, Thomas, *16:* 40-41, 43-45, 47; *YABC 1:* 107
Bezencon, Jacqueline, *48:* 40
Biamonte, Daniel, *40:* 90
Bianco, Pamela, *15:* 31; *28:* 44, 45, 46
Bible, Charles, *13:* 15
Bice, Clare, *22:* 40
Biggers, John, *2:* 123
Bileck, Marvin, *3:* 102; *40:* 36-37
Bimen, Levent, *5:* 179
Binks, Robert, *25:* 150
Binzen, Bill, *24:* 47
Birch, Reginald, *15:* 150; *19:* 33, 34, 35, 36; *37:* 196, 197; *44:* 182; *46:* 176; *YABC 1:* 84; *YABC 2:* 34, 39
Bird, Esther Brock, *1:* 36; *25:* 66
Birmingham, Lloyd, *12:* 51
Biro, Val, *1:* 26; *41:* 42
Bischoff, Ilse, *44:* 51
Bjorklund, Lorence, *3:* 188, 252; *7:* 100; *9:* 113; *10:* 66; *19:* 178; *33:* 122, 123; *35:* 36, 37, 38, 39, 41, 42, 43; *36:* 185; *38:* 93; *47:* 106; *YABC 1:* 242
Blackwell, Basil T., *YABC 1:* 68, 69
Blades, Ann, *16:* 52; *37:* 213; *50:* 41
Blair, Jay, *45:* 46; *46:* 155
Blaisdell, Elinore, *1:* 121; *3:* 134; *35:* 63
Blake, Quentin, *3:* 170; *9:* 21; *10:* 48; *13:* 38; *21:* 180; *26:* 60; *28:* 228; *30:* 29, 31; *40:* 108; *45:* 219; *46:* 165, 168; *48:* 196
Blake, Robert J., *37:* 90
Blake, William, *30:* 54, 56, 57, 58, 59, 60
Blass, Jacqueline, *8:* 215
Blegvad, Erik, *2:* 59; *3:* 98; *5:* 117; *7:* 131; *11:* 149; *14:* 34, 35; *18:* 237; *32:* 219; *YABC 1:* 201
Bliss, Corinne Demas, *37:* 38
Bloch, Lucienne, *10:* 12
Bloom, Lloyd, *35:* 180; *36:* 149; *47:* 99
Blossom, Dave, *34:* 29

Blumenschein, E. L., *YABC 1:* 113, 115
Blumer, Patt, *29:* 214
Blundell, Kim, *29:* 36
Boardman, Gwenn, *12:* 60
Bobri, *30:* 138; *47:* 27
Bock, Vera, *1:* 187; *21:* 41
Bock, William Sauts, *8:* 7; *14:* 37; *16:* 120; *21:* 141; *36:* 177
Bodecker, N. M., *8:* 13; *14:* 2; *17:* 55-57
Boehm, Linda, *40:* 31
Bohdal, Susi, *22:* 44
Bolian, Polly, *3:* 270; *4:* 30; *13:* 77; *29:* 197
Bolognese, Don, *2:* 147, 231; *4:* 176; *7:* 146; *17:* 43; *23:* 192; *24:* 50; *34:* 108; *36:* 133
Bond, Arnold, *18:* 116
Bond, Barbara Higgins, *21:* 102
Bond, Felicia, *38:* 197; *49:* 55, 56
Bonn, Pat, *43:* 40
Bonners, Susan, *41:* 40
Bonsall, Crosby, *23:* 6
Booth, Franklin, *YABC 2:* 76
Booth, Graham, *32:* 193; *37:* 41, 42
Bordier, Georgette, *16:* 54
Boren, Tinka, *27:* 128
Borja, Robert, *22:* 48
Born, Adolf, *49:* 63
Bornstein, Ruth, *14:* 44
Borten, Helen, *3:* 54; *5:* 24
Bossom, Naomi, *35:* 48
Boston, Peter, *19:* 42
Bosustow, Stephen, *34:* 202
Bottner, Barbara, *14:* 46
Boucher, Joelle, *41:* 138
Boulat, Pierre, *44:* 40
Boulet, Susan Seddon, *50:* 47
Bourke-White, Margaret, *15:* 286-287
Boutet de Monvel, M., *30:* 61, 62, 63, 65
Bowen, Richard, *42:* 134
Bowen, Ruth, *31:* 188
Bower, Ron, *29:* 33
Bowser, Carolyn Ewing, *22:* 253
Boyd, Patti, *45:* 31
Boyle, Eleanor Vere, *28:* 50, 51
Bozzo, Frank, *4:* 154
Bradford, Ron, *7:* 157
Bradley, Richard D., *26:* 182
Bradley, William, *5:* 164
Brady, Irene, *4:* 31; *42:* 37
Bragg, Michael, *32:* 78; *46:* 31
Braithwaite, Althea, *23:* 12-13
Bram, Elizabeth, *30:* 67
Bramley, Peter, *4:* 3
Brandenberg, Aliki, *2:* 36-37; *24:* 222; *35:* 49, 50, 51, 52, 53, 54, 56, 57
Brandenburg, Jim, *47:* 58
Brandi, Lillian, *31:* 158
Brandon, Brumsic, Jr., *9:* 25
Bransom, Paul, *17:* 121; *43:* 44
Brenner, Fred, *22:* 85; *36:* 34; *42:* 34
Brett, Bernard, *22:* 54
Brett, Harold M., *26:* 98, 99, 100
Brett, Jan, *30:* 135; *42:* 39
Brewer, Sally King, *33:* 44

Brewster, Patience, *40:* 68; *45:* 22, 183; *51:* 20
Brick, John, *10:* 15
Bridge, David R., *45:* 28
Bridgman, L. J., *37:* 77
Bridwell, Norman, *4:* 37
Briggs, Raymond, *10:* 168; *23:* 20, 21
Brigham, Grace A., *37:* 148
Bright, Robert, *24:* 55
Brinckloe, Julie, *13:* 18; *24:* 79, 115; *29:* 35
Brion, *47:* 116
Brisley, Joyce L., *22:* 57
Brock, Charles E., *15:* 97; *19:* 247, 249; *23:* 224, 225; *36:* 88; *42:* 41, 42, 43, 44, 45; *YABC 1:* 194, 196, 203
Brock, Emma, *7:* 21
Brock, Henry Matthew, *15:* 81; *16:* 141; *19:* 71; *34:* 115; *40:* 164; *42:* 47, 48, 49; *49:* 66
Brodkin, Gwen, *34:* 135
Bromhall, Winifred, *5:* 11; *26:* 38
Brooke, L. Leslie, *16:* 181-183, 186; *17:* 15-17; *18:* 194
Brooker, Christopher, *15:* 251
Broomfield, Maurice, *40:* 141
Brotman, Adolph E., *5:* 21
Brown, Buck, *45:* 48
Brown, David, *7:* 47; *48:* 52
Brown, Denise, *11:* 213
Brown, Ford Madox, *48:* 74
Brown, Judith Gwyn, *1:* 45; *7:* 5; *8:* 167; *9:* 182, 190; *20:* 16, 17, 18; *23:* 142; *29:* 117; *33:* 97; *36:* 23, 26; *43:* 184; *48:* 201, 223; *49:* 69
Brown, Marc Tolon, *10:* 17, 197; *14:* 263; *51:* 18
Brown, Marcia, *7:* 30; *25:* 203; *47:* 31, 32, 33, 34, 35, 36-37, 38, 39, 40, 42, 43, 44; *YABC 1:* 27
Brown, Margery W., *5:* 32-33; *10:* 3
Brown, Palmer, *36:* 40
Brown, Paul, *25:* 26; *26:* 107
Browne, Anthony, *45:* 50, 51, 52
Browne, Dik, *8:* 212
Browne, Gordon, *16:* 97
Browne, Hablot K., *15:* 65, 80; *21:* 14, 15, 16, 17, 18, 19, 20; *24:* 25
Browning, Coleen, *4:* 132
Browning, Mary Eleanor, *24:* 84
Bruce, Robert, *23:* 23
Brude, Dick, *48:* 215
Brule, Al, *3:* 135
Bruna, Dick, *43:* 48, 49, 50
Brundage, Frances, *19:* 244
Brunhoff, Jean de, *24:* 57, 58
Brunhoff, Laurent de, *24:* 60
Brunson, Bob, *43:* 135
Bryan, Ashley, *31:* 44
Brychta, Alex, *21:* 21
Bryson, Bernarda, *3:* 88, 146; *39:* 26; *44:* 185
Buba, Joy, *12:* 83; *30:* 226; *44:* 56
Buchanan, Lilian, *13:* 16
Bucholtz-Ross, Linda, *44:* 137
Buchs, Thomas, *40:* 38

Buck, Margaret Waring, *3:* 30
Buehr, Walter, *3:* 31
Buff, Conrad, *19:* 52, 53, 54
Buff, Mary, *19:* 52, 53
Bull, Charles Livingston, *18:* 207
Bullen, Anne, *3:* 166, 167
Burbank, Addison, *37:* 43
Burchard, Peter, *3:* 197; *5:* 35; *6:* 158, 218
Burger, Carl, *3:* 33; *45:* 160, 162
Burgeson, Marjorie, *19:* 31
Burgess, Gelett, *32:* 39, 42
Burkert, Nancy Ekholm, *18:* 186; *22:* 140; *24:* 62, 63, 64, 65; *26:* 53; *29:* 60, 61; *46:* 171; *YABC 1:* 46
Burn, Doris, *6:* 172
Burnett, Virgil, *44:* 42
Burningham, John, *9:* 68; *16:* 60-61
Burns, Howard M., *12:* 173
Burns, Jim, *47:* 70
Burns, M. F., *26:* 69
Burns, Raymond, *9:* 29
Burns, Robert, *24:* 106
Burr, Dane, *12:* 2
Burra, Edward, *YABC 2:* 68
Burri, René, *41:* 143
Burridge, Marge Opitz, *14:* 42
Burris, Burmah, *4:* 81
Burroughs, John Coleman, *41:* 64
Burroughs, Studley O., *41:* 65
Burton, Marilee Robin, *46:* 33
Burton, Virginia Lee, *2:* 43; *44:* 49, 51; *YABC 1:* 24
Busoni, Rafaello, *1:* 186; *3:* 224; *6:* 126; *14:* 5; *16:* 62-63
Butchkes, Sidney, *50:* 58
Butterfield, Ned, *1:* 153; *27:* 128
Buzonas, Gail, *29:* 88
Buzzell, Russ W., *12:* 177
Byard, Carole M., *39:* 44
Byars, Betsy, *46:* 35
Byfield, Barbara Ninde, *8:* 18
Byfield, Graham, *32:* 29
Byrd, Robert, *13:* 218; *33:* 46

Caddy, Alice, *6:* 41
Cady, Harrison, *17:* 21, 23; *19:* 57, 58
Caldecott, Randolph, *16:* 98, 103; *17:* 32-33, 36, 38-39; *26:* 90; *YABC 2:* 172
Calder, Alexander, *18:* 168
Calderon, W. Frank, *25:* 160
Caldwell, Doreen, *23:* 77
Caldwell, John, *46:* 225
Callahan, Kevin, *22:* 42
Callahan, Philip S., *25:* 77
Cameron, Julia Margaret, *19:* 203
Campbell, Ann, *11:* 43
Campbell, Rod, *51:* 27
Campbell, Walter M., *YABC 2:* 158
Camps, Luis, *28:* 120-121
Canright, David, *36:* 162
Caras, Peter, *36:* 64
Caraway, James, *3:* 200-201
Carbe, Nino, *29:* 183
Carigiet, Alois, *24:* 67

Carle, Eric, *4:* 42; *11:* 121; *12:* 29
Carlson, Nancy L., *41:* 116
Carr, Archie, *37:* 225
Carrick, Donald, *5:* 194; *39:* 97;
   49: 70
Carrick, Malcolm, *28:* 59, 60
Carrick, Valery, *21:* 47
Carroll, Lewis. *See* Dodgson, Charles
   L.
Carroll, Ruth, *7:* 41; *10:* 68
Carter, Barbara, *47:* 167, 169
Carter, Harry, *22:* 179
Carter, Helene, *15:* 38; *22:* 202, 203;
   YABC 2: 220-221
Cartlidge, Michelle, *49:* 65
Carty, Leo, *4:* 196; *7:* 163
Cary, *4:* 133; *9:* 32; *20:* 2; *21:* 143
Cary, Page, *12:* 41
Case, Sandra E., *16:* 2
Cassel, Lili. *See* Wronker, Lili Cassel
Cassel-Wronker, Lili.
   See also Wronker, Lili Cassel
Cassels, Jean, *8:* 50
Castellon, Federico, *48:* 45, 46, 47, 48
Castle, Jane, *4:* 80
Cather, Carolyn, *3:* 83; *15:* 203;
   34: 216
Cauley, Lorinda Bryan, *44:* 135;
   46: 49
Cayard, Bruce, *38:* 67
Cellini, Joseph, *2:* 73; *3:* 35; *16:* 116;
   47: 103
Chabrian, Debbi, *45:* 55
Chabrian, Deborah, *51:* 182
Chagnon, Mary, *37:* 158
Chalmers, Mary, *3:* 145; *13:* 148;
   33: 125
Chamberlain, Christopher, *45:* 57
Chamberlain, Margaret, *46:* 51
Chambers, C. E., *17:* 230
Chambers, Dave, *12:* 151
Chambers, Mary, *4:* 188
Chambliss, Maxie, *42:* 186
Chandler, David P., *28:* 62
Chapman, C. H., *13:* 83, 85, 87
Chapman, Frederick T., *6:* 27; *44:* 28
Chapman, Gaynor, *32:* 52, 53
Chappell, Warren, *3:* 172; *21:* 56;
   27: 125
Charles, Donald, *30:* 154, 155
Charlip, Remy, *4:* 48; *34:* 138
Charlot, Jean, *1:* 137, 138; *8:* 23;
   14: 31; *48:* 151
Charlton, Michael, *34:* 50; *37:* 39
Charmatz, Bill, *7:* 45
Chartier, Normand, *9:* 36
Chase, Lynwood M., *14:* 4
Chastain, Madye Lee, *4:* 50
Chauncy, Francis, *24:* 158
Chen, Tony, *6:* 45; *19:* 131; *29:* 126;
   34: 160
Cheney, T. A., *11:* 47
Cheng, Judith, *36:* 45; *51:* 16
Chermayeff, Ivan, *47:* 53
Cherry, Lynne, *34:* 52
Chess, Victoria, *12:* 6; *33:* 42, 48, 49;
   40: 194; *41:* 145
Chessare, Michele, *41:* 50
Chesterton, G. K., *27:* 43, 44, 45, 47

Chestnutt, David, *47:* 217
Chevalier, Christa, *35:* 66
Chew, Ruth, *7:* 46
Chifflart, *47:* 113, 127
Chin, Alex, *28:* 54
Cho, Shinta, *8:* 126
Chollick, Jay, *25:* 175
Chorao, Kay, *7:* 200-201; *8:* 25;
   11: 234; *33:* 187; *35:* 239
Christelow, Eileen, *38:* 44
Christensen, Gardell Dano, *1:* 57
Christiansen, Per, *40:* 24
Christy, Howard Chandler,
   17: 163-165, 168-169; *19:* 186,
   187; *21:* 22, 23, 24, 25
Chronister, Robert, *23:* 138
Church, Frederick, *YABC 1:* 155
Chute, Marchette, *1:* 59
Chwast, Jacqueline, *1:* 63; *2:* 275;
   6: 46-47; *11:* 125; *12:* 202;
   14: 235
Chwast, Seymour, *3:* 128-129; *18:* 43;
   27: 152
Cirlin, Edgard, *2:* 168
Clark, Victoria, *35:* 159
Clarke, Harry, *23:* 172, 173
Claverie, Jean, *38:* 46
Clayton, Robert, *9:* 181
Cleaver, Elizabeth, *8:* 204; *23:* 36
Cleland, T. M., *26:* 92
Clement, Charles, *20:* 38
Clevin, Jörgen, *7:* 50
Clifford, Judy, *34:* 163; *45:* 198
Coalson, Glo, *9:* 72, 85; *25:* 155;
   26: 42; *35:* 212
Cober, Alan E., *17:* 158; *32:* 77;
   49: 127
Cochran, Bobbye, *11:* 52
CoConis, Ted, *4:* 41; *46:* 41; *51:* 104
Coerr, Eleanor, *1:* 64
Coes, Peter, *35:* 172
Coggins, Jack, *2:* 69
Cohen, Alix, *7:* 53
Cohen, Vincent O., *19:* 243
Cohen, Vivien, *11:* 112
Coker, Paul, *51:* 172
Colbert, Anthony, *15:* 41; *20:* 193
Colby, C. B., *3:* 47
Cole, Herbert, *28:* 104
Cole, Olivia H. H., *1:* 134; *3:* 223;
   9: 111; *38:* 104
Collier, David, *13:* 127
Collier, John, *27:* 179
Collier, Steven, *50:* 52
Colonna, Bernard, *21:* 50; *28:* 103;
   34: 140; *43:* 180
Cone, Ferne Geller, *39:* 49
Cone, J. Morton, *39:* 49
Conklin, Paul, *43:* 62
Connolly, Jerome P., *4:* 128; *28:* 52
Connolly, Peter, *47:* 60
Conover, Chris, *31:* 52; *40:* 184;
   41: 51; *44:* 79
Converse, James, *38:* 70
Cook, G. R., *29:* 165
Cookburn, W. V., *29:* 204
Cooke, Donald E., *2:* 77
Coomaraswamy, A. K., *50:* 100
Coombs, Charles, *43:* 65

Coombs, Patricia, *2:* 82; *3:* 52;
   22: 119; *51:* 32, 33, 34, 35, 36-
   37, 38, 39, 40, 42, 43
Cooney, Barbara, *6:* 16-17, 50; *12:* 42;
   13: 92; *15:* 145; *16:* 74, 111;
   18: 189; *23:* 38, 89, 93; *32:* 138;
   38: 105; *YABC 2:* 10
Cooper, Heather, *50:* 39
Cooper, Mario, *24:* 107
Cooper, Marjorie, *7:* 112
Copelman, Evelyn, *8:* 61; *18:* 25
Copley, Heather, *30:* 86; *45:* 57
Corbett, Grahame, *30:* 114; *43:* 67
Corbino, John, *19:* 248
Corcos, Lucille, *2:* 223; *10:* 27; *34:* 66
Corey, Robert, *9:* 34
Corlass, Heather, *10:* 7
Cornell, James, *27:* 60
Cornell, Jeff, *11:* 58
Corrigan, Barbara, *8:* 37
Corwin, Judith Hoffman, *10:* 28
Cory, Fanny Y., *20:* 113; *48:* 29
Cosgrove, Margaret, *3:* 100; *47:* 63
Costabel, Eva Deutsch, *45:* 66, 67
Costello, David F., *23:* 55
Courtney, R., *35:* 110
Couture, Christin, *41:* 209
Covarrubias, Miguel, *35:* 118, 119,
   123, 124, 125
Coville, Katherine, *32:* 57; *36:* 167
Cox, *43:* 93
Cox, Charles, *8:* 20
Cox, Palmer, *24:* 76, 77
Craft, Kinuko, *22:* 182; *36:* 220
Craig, Helen, *49:* 76
Crane, Alan H., *1:* 217
Crane, H. M., *13:* 111
Crane, Jack, *43:* 183
Crane, Walter, *18:* 46-49, 53-54,
   56-57, 59-61; *22:* 128; *24:* 210,
   217
Crawford, Will, *43:* 77
Credle, Ellis *1:* 69
Crews, Donald, *32:* 59, 60
Crofut, Susan, *23:* 61
Crowell, Pers, *3:* 125
Cruikshank, George, *15:* 76, 83;
   22: 74, 75, 76, 77, 78, 79, 80,
   81, 82, 84, 137; *24:* 22, 23
Crump, Fred H., *11:* 62
Cruz, Ray, *6:* 55
Cstari, Joe, *44:* 82
Cuffari, Richard, *4:* 75; *5:* 98; *6:* 56;
   7: 13, 84, 153; *8:* 148, 155; *9:* 89;
   11: 19; *12:* 55, 96, 114; *15:* 51,
   202; *18:* 5; *20:* 139; *21:* 197;
   22: 14, 192; *23:* 15, 106; *25:* 97;
   27: 133; *28:* 196; *29:* 54; *30:* 85;
   31: 35; *36:* 101; *38:* 171; *42:* 97;
   44: 92, 192; *45:* 212, 213; *46:* 36,
   198; *50:* 164
Cugat, Xavier, *19:* 120
Cumings, Art, *35:* 160
Cummings, Chris, *29:* 167
Cummings, Pat, *42:* 61
Cummings, Richard, *24:* 119
Cunette, Lou, *20:* 93; *22:* 125
Cunningham, Aline, *25:* 180
Cunningham, David, *11:* 13

Cunningham, Imogene, *16:* 122, 127
Curry, John Steuart, *2:* 5; *19:* 84; *34:* 36
Curtis, Bruce, *23:* 96; *30:* 88; *36:* 22

Dabcovich, Lydia, *25:* 105; *40:* 114
Dain, Martin J., *35:* 75
Daley, Joann, *50:* 22
Dalton, Anne, *40:* 62
Daly, Niki, *37:* 53
Dalziel, Brothers, *33:* 113
D'Amato, Alex, *9:* 48; *20:* 25
D'Amato, Janet, *9:* 48; *20:* 25; *26:* 118
Daniel, Alan, *23:* 59; *29:* 110
Daniel, Lewis C., *20:* 216
Daniels, Steve, *22:* 16
Dann, Bonnie, *31:* 83
Danska, Herbert, *24:* 219
Danyell, Alice, *20:* 27
Darley, F.O.C., *16:* 145; *19:* 79, 86, 88, 185; *21:* 28, 36; *35:* 76, 77, 78, 79, 80-81; *YABC 2:* 175
Darling, Lois, *3:* 59; *23:* 30, 31
Darling, Louis, *1:* 40-41; *2:* 63; *3:* 59; *23:* 30, 31; *43:* 54, 57, 59
Darrow, Whitney, Jr., *13:* 25; *38:* 220, 221
Darwin, Beatrice, *43:* 54
Darwin, Len, *24:* 82
Dastolfo, Frank, *33:* 179
Dauber, Liz, *1:* 22; *3:* 266; *30:* 49
Daugherty, James, *3:* 66; *8:* 178; *13:* 27-28, 161; *18:* 101; *19:* 72; *29:* 108; *32:* 156; *42:* 84; *YABC 1:* 256; *YABC 2:* 174
d'Aulaire, Edgar, *5:* 51
d'Aulaire, Ingri, *5:* 51
David, Jonathan, *19:* 37
Davidson, Kevin, *28:* 154
Davidson, Raymond, *32:* 61
Davis, Allen, *20:* 11; *22:* 45; *27:* 222; *29:* 157; *41:* 99; *47:* 99; *50:* 84
Davis, Bette J., *15:* 53; *23:* 95
Davis, Dimitris, *45:* 95
Davis, Jim, *32:* 63, 64
Davis, Marguerite, *31:* 38; *34:* 69, 70; *YABC 1:* 126, 230
Davisson, Virginia H., *44:* 178
Dawson, Diane, *24:* 127; *42:* 126
Dean, Bob, *19:* 211
de Angeli, Marguerite, *1:* 77; *27:* 62, 65, 66, 67, 69, 70, 72; *YABC 1:* 166
Deas, Michael, *27:* 219, 221; *30:* 156
de Bosschère, Jean, *19:* 252; *21:* 4
De Bruyn, M(onica) G., *13:* 30-31
De Cuir, John F., *1:* 28-29
Degen, Bruce, *40:* 227, 229
De Grazia, *14:* 59; *39:* 56, 57
de Groat, Diane, *9:* 39; *18:* 7; *23:* 123; *28:* 200-201; *31:* 58, 59; *34:* 151; *41:* 152; *43:* 88; *46:* 40, 200; *49:* 163; *50:* 89
de Groot, Lee, *6:* 21
Delacre, Lulu, *36:* 66
Delaney, A., *21:* 78
Delaney, Ned, *28:* 68

de Larrea, Victoria, *6:* 119, 204; *29:* 103
Delessert, Etienne, *7:* 140; *46:* 61, 62, 63, 65, 67, 68; *YABC 2:* 209
Delulio, John, *15:* 54
Demarest, Chris L., *45:* 68-69, 70
De Mejo, Oscar, *40:* 67
Denetsosie, Hoke, *13:* 126
Dennis, Morgan, *18:* 68-69
Dennis, Wesley, *2:* 87; *3:* 111; *11:* 132; *18:* 71-74; *22:* 9; *24:* 196, 200; *46:* 178
Denslow, W. W., *16:* 84-87; *18:* 19-20, 24; *29:* 211
de Paola, Tomie, *8:* 95; *9:* 93; *11:* 69; *25:* 103; *28:* 157; *29:* 80; *39:* 52-53; *40:* 226; *46:* 187
Detmold, Edward J., *22:* 104, 105, 106, 107; *35:* 120; *YABC 2:* 203
Detrich, Susan, *20:* 133
DeVelasco, Joseph E., *21:* 51
de Veyrac, Robert, *YABC 2:* 19
DeVille, Edward A., *4:* 235
Devito, Bert, *12:* 164
Devlin, Harry, *11:* 74
Dewey, Ariane, *7:* 64; *33:* 195; *35:* 208
See also Aruego, Ariane
Dewey, Kenneth, *39:* 62; *51:* 23
de Zanger, Arie, *30:* 40
Diamond, Donna, *21:* 200; *23:* 63; *26:* 142; *35:* 83, 84, 85, 86-87, 88, 89; *38:* 78; *40:* 147; *44:* 152; *50:* 144
Dick, John Henry, *8:* 181
Dickens, Frank, *34:* 131
Dickey, Robert L., *15:* 279
DiFate, Vincent, *37:* 70
DiFiori, Lawrence, *10:* 51; *12:* 190; *27:* 97; *40:* 219
Di Grazia, Thomas, *32:* 66; *35:* 241
Dillard, Annie, *10:* 32
Dillon, Corinne B., *1:* 139
Dillon, Diane, *4:* 104, 167; *6:* 23; *13:* 29; *15:* 99; *26:* 148; *27:* 136, 201; *51:* 29, 48, 51, 52, 53, 54, 55, 56-57, 58, 59, 60, 61, 62
Dillon, Leo, *4:* 104, 167; *6:* 23; *13:* 29; *15:* 99; *26:* 148; *27:* 136, 201; *51:* 29, 48, 51, 52, 53, 54, 55, 56-57, 58, 59, 60, 61, 62
DiMaggio, Joe, *36:* 22
Dinan, Carol, *25:* 169
Dines, Glen, *7:* 66-67
Dinesen, Thomas, *44:* 37
Dinnerstein, Harvey, *42:* 63, 64, 65, 66, 67, 68; *50:* 146
Dinsdale, Mary, *10:* 65; *11:* 171
Disney, Walt, *28:* 71, 72, 73, 76, 77, 78, 79, 80, 81, 87, 88, 89, 90, 91, 94
Dixon, Maynard, *20:* 165
Doares, Robert G., *20:* 39
Dobias, Frank, *22:* 162
Dobrin, Arnold, *4:* 68
Docktor, Irv, *43:* 70
Dodd, Ed, *4:* 69
Dodd, Lynley, *35:* 92

Dodgson, Charles L., *20:* 148; *33:* 146; *YABC 2:* 98
Dodson, Bert, *9:* 138; *14:* 195; *42:* 55
Dohanos, Stevan, *16:* 10
Dolch, Marguerite P., *50:* 64
Dolesch, Susanne, *34:* 49
Dolson, Hildegarde, *5:* 57
Domanska, Janina, *6:* 66-67; *YABC 1:* 166
Domjan, Joseph, *25:* 93
Donahue, Vic, *2:* 93; *3:* 190; *9:* 44
Donald, Elizabeth, *4:* 18
Donna, Natalie, *9:* 52
Doré, Gustave, *18:* 169, 172, 175; *19:* 93, 94, 95, 96, 97, 98, 99, 100, 101, 102, 103, 104, 105; *23:* 188; *25:* 197, 199
Doremus, Robert, *6:* 62; *13:* 90; *30:* 95, 96, 97; *38:* 97
Dorfman, Ronald, *11:* 128
Doty, Roy, *28:* 98; *31:* 32; *32:* 224; *46:* 157
Dougherty, Charles, *16:* 204; *18:* 74
Douglas, Aaron, *31:* 103
Douglas, Goray, *13:* 151
Dowd, Vic, *3:* 244; *10:* 97
Dowden, Anne Ophelia, *7:* 70-71; *13:* 120
Dowdy, Mrs. Regera, *29:* 100.
See also Gorey, Edward
Doyle, Richard, *21:* 31, 32, 33; *23:* 231; *24:* 177; *31:* 87
Draper, Angie, *43:* 84
Drath, Bill, *26:* 34
Drawson, Blair, *17:* 53
Drescher, Joan, *30:* 100, 101; *35:* 245
Drew, Patricia, *15:* 100
Drummond, V. H., *6:* 70
du Bois, William Pène, *4:* 70; *10:* 122; *26:* 61; *27:* 145, 211; *35:* 243; *41:* 216
Duchesne, Janet, *6:* 162
Dudash, Michael, *32:* 122
Duer, Douglas, *34:* 177
Duffy, Joseph, *38:* 203
Duffy, Pat, *28:* 153
Duke, Chris, *8:* 195
Dulac, Edmund, *19:* 108, 109, 110, 111, 112, 113, 114, 115, 117; *23:* 187; *25:* 152; *YABC 1:* 37; *YABC 2:* 147
Dulac, Jean, *13:* 64
Dunn, Harvey, *34:* 78, 79, 80, 81
Dunn, Phoebe, *5:* 175
Dunn, Iris, *5:* 175
Dunnington, Tom, *3:* 36; *18:* 281; *25:* 61; *31:* 159; *35:* 168; *48:* 195
Dutz, *6:* 59
Duvoisin, Roger, *2:* 95; *6:* 76-77; *7:* 197; *28:* 125; *30:* 101, 102, 103, 104, 105, 107; *47:* 205
Dypold, Pat, *15:* 37

E.V.B. *See* Boyle, Eleanor Vere (Gordon)
Eachus, Jennifer, *29:* 74

Eagle, Michael, *11:* 86; *20:* 9; *23:* 18; *27:* 122; *28:* 57; *34:* 201; *44:* 189
Earle, Olive L., *7:* 75
Earle, Vana, *27:* 99
Eastman, P. D., *33:* 57
Easton, Reginald, *29:* 181
Eaton, Tom, *4:* 62; *6:* 64; *22:* 99; *24:* 124
Ebel, Alex, *11:* 89
Ebert, Len, *9:* 191; *44:* 47
Echevarria, Abe, *37:* 69
Eckersley, Maureen, *48:* 62
Ede, Janina, *33:* 59
Edens, Cooper, *49:* 81, 82, 83, 84, 85
Edgar, Sarah E., *41:* 97
Edrien, *11:* 53
Edwards, Freya, *45:* 102
Edwards, George Wharton, *31:* 155
Edwards, Gunvor, *2:* 71; *25:* 47; *32:* 71
Edwards, Jeanne, *29:* 257
Edwards, Linda Strauss, *21:* 134; *39:* 123; *49:* 88-89
Eggenhofer, Nicholas, *2:* 81
Egielski, Richard, *11:* 90; *16:* 208; *33:* 236; *38:* 35; *49:* 91, 92, 93, 95, 212, 213, 214, 216
Ehlert, Lois, *35:* 97
Ehrlich, Bettina, *1:* 83
Eichenberg, Fritz, *1:* 79; *9:* 54; *19:* 248; *23:* 170; *24:* 200; *26:* 208; *50:* 67, 68, 69, 70, 71, 72, 73, 74, 75, 77, 79, 80, 81; *YABC 1:* 104-105; *YABC 2:* 213
Einsel, Naiad, *10:* 35; *29:* 136
Einsel, Walter, *10:* 37
Einzig, Susan, *3:* 77; *43:* 78
Eitzen, Allan, *9:* 56; *12:* 212; *14:* 226; *21:* 194; *38:* 162
Eldridge, Harold, *43:* 83
Elgaard, Greta, *19:* 241
Elgin, Kathleen, *9:* 188; *39:* 69
Ellacott, S. E., *19:* 118
Elliott, Sarah M., *14:* 58
Emberley, Ed, *8:* 53
Emberley, Michael, *34:* 83
Emery, Leslie, *49:* 187
Emmett, Bruce, *49:* 147
Engle, Mort, *38:* 64
Englebert, Victor, *8:* 54
Enos, Randall, *20:* 183
Enright, Maginel Wright, *19:* 240, 243; *39:* 31, 35, 36
Enrique, Romeo, *34:* 135
Epstein, Stephen, *50:* 142, 148
Erhard, Walter, *1:* 152
Erickson, Phoebe, *11:* 83
Erikson, Mel, *31:* 69
Ernst, Lisa Campbell, *47:* 147
Escourido, Joseph, *4:* 81
Esté, Kirk, *33:* 111
Estoril, Jean, *32:* 27
Estrada, Ric, *5:* 52, 146; *13:* 174
Etchemendy, Teje, *38:* 68
Ets, Marie Hall, *2:* 102
Eulalie, *YABC 2:* 315
Evans, Katherine, *5:* 64
Ewing, Juliana Horatia, *16:* 92

Falconer, Pearl, *34:* 23
Falls, C. B., *1:* 19; *38:* 71, 72, 73, 74
Falter, John, *40:* 169, 170
Farmer, Andrew, *49:* 102
Farmer, Peter, *24:* 108; *38:* 75
Farquharson, Alexander, *46:* 75
Farrell, David, *40:* 135
Fatigati, Evelyn, *24:* 112
Faul-Jansen, Regina, *22:* 117
Faulkner, Jack, *6:* 169
Fava, Rita, *2:* 29
Fax, Elton C., *1:* 101; *4:* 2; *12:* 77; *25:* 107
Fay, *43:* 93
Federspiel, Marian, *33:* 51
Feelings, Tom, *5:* 22; *8:* 56; *12:* 153; *16:* 105; *30:* 196; *49:* 37
Fehr, Terrence, *21:* 87
Feiffer, Jules, *3:* 91; *8:* 58
Feigeles, Neil, *41:* 242
Feller, Gene, *33:* 130
Fellows, Muriel H., *10:* 42
Felts, Shirley, *33:* 71; *48:* 59
Fennelli, Maureen, *38:* 181
Fenton, Carroll Lane, *5:* 66; *21:* 39
Fenton, Mildred Adams, *5:* 66; *21:* 39
Ferguson, Walter W., *34:* 86
Fetz, Ingrid, *11:* 67; *12:* 52; *16:* 205; *17:* 59; *29:* 105; *30:* 108, 109; *32:* 149; *43:* 142
Fiammenghi, Gioia, *9:* 66; *11:* 44; *12:* 206; *13:* 57, 59
Field, Rachel, *15:* 113
Fine, Peter K., *43:* 210
Finger, Helen, *42:* 81
Fink, Sam, *18:* 119
Finlay, Winifred, *23:* 72
Fiorentino, Al, *3:* 240
Firmin, Charlotte, *29:* 75; *48:* 70
Fischel, Lillian, *40:* 204
Fischer, Hans, *25:* 202
Fisher, Leonard Everett, *3:* 6; *4:* 72, 86; *6:* 197; *9:* 59; *16:* 151, 153; *23:* 44; *27:* 134; *29:* 26; *34:* 87, 89, 90, 91, 93, 94, 95, 96; *40:* 206; *50:* 150; *YABC 2:* 169
Fisher, Lois, *20:* 62; *21:* 7
Fisk, Nicholas, *25:* 112
Fitschen, Marilyn, *2:* 20-21; *20:* 48
Fitzgerald, F. A., *15:* 116; *25:* 86-87
Fitzhugh, Louise, *1:* 94; *9:* 163; *45:* 75, 78
Fitzhugh, Susie, *11:* 117
Fitzsimmons, Arthur, *14:* 128
Fix, Philippe, *26:* 102
Flack, Marjorie, *21:* 67; *YABC 2:* 122
Flagg, James Montgomery, *17:* 227
Flax, Zeona, *2:* 245
Fleishman, Seymour, *14:* 232; *24:* 87
Fleming, Guy, *18:* 41
Floethe, Richard, *3:* 131; *4:* 90
Floherty, John J., Jr., *5:* 68
Flora, James, *1:* 96; *30:* 111, 112
Florian, Douglas, *19:* 122
Flory, Jane, *22:* 111
Floyd, Gareth, *1:* 74; *17:* 245; *48:* 63
Fluchère, Henri A., *40:* 79
Flynn, Barbara, *7:* 31; *9:* 70
Fogarty, Thomas, *15:* 89

Folger, Joseph, *9:* 100
Folkard, Charles, *22:* 132; *29:* 128, 257-258
Foott, Jeff, *42:* 202
Forberg, Ati, *12:* 71, 205; *14:* 1; *22:* 113; *26:* 22; *48:* 64, 65
Ford, George, *24:* 120; *31:* 70, 177
Ford, H. J., *16:* 185-186
Ford, Pamela Baldwin, *27:* 104
Foreman, Michael, *2:* 110-111
Forrester, Victoria, *40:* 83
Fortnum, Peggy, *6:* 29; *20:* 179; *24:* 211; *26:* 76, 77, 78; *39:* 78; *YABC 1:* 148
Foster, Brad W., *34:* 99
Foster, Genevieve, *2:* 112
Foster, Gerald, *7:* 78
Foster, Laura Louise, *6:* 79
Foster, Marian Curtis, *23:* 74; *40:* 42
Foucher, Adèle, *47:* 118
Fowler, Mel, *36:* 127
Fox, Charles Phillip, *12:* 84
Fox, Jim, *6:* 187
Fracé, Charles, *15:* 118
Frame, Paul, *2:* 45, 145; *9:* 153; *10:* 124; *21:* 71; *23:* 62; *24:* 123; *27:* 106; *31:* 48; *32:* 159; *34:* 195; *38:* 136; *42:* 55; *44:* 139
Francois, André, *25:* 117
Francoise. *See* Seignobosc, Francoise
Frank, Lola Edick, *2:* 199
Frank, Mary, *4:* 54; *34:* 100
Franké, Phil, *45:* 91
Frankel, Julie, *40:* 84, 85, 202
Frankenberg, Robert, *22:* 116; *30:* 50; *38:* 92, 94, 95
Franklin, John, *24:* 22
Frascino, Edward, *9:* 133; *29:* 229; *33:* 190; *48:* 80, 81, 82, 83, 84-85, 86
Frasconi, Antonio, *6:* 80; *27:* 208
Fraser, Betty, *2:* 212; *6:* 185; *8:* 103; *31:* 72, 73; *43:* 136
Fraser, Eric, *38:* 78; *41:* 149, 151
Fraser, F. A., *22:* 234
Frazetta, Frank, *41:* 72
Freas, John, *25:* 207
Freeman, Don, *2:* 15; *13:* 249; *17:* 62-63, 65, 67-68; *18:* 243; *20:* 195; *23:* 213, 217; *32:* 155
Fregosi, Claudia, *24:* 117
French, Fiona, *6:* 82-83
Friedman, Judith, *43:* 197
Friedman, Marvin, *19:* 59; *42:* 86
Frinta, Dagmar, *36:* 42
Frith, Michael K., *15:* 138; *18:* 120
Fritz, Ronald, *46:* 73
Fromm, Lilo, *29:* 85; *40:* 197
Frost, A. B., *17:* 6-7; *19:* 123, 124, 125, 126, 127, 128, 129, 130; *YABC 1:* 156-157, 160; *YABC 2:* 107
Fry, Guy, *2:* 224
Fry, Rosalie, *3:* 72; *YABC 2:* 180-181
Fry, Rosalind, *21:* 153, 168
Fryer, Elmer, *34:* 115
Fuchs, Erich, *6:* 84
Fuchshuber, Annegert, *43:* 96
Fufuka, Mahiri, *32:* 146

Fujikawa, Gyo, *39:* 75, 76
Fulford, Deborah, *23:* 159
Fuller, Margaret, *25:* 189
Funai, Mamoru, *38:* 105
Funk, Tom, *7:* 17, 99
Furchgott, Terry, *29:* 86
Furukawa, Mel, *25:* 42

Gaberell, J., *19:* 236
Gackenbach, Dick, *19:* 168; *41:* 81;
    48: 89, 90, 91, 92, 93, 94
Gaetano, Nicholas, *23:* 209
Gag, Flavia, *17:* 49, 52
Gág, Wanda, *YABC 1:* 135, 137-138,
    141, 143
Gagnon, Cécile, *11:* 77
Gal, Laszlo, *14:* 127
Galdone, Paul, *1:* 156, 181, 206;
    2: 40, 241; *3:* 42, 144; *4:* 141;
    10: 109, 158; *11:* 21; *12:* 118,
    210; *14:* 12; *16:* 36-37; *17:* 70-74;
    18: 111, 230; *19:* 183; *21:* 154;
    22: 150, 245; *33:* 126; *39:* 136,
    137; *42:* 57; *51:* 169
Gallagher, Sears, *20:* 112
Galloway, Ewing, *51:* 154
Galster, Robert, *1:* 66
Galsworthy, Gay John, *35:* 232
Gammell, Stephen, *7:* 48; *13:* 149;
    29: 82; *33:* 209; *41:* 88; *50:* 185,
    186-187
Gannett, Ruth Chrisman, *3:* 74;
    18: 254; *33:* 77, 78
Gantschev, Ivan, *45:* 32
Garbutt, Bernard, *23:* 68
Garcia, *37:* 71
Gardner, Earle, *45:* 167
Gardner, Joan, *40:* 87
Gardner, Joel, *40:* 87, 92
Gardner, John, *40:* 87
Gardner, Lucy, *40:* 87
Gardner, Richard. *See* Cummings,
    Richard, *24:* 119
Garland, Michael, *36:* 29; *38:* 83;
    44: 168; *48:* 78, 221, 222;
    49: 161
Garnett, Eve, *3:* 75
Garnett, Gary, *39:* 184
Garraty, Gail, *4:* 142
Garrett, Agnes, *46:* 110; *47:* 157
Garrett, Edmund H., *20:* 29
Garrison, Barbara, *19:* 133
Gates, Frieda, *26:* 80
Gaughan, Jack, *26:* 79; *43:* 185
Gaver, Becky, *20:* 61
Gay, Zhenya, *19:* 135, 136
Geary, Clifford N., *1:* 122; *9:* 104;
    51: 74
Gee, Frank, *33:* 26
Geer, Charles, *1:* 91; *3:* 179; *4:* 201;
    6: 168; *7:* 96; *9:* 58; *10:* 72;
    12: 127; *39:* 156, 157, 158, 159,
    160; *42:* 88, 89, 90, 91
Gehm, Charlie, *36:* 65
Geisel, Theodor Seuss, *1:* 104-105,
    106; *28:* 108, 109, 110, 111, 112,
    113

Geldart, William, *15:* 121; *21:* 202
Genia, *4:* 84
Gentry, Cyrille R., *12:* 66
George, Jean, *2:* 113
Gérard, Jean Ignace, *45:* 80
Gérard, Rolf, *27:* 147, 150
Geritz, Franz, *17:* 135
Gerlach, Geff, *42:* 58
Gerrard, Roy, *47:* 78
Gershinowitz, George, *36:* 27
Gerstein, Mordicai, *31:* 117; *47:* 80,
    81, 82, 83, 84, 85, 86; *51:* 173
Gervase, *12:* 27
Getz, Arthur, *32:* 148
Gibbons, Gail, *23:* 78
Gibbs, Tony, *40:* 95
Gibran, Kahlil, *32:* 116
Giesen, Rosemary, *34:* 192-193
Giguère, George, *20:* 111
Gilbert, John, *19:* 184; *YABC 2:* 287
Gilbert, W. S., *36:* 83, 85, 96
Giles, Will, *41:* 218
Gill, Margery, *4:* 57; *7:* 7; *22:* 122;
    25: 166; *26:* 146, 147
Gillen, Denver, *28:* 216
Gillette, Henry J., *23:* 237
Gilliam, Stan, *39:* 64, 81
Gilman, Esther, *15:* 124
Giovanopoulos, Paul, *7:* 104
Githens, Elizabeth M., *5:* 47
Gladstone, Gary, *12:* 89; *13:* 190
Gladstone, Lise, *15:* 273
Glanzman, Louis S., *2:* 177; *3:* 182;
    36: 97, 98; *38:* 120, 122
Glaser, Milton, *3:* 5; *5:* 156; *11:* 107;
    30: 26; *36:* 112
Glass, Andrew, *36:* 38; *44:* 133;
    48: 205
Glass, Marvin, *9:* 174
Glasser, Judy, *41:* 156
Glattauer, Ned, *5:* 84; *13:* 224; *14:* 26
Glauber, Uta, *17:* 76
Gleeson, J. M., *YABC 2:* 207
Glegg, Creina, *36:* 100
Gliewe, Unada, *3:* 78-79; *21:* 73;
    30: 220
Glovach, Linda, *7:* 105
Gobbato, Imero, *3:* 180-181; *6:* 213;
    7: 58; *9:* 150; *18:* 39; *21:* 167;
    39: 82, 83; *41:* 137, 251
Goble, Paul, *25:* 121; *26:* 86; *33:* 65
Goble, Warwick, *46:* 78, 79
Godal, Eric, *36:* 93
Godfrey, Michael, *17:* 279
Goembel, Ponder, *42:* 124
Goffstein, M. B., *8:* 71
Golbin, Andrée, *15:* 125
Goldfeder, Cheryl, *11:* 191
Goldsborough, June, *5:* 154-155;
    8: 92, *14:* 226; *19:* 139
Goldstein, Leslie, *5:* 8; *6:* 60; *10:* 106
Goldstein, Nathan, *1:* 175; *2:* 79;
    11: 41, 232; *16:* 55
Goodall, John S., *4:* 92-93; *10:* 132;
    YABC 1: 198
Goode, Diane, *15:* 126; *50:* 183
Goodelman, Aaron, *40:* 203
Goodenow, Earle, *40:* 97
Goodman, Joan Elizabeth, *50:* 86

Goodwin, Harold, *13:* 74
Goodwin, Philip R., *18:* 206
Goor, Nancy, *39:* 85, 86
Goor, Ron, *39:* 85, 86
Gordon, Gwen, *12:* 151
Gordon, Margaret, *4:* 147; *5:* 48-49;
    9: 79
Gorecka-Egan, Erica, *18:* 35
Gorey, Edward, *1:* 60-61; *13:* 169;
    18: 192; *20:* 201; *29:* 90, 91,
    92-93, 94, 95, 96, 97, 98, 99,
    100; *30:* 129; *32:* 90; *34:* 200.
    See also Dowdy, Mrs. Regera
Gorsline, Douglas, *1:* 98; *6:* 13;
    11: 113; *13:* 104; *15:* 14; *28:* 117,
    118; *YABC 1:* 15
Gosner, Kenneth, *5:* 135
Gotlieb, Jules, *6:* 127
Gough, Philip, *23:* 47; *45:* 90
Gould, Chester, *49:* 112, 113, 114,
    116, 117, 118
Govern, Elaine R., *26:* 94
Grabianski, *20:* 144
Grabiański, Janusz, *39:* 92, 93, 94, 95
Graboff, Abner, *35:* 103, 104
Graham, A. B., *11:* 61
Graham, L., *7:* 108
Graham, Margaret Bloy, *11:* 120;
    18: 305, 307
Grahame-Johnstone, Anne, *13:* 61
Grahame-Johnstone, Janet, *13:* 61
Grainger, Sam, *42:* 95
Gramatky, Hardie, *1:* 107; *30:* 116,
    119, 120, 122, 123
Grandville, J. J., *45:* 81, 82, 83, 84,
    85, 86, 87, 88; *47:* 125
Granger, Paul, *39:* 153
Grant, Gordon, *17:* 230, 234; *25:* 123,
    124, 125, 126; *YABC 1:* 164
Grant, (Alice) Leigh, *10:* 52; *15:* 131;
    20: 20; *26:* 119; *48:* 202
Graves, Elizabeth, *45:* 101
Gray, Harold, *33:* 87, 88
Gray, Reginald, *6:* 69
Green, Eileen, *6:* 97
Green, Michael, *32:* 216
Greenaway, Kate, *17:* 275; *24:* 180;
    26: 107; *41:* 222, 232;
    YABC 1: 88-89; *YABC 2:* 131,
    133, 136, 138-139, 141
Greenwald, Sheila, *1:* 34; *3:* 99; *8:* 72
Gregorian, Joyce Ballou, *30:* 125
Gregory, Frank M., *29:* 107
Greiffenhagen, Maurice, *16:* 137;
    27: 57; *YABC 2:* 288
Greiner, Robert, *6:* 86
Gretter, J. Clemens, *31:* 134
Gretz, Susanna, *7:* 114
Gretzer, John, *1:* 54; *3:* 26; *4:* 162;
    7: 125; *16:* 247; *18:* 117; *28:* 66;
    30: 85, 211; *33:* 235
Grey Owl, *24:* 41
Gri, *25:* 90
Grieder, Walter *9:* 84
Grifalconi, Ann, *2:* 126; *3:* 248;
    11: 18; *13:* 182; *46:* 38; *50:* 145
Griffin, Gillett Good, *26:* 96
Griffin, James, *30:* 166
Griffiths, Dave, *29:* 76

Gringhuis, Dirk, *6:* 98; *9:* 196
Gripe, Harald, *2:* 127
Grisha, *3:* 71
Gropper, William, *27:* 93; *37:* 193
Grose, Helen Mason, *YABC 1:* 260; *YABC 2:* 150
Grossman, Nancy, *24:* 130; *29:* 101
Grossman, Robert, *11:* 124; *46:* 39
Groth, John, *15:* 79; *21:* 53, 54
Gruelle, Johnny, *35:* 107
Gschwind, William, *11:* 72
Guggenheim, Hans, *2:* 10; *3:* 37; *8:* 136
Guilbeau, Honoré, *22:* 69
Gundersheimer, Karen, *35:* 240
Gusman, Annie, *38:* 62
Gustafson, Scott, *34:* 111; *43:* 40
Guthrie, Robin, *20:* 122
Gwynne, Fred, *41:* 94, 95
Gyberg, Bo-Erik, *38:* 131

Haas, Irene, *17:* 77
Hack, Konrad, *51:* 127
Hader, Berta H., *16:* 126
Hader, Elmer S., *16:* 126
Hafner, Marylin, *22:* 196, 216; *24:* 44; *30:* 51; *35:* 95; *51:* 25, 160, 164
Hague, Michael, *32:* 128; *48:* 98, 99, 100-101, 103, 105, 106-107, 108, 109, 110; *49:* 121; *51:* 105
Halas, John, *29:* 41, 47, 48
Haldane, Roger, *13:* 76; *14:* 202
Hale, Irina, *26:* 97
Hale, Kathleen, *17:* 79
Haley, Gail E., *43:* 102, 103, 104, 105
Hall, Chuck, *30:* 189
Hall, Douglas, *15:* 184; *43:* 106, 107
Hall, H. Tom, *1:* 227; *30:* 210
Hall, Sydney P., *31:* 89
Hall, Vicki, *20:* 24
Hallinan, P. K., *39:* 98
Halpern, Joan, *10:* 25
Halverson, Janet, *49:* 38, 42, 44
Hamberger, John, *6:* 8; *8:* 32; *14:* 79; *34:* 136
Hamil, Tom, *14:* 80; *43:* 163
Hamilton, Bill and Associates, *26:* 215
Hamilton, Helen S., *2:* 238
Hamilton, J., *19:* 83, 85, 87
Hammond, Chris, *21:* 37
Hammond, Elizabeth, *5:* 36, 203
Hampshire, Michael, *5:* 187; *7:* 110-111; *48:* 150; *51:* 129
Hampson, Denman, *10:* 155; *15:* 130
Hampton, Blake, *41:* 244
Handforth, Thomas, *42:* 100, 101, 102, 103, 104, 105, 107
Handville, Robert, *1:* 89; *38:* 76; *45:* 108, 109
Hane, Roger, *17:* 239; *44:* 54
Haney, Elizabeth Mathieu, *34:* 84
Hanley, Catherine, *8:* 161
Hann, Jacquie, *19:* 144
Hannon, Mark, *38:* 37
Hanson, Joan, *8:* 76; *11:* 139
Hardy, David A., *9:* 96
Hardy, Paul, *YABC 2:* 245

Harlan, Jerry, *3:* 96
Harnischfeger, *18:* 121
Harper, Arthur, *YABC 2:* 121
Harrington, Richard, *5:* 81
Harris, Susan Yard, *42:* 121
Harrison, Florence, *20:* 150, 152
Harrison, Harry, *4:* 103
Harrison, Jack, *28:* 149
Hart, William, *13:* 72
Hartelius, Margaret, *10:* 24
Hartshorn, Ruth, *5:* 115; *11:* 129
Harvey, Bob, *48:* 219
Harvey, Gerry, *7:* 180
Hassall, Joan, *43:* 108, 109
Hassell, Hilton, *YABC 1:* 187
Hasselriis, Else, *18:* 87; *YABC 1:* 96
Hauman, Doris, *2:* 184; *29:* 58, 59; *32:* 85, 86, 87
Hauman, George, *2:* 184; *29:* 58, 59; *32:* 85, 86, 87
Hausherr, Rosmarie, *15:* 29
Hawkinson, John, *4:* 109; *7:* 83; *21:* 64
Hawkinson, Lucy, *21:* 64
Haxton, Elaine, *28:* 131
Haydock, Robert, *4:* 95
Hayes, Geoffrey, *26:* 111; *44:* 133
Haywood, Carolyn, *1:* 112; *29:* 104
Healy, Daty, *12:* 143
Hearon, Dorothy, *34:* 69
Hechtkopf, H., *11:* 110
Hedderwick, Mairi, *30:* 127; *32:* 47; *36:* 104
Hefter, Richard, *28:* 170; *31:* 81, 82; *33:* 183
Heigh, James, *22:* 98
Heighway, Richard, *25:* 160
Heinly, John, *45:* 113
Hellebrand, Nancy, *26:* 57
Heller, Linda, *46:* 86
Hellmuth, Jim, *38:* 164
Helms, Georgeann, *33:* 62
Helweg, Hans, *41:* 118; *50:* 93
Henderson, Keith, *35:* 122
Henkes, Kevin, *43:* 111
Henneberger, Robert, *1:* 42; *2:* 237; *25:* 83
Henriksen, Harold, *35:* 26; *48:* 68
Henry, Everett, *29:* 191
Henry, Thomas, *5:* 102
Hensel, *27:* 119
Henstra, Friso, *8:* 80; *36:* 70; *40:* 222; *41:* 250
Hepple, Norman, *28:* 198
Herbert, Wally, *23:* 101
Herbster, Mary Lee, *9:* 33
Hergé. *See* Rémi, Georges
Hermanson, Dennis, *10:* 55
Herrington, Roger, *3:* 161
Heslop, Mike, *38:* 60; *40:* 130
Hess, Richard, *42:* 31
Hester, Ronnie, *37:* 85
Heustis, Louise L., *20:* 28
Heyduck-Huth, Hilde, *8:* 82
Heyer, Hermann, *20:* 114, 115
Heyman, Ken, *8:* 33; *34:* 113
Heywood, Karen, *48:* 114
Hickling, P. B., *40:* 165

Higginbottom, J. Winslow, *8:* 170; *29:* 105, 106
Higham, David, *50:* 104
Hildebrandt, Greg, *8:* 191
Hildebrandt, Tim, *8:* 191
Hilder, Rowland, *19:* 207
Hill, Gregory, *35:* 190
Hill, Pat, *49:* 120
Hillier, Matthew, *45:* 205
Hillman, Priscilla, *48:* 115
Himler, Ronald, *6:* 114; *7:* 162; *8:* 17, 84, 125; *14:* 76; *19:* 145; *26:* 160; *31:* 43; *38:* 116; *41:* 44, 79; *43:* 52; *45:* 120; *46:* 43
Himmelman, John, *47:* 109
Hinds, Bill, *37:* 127, 130
Hines, Anna Grossnickle, *51:* 90
Hiroshige, *25:* 71
Hirsh, Marilyn, *7:* 126
Hitz, Demi, *11:* 135; *15:* 245
Hnizdovsky, Jacques, *32:* 96
Ho, Kwoncjan, *15:* 132
Hoban, Lillian, *1:* 114; *22:* 157; *26:* 72; *29:* 53; *40:* 105, 107, 195; *41:* 80
Hoban, Tana, *22:* 159
Hoberman, Norman, *5:* 82
Hockerman, Dennis, *39:* 22
Hodgell, P. C., *42:* 114
Hodges, C. Walter, *2:* 139; *11:* 15; *12:* 25; *23:* 34; *25:* 96; *38:* 165; *44:* 197; *45:* 95; *YABC 2:* 62-63
Hodges, David, *9:* 98
Hodgetts, Victoria, *43:* 132
Hofbauer, Imre, *2:* 162
Hoff, Syd, *9:* 107; *10:* 128; *33:* 94
Hoffman, Rosekrans, *15:* 133; *50:* 219
Hoffman, Sanford, *38:* 208
Hoffmann, Felix, *9:* 109
Hofsinde, Robert, *21:* 70
Hogan, Inez, *2:* 141
Hogarth, Burne, *41:* 58
Hogarth, Paul, *41:* 102, 103, 104; *YABC 1:* 16
Hogarth, William, *42:* 33
Hogenbyl, Jan, *1:* 35
Hogner, Nils, *4:* 122; *25:* 144
Hogrogian, Nonny, *3:* 221; *4:* 106-107; *5:* 166; *7:* 129; *15:* 2; *16:* 176; *20:* 154; *22:* 146; *25:* 217; *27:* 206; *YABC 2:* 84, 94
Hokusai, *25:* 71
Holberg, Richard, *2:* 51
Holdcroft, Tina, *38:* 109
Holder, Heidi, *36:* 99
Holiday, Henry, *YABC 2:* 107
Holl, F., *36:* 91
Holland, Brad, *45:* 59, 159
Holland, Janice, *18:* 118
Holland, Marion, *6:* 116
Holldobler, Turid, *26:* 120
Holling, Holling C., *15:* 136-137
Hollinger, Deanne, *12:* 116
Holmes, B., *3:* 82
Holmes, Bea, *7:* 74; *24:* 156; *31:* 93
Holmgren, George Ellen, *45:* 112
Holt, Norma, *44:* 106
Holtan, Gene, *32:* 192
Holz, Loretta, *17:* 81

Homar, Lorenzo, *6:* 2
Homer, Winslow, *YABC 2:* 87
Honigman, Marian, *3:* 2
Honoré, Paul, *42:* 77, 79, 81, 82
Hood, Susan, *12:* 43
Hook, Frances, *26:* 188; *27:* 127
Hook, Jeff, *14:* 137
Hook, Richard, *26:* 188
Hoover, Carol A., *21:* 77
Hoover, Russell, *12:* 95; *17:* 2;
   34: 156
Hoppin, Augustus, *34:* 66
Horder, Margaret, *2:* 108
Horen, Michael, *45:* 121
Horvat, Laurel, *12:* 201
Horvath, Ferdinand Kusati, *24:* 176
Hotchkiss, De Wolfe, *20:* 49
Hough, Charlotte, *9:* 112; *13:* 98;
   17: 83; *24:* 195
Houlihan, Ray, *11:* 214
Housman, Laurence, *25:* 146, 147
Houston, James, *13:* 107
How, W. E., *20:* 47
Howard, Alan, *16:* 80; *34:* 58; *45:* 114
Howard, J. N., *15:* 234
Howard, John, *33:* 179
Howard, Rob, *40:* 161
Howe, Stephen, *1:* 232
Howell, Pat, *15:* 139
Howell, Troy, *23:* 24; *31:* 61; *36:* 158;
   37: 184; *41:* 76, 235; *48:* 112
Howes, Charles, *22:* 17
Hubley, Faith, *48:* 120-121, 125, 130,
   131, 132, 134
Hubley, John, *48:* 125, 130, 131, 132,
   134
Hudnut, Robin, *14:* 62
Huffaker, Sandy, *10:* 56
Huffman, Joan, *13:* 33
Huffman, Tom, *13:* 180; *17:* 212;
   21: 116; *24:* 132; *33:* 154; *38:* 59;
   42: 147
Hughes, Arthur, *20:* 148, 149, 150;
   33: 114, 148, 149
Hughes, David, *36:* 197
Hughes, Shirley, *1:* 20, 21; *7:* 3;
   12: 217; *16:* 163; *29:* 154
Hugo, Victor, *47:* 112
Hülsmann, Eva, *16:* 166
Hummel, Berta, *43:* 137, 138, 139
Hummel, Lisl, *29:* 109;
   YABC 2: 333-334
Humphrey, Henry, *16:* 167
Humphreys, Graham, *25:* 168
Hunt, James, *2:* 143
Hurd, Clement, *2:* 148, 149
Hurd, Peter; *24:* 30, 31; *YABC 2:* 56
Hurd, Thacher, *46:* 88-89
Hugo, Victor, *47:* 112
Hürlimann, Ruth, *32:* 99
Hustler, Tom, *6:* 105
Hutchins, Pat, *15:* 142
Hutchinson, William M., *6:* 3, 138;
   46: 70
Hutchison, Paula, *23:* 10
Hutton, Clarke, *YABC 2:* 335
Hutton, Kathryn, *35:* 155
Hutton, Warwick, *20:* 91
Huyette, Marcia, *29:* 188

Hyman, Trina Schart, *1:* 204; *2:* 194;
   5: 153; *6:* 106; *7:* 138, 145; *8:* 22;
   10: 196; *13:* 96; *14:* 114; *15:* 204;
   16: 234; *20:* 82; *22:* 133; *24:* 151;
   25: 79, 82; *26:* 82; *29:* 83; *31:* 37,
   39; *34:* 104; *38:* 84, 100, 128;
   41: 49; *43:* 146; *46:* 91, 92, 93,
   95, 96, 97, 98, 99, 100, 101, 102,
   103, 104-105, 108, 109, 111, 197;
   48: 60, 61

Ichikawa, Satomi, *29:* 152; *41:* 52;
   47: 133, 134, 135, 136
Ide, Jacqueline, *YABC 1:* 39
Ilsley, Velma, *3:* 1; *7:* 55; *12:* 109;
   37: 62; *38:* 184
Inga, *1:* 142
Ingraham, Erick, *21:* 177
Innocenti, Roberto, *21:* 123
Inoue, Yosuke, *24:* 118
Ipcar, Dahlov, *1:* 124-125; *49:* 137,
   138, 139, 140-141, 142, 143, 144,
   145
Irvin, Fred, *13:* 166; *15:* 143-144;
   27: 175
Irving, Jay, *45:* 72
Irving, Laurence, *27:* 50
Isaac, Joanne, *21:* 76
Isadora, Rachel, *43:* 159, 160
Ishmael, Woodi, *24:* 111; *31:* 99
Ives, Ruth, *15:* 257

Jackson, Michael, *43:* 42
Jacobs, Barbara, *9:* 136
Jacobs, Lou, Jr., *9:* 136; *15:* 128
Jacques, Robin, *1:* 70; *2:* 1; *8:* 46;
   9: 20; *15:* 187; *19:* 253; *32:* 102,
   103, 104; *43:* 184; *YABC 1:* 42
Jagr, Miloslav, *13:* 197
Jakubowski, Charles, *14:* 192
Jambor, Louis, *YABC 1:* 11
James, Derek, *35:* 187; *44:* 91
James, Gilbert, *YABC 1:* 43
James, Harold, *2:* 151; *3:* 62; *8:* 79;
   29: 113; *51:* 195
James, Robin, *50:* 106
James, Will, *19:* 150, 152, 153, 155,
   163
Janosch. *See* Eckert, Horst
Jansons, Inese, *48:* 117
Jansson, Tove, *3:* 90; *41:* 106, 108,
   109, 110, 111, 113, 114
Jaques, Faith, *7:* 11, 132-33; *21:* 83,
   84
Jaques, Frances Lee, *29:* 224
Jauss, Anne Marie, *1:* 139; *3:* 34;
   10: 57, 119; *11:* 205; *23:* 194
Jeffers, Susan, *17:* 86-87; *25:* 164-165;
   26: 112; *50:* 132, 134-135
Jefferson, Louise E., *4:* 160
Jenkyns, Chris, *51:* 97
Jeruchim, Simon, *6:* 173; *15:* 250
Jeschke, Susan, *20:* 89; *39:* 161;
   41: 84; *42:* 120
Jessel, Camilla, *29:* 115

Joerns, Consuelo, *38:* 36; *44:* 94
John, Diana, *12:* 209
John, Helen, *1:* 215; *28:* 204
Johns, Jeanne, *24:* 114
Johnson, Bruce, *9:* 47
Johnson, Crockett. *See* Leisk, David
Johnson, D. William, *23:* 104
Johnson, Harper, *1:* 27; *2:* 33; *18:* 302;
   19: 61; *31:* 181; *44:* 46, 50, 95
Johnson, Ingrid, *37:* 118
Johnson, James David, *12:* 195
Johnson, James Ralph, *1:* 23, 127
Johnson, Jane, *48:* 136
Johnson, John E., *34:* 133
Johnson, Larry, *47:* 56
Johnson, Margaret S., *35:* 131
Johnson, Milton, *1:* 67; *2:* 71; *26:* 45;
   31: 107
Johnson, Pamela, *16:* 174
Johnson, William R., *38:* 91
Johnston, David McCall, *50:* 131, 133
Johnstone, Anne, *8:* 120; *36:* 89
Johnstone, Janet Grahame, *8:* 120;
   36: 89
Jonas, Ann, *50:* 107, 108, 109
Jones, Carol, *5:* 131
Jones, Elizabeth Orton, *18:* 124, 126,
   128-129
Jones, Harold, *14:* 88
Jones, Jeff, *41:* 64
Jones, Laurian, *25:* 24, 27
Jones, Robert, *25:* 67
Jones, Wilfred, *35:* 115; *YABC 1:* 163
Joyner, Jerry, *34:* 138
Jucker, Sita, *5:* 93
Judkis, Jim, *37:* 38
Juhasz, Victor, *31:* 67
Jullian, Philippe, *24:* 206; *25:* 203
Jupo, Frank, *7:* 148-149
Justice, Martin, *34:* 72

Kahl, M. P., *37:* 83
Kahl, Virginia, *48:* 138
Kakimoo, Kozo, *11:* 148
Kalett, Jim, *48:* 159, 160, 161
Kalin, Victor, *39:* 186
Kalmenoff, Matthew, *22:* 191
Kalow, Gisela, *32:* 105
Kamen, Gloria, *1:* 41; *9:* 119; *10:* 178;
   35: 157
Kandell, Alice, *35:* 133
Kane, Henry B., *14:* 90; *18:* 219-220
Kane, Robert, *18:* 131
Kappes, Alfred, *28:* 104
Karalus, Bob, *41:* 157
Karlin, Eugene, *10:* 63; *20:* 131
Kasuya, Masahiro, *41:* 206-207;
   51: 100
Katona, Robert, *21:* 85; *24:* 126
Kauffer, E. McKnight, *33:* 103;
   35: 127
Kaufman, Angelika, *15:* 156
Kaufman, Joe, *33:* 119
Kaufman, John, *13:* 158
Kaufmann, John, *1:* 174; *4:* 159;
   8: 43, 1; *10:* 102; *18:* 133-134;
   22: 251

Kaye, Graham, *1:* 9
Kazalovski, Nata, *40:* 205
Keane, Bil, *4:* 135
Keats, Ezra Jack, *3:* 18, 105, 257;
    14: 101, 102; *33:* 129
Keegan, Marcia, *9:* 122; *32:* 93
Keely, John, *26:* 104; *48:* 214
Keen, Eliot, *25:* 213
Keeping, Charles, *9:* 124, 185; *15:* 28,
    134; *18:* 115; *44:* 194, 196; *47:* 25
Keith, Eros, *4:* 98; *5:* 138; *31:* 29;
    43: 220
Kelen, Emery, *13:* 115
Keller, Arthur I., *26:* 106
Keller, Dick, *36:* 123, 125
Keller, Holly, *45:* 79
Keller, Ronald, *45:* 208
Kelley, True, *41:* 114, 115; *42:* 137
Kellogg, Steven, *8:* 96; *11:* 207;
    14: 130; *20:* 58; *29:* 140-141;
    30: 35; *41:* 141; *YABC 1:* 65, 73
Kelly, Walt, *18:* 136-141, 144-146,
    148-149
Kemble, E. W., *34:* 75; *44:* 178;
    YABC 2: 54, 59
Kemp-Welsh, Lucy, *24:* 197
Kennedy, Paul Edward, *6:* 190; *8:* 132;
    33: 120
Kennedy, Richard, *3:* 93; *12:* 179;
    44: 193; *YABC 1:* 57
Kent, Jack, *24:* 136; *37:* 37; *40:* 81
Kent, Rockwell, *5:* 166; *6:* 129;
    20: 225, 226, 227, 229
Kepes, Juliet, *13:* 119
Kerr, Judity, *24:* 137
Kessler, Leonard, *1:* 108; *7:* 139;
    14: 107, 227; *22:* 101; *44:* 96
Kesteven, Peter, *35:* 189
Ketcham, Hank, *28:* 140, 141, 142
Kettelkamp, Larry, *2:* 164
Key, Alexander, *8:* 99
Kiakshuk, *8:* 59
Kiddell-Monroe, Joan, *19:* 201
Kidder, Harvey, *9:* 105
Kidwell, Carl, *43:* 145
Kieffer, Christa, *41:* 89
Kiff, Ken, *40:* 45
Kilbride, Robert, *37:* 100
Kimball, Yeffe, *23:* 116; *37:* 88
Kincade, Orin, *34:* 116
Kindred, Wendy, *7:* 151
King, Robin, *10:* 164-165
King, Tony, *39:* 121
Kingman, Dong, *16:* 287; *44:* 100,
    102, 104
Kingsley, Charles, *YABC 2:* 182
Kipling, John Lockwood, *YABC 2:* 198
Kipling, Rudyard, *YABC 2:* 196
Kipniss, Robert, *29:* 59
Kirchhoff, Art, *28:* 136
Kirk, Ruth, *5:* 96
Kirk, Tim, *32:* 209, 211
Kirmse, Marguerite, *15:* 283; *18:* 153
Kirschner, Ruth, *22:* 154
Klapholz, Mel, *13:* 35
Kleinman, Zalman, *28:* 143
Kliban, B., *35:* 137, 138
Knight, Ann, *34:* 143
Knight, Christopher, *13:* 125

Knight, Hilary, *1:* 233; *3:* 21; *15:* 92,
    158-159; *16:* 258-260; *18:* 235;
    19: 169; *35:* 242; *46:* 167;
    YABC 1: 168-169, 172
Knotts, Howard, *20:* 4; *25:* 170;
    36: 163
Kobayashi, Ann, *39:* 58
Kocsis, J. C. *See* Paul, James
Koehn, Ilse, *34:* 198
Koering, Ursula, *3:* 28; *4:* 14; *44:* 53
Koerner, Henry. *See* Koerner, W.H.D.
Koerner, W.H.D., *14:* 216; *21:* 88,
    89, 90, 91; *23:* 211
Koffler, Camilla, *36:* 113
Kogan, Deborah, *8:* 164; *29:* 238;
    50: 112, 113
Koide, Yasuko, *50:* 114
Komoda, Kiyo, *9:* 128; *13:* 214
Konashevicha, V., *YABC 1:* 26
Konigsburg, E. L., *4:* 138; *48:* 141,
    142, 144, 145
Kooiker, Leonie, *48:* 148
Korach, Mimi, *1:* 128-129; *2:* 52;
    4: 39; *5:* 159; *9:* 129; *10:* 21;
    24: 69
Koren, Edward, *5:* 100
Kossin, Sandy, *10:* 71; *23:* 105
Kostin, Andrej, *26:* 204
Kovacević, Zivojin, *13:* 247
Krahn, Fernando, *2:* 257; *34:* 206;
    49: 152
Kramer, Anthony, *33:* 81
Kramer, Frank, *6:* 121
Krantz, Kathy, *35:* 83
Kraus, Robert, *13:* 217
Kredel, Fritz, *6:* 35; *17:* 93-96;
    22: 147; *24:* 175; *29:* 130; *35:* 77;
    YABC 2: 166, 300
Krementz, Jill, *17:* 98; *49:* 41
Kresin, Robert, *23:* 19
Krush, Beth, *1:* 51, 85; *2:* 233; *4:* 115;
    9: 61; *10:* 191; *11:* 196;
    18: 164-165; *32:* 72; *37:* 203;
    43: 57
Krush, Joe, *2:* 233; *4:* 115; *9:* 61;
    10: 191; *11:* 196; *18:* 164-165;
    32: 72, 91; *37:* 203; *43:* 57
Kubinyi, Laszlo, *4:* 116; *6:* 113;
    16: 118; *17:* 100; *28:* 227;
    30: 172; *49:* 24, 28
Kuhn, Bob, *17:* 91; *35:* 235
Künstler, Mort, *10:* 73; *32:* 143
Kurchevsky, V., *34:* 61
Kurelek, William, *8:* 107
Kuriloff, Ron, *13:* 19
Kuskin, Karla, *2:* 170
Kutzer, Ernst, *19:* 249

LaBlanc, André, *24:* 146
Laboccetta, Mario, *27:* 120
Laceky, Adam, *32:* 121
La Croix, *YABC 2:* 4
La Farge, Margaret, *47:* 141
Laimgruber, Monika, *11:* 153
Laite, Gordon, *1:* 130-131; *8:* 209;
    31: 113; *40:* 63; *46:* 117
Lamarche, Jim, *46:* 204

Lamb, Jim, *10:* 117
Lambert, J. K., *38:* 129; *39:* 24
Lambert, Saul, *23:* 112; *33:* 107
Lambo, Don, *6:* 156; *35:* 115; *36:* 146
Landa, Peter, *11:* 95; *13:* 177
Landau, Jacob, *38:* 111
Landshoff, Ursula, *13:* 124
Lane, John, *15:* 176-177; *30:* 146
Lane, John R., *8:* 145
Lang, G. D., *48:* 56
Lang, Jerry, *18:* 295
Lange, Dorothea, *50:* 141
Langner, Nola, *8:* 110; *42:* 36
Lantz, Paul, *1:* 82, 102; *27:* 88;
    34: 102; *45:* 123
Larrecq, John, *44:* 108
Larsen, Suzanne, *1:* 13
Larsson, Carl, *35:* 144, 145, 146, 147,
    148-149, 150, 152, 153, 154
Larsson, Karl, *19:* 177
La Rue, Michael D., *13:* 215
Lasker, Joe, *7:* 186-187; *14:* 55;
    38: 115; *39:* 47
Latham, Barbara, *16:* 188-189; *43:* 71
Lathrop, Dorothy, *14:* 117, 118-119;
    15: 109; *16:* 78-79, 81; *32:* 201,
    203; *33:* 112; *YABC 2:* 301
Lattimore, Eleanor Frances, *7:* 156
Lauden, Claire, *16:* 173
Lauden, George, Jr., *16:* 173
Laune, Paul, *2:* 235; *34:* 31
Lauré, Jason, *49:* 53; *50:* 122
Lavis, Stephen, *43:* 143
Lawrence, John, *25:* 131; *30:* 141;
    44: 198, 200
Lawrence, Stephen, *20:* 195
Lawson, Carol, *6:* 38; *42:* 93, 131
Lawson, George, *17:* 280
Lawson, Robert, *5:* 26; *6:* 94; *13:* 39;
    16: 11; *20:* 100, 102, 103;
    YABC 2: 222,
    224-225, 227-235, 237-241
Lazare, Jerry, *44:* 109
Lazarevich, Mila, *17:* 118
Lazarus, Keo Felker, *21:* 94
Lazzaro, Victor, *11:* 126
Lea, Tom, *43:* 72, 74
Leacroft, Richard, *6:* 140
Leaf, Munro, *20:* 99
Leander, Patricia, *23:* 27
Lear, Edward, *18:* 183-185
Lebenson, Richard, *6:* 209; *7:* 76;
    23: 145; *44:* 191
Le Cain, Errol, *6:* 141; *9:* 3; *22:* 142;
    25: 198; *28:* 173
Lee, Doris, *13:* 246; *32:* 183; *44:* 111
Lee, Manning de V., *2:* 200; *17:* 12;
    27: 87; *37:* 102, 103, 104;
    YABC 2: 304
Lee, Robert J., *3:* 97
Leech, John, *15:* 59
Leeman, Michael, *44:* 157
Lees, Harry, *6:* 112
Legènisel, *47:* 111
Legrand, Edy, *18:* 89, 93
Lehrman, Rosalie, *2:* 180
Leichman, Seymour, *5:* 107
Leighton, Clare, *25:* 130; *33:* 168;
    37: 105, 106, 108, 109

Leisk, David, *1:* 140-141; *11:* 54; *30:* 137, 142, 143, 144
Leloir, Maurice, *18:* 77, 80, 83, 99
Lemke, Horst, *14:* 98; *38:* 117, 118, 119
Lemke, R. W., *42:* 162
Lemon, David Gwynne, *9:* 1
Lenski, Lois, *1:* 144; *26:* 135, 137, 139, 141
Lent, Blair, *1:* 116-117; *2:* 174; *3:* 206-207; *7:* 168-169; *34:* 62
Leone, Leonard, *49:* 190
Lerner, Sharon, *11:* 157; *22:* 56
Leslie, Cecil, *19:* 244
Lester, Alison, *50:* 124
Le Tord, Bijou, *49:* 156
Levai, Blaise, *39:* 130
Levin, Ted, *12:* 148
Levine, David, *43:* 147, 149, 150, 151, 152
Levit, Herschel, *24:* 223
Levy, Jessica Ann, *19:* 225; *39:* 191
Lewin, Betsy, *32:* 114; *48:* 177
Lewin, Ted, *4:* 77; *8:* 168; *20:* 110; *21:* 99, 100; *27:* 110; *28:* 96, 97; *31:* 49; *45:* 55; *48:* 223
Lewis, Allen, *15:* 112
Leydon, Rita Flodén, *21:* 101
Lieblich, Irene, *22:* 173; *27:* 209, 214
Liese, Charles, *4:* 222
Lightfoot, Norman R., *45:* 47
Lignell, Lois, *37:* 114
Lilly, Charles, *8:* 73; *20:* 127; *48:* 53
Lilly, Ken, *37:* 224
Lim, John, *43:* 153
Limona, Mercedes, *51:* 183
Lincoln, Patricia Henderson, *27:* 27
Lindberg, Howard, *10:* 123; *16:* 190
Linden, Seymour, *18:* 200-201; *43:* 140
Linder, Richard, *27:* 119
Lindman, Maj, *43:* 154
Lindsay, Vachel, *40:* 118
Line, Les, *27:* 143
Linell. *See* Smith, Linell
Lionni, Leo, *8:* 115
Lipinsky, Lino, *2:* 156; *22:* 175
Lippman, Peter, *8:* 31; *31:* 119, 120, 160
Lisker, Sonia O., *16:* 274; *31:* 31; *44:* 113, 114
Lisowski, Gabriel, *47:* 144; *49:* 157
Lissim, Simon, *17:* 138
Little, Harold, *16:* 72
Little, Mary E., *28:* 146
Lively, Lorna, *19:* 216
Llerena, Carlos Antonio, *19:* 181
Lloyd, Errol, *11:* 39; *22:* 178
Lo, Koon-chiu, *7:* 134
Lobel, Anita, *6:* 87; *9:* 141; *18:* 248
Lobel, Arnold, *1:* 188-189; *5:* 12; *6:* 147; *7:* 167, 209; *18:* 190-191; *25:* 39, 43; *27:* 40; *29:* 174
Loefgren, Ulf, *3:* 108
Loescher, Ann, *20:* 108
Loescher, Gil, *20:* 108
Lofting, Hugh, *15:* 182-183
Loh, George, *38:* 88

Lonette, Reisie, *11:* 211; *12:* 168; *13:* 56; *36:* 122; *43:* 155
Long, Sally, *42:* 184
Longtemps, Ken, *17:* 123; *29:* 221
Looser, Heinz, *YABC 2:* 208
Lopshire, Robert, *6:* 149; *21:* 117; *34:* 166
Lord, John Vernon, *21:* 104; *23:* 25; *51:* 22
Lorenz, Al, *40:* 146
Loretta, Sister Mary, *33:* 73
Lorraine, Walter H., *3:* 110; *4:* 123; *16:* 192
Loss, Joan, *11:* 163
Louderback, Walt, *YABC 1:* 164
Lousada, Sandra, *40:* 138
Low, Joseph, *14:* 124, 125; *18:* 68; *19:* 194; *31:* 166
Lowenheim, Alfred, *13:* 65-66
Lowitz, Anson, *17:* 124; *18:* 215
Lowrey, Jo, *8:* 133
Lubell, Winifred, *1:* 207; *3:* 15; *6:* 151
Lubin, Leonard B., *19:* 224; *36:* 79, 80; *45:* 128, 129, 131, 132, 133, 134, 135, 136, 137, 139, 140, 141; *YABC 2:* 96
Ludwig, Helen, *33:* 144, 145
Lufkin, Raymond, *38:* 138; *44:* 48
Luhrs, Henry, *7:* 123; *11:* 120
Lupo, Dom, *4:* 204
Lustig, Loretta, *30:* 186; *46:* 134, 135, 136, 137
Lydecker, Laura, *21:* 113; *42:* 53
Lynch, Charles, *16:* 33
Lynch, Marietta, *29:* 137; *30:* 171
Lyon, Elinor, *6:* 154
Lyon, Fred, *14:* 16
Lyons, Oren, *8:* 193
Lyster, Michael, *26:* 41

Maas, Dorothy, *6:* 175
Maas, Julie, *47:* 61
Macaulay, David, *46:* 139, 140-141, 142, 143, 144-145, 147, 149, 150
Macdonald, Alister, *21:* 55
MacDonald, Norman, *13:* 99
MacDonald, Roberta, *19:* 237
Mace, Varian, *49:* 159
Macguire, Robert Reid, *18:* 67
Machetanz, Fredrick, *34:* 147, 148
MacInnes, Ian, *35:* 59
MacIntyre, Elisabeth, *17:* 127-128
Mack, Stan, *17:* 129
Mackay, Donald, *17:* 60
MacKaye, Arvia, *32:* 119
MacKenzie, Garry, *33:* 159
Mackinlay, Miguel, *27:* 22
MacKinstry, Elizabeth, *15:* 110; *42:* 139, 140, 141, 142, 143, 144, 145
Maclise, Daniel, *YABC 2:* 257
Madden, Don, *3:* 112-113; *4:* 33, 108, 155; *7:* 193; *YABC 2:* 211
Maddison, Angela Mary, *10:* 83
Maestro, Giulio, *8:* 124; *12:* 17; *13:* 108; *25:* 182

Magnuson, Diana, *28:* 102; *34:* 190; *41:* 175
Maguire, Sheila, *41:* 100
Mahony, Will, *37:* 120
Mahood, Kenneth, *24:* 141
Maik, Henri, *9:* 102
Maisto, Carol, *29:* 87
Maitland, Antony, *1:* 100, 176; *8:* 41; *17:* 246; *24:* 46; *25:* 177, 178; *32:* 74
Makie, Pam, *37:* 117
Malsberg, Edward, *51:* 175
Malvern, Corinne, *2:* 13; *34:* 148, 149
Mandelbaum, Ira, *31:* 115
Manet, Edouard, *23:* 170
Mangurian, David, *14:* 133
Manham, Allan, *42:* 109
Manniche, Lise, *31:* 121
Manning, Samuel F., *5:* 75
Maraja, *15:* 86; *YABC 1:* 28; *YABC 2:* 115
Marcellino, Fred, *20:* 125; *34:* 222
Marchesi, Stephen, *34:* 140; *46:* 72; *50:* 147
Marchiori, Carlos, *14:* 60
Margules, Gabriele, *21:* 120
Mariana. *See* Foster, Marian Curtis
Marino, Dorothy, *6:* 37; *14:* 135
Markham, R. L., *17:* 240
Marokvia, Artur, *31:* 122
Marriott, Pat, *30:* 30; *34:* 39; *35:* 164, 165, 166; *44:* 170; *48:* 186, 187, 188, 189, 191, 192, 193
Mars, W. T., *1:* 161; *3:* 115; *4:* 208, 225; *5:* 92, 105, 186; *8:* 214; *9:* 12; *13:* 121; *27:* 151; *31:* 180; *38:* 102; *48:* 66
Marsh, Christine, *3:* 164
Marsh, Reginald, *17:* 5; *19:* 89; *22:* 90, 96
Marshall, Anthony D., *18:* 216
Marshall, James, *6:* 160; *40:* 221; *42:* 24, 25, 29; *51:* 111, 112, 113, 114, 115, 116, 117, 118, 119, 120, 121
Martchenko, Michael, *50:* 129, 153, 155, 156, 157
Martin, David Stone, *23:* 232
Martin, Fletcher, *18:* 213; *23:* 151
Martin, René, *7:* 144; *42:* 148, 149, 150
Martin, Richard E., *51:* 157
Martin, Ron, *32:* 81
Martin, Stefan, *8:* 68; *32:* 124, 126
Martinez, John, *6:* 113
Marx, Robert F., *24:* 143
Masefield, Judith, *19:* 208, 209
Mason, George F., *14:* 139
Massie, Diane Redfield, *16:* 194
Massie, Kim, *31:* 43
Mathewuse, James, *51:* 143
Mathieu, Joseph, *14:* 33; *39:* 206; *43:* 167
Matsubara, Naoko, *12:* 121
Matsuda, Shizu, *13:* 167
Matte, L'Enc, *22:* 183
Mattelson, Marvin, *36:* 50, 51
Matthews, F. Leslie, *4:* 216
Matulay, Laszlo, *5:* 18; *43:* 168

Matus, Greta, *12:* 142
Mauldin, Bill, *27:* 23
Mawicke, Tran, *9:* 137; *15:* 191; *47:* 100
Max, Peter, *45:* 146, 147, 148-149, 150
Maxie, Betty, *40:* 135
Maxwell, John Alan, *1:* 148
Mayan, Earl, *7:* 193
Mayer, Marianna, *32:* 132
Mayer, Mercer, *11:* 192; *16:* 195-196; *20:* 55, 57; *32:* 129, 130, 132, 133, 134; *41:* 144, 248, 252
Mayhew, Richard, *3:* 106
Mayo, Gretchen, *38:* 81
Mays, Victor, *5:* 127; *8:* 45, 153; *14:* 245; *23:* 50; *34:* 155; *40:* 79; *45:* 158
Mazal, Chanan, *49:* 104
Mazza, Adriana Saviozzi, *19:* 215
Mazzetti, Alan, *45:* 210
McBride, Angus, *28:* 49
McBride, Will, *30:* 110
McCaffery, Janet, *38:* 145
McCann, Gerald, *3:* 50; *4:* 94; *7:* 54; *41:* 121
McCay, Winsor, *41:* 124, 126, 128-129, 130-131
McClary, Nelson, *1:* 111
McClintock, Theodore, *14:* 141
McCloskey, Robert, *1:* 184-185; *2:* 186-187; *17:* 209; *39:* 139, 140, 141, 142, 143, 146, 147, 148
McClung, Robert, *2:* 189
McClure, Gillian, *31:* 132
McConnel, Jerry, *31:* 75, 187
McCormick, A. D., *35:* 119
McCormick, Dell J., *19:* 216
McCrady, Lady, *16:* 198; *39:* 127
McCrea, James, *3:* 122; *33:* 216
McCrea, Ruth, *3:* 122; *27:* 102; *33:* 216
McCully, Emily Arnold, *2:* 89; *4:* 120-121, 146, 197; *5:* 2, 129; *7:* 191; *11:* 122; *15:* 210; *33:* 23; *35:* 244; *37:* 122; *39:* 88; *40:* 103; *50:* 30, 31, 32, 33, 34, 35, 36-37
McCurdy, Michael, *13:* 153; *24:* 85
McDermott, Beverly Brodsky, *11:* 180
McDermott, Gerald, *16:* 201
McDonald, Jill, *13:* 155; *26:* 128
McDonald, Ralph J., *5:* 123, 195
McDonough, Don, *10:* 163
McEntee, Dorothy, *37:* 124
McFall, Christie, *12:* 144
McGee, Barbara, *6:* 165
McGregor, Malcolm, *23:* 27
McHugh, Tom, *23:* 64
McIntosh, Jon, *42:* 56
McKay, Donald, *2:* 118; *32:* 157; *45:* 151, 152
McKeating, Eileen, *44:* 58
McKee, David, *10:* 48; *21:* 9
McKie, Roy, *7:* 44
McKillip, Kathy, *30:* 153
McKinney, Ena, *26:* 39
McLachlan, Edward, *5:* 89
McLean, Sammis, *32:* 197
McLoughlin, John C., *47:* 149

McMahon, Robert, *36:* 155
McMillan, Bruce, *22:* 184
McMullan, James, *40:* 33
McNaught, Harry, *12:* 80; *32:* 136
McNaughton, Colin, *39:* 149; *40:* 108
McNicholas, Maureen, *38:* 148
McPhail, David, *14:* 105; *23:* 135; *37:* 217, 218, 220, 221; *47:* 151, 152, 153, 154, 155, 156, 158-159, 160, 162-163, 164
McPhee, Richard B., *41:* 133
McQueen, Lucinda, *28:* 149; *41:* 249; *46:* 206
McVay, Tracy, *11:* 68
McVicker, Charles, *39:* 150
Mead, Ben Carlton, *43:* 75
Mecray, John, *33:* 62
Meddaugh, Susan, *20:* 42; *29:* 143; *41:* 241
Melo, John, *16:* 285
Mcnasco, Milton, *43:* 85
Mendelssohn, Felix, *19:* 170
Meng, Heinz, *13:* 158
Mero, Lee, *34:* 68
Merrill, Frank T., *16:* 147; *19:* 71; *YABC 1:* 226, 229, 273
Meryman, Hope, *27:* 41
Meryweather, Jack, *10:* 179
Meth, Harold, *24:* 203
Meyer, Herbert, *19:* 189
Meyer, Renate, *6:* 170
Meyers, Bob, *11:* 136
Meynell, Louis, *37:* 76
Micale, Albert, *2:* 65; *22:* 185
Middleton-Sandford, Betty, *2:* 125
Mieke, Anne, *45:* 74
Mighell, Patricia, *43:* 134
Mikolaycak, Charles, *9:* 144; *12:* 101; *13:* 212; *21:* 121; *22:* 168; *30:* 187; *34:* 103, 150; *37:* 183; *43:* 179; *44:* 90; *46:* 115, 118-119; *49:* 25
Miles, Jennifer, *17:* 278
Milhous, Katherine, *15:* 193; *17:* 51
Millais, John E., *22:* 230, 231
Millar, H. R., *YABC 1:* 194-195, 203
Millard, C. E., *28:* 186
Miller, Don, *15:* 195; *16:* 71; *20:* 106; *31:* 178
Miller, Edna, *29:* 148
Miller, Frank J., *25:* 94
Miller, Grambs, *18:* 38; *23:* 16
Miller, Jane, *15:* 196
Miller, Marcia, *13:* 233
Miller, Marilyn, *1:* 87; *31:* 69; *33:* 157
Miller, Mitchell, *28:* 183; *34:* 207
Miller, Shane, *5:* 140
Mills, Yaroslava Surmach, *35:* 169, 170; *46:* 114
Millsap, Darrel, *51:* 102
Minor, Wendell, *39:* 188
Mitsuhashi, Yoko, *45:* 153
Miyake, Yoshi, *38:* 141
Mizumura, Kazue, *10:* 143; *18:* 223; *36:* 159
Mochi, Ugo, *8:* 122; *38:* 150
Modell, Frank, *39:* 152
Mohr, Nicholasa, *8:* 139
Moldon, Peter L., *49:* 168

Momaday, N. Scott, *48:* 159
Montresor, Beni, *2:* 91; *3:* 138; *38:* 152, 153, 154, 155, 156-157, 158, 159, 160
Moon, Carl, *25:* 183, 184, 185
Moon, Eliza, *14:* 40
Moon, Ivan, *22:* 39; *38:* 140
Moore, Agnes Kay Randall, *43:* 187
Moore, Mary, *29:* 160
Mora, Raul Mina, *20:* 41
Mordvinoff, Nicolas, *15:* 179
Morgan, Tom, *42:* 157
Morrill, Les, *42:* 127
Morrill, Leslie, *18:* 218; *29:* 177; *33:* 84; *38:* 147; *44:* 93; *48:* 164, 165, 167, 168, 169, 170, 171; *49:* 162
Morris, *47:* 91
Morrison, Bill, *42:* 116
Morrow, Gray, *2:* 64; *5:* 200; *10:* 103, 114; *14:* 175
Morton, Lee Jack, *32:* 140
Morton, Marian, *3:* 185
Moses, Grandma, *18:* 228
Moskof, Martin Stephen, *27:* 152
Moss, Donald, *11:* 184
Moss, Geoffrey, *32:* 198
Most, Bernard, *48:* 173
Mowry, Carmen, *50:* 62
Moyers, William, *21:* 65
Moyler, Alan, *36:* 142
Mozley, Charles, *9:* 87; *20:* 176, 192, 193; *22:* 228; *25:* 205; *33:* 150; *43:* 170, 171, 172, 173, 174; *YABC 2:* 89
Mueller, Hans Alexander, *26:* 64; *27:* 52, 53
Mugnaini, Joseph, *11:* 35; *27:* 52, 53; *35:* 62
Müller, Jörg, *35:* 215
Muller, Steven, *32:* 167
Mullins, Edward S., *10:* 101
Mullins, Patricia, *51:* 68
Munari, Bruno, *15:* 200
Munowitz, Ken, *14:* 148
Muñoz, William, *42:* 160
Munsinger, Lynn, *33:* 161; *46:* 126
Munson, Russell, *13:* 9
Murphy, Bill, *5:* 138
Murphy, Jill, *37:* 142
Murr, Karl, *20:* 62
Murray, Ossie, *43:* 176
Mussino, Attilio, *29:* 131
Mutchler, Dwight, *1:* 25
Myers, Bernice, *9:* 147; *36:* 75
Myers, Lou, *11:* 2

Nachreiner, Tom, *29:* 182
Nakai, Michael, *30:* 217
Nakatani, Chiyoko, *12:* 124
Nash, Linell, *46:* 175
Naso, John, *33:* 183
Nason, Thomas W., *14:* 68
Nasser, Muriel, *48:* 74
Nast, Thomas, *21:* 29; *28:* 23; *51:* 132, 133, 134, 135, 136, 137, 138, 139, 141

Natti, Susanna, *20:* 146; *32:* 141, 142; *35:* 178; *37:* 143
Navarra, Celeste Scala, *8:* 142
Naylor, Penelope, *10:* 104
Nebel, M., *45:* 154
Neebe, William, *7:* 93
Needler, Jerry, *12:* 93
Neel, Alice, *31:* 23
Neely, Keith R., *46:* 124
Negri, Rocco, *3:* 213; *5:* 67; *6:* 91, 108; *12:* 159
Neill, John R., *18:* 8, 10-11, 21, 30
Ness, Evaline, *1:* 164-165; *2:* 39; *3:* 8; *10:* 147; *12:* 53; *26:* 150, 151, 152, 153; *49:* 30, 31, 32
Neville, Vera, *2:* 182
Newberry, Clare Turlay, *1:* 170
Newfeld, Frank, *14:* 121; *26:* 154
Newman, Ann, *43:* 90
Newsom, Carol, *40:* 159; *44:* 60; *47:* 189
Newsom, Tom, *49:* 149
Ng, Michael, *29:* 171
Nicholson, William, *15:* 33-34; *16:* 48
Nicklaus, Carol, *45:* 194
Nickless, Will, *16:* 139
Nicolas, *17:* 130, 132-133; *YABC 2:* 215
Niebrugge, Jane, *6:* 118
Nielsen, Jon, *6:* 100; *24:* 202
Nielsen, Kay, *15:* 7; *16:* 211-213, 215, 217; *22:* 143; *YABC 1:* 32-33
Niland, Deborah, *25:* 191; *27:* 156
Niland, Kilmeny, *25:* 191
Ninon, *1:* 5; *38:* 101, 103, 108
Nissen, Rie, *44:* 35
Nixon, K., *14:* 152
Noble, Trinka Hakes, *39:* 162
Noguchi, Yoshie, *30:* 99
Nolan, Dennis, *42:* 163
Noonan, Julia, *4:* 163; *7:* 207; *25:* 151
Nordenskjold, Birgitta, *2:* 208
Norman, Mary, *36:* 138, 147
Norman, Michael, *12:* 117; *27:* 168
Numeroff, Laura Joffe, *28:* 161; *30:* 177
Nussbaumer, Paul, *16:* 219; *39:* 117
Nyce, Helene, *19:* 219
Nygren, Tord, *30:* 148

Oakley, Graham, *8:* 112; *30:* 164, 165
Oakley, Thornton, *YABC 2:* 189
Obligado, Lilian, *2:* 28, 66-67; *6:* 30; *14:* 179; *15:* 103; *25:* 84
Obrant, Susan, *11:* 186
O'Brien, John, *41:* 253
Odell, Carole, *35:* 47
O'Donohue, Thomas, *40:* 89
Oechsli, Kelly, *5:* 144-145; *7:* 115; *8:* 83, 183; *13:* 117; *20:* 94
Offen, Hilda, *42:* 207
Ogden, Bill, *42:* 59; *47:* 55
Ogg, Oscar, *33:* 34
Ohlsson, Ib, *4:* 152; *7:* 57; *10:* 20; *11:* 90; *19:* 217; *41:* 246
Ohtomo, Yasuo, *37:* 146; *39:* 212, 213
O'Kelley, Mattie Lou, *36:* 150

Oliver, Jenni, *23:* 121; *35:* 112
Olschewski, Alfred, *7:* 172
Olsen, Ib Spang, *6:* 178-179
Olugebefola, Ademola, *15:* 205
O'Neil, Dan IV, *7:* 176
O'Neill, Jean, *22:* 146
O'Neill, Rose, *48:* 30, 31
O'Neill, Steve, *21:* 118
Ono, Chiyo, *7:* 97
Orbaan, Albert, *2:* 31; *5:* 65, 171; *9:* 8; *14:* 241; *20:* 109
Orbach, Ruth, *21:* 112
Orfe, Joan, *20:* 81
Ormsby, Virginia H., *11:* 187
Orozco, José Clemente, *9:* 177
Orr, Forrest W., *23:* 9
Orr, N., *19:* 70
Osborne, Billie Jean, *35:* 209
Osmond, Edward, *10:* 111
O'Sullivan, Tom, *3:* 176; *4:* 55
Otto, Svend, *22:* 130, 141
Oudry, J. B., *18:* 167
Oughton, Taylor, *5:* 23
Övereng, Johannes, *44:* 36
Overlie, George, *11:* 156
Owens, Carl, *2:* 35; *23:* 521
Owens, Gail, *10:* 170; *12:* 157; *19:* 16; *22:* 70; *25:* 81; *28:* 203, 205; *32:* 221, 222; *36:* 132; *46:* 40; *47:* 57
Oxenbury, Helen, *3:* 150-151; *24:* 81

Padgett, Jim, *12:* 165
Page, Homer, *14:* 145
Paget, Sidney, *24:* 90, 91, 93, 95, 97
Pak, *12:* 76
Palazzo, Tony, *3:* 152-153
Palladini, David, *4:* 113; *40:* 176, 177, 178-179, 181, 224-225; *50:* 138
Pallarito, Don, *43:* 36
Palmer, Heidi, *15:* 207; *29:* 102
Palmer, Jan, *42:* 153
Palmer, Juliette, *6:* 89; *15:* 208
Palmer, Lemuel, *17:* 25, 29
Palmquist, Eric, *38:* 133
Panesis, Nicholas, *3:* 127
Papas, William, *11:* 223; *50:* 160
Papin, Joseph, *26:* 113
Papish, Robin Lloyd, *10:* 80
Paradis, Susan, *40:* 216
Paraquin, Charles H., *18:* 166
Paris, Peter, *31:* 127
Park, Seho, *39:* 110
Park, W. B., *22:* 189
Parker, Lewis, *2:* 179
Parker, Nancy Winslow, *10:* 113; *22:* 164; *28:* 47, 144
Parker, Robert, *4:* 161; *5:* 74; *9:* 136; *29:* 39
Parker, Robert Andrew, *11:* 81; *29:* 186; *39:* 165; *40:* 25; *41:* 78; *42:* 123; *43:* 144; *48:* 182
Parks, Gordon, Jr., *33:* 228
Parnall, Peter, *5:* 137; *16:* 221; *24:* 70; *40:* 78; *51:* 130
Parnall, Virginia, *40:* 78
Parrish, Anne, *27:* 159, 160

Parrish, Dillwyn, *27:* 159
Parrish, Maxfield, *14:* 160, 161, 164, 165; *16:* 109; *18:* 12-13; *YABC 1:* 149, 152, 267; *YABC 2:* 146, 149
Parry, David, *26:* 156
Parry, Marian, *13:* 176; *19:* 179
Partch, Virgil, *45:* 163, 165
Pascal, David, *14:* 174
Pasquier, J. A., *16:* 91
Paterson, Diane, *13:* 116; *39:* 163
Paterson, Helen, *16:* 93
Paton, Jane, *15:* 271; *35:* 176
Patterson, Robert, *25:* 118
Paul, James, *4:* 130; *23:* 161
Paull, Grace, *24:* 157
Payne, Joan Balfour, *1:* 118
Payson, Dale, *7:* 34; *9:* 151; *20:* 140; *37:* 22
Payzant, Charles, *21:* 147
Peake, Mervyn, *22:* 136, 149; *23:* 162, 163, 164; *YABC 2:* 307
Pearson, Larry, *38:* 225
Peat, Fern B., *16:* 115
Peck, Anne Merriman, *18:* 241; *24:* 155
Pederson, Sharleen, *12:* 92
Pedersen, Vilhelm, *YABC 1:* 40
Peek, Merle, *39:* 168
Peet, Bill, *2:* 203; *41:* 159, 160, 161, 162, 163
Peltier, Leslie C., *13:* 178
Pendle, Alexy, *7:* 159; *13:* 34; *29:* 161; *33:* 215
Pennington, Eunice, *27:* 162
Peppé, Mark, *28:* 142
Peppe, Rodney, *4:* 164-165
Perl, Susan, *2:* 98; *4:* 231; *5:* 44-45, 118; *6:* 199; *8:* 137; *12:* 88; *22:* 193; *34:* 54-55; *YABC 1:* 176
Perry, Patricia, *29:* 137; *30:* 171
Perry, Roger, *27:* 163
Perske, Martha, *46:* 83; *51:* 108, 147
Pesek, Ludek, *15:* 237
Petersham, Maud, *17:* 108, 147-153
Petersham, Miska, *17:* 108, 147-153
Peterson, R. F., *7:* 101
Peterson, Russell, *7:* 130
Petie, Haris, *2:* 3; *10:* 41, 118; *11:* 227; *12:* 70
Petrides, Heidrun, *19:* 223
Peyo, *40:* 56, 57
Peyton, K. M., *15:* 212
Pfeifer, Herman, *15:* 262
Phillips, Douglas, *1:* 19
Phillips, F. D., *6:* 202
Phillips, Thomas, *30:* 55
"Phiz." *See* Browne, Hablot K.
Piatti, Celestino, *16:* 223
Picarella, Joseph, *13:* 147
Pickard, Charles, *12:* 38; *18:* 203; *36:* 152
Picken, George A., *23:* 150
Pickens, David, *22:* 156
Pienkowski, Jan, *6:* 183; *30:* 32
Pimlott, John, *10:* 205
Pincus, Harriet, *4:* 186; *8:* 179; *22:* 148; *27:* 164, 165

Pinkney, Jerry, *8:* 218; *10:* 40; *15:* 276; *20:* 66; *24:* 121; *33:* 109; *36:* 222; *38:* 200; *41:* 165, 166, 167, 168, 169, 170, 171, 173, 174; *44:* 198; *48:* 51
Pinkwater, Daniel Manus, *46:* 180, 181, 182, 185, 188, 189, 190
Pinkwater, Manus, *8:* 156; *46:* 180
Pinto, Ralph, *10:* 131; *45:* 93
Pitz, Henry C., *4:* 168; *19:* 165; *35:* 128; *42:* 80; *YABC 2:* 95, 176
Pitzenberger, Lawrence J., *26:* 94
Plummer, William, *32:* 31
Pogány, Willy, *15:* 46, 49; *19:* 222, 256; *25:* 214; *44:* 142, 143, 144, 145, 146, 147, 148
Poirson, V. A., *26:* 89
Polgreen, John, *21:* 44
Politi, Leo, *1:* 178; *4:* 53; *21:* 48; *47:* 173, 174, 176, 178, 179, 180, 181
Polonsky, Arthur, *34:* 168
Polseno, Jo, *1:* 53; *3:* 117; *5:* 114; *17:* 154; *20:* 87; *32:* 49; *41:* 245
Ponter, James, *5:* 204
Poortvliet, Rien, *6:* 212
Portal, Colette, *6:* 186; *11:* 203
Porter, George, *7:* 181
Potter, Beatrix, *YABC 1:* 208-210, 212, 213
Potter, Miriam Clark, *3:* 162
Powers, Richard M., *1:* 230; *3:* 218; *7:* 194; *26:* 186
Powledge, Fred, *37:* 154
Pratt, Charles, *23:* 29
Price, Christine, *2:* 247; *3:* 163, 253; *8:* 166
Price, Edward, *33:* 34
Price, Garrett, *1:* 76; *2:* 42
Price, Hattie Longstreet, *17:* 13
Price, Norman, *YABC 1:* 129
Price, Willard, *48:* 184
Primavera, Elise, *26:* 95
Primrose, Jean, *36:* 109
Prince, Leonora E., *7:* 170
Prittie, Edwin J., *YABC 1:* 120
Provensen, Alice, *37:* 204, 215, 222
Provensen, Martin, *37:* 204, 215, 222
Pucci, Albert John, *44:* 154
Pudlo, *8:* 59
Purdy, Susan, *8:* 162
Puskas, James, *5:* 141
Pyk, Jan, *7:* 26; *38:* 123
Pyle, Howard, *16:* 225-228, 230-232, 235; *24:* 27; *34:* 124, 125, 127, 128

Quackenbush, Robert, *4:* 190; *6:* 166; *7:* 175, 178; *9:* 86; *11:* 65, 221; *41:* 154; *43:* 157
Quennell, Marjorie (Courtney), *29:* 163, 164
Quidor, John, *19:* 82
Quirk, Thomas, *12:* 81

Rackham, Arthur, *15:* 32, 78, 214-227; *17:* 105, 115; *18:* 233; *19:* 254; *20:* 151; *22:* 129, 131, 132, 133; *23:* 175; *24:* 161, 181; *26:* 91; *32:* 118; *YABC 1:* 25, 45, 55, 147; *YABC 2:* 103, 142, 173, 210
Rafilson, Sidney, *11:* 172
Raible, Alton, *1:* 202-203; *28:* 193; *35:* 181
Ramsey, James, *16:* 41
Ramus, Michael, *51:* 171
Rand, Paul, *6:* 188
Ransome, Arthur, *22:* 201
Rao, Anthony, *28:* 126
Raphael, Elaine, *23:* 192
Rappaport, Eva, *6:* 190
Raskin, Ellen, *2:* 208-209; *4:* 142; *13:* 183; *22:* 68; *29:* 139; *36:* 134; *38:* 173, 174, 175, 176, 177, 178, 179, 180, 181
Ratzkin, Lawrence, *40:* 143
Rau, Margaret, *9:* 157
Raverat, Gwen, *YABC 1:* 152
Ravielli, Anthony, *1:* 198; *3:* 168; *11:* 143
Ray, Deborah. *See* Kogan, Deborah Ray.
Ray, Ralph, *2:* 239; *5:* 73
Raymond, Larry, *31:* 108
Rayner, Mary, *22:* 207; *47:* 140
Raynor, Dorka, *28:* 168
Raynor, Paul, *24:* 73
Razzi, James, *10:* 127
Read, Alexander D. "Sandy," *20:* 45
Reed, Tom, *34:* 171
Reid, Stephen, *19:* 213; *22:* 89
Reinertson, Barbara, *44:* 150
Reiniger, Lotte, *40:* 185
Reiss, John J., *23:* 193
Relf, Douglas, *3:* 63
Relyea, C. M., *16:* 29; *31:* 153
Rémi, Georges, *13:* 184
Remington, Frederic, *19:* 188; *41:* 178, 179, 180, 181, 183, 184, 185, 186, 187, 188
Renlie, Frank, *11:* 200
Reschofsky, Jean, *7:* 118
Réthi, Lili, *2:* 153; *36:* 156
Reusswig, William, *3:* 267
Rey, H. A., *1:* 182; *26:* 163, 164, 166, 167, 169; *YABC 2:* 17
Reynolds, Doris, *5:* 71; *31:* 77
Rhead, Louis, *31:* 91
Rhodes, Andrew, *38:* 204; *50:* 163
Ribbons, Ian, *3:* 10; *37:* 161; *40:* 76
Rice, Elizabeth, *2:* 53, 214
Rice, James, *22:* 210
Rice, Eve, *34:* 174, 175
Richards, George, *40:* 116, 119, 121; *44:* 179
Richards, Henry, *YABC 1:* 228, 231
Richardson, Ernest, *2:* 144
Richardson, Frederick, *18:* 27, 31
Richman, Hilda, *26:* 132
Richmond, George, *24:* 179
Rieniets, Judy King, *14:* 28
Riger, Bob, *2:* 166
Riley, Kenneth, *22:* 230
Ringi, Kjell, *12:* 171

Rios, Tere. *See* Versace, Marie
Ripper, Charles L., *3:* 175
Ritz, Karen, *41:* 117
Rivkin, Jay, *15:* 230
Rivoche, Paul, *45:* 125
Roach, Marilynne, *9:* 158
Robbin, Jodi, *44:* 156, 159
Robbins, Frank, *42:* 167
Roberts, Cliff, *4:* 126
Roberts, Doreen, *4:* 230; *28:* 105
Roberts, Jim, *22:* 166; *23:* 69; *31:* 110
Roberts, W., *22:* 2, 3
Robinson, Charles, *3:* 53; *5:* 14; *6:* 193; *7:* 150; *7:* 183; *8:* 38; *9:* 81; *13:* 188; *14:* 248-249; *23:* 149; *26:* 115; *27:* 48; *28:* 191; *32:* 28; *35:* 210; *36:* 37; *48:* 96
Robinson, Charles [1870-1937], *17:* 157, 171-173, 175-176; *24:* 207; *25:* 204; *YABC 2:* 308-310, 331
Robinson, Jerry, *3:* 262
Robinson, Joan G., *7:* 184
Robinson, T. H., *17:* 179, 181-183; *29:* 254
Robinson, W. Heath, *17:* 185, 187, 189, 191, 193, 195, 197, 199, 202; *23:* 167; *25:* 194; *29:* 150; *YABC 1:* 44; *YABC 2:* 183
Roche, Christine, *41:* 98
Rocker, Fermin, *7:* 34; *13:* 21; *31:* 40; *40:* 190, 191
Rockwell, Anne, *5:* 147; *33:* 171, 173
Rockwell, Gail, *7:* 186
Rockwell, Harlow, *33:* 171, 173, 175
Rockwell, Norman, *23:* 39, 196, 197, 199, 200, 203, 204, 207; *41:* 140, 143; *YABC 2:* 60
Rodegast, Roland, *43:* 100
Rodriguez, Joel, *16:* 65
Roever, J. M., *4:* 119; *26:* 170
Roffey, Maureen, *33:* 142, 176, 177
Rogasky, Barbara, *46:* 90
Rogers, Carol, *2:* 262; *6:* 164; *26:* 129
Rogers, Frances, *10:* 130
Rogers, Walter S., *31:* 135, 138
Rogers, William A., *15:* 151, 153-154; *33:* 35
Rojankovsky, Feodor, *6:* 134, 136; *10:* 183; *21:* 128, 129, 130; *25:* 110; *28:* 42
Rorer, Abigail, *43:* 222
Rosamilia, Patricia, *36:* 120
Rose, Carl, *5:* 62
Rose, David S., *29:* 109
Rosenbaum, Jonathan, *50:* 46
Rosenblum, Richard, *11:* 202; *18:* 18
Rosier, Lydia, *16:* 236; *20:* 104; *21:* 109; *22:* 125; *30:* 151, 158; *42:* 128; *45:* 214
Ross. *See* Thomson, Ross
Ross, Clare Romano, *3:* 123; *21:* 45; *48:* 199
Ross, Dave, *32:* 152
Ross, Herbert, *37:* 78
Ross, John, *3:* 123; *21:* 45
Ross, Johnny, *32:* 190
Ross, Larry, *47:* 168
Ross, Tony, *17:* 204

Rossetti, Dante Gabriel, *20:* 151, 153
Roth, Arnold, *4:* 238; *21:* 133
Rotondo, Pat, *32:* 158
Roughsey, Dick, *35:* 186
Rouille, M., *11:* 96
Rounds, Glen, *8:* 173; *9:* 171; *12:* 56;
   32: 194; *40:* 230; *51:* 161, 162,
   166; *YABC 1:* 1-3
Rowe, Gavin, *27:* 144
Rowell, Kenneth, *40:* 72
Roy, Jeroo, *27:* 229; *36:* 110
Rubel, Nicole, *18:* 255; *20:* 59
Rubel, Reina, *33:* 217
Rud, Borghild, *6:* 15
Rudolph, Norman Guthrie, *17:* 13
Rue, Leonard Lee III, *37:* 164
Ruff, Donna, *50:* 173
Ruffins, Reynold, *10:* 134-135;
   41: 191, 192-193, 194-195, 196
Ruhlin, Roger, *34:* 44
Ruse, Margaret, *24:* 155
Rush, Peter, *42:* 75
Russell, E. B., *18:* 177, 182
Russo, Susan, *30:* 182; *36:* 144
Ruth, Rod, *9:* 161
Rutherford, Meg, *25:* 174; *34:* 178,
   179
Rutland, Jonathan, *31:* 126
Ryden, Hope, *8:* 176
Rymer, Alta M., *34:* 181
Rystedt, Rex, *49:* 80

Saaf, Chuck, *49:* 179
Sabaka, Donna R., *21:* 172
Sabin, Robert, *45:* 35
Sacker, Amy, *16:* 100
Saffioti, Lino, *36:* 176; *48:* 60
Sagsoorian, Paul, *12:* 183; *22:* 154;
   33: 106
Saint Exupéry, Antoine de, *20:* 157
St. John, J. Allen, *41:* 62
Saldutti, Denise, *39:* 186
Sale, Morton, *YABC 2:* 31
Sambourne, Linley, *YABC 2:* 181
Sampson, Katherine, *9:* 197
Samson, Anne S., *2:* 216
Sancha, Sheila, *38:* 185
Sand, George X., *45:* 182
Sandberg, Lasse, *15:* 239, 241
Sanders, Beryl, *39:* 173
Sanderson, Ruth, *21:* 126; *24:* 53;
   28: 63; *33:* 67; *41:* 48, 198, 199,
   200, 201, 202, 203; *43:* 79;
   46: 36, 44; *47:* 102; *49:* 58
Sandin, Joan, *4:* 36; *6:* 194; *7:* 177;
   12: 145, 185; *20:* 43; *21:* 74;
   26: 144; *27:* 142; *28:* 224, 225;
   38: 86; *41:* 46; *42:* 35
Sandland, Reg, *39:* 215
Sandoz, Edouard, *26:* 45, 47
San Souci, Daniel, *40:* 200
Sapieha, Christine, *1:* 180
Sarg, Tony, *YABC 2:* 236
Sargent, Robert, *2:* 217
Saris, *1:* 33
Sarony, *YABC 2:* 170
Sasek, Miroslav, *16:* 239-242

Sassman, David, *9:* 79
Sätty, *29:* 203, 205
Sauber, Rob, *40:* 183
Savage, Steele, *10:* 203; *20:* 77; *35:* 28
Savitt, Sam, *8:* 66, 182; *15:* 278;
   20: 96; *24:* 192; *28:* 98
Say, Allen, *28:* 178
Scabrini, Janet, *13:* 191; *44:* 128
Scarry, Huck, *35:* 204-205
Scarry, Richard, *2:* 220-221; *18:* 20;
   35: 193, 194-195, 196, 197, 198,
   199, 200-201, 202
Schaeffer, Mead, *18:* 81, 94; *21:* 137,
   138, 139; *47:* 128
Scharl, Josef, *20:* 132; *22:* 128
Scheel, Lita, *11:* 230
Scheib, Ida, *29:* 28
Schermer, Judith, *30:* 184
Schick, Joel, *16:* 160; *17:* 167; *22:* 12;
   27: 176; *31:* 147, 148; *36:* 23;
   38: 64; *45:* 116, 117
Schindelman, Joseph, *1:* 74; *4:* 101;
   12: 49; *26:* 51; *40:* 146
Schindler, Edith, *7:* 22
Schindler, S. D., *38:* 107; *46:* 196
Schlesinger, Bret, *7:* 77
Schmid, Eleanore, *12:* 188
Schmiderer, Dorothy, *19:* 224
Schmidt, Elizabeth, *15:* 242
Schneider, Rex, *29:* 64; *44:* 171
Schoenherr, Ian, *32:* 83
Schoenherr, John, *1:* 146-147, 173;
   3: 39, 139; *17:* 75; *29:* 72; *32:* 83;
   37: 168, 169, 170; *43:* 164, 165;
   45: 160, 162; *51:* 127
Schomburg, Alex, *13:* 23
Schongut, Emanuel, *4:* 102; *15:* 186;
   47: 218, 219
Schoonover, Frank, *17:* 107; *19:* 81,
   190, 233; *22:* 88, 129; *24:* 189;
   31: 88; *41:* 69; *YABC 2:* 282, 316
Schottland, Miriam, *22:* 172
Schramm, Ulrik, *2:* 16; *14:* 112
Schreiber, Elizabeth Anne, *13:* 193
Schreiber, Ralph W., *13:* 193
Schreiter, Rick, *14:* 97; *23:* 171;
   41: 247; *49:* 131
Schroeder, E. Peter, *12:* 112
Schroeder, Ted, *11:* 160; *15:* 189;
   30: 91; *34:* 43
Schrotter, Gustav, *22:* 212; *30:* 225
Schucker, James, *31:* 163
Schulz, Charles M., *10:* 137-142
Schwark, Mary Beth, *51:* 155
Schwartz, Amy, *47:* 191
Schwartz, Charles, *8:* 184
Schwartz, Daniel, *46:* 37
Schwartzberg, Joan, *3:* 208
Schweitzer, Iris, *2:* 137; *6:* 207
Schweninger, Ann, *29:* 172
Scott, Anita Walker, *7:* 38
Scott, Art, *39:* 41
Scott, Frances Gruse, *38:* 43
Scott, Julian, *34:* 126
Scott, Roszel, *33:* 238
Scott, Trudy, *27:* 172
Scribner, Joanne, *14:* 236; *29:* 78;
   33: 185; *34:* 208
Scrofani, Joseph, *31:* 65

Seaman, Mary Lott, *34:* 64
Searle, Ronald, *24:* 98; *42:* 172, 173,
   174, 176, 177, 179
Searle, Townley, *36:* 85
Sebree, Charles, *18:* 65
Sedacca, Joseph M., *11:* 25; *22:* 36
Ségur, Adrienne, *27:* 121
Seignobosc, Francoise, *21:* 145, 146
Sejima, Yoshimasa, *8:* 187
Selig, Sylvie, *13:* 199
Seltzer, Isadore, *6:* 18
Seltzer, Meyer, *17:* 214
Sempé, Jean-Jacques, *47:* 92;
   YABC 2: 109
Sendak, Maurice, *1:* 135, 190; *3:* 204;
   7: 142; *15:* 199; *17:* 210; *27:* 181,
   182, 183, 185, 186, 187, 189,
   190-191, 192, 193, 194, 195, 197,
   198, 199, 203; *28:* 181, 182;
   32: 108; *33:* 148, 149; *35:* 238;
   44: 180, 181; *45:* 97, 99; *46:* 174;
   YABC 1: 167
Sengler, Johanna, *18:* 256
Seredy, Kate, *1:* 192; *14:* 20-21;
   17: 210
Sergeant, John, *6:* 74
Servello, Joe, *10:* 144; *24:* 139; *40:* 91
Seton, Ernest Thompson, *18:* 260-269,
   271
Seuss, Dr. *See* Geisel, Theodor
Severin, John Powers, *7:* 62
Sewall, Marcia, *15:* 8; *22:* 170;
   37: 171, 172, 173; *39:* 73;
   45: 209
Seward, Prudence, *16:* 243
Sewell, Helen, *3:* 186; *15:* 308;
   33: 102; *38:* 189, 190, 191, 192
Shahn, Ben, *39:* 178; *46:* 193
Shalansky, Len, *38:* 167
Shanks, Anne Zane, *10:* 149
Sharp, William, *6:* 131; *19:* 241;
   20: 112; *25:* 141
Shaw, Charles, *21:* 135; *38:* 187;
   47: 124
Shaw, Charles G., *13:* 200
Shearer, Ted, *43:* 193, 194, 195, 196
Shecter, Ben, *16:* 244; *25:* 109;
   33: 188, 191; *41:* 77
Shefcik, James, *48:* 221, 222
Shefts, Joelle, *48:* 210
Shekerjian, Haig, *16:* 245
Shekerjian, Regina, *16:* 245; *25:* 73
Shenton, Edward, *45:* 187, 188, 189;
   YABC 1: 218-219, 221
Shepard, Ernest H., *3:* 193; *4:* 74;
   16: 101; *17:* 109; *25:* 148;
   33: 152, 199, 200, 201, 202, 203,
   204, 205, 206, 207; *46:* 194;
   YABC 1: 148, 153, 174, 176,
   180-181
Shepard, Mary, *4:* 210; *22:* 205;
   30: 132, 133
Sherman, Theresa, *27:* 167
Sherwan, Earl, *3:* 196
Shields, Charles, *10:* 150; *36:* 63
Shields, Leonard, *13:* 83, 85, 87
Shillabeer, Mary, *35:* 74
Shilston, Arthur, *49:* 61

Shimin, Symeon, *1:* 93; *2:* 128-129; *3:* 202; *7:* 85; *11:* 177; *12:* 139; *13:* 202-203; *27:* 138; *28:* 65; *35:* 129; *36:* 130; *48:* 151; *49:* 59
Shinn, Everett, *16:* 148; *18:* 229; *21:* 149, 150, 151; *24:* 218
Shore, Robert, *27:* 54; *39:* 192, 193; *YABC 2:* 200
Shortall, Leonard, *4:* 144; *8:* 196; *10:* 166; *19:* 227, 228-229, 230; *25:* 78; *28:* 66, 167; *33:* 127
Shortt, T. M., *27:* 36
Shtainments, Leon, *32:* 161
Shulevitz, Uri, *3:* 198-199; *17:* 85; *22:* 204; *27:* 212; *28:* 184; *50:* 190, 191, 192, 193, 194-195, 196, 197, 198, 199, 201
Shute, Linda, *46:* 59
Siberell, Anne, *29:* 193
Sibley, Don, *1:* 39; *12:* 196; *31:* 47
Sidjakov, Nicolas, *18:* 274
Siebel, Fritz, *3:* 120; *17:* 145
Siegl, Helen, *12:* 166; *23:* 216; *34:* 185, 186
Sills, Joyce, *5:* 199
Silverstein, Alvin, *8:* 189
Silverstein, Shel, *33:* 211
Silverstein, Virginia, *8:* 189
Simon, Eric M., *7:* 82
Simon, Hilda, *28:* 189
Simon, Howard, *2:* 175; *5:* 132; *19:* 199; *32:* 163, 164, 165
Simont, Marc, *2:* 119; *4:* 213; *9:* 168; *13:* 238, 240; *14:* 262; *16:* 179; *18:* 221; *26:* 210; *33:* 189, 194; *44:* 132
Sims, Blanche, *44:* 116
Singer, Edith G., *2:* 30
Singer, Gloria, *34:* 56; *36:* 43
Singer, Julia, *28:* 190
Sivard, Robert, *26:* 124
Skardinski, Stanley, *23:* 144; *32:* 84
Slackman, Charles B., *12:* 201
Slater, Rod, *25:* 167
Sloan, Joseph, *16:* 68
Sloane, Eric, *21:* 3
Slobodkin, Louis, *1:* 200; *3:* 232; *5:* 168; *13:* 251; *15:* 13, 88; *26:* 173, 174, 175, 176, 178, 179
Slobodkina, Esphyr, *1:* 201
Small, David, *50:* 204-205
Small, W., *33:* 113
Smalley, Janet, *1:* 154
Smedley, William T., *34:* 129
Smee, David, *14:* 78
Smith, A. G., Jr., *35:* 182
Smith, Alvin, *1:* 31, 229; *13:* 187; *27:* 216; *28:* 226; *48:* 149; *49:* 60
Smith, Anne Warren, *41:* 212
Smith, Carl, *36:* 41
Smith, Doris Susan, *41:* 139
Smith, E. Boyd, *19:* 70; *22:* 89; *26:* 63; *YABC 1:* 4-5, 240, 248-249
Smith, Edward J., *4:* 224
Smith, Eunice Young, *5:* 170
Smith, Howard, *19:* 196
Smith, Jacqueline Bardner, *27:* 108; *39:* 197

Smith, Jessie Willcox, *15:* 91; *16:* 95; *18:* 231; *19:* 57, 242; *21:* 29, 156, 157, 158, 159, 160, 161; *34:* 65; *YABC 1:* 6; *YABC 2:* 180, 185, 191, 311, 325
Smith, Kenneth R., *47:* 182
Smith, L. H., *35:* 174
Smith, Lee, *29:* 32
Smith, Linell Nash, *2:* 195
Smith, Maggie Kaufman, *13:* 205; *35:* 191
Smith, Moishe, *33:* 155
Smith, Philip, *44:* 134; *46:* 203
Smith, Ralph Crosby, *2:* 267; *49:* 203
Smith, Robert D., *5:* 63
Smith, Susan Carlton, *12:* 208
Smith, Terry, *12:* 106; *33:* 158
Smith, Virginia, *3:* 157; *33:* 72
Smith, William A., *1:* 36; *10:* 154; *25:* 65
Smollin, Mike, *39:* 203
Smyth, M. Jane, *12:* 15
Snyder, Andrew A., *30:* 212
Snyder, Jerome, *13:* 207; *30:* 173
Snyder, Joel, *28:* 163
Sofia, *1:* 62; *5:* 90; *32:* 166
Sokol, Bill, *37:* 178; *49:* 23
Sokolov, Kirill, *34:* 188
Solbert, Ronni, *1:* 159; *2:* 232; *5:* 121; *6:* 34; *17:* 249
Solonevich, George, *15:* 246; *17:* 47
Sommer, Robert, *12:* 211
Sorel, Edward, *4:* 61; *36:* 82
Sotomayor, Antonio, *11:* 215
Soyer, Moses, *20:* 177
Spaenkuch, August, *16:* 28
Spanfeller, James, *1:* 72, 149; *2:* 183; *19:* 230, 231, 232; *22:* 66; *36:* 160, 161; *40:* 75
Sparks, Mary Walker, *15:* 247
Spence, Geraldine, *21:* 163; *47:* 196
Spence, Jim, *38:* 89; *50:* 102
Spiegel, Doris, *29:* 111
Spier, Jo, *10:* 30
Spier, Peter, *3:* 155; *4:* 200; *7:* 61; *11:* 78; *38:* 106
Spilka, Arnold, *5:* 120; *6:* 204; *8:* 131
Spivak, I. Howard, *8:* 10
Spollen, Christopher J., *12:* 214
Spooner, Malcolm, *40:* 142
Sprattler, Rob, *12:* 176
Spring, Bob, *5:* 60
Spring, Ira, *5:* 60
Springer, Harriet, *31:* 92
Spurrier, Steven, *28:* 198
Spy. *See* Ward, Leslie
Staffan, Alvin E., *11:* 56; *12:* 187
Stahl, Ben, *5:* 181; *12:* 91; *49:* 122
Stair, Gobin, *35:* 214
Stamaty, Mark Alan, *12:* 215
Stampnick, Ken, *51:* 142
Stanley, Diane, *3:* 45; *37:* 180
Stasiak, Krystyna, *49:* 181
Steadman, Ralph, *32:* 180
Steichen, Edward, *30:* 79
Steig, William, *18:* 275-276
Stein, Harve, *1:* 109
Steinberg, Saul, *47:* 193
Steinel, William, *23:* 146

Steiner, Charlotte, *45:* 196
Stephens, Charles H., *YABC 2:* 279
Stephens, William M., *21:* 165
Steptoe, John, *8:* 197
Stern, Simon, *15:* 249-250; *17:* 58; *34:* 192-193
Stevens, Janet, *40:* 126
Stevens, Mary, *11:* 193; *13:* 129; *43:* 95
Stevenson, James, *42:* 182, 183; *51:* 163
Stewart, Arvis, *33:* 98; *36:* 69
Stewart, Charles, *2:* 205
Stiles, Fran, *26:* 85
Stillman, Susan, *44:* 130
Stimpson, Tom, *49:* 171
Stinemetz, Morgan, *40:* 151
Stirnweis, Shannon, *10:* 164
Stobbs, William, *1:* 48-49; *3:* 68; *6:* 20; *17:* 117, 217; *24:* 150; *29:* 250
Stock, Catherine, *37:* 55
Stolp, Jaap, *49:* 98
Stone, David, *9:* 173
Stone, David K., *4:* 38; *6:* 124; *9:* 180; *43:* 182
Stone, Helen, *44:* 121, 122, 126
Stone, Helen V., *6:* 209
Stratton, Helen, *33:* 151
Stratton-Porter, Gene, *15:* 254, 259, 263-264, 268-269
Streano, Vince, *20:* 173
Strodl, Daniel, *47:* 95
Strong, Joseph D., Jr., *YABC 2:* 330
Ströyer, Poul, *13:* 221
Strugnell, Ann, *27:* 38
Stubis, Talivaldis, *5:* 182, 183; *10:* 45; *11:* 9; *18:* 304; *20:* 127
Stubley, Trevor, *14:* 43; *22:* 219; *23:* 37; *28:* 61
Stuecklen, Karl W., *8:* 34, 65; *23:* 103
Stull, Betty, *11:* 46
Suba, Susanne, *4:* 202-203; *14:* 261; *23:* 134; *29:* 222; *32:* 30
Sugarman, Tracy, *3:* 76; *8:* 199; *37:* 181, 182
Sugita, Yutaka, *36:* 180-181
Sullivan, Edmund J., *31:* 86
Sullivan, James F., *19:* 280; *20:* 192
Sumichrast, Jözef, *14:* 253; *29:* 168, 213
Sumiko, *46:* 57
Summers, Leo, *1:* 177; *2:* 273; *13:* 22
Svolinsky, Karel, *17:* 104
Swain, Su Zan Noguchi, *21:* 170
Swan, Susan, *22:* 220-221; *37:* 66
Sweat, Lynn, *25:* 206
Sweet, Darryl, *1:* 163; *4:* 136
Sweet, Ozzie, *31:* 149, 151, 152
Sweetland, Robert, *12:* 194
Swope, Martha, *43:* 160
Sylvester, Natalie G., *22:* 222
Szafran, Gene, *24:* 144
Szasz, Susanne, *13:* 55, 226; *14:* 48
Szekeres, Cyndy, *2:* 218; *5:* 185; *8:* 85; *11:* 166; *14:* 19; *16:* 57, 159; *26:* 49, 214; *34:* 205

Taback, Simms, *40:* 207
Tafuri, Nancy, *39:* 210
Tait, Douglas, *12:* 220
Takakjian, Portia, *15:* 274
Takashima, Shizuye, *13:* 228
Talarczyk, June, *4:* 173
Tallon, Robert, *2:* 228; *43:* 200, 201,
    202, 203, 204, 205, 206, 207, 209
Tamas, Szecskó, *29:* 135
Tamburine, Jean, *12:* 222
Tandy, H. R., *13:* 69
Tannenbaum, Robert, *48:* 181
Tanobe, Miyuki, *23:* 221
Tarkington, Booth, *17:* 224-225
Taylor, Ann, *41:* 226
Taylor, Isaac, *41:* 228
Teale, Edwin Way, *7:* 196
Teason, James, *1:* 14
Teeple, Lyn, *33:* 147
Tee-Van, Helen Damrosch, *10:* 176;
    11: 182
Teicher, Dick, *50:* 211
Tempest, Margaret, *3:* 237, 238
Temple, Herbert, *45:* 201
Templeton, Owen, *11:* 77
Tenggren, Gustaf, *18:* 277-279; *19:* 15;
    28: 86; *YABC 2:* 145
Tenney, Gordon, *24:* 204
Tenniel, John, *YABC 2:* 99
Thacher, Mary M., *30:* 72
Thackeray, William Makepeace,
    23: 224, 228
Thamer, Katie, *42:* 187
Thelwell, Norman, *14:* 201
Theobalds, Prue, *40:* 23
Theurer, Marilyn Churchill, *39:* 195
Thistlethwaite, Miles, *12:* 224
Thollander, Earl, *11:* 47; *18:* 112;
    22: 224
Thomas, Allan, *22:* 13
Thomas, Art, *48:* 217
Thomas, Eric, *28:* 49
Thomas, Harold, *20:* 98
Thomas, Mark, *42:* 136
Thomas, Martin, *14:* 255
Thompson, Arthur, *34:* 107
Thompson, Ellen, *51:* 88, 151
Thompson, George, *22:* 18; *28:* 150;
    33: 135
Thompson, George, W., *33:* 135
Thompson, Julie, *44:* 158
Thomson, Arline K., *3:* 264
Thomson, Hugh, *26:* 88
Thomson, Ross, *36:* 179
Thorne, Diana, *25:* 212
Thorvall, Kerstin, *13:* 235
Thurber, James, *13:* 239, 242-245,
    248-249
Tibbles, Paul, *45:* 23
Tichenor, Tom, *14:* 207
Tiegreen, Alan, *36:* 143; *43:* 55, 56,
    58
Tilney, F. C., *22:* 231
Timbs, Gloria, *36:* 90
Timmins, Harry, *2:* 171
Tinkelman, Murray, *12:* 225; *35:* 44
Titherington, Jeanne, *39:* 90
Tolford, Joshua, *1:* 221
Tolkien, J. R. R., *2:* 243; *32:* 215

Tolmie, Ken, *15:* 292
Tomei, Lorna, *47:* 168, 171
Tomes, Jacqueline, *2:* 117; *12:* 139
Tomes, Margot, *1:* 224; *2:* 120-121;
    16: 207; *18:* 250; *20:* 7; *25:* 62;
    27: 78, 79; *29:* 81, 199; *33:* 82;
    36: 186, 187, 188, 189, 190;
    46: 129
Toner, Raymond John, *10:* 179
Toothill, Harry, *6:* 54; *7:* 49; *25:* 219;
    42: 192
Toothill, Ilse, *6:* 54
Topolski, Feliks, *44:* 48
Torbert, Floyd James, *22:* 226
Torrey, Marjorie, *34:* 105
Toschik, Larry, *6:* 102
Totten, Bob, *13:* 93
Travers, Bob, *49:* 100
Tremain, Ruthven, *17:* 238
Tresilian, Stuart, *25:* 53; *40:* 212
Trez, Alain, *17:* 236
Trier, Walter, *14:* 96
Trimby, Elisa, *47:* 199
Tripp, F. J., *24:* 167
Tripp, Wallace, *2:* 48; *7:* 28; *8:* 94;
    10: 54, 76; *11:* 92; *31:* 170, 171;
    34: 203; *42:* 57
Trnka, Jiri, *22:* 151; *43:* 212, 213,
    214, 215; *YABC 1:* 30-31
Troughton, Joanna, *37:* 186; *48:* 72
Troyer, Johannes, *3:* 16; *7:* 18
Trudeau, G. B., *35:* 220, 221, 222;
    48: 119, 123, 126, 127, 128-129,
    133
Tsinajinie, Andy, *2:* 62
Tsugami, Kyuzo, *18:* 198-199
Tuckwell, Jennifer, *17:* 205
Tudor, Bethany, *7:* 103
Tudor, Tasha, *18:* 227; *20:* 185, 186,
    187; *36:* 111; *YABC 2:* 46, 314
Tulloch, Maurice, *24:* 79
Tunis, Edwin, *1:* 218-219; *28:* 209,
    210, 211, 212
Turkle, Brinton, *1:* 211, 213; *2:* 249;
    3: 226; *11:* 3; *16:* 209; *20:* 22;
    50: 23; *YABC 1:* 79
Turska, Krystyna, *12:* 103; *31:* 173,
    174-175
Tusan, Stan, *6:* 58; *22:* 236-237
Tworkov, Jack, *47:* 207
Tzimoulis, Paul, *12:* 104

Uchida, Yoshiko, *1:* 220
Uderzo, *47:* 88
Ulm, Robert, *17:* 238
Unada. *See* Gliewe, Unada
Underwood, Clarence, *40:* 166
Ungerer, Tomi, *5:* 188; *9:* 40; *18:* 188;
    29: 175; *33:* 221, 222-223, 225
Unwin, Nora S., *3:* 65, 234-235;
    4: 237; *44:* 173, 174; *YABC 1:* 59;
    YABC 2: 301
Uris, Jill, *49:* 188, 197
Ursell, Martin, *50:* 51
Utpatel, Frank, *18:* 114
Utz, Lois, *5:* 190

Van Abbé, S., *16:* 142; *18:* 282;
    31: 90; *YABC 2:* 157, 161
Van Allsburg, Chris, *37:* 205, 206
Vandivert, William, *21:* 175
Van Everen, Jay, *13:* 160;
    YABC 1: 121
Van Horn, William, *43:* 218
Van Loon, Hendrik Willem, *18:* 285,
    289, 291
Van Sciver, Ruth, *37:* 162
Van Stockum, Hilda, *5:* 193
Van Wely, Babs, *16:* 50
Varga, Judy, *29:* 196
Vasiliu, Mircea, *2:* 166, 253; *9:* 166;
    13: 58
Vaughn, Frank, *34:* 157
Vavra, Robert, *8:* 206
Vawter, Will, *17:* 163
Veeder, Larry, *18:* 4
Velasquez, Eric, *45:* 217
Vendrell, Carme Solé, *42:* 205
Ver Beck, Frank, *18:* 16-17
Verney, John, *14:* 225
Verrier, Suzanne, *5:* 20; *23:* 212
Versace, Marie, *2:* 255
Vestal, H. B., *9:* 134; *11:* 101; *27:* 25;
    34: 158
Vickrey, Robert, *45:* 59, 64
Victor, Joan Berg, *30:* 193
Viereck, Ellen, *3:* 242; *14:* 229
Vigna, Judith, *15:* 293
Vilato, Gaspar E., *5:* 41
Villiard, Paul, *51:* 178
Vimnèra, A., *23:* 154
Vincent, Eric, *34:* 98
Vincent, Félix, *41:* 237
Vip, *45:* 164
Vivas, Julie, *51:* 67, 69
Vo-Dinh, Mai, *16:* 272
Vogel, Ilse-Margret, *14:* 230
Voigt, Erna, *35:* 228
Vojtech, Anna, *42:* 190
von Schmidt, Eric, *8:* 62; *50:* 209, 210
von Schmidt, Harold, *30:* 80
Vosburgh, Leonard, *1:* 161; *7:* 32;
    15: 295-296; *23:* 110; *30:* 214;
    43: 181
Voter, Thomas W., *19:* 3, 9
Vroman, Tom, *10:* 29

Waber, Bernard, *47:* 209, 210, 211,
    212, 213, 214
Wagner, John, *8:* 200
Wagner, Ken, *2:* 59
Waide, Jan, *29:* 225; *36:* 139
Wainwright, Jerry, *14:* 85
Wakeen, Sandra, *47:* 97
Waldman, Bruce, *15:* 297; *43:* 178
Waldman, Neil, *35:* 141; *50:* 163;
    51: 180
Walker, Charles, *1:* 46; *4:* 59; *5:* 177;
    11: 115; *19:* 45; *34:* 74
Walker, Dugald Stewart, *15:* 47;
    32: 202; *33:* 112
Walker, Gil, *8:* 49; *23:* 132; *34:* 42
Walker, Jim, *10:* 94
Walker, Mort, *8:* 213

Walker, Norman, *41:* 37; *45:* 58
Walker, Stephen, *12:* 229; *21:* 174
Wallace, Beverly Dobrin, *19:* 259
Waller, S. E., *24:* 36
Wallner, Alexandra, *15:* 120
Wallner, John C., *9:* 77; *10:* 188; *11:* 28; *14:* 209; *31:* 56, 118; *37:* 64; *51:* 186, 187, 188-189, 190-191, 192-193, 194, 195
Wallower, Lucille, *11:* 226
Walters, Audrey, *18:* 294
Walther, Tom, *31:* 179
Walton, Tony, *11:* 164; *24:* 209
Waltrip, Lela, *9:* 195
Waltrip, Mildred, *3:* 209; *37:* 211
Waltrip, Rufus, *9:* 195
Wan, *12:* 76
Ward, John, *42:* 191
Ward, Keith, *2:* 107
Ward, Leslie, *34:* 126; *36:* 87
Ward, Lynd, *1:* 99, 132, 133, 150; *2:* 108, 158, 196, 259; *18:* 86; *27:* 56; *29:* 79, 187, 253, 255; *36:* 199, 200, 201, 202, 203, 204, 205, 206, 207, 209; *43:* 34
Ward, Peter, *37:* 116
Warner, Peter, *14:* 87
Warren, Betsy, *2:* 101
Warren, Marion Cray, *14:* 215
Warshaw, Jerry, *30:* 197, 198; *42:* 165
Washington, Nevin, *20:* 123
Washington, Phyllis, *20:* 123
Waterman, Stan, *11:* 76
Watkins-Pitchford, D. J., *6:* 215, 217
Watson, Aldren A., *2:* 267; *5:* 94; *13:* 71; *19:* 253; *32:* 220; *42:* 193, 194, 195, 196, 197, 198, 199, 200, 201; *YABC 2:* 202
Watson, Gary, *19:* 147; *36:* 68; *41:* 122; *47:* 139
Watson, J. D., *22:* 86
Watson, Karen, *11:* 26
Watson, Wendy, *5:* 197; *13:* 101; *33:* 116; *46:* 163
Watts, Bernadette, *4:* 227
Watts, John, *37:* 149
Webber, Helen, *3:* 141
Webber, Irma E., *14:* 238
Weber, Florence, *40:* 153
Weber, William J., *14:* 239
Webster, Jean, *17:* 241
Wegner, Fritz, *14:* 250; *20:* 189; *44:* 165
Weidenear, Reynold H., *21:* 122
Weihs, Erika, *4:* 21; *15:* 299
Weil, Lisl, *7:* 203; *10:* 58; *21:* 95; *22:* 188, 217; *33:* 193
Weiman, Jon, *50:* 162, 165
Weiner, Sandra, *14:* 240
Weisgard, Leonard, *1:* 65; *2:* 191, 197, 204, 264-265; *5:* 108; *21:* 42; *30:* 200, 201, 203, 204; *41:* 47; *44:* 125; *YABC 2:* 13
Weiss, Ellen, *44:* 202
Weiss, Emil, *1:* 168; *7:* 60
Weiss, Harvey, *1:* 145, 223; *27:* 224, 227
Weiss, Nicki, *33:* 229
Weissman, Bari, *49:* 72

Wells, Frances, *1:* 183
Wells, H. G., *20:* 194, 200
Wells, Rosemary, *6:* 49; *18:* 297
Wells, Susan, *22:* 43
Wendelin, Rudolph, *23:* 234
Wengenroth, Stow, *37:* 47
Werenskiold, Erik, *15:* 6
Werner, Honi, *24:* 110; *33:* 41
Werth, Kurt, *7:* 122; *14:* 157; *20:* 214; *39:* 128
Westerberg, Christine, *29:* 226
Weston, Martha, *29:* 116; *30:* 213; *33:* 85, 100
Wetherbee, Margaret, *5:* 3
Wexler, Jerome, *49:* 73
Whalley, Peter, *50:* 49
Wheatley, Arabelle, *11:* 231; *16:* 276
Wheeler, Cindy, *49:* 205
Wheeler, Dora, *44:* 179
Wheelright, Rowland, *15:* 81; *YABC 2:* 286
Whistler, Rex, *16:* 75; *30:* 207, 208
White, David Omar, *5:* 56; *18:* 6
White, Martin, *51:* 197
Whitear, *32:* 26
Whithorne, H. S., *7:* 49
Whitney, George Gillett, *3:* 24
Whittam, Geoffrey, *30:* 191
Wiberg, Harald, *38:* 127
Wiese, Kurt, *3:* 255; *4:* 206; *14:* 17; *17:* 18-19; *19:* 47; *24:* 152; *25:* 212; *32:* 184; *36:* 211, 213, 214, 215, 216, 217, 218; *45:* 161
Wiesner, David, *33:* 47; *51:* 106
Wiesner, William, *4:* 100; *5:* 200, 201; *14:* 262
Wiggins, George, *6:* 133
Wikkelsoe, Otto, *45:* 25, 26
Wikland, Ilon, *5:* 113; *8:* 150; *38:* 124, 125, 130
Wilbur, C. Keith, M.D., *27:* 228
Wilcox, J.A.J., *34:* 122
Wilcox, R. Turner, *36:* 219
Wild, Jocelyn, *46:* 220-221, 222
Wilde, George, *7:* 139
Wildsmith, Brian, *16:* 281-282; *18:* 170-171
Wilkin, Eloise, *36:* 173; *49:* 208, 209, 210
Wilkinson, Barry, *50:* 213
Wilkinson, Gerald, *3:* 40
Wilkoń, Józef, *31:* 183, 184
Wilks, Mike, *34:* 24; *44:* 203
Williams, Ferelith Eccles, *22:* 238
Williams, Garth, *1:* 197; *2:* 49, 270; *4:* 205; *15:* 198, 302-304, 307; *16:* 34; *18:* 283, 298-301; *29:* 177, 178, 179, 232-233, 241-245, 248; *40:* 106; *YABC 2:* 15-16, 19
Williams, J. Scott, *48:* 28
Williams, Kit, *44:* 206-207, 208, 209, 211, 212
Williams, Maureen, *12:* 238
Williams, Patrick, *14:* 218
Williams, Richard, *44:* 93
Wilson, Charles Banks, *17:* 92; *43:* 73
Wilson, Dagmar, *10:* 47

Wilson, Edward A., *6:* 24; *16:* 149; *20:* 220-221; *22:* 87; *26:* 67; *38:* 212, 214, 215, 216, 217
Wilson, Forrest, *27:* 231
Wilson, Gahan, *35:* 234; *41:* 136
Wilson, Jack, *17:* 139
Wilson, John, *22:* 240
Wilson, Maurice, *46:* 224
Wilson, Patten, *35:* 61
Wilson, Peggy, *15:* 4
Wilson, Rowland B., *30:* 170
Wilson, Sarah, *50:* 215
Wilson, Tom, *33:* 232
Wilson, W. N., *22:* 26
Wilwerding, Walter J., *9:* 202
Winchester, Linda, *13:* 231
Wind, Betty, *28:* 158
Windham, Kathryn Tucker, *14:* 260
Wing, Ron, *50:* 85
Winslow, Will, *21:* 124
Winsten, Melanie Willa, *41:* 41
Winter, Milo, *15:* 97; *19:* 221; *21:* 181, 203, 204, 205; *YABC 2:* 144
Winter, Paula, *48:* 227
Wise, Louis, *13:* 68
Wiseman, Ann, *31:* 187
Wiseman, B., *4:* 233
Wishnefsky, Phillip, *3:* 14
Wiskur, Darrell, *5:* 72; *10:* 50; *18:* 246
Wittman, Sally, *30:* 219
Woehr, Lois, *12:* 5
Wohlberg, Meg, *12:* 100; *14:* 197; *41:* 255
Woldin, Beth Weiner, *34:* 211
Wolf, J., *16:* 91
Wolf, Linda, *33:* 163
Wolff, Ashley, *50:* 217
Wondriska, William, *6:* 220
Wonsetler, John C., *5:* 168
Wood, Audrey, *50:* 221, 222, 223
Wood, Don, *50:* 220, 225, 226, 228-229
Wood, Grant, *19:* 198
Wood, Muriel, *36:* 119
Wood, Myron, *6:* 220
Wood, Owen, *18:* 187
Wood, Ruth, *8:* 11
Woodson, Jack, *10:* 201
Woodward, Alice, *26:* 89; *36:* 81
Wool, David, *26:* 27
Wooten, Vernon, *23:* 70; *51:* 170
Worboys, Evelyn, *1:* 166-167
Worth, Jo, *34:* 143
Worth, Wendy, *4:* 133
Wosmek, Frances, *29:* 251
Wrenn, Charles L., *38:* 96; *YABC 1:* 20, 21
Wright, Dare, *21:* 206
Wright, George, *YABC 1:* 268
Wright, Joseph, *30:* 160
Wronker, Lili Cassel, *3:* 247; *10:* 204; *21:* 10
Wyatt, Stanley, *46:* 210
Wyeth, Andrew, *13:* 40; *YABC 1:* 133-134
Wyeth, Jamie, *41:* 257

Wyeth, N. C., *13:* 41; *17:* 252-259, 264-268; *18:* 181; *19:* 80, 191, 200; *21:* 57, 183; *22:* 91; *23:* 152; *24:* 28, 99; *35:* 61; *41:* 65; *YABC 1:* 133, 223; *YABC 2:* 53, 75, 171, 187, 317

Yang, Jay, *1:* 8; *12:* 239
Yap, Weda, *6:* 176
Yaroslava. *See* Mills, Yaroslava Surmach
Yashima, Taro, *14:* 84
Ylla. *See* Koffler, Camilla
Yohn, F. C., *23:* 128; *YABC 1:* 269

Young, Ed, *7:* 205; *10:* 206; *40:* 124; *YABC 2:* 242
Young, Noela, *8:* 221

Zacks, Lewis, *10:* 161
Zadig, *50:* 58
Zaffo, George, *42:* 208
Zaid, Barry, *50:* 127; *51:* 201
Zaidenberg, Arthur, *34:* 218, 219, 220
Zalben, Jane Breskin, *7:* 211
Zallinger, Jean, *4:* 192; *8:* 8, 129; *14:* 273
Zallinger, Rudolph F., *3:* 245
Zeck, Gerry, *40:* 232

Zeiring, Bob, *42:* 130
Zeldich, Arieh, *49:* 124
Zelinsky, Paul O., *14:* 269; *43:* 56; *49:* 218, 219, 220, 221, 222-223
Zemach, Margot, *3:* 270; *8:* 201; *21:* 210-211; *27:* 204, 205, 210; *28:* 185; *49:* 22, 183, 224
Zemsky, Jessica, *10:* 62
Zepelinsky, Paul, *35:* 93
Zimmer, Dirk, *38:* 195; *49:* 71
Zimnik, Reiner, *36:* 224
Zinkeisen, Anna, *13:* 106
Zoellick, Scott, *33:* 231
Zonia, Dhimitri, *20:* 234-235
Zweifel, Francis, *14:* 274; *28:* 187
Zwinger, Herman H., *46:* 227

Author Index

The following index gives the number of the volume in which an author's biographical sketch, Brief Entry, or Obituary appears.

This index includes references to all entries in the following series, which are also published by Gale Research Company.

YABC—*Yesterday's Authors of Books for Children: Facts and Pictures about Authors and Illustrators of Books for Young People from Early Times to 1960*, Volumes 1-2

CLR—*Children's Literature Review: Excerpts from Reviews, Criticism, and Commentary on Books for Children*, Volumes 1-13

SAAS—*Something about the Author Autobiography Series*, Volumes 1-5

A

Aardema, Verna 1911- 4
Aaron, Chester 1923- 9
Aaseng, Nate
  See Aaseng, Nathan
Aaseng, Nathan 1938- 51
  Brief Entry 38
Abbott, Alice
  See Borland, Kathryn Kilby
Abbott, Alice
  See Speicher, Helen Ross (Smith)
Abbott, Jacob 1803-1879 22
Abbott, Manager Henry
  See Stratemeyer, Edward L.
Abbott, Sarah
  See Zolotow, Charlotte S.
Abdul, Raoul 1929- 12
Abel, Raymond 1911- 12
Abell, Kathleen 1938- 9
Abels, Harriette S(heffer)
  1926- 50
Abercrombie, Barbara (Mattes)
  1939- 16
Abernethy, Robert G. 1935- 5
Abisch, Roslyn Kroop 1927- 9
Abisch, Roz
  See Abisch, Roslyn Kroop
Abodaher, David J. (Naiph)
  1919- 17
Abolafia, Yossi
  Brief Entry 46
Abrahall, C. H.
  See Hoskyns-Abrahall, Clare
Abrahall, Clare Hoskyns
  See Hoskyns-Abrahall, Clare
Abrahams, Hilary (Ruth)
  1938- 29
Abrahams, Robert D(avid)
  1905- 4
Abrams, Joy 1941- 16
Abrams, Lawrence F.
  Brief Entry 47
Abrashkin, Raymond
  1911-1960 50
Achebe, Chinua 1930- 40
  Brief Entry 38
Ackerman, Eugene 1888-1974 10
Acs, Laszlo (Bela) 1931- 42
  Brief Entry 32
Acuff, Selma Boyd 1924- 45
Ada, Alma Flor 1938- 43

Adair, Margaret Weeks
  (?)-1971 10
Adam, Cornel
  See Lengyel, Cornel Adam
Adams, Adrienne 1906- 8
Adams, Andy
  1859-1935 ....*YABC 1*
Adams, Dale
  See Quinn, Elisabeth
Adams, Harriet S(tratemeyer)
  1893(?)-1982 1
  Obituary 29
Adams, Harrison
  See Stratemeyer, Edward L.
Adams, Hazard 1926- 6
Adams, Laurie 1941- 33
Adams, Richard 1920- 7
Adams, Ruth Joyce 14
Adams, William Taylor
  1822-1897 28
Adamson, Gareth 1925-1982 46
  Obituary 30
Adamson, George Worsley
  1913- 30
Adamson, Graham
  See Groom, Arthur William
Adamson, Joy 1910-1980 11
  Obituary 22
Adamson, Wendy Wriston
  1942- 22
Addona, Angelo F. 1925- 14
Addy, Ted
  See Winterbotham, R(ussell)
  R(obert)
Adelberg, Doris
  See Orgel, Doris
Adelson, Leone 1908- 11
Adkins, Jan 1944- 8
  See also CLR 7
Adler, C(arole) S(chwerdtfeger)
  1932- 26
Adler, David A. 1947- 14
Adler, Irene
  See Penzler, Otto
  See Storr, Catherine (Cole)
Adler, Irving 1913- 29
  Earlier sketch in SATA 1
Adler, Larry 1939- 36
Adler, Peggy 22
Adler, Ruth 1915-1968 1
Adoff, Arnold 1935- 5
  See also CLR 7

Adorjan, Carol 1934- 10
Adrian, Mary
  See Jorgensen, Mary Venn
Adshead, Gladys L. 1896- 3
Aesop, Abraham
  See Newbery, John
Agapida, Fray Antonio
  See Irving, Washington
Agard, Nadema 1948- 18
Agle, Nan Hayden 1905- 3
Agnew, Edith J(osephine)
  1897- 11
Ahern, Margaret McCrohan
  1921- 10
Ahl, Anna Maria 1926- 32
Ahlberg, Allan
  Brief Entry 35
Ahlberg, Janet
  Brief Entry 32
Aichinger, Helga 1937- 4
Aiken, Clarissa (Lorenz)
  1899- 12
Aiken, Conrad (Potter)
  1889-1973 30
  Earlier sketch in SATA 3
Aiken, Joan 1924- 30
  Earlier sketch in SATA 2
  See also CLR 1
  See also SAAS 1
Ainsworth, Norma 9
Ainsworth, Ruth 1908- 7
Ainsworth, William Harrison
  1805-1882 24
Aistrop, Jack 1916- 14
Aitken, Amy 1952-
  Brief Entry 40
Aitken, Dorothy 1916- 10
Akaba, Suekichi 1910- 46
Akers, Floyd
  See Baum, L(yman) Frank
Alain
  See Brustlein, Daniel
Albert, Burton, Jr. 1936- 22
Alberts, Frances Jacobs 1907- 14
Albion, Lee Smith 29
Albrecht, Lillie (Vanderveer)
  1894- 12
Alcock, Gudrun
  Brief Entry 33
Alcock, Vivien 1924- 45
  Brief Entry 38

Alcorn, John 1935- *31*
Brief Entry *30*
Alcott, Louisa May
1832-1888 ....*YABC 1*
See also CLR 1
Alda, Arlene 1933- *44*
Brief Entry *36*
Alden, Isabella (Macdonald)
1841-1930 ....*YABC 2*
Alderman, Clifford Lindsey
1902- *3*
Alderson, Sue Ann 1940-
Brief Entry *48*
Aldis, Dorothy (Keeley)
1896-1966 .... *2*
Aldiss, Brian W(ilson) 1925- *34*
Aldon, Adair
See Meigs, Cornelia
Aldous, Allan (Charles) 1911- *27*
Aldrich, Ann
See Meaker, Marijane
Aldrich, Thomas Bailey
1836-1907 .... *17*
Aldridge, Alan 1943(?)-
Brief Entry *33*
Aldridge, Josephine Haskell *14*
Alegria, Ricardo E. 1921- *6*
Aleksin, Anatolii (Georgievich)
1924- *36*
Alex, Ben [a pseudonym]
1946- *45*
Alex, Marlee [a pseudonym]
1948- *45*
Alexander, Anna Cooke 1913- *1*
Alexander, Frances 1888- *4*
Alexander, Jocelyn (Anne) Arundel
1930- *22*
Alexander, Linda 1935- *2*
Alexander, Lloyd 1924- *49*
Earlier sketch in SATA 3
See also CLR 1, 5
Alexander, Martha 1920- *11*
Alexander, Rae Pace
See Alexander, Raymond Pace
Alexander, Raymond Pace
1898-1974 .... *22*
Alexander, Sue 1933- *12*
Alexander, Vincent Arthur 1925-1980
Obituary *23*
Alexeieff, Alexandre A.
1901- *14*
Alger, Horatio, Jr. 1832-1899 ..... *16*
Alger, Leclaire (Gowans)
1898-1969 .... *15*
Aliki
See Brandenberg, Aliki
See also CLR 9
Alkema, Chester Jay 1932- *12*
Allamand, Pascale 1942- *12*
Allan, Mabel Esther 1915- *32*
Earlier sketch in SATA 5
Allard, Harry
See Allard, Harry G(rover), Jr.
Allard, Harry G(rover), Jr.
1928- *42*
Allee, Marjorie Hill
1890-1945 .... *17*

Allen, Adam [Joint pseudonym]
See Epstein, Beryl and Epstein, Samuel
Allen, Alex B.
See Heide, Florence Parry
Allen, Allyn
See Eberle, Irmengarde
Allen, Betsy
See Cavanna, Betty
Allen, Gertrude E(lizabeth)
1888- *9*
Allen, Jack 1899-
Brief Entry *29*
Allen, Jeffrey (Yale) 1948- *42*
Allen, Leroy 1912- *11*
Allen, Linda 1925- *33*
Allen, Marjorie 1931- *22*
Allen, Maury 1932- *26*
Allen, Merritt Parmelee
1892-1954 .... *22*
Allen, Nina (Strömgren)
1935- *22*
Allen, Pamela 1934- *50*
Allen, Rodney F. 1938- *27*
Allen, Ruth
See Peterson, Esther (Allen)
Allen, Samuel (Washington)
1917- *9*
Allen, T. D. [Joint pseudonym]
See Allen, Terril Diener
Allen, Terril Diener 1908- *35*
Allen, Terry D.
See Allen, Terril Diener
Allen, Thomas B(enton)
1929- *45*
Allen, Tom
See Allen, Thomas B(enton)
Allerton, Mary
See Govan, Christine Noble
Alleyn, Ellen
See Rossetti, Christina (Georgina)
Allington, Richard L(loyd)
1947- *39*
Brief Entry *35*
Allison, Bob *14*
Allison, Linda 1948- *43*
Allmendinger, David F(rederick), Jr.
1938- *35*
Allred, Gordon T. 1930- *10*
Allsop, Kenneth 1920-1973 .... *17*
Almedingen, E. M.
1898-1971 .... *3*
Almedingen, Martha Edith von
See Almedingen, E. M.
Almond, Linda Stevens 1881(?)-1987
Obituary *50*
Almquist, Don 1929- *11*
Alsop, Mary O'Hara
1885-1980 .... *34*
Obituary *24*
Earlier sketch in SATA 5
Alter, Robert Edmond
1925-1965 .... *9*
Althea
See Braithwaite, Althea *23*
Altschuler, Franz 1923- *45*
Altsheler, Joseph A(lexander)
1862-1919 ....*YABC 1*
Alvarez, Joseph A. 1930- *18*

Ambler, C(hristopher) Gifford 1886-
Brief Entry *29*
Ambrose, Stephen E(dward)
1936- *40*
Ambrus, Gyozo (Laszlo)
1935- *41*
Earlier sketch in SATA 1
Ambrus, Victor G.
See Ambrus, Gyozo (Laszlo)
See also SAAS 4
Amerman, Lockhart
1911-1969 .... *3*
Ames, Evelyn 1908- *13*
Ames, Gerald 1906- *11*
Ames, Lee J. 1921- *3*
Ames, Mildred 1919- *22*
Amon, Aline 1928- *9*
Amoss, Berthe 1925- *5*
Anastasio, Dina 1941- *37*
Brief Entry *30*
Anckarsvard, Karin
1915-1969 .... *6*
Ancona, George 1929- *12*
Andersdatter, Karla M(argaret)
1938- *34*
Andersen, Hans Christian
1805-1875 ....*YABC 1*
See also CLR 6
Andersen, Ted
See Boyd, Waldo T.
Andersen, Yvonne 1932- *27*
Anderson, Bernice G(oudy)
1894- *33*
Anderson, Brad(ley Jay)
1924- *33*
Brief Entry *31*
Anderson, C(larence) W(illiam)
1891-1971 .... *11*
Anderson, Clifford [Joint pseudonym]
See Gardner, Richard
Anderson, Ella
See MacLeod, Ellen Jane (Anderson)
Anderson, Eloise Adell 1927- *9*
Anderson, George
See Groom, Arthur William
Anderson, Grace Fox 1932- *43*
Anderson, J(ohn) R(ichard) L(ane)
1911-1981 .... *15*
Obituary *27*
Anderson, Joy 1928- *1*
Anderson, LaVere (Francis Shoenfelt)
1907- *27*
Anderson, Leone Castell 1923-
Brief Entry *49*
Anderson, (John) Lonzo
1905- *2*
Anderson, Lucia (Lewis)
1922- *10*
Anderson, Madelyn Klein *28*
Anderson, Margaret J(ean)
1931- *27*
Anderson, Mary 1939- *7*
Anderson, Mona 1910- *40*
Anderson, Norman D(ean)
1928- *22*
Anderson, Poul (William) 1926-
Brief Entry *39*
Anderson, Rachel 1943- *34*
Andre, Evelyn M(arie) 1924- *27*

Andree, Louise
  See Coury, Louise Andree
Andrews, Benny 1930- *31*
Andrews, F(rank) Emerson
  1902-1978 .... *22*
Andrews, J(ames) S(ydney)
  1934- *4*
Andrews, Jan 1942-
  Brief Entry *49*
Andrews, Julie 1935- *7*
Andrews, Laura
  See Coury, Louise Andree
Andrews, Roy Chapman
  1884-1960 .... *19*
Andrews, V(irginia) C(leo) (?)-1986
  Obituary *50*
Andrézel, Pierre
  See Blixen, Karen (Christentze
  Dinesen)
Andriola, Alfred J. 1912-1983
  Obituary *34*
Andrist, Ralph K. 1914- *45*
Anfousse, Ginette 1944-
  Brief Entry *48*
Angel, Marie (Felicity) 1923- *47*
Angeles, Peter A. 1931- *40*
Angell, Judie 1937- *22*
Angell, Madeline 1919- *18*
Angelo, Valenti 1897- *14*
Angelou, Maya 1928- *49*
Angier, Bradford *12*
Angle, Paul M(cClelland) 1900-1975
  Obituary *20*
Anglund, Joan Walsh 1926- *2*
  See also CLR 1
Angrist, Stanley W(olff)
  1933- *4*
Anita
  See Daniel, Anita
Annett, Cora
  See Scott, Cora Annett
Annixter, Jane
  See Sturtzel, Jane Levington
Annixter, Paul
  See Sturtzel, Howard A.
Anno, Mitsumasa 1926- *38*
  Earlier sketch in SATA 5
  See also CLR 2
Anrooy, Frans van
  See Van Anrooy, Francine
Antell, Will D. 1935- *31*
Anthony, Barbara 1932- *29*
Anthony, C. L.
  See Smith, Dodie
Anthony, Edward 1895-1971 ...... *21*
Anticaglia, Elizabeth 1939- *12*
Antolini, Margaret Fishback
  1904-1985
  Obituary *45*
Anton, Michael (James) 1940- *12*
Antonacci, Robert J(oseph)
  1916- *45*
  Brief Entry *37*
Aoki, Hisako 1942- *45*
Apfel, Necia H(alpern) 1930- *51*
  Brief Entry *41*
Aphrodite, J.
  See Livingston, Carole

Appel, Benjamin 1907-1977 ...... *39*
  Obituary *21*
Appel, Martin E(liot) 1948- *45*
Appel, Marty
  See Appel, Martin E(liot)
Appiah, Peggy 1921- *15*
Apple, Margot
  Brief Entry *42*
Applebaum, Stan 1929- *45*
Appleton, Victor [Collective
  pseudonym] *1*
Appleton, Victor II [Collective
  pseudonym] *1*
  See also Adams, Harriet
  S(tratemeyer)
Apsler, Alfred 1907- *10*
Aquillo, Don
  See Prince, J(ack) H(arvey)
Aragonés, Sergio 1937- *48*
  Brief Entry *39*
Arbuckle, Dorothy Fry 1910-1982
  Obituary *33*
Arbuthnot, May Hill
  1884-1969 .... *2*
Archer, Frank
  See O'Connor, Richard
Archer, Jules 1915- *4*
  See also SAAS 5
Archer, Marion Fuller 1917- *11*
Archibald, Joe
  See Archibald, Joseph S(topford)
Archibald, Joseph S(topford)
  1898-1986 .... *3*
  Obituary *47*
Arden, Barbie
  See Stoutenburg, Adrien
Arden, William
  See Lynds, Dennis
Ardizzone, Edward 1900-1979 .... *28*
  Obituary *21*
  Earlier sketch in SATA 1
  See also CLR 3
Ardley, Neil (Richard) 1937- *43*
Arehart-Treichel, Joan 1942- *22*
Arenella, Roy 1939- *14*
Arkin, Alan (Wolf) 1934-
  Brief Entry *32*
Armer, Alberta (Roller) 1904- *9*
Armer, Laura Adams
  1874-1963 .... *13*
Armitage, David 1943-
  Brief Entry *38*
Armitage, Ronda (Jacqueline)
  1943- *47*
  Brief Entry *38*
Armour, Richard 1906- *14*
Armstrong, George D. 1927- *10*
Armstrong, Gerry (Breen)
  1929- *10*
Armstrong, Louise *43*
  Brief Entry *33*
Armstrong, Richard 1903- *11*
Armstrong, William H. 1914- *4*
  See also CLR 1
Arndt, Ursula (Martha H.)
  Brief Entry *39*
Arneson, D(on) J(on) 1935- *37*
Arnett, Carolyn
  See Cole, Lois Dwight

Arno, Enrico 1913-1981 .... *43*
  Obituary *28*
Arnold, Caroline 1944- *36*
  Brief Entry *34*
Arnold, Elliott 1912-1980 .... *5*
  Obituary *22*
Arnold, Emily 1939- *50*
Arnold, Oren 1900- *4*
Arnoldy, Julie
  See Bischoff, Julia Bristol
Arnosky, Jim 1946- *22*
Arnott, Kathleen 1914- *20*
Arnov, Boris, Jr. 1926- *12*
Arnow, Harriette (Louisa Simpson)
  1908-1986 .... *42*
  Obituary *47*
Arnstein, Helene S(olomon)
  1915- *12*
Arntson, Herbert E(dward)
  1911- *12*
Aronin, Ben 1904-1980
  Obituary *25*
Arora, Shirley (Lease) 1930- *2*
Arquette, Lois S(teinmetz)
  1934- *1*
  See also Duncan, Lois S(teinmetz)
Arrowood, (McKendrick Lee) Clinton
  1939- *19*
Arthur, Robert
  See Feder, Robert Arthur
Arthur, Ruth M(abel)
  1905-1979 .... *7*
  Obituary *26*
Artis, Vicki Kimmel 1945- *12*
Artzybasheff, Boris (Miklailovich)
  1899-1965 .... *14*
Aruego, Ariane
  See Dewey, Ariane
Aruego, Jose 1932- *6*
  See also CLR 5
Arundel, Honor (Morfydd)
  1919-1973 .... *4*
  Obituary *24*
Arundel, Jocelyn
  See Alexander, Jocelyn (Anne)
  Arundel
Asbjörnsen, Peter Christen
  1812-1885 .... *15*
Asch, Frank 1946- *5*
Ash, Jutta 1942- *38*
Ashabranner, Brent (Kenneth)
  1921- *1*
Ashby, Gwynneth 1922- *44*
Ashe, Geoffrey (Thomas)
  1923- *17*
Asher, Sandy (Fenichel)
  1942- *36*
  Brief Entry *34*
Ashey, Bella
  See Breinburg, Petronella
Ashford, Daisy
  See Ashford, Margaret Mary
Ashford, Margaret Mary
  1881-1972 .... *10*
Ashley, Bernard 1935- *47*
  Brief Entry *39*
  See also CLR 4
Ashley, Elizabeth
  See Salmon, Annie Elizabeth

Ashley, Ray
   See Abrashkin, Raymond
Ashton, Warren T.
   See Adams, William Taylor
Asimov, Issac 1920- 26
   Earlier sketch in SATA 1
   See also CLR 12
Asimov, Janet
   See Jeppson, J(anet) O(pal)
Asinof, Eliot 1919- 6
Astley, Juliet
   See Lofts, Nora (Robinson)
Aston, James
   See White, T(erence) H(anbury)
Atene, Ann
   See Atene, (Rita) Anna
Atene, (Rita) Anna 1922- 12
Atkinson, Allen
   Brief Entry 46
Atkinson, M. E.
   See Frankau, Mary Evelyn
Atkinson, Margaret Fleming 14
Atticus
   See Davies, (Edward) Hunter
   See Fleming, Ian (Lancaster)
Atwater, Florence (Hasseltine
   Carroll) 16
Atwater, Montgomery Meigs
   1904- 15
Atwater, Richard Tupper 1892-1948
   Brief Entry 27
Atwood, Ann 1913- 7
Atwood, Margaret (Eleanor)
   1939- 50
Aubry, Claude B. 1914-1984 29
   Obituary 40
Augarde, Steve 1950- 25
Augelli, John P(at) 1921- 46
Ault, Phillip H. 1914- 23
Ault, Rosalie Sain 1942- 38
Ault, Roz
   See Ault, Rosalie Sain
Aung, (Maung) Htin 1910- 21
Aung, U. Htin
   See Aung, (Maung) Htin
Auntie Deb
   See Coury, Louise Andree
Auntie Louise
   See Coury, Louise Andree
Austin, Elizabeth S. 1907- 5
Austin, Margot 11
Austin, Oliver L., Jr. 1903- 7
Austin, R. G.
   See Gelman, Rita Golden
Austin, Tom
   See Jacobs, Linda C.
Auth, Tony
   See Auth, William Anthony, Jr.
Auth, William Anthony, Jr.
   1942- 51
Averill, Esther 1902- 28
   Earlier sketch in SATA 1
Avery, Al
   See Montgomery, Rutherford
Avery, Gillian 1926- 7
Avery, Kay 1908- 5
Avery, Lynn
   See Cole, Lois Dwight

Avi
   See Wortis, Avi
Ayars, James S(terling) 1898- 4
Ayer, Jacqueline 1930- 13
Ayer, Margaret 15
Aylesworth, Jim 1943- 38
Aylesworth, Thomas G(ibbons)
   1927- 4
   See also CLR 6
Aymar, Brandt 1911- 22
Ayres, Carole Briggs
   See Briggs, Carole S(uzanne)
Ayres, Patricia Miller 1923-1985
   Obituary 46
Azaid
   See Zaidenberg, Arthur

B

B
   See Gilbert, W(illiam) S(chwenk)
B., Tania
   See Blixen, Karen (Christentze
   Dinesen)
BB
   See Watkins-Pitchford, D. J.
Baastad, Babbis Friis
   See Friis-Baastad, Babbis
Bab
   See Gilbert, W(illiam) S(chwenk)
Babbis, Eleanor
   See Friis-Baastad, Babbis
Babbitt, Natalie 1932- 6
   See also CLR 2
   See also SAAS 5
Babcock, Dennis Arthur
   1948- 22
Bach, Alice (Hendricks)
   1942- 30
   Brief Entry 27
Bach, Richard David 1936- 13
Bachman, Fred 1949- 12
Bacmeister, Rhoda W(arner)
   1893- 11
Bacon, Elizabeth 1914- 3
Bacon, Joan Chase
   See Bowden, Joan Chase
Bacon, Josephine Dodge (Daskam)
   1876-1961 48
Bacon, Margaret Frances 1895-1987
   Obituary 50
Bacon, Margaret Hope 1921- 6
Bacon, Martha Sherman
   1917-1981 18
   Obituary 27
   See also CLR 3
Bacon, Peggy 1895- 2
   See also Bacon, Margaret Frances
Bacon, R(onald) L(eonard)
   1924- 26
Baden-Powell, Robert (Stephenson
   Smyth) 1857-1941 16
Baerg, Harry J(ohn) 1909- 12
Bagnold, Enid 1889-1981 25
   Earlier sketch in SATA 1
Bahr, Robert 1940- 38
Bahti, Tom
   Brief Entry 31

Bailey, Alice Cooper 1890- 12
Bailey, Bernadine Freeman 14
Bailey, Carolyn Sherwin
   1875-1961 14
Bailey, Jane H(orton) 1916- 12
Bailey, Maralyn Collins (Harrison)
   1941- 12
Bailey, Matilda
   See Radford, Ruby L.
Bailey, Maurice Charles
   1932- 12
Bailey, Ralph Edgar 1893- 11
Baird, Bil 1904- 30
Baird, Thomas P. 1923- 45
   Brief Entry 39
Baity, Elizabeth Chesley
   1907- 1
Bakeless, John (Edwin) 1894- 9
Bakeless, Katherine Little
   1895- 9
Baker, Alan 1951- 22
Baker, Augusta 1911- 3
Baker, Betty (Lou) 1928- 5
Baker, Charlotte 1910- 2
Baker, Elizabeth 1923- 7
Baker, Eugene H.
   Brief Entry 50
Baker, Gayle C(unningham)
   1950- 39
Baker, James W. 1924- 22
Baker, Janice E(dla) 1941- 22
Baker, Jeannie 1950- 23
Baker, Jeffrey J(ohn) W(heeler)
   1931- 5
Baker, Jim
   See Baker, James W.
Baker, Laura Nelson 1911- 3
Baker, Margaret 1890- 4
Baker, Margaret J(oyce)
   1918- 12
Baker, Mary Gladys Steel
   1892-1974 12
Baker, (Robert) Michael
   1938- 4
Baker, Nina (Brown)
   1888-1957 15
Baker, Rachel 1904-1978 2
   Obituary 26
Baker, Samm Sinclair 1909- 12
Baker, Susan (Catherine)
   1942- 29
Balaam
   See Lamb, G(eoffrey) F(rederick)
Balch, Glenn 1902- 3
Baldridge, Cyrus LeRoy 1889-
   Brief Entry 29
Balducci, Carolyn Feleppa
   1946- 5
Baldwin, Anne Norris 1938- 5
Baldwin, Clara 11
Baldwin, Gordo
   See Baldwin, Gordon C.
Baldwin, Gordon C. 1908- 12
Baldwin, James 1841-1925 24
Baldwin, James (Arthur)
   1924- 9
Baldwin, Margaret
   See Weis, Margaret (Edith)

Baldwin, Stan(ley C.) 1929-
  Brief Entry 28
Bales, Carol Ann 1940-
  Brief Entry 29
Balet, Jan (Bernard) 1913- 11
Balian, Lorna 1929- 9
Ball, Zachary
  See Masters, Kelly R.
Ballantine, Lesley Frost
  See Frost, Lesley
Ballantyne, R(obert) M(ichael)
  1825-1894 24
Ballard, Lowell Clyne
  1904-1986 12
  Obituary 49
Ballard, (Charles) Martin
  1929- 1
Ballard, Mignon Franklin 1934-
  Brief Entry 49
Balogh, Penelope 1916-1975 1
  Obituary 34
Balow, Tom 1931- 12
Baltzer, Hans (Adolf) 1900- 40
Bamfylde, Walter
  See Bevan, Tom
Bamman, Henry A. 1918- 12
Bancroft, Griffing 1907- 6
Bancroft, Laura
  See Baum, L(yman) Frank
Bandel, Betty 1912- 47
Baner, Skulda V(anadis)
  1897-1964 10
Bang, Betsy (Garrett) 1912- 48
  Brief Entry 37
Bang, Garrett
  See Bang, Molly Garrett
Bang, Molly Garrett 1943- 24
  See also CLR 8
Banks, Laura Stockton Voorhees
  1908(?)-1980
  Obituary 23
Banks, Sara (Jeanne Gordon Harrell)
  1937- 26
Banner, Angela
  See Maddison, Angela Mary
Bannerman, Helen (Brodie Cowan
  Watson) 1863(?)-1946 19
Banning, Evelyn I. 1903- 36
Bannon, Laura (?)-1963 6
Barbary, James
  See Baumann, Amy (Brown)
Barbary, James
  See Beeching, Jack
Barbe, Walter Burke 1926- 45
Barber, Antonia
  See Anthony, Barbara
Barber, Linda
  See Graham-Barber, Lynda
Barber, Richard (William)
  1941- 35
Barbera, Joe
  See Barbera, Joseph Roland
Barbera, Joseph Roland 1911- 51
Barbour, Ralph Henry
  1870-1944 16
Barclay, Isabel
  See Dobell, I.M.B.
Bare, Arnold Edwin 1920- 16
Bare, Colleen Stanley 32

Barish, Matthew 1907- 12
Barker, Albert W. 1900- 8
Barker, Carol (Minturn) 1938- 31
Barker, Cicely Mary
  1895-1973 49
  Brief Entry 39
Barker, Melvern 1907- 11
Barker, S. Omar 1894- 10
Barker, Will 1908- 8
Barkhouse, Joyce 1913-
  Brief Entry 48
Barkley, James Edward 1941- 6
Barks, Carl 1901- 37
Barnaby, Ralph S(tanton)
  1893- 9
Barner, Bob 1947- 29
Barnes, (Frank) Eric Wollencott
  1907-1962 22
Barnes, Malcolm 1909(?)-1984
  Obituary 41
Barnett, Lincoln (Kinnear)
  1909-1979 36
Barnett, Moneta 1922-1976 33
Barnett, Naomi 1927- 40
Barney, Maginel Wright
  1881-1966 39
  Brief Entry 32
Barnhart, Clarence L(ewis)
  1900- 48
Barnouw, Adriaan Jacob 1877-1968
  Obituary 27
Barnouw, Victor 1915- 43
  Brief Entry 28
Barnstone, Willis 1927- 20
Barnum, Jay Hyde
  1888(?)-1962 20
Barnum, Richard [Collective
  pseudonym] 1
Baron, Virginia Olsen 1931- 46
  Brief Entry 28
Barr, Donald 1921- 20
Barr, George 1907- 2
Barr, Jene 1900-1985 16
  Obituary 42
Barrer, Gertrude
  See Barrer-Russell, Gertrude
Barrer-Russell, Gertrude
  1921- 27
Barrett, Ethel
  Brief Entry 44
Barrett, Judith 1941- 26
Barrett, Ron 1937- 14
Barrett, William E(dmund) 1900-1986
  Obituary 49
Barrie, J(ames) M(atthew)
  1860-1937 .... YABC 1
Barris, George 1925- 47
Barrol, Grady
  See Bograd, Larry
Barry, James P(otvin) 1918- 14
Barry, Katharina (Watjen)
  1936- 4
Barry, Robert 1931- 6
Barry, Scott 1952- 32
Bartenbach, Jean 1918- 40
Barth, Edna 1914-1980 7
  Obituary 24
Barthelme, Donald 1931- 7

Bartholomew, Barbara 1941-
  Brief Entry 42
Bartlett, Philip A. [Collective
  pseudonym] 1
Bartlett, Robert Merill 1899- 12
Barton, Byron 1930- 9
Barton, Harriett
  Brief Entry 43
Barton, May Hollis [Collective
  pseudonym] 1
  See also Adams, Harriet
  S(tratemeyer)
Bartos-Hoeppner, Barbara
  1923- 5
Bartsch, Jochen 1906- 39
Baruch, Dorothy W(alter)
  1899-1962 21
Bas, Rutger
  See Rutgers van der Loeff, An(na)
  Basenau
Bashevis, Isaac
  See Singer, Isaac Bashevis
Baskin, Leonard 1922- 30
  Brief Entry 27
Bason, Lillian 1913- 20
Bassett, Jeni 1960(?)-
  Brief Entry 43
Bassett, John Keith
  See Keating, Lawrence A.
Batchelor, Joy 1914-
  Brief Entry 29
Bate, Lucy 1939- 18
Bate, Norman 1916- 5
Bates, Barbara S(nedeker)
  1919- 12
Bates, Betty 1921- 19
Batey, Tom 1946-
  Brief Entry 41
Batherman, Muriel
  See Sheldon, Muriel
Batiuk, Thomas M(artin) 1947-
  Brief Entry 40
Batson, Larry 1930- 35
Battaglia, Aurelius 1910- 50
  Brief Entry 33
Batten, H(arry) Mortimer
  1888-1958 25
Batten, Mary 1937- 5
Batterberry, Ariane Ruskin
  1935- 13
Batterberry, Michael (Carver)
  1932- 32
Battles, Edith 1921- 7
Baudouy, Michel-Aime 1909- 7
Bauer, Caroline Feller 1935-
  Brief Entry 46
Bauer, Fred 1934- 36
Bauer, Helen 1900- 2
Bauer, Marion Dane 1938- 20
Bauernschmidt, Marjorie
  1926- 15
Baum, Allyn Z(elton) 1924- 20
Baum, L(yman) Frank
  1856-1919 18
Baum, Willi 1931- 4
Baumann, Amy (Brown)
  1922- 10
Baumann, Elwood D.
  Brief Entry 33

Baumann, Hans 1914- 2
Baumann, Kurt 1935- *21*
Bawden, Nina
  See Kark, Nina Mary
  See also CLR 2
Bayer, Jane E. (?)-1985
  Obituary *44*
Bayley, Nicola 1949- *41*
Baylor, Byrd 1924- *16*
  See also CLR 3
Baynes, Pauline (Diana)
  1922- *19*
Beach, Charles
  See Reid, (Thomas) Mayne
Beach, Charles Amory [Collective
  pseudonym] *1*
Beach, Edward L(atimer)
  1918- *12*
Beach, Stewart Taft 1899- *23*
Beachcroft, Nina 1931- *18*
Bealer, Alex W(inkler III)
  1921-1980 8
  Obituary *22*
Beals, Carleton 1893- *12*
Beals, Frank Lee 1881-1972
  Obituary *26*
Beame, Rona 1934- *12*
Beamer, (G.) Charles, (Jr.)
  1942- *43*
Beaney, Jan
  See Udall, Jan Beaney
Beard, Charles Austin
  1874-1948 .... *18*
Beard, Dan(iel Carter)
  1850-1941 .... *22*
Bearden, Romare (Howard)
  1914- *22*
Beardmore, Cedric
  See Beardmore, George
Beardmore, George
  1908-1979 .... *20*
Bearman, Jane (Ruth) 1917- *29*
Beatty, Elizabeth
  See Holloway, Teresa (Bragunier)
Beatty, Hetty Burlingame
  1907-1971 5
Beatty, Jerome, Jr. 1918- 5
Beatty, John (Louis)
  1922-1975 6
  Obituary *25*
Beatty, Patricia (Robbins)
  1922- *30*
  Earlier sketch in SATA 1
  See also SAAS 4
Bechtel, Louise Seaman
  1894-1985 4
  Obituary *43*
Beck, Barbara L. 1927- *12*
Becker, Beril 1901- *11*
Becker, John (Leonard) 1901- *12*
Becker, Joyce 1936- *39*
Becker, May Lamberton
  1873-1958 .... *33*
Beckett, Sheilah 1913- *33*
Beckman, Delores 1914- *51*
Beckman, Gunnel 1910- 6
Beckman, Kaj
  See Beckman, Karin
Beckman, Karin 1913- *45*

Beckman, Per (Frithiof) 1913- *45*
Bedford, A. N.
  See Watson, Jane Werner
Bedford, Annie North
  See Watson, Jane Werner
Beebe, B(urdetta) F(aye)
  1920- *1*
Beebe, (Charles) William
  1877-1962 .... *19*
Beeby, Betty 1923- *25*
Beech, Webb
  See Butterworth, W. E.
Beeching, Jack 1922- *14*
Beeler, Nelson F(rederick)
  1910- *13*
Beers, Dorothy Sands 1917- 9
Beers, Lorna 1897- *14*
Beers, V(ictor) Gilbert 1928- 9
Begley, Kathleen A(nne)
  1948- *21*
Behn, Harry 1898-1973 2
  Obituary *34*
Behnke, Frances L. 8
Behr, Joyce 1929- *15*
Behrens, June York 1925- *19*
Behrman, Carol H(elen) 1925- *14*
Beiser, Arthur 1931- *22*
Beiser, Germaine 1931- *11*
Belair, Richard L. 1934- *45*
Belaney, Archibald Stansfeld
  1888-1938 .... *24*
Belknap, B. H.
  See Ellis, Edward S(ylvester)
Bell, Corydon 1894- 3
Bell, Emily Mary
  See Cason, Mabel Earp
Bell, Gertrude (Wood) 1911- *12*
Bell, Gina
  See Iannone, Jeanne
Bell, Janet
  See Clymer, Eleanor
Bell, Margaret E(lizabeth)
  1898- 2
Bell, Neill 1946-
  Brief Entry *50*
Bell, Norman (Edward) 1899- *11*
Bell, Raymond Martin 1907- *13*
Bell, Robert S(tanley) W(arren)
  1871-1921
  Brief Entry *27*
Bell, Thelma Harrington
  1896- 3
Bellairs, John 1938- 2
Bellingham, Brenda 1931-
  Brief Entry *51*
Belloc, (Joseph) Hilaire (Pierre)
  1870-1953 ....*YABC 1*
Bellville, Cheryl Walsh 1944-
  Brief Entry *49*
Bell-Zano, Gina
  See Iannone, Jeanne
Belpré, Pura 1899-1982 .... *16*
  Obituary *30*
Belting, Natalie Maree 1915- 6
Belton, John Raynor 1931- *22*
Beltran, Alberto 1923- *43*
Belvedere, Lee
  See Grayland, Valerie

Bemelmans, Ludwig
  1898-1962 .... *15*
  See also CLR 6
Benary, Margot
  See Benary-Isbert, Margot
Benary-Isbert, Margot
  1889-1979 2
  Obituary *21*
  See also CLR 12
Benasutti, Marion 1908- 6
Benchley, Nathaniel (Goddard)
  1915-1981 .... *25*
  Obituary *28*
  Earlier sketch in SATA 3
Benchley, Peter 1940- 3
Bender, Lucy Ellen 1942- *22*
Bendick, Jeanne 1919- 2
  See also CLR 5
  See also SAAS 4
Bendick, Robert L(ouis)
  1917- *11*
Benedict, Dorothy Potter
  1889-1979 .... *11*
  Obituary *23*
Benedict, Lois Trimble
  1902-1967 .... *12*
Benedict, Rex 1920- 8
Benedict, Stewart H(urd)
  1924- *26*
Benét, Laura 1884-1979 3
  Obituary *23*
Benét, Stephen Vincent
  1898-1943 ....*YABC 1*
Benet, Sula 1903(?)-1982 .... *21*
  Obituary *33*
Benezra, Barbara 1921- *10*
Benham, Leslie 1922- *48*
Benham, Lois (Dakin) 1924- *48*
Benjamin, Nora
  See Kubie, Nora (Gottheil) Benjamin
Bennett, Dorothea
  See Young, Dorothea Bennett
Bennett, Jay 1912- *41*
  Brief Entry *27*
  See also SAAS 4
Bennett, Jill (Crawford) 1934- *41*
Bennett, John 1865-1956 .....*YABC 1*
Bennett, Rachel
  See Hill, Margaret (Ohler)
Bennett, Rainey 1907- *15*
Bennett, Richard 1899- *21*
Bennett, Russell H(oradley)
  1896- *25*
Benson, Sally 1900-1972 .... *35*
  Obituary *27*
  Earlier sketch in SATA 1
Bentley, Judith (McBride)
  1945- *40*
Bentley, Nicolas Clerihew 1907-1978
  Obituary *24*
Bentley, Phyllis (Eleanor)
  1894-1977 6
  Obituary *25*
Bentley, Roy 1947- *46*
Berelson, Howard 1940- 5
Berends, Polly B(errien)
  1939- *50*
  Brief Entry *38*
Berenstain, Janice *12*

Berenstain, Michael 1951-
   Brief Entry 45
Berenstain, Stan(ley) 1923- 12
Beresford, Elisabeth 25
Berg, Björn 1923-
   Brief Entry 47
Berg, Dave
   See Berg, David
Berg, David 1920- 27
Berg, Jean Horton 1913- 6
Berg, Joan
   See Victor, Joan Berg
Berg, Ron 1952- 48
Bergaust, Erik 1925-1978 20
Berger, Gilda
   Brief Entry 42
Berger, Josef 1903-1971 36
Berger, Melvin H. 1927- 5
   See also SAAS 2
Berger, Terry 1933- 8
Bergey, Alyce (Mae) 1934- 45
Berkebile, Fred D(onovan) 1900-1978
   Obituary 26
Berkey, Barry Robert 1935- 24
Berkowitz, Freda Pastor 1910- 12
Berliner, Don 1930- 33
Berliner, Franz 1930- 13
Berlitz, Charles L. (Frambach)
   1913- 32
Berman, Linda 1948- 38
Berna, Paul 1910- 15
Bernadette
   See Watts, Bernadette
Bernard, George I. 1949- 39
Bernard, Jacqueline (de Sieyes)
   1921-1983 8
   Obituary 45
Bernays, Anne
   See Kaplan, Anne Bernays
Bernstein, Joanne E(ckstein)
   1943- 15
Bernstein, Theodore M(enline)
   1904-1979 12
   Obituary 27
Berrien, Edith Heal
   See Heal, Edith
Berrill, Jacquelyn (Batsel)
   1905- 12
Berrington, John
   See Brownjohn, Alan
Berry, B. J.
   See Berry, Barbara J.
Berry, Barbara J. 1937- 7
Berry, Erick
   See Best, Allena Champlin
Berry, Jane Cobb 1915(?)-1979
   Obituary 22
Berry, Joy Wilt
   Brief Entry 46
Berry, William D(avid) 1926- 14
Berson, Harold 1926- 4
Berwick, Jean
   See Meyer, Jean Shepherd
Beskow, Elsa (Maartman)
   1874-1953 20
Best, (Evangel) Allena Champlin
   1892-1974 2
   Obituary 25
Best, (Oswald) Herbert 1894- 2

Bestall, Alfred (Edmeades) 1892-1986
   Obituary 48
Betancourt, Jeanne 1941-
   Brief Entry 43
Beth, Mary
   See Miller, Mary Beth
Bethancourt, T. Ernesto 1932- 11
   See also CLR 3
Bethell, Jean (Frankenberry)
   1922- 8
Bethers, Ray 1902- 6
Bethune, J. G.
   See Ellis, Edward S(ylvester)
Betteridge, Anne
   See Potter, Margaret (Newman)
Bettina
   See Ehrlich, Bettina
Bettmann, Otto Ludwig 1903- 46
Betts, James [Joint pseudonym]
   See Haynes, Betsy
Betz, Eva Kelly 1897-1968 10
Bevan, Tom
   1868-1930(?) .... YABC 2
Bewick, Thomas 1753-1828 16
Beyer, Audrey White 1916- 9
Bezencon, Jacqueline (Buxcel)
   1924- 48
Bhatia, June
   See Forrester, Helen
Bialk, Elisa 1
Bianco, Margery (Williams)
   1881-1944 15
Bianco, Pamela 1906- 28
Bibby, Violet 1908- 24
Bible, Charles 1937- 13
Bice, Clare 1909-1976 22
Bickerstaff, Isaac
   See Swift, Jonathan
Biegel, Paul 1925- 16
Biemiller, Carl L(udwig)
   1912-1979 40
   Obituary 21
Bienenfeld, Florence L(ucille)
   1929- 39
Bierhorst, John 1936- 6
Bileck, Marvin 1920- 40
Bill, Alfred Hoyt 1879-1964 44
Billings, Charlene W(interer)
   1941- 41
Billington, Elizabeth T(hain) 50
   Brief Entry 43
Billout, Guy René 1941- 10
Binkley, Anne
   See Rand, Ann (Binkley)
Binzen, Bill 24
Binzen, William
   See Binzen, Bill
Birch, Reginald B(athurst)
   1856-1943 19
Birmingham, Lloyd 1924- 12
Biro, Val 1921- 1
Bischoff, Julia Bristol
   1909-1970 12
Bishop, Bonnie 1943- 37
Bishop, Claire (Huchet) 14
Bishop, Curtis 1912-1967 6
Bishop, Elizabeth 1911-1979
   Obituary 24
Bisset, Donald 1910- 7

Bitter, Gary G(len) 1940- 22
Bixby, William (Courtney)
   1920-1986 6
   Obituary 47
Bjerregaard-Jensen, Vilhelm Hans
   See Hillcourt, William
Bjorklund, Lorence F.
   1913-1978 35
   Brief Entry 32
Black, Algernon David 1900- 12
Black, Irma S(imonton)
   1906-1972 2
   Obituary 25
Black, Mansell
   See Trevor, Elleston
Black, Susan Adams 1953- 40
Blackburn, Claire
   See Jacobs, Linda C.
Blackburn, John(ny) Brewton
   1952- 15
Blackburn, Joyce Knight
   1920- 29
Blackett, Veronica Heath
   1927- 12
Blackton, Peter
   See Wilson, Lionel
Blades, Ann 1947- 16
Bladow, Suzanne Wilson
   1937- 14
Blaine, John
   See Goodwin, Harold Leland
Blaine, John
   See Harkins, Philip
Blaine, Margery Kay 1937- 11
Blair, Anne Denton 1914- 46
Blair, Eric Arthur 1903-1950 29
Blair, Helen 1910-
   Brief Entry 29
Blair, Jay 1953- 45
Blair, Ruth Van Ness 1912- 12
Blair, Walter 1900- 12
Blake, Olive
   See Supraner, Robyn
Blake, Quentin 1932- 9
Blake, Robert 1949- 42
Blake, Walker E.
   See Butterworth, W. E.
Blake, William 1757-1827 30
Bland, Edith Nesbit
   See Nesbit, E(dith)
Bland, Fabian [Joint pseudonym]
   See Nesbit, E(dith)
Blane, Gertrude
   See Blumenthal, Gertrude
Blassingame, Wyatt Rainey
   1909-1985 34
   Obituary 41
   Earlier sketch in SATA 1
Blauer, Ettagale 1940- 49
Bleeker, Sonia 1909-1971 2
   Obituary 26
Blegvad, Erik 1923- 14
Blegvad, Lenore 1926- 14
Blishen, Edward 1920- 8
Bliss, Corinne D(emas) 1947- 37
Bliss, Reginald
   See Wells, H(erbert) G(eorge)
Bliss, Ronald G(ene) 1942- 12
Bliven, Bruce, Jr. 1916- 2

Blixen, Karen (Christentze Dinesen)
1885-1962 44
Bloch, Luciennc 1909- 10
Bloch, Marie Halun 1910- 6
Bloch, Robert 1917- 12
Blochman, Lawrence G(oldtree)
1900-1975 22
Block, Irvin 1917- 12
Blocksma, Mary
Brief Entry 44
Blood, Charles Lewis 1929- 28
Bloom, Freddy 1914- 37
Bloom, Lloyd
Brief Entry 43
Blos, Joan W(insor) 1928- 33
Brief Entry 27
Blough, Glenn O(rlando)
1907- 1
Blue, Rose 1931- 5
Blumberg, Rhoda 1917- 35
Blume, Judy (Sussman) 1938- 31
Earlier sketch in SATA 2
See also CLR 2
Blumenthal, Gertrude 1907-1971
Obituary 27
Blumenthal, Shirley 1943- 46
Blutig, Eduard
See Gorey, Edward St. John
Bly, Janet Chester 1945- 43
Bly, Robert W(ayne) 1957-
Brief Entry 48
Bly, Stephen A(rthur) 1944- 43
Blyton, Carey 1932- 9
Blyton, Enid (Mary)
1897-1968 25
Boardman, Fon Wyman, Jr.
1911- 6
Boardman, Gwenn R. 1924- 12
Boase, Wendy 1944- 28
Boatner, Mark Mayo III
1921- 29
Bobbe, Dorothie 1905-1975 1
Obituary 25
Bobri
See Bobritsky, Vladimir
Bobri, Vladimir
See Bobritsky, Vladimir
Bobritsky, Vladimir 1898- 47
Brief Entry 32
Bock, Hal
See Bock, Harold I.
Bock, Harold I. 1939- 10
Bock, William Sauts
Netamux'we 14
Bodecker, N. M. 1922- 8
Boden, Hilda
See Bodenham, Hilda Esther
Bodenham, Hilda Esther
1901- 13
Bodie, Idella F(allaw) 1925- 12
Bodker, Cecil 1927- 14
Bodsworth, (Charles) Fred(erick)
1918- 27
Boeckman, Charles 1920- 12
Boegehold, Betty (Doyle) 1913-1985
Obituary 42
Boesch, Mark J(oseph) 1917- 12
Boesen, Victor 1908- 16
Boggs, Ralph Steele 1901- 7

Bograd, Larry 1953- 33
Bohdal, Susi 1951- 22
Boles, Paul Darcy 1916-1984 9
Obituary 38
Bolian, Polly 1925- 4
Bollen, Roger 1941(?)-
Brief Entry 29
Bolliger, Max 1929- 7
Bolognese, Don(ald Alan)
1934- 24
Bolton, Carole 1926- 6
Bolton, Elizabeth
See Johnston, Norma
Bolton, Evelyn
See Bunting, Anne Evelyn
Bond, Felicia 1954- 49
Bond, Gladys Baker 1912- 14
Bond, J. Harvey
See Winterbotham, R(ussell)
R(obert)
Bond, Michael 1926- 6
See also CLR 1
See also SAAS 3
Bond, Nancy (Barbara) 1945- 22
See also CLR 11
Bond, Ruskin 1934- 14
Bonehill, Captain Ralph
See Stratemeyer, Edward L.
Bonestell, Chesley 1888-1986
Obituary 48
Bonham, Barbara 1926- 7
Bonham, Frank 1914- 49
Earlier sketch in SATA 1
See also SAAS 3
Bonn, Pat
See Bonn, Patricia Carolyn
Bonn, Patricia Carolyn 1948- 43
Bonner, Mary Graham
1890-1974 19
Bonners, Susan
Brief Entry 48
Bonsall, Crosby (Barbara Newell)
1921- 23
Bontemps, Arna 1902-1973 44
Obituary 24
Earlier sketch in SATA 2
See also CLR 6
Bonzon, Paul-Jacques 1908- 22
Booher, Dianna Daniels 1948- 33
Bookman, Charlotte
See Zolotow, Charlotte S.
Boone, Pat 1934- 7
Boorman, Linda (Kay) 1940- 46
Booth, Ernest Sheldon
1915-1984 43
Booth, Graham (Charles)
1935- 37
Bordier, Georgette 1924- 16
Boring, Mel 1939- 35
Borja, Corinne 1929- 22
Borja, Robert 1923- 22
Borland, Hal 1900-1978 5
Obituary 24
Borland, Harold Glen
See Borland, Hal
Borland, Kathryn Kilby 1916- 16
Born, Adolf 1930- 49
Bornstein, Ruth 1927- 14
Borski, Lucia Merecka 18

Borten, Helen Jacobson 1930- 5
Borton, Elizabeth
See Treviño, Elizabeth B. de
Bortstein, Larry 1942- 16
Bosco, Jack
See Holliday, Joseph
Boshell, Gordon 1908- 15
Boshinski, Blanche 1922- 10
Bosse, Malcolm J(oseph)
1926- 35
Bossom, Naomi 1933- 35
Boston, Lucy Maria (Wood)
1892- 19
See also CLR 3
Bosworth, J. Allan 1925- 19
Bothwell, Jean 2
Botkin, B(enjamin) A(lbert)
1901-1975 40
Botting, Douglas (Scott)
1934- 43
Bottner, Barbara 1943- 14
Boulet, Susan Seddon 1941- 50
Boulle, Pierre (Francois Marie-Louis)
1912- 22
Bourdon, David 1934- 46
Bourne, Leslie
See Marshall, Evelyn
Bourne, Miriam Anne 1931- 16
Boutet De Monvel, (Louis) M(aurice)
1850(?)-1913 30
Bova, Ben 1932- 6
See also CLR 3
Bowden, Joan Chase 1925- 51
Brief Entry 38
Bowen, Betty Morgan
See West, Betty
Bowen, Catherine Drinker
1897-1973 7
Bowen, David
See Bowen, Joshua David
Bowen, Joshua David 1930- 22
Bowen, Robert Sidney 1900(?)-1977
Obituary 21
Bowie, Jim
See Stratemeyer, Edward L.
Bowler, Jan Brett
See Brett, Jan
Bowman, James Cloyd
1880-1961 23
Bowman, John S(tewart)
1931- 16
Bowman, Kathleen (Gill) 1942-
Brief Entry 40
Boyce, George A(rthur) 1898- 19
Boyd, Pauline
See Schock, Pauline
Boyd, Selma
See Acuff, Selma Boyd
Boyd, Waldo T. 1918- 18
Boyer, Robert E(rnst) 1929- 22
Boyle, Ann (Peters) 1916- 10
Boyle, Eleanor Vere (Gordon)
1825-1916 28
Boylston, Helen (Dore)
1895-1984 23
Obituary 39
Boynton, Sandra 1953-
Brief Entry 38

Boz
  See Dickens, Charles
Bradbury, Bianca 1908- 3
Bradbury, Ray (Douglas)
  1920- 11
Bradford, Ann (Liddell) 1917-
  Brief Entry 38
Bradford, Karleen 1936- 48
Bradford, Lois J(ean) 1936- 36
Bradley, Duane
  See Sanborn, Duane
Bradley, Virginia 1912- 23
Brady, Esther Wood 1905- 31
Brady, Irene 1943- 4
Brady, Lillian 1902- 28
Bragdon, Elspeth 1897- 6
Bragdon, Lillian (Jacot) 24
Bragg, Mabel Caroline
  1870-1945 24
Bragg, Michael 1948- 46
Braithwaite, Althea 1940- 23
Bram, Elizabeth 1948- 30
Brancato, Robin F(idler)
  1936- 23
Brandenberg, Aliki (Liacouras)
  1929- 35
  Earlier sketch in SATA 2
Brandenberg, Franz 1932- 35
  Earlier sketch in SATA 8
Brandhorst, Carl T(heodore)
  1898- 23
Brandon, Brumsic, Jr. 1927- 9
Brandon, Curt
  See Bishop, Curtis
Brandreth, Gyles 1948- 28
Brandt, Catharine 1905- 40
Brandt, Keith
  See Sabin, Louis
Branfield, John (Charles)
  1931- 11
Branley, Franklyn M(ansfield)
  1915- 4
  See also CLR 13
Branscum, Robbie 1937- 23
Bransom, (John) Paul
  1885-1979 43
Bratton, Helen 1899- 4
Braude, Michael 1936- 23
Braymer, Marjorie 1911- 6
Brecht, Edith 1895-1975 6
  Obituary 25
Breck, Vivian
  See Breckenfeld, Vivian Gurney
Breckenfeld, Vivian Gurney
  1895- 1
Breda, Tjalmar
  See DeJong, David C(ornel)
Breinburg, Petronella 1927- 11
Breisky, William J(ohn) 1928- 22
Brennan, Joseph L. 1903- 6
Brennan, Tim
  See Conroy, Jack (Wesley)
Brenner, Barbara (Johnes)
  1925- 42
  Earlier sketch in SATA 4
Brenner, Fred 1920- 36
  Brief Entry 34
Brent, Hope 1935(?)-1984
  Obituary 39

Brent, Stuart 14
Brett, Bernard 1925- 22
Brett, Grace N(eff) 1900-1975 23
Brett, Hawksley
  See Bell, Robert S(tanley) W(arren)
Brett, Jan 1949- 42
Brewer, Sally King 1947- 33
Brewster, Benjamin
  See Folsom, Franklin
Brewster, Patience 1952- 51
Brewton, John E(dmund)
  1898- 5
Brick, John 1922-1973 10
Bridgers, Sue Ellen 1942- 22
  See also SAAS 1
Bridges, Laurie
  See Bruck, Lorraine
Bridges, William (Andrew)
  1901- 5
Bridwell, Norman 1928- 4
Brier, Howard M(axwell)
  1903-1969 8
Briggs, Carole S(uzanne) 1950-
  Brief Entry 47
Briggs, Katharine Mary 1898-1980
  Obituary 25
Briggs, Peter 1921-1975 39
  Obituary 31
Briggs, Raymond (Redvers)
  1934- 23
  See also CLR 10
Bright, Robert 1902- 24
Brightwell, L(eonard) R(obert) 1889-
  Brief Entry 29
Brimberg, Stanlee 1947- 9
Brin, Ruth F(irestone) 1921- 22
Brinckloe, Julie (Lorraine)
  1950- 13
Brindel, June (Rachuy) 1919- 7
Brindze, Ruth 1903- 23
Brink, Carol Ryrie 1895-1981 31
  Obituary 27
  Earlier sketch in SATA 1
Brinsmead, H(esba) F(ay)
  1922- 18
  See also SAAS 5
Briquebec, John
  See Rowland-Entwistle, (Arthur)
  Theodore (Henry)
Brisco, Pat A.
  See Matthews, Patricia
Brisco, Patty
  See Matthews, Patricia
Briscoe, Jill (Pauline) 1935-
  Brief Entry 47
Brisley, Joyce Lankester
  1896- 22
Britt, Albert 1874-1969
  Obituary 28
Britt, Dell 1934- 1
Brittain, William 1930- 36
Britton, Kate
  See Stegeman, Janet Allais
Britton, Louisa
  See McGuire, Leslie (Sarah)
Bro, Marguerite (Harmon)
  1894-1977 19
  Obituary 27

Broadhead, Helen Cross
  1913- 25
Brochmann, Elizabeth (Anne)
  1938- 41
Brock, Betty 1923- 7
Brock, C(harles) E(dmund)
  1870-1938 42
  Brief Entry 32
Brock, Delia
  See Ephron, Delia
Brock, Emma L(illian)
  1886-1974 8
Brock, H(enry) M(atthew)
  1875-1960 42
Brockett, Eleanor Hall
  1913-1967 10
Brockman, C(hristian) Frank
  1902- 26
Broderick, Dorothy M. 1929- 5
Brodie, Sally
  See Cavin, Ruth (Brodie)
Broekel, Rainer Lothar 1923- 38
Broekel, Ray
  See Broekel, Rainer Lothar
Bröger, Achim 1944- 31
Brokamp, Marilyn 1920- 10
Bromhall, Winifred 26
Bromley, Dudley 1948-
  Brief Entry 51
Brommer, Gerald F(rederick)
  1927- 28
Brondfield, Jerome 1913- 22
Brondfield, Jerry
  See Brondfield, Jerome
Bronson, Lynn
  See Lampman, Evelyn Sibley
Bronson, Wilfrid Swancourt
  1894-1985
  Obituary 43
Brook, Judith Penelope 1926-
  Brief Entry 51
Brook, Judy
  See Brook, Judith Penelope
Brooke, L(eonard) Leslie
  1862-1940 17
Brooke-Haven, P.
  See Wodehouse, P(elham)
  G(renville)
Brookins, Dana 1931- 28
Brooks, Anita 1914- 5
Brooks, Barbara
  See Simons, Barbara B(rooks)
Brooks, Charlotte K. 24
Brooks, Gwendolyn 1917- 6
Brooks, Jerome 1931- 23
Brooks, Lester 1924- 7
Brooks, Maurice (Graham)
  1900- 45
Brooks, Polly Schoyer 1912- 12
Brooks, Ron(ald George) 1948-
  Brief Entry 33
Brooks, Walter R(ollin)
  1886-1958 17
Brosnan, James Patrick 1929- 14
Brosnan, Jim
  See Brosnan, James Patrick
Broun, Emily
  See Sterne, Emma Gelders
Brower, Millicent 8

Brower, Pauline (York) 1929- 22
Browin, Frances Williams
1898- 5
Brown, Alexis
See Baumann, Amy (Brown)
Brown, Bill
See Brown, William L.
Brown, Billye Walker
See Cutchen, Billye Walker
Brown, Bob
See Brown, Robert Joseph
Brown, Buck 1936- 45
Brown, Conrad 1922- 31
Brown, David
See Myller, Rolf
Brown, Dee (Alexander)
1908- 5
Brown, Eleanor Frances 1908- 3
Brown, Elizabeth M(yers)
1915- 43
Brown, Fern G. 1918- 34
Brown, (Robert) Fletch 1923- 42
Brown, George Earl
1883-1964 11
Brown, George Mackay 1921- ... 35
Brown, Irene Bennett 1932- 3
Brown, Irving
See Adams, William Taylor
Brown, Ivor (John Carnegie)
1891-1974 5
Obituary 26
Brown, Joe David 1915-1976 44
Brown, Joseph E(dward) 1929-
Brief Entry 51
Brown, Judith Gwyn 1933- 20
Brown, Lloyd Arnold
1907-1966 36
Brown, Marc Tolon 1946- 10
Brown, Marcia 1918- 47
Earlier sketch in SATA 7
See also CLR 12
Brown, Margaret Wise
1910-1952 .... YABC 2
See also CLR 10
Brown, Margery 5
Brown, Marion Marsh 1908- 6
Brown, Myra Berry 1918- 6
Brown, Palmer 1919- 36
Brown, Pamela 1924- 5
Brown, Robert Joseph 1907- 14
Brown, Rosalie (Gertrude) Moore
1910- 9
Brown, Roswell
See Webb, Jean Francis (III)
Brown, Roy (Frederick)
1921-1982 51
Obituary 39
Brown, Vinson 1912- 19
Brown, Walter R(eed) 1929- 19
Brown, Will
See Ainsworth, William Harrison
Brown, William L(ouis)
1910-1964 5
Browne, Anthony (Edward Tudor)
1946- 45
Brief Entry 44
Browne, Dik
See Browne, Richard

Browne, Hablot Knight
1815-1882 21
Browne, Matthew
See Rands, William Brighty
Browne, Richard 1917-
Brief Entry 38
Browning, Robert
1812-1889 .... YABC 1
Brownjohn, Alan 1931- 6
Bruce, Dorita Fairlie 1885-1970
Obituary 27
Bruce, Mary 1927- 1
Bruchac, Joseph III 1942- 42
Bruck, Lorraine 1921-
Brief Entry 46
Bruemmer, Fred 1929- 47
Bruna, Dick 1927- 43
Brief Entry 30
See also CLR 7
Brunhoff, Jean de 1899-1937 24
See also CLR 4
Brunhoff, Laurent de 1925- 24
See also CLR 4
Brustlein, Daniel 1904- 40
Brustlein, Janice Tworkov 40
Bryan, Ashley F. 1923- 31
Bryan, Dorothy (Marie) 1896(?)-1984
Obituary 39
Bryant, Bernice (Morgan)
1908- 11
Brychta, Alex 1956- 21
Bryson, Bernarda 1905- 9
Buba, Joy Flinsch 1904- 44
Buchan, Bryan 1945- 36
Buchan, John 1875-1940 ..... YABC 2
Buchheimer, Naomi Barnett
See Barnett, Naomi
Buchwald, Art(hur) 1925- 10
Buchwald, Emilie 1935- 7
Buck, Lewis 1925- 18
Buck, Margaret Waring 1910- 3
Buck, Pearl S(ydenstricker)
1892-1973 25
Earlier sketch in SATA 1
Buckeridge, Anthony 1912- 6
Buckholtz, Eileen (Garber) 1949-
Brief Entry 47
Buckler, Ernest 1908-1984 47
Buckley, Helen E(lizabeth)
1918- 2
Buckmaster, Henrietta 6
Budd, Lillian 1897- 7
Buehr, Walter 1897-1971 3
Buff, Conrad 1886-1975 19
Buff, Mary Marsh 1890-1970 19
Bugbee, Emma 1888(?)-1981
Obituary 29
Bulfinch, Thomas 1796-1867 35
Bull, Angela (Mary) 1936- 45
Bull, Norman John 1916- 41
Bull, Peter (Cecil) 1912-1984
Obituary 39
Bulla, Clyde Robert 1914- 41
Earlier sketch in SATA 2
Bunin, Catherine 1967- 30
Bunin, Sherry 1925- 30
Bunting, A. E.
See Bunting, Anne Evelyn
Bunting, Anne Evelyn 1928- 18

Bunting, Eve
See Bunting, Anne Evelyn
Bunting, Glenn (Davison)
1957- 22
Burack, Sylvia K. 1916- 35
Burbank, Addison (Buswell)
1895-1961 37
Burch, Robert J(oseph) 1925- 1
Burchard, Peter D(uncan) 5
Burchard, Sue 1937- 22
Burchardt, Nellie 1921- 7
Burdick, Eugene (Leonard)
1918-1965 22
Burford, Eleanor
See Hibbert, Eleanor
Burger, Carl 1888-1967 9
Burgess, Anne Marie
See Gerson, Noel B(ertram)
Burgess, Em
See Burgess, Mary Wyche
Burgess, (Frank) Gelett
1866-1951 32
Brief Entry 30
Burgess, Mary Wyche 1916- 18
Burgess, Michael
See Gerson, Noel B(ertram)
Burgess, Robert F(orrest)
1927- 4
Burgess, Thornton W(aldo)
1874-1965 17
Burgess, Trevor
See Trevor, Elleston
Burgwyn, Mebane H. 1914- 7
Burke, David 1927- 46
Burke, John
See O'Connor, Richard
Burkert, Nancy Ekholm 1933- 24
Burland, Brian (Berkeley)
1931- 34
Burland, C. A.
See Burland, Cottie A.
Burland, Cottie A. 1905- 5
Burlingame, (William) Roger
1889-1967 2
Burman, Alice Caddy 1896(?)-1977
Obituary 24
Burman, Ben Lucien
1896-1984 6
Obituary 40
Burn, Doris 1923- 1
Burnett, Constance Buel
1893-1975 36
Burnett, Frances (Eliza) Hodgson
1849-1924 .... YABC 2
Burnford, S. D.
See Burnford, Sheila
Burnford, Sheila 1918-1984 3
Obituary 38
See also CLR 2
Burningham, John (Mackintosh)
1936- 16
See also CLR 9
Burns, Marilyn
Brief Entry 33
Burns, Paul C. 5
Burns, Raymond (Howard)
1924- 9
Burns, William A. 1909- 5
Burr, Lonnie 1943- 47

Burroughs, Edgar Rice
  1875-1950 .... *41*
Burroughs, Jean Mitchell
  1908- *28*
Burroughs, Polly 1925- *2*
Burroway, Janet (Gay) 1936- *23*
Burstein, John 1949-
  Brief Entry *40*
Burt, Jesse Clifton 1921-1976 ..... *46*
  Obituary *20*
Burt, Olive Woolley 1894- *4*
Burton, Hester 1913- *7*
  See also CLR 1
Burton, Leslie
  See McGuire, Leslie (Sarah)
Burton, Marilee Robin 1950- *46*
Burton, Maurice 1898- *23*
Burton, Robert (Wellesley)
  1941- *22*
Burton, Virginia Lee
  1909-1968 .... *2*
  See also CLR 11
Burton, William H(enry)
  1890-1964 .... *11*
Busby, Edith (?)-1964
  Obituary *29*
Busch, Phyllis S. 1909- *30*
Bushmiller, Ernie 1905-1982
  Obituary *31*
Busoni, Rafaello 1900-1962 .... *16*
Butler, Beverly 1932- *7*
Butler, Suzanne
  See Perreard, Suzanne Louise Butler
Butters, Dorothy Gilman
  1923- *5*
Butterworth, Emma Macalik
  1928- *43*
Butterworth, Oliver 1915- *1*
Butterworth, W(illiam) E(dmund III)
  1929- *5*
Byars, Betsy (Cromer) 1928- *46*
  Earlier sketch in SATA 4
  See also CLR 1
  See also SAAS 1
Byfield, Barbara Ninde 1930- *8*
Byrd, Elizabeth 1912- *34*
Byrd, Robert (John) 1942- *33*

C

C.3.3.
  See Wilde, Oscar (Fingal O'Flahertie
    Wills)
Cable, Mary 1920- *9*
Cabral, O. M.
  See Cabral, Olga
Cabral, Olga 1909- *46*
Caddy, Alice
  See Burman, Alice Caddy
Cadwallader, Sharon 1936- *7*
Cady, (Walter) Harrison
  1877-1970 .... *19*
Cagle, Malcolm W(infield)
  1918- *32*
Cahn, Rhoda 1922- *37*
Cahn, William 1912-1976 .... *37*
Cain, Arthur H. 1913- *3*

Cain, Christopher
  See Fleming, Thomas J(ames)
Caines, Jeanette (Franklin)
  Brief Entry *43*
Cairns, Trevor 1922- *14*
Caldecott, Moyra 1927- *22*
Caldecott, Randolph (J.)
  1846-1886 .... *17*
Calder, Lyn
  See Calmenson, Stephanie
Caldwell, John C(ope) 1913- *7*
Calhoun, Mary (Huiskamp)
  1926- *2*
Calkins, Franklin
  See Stratemeyer, Edward L.
Call, Hughie Florence
  1890-1969 .... *1*
Callahan, Dorothy M. 1934- *39*
  Brief Entry *35*
Callahan, Philip S(erna) 1923- *25*
Callaway, Bernice (Anne)
  1923- *48*
Callaway, Kathy 1943- *36*
Callen, Larry
  See Callen, Lawrence Willard, Jr.
Callen, Lawrence Willard, Jr.
  1927- *19*
Calmenson, Stephanie 1952- *51*
  Brief Entry *37*
Calvert, John
  See Leaf, (Wilbur) Munro
Calvert, Patricia 1931- *45*
Cameron, Ann 1943- *27*
Cameron, Edna M. 1905- *3*
Cameron, Eleanor (Butler)
  1912- *25*
  Earlier sketch in SATA 1
  See also CLR 1
Cameron, Elizabeth
  See Nowell, Elizabeth Cameron
Cameron, Elizabeth Jane
  1910-1976 .... *32*
  Obituary *30*
Cameron, Ian
  See Payne, Donald Gordon
Cameron, Polly 1928- *2*
Camp, Charles Lewis 1893-1975
  Obituary *31*
Camp, Walter (Chauncey)
  1859-1925 .... YABC *1*
Campbell, (Elizabeth) Andréa
  1963- *50*
Campbell, Ann R. 1925- *11*
Campbell, Bruce
  See Epstein, Samuel
Campbell, Camilla 1905- *26*
Campbell, Hope *20*
Campbell, Jane
  See Edwards, Jane Campbell
Campbell, Patricia J(ean)
  1930- *45*
Campbell, Patty
  See Campbell, Patricia J(ean)
Campbell, R. W.
  See Campbell, Rosemae Wells
Campbell, Rod 1945- *51*
  Brief Entry *44*
Campbell, Rosemae Wells
  1909- *1*

Campion, Nardi Reeder 1917- *22*
Candell, Victor 1903-1977
  Obituary *24*
Canfield, Dorothy
  See Fisher, Dorothy Canfield
Canfield, Jane White
  1897-1984 .... *32*
  Obituary *38*
Cannon, Cornelia (James) 1876-1969
  Brief Entry *28*
Cannon, Ravenna
  See Mayhar, Ardath
Canusi, Jose
  See Barker, S. Omar
Caplin, Alfred Gerald 1909-1979
  Obituary *21*
Capp, Al
  See Caplin, Alfred Gerald
Cappel, Constance 1936- *22*
Capps, Benjamin (Franklin)
  1922- *9*
Captain Kangaroo
  See Keeshan, Robert J.
Carafoli, Marci
  See Ridlon, Marci
Caras, Roger A(ndrew) 1928- *12*
Carbonnier, Jeanne 1894-1974 .... *3*
  Obituary *34*
Care, Felicity
  See Coury, Louise Andree
Carew, Jan (Rynveld) 1925- *51*
  Brief Entry *40*
Carey, Bonnie 1941- *18*
Carey, Ernestine Gilbreth
  1908- *2*
Carey, M. V.
  See Carey, Mary (Virginia)
Carey, Mary (Virginia) 1925- *44*
  Brief Entry *39*
Carigiet, Alois 1902-1985 .... *24*
  Obituary *47*
Carini, Edward 1923- *9*
Carle, Eric 1929- *4*
  See CLR 10
Carleton, Captain L. C.
  See Ellis, Edward S(ylvester)
Carley, V(an Ness) Royal 1906-1976
  Obituary *20*
Carlisle, Clark, Jr.
  See Holding, James
Carlisle, Olga A(ndreyev)
  1930- *35*
Carlsen, G(eorge) Robert
  1917- *30*
Carlsen, Ruth C(hristoffer) *2*
Carlson, Bernice Wells 1910- *8*
Carlson, Dale Bick 1935- *1*
Carlson, Daniel 1960- *27*
Carlson, Nancy L(ee) 1953-
  Brief Entry *45*
Carlson, Natalie Savage 1906- *2*
  See also SAAS 4
Carlson, Vada F. 1897- *16*
Carlstrom, Nancy White 1948-
  Brief Entry *48*
Carmer, Carl (Lamson)
  1893-1976 .... *37*
  Obituary *30*

Carmer, Elizabeth Black
  1904- 24
Carmichael, Carrie 40
Carmichael, Harriet
  See Carmichael, Carrie
Carol, Bill J.
  See Knott, William Cecil, Jr.
Caroselli, Remus F(rancis)
  1916- 36
Carpelan, Bo (Gustaf Bertelsson)
  1926- 8
Carpenter, Allan 1917- 3
Carpenter, Frances 1890-1972 3
  Obituary 27
Carpenter, Patricia (Healy Evans)
  1920- 11
Carr, Glyn
  See Styles, Frank Showell
Carr, Harriett Helen 1899- 3
Carr, Mary Jane 2
Carrick, Carol 1935- 7
Carrick, Donald 1929- 7
Carrick, Malcolm 1945- 28
Carrier, Lark 1947-
  Brief Entry 50
Carrighar, Sally 24
Carris, Joan Davenport 1938- 44
  Brief Entry 42
Carroll, Curt
  See Bishop, Curtis
Carroll, Latrobe 7
Carroll, Laura
  See Parr, Lucy
Carroll, Lewis
  See Dodgson, Charles Lutwidge
  See also CLR 2
Carroll, Raymond
  Brief Entry 47
Carruth, Hayden 1921- 47
Carse, Robert 1902-1971 5
Carson, Captain James
  See Stratemeyer, Edward L.
Carson, John F. 1920- 1
Carson, Rachel (Louise)
  1907-1964 23
Carson, Rosalind
  See Chittenden, Margaret
Carson, S. M.
  See Gorsline, (Sally) Marie
Carter, Bruce
  See Hough, Richard (Alexander)
Carter, Dorothy Sharp 1921- 8
Carter, Forrest 1927(?)-1979 32
Carter, Helene 1887-1960 15
Carter, (William) Hodding
  1907-1972 2
  Obituary 27
Carter, Katharine J(ones)
  1905- 2
Carter, Nick
  See Lynds, Dennis
Carter, Phyllis Ann
  See Eberle, Irmengarde
Carter, Samuel III 1904- 37
Carter, William E. 1926-1983 1
  Obituary 35
Cartlidge, Michelle 1950- 49
  Brief Entry 37

Cartner, William Carruthers
  1910- 11
Cartwright, Sally 1923- 9
Carver, John
  See Gardner, Richard
Carwell, L'Ann
  See McKissack, Patricia (L'Ann)
  C(arwell)
Cary
  See Cary, Louis F(avreau)
Cary, Barbara Knapp 1912(?)-1975
  Obituary 31
Cary, Louis F(avreau) 1915- 9
Caryl, Jean
  See Kaplan, Jean Caryl Korn
Case, Marshal T(aylor) 1941- 9
Case, Michael
  See Howard, Robert West
Casewit, Curtis 1922- 4
Casey, Brigid 1950- 9
Casey, Winifred Rosen
  See Rosen, Winifred
Cason, Mabel Earp 1892-1965 10
Cass, Joan E(velyn) 1
Cassedy, Sylvia 1930- 27
Cassel, Lili
  See Wronker, Lili Cassell
Cassel-Wronker, Lili
  See Wronker, Lili Cassell
Castellanos, Jane Mollie (Robinson)
  1913- 9
Castellon, Federico 1914-1971 48
Castillo, Edmund L. 1924- 1
Castle, Lee [Joint pseudonym]
  See Ogan, George F. and Ogan,
  Margaret E. (Nettles)
Castle, Paul
  See Howard, Vernon (Linwood)
Caswell, Helen (Rayburn)
  1923- 12
Cate, Dick
  See Cate, Richard (Edward Nelson)
Cate, Richard (Edward Nelson)
  1932- 28
Cather, Willa (Sibert)
  1873-1947 30
Catherall, Arthur 1906- 3
Cathon, Laura E(lizabeth)
  1908- 27
Catlin, Wynelle 1930- 13
Catton, (Charles) Bruce
  1899-1978 2
  Obituary 24
Catz, Max
  See Glaser, Milton
Caudill, Rebecca 1899-1985 1
  Obituary 44
Cauley, Lorinda Bryan 1951- 46
  Brief Entry 43
Cauman, Samuel 1910-1971 48
Causley, Charles 1917- 3
Cavallo, Diana 1931- 7
Cavanagh, Helen (Carol)
  1939- 48
  Brief Entry 37
Cavanah, Frances 1899-1982 31
  Earlier sketch in SATA 1

Cavanna, Betty 1909- 30
  Earlier sketch in SATA 1
  See also SAAS 4
Cavin, Ruth (Brodie) 1918- 38
Cawley, Winifred 1915- 13
Caxton, Pisistratus
  See Lytton, Edward G(eorge) E(arle)
  L(ytton) Bulwer-Lytton, Baron
Cazet, Denys 1938-
  Brief Entry 41
Cebulash, Mel 1937- 10
Ceder, Georgiana Dorcas 10
Celestino, Martha Laing
  1951- 39
Cerf, Bennett 1898-1971 7
Cerf, Christopher (Bennett)
  1941- 2
Cervon, Jacqueline
  See Moussard, Jacqueline
Cetin, Frank (Stanley) 1921- 2
Chadwick, Lester [Collective
  pseudonym] 1
Chaffee, Allen 3
Chaffin, Lillie D(orton) 1925- ... 4
Chaikin, Miriam 1928- 24
Challans, Mary 1905-1983 23
  Obituary 36
Chalmers, Mary 1927- 6
Chamberlain, Margaret 1954- 46
Chambers, Aidan 1934- 1
Chambers, Bradford 1922-1984
  Obituary 39
Chambers, Catherine E.
  See Johnston, Norma
Chambers, John W. 1933-
  Brief Entry 46
Chambers, Margaret Ada Eastwood
  1911- 2
Chambers, Peggy
  See Chambers, Margaret Ada
  Eastwood
Chandler, Caroline A(ugusta)
  1906-1979 22
  Obituary 24
Chandler, David Porter 1933- 28
Chandler, Edna Walker
  1908-1982 11
  Obituary 31
Chandler, Linda S(mith)
  1929- 39
Chandler, Robert 1953- 40
Chandler, Ruth Forbes
  1894-1978 2
  Obituary 26
Channel, A. R.
  See Catherall, Arthur
Chapian, Marie 1938- 29
Chapin, Alene Olsen Dalton
  1915(?)-1986
  Obituary 47
Chapman, Allen [Collective
  pseudonym] 1
Chapman, (Constance) Elizabeth
  (Mann) 1919- 10
Chapman, Gaynor 1935- 32
Chapman, Jean 34
Chapman, John Stanton Higham
  1891-1972
  Obituary 27

Chapman, Maristan [Joint pseudonym]
  See Chapman, John Stanton Higham
Chapman, Vera 1898- 33
Chapman, Walker
  See Silverberg, Robert
Chappell, Warren 1904- 6
Chardiet, Bernice (Kroll) 27
Charles, Donald
  See Meighan, Donald Charles
Charles, Louis
  See Stratemeyer, Edward L.
Charlip, Remy 1929- 4
  See also CLR 8
Charlot, Jean 1898-1979 8
  Obituary 31
Charlton, Michael (Alan)
  1923- 34
Charmatz, Bill 1925- 7
Charosh, Mannis 1906- 5
Chase, Alice
  See McHargue, Georgess
Chase, Emily
  See Sachs, Judith
Chase, Mary (Coyle)
  1907-1981 17
  Obituary 29
Chase, Mary Ellen 1887-1973 10
Chastain, Madye Lee 1908- 4
Chauncy, Nan 1900 1970 6
  See also CLR 6
Chaundler, Christine
  1887-1972 1
  Obituary 25
Chen, Tony 1929- 6
Chenault, Nell
  See Smith, Linell Nash
Chenery, Janet (Dai) 1923- 25
Cheney, Cora 1916- 3
Cheney, Ted
  See Cheney, Theodore Albert
Cheney, Theodore Albert
  1928- 11
Cheng, Judith 1955- 36
Chermayeff, Ivan 1932- 47
Chernoff, Dorothy A.
  See Ernst, (Lyman) John
Chernoff, Goldie Taub 1909- 10
Cherry, Lynne 1952- 34
Cherryholmes, Anne
  See Price, Olive
Chess, Victoria (Dickerson)
  1939- 33
Chessare, Michele
  Brief Entry 42
Chesterton, G(ilbert) K(eith)
  1874-1936 27
Chetin, Helen 1922- 6
Chetwin, Grace
  Brief Entry 50
Chevalier, Christa 1937- 35
Chew, Ruth 7
Chidsey, Donald Barr
  1902-1981 3
  Obituary 27
Child, Philip 1898-1978 47
Childress, Alice 1920- 48
  Earlier sketch in SATA 7

Childs, (Halla) Fay (Cochrane)
  1890-1971 1
  Obituary 25
Chimaera
  See Farjeon, Eleanor
Chinery, Michael 1938- 26
Chipperfield, Joseph E(ugene)
  1912- 2
Chittenden, Elizabeth F.
  1903- 9
Chittenden, Margaret 1933- 28
Chittum, Ida 1918- 7
Choate, Judith (Newkirk)
  1940- 30
Chorao, (Ann Mc)Kay (Sproat)
  1936- 8
Chorpenning, Charlotte (Lee Barrows)
  1872-1955
  Brief Entry 37
Chrisman, Arthur Bowie
  1889-1953 ....YABC 1
Christelow, Eileen 1943- 38
  Brief Entry 35
Christensen, Gardell Dano
  1907- 1
Christesen, Barbara 1940- 40
Christgau, Alice Erickson
  1902- 13
Christian, Mary Blount 1933- 9
Christie, Agatha (Mary Clarissa)
  1890-1976 36
Christopher, John
  See Youd, (Christopher) Samuel
  See also CLR 2
Christopher, Louise
  See Hale, Arlene
Christopher, Matt(hew F.)
  1917- 47
  Earlier sketch in SATA 2
Christopher, Milbourne
  1914(?)-1984 46
Christy, Howard Chandler
  1873-1952 21
Chu, Daniel 1933- 11
Chukovsky, Kornei (Ivanovich)
  1882-1969 34
  Earlier sketch in SATA 5
Church, Richard 1893-1972 3
Churchill, E. Richard 1937- 11
Chute, B(eatrice) J(oy) 1913- 2
Chute, Marchette (Gaylord)
  1909- 1
Chwast, Jacqueline 1932- 6
Chwast, Seymour 1931- 18
Ciardi, John (Anthony)
  1916-1986 1
  Obituary 46
Clair, Andrée 19
Clampett, Bob
  Obituary 38
  See also Clampett, Robert
Clampett, Robert
  1914(?)-1984 44
Clapp, Patricia 1912- 4
  See also SAAS 4
Clare, Helen
  See Hunter, Blair Pauline
Clark, Ann Nolan 1898- 4
Clark, Champ 1923- 47

Clark, David
  See Hardcastle, Michael
Clark, David Allen
  See Ernst, (Lyman) John
Clark, Frank J(ames) 1922- 18
Clark, Garel [Joint pseudonym]
  See Garelick, May
Clark, Leonard 1905-1981 30
  Obituary 29
Clark, Margaret Goff 1913- 8
Clark, Mary Higgins 46
Clark, Mavis Thorpe 8
  See also SAAS 5
Clark, Merle
  See Gessner, Lynne
Clark, Patricia (Finrow) 1929- 11
Clark, Ronald William 1916- 2
Clark, Van D(eusen) 1909- 2
Clark, Virginia
  See Gray, Patricia
Clark, Walter Van Tilburg
  1909-1971 8
Clarke, Arthur C(harles)
  1917- 13
Clarke, Clorinda 1917- 7
Clarke, Joan 1921- 42
  Brief Entry 27
Clarke, John
  See Laklan, Carli
Clarke, Mary Stetson 1911- 5
Clarke, Michael
  See Newlon, Clarke
Clarke, Pauline
  See Hunter Blair, Pauline
Clarkson, E(dith) Margaret
  1915- 37
Clarkson, Ewan 1929- 9
Claverie, Jean 1946- 38
Clay, Patrice 1947- 47
Claypool, Jane
  See Miner, Jane Claypool
Cleary, Beverly (Bunn) 1916- 43
  Earlier sketch in SATA 2
  See also CLR 2, 8
Cleaver, Bill 1920-1981 22
  Obituary 27
  See also CLR 6
Cleaver, Carole 1934- 6
Cleaver, Elizabeth (Mrazik)
  1939-1985 23
  Obituary 43
  See also CLR 13
Cleaver, Hylton (Reginald)
  1891-1961 49
Cleaver, Vera 22
  See also CLR 6
Cleishbotham, Jebediah
  See Scott, Sir Walter
Cleland, Mabel
  See Widdemer, Mabel Cleland
Clemens, Samuel Langhorne
  1835-1910 ....YABC 2
Clemens, Virginia Phelps
  1941- 35
Clements, Bruce 1931- 27
Clemons, Elizabeth
  See Nowell, Elizabeth Cameron
Clerk, N. W.
  See Lewis, C. S.

Cleveland, Bob
See Cleveland, George
Cleveland, George 1903(?)-1985
Obituary *43*
Cleven, Cathrine
See Cleven, Kathryn Seward
Cleven, Kathryn Seward *2*
Clevin, Jörgen 1920- *7*
Clewes, Dorothy (Mary)
1907- *1*
Clifford, Eth
See Rosenberg, Ethel
Clifford, Harold B. 1893- *10*
Clifford, Margaret Cort 1929- *1*
Clifford, Martin
See Hamilton, Charles H. St. John
Clifford, Mary Louise (Beneway)
1926- *23*
Clifford, Peggy
See Clifford, Margaret Cort
Clifton, Harry
See Hamilton, Charles H. St. John
Clifton, Lucille 1936- *20*
See also CLR 5
Clifton, Martin
See Hamilton, Charles H. St. John
Climo, Shirley 1928- *39*
Brief Entry *35*
Clinton, Jon
See Prince, J(ack) H(arvey)
Clish, (Lee) Marian 1946- *43*
Clive, Clifford
See Hamilton, Charles H. St. John
Cloudsley-Thompson, J(ohn) L(eonard)
1921- *19*
Clymer, Eleanor 1906- *9*
Clyne, Patricia Edwards *31*
Coalson, Glo 1946- *26*
Coates, Belle 1896- *2*
Coates, Ruth Allison 1915- *11*
Coats, Alice M(argaret) 1905- *11*
Coatsworth, Elizabeth
1893-1986 .... *2*
Obituary *49*
See also CLR 2
Cobb, Jane
See Berry, Jane Cobb
Cobb, Vicki 1938- *8*
See also CLR 2
Cobbett, Richard
See Pluckrose, Henry (Arthur)
Cober, Alan E. 1935- *7*
Cobham, Sir Alan
See Hamilton, Charles H. St. John
Cocagnac, A(ugustin) M(aurice-Jean)
1924- *7*
Cochran, Bobbye A. 1949- *11*
Cockett, Mary *3*
Coe, Douglas [Joint pseudonym]
See Epstein, Beryl and Epstein,
Samuel
Coe, Lloyd 1899-1976
Obituary *30*
Coen, Rena Neumann 1925- *20*
Coerr, Eleanor 1922- *1*
Coffin, Geoffrey
See Mason, F. van Wyck
Coffman, Ramon Peyton
1896- *4*

Coggins, Jack (Banham)
1911- *2*
Cohen, Barbara 1932- *10*
Cohen, Daniel 1936- *8*
See also CLR 3
See also SAAS 4
Cohen, Jene Barr
See Barr, Jene
Cohen, Joan Lebold 1932- *4*
Cohen, Miriam 1926- *29*
Cohen, Peter Zachary 1931- *4*
Cohen, Robert Carl 1930- *8*
Cohn, Angelo 1914- *19*
Coit, Margaret L(ouise) *2*
Colbert, Anthony 1934- *15*
Colby, C(arroll) B(urleigh)
1904-1977 .... *35*
Earlier sketch in SATA 3
Colby, Jean Poindexter 1909- *23*
Cole, Annette
See Steiner, Barbara A(nnette)
Cole, Davis
See Elting, Mary
Cole, Jack
See Stewart, John (William)
Cole, Jackson
See Schisgall, Oscar
Cole, Jennifer
See Zach, Cheryl (Byrd)
Cole, Joanna 1944- *49*
Brief Entry *37*
See also CLR 5
Cole, Lois Dwight
1903(?)-1979 .... *10*
Obituary *26*
Cole, Sheila R(otenberg)
1939- *24*
Cole, William (Rossa) 1919- *9*
Coleman, William L(eRoy)
1938- *49*
Brief Entry *34*
Coles, Robert (Martin) 1929- *23*
Colin, Ann
See Ure, Jean
Collier, Christopher 1930- *16*
Collier, Ethel 1903- *22*
Collier, James Lincoln 1928- *8*
See also CLR 3
Collier, Jane
See Collier, Zena
Collier, Zena 1926- *23*
Collins, David 1940- *7*
Collins, Hunt
See Hunter, Evan
Collins, Michael
See Lynds, Dennis
Collins, Pat Lowery 1932- *31*
Collins, Ruth Philpott 1890-1975
Obituary *30*
Collodi, Carlo
See Lorenzini, Carlo
See also CLR 5
Colloms, Brenda 1919- *40*
Colman, Hila *1*
Colman, Morris 1899(?)-1981
Obituary *25*
Colombo, John Robert 1936- *50*
Colonius, Lillian 1911- *3*

Colorado (Capella), Antonio J(ulio)
1903- *23*
Colt, Martin [Joint pseudonym]
See Epstein, Beryl and Epstein,
Samuel
Colum, Padraic 1881-1972 .... *15*
Columella
See Moore, Clement Clarke
Colver, Anne 1908- *7*
Colwell, Eileen (Hilda) 1904- *2*
Combs, Robert
See Murray, John
Comfort, Jane Levington
See Sturtzel, Jane Levington
Comfort, Mildred Houghton
1886- *3*
Comins, Ethel M(ae) *11*
Comins, Jeremy 1933- *28*
Commager, Henry Steele
1902- *23*
Comus
See Ballantyne, R(obert) M(ichael)
Conan Doyle, Arthur
See Doyle, Arthur Conan
Condit, Martha Olson 1913- *28*
Cone, Ferne Geller 1921- *39*
Cone, Molly (Lamken) 1918- *28*
Earlier sketch in SATA 1
Conford, Ellen 1942- *6*
See also CLR 10
Conger, Lesley
See Suttles, Shirley (Smith)
Conklin, Gladys (Plemon)
1903- *2*
Conklin, Paul S. *43*
Brief Entry *33*
Conkling, Hilda 1910- *23*
Conly, Robert Leslie
1918(?)-1973 .... *23*
Connell, Kirk [Joint pseudonym]
See Chapman, John Stanton Higham
Connelly, Marc(us Cook) 1890-1980
Obituary *25*
Connolly, Jerome P(atrick)
1931- *8*
Connolly, Peter 1935- *47*
Conover, Chris 1950- *31*
Conquest, Owen
See Hamilton, Charles H. St. John
Conrad, Joseph 1857-1924 .... *27*
Conrad, Pam(ela) 1947-
Brief Entry *49*
Conroy, Jack (Wesley) 1899- *19*
Conroy, John
See Conroy, Jack (Wesley)
Constant, Alberta Wilson
1908-1981 .... *22*
Obituary *28*
Conway, Gordon
See Hamilton, Charles H. St. John
Cook, Bernadine 1924- *11*
Cook, Fred J(ames) 1911- *2*
Cook, Joseph J(ay) 1924- *8*
Cook, Lyn
See Waddell, Evelyn Margaret
Cooke, Ann
See Cole, Joanna
Cooke, David Coxe 1917- *2*

Cooke, Donald Ewin
1916-1985 2
Obituary 45
Cookson, Catherine (McMullen)
1906- 9
Coolidge, Olivia E(nsor)
1908- 26
Earlier sketch in SATA 1
Coombs, Charles I(ra) 1914- 43
Earlier sketch in SATA 3
Coombs, Chick
See Coombs, Charles I(ra)
Coombs, Patricia 1926- 51
Earlier sketch in SATA 3
Cooney, Barbara 1917- 6
Cooney, Caroline B. 1947- 48
Brief Entry 41
Cooney, Nancy Evans 1932- 42
Coontz, Otto 1946- 33
Cooper, Elizabeth Keyser 47
Cooper, Gordon 1932- 23
Cooper, James Fenimore
1789-1851 19
Cooper, James R.
See Stratemeyer, Edward L.
Cooper, John R. [Collective
pseudonym] 1
Cooper, Kay 1941- 11
Cooper, Lee (Pelham) 5
Cooper, Lester (Irving)
1919-1985 32
Obituary 43
Cooper, Lettice (Ulpha) 1897- 35
Cooper, Susan 1935- 4
See also CLR 4
Copeland, Helen 1920- 4
Copeland, Paul W. 23
Copley, (Diana) Heather Pickering
1918- 45
Coppard, A(lfred) E(dgar)
1878-1957 ....YABC 1
Corbett, Grahame 43
Brief Entry 36
Corbett, Scott 1913- 42
Earlier sketch in SATA 2
See also CLR 1
See also SAAS 2
Corbett, W(illiam) J(esse)
1938- 50
Brief Entry 44
Corbin, Sabra Lee
See Malvern, Gladys
Corbin, William
See McGraw, William Corbin
Corby, Dan
See Catherall, Arthur
Corcoran, Barbara 1911- 3
Corcos, Lucille 1908-1973 10
Cordell, Alexander
See Graber, Alexander
Coren, Alan 1938- 32
Corey, Dorothy 23
Corfe, Thomas Howell 1928- 27
Corfe, Tom
See Corfe, Thomas Howell
Corlett, William 1938- 46
Brief Entry 39
Cormack, M(argaret) Grant
1913- 11

Cormack, Maribelle B.
1902-1984 39
Cormier, Robert (Edmund)
1925- 45
Earlier sketch in SATA 10
See also CLR 12
Cornelius, Carol 1942- 40
Cornell, J.
See Cornell, Jeffrey
Cornell, James (Clayton, Jr.)
1938- 27
Cornell, Jean Gay 1920- 23
Cornell, Jeffrey 1945- 11
Cornish, Samuel James 1935- 23
Cornwall, Nellie
See Sloggett, Nellie
Correy, Lee
See Stine, G. Harry
Corrigan, (Helen) Adeline
1909- 23
Corrigan, Barbara 1922- 8
Corrin, Sara 1918-
Brief Entry 48
Corrin, Stephen
Brief Entry 48
Cort, M. C.
See Clifford, Margaret Cort
Corwin, Judith Hoffman
1946- 10
Cosgrave, John O'Hara II 1908-1968
Obituary 21
Cosgrove, Margaret (Leota)
1926- 47
Cosgrove, Stephen E(dward) 1945-
Brief Entry 40
Coskey, Evelyn 1932- 7
Cosner, Shaaron 1940- 43
Costabel, Eva Deutsch 1924- 45
Costello, David F(rancis)
1904- 23
Cott, Jonathan 1942- 23
Cottam, Clarence 1899-1974 25
Cottler, Joseph 1899- 22
Cottrell, Leonard 1913-1974 24
The Countryman
See Whitlock, Ralph
Courlander, Harold 1908- 6
Courtis, Stuart Appleton 1874-1969
Obituary 29
Coury, Louise Andree 1895(?)-1983
Obituary 34
Cousins, Margaret 1905- 2
Cousteau, Jacques-Yves 1910- 38
Coville, Bruce 1950- 32
Cowen, Eve
See Werner, Herma
Cowie, Leonard W(allace)
1919- 4
Cowles, Kathleen
See Krull, Kathleen
Cowley, Joy 1936- 4
Cox, Donald William 1921- 23
Cox, Jack
See Cox, John Roberts
Cox, John Roberts 1915- 9
Cox, Palmer 1840-1924 24
Cox, Victoria
See Garretson, Victoria Diane
Cox, Wally 1924-1973 25

Cox, William R(obert) 1901- 46
Brief Entry 31
Coy, Harold 1902- 3
Craft, Ruth
Brief Entry 31
Craig, A. A.
See Anderson, Poul (William)
Craig, Alisa
See MacLeod, Charlotte (Matilda
Hughes)
Craig, Helen 1934- 49
Brief Entry 46
Craig, John Eland
See Chipperfield, Joseph
Craig, John Ernest 1921- 23
Craig, M. Jean 17
Craig, Margaret Maze
1911-1964 9
Craig, Mary Francis 1923- 6
Craik, Dinah Maria (Mulock)
1826-1887 34
Crane, Barbara J. 1934- 31
Crane, Caroline 1930- 11
Crane, M. A.
See Wartski, Maureen (Ann Crane)
Crane, Roy
See Crane, Royston Campbell
Crane, Royston Campbell 1901-1977
Obituary 22
Crane, Stephen (Townley)
1871-1900 ....YABC 2
Crane, Walter 1845-1915 18
Crane, William D(wight)
1892- 1
Crary, Elizabeth (Ann) 1942-
Brief Entry 43
Crary, Margaret (Coleman)
1906- 9
Craven, Thomas 1889-1969 22
Crawford, Charles P. 1945- 28
Crawford, Deborah 1922- 6
Crawford, John E. 1904-1971 3
Crawford, Mel 1925- 44
Brief Entry 33
Crawford, Phyllis 1899- 3
Craz, Albert G. 1926- 24
Crayder, Dorothy 1906- 7
Crayder, Teresa
See Colman, Hila
Crayon, Geoffrey
See Irving, Washington
Crecy, Jeanne
See Williams, Jeanne
Credle, Ellis 1902- 1
Cresswell, Helen 1934- 48
Earlier sketch in SATA 1
Cretan, Gladys (Yessayan)
1921- 2
Crew, Helen (Cecilia) Coale
1866-1941 ....YABC 2
Crews, Donald 1938- 32
Brief Entry 30
See also CLR 7
Crichton, (J.) Michael 1942- 9
Crofut, Bill
See Crofut, William E. III
Crofut, William E. III 1934- 23
Croman, Dorothy Young
See Rosenberg, Dorothy

Cromie, Alice Hamilton 1914- *24*
Cromie, William J(oseph)
  1930- *4*
Crompton, Anne Eliot 1930- *23*
Crompton, Richmal
  See Lamburn, Richmal Crompton
Cronbach, Abraham
  1882-1965 .... *11*
Crone, Ruth 1919- *4*
Cronin, A(rchibald) J(oseph)
  1896-1981 .... *47*
  Obituary *25*
Crook, Beverly Courtney *38*
  Brief Entry *35*
Cros, Earl
  See Rose, Carl
Crosby, Alexander L.
  1906-1980 .... *2*
  Obituary *23*
Crosher, G(eoffry) R(obins)
  1911- *14*
Cross, Gilbert B. 1939-
  Brief Entry *51*
Cross, Gillian (Clare) 1945- *38*
Cross, Helen Reeder
  See Broadhead, Helen Cross
Cross, Wilbur Lucius III
  1918- *2*
Crossley-Holland, Kevin *5*
Crouch, Marcus 1913- *4*
Crout, George C(lement)
  1917- *11*
Crow, Donna Fletcher 1941- *40*
Crowe, Bettina Lum 1911- *6*
Crowe, John
  See Lynds, Dennis
Crowell, Grace Noll
  1877-1969 .... *34*
Crowell, Pers 1910- *2*
Crowfield, Christopher
  See Stowe, Harriet (Elizabeth)
  Beecher
Crowley, Arthur M(cBlair)
  1945- *38*
Crownfield, Gertrude
  1867-1945 .... *YABC 1*
Crowther, James Gerald 1899- *14*
Cruikshank, George
  1792-1878 .... *22*
Crump, Fred H., Jr. 1931- *11*
Crump, J(ames) Irving 1887-1979
  Obituary *21*
Crunden, Reginald
  See Cleaver, Hylton (Reginald)
Cruz, Ray 1933- *6*
Ctvrtek, Vaclav 1911-1976
  Obituary *27*
Cuffari, Richard 1925-1978 ...... *6*
  Obituary *25*
Cullen, Countee 1903-1946 .... *18*
Culliford, Pierre 1928- *40*
Culp, Louanna McNary
  1901-1965 .... *2*
Cumming, Primrose (Amy)
  1915- *24*
Cummings, Betty Sue 1918- *15*
Cummings, Parke 1902- *2*
Cummings, Pat 1950- *42*

Cummings, Richard
  See Gardner, Richard
Cummins, Maria Susanna
  1827-1866 .... *YABC 1*
Cunliffe, John Arthur 1933- *11*
Cunliffe, Marcus (Falkner)
  1922- *37*
Cunningham, Captain Frank
  See Glick, Carl (Cannon)
Cunningham, Cathy
  See Cunningham, Chet
Cunningham, Chet 1928- *23*
Cunningham, Dale S(peers)
  1932- *11*
Cunningham, E.V.
  See Fast, Howard
Cunningham, Julia W(oolfolk)
  1916- *26*
  Earlier sketch in SATA 1
  See also SAAS 2
Cunningham, Virginia
  See Holmgren, Virginia
  C(unningham)
Curiae, Amicus
  See Fuller, Edmund (Maybank)
Curie, Eve 1904- *1*
Curley, Daniel 1918- *23*
Curry, Jane L(ouise) 1932- *1*
Curry, Peggy Simson
  1911-1987 .... *8*
  Obituary *50*
Curtis, Bruce (Richard) 1944- *30*
Curtis, Patricia 1921- *23*
Curtis, Peter
  See Lofts, Norah (Robinson)
Curtis, Richard (Alan) 1937- *29*
Curtis, Wade
  See Pournelle, Jerry (Eugene)
Cushman, Jerome *2*
Cutchen, Billye Walker 1930- *15*
Cutler, (May) Ebbitt 1923- *9*
Cutler, Ivor 1923- *24*
Cutler, Samuel
  See Folsom, Franklin
Cutt, W(illiam) Towrie 1898- *16*
Cuyler, Margery Stuyvesant
  1948- *39*
Cuyler, Stephen
  See Bates, Barbara S(nedeker)

D

Dabcovich, Lydia
  Brief Entry *47*
Dahl, Borghild 1890-1984 .... *7*
  Obituary *37*
Dahl, Roald 1916- *26*
  Earlier sketch in SATA 1
  See also CLR 1; 7
Dahlstedt, Marden 1921- *8*
Dain, Martin J. 1924- *35*
Dale, Jack
  See Holliday, Joseph
Dale, Margaret J(essy) Miller
  1911- *39*
Dale, Norman
  See Denny, Norman (George)

Dalgliesh, Alice 1893-1979 .... *17*
  Obituary *21*
Dalton, Alene
  See Chapin, Alene Olsen Dalton
Dalton, Anne 1948- *40*
Daly, Jim
  See Stratemeyer, Edward L.
Daly, Kathleen N(orah)
  Brief Entry *37*
Daly, Maureen *2*
  See also SAAS 1
Daly, Nicholas 1946- *37*
Daly, Niki
  See Daly, Nicholas
D'Amato, Alex 1919- *20*
D'Amato, Janet 1925- *9*
Damrosch, Helen Therese
  See Tee-Van, Helen Damrosch
Dana, Barbara 1940- *22*
Dana, Richard Henry, Jr.
  1815-1882 .... *26*
Danachair, Caoimhin O.
  See Danaher, Kevin
Danaher, Kevin 1913- *22*
D'Andrea, Kate
  See Steiner, Barbara A(nnette)
Dangerfield, Balfour
  See McCloskey, Robert
Daniel, Anita 1893(?)-1978 .... *23*
  Obituary *24*
Daniel, Anne
  See Steiner, Barbara A(nnette)
Daniel, Hawthorne 1890- *8*
Daniels, Guy 1919- *11*
Dank, Gloria Rand 1955-
  Brief Entry *46*
Dank, Leonard D(ewey)
  1929- *44*
Dank, Milton 1920- *31*
Danziger, Paula 1944- *36*
  Brief Entry *30*
Darby, J. N.
  See Govan, Christine Noble
Darby, Patricia (Paulsen) *14*
Darby, Ray K. 1912- *7*
Daringer, Helen Fern 1892- *1*
Darke, Marjorie 1929- *16*
Darley, F(elix) O(ctavius) C(arr)
  1822-1888 .... *35*
Darling, David J.
  Brief Entry *44*
Darling, Kathy
  See Darling, Mary Kathleen
Darling, Lois M. 1917- *3*
Darling, Louis, Jr. 1916-1970 ..... *3*
  Obituary *23*
Darling, Mary Kathleen 1943- *9*
Darrow, Whitney, Jr. 1909- *13*
Darwin, Len
  See Darwin, Leonard
Darwin, Leonard 1916- *24*
Dasent, Sir George Webbe 1817-1896
  Brief Entry *29*
Daskam, Josephine Dodge
  See Bacon, Josephine Dodge
  (Daskam)
Dauer, Rosamond 1934- *23*
Daugherty, Charles Michael
  1914- *16*

Daugherty, James (Henry)
  1889-1974 .... *13*
Daugherty, Richard D(eo)
  1922- *35*
Daugherty, Sonia Medwedeff (?)-1971
  Obituary *27*
d'Aulaire, Edgar Parin
  1898-1986 .... *5*
  Obituary *47*
d'Aulaire, Ingri (Maartenson Parin)
  1904-1980 .... *5*
  Obituary *24*
Daveluy, Paule Cloutier 1919- *11*
Davenport, Spencer
  See Stratemeyer, Edward L.
Daves, Michael 1938- *40*
David, Jonathan
  See Ames, Lee J.
Davidson, Alice Joyce 1932-
  Brief Entry *45*
Davidson, Basil 1914- *13*
Davidson, Jessica 1915- *5*
Davidson, Judith 1953- *40*
Davidson, Margaret 1936- *5*
Davidson, Marion
  See Garis, Howard R(oger)
Davidson, Mary R.
  1885-1973 .... *9*
Davidson, R.
  See Davidson, Raymond
Davidson, Raymond 1926- *32*
Davidson, Rosalie 1921- *23*
Davies, Andrew (Wynford)
  1936- *27*
Davies, Bettilu D(onna) 1942- *33*
Davies, (Edward) Hunter 1936-
  Brief Entry *45*
Davies, Joan 1934- *50*
  Brief Entry *47*
Davies, Sumiko 1942- *46*
Davis, Bette J. 1923- *15*
Davis, Burke 1913- *4*
Davis, Christopher 1928- *6*
Davis, D(elbert) Dwight
  1908-1965 .... *33*
Davis, Daniel S(heldon) 1936- *12*
Davis, Gibbs 1953- *46*
  Brief Entry *41*
Davis, Grania 1943-
  Brief Entry *50*
Davis, Hubert J(ackson) 1904- *31*
Davis, James Robert 1945- *32*
Davis, Jim
  See Davis, James Robert
Davis, Julia 1904- *6*
Davis, Louise Littleton 1921- *25*
Davis, Marguerite 1889- *34*
Davis, Mary L(ee) 1935- *9*
Davis, Mary Octavia 1901- *6*
Davis, Paxton 1925- *16*
Davis, Robert
  1881-1949 .... *YABC 1*
Davis, Russell G. 1922- *3*
Davis, Verne T. 1889-1973 .... *6*
Dawson, Elmer A. [Collective
  pseudonym] *1*
Dawson, Mary 1919- *11*
Day, Beth (Feagles) 1924- *33*

Day, Maurice 1892-
  Brief Entry *30*
Day, Thomas 1748-1789 ..... *YABC 1*
Dazey, Agnes J(ohnston) *2*
Dazey, Frank M. *2*
Deacon, Eileen
  See Geipel, Eileen
Deacon, Richard
  See McCormick, (George) Donald
  (King)
Dean, Anabel 1915- *12*
Dean, Karen Strickler 1923- *49*
de Angeli, Marguerite
  1889-1987 .... *27*
  Obituary *51*
  Earlier sketch in SATA 1
  See also CLR 1
DeArmand, Frances Ullmann
  1904(?)-1984 .... *10*
  Obituary *38*
Deary, Terry 1946- *51*
  Brief Entry *41*
deBanke, Cecile 1889-1965 .... *11*
De Bruyn, Monica 1952- *13*
de Camp, Catherine C(rook)
  1907- *12*
DeCamp, L(yon) Sprague
  1907- *9*
Decker, Duane 1910-1964 .... *5*
DeClements, Barthe 1920- *35*
Deedy, John 1923- *24*
Deegan, Paul Joseph 1937- *48*
  Brief Entry *38*
Defoe, Daniel 1660(?)-1731 ...... *22*
deFrance, Anthony
  See Di Franco, Anthony (Mario)
Degen, Bruce
  Brief Entry *47*
DeGering, Etta 1898- *7*
De Grazia
  See De Grazia, Ted
De Grazia, Ted 1909-1982 .... *39*
De Grazia, Ettore
  See De Grazia, Ted
De Groat, Diane 1947- *31*
deGros, J. H.
  See Villiard, Paul
de Grummond, Lena Young *6*
Deiss, Joseph J. 1915- *12*
DeJong, David C(ornel)
  1905-1967 .... *10*
de Jong, Dola *7*
De Jong, Meindert 1906- *2*
  See also CLR 1
de Kay, Ormonde, Jr. 1923- *7*
de Kiriline, Louise
  See Lawrence, Louise de Kiriline
Dekker, Carl
  See Laffin, John (Alfred Charles)
Dekker, Carl
  See Lynds, Dennis
deKruif, Paul (Henry)
  1890-1971 .... *50*
  Earlier sketch in SATA 5
Delacre, Lulu 1957- *36*
De Lage, Ida 1918- *11*
de la Mare, Walter 1873-1956 .... *16*
Delaney, Harry 1932- *3*
Delaney, Ned 1951- *28*

Delano, Hugh 1933- *20*
De La Ramée, (Marie) Louise
  1839-1908 .... *20*
Delaune, Lynne *7*
DeLaurentis, Louise Budde
  1920- *12*
Delderfield, Eric R(aymond)
  1909- *14*
Delderfield, R(onald) F(rederick)
  1912-1972 .... *20*
De Leeuw, Adele Louise
  1899- *30*
  Earlier sketch in SATA 1
Delessert, Etienne 1941- *46*
  Brief Entry *27*
Delmar, Roy
  See Wexler, Jerome (LeRoy)
Deloria, Vine (Victor), Jr.
  1933- *21*
Del Rey, Lester 1915- *22*
Delton, Judy 1931- *14*
Delulio, John 1938- *15*
Delving, Michael
  See Williams, Jay
Demarest, Chris(topher) L(ynn)
  1951- *45*
  Brief Entry *44*
Demarest, Doug
  See Barker, Will
Demas, Vida 1927- *9*
De Mejo, Oscar 1911- *40*
de Messières, Nicole 1930- *39*
Deming, Richard 1915- *24*
Demuth, Patricia Brennan 1948-
  Brief Entry *51*
Dengler, Sandy 1939-
  Brief Entry *40*
Denmark, Harrison
  See Zelazny, Roger (Joseph
  Christopher)
Denney, Diana 1910- *25*
Dennis, Morgan 1891(?)-1960 ..... *18*
Dennis, Wesley 1903-1966 .... *18*
Denniston, Elinore 1900-1978
  Obituary *24*
Denny, Norman (George)
  1901-1982 .... *43*
Denslow, W(illiam) W(allace)
  1856-1915 .... *16*
Denzel, Justin F(rancis) 1917- *46*
  Brief Entry *38*
Denzer, Ann Wiseman
  See Wiseman, Ann (Sayre)
de Paola, Thomas Anthony
  1934- *11*
de Paola, Tomie
  See de Paola, Thomas Anthony
  See also CLR 4
DePauw, Linda Grant 1940- *24*
deRegniers, Beatrice Schenk
  (Freedman) 1914- *2*
Derleth, August (William)
  1909-1971 .... *5*
Derman, Sarah Audrey 1915- *11*
de Roo, Anne Louise 1931- *25*
De Roussan, Jacques 1929-
  Brief Entry *31*
Derry Down Derry
  See Lear, Edward

Author Index

Derwent, Lavinia *14*
Desbarats, Peter 1933- *39*
De Selincourt, Aubrey
1894-1962 .... *14*
Desmond, Adrian J(ohn)
1947- *51*
Desmond, Alice Curtis 1897- *8*
Detine, Padre
See Olsen, Ib Spang
Deutsch, Babette 1895-1982 ...... *1*
Obituary *33*
De Valera, Sinead 1870(?)-1975
Obituary *30*
Devaney, John 1926- *12*
Devereux, Frederick L(eonard), Jr.
1914- *9*
Devlin, Harry 1918- *11*
Devlin, (Dorothy) Wende
1918- *11*
DeWaard, E. John 1935- *7*
DeWeese, Gene
See DeWeese, Thomas Eugene
DeWeese, Jean
See DeWeese, Thomas Eugene
DeWeese, Thomas Eugene
1934- *46*
Brief Entry *45*
Dewey, Ariane 1937- *7*
Dewey, Jennifer (Owings)
Brief Entry *48*
Dewey, Ken(neth Francis)
1940- *39*
DeWit, Dorothy (May Knowles)
1916-1980 .... *39*
Obituary *28*
Deyneka, Anita 1943- *24*
Deyrup, Astrith Johnson
1923- *24*
Diamond, Donna 1950- *35*
Brief Entry *30*
Diamond, Petra
See Sachs, Judith
Diamond, Rebecca
See Sachs, Judith
Dias, Earl Joseph 1916- *41*
Dick, Cappy
See Cleveland, George
Dick, Trella Lamson
1889-1974 .... *9*
Dickens, Charles 1812-1870 ..... *15*
Dickens, Frank
See Huline-Dickens, Frank William
Dickens, Monica 1915- *4*
Dickerson, Roy Ernest 1886-1965
Obituary *26*
Dickinson, Emily (Elizabeth)
1830-1886 .... *29*
Dickinson, Mary 1949- *48*
Brief Entry *41*
Dickinson, Peter 1927- *5*
Dickinson, Susan 1931- *8*
Dickinson, William Croft
1897-1973 .... *13*
Dickmeyer, Lowell A. 1939-
Brief Entry *51*
Dickson, Helen
See Reynolds, Helen Mary
Greenwood Campbell
Dickson, Naida 1916- *8*

Dietz, David H(enry)
1897-1984 .... *10*
Obituary *41*
Dietz, Lew 1907- *11*
Di Franco, Anthony (Mario)
1945- *42*
Digges, Jeremiah
See Berger, Josef
D'Ignazio, Fred 1949- *39*
Brief Entry *35*
Di Grazia, Thomas (?)-1983 ..... *32*
Dillard, Annie 1945- *10*
Dillard, Polly (Hargis) 1916- *24*
Dillon, Barbara 1927- *44*
Brief Entry *39*
Dillon, Diane 1933- *51*
Earlier sketch in SATA 15
Dillon, Eilis 1920- *2*
Dillon, Leo 1933- *51*
Earlier sketch in SATA 15
Dilson, Jesse 1914- *24*
Dinan, Carolyn
Brief Entry *47*
Dines, Glen 1925- *7*
Dinesen, Isak
See Blixen, Karen (Christentze
Dinesen)
Dinnerstein, Harvey 1928- *42*
Dinsdale, Tim 1924- *11*
Dirks, Rudolph 1877-1968
Brief Entry *31*
Disney, Walt(er Elias)
1901-1966 .... *28*
Brief Entry *27*
DiValentin, Maria 1911- *7*
Dixon, Dougal 1947- *45*
Dixon, Franklin W. [Collective
pseudonym] *1*
See also Adams, Harriet
S(tratemeyer); McFarlane, Leslie;
Stratemeyer, Edward L.; Svenson,
Andrew E.
Dixon, Jeanne 1936- *31*
Dixon, Peter L. 1931- *6*
Doane, Pelagie 1906-1966 .... *7*
Dobell, I(sabel) M(arian) B(arclay)
1909- *11*
Dobie, J(ames) Frank
1888-1964 .... *43*
Dobkin, Alexander 1908-1975
Obituary *30*
Dobler, Lavinia G. 1910- *6*
Dobrin, Arnold 1928- *4*
Dobson, Julia 1941- *48*
Dockery, Wallene T. 1941- *27*
"Dr. A"
See Silverstein, Alvin
Dr. X
See Nourse, Alan E(dward)
Dodd, Ed(ward) Benton 1902- *4*
Dodd, Lynley (Stuart) 1941- *35*
Dodge, Bertha S(anford)
1902- *8*
Dodge, Mary (Elizabeth) Mapes
1831-1905 .... *21*
Dodgson, Charles Lutwidge
1832-1898 .... *YABC 2*
Dodson, Kenneth M(acKenzie)
1907- *11*

Dodson, Susan 1941- *50*
Brief Entry *40*
Doerksen, Nan 1934-
Brief Entry *50*
Doherty, C. H. 1913- *6*
Dolan, Edward F(rancis), Jr.
1924- *45*
Brief Entry *31*
Dolch, Edward William
1889-1961 .... *50*
Dolch, Marguerite Pierce
1891-1978 .... *50*
Dolson, Hildegarde 1908- *5*
Domanska, Janina *6*
Domino, John
See Averill, Esther
Domjan, Joseph 1907- *25*
Donalds, Gordon
See Shirreffs, Gordon D.
Donna, Natalie 1934- *9*
Donovan, Frank (Robert) 1906-1975
Obituary *30*
Donovan, John 1928-
Brief Entry *29*
See also CLR 3
Donovan, William
See Berkebile, Fred D(onovan)
Doob, Leonard W(illiam)
1909- *8*
Dor, Ana
See Ceder, Georgiana Dorcas
Doré, (Louis Christophe Paul) Gustave
1832-1883 .... *19*
Doremus, Robert 1913- *30*
Dorian, Edith M(cEwen)
1900- *5*
Dorian, Harry
See Hamilton, Charles H. St. John
Dorian, Marguerite *7*
Dorman, Michael 1932- *7*
Dorman, N. B. 1927- *39*
Dorson, Richard M(ercer)
1916-1981 .... *30*
Doss, Helen (Grigsby) 1918- *20*
Doss, Margot Patterson *6*
dos Santos, Joyce Audy
Brief Entry *42*
Dottig
See Grider, Dorothy
Dotts, Maryann J. 1933- *35*
Doty, Jean Slaughter 1929- *28*
Doty, Roy 1922- *28*
Doubtfire, Dianne (Abrams)
1918- *29*
Dougherty, Charles 1922- *18*
Douglas, James McM.
See Butterworth, W. E.
Douglas, Kathryn
See Ewing, Kathryn
Douglas, Marjory Stoneman
1890- *10*
Douglass, Barbara 1930- *40*
Douglass, Frederick
1817(?)-1895 .... *29*
Douty, Esther M(orris)
1911-1978 .... *8*
Obituary *23*
Dow, Emily R. 1904- *10*

Dowdell, Dorothy (Florence) Karns
  1910- *12*
Dowden, Anne Ophelia 1907- *7*
Dowdey, Landon Gerald
  1923- *11*
Dowdy, Mrs. Regera
  See Gorey, Edward St. John
Downer, Marion 1892(?)-1971 .... *25*
Downey, Fairfax 1893- *3*
Downie, Mary Alice 1934- *13*
Doyle, Arthur Conan
  1859-1930 .... *24*
Doyle, Donovan
  See Boegehold, Betty (Doyle)
Doyle, Richard 1824-1883 .... *21*
Drabble, Margaret 1939- *48*
Draco, F.
  See Davis, Julia
Drager, Gary
  See Edens, Cooper
Dragonwagon, Crescent 1952- *41*
  Earlier sketch in SATA 11
Drake, Frank
  See Hamilton, Charles H. St. John
Drapier, M. B.
  See Swift, Jonathan
Drawson, Blair 1943- *17*
Dresang, Eliza (Carolyn Timberlake)
  1941- *19*
Drescher, Joan E(lizabeth)
  1939- *30*
Dreves, Veronica R. 1927-1986
  Obituary *50*
Drew, Patricia (Mary) 1938- *15*
Drewery, Mary 1918- *6*
Drial, J. E.
  See Laird, Jean E(louise)
Drucker, Malka 1945- *39*
  Brief Entry *29*
Drummond, V(iolet) H. 1911- *6*
Drummond, Walter
  See Silverberg, Robert
Drury, Roger W(olcott) 1914- *15*
Dryden, Pamela
  See Johnston, Norma
Duane, Diane (Elizabeth) 1952-
  Brief Entry *46*
du Blanc, Daphne
  See Groom, Arthur William
DuBois, Rochelle Holt
  See Holt, Rochelle Lynn
Du Bois, Shirley Graham
  1907-1977 .... *24*
Du Bois, W(illiam) E(dward)
  B(urghardt) 1868-1963 .... *42*
du Bois, William Pène 1916- *4*
  See also CLR 1
DuBose, LaRocque (Russ)
  1926- *2*
Du Chaillu, Paul (Belloni)
  1831(?)-1903 .... *26*
Duchesne, Janet 1930-
  Brief Entry *32*
Ducornet, Erica 1943- *7*
Dudley, Martha Ward 1909(?)-1985
  Obituary *45*
Dudley, Nancy
  See Cole, Lois Dwight

Dudley, Robert
  See Baldwin, James
Dudley, Ruth H(ubbell) 1905- *11*
Dueland, Joy V(ivian) *27*
Duff, Annis (James) 1904(?)-1986
  Obituary *49*
Duff, Maggie
  See Duff, Margaret K.
Duff, Margaret K. *37*
Dugan, Michael (Gray) 1947- *15*
Duggan, Alfred Leo
  1903-1964 .... *25*
Duggan, Maurice (Noel)
  1922-1974 .... *40*
  Obituary *30*
du Jardin, Rosamond (Neal)
  1902-1963 .... *2*
Dulac, Edmund 1882-1953 .... *19*
Dumas, Alexandre (the elder)
  1802-1870 .... *18*
du Maurier, Daphne 1907- *27*
Dunbar, Paul Laurence
  1872-1906 .... *34*
Dunbar, Robert E(verett)
  1926- *32*
Duncan, Frances (Mary) 1942-
  Brief Entry *48*
Duncan, Gregory
  See McClintock, Marshall
Duncan, Jane
  See Cameron, Elizabeth Jane
Duncan, Julia K. [Collective
  pseudonym] *1*
Duncan, Lois S(teinmetz)
  1934- *36*
  Earlier sketch in SATA 1
  See also SAAS 2
Duncan, Norman
  1871-1916 .... *YABC 1*
Duncombe, Frances (Riker)
  1900- *25*
Dunlop, Agnes M.R. *3*
Dunlop, Eileen (Rhona) 1938- *24*
Dunn, Harvey T(homas)
  1884-1952 .... *34*
Dunn, Judy
  See Spangenberg, Judith Dunn
Dunn, Mary Lois 1930- *6*
Dunnahoo, Terry 1927- *7*
Dunne, Mary Collins 1914- *11*
Dunnett, Margaret (Rosalind)
  1909-1977 .... *42*
Dunrea, Olivier 1953-
  Brief Entry *46*
Dupuy, T(revor) N(evitt)
  1916- *4*
Durant, John 1902- *27*
Durrell, Gerald (Malcolm)
  1925- *8*
Du Soe, Robert C.
  1892-1958 .... *YABC 2*
Dutz
  See Davis, Mary Octavia
Duvall, Evelyn Millis 1906- *9*
Duvoisin, Roger (Antoine)
  1904-1980 .... *30*
  Obituary *23*
  Earlier sketch in SATA 2
Dwiggins, Don 1913- *4*

Dwight, Allan
  See Cole, Lois Dwight
Dyer, James (Frederick) 1934- *37*
Dygard, Thomas J. 1931- *24*
Dyke, John 1935- *35*

E

E.V.B.
  See Boyle, Eleanor Vere (Gordon)
Eagar, Frances 1940- *11*
Eager, Edward (McMaken)
  1911-1964 .... *17*
Eagle, Mike 1942- *11*
Earle, Olive L. *7*
Earnshaw, Brian 1929- *17*
Eastman, Charles A(lexander)
  1858-1939 .... *YABC 1*
Eastman, P(hilip) D(ey)
  1909-1986 .... *33*
  Obituary *46*
Eastwick, Ivy O. *3*
Eaton, Anne T(haxter)
  1881-1971 .... *32*
Eaton, George L.
  See Verral, Charles Spain
Eaton, Jeanette 1886-1968 .... *24*
Eaton, Tom 1940- *22*
Ebel, Alex 1927- *11*
Eber, Dorothy (Margaret) Harley
  1930- *27*
Eberle, Irmengarde 1898-1979 .... *2*
  Obituary *23*
Eccles
  See Williams, Ferelith Eccles
Eckblad, Edith Berven 1923- *23*
Ecke, Wolfgang 1927-1983
  Obituary *37*
Eckert, Allan W. 1931- *29*
  Brief Entry *27*
Eckert, Horst 1931- *8*
Ede, Janina 1937- *33*
Edell, Celeste *12*
Edelman, Elaine
  Brief Entry *50*
Edelman, Lily (Judith) 1915- *22*
Edelson, Edward 1932- *51*
Edens, Cooper 1945- *49*
Edens, (Bishop) David 1926- *39*
Edey, Maitland A(rmstrong)
  1910- *25*
Edgeworth, Maria 1767-1849 ..... *21*
Edmonds, I(vy) G(ordon)
  1917- *8*
Edmonds, Walter D(umaux)
  1903- *27*
  Earlier sketch in SATA 1
  See also SAAS 4
Edmund, Sean
  See Pringle, Laurence
Edsall, Marian S(tickney)
  1920- *8*
Edwards, Al
  See Nourse, Alan E(dward)
Edwards, Alexander
  See Fleischer, Leonore
Edwards, Anne 1927- *35*

Edwards, Audrey 1947-
 Brief Entry 31
Edwards, Bertram
 See Edwards, Herbert Charles
Edwards, Bronwen Elizabeth
 See Rose, Wendy
Edwards, Cecile (Pepin)
 1916- 25
Edwards, Dorothy 1914-1982 4
 Obituary 31
Edwards, Gunvor 32
Edwards, Harvey 1929- 5
Edwards, Herbert Charles
 1912- 12
Edwards, Jane Campbell
 1932- 10
Edwards, Julic
 See Andrews, Julie
Edwards, Julie
 See Stratemeyer, Edward L.
Edwards, June
 See Forrester, Helen
Edwards, Linda Strauss 1948- 49
 Brief Entry 42
Edwards, Monica le Doux Newton
 1912- 12
Edwards, Olwen
 See Gater, Dilys
Edwards, Sally 1929- 7
Edwards, Samuel
 See Gerson, Noel B(ertram)
Egan, E(dward) W(elstead)
 1922- 35
Eggenberger, David 1918- 6
Eggleston, Edward 1837-1902 27
Egielski, Richard 1952- 49
 Earlier sketch in SATA 11
Egypt, Ophelia Settle
 1903-1984 16
 Obituary 38
Ehlert, Lois (Jane) 1934- 35
Ehrlich, Amy 1942- 25
Ehrlich, Bettina (Bauer) 1903- 1
Eichberg, James Bandman
 See Garfield, James B.
Eichenberg, Fritz 1901- 50
 Earlier sketch in SATA 9
Eichler, Margrit 1942- 35
Eichner, James A. 1927- 4
Eifert, Virginia S(nider)
 1911-1966 2
Einsel, Naiad 10
Einsel, Walter 1926- 10
Einzig, Susan 1922- 43
Eiseman, Alberta 1925- 15
Eisenberg, Azriel 1903- 12
Eisenberg, Lisa 1949-
 Brief Entry 50
Eisenberg, Phyllis Rose 1924- 41
Eisner, Vivienne
 See Margolis, Vivienne
Eisner, Will(iam Erwin) 1917- 31
Eitzen, Allan 1928- 9
Eitzen, Ruth (Carper) 1924- 9
Elam, Richard M(ace, Jr.)
 1920- 9
Elfman, Blossom 1925- 8
Elgin, Kathleen 1923- 39

Elia
 See Lamb, Charles
Eliot, Anne
 See Cole, Lois Dwight
Elisofon, Eliot 1911-1973
 Obituary 21
Elkin, Benjamin 1911- 3
Elkins, Dov Peretz 1937- 5
Ellacott, S(amuel) E(rnest)
 1911- 19
Elliott, Sarah M(cCarn) 1930- 14
Ellis, Anyon
 See Rowland-Entwistle, (Arthur)
 Theodore (Henry)
Ellis, Edward S(ylvester)
 1840-1916 .... YABC 1
Ellis, Ella Thorp 1928- 7
Ellis, Harry Bearse 1921- 9
Ellis, Herbert
 See Wilson, Lionel
Ellis, Mel 1912-1984 7
 Obituary 39
Ellison, Lucile Watkins
 1907(?)-1979 50
 Obituary 22
Ellison, Virginia Howell
 1910- 4
Ellsberg, Edward 1891- 7
Elmore, (Carolyn) Patricia
 1933- 38
 Brief Entry 35
Elspeth
 See Bragdon, Elspeth
Elting, Mary 1906- 2
Elwart, Joan Potter 1927- 2
Emberley, Barbara A(nne) 8
 See also CLR 5
Emberley, Ed(ward Randolph)
 1931- 8
 See also CLR 5
Emberley, Michael 1960- 34
Embry, Margaret (Jacob)
 1919- 5
Emerson, Alice B. [Collective
 pseudonym] 1
Emerson, William K(eith)
 1925- 25
Emery, Anne (McGuigan)
 1907- 33
 Earlier sketch in SATA 1
Emmens, Carol Ann 1944- 39
Emmons, Della (Florence) Gould
 1890-1983
 Obituary 39
Emrich, Duncan (Black Macdonald)
 1908- 11
Emslie, M. L.
 See Simpson, Myrtle L(illias)
Ende, Michael 1930(?)-
 Brief Entry 42
Enderle, Judith (Ann) 1941- 38
Enfield, Carrie
 See Smith, Susan Vernon
Engdahl, Sylvia Louise 1933- 4
 See also CLR 2
 See also SAAS 5
Engle, Eloise Katherine 1923- 9
Englebert, Victor 1933- 8

English, James W(ilson)
 1915- 37
Enright, D(ennis) J(oseph)
 1920- 25
Enright, Elizabeth 1909-1968 9
 See also CLR 4
Enright, Maginel Wright
 See Barney, Maginel Wright
Enys, Sarah L.
 See Sloggett, Nellie
Ephron, Delia 1944-
 Brief Entry 50
Epp, Margaret A(gnes) 20
Epple, Anne Orth 1927- 20
Epstein, Anne Merrick 1931- 20
Epstein, Beryl (Williams)
 1910- 31
 Earlier sketch in SATA 1
Epstein, Perle S(herry) 1938- 27
Epstein, Samuel 1909- 31
 Earlier sketch in SATA 1
Erdman, Loula Grace 1
Erdoes, Richard 1912- 33
 Brief Entry 28
Erhard, Walter 1920-
 Brief Entry 30
Erickson, Russell E(verett)
 1932- 27
Erickson, Sabra R(ollins)
 1912- 35
Ericson, Walter
 See Fast, Howard
Erikson, Mel 1937- 31
Erlanger, Baba
 See Trahey, Jane
Erlich, Lillian (Feldman)
 1910- 10
Ernest, William
 See Berkebile, Fred D(onovan)
Ernst, (Lyman) John 1940- 39
Ernst, Kathryn (Fitzgerald)
 1942- 25
Ernst, Lisa Campbell 1957-
 Brief Entry 44
Ervin, Janet Halliday 1923- 4
Erwin, Will
 See Eisner, Will(iam Erwin)
Eshmeyer, R(einhart) E(rnst)
 1898- 29
Espeland, Pamela (Lee) 1951-
 Brief Entry 38
Espy, Willard R(ichardson)
 1910- 38
Estep, Irene (Compton) 5
Estes, Eleanor 1906- 7
 See also CLR 2
Estoril, Jean
 See Allan, Mabel Esther
Etchemendy, Nancy 1952- 38
Etchison, Birdie L(ee) 1937- 38
Ets, Marie Hall 2
Eunson, Dale 1904- 5
Evans, Eva Knox 1905- 27
Evans, Hubert Reginald 1892-1986
 Obituary 48
Evans, Katherine (Floyd)
 1901-1964 5
Evans, Mari 10
Evans, Mark 19

Evans, Patricia Healy
   See Carpenter, Patricia
Evarts, Esther
   See Benson, Sally
Evarts, Hal G. (Jr.) 1915- 6
Everett, Gail
   See Hale, Arlene
Evernden, Margery 1916- 5
Evslin, Bernard 1922- 45
   Brief Entry 28
Ewen, David 1907-1985 4
   Obituary 47
Ewing, Juliana (Horatia Gatty)
   1841-1885 16
Ewing, Kathryn 1921- 20
Eyerly, Jeannette Hyde 1908- 4
Eyre, Dorothy
   See McGuire, Leslie (Sarah)
Eyre, Katherine Wigmore
   1901-1970 26
Ezzell, Marilyn 1937- 42
   Brief Entry 38

F

Fabe, Maxene 1943- 15
Faber, Doris 1924- 3
Faber, Harold 1919- 5
Fabre, Jean Henri (Casimir)
   1823-1915 22
Facklam, Margery Metz 1927- 20
Fadiman, Clifton (Paul) 1904- 11
Fair, Sylvia 1933- 13
Fairfax-Lucy, Brian (Fulke Cameron-
   Ramsay) 1898-1974 6
   Obituary 26
Fairlie, Gerard 1899-1983
   Obituary 34
Fairman, Joan A(lexandra)
   1935- 10
Faithfull, Gail 1936- 8
Falconer, James
   See Kirkup, James
Falkner, Leonard 1900- 12
Fall, Thomas
   See Snow, Donald Clifford
Falls, C(harles) B(uckles)
   1874-1960 38
   Brief Entry 27
Falstein, Louis 1909- 37
Fanning, Leonard M(ulliken)
   1888-1967 5
Faralla, Dana 1909- 9
Faralla, Dorothy W.
   See Faralla, Dana
Farb, Peter 1929-1980 12
   Obituary 22
Farber, Norma 1909-1984 25
   Obituary 38
Farge, Monique
   See Grée, Alain
Farjeon, (Eve) Annabel 1919- 11
Farjeon, Eleanor 1881-1965 2
Farley, Carol 1936- 4
Farley, Walter 1920- 43
   Earlier sketch in SATA 2

Farmer, Penelope (Jane)
   1939- 40
   Brief Entry 39
   See also CLR 8
Farmer, Peter 1950- 38
Farnham, Burt
   See Clifford, Harold B.
Farquhar, Margaret C(utting)
   1905- 13
Farquharson, Alexander 1944- 46
Farquharson, Martha
   See Finley, Martha
Farr, Finis (King) 1904- 10
Farrar, Susan Clement 1917- 33
Farrell, Ben
   See Cebulash, Mel
Farrington, Benjamin 1891-1974
   Obituary 20
Farrington, Selwyn Kip, Jr.
   1904- 20
Farthing, Alison 1936- 45
   Brief Entry 36
Fassler, Joan (Grace) 1931- 11
Fast, Howard 1914- 7
Fatchen, Max 1920- 20
Father Xavier
   See Hurwood, Bernhardt J.
Fatigati, (Frances) Evelyn de Buhr
   1948- 24
Fatio, Louise 6
Faulhaber, Martha 1926- 7
Faulkner, Anne Irvin 1906- 23
Faulkner, Nancy
   See Faulkner, Anne Irvin
Fax, Elton Clay 1909- 25
Feagles, Anita MacRae 9
Feagles, Elizabeth
   See Day, Beth (Feagles)
Feague, Mildred H. 1915- 14
Fecher, Constance 1911- 7
Feder, Paula (Kurzband)
   1935- 26
Feder, Robert Arthur 1909-1969
   Brief Entry 35
Feelings, Muriel (Grey) 1938- 16
   See also CLR 5
Feelings, Thomas 1933- 8
Feelings, Tom
   See Feelings, Thomas
   See also CLR 5
Fehrenbach, T(heodore) R(eed, Jr.)
   1925- 33
Feiffer, Jules 1929- 8
Feig, Barbara Krane 1937- 34
Feikema, Feike
   See Manfred, Frederick F(eikema)
Feil, Hila 1942- 12
Feilen, John
   See May, Julian
Feldman, Anne (Rodgers)
   1939- 19
Félix
   See Vincent, Félix
Fellows, Muriel H. 10
Felsen, Henry Gregor 1916- 1
   See also SAAS 2
Felton, Harold William 1902- 1
Felton, Ronald Oliver 1909- 3
Felts, Shirley 1934- 33

Fenderson, Lewis H.
   1907-1983 47
   Obituary 37
Fenner, Carol 1929- 7
Fenner, Phyllis R(eid)
   1899-1982 1
   Obituary 29
Fenten, Barbara D(oris) 1935- 26
Fenten, D. X. 1932- 4
Fenton, Carroll Lane
   1900-1969 5
Fenton, Edward 1917- 7
Fenton, Mildred Adams 1899- 21
Fenwick, Patti
   See Grider, Dorothy
Feravolo, Rocco Vincent
   1922- 10
Ferber, Edna 1887-1968 7
Ferguson, Bob
   See Ferguson, Robert Bruce
Ferguson, Cecil 1931- 45
Ferguson, Robert Bruce 1927- 13
Ferguson, Walter (W.) 1930- 34
Fergusson, Erna 1888-1964 5
Fermi, Laura (Capon)
   1907-1977 6
   Obituary 28
Fern, Eugene A. 1919- 10
Ferrier, Lucy
   See Penzler, Otto
Ferris, Helen Josephine
   1890-1969 21
Ferris, James Cody [Collective
   pseudonym] 1
   See also McFarlane, Leslie;
   Stratemeyer, Edward L.
Ferris, Jean 1939-
   Brief Entry 50
Ferry, Charles 1927- 43
Fetz, Ingrid 1915- 30
Feydy, Anne Lindbergh
   Brief Entry 32
   See Sapieyevski, Anne Lindbergh
Fiammenghi, Gioia 1929- 9
Fiarotta, Noel 1944- 15
Fiarotta, Phyllis 1942- 15
Fichter, George S. 1922- 7
Fidler, Kathleen (Annie)
   1899-1980 3
   Obituary 45
Fiedler, Jean 4
Field, Edward 1924- 8
Field, Elinor Whitney 1889-1980
   Obituary 28
Field, Eugene 1850-1895 16
Field, Gans T.
   See Wellman, Manly Wade
Field, Rachel (Lyman)
   1894-1942 15
Fife, Dale (Odile) 1910- 18
Fighter Pilot, A
   See Johnston, H(ugh) A(nthony)
   S(tephen)
Figueroa, Pablo 1938- 9
Fijan, Carol 1918- 12
Fillmore, Parker H(oysted)
   1878-1944 .... YABC 1
Filstrup, Chris
   See Filstrup, E(dward) Christian

Filstrup, E(dward) Christian
1942- 43
Filstrup, Jane Merrill
See Merrill, Jane
Filstrup, Janie
See Merrill, Jane
Finder, Martin
See Salzmann, Siegmund
Fine, Anne 1947- 29
Finger, Charles J(oseph)
1869(?)-1941 42
Fink, William B(ertrand)
1916- 22
Finke, Blythe F(oote) 1922- 26
Finkel, George (Irvine)
1909-1975 8
Finlay, Winifred 1910- 23
Finlayson, Ann 1925- 8
Finley, Martha 1828-1909 43
Firmin, Charlotte 1954- 29
Firmin, Peter 1928- 15
Fischbach, Julius 1894- 10
Fischler, Stan(ley I.)
Brief Entry 36
Fishback, Margaret
See Antolini, Margaret Fishback
Fisher, Aileen (Lucia) 1906- 25
Earlier sketch in SATA 1
Fisher, Barbara 1940- 44
Brief Entry 34
Fisher, Clavin C(argill) 1912- 24
Fisher, Dorothy Canfield
1879-1958 .... YABC 1
Fisher, John (Oswald Hamilton)
1909- 15
Fisher, Laura Harrison 1934- 5
Fisher, Leonard Everett 1924- 34
Earlier sketch in SATA 4
See also SAAS 1
Fisher, Lois I. 1948- 38
Brief Entry 35
Fisher, Margery (Turner)
1913- 20
Fisher, Robert (Tempest)
1943- 47
Fisk, Nicholas 1923- 25
Fitch, Clarke
See Sinclair, Upton (Beall)
Fitch, John IV
See Cormier, Robert (Edmund)
Fitschen, Dale 1937- 20
Fitzalan, Roger
See Trevor, Elleston
Fitzgerald, Captain Hugh
See Baum, L(yman) Frank
FitzGerald, Cathleen 1932-1987
Obituary 50
Fitzgerald, Edward Earl 1919- 20
Fitzgerald, F(rancis) A(nthony)
1940- 15
Fitzgerald, John D(ennis)
1907- 20
See also CLR 1
Fitzhardinge, Joan Margaret
1912- 2
Fitzhugh, Louise (Perkins)
1928-1974 45
Obituary 24
Earlier sketch in SATA 1
See also CLR 1

Fitz-Randolph, Jane (Currens)
1915- 51
Flack, Marjorie
1899-1958 .... YABC 2
Flack, Naomi John (White) 40
Brief Entry 35
Flash Flood
See Robinson, Jan M.
Fleischer, Leonore 1934(?)-
Brief Entry 47
Fleischer, Max 1889-1972
Brief Entry 30
Fleischhauer-Hardt, Helga
1936- 30
Fleischman, Paul 1952- 39
Brief Entry 32
Fleischman, (Albert) Sid(ney)
1920- 8
See also CLR 1
Fleisher, Robbin 1951-1977
Brief Entry 49
Fleishman, Seymour 1918-
Brief Entry 32
Fleming, Alice Mulcahey
1928- 9
Fleming, Elizabeth P. 1888-1985
Obituary 48
Fleming, Ian (Lancaster)
1908-1964 9
Fleming, Susan 1932- 32
Fleming, Thomas J(ames)
1927- 8
Fletcher, Charlie May 1897- 3
Fletcher, Colin 1922- 28
Fletcher, Helen Jill 1911- 13
Fletcher, Richard E. 1917(?)-1983
Obituary 34
Fletcher, Rick
See Fletcher, Richard E.
Fleur, Anne 1901-
Brief Entry 31
Flexner, James Thomas 1908- 9
Flitner, David P. 1949- 7
Floethe, Louise Lee 1913- 4
Floethe, Richard 1901- 4
Floherty, John Joseph
1882-1964 25
Flood, Flash
See Robinson, Jan M.
Flora, James (Royer) 1914- 30
Earlier sketch in SATA 1
Florian, Douglas 1950- 19
Flory, Jane Trescott 1917- 22
Flowerdew, Phyllis 33
Floyd, Gareth 1940-
Brief Entry 31
Fluchère, Henri A(ndré) 1914- 40
Flynn, Barbara 1928- 9
Flynn, Jackson
See Shirreffs, Gordon D.
Flynn, Mary
See Welsh, Mary Flynn
Fodor, Ronald V(ictor) 1944- 25
Foley, (Anna) Bernice Williams
1902- 28
Foley, June 1944- 44
Foley, (Mary) Louise Munro 1933-
Brief Entry 40

Foley, Rae
See Denniston, Elinore
Folkard, Charles James 1878-1963
Brief Entry 28
Follett, Helen (Thomas) 1884(?)-1970
Obituary 27
Folsom, Franklin (Brewster)
1907- 5
Folsom, Michael (Brewster)
1938- 40
Fontenot, Mary Alice 1910- 34
Fooner, Michael 22
Forberg, Ati 1925- 22
Forbes, Bryan 1926- 37
Forbes, Cabot L.
See Hoyt, Edwin P(almer), Jr.
Forbes, Esther 1891-1967 2
Forbes, Graham B. [Collective
pseudonym] 1
Forbes, Kathryn
See McLean, Kathryn (Anderson)
Ford, Albert Lee
See Stratemeyer, Edward L.
Ford, Barbara
Brief Entry 34
Ford, Brian J(ohn) 1939- 49
Ford, Elbur
See Hibbert, Eleanor
Ford, George (Jr.) 31
Ford, Hilary
See Youd, (Christopher) Samuel
Ford, Hildegarde
See Morrison, Velma Ford
Ford, Marcia
See Radford, Ruby L.
Ford, Nancy K(effer) 1906-1961
Obituary 29
Foreman, Michael 1938- 2
Forest, Antonia 29
Forester, C(ecil) S(cott)
1899-1966 13
Forman, Brenda 1936- 4
Forman, James Douglas 1932- 8
Forrest, Sybil
See Markun, Patricia M(aloney)
Forrester, Helen 1919- 48
Forrester, Marian
See Schachtel, Roger
Forrester, Victoria 1940- 40
Brief Entry 35
Forsee, (Frances) Aylesa 1
Fort, Paul
See Stockton, Francis Richard
Fortnum, Peggy 1919- 26
Fortune, Brad W. 1955- 34
Foster, Brad W. 1955- 34
Foster, Doris Van Liew 1899- 10
Foster, E(lizabeth) C(onnell)
1902- 9
Foster, Elizabeth 1905-1963 10
Foster, Elizabeth Vincent
1902- 12
Foster, F. Blanche 1919- 11
Foster, G(eorge) Allen
1907-1969 26
Foster, Genevieve (Stump)
1893-1979 2
Obituary 23
See also CLR 7

Foster, Hal
  See Foster, Harold Rudolf
Foster, Harold Rudolf 1892-1982
  Obituary 31
Foster, John T(homas) 1925- 8
Foster, Laura Louise 1918- 6
Foster, Margaret Lesser 1899-1979
  Obituary 21
Foster, Marian Curtis
  1909-1978 23
Fourth Brother, The
  See Aung, (Maung) Htin
Fowke, Edith (Margaret)
  1913- 14
Fowles, John 1926- 22
Fox, Charles Philip 1913- 12
Fox, Eleanor
  See St. John, Wylly Folk
Fox, Fontaine Talbot, Jr. 1884-1964
  Obituary 23
Fox, Fred 1903(?)-1981
  Obituary 27
Fox, Freeman
  See Hamilton, Charles H. St. John
Fox, Grace
  See Anderson, Grace Fox
Fox, Larry 30
Fox, Lorraine 1922-1975 11
  Obituary 27
Fox, Mary Virginia 1919- 44
  Brief Entry 39
Fox, Mem
  See Fox, Merrion Frances
Fox, Merrion Frances 1946- 51
Fox, Michael Wilson 1937- 15
Fox, Paula 1923- 17
  See also CLR 1
Fox, Petronella
  See Balogh, Penelope
Fox, Robert J. 1927- 33
Fradin, Dennis Brindel 1945- 29
Frame, Paul 1913-
  Brief Entry 33
Franchere, Ruth 18
Francis, Charles
  See Holme, Bryan
Francis, Dee
  See Haas, Dorothy F.
Francis, Dorothy Brenner
  1926- 10
Francis, Pamela (Mary) 1926- 11
Franco, Marjorie 38
Francois, André 1915- 25
Francoise
  See Seignobosc, Francoise
Frank, Anne 1929-1945(?)
  Brief Entry 42
Frank, Josette 1893- 10
Frank, Mary 1933- 34
Frank, R., Jr.
  See Ross, Frank (Xavier), Jr.
Frankau, Mary Evelyn 1899- 4
Frankel, Bernice 9
Frankel, Edward 1910- 44
Frankel, Julie 1947- 40
  Brief Entry 34
Frankenberg, Robert 1911- 22
Franklin, Harold 1920- 13

Franklin, Max
  See Deming, Richard
Franklin, Steve
  See Stevens, Franklin
Franzén, Nils-Olof 1916- 10
Frascino, Edward 1938- 48
  Brief Entry 33
Frasconi, Antonio 1919- 6
Fraser, Antonia (Pakenham) 1932-
  Brief Entry 32
Fraser, Betty
  See Fraser, Elizabeth Marr
Fraser, Elizabeth Marr 1928- 31
Fraser, Eric (George)
  1902-1983 38
Frazier, Neta Lohnes 7
Freed, Alvyn M. 1913- 22
Freedman, Benedict 1919- 27
Freedman, Nancy 1920- 27
Freedman, Russell (Bruce)
  1929- 16
Freeman, Barbara C(onstance)
  1906- 28
Freeman, Bill
  See Freeman, William Bradford
Freeman, Don 1908-1978 17
Freeman, Ira M(aximilian)
  1905- 21
Freeman, Lucy (Greenbaum)
  1916- 24
Freeman, Mae (Blacker)
  1907- 25
Freeman, Peter J.
  See Calvert, Patricia
Freeman, Tony
  Brief Entry 44
Freeman, William Bradford 1938-
  Brief Entry 48
Fregosi, Claudia (Anne Marie)
  1946- 24
French, Allen 1870-1946 .....YABC 1
French, Dorothy Kayser 1926- 5
French, Fiona 1944- 6
French, Kathryn
  See Mosesson, Gloria R(ubin)
French, Michael 1944- 49
  Brief Entry 38
French, Paul
  See Asimov, Isaac
Freund, Rudolf 1915-1969
  Brief Entry 28
Frewer, Glyn 1931- 11
Frick, C. H.
  See Irwin, Constance Frick
Frick, Constance
  See Irwin, Constance Frick
Friedlander, Joanne K(ohn)
  1930- 9
Friedman, Estelle 1920- 7
Friedman, Frieda 1905- 43
Friedman, Ina R(osen) 1926- 49
  Brief Entry 41
Friedman, Marvin 1930- 42
  Brief Entry 33
Friedrich, Otto (Alva) 1929- 33
Friedrich, Priscilla 1927- 39
Friendlich, Dick
  See Friendlich, Richard J.
Friendlich, Richard J. 1909- 11

Friermood, Elisabeth Hamilton
  1903- 5
Friis, Babbis
  See Friis-Baastad, Babbis
Friis-Baastad, Babbis
  1921-1970 7
Frimmer, Steven 1928- 31
Friskey, Margaret Richards
  1901- 5
Fritz, Jean (Guttery) 1915- 29
  Earlier sketch in SATA 1
  See also CLR 2
  See also SAAS 2
Froissart, Jean
  1338(?)-1410(?) 28
Froman, Elizabeth Hull
  1920-1975 10
Froman, Robert (Winslow)
  1917- 8
Fromm, Lilo 1928- 29
Frommer, Harvey 1937- 41
Frost, A(rthur) B(urdett)
  1851-1928 19
Frost, Erica
  See Supraner, Robyn
Frost, Lesley 1899(?)-1983 14
  Obituary 34
Frost, Robert (Lee) 1874-1963 14
Fry, Edward Bernard 1925- 35
Fry, Rosalie 1911- 3
Fuchs, Erich 1916- 6
Fuchshuber, Annegert 1940- 43
Fujikawa, Gyo 1908- 39
  Brief Entry 30
Fujita, Tamao 1905- 7
Fujiwara, Michiko 1946- 15
Fuka, Vladimir 1926-1977
  Obituary 27
Fuller, Catherine L(euthold)
  1916- 9
Fuller, Edmund (Maybank)
  1914- 21
Fuller, Iola
  See McCoy, Iola Fuller
Fuller, Lois Hamilton 1915- 11
Fuller, Margaret
  See Ossoli, Sarah Margaret (Fuller)
  marchesa d'
Fults, John Lee 1932- 33
Funai, Mamoru (Rolland) 1932-
  Brief Entry 46
Funk, Thompson
  See Funk, Tom
Funk, Tom 1911- 7
Funke, Lewis 1912- 11
Furchgott, Terry 1948- 29
Furniss, Tim 1948- 49
Furukawa, Toshi 1924- 24
Fyleman, Rose 1877-1957 21
Fyson, J(enny) G(race) 1904- 42

G

Gackenbach, Dick 48
  Brief Entry 30
Gaddis, Vincent H. 1913- 35
Gadler, Steve J. 1905- 36

Gaeddert, Lou Ann (Bigge)
1931- 20
Gàg, Flavia 1907-1979
Obituary 24
Gàg, Wanda (Hazel)
1893-1946 .... YABC 1
See also CLR 4
Gage, Wilson
See Steele, Mary Q(uintard Govan)
Gagliardo, Ruth Garver 1895(?)-1980
Obituary 22
Gal, Laszlo 1933-
Brief Entry 32
Galdone, Paul 1914-1986 17
Obituary 49
Galinsky, Ellen 1942- 23
Gallant, Roy (Arthur) 1924- 4
Gallico, Paul 1897-1976 13
Galt, Thomas Franklin, Jr.
1908- 5
Galt, Tom
See Galt, Thomas Franklin, Jr.
Gamerman, Martha 1941- 15
Gannett, Ruth Chrisman (Arens)
1896-1979 33
Gannett, Ruth Stiles 1923- 3
Gannon, Robert (Haines)
1931- 8
Gans, Roma 1894- 45
Gantos, Jack
See Gantos, John (Bryan), Jr.
Gantos, John (Bryan), Jr.
1951- 20
Garbutt, Bernard 1900-
Brief Entry 31
Gard, Joyce
See Reeves, Joyce
Gard, Robert Edward 1910- 18
Gard, (Sanford) Wayne 1899-1986
Obituary 49
Gardam, Jane 1928- 39
Brief Entry 28
See also CLR 12
Garden, Nancy 1938- 12
Gardner, Beau
Brief Entry 50
Gardner, Dic
See Gardner, Richard
Gardner, Hugh 1910-1986
Obituary 49
Gardner, Jeanne LeMonnier 5
Gardner, John (Champlin, Jr.)
1933-1982 40
Obituary 31
Gardner, Martin 1914- 16
Gardner, Richard 1931- 24
Gardner, Richard A. 1931- 13
Gardner, Robert 1929-
Brief Entry 43
Gardner, Sheldon 1934- 33
Garelick, May 19
Garfield, James B. 1881-1984 6
Obituary 38
Garfield, Leon 1921- 32
Earlier sketch in SATA 1
Garis, Howard R(oger)
1873-1962 13
Garner, Alan 1934- 18
Garnett, Eve C. R. 3

Garraty, John A. 1920- 23
Garret, Maxwell R. 1917- 39
Garretson, Victoria Diane
1945- 44
Garrett, Helen 1895- 21
Garrigue, Sheila 1931- 21
Garrison, Barbara 1931- 19
Garrison, Frederick
See Sinclair, Upton (Beall)
Garrison, Webb B(lack) 1919- 25
Garst, Doris Shannon 1894- 1
Garst, Shannon
See Garst, Doris Shannon
Garthwaite, Marion H. 1893- 7
Garton, Malinda D(ean) (?)-1976
Obituary 26
Gasperini, Jim 1952-
Brief Entry 49
Gater, Dilys 1944- 41
Gates, Doris 1901- 34
Earlier sketch in SATA 1
See also SAAS 1
Gates, Frieda 1933- 26
Gathorne-Hardy, Jonathan G.
1933- 26
Gatty, Juliana Horatia
See Ewing, Juliana (Horatia Gatty)
Gatty, Margaret Scott 1809-1873
Brief Entry 27
Gauch, Patricia Lee 1934- 26
Gault, Clare S. 1925- 36
Gault, Frank 1926-1982 36
Brief Entry 30
Gault, William Campbell
1910- 8
Gaver, Becky
See Gaver, Rebecca
Gaver, Rebecca 1952- 20
Gay, Francis
See Gee, H(erbert) L(eslie)
Gay, Kathlyn 1930- 9
Gay, Zhenya 1906-1978 19
Gee, H(erbert) L(eslie) 1901-1977
Obituary 26
Gee, Maurice (Gough) 1931- 46
Geer, Charles 1922- 42
Brief Entry 32
Gehr, Mary 32
Geipel, Eileen 1932- 30
Geis, Darlene 7
Geisel, Helen 1898-1967 26
Geisel, Theodor Seuss 1904- 28
Earlier sketch in SATA 1
See also CLR 1
Geldart, William 1936- 15
Gelinas, Paul J. 1911- 10
Gelman, Rita Golden 1937-
Brief Entry 51
Gelman, Steve 1934- 3
Gemming, Elizabeth 1932- 11
Gendel, Evelyn W. 1916(?)-1977
Obituary 27
Gentle, Mary 1956- 48
Gentleman, David 1930- 7
George, Jean Craighead 1919- 2
See also CLR 1
George, John L(othar) 1916- 2
George, S(idney) C(harles)
1898- 11

George, W(illiam) Lloyd 1900(?)-1975
Obituary 30
Georgiou, Constantine 1927- 7
Gérard, Jean Ignace Isidore
1803-1847 45
Geras, Adele (Daphne) 1944- 23
Gergely, Tibor 1900-1978
Obituary 20
Geringer, Laura 1948- 29
Gerler, William R(obert)
1917- 47
Gerrard, Jean 1933- 51
Gerrard, Roy 1935- 47
Brief Entry 45
Gerson, Corinne 37
Gerson, Noel B(ertram) 1914- 22
Gerstein, Mordicai 1935- 47
Brief Entry 36
Gesner, Clark 1938- 40
Gessner, Lynne 1919- 16
Gevirtz, Eliezer 1950- 49
Gewe, Raddory
See Gorey, Edward St. John
Gibbons, Gail 1944- 23
See also CLR 8
Gibbs, Alonzo (Lawrence)
1915- 5
Gibbs, (Cecilia) May 1877-1969
Obituary 27
Gibbs, Tony
See Gibbs, Wolcott, Jr.
Gibbs, Wolcott, Jr. 1935- 40
Giblin, James Cross 1933- 33
Gibson, Josephine
See Joslin, Sesyle
Gidal, Sonia 1922- 2
Gidal, Tim N(ahum) 1909- 2
Giegling, John A(llan) 1935- 17
Giff, Patricia Reilly 1935- 33
Gifford, Griselda 1931- 42
Gilbert, Ann
See Taylor, Ann
Gilbert, Harriett 1948- 30
Gilbert, (Agnes) Joan (Sewell)
1931- 10
Gilbert, John (Raphael) 1926- ... 36
Gilbert, Miriam
See Presberg, Miriam Goldstein
Gilbert, Nan
See Gilbertson, Mildred
Gilbert, Sara (Dulaney) 1943- ... 11
Gilbert, W(illiam) S(chwenk)
1836-1911 36
Gilbertson, Mildred Geiger
1908- 2
Gilbreath, Alice (Thompson)
1921- 12
Gilbreth, Frank B., Jr. 1911- ... 2
Gilfond, Henry 2
Gilge, Jeanette 1924- 22
Gill, Derek L(ewis) T(heodore)
1919- 9
Gill, Margery Jean 1925- 22
Gillett, Mary 7
Gillette, Henry Sampson
1915- 14
Gillham, Bill
See Gillham, William Edwin Charles

Gillham, William Edwin Charles
1936- *42*
Gilliam, Stan 1946- *39*
  Brief Entry *35*
Gilman, Dorothy
  See Butters, Dorothy Gilman
Gilman, Esther 1925- *15*
Gilmore, Iris 1900- *22*
Gilmore, Mary (Jean Cameron)
1865-1962 .... *49*
Gilson, Barbara
  See Gilson, Charles James Louis
Gilson, Charles James Louis
1878-1943 ....*YABC 2*
Gilson, Jamie 1933- *37*
  Brief Entry *34*
Ginsburg, Mirra *6*
Giovanni, Nikki 1943- *24*
  See also CLR 6
Giovanopoulos, Paul 1939- *7*
Gipson, Frederick B.
1908-1973 .... *2*
  Obituary *24*
Girard, Linda Walvoord 1942- *41*
Girion, Barbara 1937- *26*
Gittings, Jo Manton 1919- *3*
Gittings, Robert 1911- *6*
Gladstone, Eve
  See Werner, Herma
Gladstone, Gary 1935- *12*
Gladstone, M(yron) J. 1923- *37*
Gladwin, William Zachary
  See Zollinger, Gulielma
Glanville, Brian (Lester)
1931- *42*
Glanzman, Louis S. 1922- *36*
Glaser, Dianne E(lizabeth)
1937- *50*
  Brief Entry *31*
Glaser, Milton 1929- *11*
Glaspell, Susan
1882-1948 ....*YABC 2*
Glass, Andrew
  Brief Entry *46*
Glauber, Uta (Heil) 1936- *17*
Glazer, Tom 1914- *9*
Gleasner, Diana (Cottle)
1936- *29*
Gleason, Judith 1929- *24*
Glendinning, Richard 1917- *24*
Glendinning, Sally
  See Glendinning, Sara W(ilson)
Glendinning, Sara W(ilson)
1913- *24*
Glenn, Mel 1943- *51*
  Brief Entry *45*
Gles, Margaret Breitmaier
1940- *22*
Glick, Carl (Cannon)
1890-1971 .... *14*
Glick, Virginia Kirkus 1893-1980
  Obituary *23*
Gliewe, Unada 1927- *3*
Glines, Carroll V(ane), Jr.
1920- *19*
Globe, Leah Ain 1900- *41*
Glovach, Linda 1947- *7*
Glubok, Shirley *6*
  See also CLR 1

Gluck, Felix 1924(?)-1981
  Obituary *25*
Glynne-Jones, William 1907- *11*
Gobbato, Imero 1923- *39*
Goble, Dorothy *26*
Goble, Paul 1933- *25*
Goble, Warwick (?)-1943 .... *46*
Godden, Rumer 1907- *36*
  Earlier sketch in SATA 3
Gode, Alexander
  See Gode von Aesch, Alexander
  (Gottfried Friedrich)
Gode von Aesch, Alexander (Gottfried
  Friedrich) 1906-1970 .... *14*
Godfrey, Jane
  See Bowden, Joan Chase
Godfrey, William
  See Youd, (Christopher) Samuel
Goettel, Elinor 1930- *12*
Goetz, Delia 1898- *22*
Goffstein, M(arilyn) B(rooke)
1940- *8*
  See also CLR 3
Golann, Cecil Paige 1921- *11*
Golbin, Andrée 1923- *15*
Gold, Phyllis 1941- *21*
Gold, Sharlya *9*
Goldberg, Herbert S. 1926- *25*
Goldberg, Stan J. 1939- *26*
Goldfeder, Cheryl
  See Pahz, Cheryl Suzanne
Goldfeder, Jim
  See Pahz, James Alon
Goldfrank, Helen Colodny
1912- *6*
Goldin, Augusta 1906- *13*
Goldsborough, June 1923- *19*
Goldsmith, Howard 1943- *24*
Goldsmith, Oliver 1728-1774 ..... *26*
Goldstein, Nathan 1927- *47*
Goldstein, Philip 1910- *23*
Goldston, Robert (Conroy)
1927- *6*
Goll, Reinhold W(eimar)
1897- *26*
Gonzalez, Gloria 1940- *23*
Goodall, John S(trickland)
1908- *4*
Goodbody, Slim
  See Burstein, John
Goode, Diane 1949- *15*
Goode, Stephen 1943-
  Brief Entry *40*
Goodenow, Earle 1913- *40*
Goodman, Deborah Lerme
1956- *50*
  Brief Entry *49*
Goodman, Elaine 1930- *9*
Goodman, Joan Elizabeth
1950- *50*
Goodman, Walter 1927- *9*
Goodrich, Samuel Griswold
1793-1860 .... *23*
Goodwin, Hal
  See Goodwin, Harold Leland
Goodwin, Harold Leland
1914- *51*
  Earlier sketch in SATA 13

Goor, Nancy (Ruth Miller)
1944- *39*
  Brief Entry *34*
Goor, Ron(ald Stephen) 1940- *39*
  Brief Entry *34*
Goossen, Agnes
  See Epp, Margaret A(gnes)
Gordon, Bernard Ludwig
1931- *27*
Gordon, Colonel H. R.
  See Ellis, Edward S(ylvester)
Gordon, Donald
  See Payne, Donald Gordon
Gordon, Dorothy 1893-1970 ...... *20*
Gordon, Esther S(aranga)
1935- *10*
Gordon, Frederick [Collective
  pseudonym] *1*
Gordon, Hal
  See Goodwin, Harold Leland
Gordon, John 1925- *6*
Gordon, John
  See Gesner, Clark
Gordon, Lew
  See Baldwin, Gordon C.
Gordon, Margaret (Anna)
1939- *9*
Gordon, Mildred 1912-1979
  Obituary *24*
Gordon, Selma
  See Lanes, Selma G.
Gordon, Shirley 1921- *48*
  Brief Entry *41*
Gordon, Sol 1923- *11*
Gordon, Stewart
  See Shirreffs, Gordon D.
Gordons, The [Joint pseudonym]
  See Gordon, Mildred
Gorelick, Molly C. 1920- *9*
Gorey, Edward St. John
1925- *29*
  Brief Entry *27*
Gorham, Charles Orson
1911-1975 .... *36*
Gorham, Michael
  See Folsom, Franklin
Gormley, Beatrice 1942- *39*
  Brief Entry *35*
Gorog, Judith (Allen) 1938- *39*
Gorsline, Douglas (Warner)
1913-1985 .... *11*
  Obituary *43*
Gorsline, (Sally) Marie 1928- *28*
Gorsline, S. M.
  See Gorsline, (Sally) Marie
Goryan, Sirak
  See Saroyan, William
Goscinny, René 1926-1977 .... *47*
  Brief Entry *39*
Gottlieb, Bill
  See Gottlieb, William P(aul)
Gottlieb, Gerald 1923- *7*
Gottlieb, William P(aul) *24*
Goudey, Alice E. 1898- *20*
Goudge, Elizabeth 1900-1984 ..... *2*
  Obituary *38*
Gough, Catherine 1931- *24*
Gough, Philip 1908- *45*
Goulart, Ron 1933- *6*

Gould, Chester 1900-1985 49
  Obituary 43
Gould, Jean R(osalind) 1919- 11
Gould, Lilian 1920- 6
Gould, Marilyn 1923- 15
Govan, Christine Noble 1898- 9
Govern, Elaine 1939- 26
Graaf, Peter
  See Youd, (Christopher) Samuel
Graber, Alexander 7
Graber, Richard (Fredrick)
  1927- 26
Grabiański, Janusz 1929-1976 39
  Obituary 30
Graboff, Abner 1919- 35
Grace, F(rances Jane) 45
Graeber, Charlotte Towner
  Brief Entry 44
Graff, Polly Anne
  See Colver, Anne
Graff, (S.) Stewart 1908- 9
Graham, Ada 1931- 11
Graham, Brenda Knight 1942- 32
Graham, Charlotte
  See Bowden, Joan Chase
Graham, Eleanor 1896-1984 18
  Obituary 38
Graham, Frank, Jr. 1925- 11
Graham, John 1926- 11
Graham, Kennon
  See Harrison, David Lee
Graham, Lorenz B(ell) 1902- 2
  See also CLR 10
  See also SAAS 5
Graham, Margaret Bloy 1920- 11
Graham, Robin Lee 1949- 7
Graham, Shirley
  See Du Bois, Shirley Graham
Graham-Barber, Lynda 1944- 42
Graham-Cameron, M(alcolm) G(ordon)
  1931-
  Brief Entry 45
Graham-Cameron, Mike
  See Graham-Cameron, M(alcolm)
  G(ordon)
Grahame, Kenneth
  1859-1932 ....YABC 1
  See also CLR 5
Gramatky, Hardie 1907-1979 30
  Obituary 23
  Earlier sketch in SATA 1
Grand, Samuel 1912- 42
Grandville, J. J.
  See Gérard, Jean Ignace Isidore
Grandville, Jean Ignace Isidore Gérard
  See Gérard, Jean Ignace Isidore
Grange, Peter
  See Nicole, Christopher Robin
Granger, Margaret Jane 1925(?)-1977
  Obituary 27
Granger, Peggy
  See Granger, Margaret Jane
Granstaff, Bill 1925- 10
Grant, Bruce 1893-1977 5
  Obituary 25
Grant, Cynthia D. 1950- 33
Grant, Eva 1907- 7
Grant, Evva H. 1913-1977
  Obituary 27

Grant, Gordon 1875-1962 25
Grant, Gwen(doline Ellen)
  1940- 47
Grant, (Alice) Leigh 1947- 10
Grant, Matthew C.
  See May, Julian
Grant, Maxwell
  See Lynds, Dennis
Grant, Myrna (Lois) 1934- 21
Grant, Neil 1938- 14
Gravel, Fern
  See Hall, James Norman
Graves, Charles Parlin
  1911-1972 4
Graves, Robert (von Ranke)
  1895-1985 45
Gray, Elizabeth Janet 1902- 6
Gray, Genevieve S. 1920- 4
Gray, Harold (Lincoln)
  1894-1968 33
  Brief Entry 32
Gray, Jenny
  See Gray, Genevieve S.
Gray, Marian
  See Pierce, Edith Gray
Gray, Nicholas Stuart
  1922-1981 4
  Obituary 27
Gray, Nigel 1941- 33
Gray, (Lucy) Noel (Clervaux)
  1898-1983 47
Gray, Patricia 7
Gray, Patsey
  See Gray, Patricia
Grayland, V. Merle
  See Grayland, Valerie
Grayland, Valerie 7
Great Comte, The
  See Hawkesworth, Eric
Greaves, Margaret 1914- 7
Grée, Alain 1936- 28
Green, Adam
  See Weisgard, Leonard
Green, D.
  See Casewit, Curtis
Green, Hannah
  See Greenberg, Joanne (Goldenberg)
Green, Jane 1937- 9
Green, Mary Moore 1906- 11
Green, Morton 1937- 8
Green, Norma B(erger) 1925- 11
Green, Phyllis 1932- 20
Green, Roger (Gilbert) Lancelyn
  1918- 2
Green, Sheila Ellen 1934- 8
Greenaway, Kate
  1846-1901 ....YABC 2
  See also CLR 6
Greenbank, Anthony Hunt
  1933- 39
Greenberg, Harvey R. 1935- 5
Greenberg, Joanne (Goldenberg)
  1932- 25
Greenberg, Polly 1932-
  Brief Entry 43
Greene, Bette 1934- 8
  See also CLR 2
Greene, Carla 1916- 1

Greene, Carol
  Brief Entry 44
Greene, Constance C(larke)
  1924- 11
Greene, Ellin 1927- 23
Greene, Graham 1904- 20
Greene, Laura 1935- 38
Greene, Wade 1933- 11
Greenfeld, Howard 19
Greenfield, Eloise 1929- 19
  See also CLR 4
Greenhaus, Thelma Nurenberg
  1903-1984 45
Greening, Hamilton
  See Hamilton, Charles H. St. John
Greenleaf, Barbara Kaye
  1942- 6
Greenleaf, Peter 1910- 33
Greenwald, Sheila
  See Green, Sheila Ellen
Gregg, Walter H(arold) 1919- 20
Gregor, Arthur 1923- 36
Gregori, Leon 1919- 15
Gregorian, Joyce Ballou
  1946- 30
Gregorowski, Christopher
  1940- 30
Gregory, Diana (Jean) 1933- 49
  Brief Entry 42
Gregory, Jean
  See Ure, Jean
Gregory, Stephen
  See Penzler, Otto
Greisman, Joan Ruth 1937- 31
Grendon, Stephen
  See Derleth, August (William)
Grenville, Pelham
  See Wodehouse, P(elham)
  G(renville)
Gretz, Susanna 1937- 7
Gretzer, John 18
Grey, Jerry 1926- 11
Grey Owl
  See Belaney, Archibald Stansfeld
Gri
  See Denney, Diana
Grice, Frederick 1910- 6
Grider, Dorothy 1915- 31
Gridley, Marion E(leanor)
  1906-1974 35
  Obituary 26
Grieder, Walter 1924- 9
Griese, Arnold A(lfred) 1921- 9
Grifalconi, Ann 1929- 2
Griffin, Gillett Good 1928- 26
Griffin, Judith Berry 34
Griffith, Helen V(irginia)
  1934- 39
Griffith, Jeannette
  See Eyerly, Jeanette
Griffiths, G(ordon) D(ouglas)
  1910-1973
  Obituary 20
Griffiths, Helen 1939- 5
  See also SAAS 5
Grimm, Cherry Barbara Lockett 1930-
  Brief Entry 43
Grimm, Jacob Ludwig Karl
  1785-1863 22

Grimm, Wilhelm Karl
  1786-1859 22
Grimm, William C(arey)
  1907- .... _14_
Grimshaw, Nigel (Gilroy)
  1925- 23
Grimsley, Gordon
  See Groom, Arthur William
Gringhuis, Dirk
  See Gringhuis, Richard H.
Gringhuis, Richard H.
  1918-1974 6
  Obituary 25
Grinnell, George Bird
  1849-1938 .... _16_
Gripe, Maria (Kristina) 1923- 2
  See also CLR 5
Groch, Judith (Goldstein)
  1929- 25
Grode, Redway
  See Gorey, Edward St. John
Grohskopf, Bernice 7
Grol, Lini Richards 1913- .... _9_
Grollman, Earl A. 1925- 22
Groom, Arthur William
  1898-1964 .... _10_
Gross, Alan 1947-
  Brief Entry .... _43_
Gross, Ruth Belov 1929- .... _33_
Gross, Sarah Chokla
  1906-1976 .... _9_
  Obituary 26
Grossman, Nancy 1940- 29
Grossman, Robert 1940- .... _11_
Groth, John 1908- 21
Groves, Georgina
  See Symons, (Dorothy) Geraldine
Gruelle, John (Barton)
  1880-1938 .... _35_
  Brief Entry .... _32_
Gruelle, Johnny
  See Gruelle, John
Gruenberg, Sidonie M(atsner)
  1881-1974 2
  Obituary 27
Grummer, Arnold E(dward)
  1923- .... _49_
Guck, Dorothy 1913- 27
Gugliotta, Bobette 1918- 7
Guillaume, Jeanette G. (Flierl)
  1899- 8
Guillot, Rene 1900-1969 7
Gundersheimer, Karen
  Brief Entry .... _44_
Gundrey, Elizabeth 1924- 23
Gunn, James E(dwin) 1923- .... _35_
Gunston, Bill
  See Gunston, William Tudor
Gunston, William Tudor
  1927- 9
Gunterman, Bertha Lisette
  1886(?)-1975
  Obituary 27
Gunther, John 1901-1970 2
Gurko, Leo 1914- .... _9_
Gurko, Miriam .... _9_
Gustafson, Anita 1942-
  Brief Entry .... _45_

Gustafson, Sarah R.
  See Riedman, Sarah R.
Gustafson, Scott 1956- .... _34_
Guthrie, Anne 1890-1979 28
Gutman, Bill
  Brief Entry .... _43_
Gutman, Naham 1899(?)-1981
  Obituary 25
Guy, Rosa (Cuthbert) 1928- ...... _14_
  See also CLR 13
Guymer, (Wilhelmina) Mary
  1909- 50
Gwynne, Fred(erick Hubbard)
  1926- .... _41_
  Brief Entry 27

H

Haas, Carolyn Buhai 1926- .... _43_
Haas, Dorothy F. 46
  Brief Entry .... _43_
Haas, Irene 1929- 17
Haas, James E(dward) 1943- 40
Haas, Merle S. 1896(?)-1985
  Obituary .... _41_
Habenstreit, Barbara 1937- .... _5_
Haber, Louis 1910- 12
Hader, Berta (Hoerner)
  1891(?)-1976 .... _16_
Hader, Elmer (Stanley)
  1889-1973 .... _16_
Hadley, Franklin
  See Winterbotham, R(ussell)
  R(obert)
Hadley, Lee 1934- 47
  Brief Entry 38
Hafner, Marylin 1925- 7
Hager, Alice Rogers 1894-1969
  Obituary 26
Haggard, H(enry) Rider
  1856-1925 .... _16_
Haggerty, James J(oseph)
  1920- .... _5_
Hagon, Priscilla
  See Allan, Mabel Esther
Hague, (Susan) Kathleen
  1949- 49
  Brief Entry 45
Hague, Michael (Riley) 1948- 48
  Brief Entry 32
Hahn, Emily 1905- .... _3_
Hahn, Hannelore 1926- 8
Hahn, James (Sage) 1947- .... _9_
Hahn, (Mona) Lynn 1949- .... _9_
Hahn, Mary Downing 1937- 50
  Brief Entry 44
Haig-Brown, Roderick (Langmere)
  1909-1976 12
Haight, Anne Lyon 1895-1977
  Obituary 30
Haines, Gail Kay 1943- .... _11_
Haining, Peter 1940- .... _14_
Halacy, D(aniel) S(tephen), Jr.
  1919- 36
Haldane, Roger John 1945- .... _13_
Hale, Arlene 1924-1982 .... _49_
Hale, Edward Everett
  1822-1909 .... _16_

Hale, Helen
  See Mulcahy, Lucille Burnett
Hale, Irina 1932- 26
Hale, Kathleen 1898- .... _17_
Hale, Linda 1929- 6
Hale, Lucretia Peabody
  1820-1900 26
Hale, Nancy 1908- .... _31_
Haley, Gail E(inhart) 1939- .... _43_
  Brief Entry 28
Hall, Adam
  See Trevor, Elleston
Hall, Adele 1910- 7
Hall, Anna Gertrude
  1882-1967 8
Hall, Borden
  See Yates, Raymond F(rancis)
Hall, Brian P(atrick) 1935- .... _31_
Hall, Caryl
  See Hansen, Caryl (Hall)
Hall, Donald (Andrew, Jr.)
  1928- 23
Hall, Douglas 1931- .... _43_
Hall, Elvajean 6
Hall, James Norman
  1887-1951 21
Hall, Jesse
  See Boesen, Victor
Hall, Katy
  See McMullan, Kate (Hall)
Hall, Lynn 1937- 47
  Earlier sketch in SATA 2
  See also SAAS 4
Hall, Malcolm 1945- 7
Hall, Marjory
  See Yeakley, Marjory Hall
Hall, Rosalys Haskell 1914- 7
Hallard, Peter
  See Catherall, Arthur
Hallas, Richard
  See Knight, Eric (Mowbray)
Hall-Clarke, James
  See Rowland-Entwistle, (Arthur)
  Theodore (Henry)
Haller, Dorcas Woodbury
  1946- 46
Halliburton, Warren J. 1924- ...... _19_
Hallin, Emily Watson 1919- 6
Hallinan, P(atrick) K(enneth)
  1944- 39
  Brief Entry 37
Hallman, Ruth 1929- .... _43_
  Brief Entry 28
Hall-Quest, (Edna) Olga W(ilbourne)
  1899-1986 .... _11_
  Obituary 47
Hallstead, William F(inn) III
  1924- .... _11_
Hallward, Michael 1889- .... _12_
Halsell, Grace 1923- .... _13_
Halsted, Anna Roosevelt 1906-1975
  Obituary 30
Halter, Jon C(harles) 1941- 22
Hamalian, Leo 1920- .... _41_
Hamberger, John 1934- .... _14_
Hamblin, Dora Jane 1920- 36
Hamerstrom, Frances 1907- 24
Hamil, Thomas Arthur 1928- ..... _14_

Hamil, Tom
  See Hamil, Thomas Arthur
Hamill, Ethel
  See Webb, Jean Francis (III)
Hamilton, Alice
  See Cromie, Alice Hamilton
Hamilton, Charles Harold St. John
  1875-1961 .... *13*
Hamilton, Clive
  See Lewis, C. S.
Hamilton, Dorothy 1906-1983 ..... *12*
  Obituary *35*
Hamilton, Edith 1867-1963 .... *20*
Hamilton, Elizabeth 1906- *23*
Hamilton, Morse 1943- *35*
Hamilton, Robert W.
  See Stratemeyer, Edward L.
Hamilton, Virginia 1936- *4*
  See also CLR 1, 11
Hamley, Dennis 1935- *39*
Hammer, Richard 1928- *6*
Hammerman, Gay M(orenus)
  1926- *9*
Hammond, Winifred G(raham)
  1899- *29*
Hammontree, Marie (Gertrude)
  1913- *13*
Hampson, (Richard) Denman
  1929- *15*
Hampson, Frank 1918(?)-1985
  Obituary *46*
Hamre, Leif 1914- *5*
Hamsa, Bobbie 1944-
  Brief Entry *38*
Hancock, Mary A. 1923- *31*
Hancock, Sibyl 1940- *9*
Handforth, Thomas (Schofield)
  1897-1948 .... *42*
Handville, Robert (Tompkins)
  1924- *45*
Hane, Roger 1940-1974
  Obituary *20*
Haney, Lynn 1941- *23*
Hanff, Helene *11*
Hanlon, Emily 1945- *15*
Hann, Jacquie 1951- *19*
Hanna, Bill
  See Hanna, William
Hanna, Paul R(obert) 1902- *9*
Hanna, William 1910- *51*
Hannam, Charles 1925- *50*
Hano, Arnold 1922- *12*
Hansen, Caryl (Hall) 1929- *39*
Hansen, Joyce 1942- *46*
  Brief Entry *39*
Hanser, Richard (Frederick)
  1909- *13*
Hanson, Joan 1938- *8*
Hanson, Joseph E. 1894(?)-1971
  Obituary *27*
Harald, Eric
  See Boesen, Victor
Harcourt, Ellen Knowles 1890(?)-1984
  Obituary *36*
Hardcastle, Michael 1933- *47*
  Brief Entry *38*
Harding, Lee 1937- *32*
  Brief Entry *31*

Hardwick, Richard Holmes, Jr.
  1923- *12*
Hardy, Alice Dale [Collective
  pseudonym] *1*
Hardy, David A(ndrews)
  1936- *9*
Hardy, Stuart
  See Schisgall, Oscar
Hardy, Thomas 1840-1928 .... *25*
Hare, Norma Q(uarles) 1924- *46*
  Brief Entry *41*
Harford, Henry
  See Hudson, W(illiam) H(enry)
Hargrove, James 1947-
  Brief Entry *50*
Hargrove, Jim
  See Hargrove, James
Hark, Mildred
  See McQueen, Mildred Hark
Harkaway, Hal
  See Stratemeyer, Edward L.
Harkins, Philip 1912- *6*
Harlan, Elizabeth 1945- *41*
  Brief Entry *35*
Harlan, Glen
  See Cebulash, Mel
Harman, Fred 1902(?)-1982
  Obituary *30*
Harman, Hugh 1903-1982
  Obituary *33*
Harmelink, Barbara (Mary) *9*
Harmer, Mabel 1894- *45*
Harmon, Margaret 1906- *20*
Harnan, Terry 1920- *12*
Harnett, Cynthia (Mary)
  1893-1981 .... *5*
  Obituary *32*
Harper, Anita 1943- *41*
Harper, Mary Wood
  See Dixon, Jeanne
Harper, Wilhelmina
  1884-1973 .... *4*
  Obituary *26*
Harrah, Michael 1940- *41*
Harrell, Sara Gordon
  See Banks, Sara (Jeanne Gordon
  Harrell)
Harries, Joan 1922- *39*
Harrington, Lyn 1911- *5*
Harris, Aurand 1915- *37*
Harris, Christie 1907- *6*
Harris, Colver
  See Colver, Anne
Harris, Dorothy Joan 1931- *13*
Harris, Janet 1932-1979 .... *4*
  Obituary *23*
Harris, Joel Chandler
  1848-1908 .... *YABC 1*
Harris, Lavinia
  See Johnston, Norma
Harris, Leon A., Jr. 1926- *4*
Harris, Lorle K(empe) 1912- *22*
Harris, Marilyn
  See Springer, Marilyn Harris
Harris, Mark Jonathan 1941- *32*
Harris, Rosemary (Jeanne) *4*
Harris, Sherwood 1932- *25*
Harrison, C. William 1913- *35*
Harrison, David Lee 1937- *26*

Harrison, Deloris 1938- *9*
Harrison, Harry 1925- *4*
Harrison, Molly 1909- *41*
Harshaw, Ruth H(etzel)
  1890-1968 .... *27*
Hart, Bruce 1938-
  Brief Entry *39*
Hart, Carole 1943-
  Brief Entry *39*
Harte, (Francis) Bret(t)
  1836-1902 .... *26*
Hartley, Ellen (Raphael)
  1915- *23*
Hartley, Fred Allan III 1953- *41*
Hartley, William B(rown)
  1913- *23*
Hartman, Evert 1937- *38*
  Brief Entry *35*
Hartman, Jane E(vangeline)
  1928- *47*
Hartman, Louis F(rancis)
  1901-1970 .... *22*
Hartshorn, Ruth M. 1928- *11*
Harvey, Edith 1908(?)-1972
  Obituary *27*
Harwin, Brian
  See Henderson, LeGrand
Harwood, Pearl Augusta (Bragdon)
  1903- *9*
Haseley, Dennis
  Brief Entry *44*
Haskell, Arnold 1903- *6*
Haskins, James 1941- *9*
  See also CLR 3
Haskins, Jim
  See Haskins, James
  See also SAAS 4
Hasler, Joan 1931- *28*
Hassall, Joan 1906- *43*
Hassler, Jon (Francis) 1933- *19*
Hatch, Mary Cottam 1912-1970
  Brief Entry *28*
Hatlo, Jimmy 1898-1963
  Obituary *23*
Haugaard, Erik Christian
  1923- *4*
  See also CLR 11
Hauman, Doris 1898- *32*
Hauman, George 1890-1961 ...... *32*
Hauser, Margaret L(ouise)
  1909- *10*
Hausman, Gerald 1945- *13*
Hausman, Gerry
  See Hausman, Gerald
Hautzig, Deborah 1956- *31*
Hautzig, Esther 1930- *4*
Havenhand, John
  See Cox, John Roberts
Havighurst, Walter (Edwin)
  1901- *1*
Haviland, Virginia 1911- *6*
Hawes, Judy 1913- *4*
Hawk, Virginia Driving
  See Sneve, Virginia Driving Hawk
Hawkesworth, Eric 1921- *13*
Hawkins, Arthur 1903- *19*
Hawkins, Quail 1905- *6*
Hawkinson, John 1912- *4*

Hawkinson, Lucy (Ozone)
1924-1971 .... *21*
Hawley, Mable C. [Collective
pseudonym] *1*
Hawthorne, Captain R. M.
See Ellis, Edward S(ylvester)
Hawthorne, Nathaniel
1804-1864 .... *YABC 2*
Hay, John 1915- *13*
Hay, Timothy
See Brown, Margaret Wise
Haycraft, Howard 1905- *6*
Haycraft, Molly Costain
1911- *6*
Hayden, Gwendolen Lampshire
1904- *35*
Hayden, Robert C(arter), Jr.
1937- *47*
Brief Entry *28*
Hayden, Robert E(arl)
1913-1980 .... *19*
Obituary *26*
Hayes, Carlton J. H.
1882-1964 .... *11*
Hayes, Geoffrey 1947- *26*
Hayes, John F. 1904- *11*
Hayes, Sheila 1937- *51*
Brief Entry *50*
Hayes, Will *7*
Hayes, William D(imitt)
1913- *8*
Haynes, Betsy 1937- *48*
Brief Entry *37*
Hays, H(offman) R(eynolds)
1904-1980 .... *26*
Hays, Wilma Pitchford 1909- *28*
Earlier sketch in SATA 1
See also SAAS 3
Hayward, Linda 1943-
Brief Entry *39*
Haywood, Carolyn 1898- *29*
Earlier sketch in SATA 1
Hazen, Barbara Shook 1930- *27*
Head, Gay
See Hauser, Margaret L(ouise)
Headley, Elizabeth
See Cavanna, Betty
Headstrom, Richard 1902- *8*
Heady, Eleanor B(utler) 1917- ... *8*
Heal, Edith 1903- *7*
Healey, Brooks
See Albert, Burton, Jr.
Healey, Larry 1927- *44*
Brief Entry *42*
Heaps, Willard (Allison)
1909- *26*
Hearn, Emily
See Valleau, Emily
Hearne, Betsy Gould 1942- *38*
Heath, Charles D(ickinson)
1941- *46*
Heath, Veronica
See Blackett, Veronica Heath
Heaven, Constance
See Fecher, Constance
Hecht, George J(oseph) 1895-1980
Obituary *22*
Hecht, Henri Joseph 1922- *9*
Hechtkopf, Henryk 1910- *17*

Heck, Bessie Holland 1911- *26*
Hedderwick, Mairi 1939- *30*
Hedges, Sid(ney) G(eorge)
1897-1974 .... *28*
Hefter, Richard 1942- *31*
Hegarty, Reginald Beaton
1906-1973 .... *10*
Heide, Florence Parry 1919- *32*
Heiderstadt, Dorothy 1907- *6*
Heilman, Joan Rattner *50*
Hein, Lucille Eleanor 1915- *20*
Heinemann, George Alfred 1918-
Brief Entry *31*
Heinlein, Robert A(nson)
1907- *9*
Heins, Paul 1909- *13*
Heintze, Carl 1922- *26*
Heinz, W(ilfred) C(harles)
1915- *26*
Heinzen, Mildred
See Masters, Mildred
Helfman, Elizabeth S(eaver)
1911- *3*
Helfman, Harry 1910- *3*
Hellberg, Hans-Eric 1927- *38*
Heller, Linda 1944- *46*
Brief Entry *40*
Hellman, Hal
See Hellman, Harold
Hellman, Harold 1927- *4*
Helps, Racey 1913-1971 .... *2*
Obituary *25*
Helweg, Hans H. 1917- *50*
Brief Entry *33*
Hemming, Roy 1928- *11*
Hemphill, Martha Locke
1904-1973 .... *37*
Henderley, Brooks [Collective
pseudonym] *1*
Henderson, LeGrand
1901-1965 .... *9*
Henderson, Nancy Wallace
1916- *22*
Henderson, Zenna (Chlarson)
1917- *5*
Hendrickson, Walter Brookfield, Jr.
1936- *9*
Henkes, Kevin 1960- *43*
Henriod, Lorraine 1925- *26*
Henry, Joanne Landers 1927- *6*
Henry, Marguerite *11*
See also CLR 4
Henry, O.
See Porter, William Sydney
Henry, Oliver
See Porter, William Sydney
Henry, T. E.
See Rowland-Entwistle, (Arthur)
Theodore (Henry)
Henson, James Maury 1936- *43*
Henson, Jim
See Henson, James Maury
Henstra, Friso 1928- *8*
Hentoff, Nat(han Irving)
1925- *42*
Brief Entry *27*
See also CLR 1
Herald, Kathleen
See Peyton, Kathleen (Wendy)

Herbert, Cecil
See Hamilton, Charles H. St. John
Herbert, Don 1917- *2*
Herbert, Frank (Patrick)
1920-1986 .... *37*
Obituary *47*
Earlier sketch in SATA 9
Herbert, Wally
See Herbert, Walter William
Herbert, Walter William
1934- *23*
Hergé
See Rémi, Georges
See also CLR 6
Herkimer, L(awrence) R(ussell)
1925- *42*
Herman, Charlotte 1937- *20*
Hermanson, Dennis (Everett)
1947- *10*
Hermes, Patricia 1936- *31*
Herriot, James
See Wight, James Alfred
Herrmanns, Ralph 1933- *11*
Herron, Edward A(lbert)
1912- *4*
Hersey, John (Richard) 1914- *25*
Hertz, Grete Janus 1915- *23*
Hess, Lilo 1916- *4*
Hesse, Hermann 1877-1962 ...... *50*
Heuer, Kenneth John 1927- *44*
Heuman, William 1912-1971 ..... *21*
Hewes, Agnes Danforth
1874-1963 .... *35*
Hewett, Anita 1918- *13*
Hext, Harrington
See Phillpotts, Eden
Hey, Nigel S(tewart) 1936- *20*
Heyduck-Huth, Hilde 1929- *8*
Heyerdahl, Thor 1914- *2*
Heyliger, William
1884-1955 .... *YABC 1*
Heyman, Ken(neth Louis)
1930- *34*
Heyward, Du Bose 1885-1940 .... *21*
Heywood, Karen 1946- *48*
Hibbert, Christopher 1924- *4*
Hibbert, Eleanor Burford
1906- *2*
Hickman, Janet 1940- *12*
Hickman, Martha Whitmore
1925- *26*
Hickok, Lorena A.
1892(?)-1968 .... *20*
Hickok, Will
See Harrison, C. William
Hicks, Clifford B. 1920- *50*
Hicks, Eleanor B.
See Coerr, Eleanor
Hicks, Harvey
See Stratemeyer, Edward L.
Hieatt, Constance B(artlett)
1928- *4*
Hiebert, Ray Eldon 1932- *13*
Higdon, Hal 1931- *4*
Higginbottom, J(effrey) Winslow
1945- *29*
Higham, David (Michael)
1949- *50*

Highet, Helen
  See MacInnes, Helen
Hightower, Florence Cole
  1916-1981 .... *4*
  Obituary *27*
Highwater, Jamake 1942- *32*
  Brief Entry *30*
Hildebrandt, Greg 1939-
  Brief Entry *33*
Hildebrandt, Tim 1939-
  Brief Entry *33*
Hilder, Rowland 1905- *36*
Hildick, E. W.
  See Hildick, Wallace
Hildick, (Edmund) Wallace
  1925- *2*
Hill, Donna (Marie) *24*
Hill, Douglas (Arthur) 1935- *39*
Hill, Elizabeth Starr 1925- *24*
Hill, Eric 1927-
  See CLR 13
Hill, Grace Brooks [Collective
  pseudonym] *1*
Hill, Grace Livingston
  1865-1947 ....*YABC 2*
Hill, Helen M(orey) 1915- *27*
Hill, Kathleen Louise 1917- *4*
Hill, Kay
  See Hill, Kathleen Louise
Hill, Lorna 1902- *12*
Hill, Margaret (Ohler) 1915- *36*
Hill, Meg
  See Hill, Margaret (Ohler)
Hill, Monica
  See Watson, Jane Werner
Hill, Robert W(hite)
  1919-1982 .... *12*
  Obituary *31*
Hill, Ruth A.
  See Viguers, Ruth Hill
Hill, Ruth Livingston
  See Munce, Ruth Hill
Hillcourt, William 1900- *27*
Hillerman, Tony 1925- *6*
Hillert, Margaret 1920- *8*
Hillman, Martin
  See Hill, Douglas (Arthur)
Hillman, Priscilla 1940- *48*
  Brief Entry *39*
Hills, C(harles) A(lbert) R(eis)
  1955- *39*
Hilton, Irene (P.) 1912- *7*
Hilton, James 1900-1954 .... *34*
Hilton, Ralph 1907- *8*
Hilton, Suzanne 1922- *4*
Him, George 1900-1982
  Obituary *30*
Himler, Ann 1946- *8*
Himler, Ronald 1937- *6*
Himmelman, John (Carl)
  1959- *47*
Hinckley, Helen
  See Jones, Helen Hinckley
Hind, Dolores (Ellen) 1931-
  Brief Entry *49*
Hines, Anna G(rossnickle)
  1946- *51*
  Brief Entry *45*

Hinton, S(usan) E(loise)
  1950- *19*
  See also CLR 3
Hinton, Sam 1917- *43*
Hintz, (Loren) Martin 1945- *47*
  Brief Entry *39*
Hirsch, Phil 1926- *35*
Hirsch, S. Carl 1913- *2*
Hirschmann, Linda (Ann)
  1941- *40*
Hirsh, Marilyn 1944- *7*
Hirshberg, Al(bert Simon)
  1909-1973 .... *38*
Hiser, Iona Seibert 1901- *4*
Hitchcock, Alfred (Joseph)
  1899-1980 .... *27*
  Obituary *24*
Hitte, Kathryn 1919- *16*
Hitz, Demi 1942- *11*
Hnizdovsky, Jacques 1915- *32*
Ho, Minfong 1951- *15*
Hoagland, Edward 1932- *51*
Hoare, Robert J(ohn)
  1921-1975 .... *38*
Hoban, Lillian 1925- *22*
Hoban, Russell C(onwell)
  1925- *40*
  Earlier sketch in SATA 1
  See also CLR 3
Hoban, Tana *22*
  See also CLR 13
Hobart, Lois *7*
Hoberman, Mary Ann 1930- *5*
Hobson, Burton (Harold)
  1933- *28*
Hochschild, Arlie Russell
  1940- *11*
Hockaby, Stephen
  See Mitchell, Gladys (Maude
  Winifred)
Hockenberry, Hope
  See Newell, Hope (Hockenberry)
Hodge, P(aul) W(illiam)
  1934- *12*
Hodgell, P(atricia) C(hristine)
  1951- *42*
Hodges, C(yril) Walter 1909- *2*
Hodges, Carl G. 1902-1964 .... *10*
Hodges, Elizabeth Jamison *1*
Hodges, Margaret Moore
  1911- *33*
  Earlier sketch in SATA 1
Hodgetts, Blake Christopher
  1967- *43*
Hoexter, Corinne K. 1927- *6*
Hoff, Carol 1900- *11*
Hoff, Syd(ney) 1912- *9*
  See also SAAS 4
Hoffman, Edwin D. *49*
Hoffman, Phyllis M. 1944- *4*
Hoffman, Rosekrans 1926- *15*
Hoffmann, E(rnst) T(heodor)
  A(madeus) 1776-1822 .... *27*
Hoffmann, Felix 1911-1975 .... *9*
Hoffmann, Margaret Jones
  1910- *48*
Hoffmann, Peggy
  See Hoffmann, Margaret Jones
Hofsinde, Robert 1902-1973 ...... *21*

Hogan, Bernice Harris 1929- *12*
Hogan, Inez 1895- *2*
Hogarth, Jr.
  See Kent, Rockwell
Hogarth, Paul 1917- *41*
Hogg, Garry 1902- *2*
Hogner, Dorothy Childs *4*
Hogner, Nils 1893-1970 .... *25*
Hogrogian, Nonny 1932- *7*
  See also CLR 2
  See also SAAS 1
Hoh, Diane 1937-
  Brief Entry *48*
Hoke, Helen (L.) 1903- *15*
Hoke, John 1925- *7*
Holbeach, Henry
  See Rands, William Brighty
Holberg, Ruth Langland
  1889- *1*
Holbrook, Peter
  See Glick, Carl (Cannon)
Holbrook, Sabra
  See Erickson, Sabra R(ollins)
Holbrook, Stewart Hall
  1893-1964 .... *2*
Holden, Elizabeth Rhoda
  See Lawrence, Louise
Holding, James 1907- *3*
Holisher, Desider 1901-1972 ...... *6*
Holl, Adelaide (Hinkle) *8*
Holl, Kristi D(iane) 1951- *51*
Holland, Isabelle 1920- *8*
Holland, Janice 1913-1962 .... *18*
Holland, John L(ewis) 1919- *20*
Holland, Lys
  See Gater, Dilys
Holland, Marion 1908- *6*
Hollander, John 1929- *13*
Hollander, Phyllis 1928- *39*
Holldobler, Turid 1939- *26*
Holliday, Joe
  See Holliday, Joseph
Holliday, Joseph 1910- *11*
Holling, Holling C(lancy)
  1900-1973 .... *15*
  Obituary *26*
Hollingsworth, Alvin C(arl)
  1930- *39*
Holloway, Teresa (Bragunier)
  1906- *26*
Holm, (Else) Anne (Lise)
  1922- *1*
Holman, Felice 1919- *7*
Holme, Bryan 1913- *26*
Holmes, Marjorie 1910- *43*
Holmes, Oliver Wendell
  1809-1894 .... *34*
Holmes, Rick
  See Hardwick, Richard Holmes, Jr.
Holmgren, George Ellen
  See Holmgren, Helen Jean
Holmgren, Helen Jean 1930- *45*
Holmgren, Virginia C(unningham)
  1909- *26*
Holmquist, Eve 1921- *11*
Holt, Margaret 1937- *4*
Holt, Margaret Van Vechten
  (Saunders) 1899-1963 .... *32*
Holt, Michael (Paul) 1929- *13*

Holt, Rackham
  See Holt, Margaret Van Vechten
    (Saunders)
Holt, Rochelle Lynn 1946- *41*
Holt, Stephen
  See Thompson, Harlan H.
Holt, Victoria
  See Hibbert, Eleanor
Holton, Leonard
  See Wibberley, Leonard (Patrick
    O'Connor)
Holyer, Erna Maria 1925- *22*
Holyer, Ernie
  See Holyer, Erna Maria
Holz, Loretta (Marie) 1943- *17*
Homze, Alma C. 1932- *17*
Honig, Donald 1931- *18*
Honness, Elizabeth H. 1904- *2*
Hoobler, Dorothy *28*
Hoobler, Thomas *28*
Hood, Joseph F. 1925- *4*
Hood, Robert E. 1926- *21*
Hook, Frances 1912- *27*
Hook, Martha 1936- *27*
Hooker, Ruth 1920- *21*
Hooks, William H(arris)
  1921- *16*
Hooper, Byrd
  See St. Clair, Byrd Hooper
Hooper, Meredith (Jean)
  1939- *28*
Hoopes, Lyn L(ittlefield)
  1953- *49*
  Brief Entry *44*
Hoopes, Ned E(dward) 1932- *21*
Hoopes, Roy 1922- *11*
Hoople, Cheryl G.
  Brief Entry *32*
Hoover, H(elen) M(ary) 1935- *44*
  Brief Entry *33*
Hoover, Helen (Drusilla Blackburn)
  1910-1984 .... *12*
  Obituary *39*
Hope, Laura Lee [Collective
  pseudonym] *1*
  See also Adams, Harriet
    S(tratemeyer)
Hope Simpson, Jacynth 1930- *12*
Hopf, Alice L(ightner) 1904- *5*
Hopkins, A. T.
  See Turngren, Annette
Hopkins, Clark 1895-1976
  Obituary *34*
Hopkins, Joseph G(erard) E(dward)
  1909- *11*
Hopkins, Lee Bennett 1938- *3*
  See also SAAS 4
Hopkins, Lyman
  See Folsom, Franklin
Hopkins, Marjorie 1911- *9*
Hoppe, Joanne 1932- *42*
Hopper, Nancy J. 1937- *38*
  Brief Entry *35*
Horgan, Paul 1903- *13*
Hornblow, Arthur (Jr.)
  1893-1976 .... *15*
Hornblow, Leonora (Schinasi)
  1920- *18*

Horne, Richard Henry
  1803-1884 .... *29*
Horner, Althea (Jane) 1926- *36*
Horner, Dave 1934- *12*
Hornos, Axel 1907- *20*
Horvath, Betty 1927- *4*
Horwich, Frances R(appaport)
  1908- *11*
Horwitz, Elinor Lander *45*
  Brief Entry *33*
Hosford, Dorothy (Grant)
  1900-1952 .... *22*
Hosford, Jessie 1892- *5*
Hoskyns-Abrahall, Clare *13*
Houck, Carter 1924- *22*
Hough, (Helen) Charlotte
  1924- *9*
Hough, Judy Taylor 1932-
  Brief Entry *51*
Hough, Richard (Alexander)
  1922- *17*
Houghton, Eric 1930- *7*
Houlehen, Robert J. 1918- *18*
Household, Geoffrey (Edward West)
  1900- *14*
Houselander, (Frances) Caryll
  1900-1954
  Brief Entry *31*
Housman, Laurence
  1865-1959 .... *25*
Houston, James A(rchibald)
  1921- *13*
  See also CLR 3
Houton, Kathleen
  See Kilgore, Kathleen
Howard, Alan 1922- *45*
Howard, Alyssa
  See Buckholtz, Eileen (Garber)
Howard, Elizabeth
  See Mizner, Elizabeth Howard
Howard, Prosper
  See Hamilton, Charles H. St. John
Howard, Robert West 1908- *5*
Howard, Vernon (Linwood)
  1918- *40*
Howarth, David 1912- *6*
Howe, Deborah 1946-1978 .... *29*
Howe, James 1946- *29*
  See also CLR 9
Howell, Pat 1947- *15*
Howell, S.
  See Styles, Frank Showell
Howell, Virginia Tier
  See Ellison, Virginia Howell
Howes, Barbara 1914- *5*
Howker, Janni
  Brief Entry *46*
Hoy, Nina
  See Roth, Arthur J(oseph)
Hoyle, Geoffrey 1942- *18*
Hoyt, Edwin P(almer), Jr.
  1923- *28*
Hoyt, Olga (Gruhzit) 1922- *16*
Hubbell, Patricia 1928- *8*
Hubley, Faith (Elliot) 1924- *48*
Hubley, John 1914-1977 .... *48*
  Obituary *24*
Hudson, Jeffrey
  See Crichton, (J.) Michael

Hudson, (Margaret) Kirsty
  1947- *32*
Hudson, W(illiam) H(enry)
  1841-1922 .... *35*
Huffaker, Sandy 1943- *10*
Huffman, Tom *24*
Hughes, Dean 1943- *33*
Hughes, (James) Langston
  1902-1967 .... *33*
  Earlier sketch in SATA 4
Hughes, Matilda
  See MacLeod, Charlotte (Matilda
    Hughes)
Hughes, Monica 1925- *15*
  See also CLR 9
Hughes, Richard (Arthur Warren)
  1900-1976 .... *8*
  Obituary *25*
Hughes, Sara
  See Saunders, Susan
Hughes, Shirley 1929- *16*
Hughes, Ted 1930- *49*
  Brief Entry *27*
  See also CLR 3
Hughes, Thomas 1822-1896 .... *31*
Hughes, Walter (Llewellyn)
  1910- *26*
Hugo, Victor (Marie)
  1802-1885 .... *47*
Huline-Dickens, Frank William
  1931- *34*
Hull, Eleanor (Means) 1913- *21*
Hull, Eric Traviss
  See Harnan, Terry
Hull, H. Braxton
  See Jacobs, Helen Hull
Hull, Jesse Redding
  See Hull, Jessie Redding
Hull, Jessie Redding 1932- *51*
Hull, Katharine 1921-1977 .... *23*
Hülsmann, Eva 1928- *16*
Hults, Dorothy Niebrugge
  1898- *6*
Hume, Lotta Carswell *7*
Hume, Ruth (Fox) 1922-1980 ..... *26*
  Obituary *22*
Hummel, Berta 1909-1946 .... *43*
Hummel, Sister Maria Innocentia
  See Hummel, Berta
Humphrey, Henry (III) 1930- *16*
Humphreys, Graham 1945-
  Brief Entry *32*
Hungerford, Pixie
  See Brinsmead, H(esba) F(ay)
Hunt, Francis
  See Stratemeyer, Edward L.
Hunt, Irene 1907- *2*
  See also CLR 1
Hunt, Joyce 1927- *31*
Hunt, Linda Lawrence 1940- *39*
Hunt, Mabel Leigh 1892-1971 .... *1*
  Obituary *26*
Hunt, Morton 1920- *22*
Hunt, Nigel
  See Greenbank, Anthony Hunt
Hunter, Bernice Thurman 1922-
  Brief Entry *45*
Hunter, Clingham, M.D.
  See Adams, William Taylor

Hunter, Dawe
  See Downie, Mary Alice
Hunter, Edith Fisher 1919- *31*
Hunter, Evan 1926- *25*
Hunter, Hilda 1921- *7*
Hunter, Kristin (Eggleston)
  1931- *12*
  See also CLR 3
Hunter, Leigh
  See Etchison, Birdie L(ee)
Hunter, Mel 1927- *39*
Hunter, Mollie
  See McIllwraith, Maureen
Hunter, Norman (George Lorimer)
  1899- *26*
Hunter Blair, Pauline 1921- *3*
Huntington, Harriet E(lizabeth)
  1909- *1*
Huntsberry, William E(mery)
  1916- *5*
Hurd, Clement 1908- *2*
Hurd, Edith Thacher 1910- *2*
Hurd, Thacher 1949- *46*
  Brief Entry *45*
Hürlimann, Bettina 1909-1983 .... *39*
  Obituary *34*
Hürlimann, Ruth 1939- *32*
  Brief Entry *31*
Hurwitz, Johanna 1937- *20*
Hurwood, Bernhardt J.
  1926-1987 .... *12*
  Obituary *50*
Hutchens, Paul 1902-1977 .... *31*
Hutchins, Carleen Maley
  1911- *9*
Hutchins, Hazel J. 1952-
  Brief Entry *51*
Hutchins, Pat 1942- *15*
Hutchins, Ross E(lliott) 1906- *4*
Hutchmacher, J. Joseph 1929- *5*
Hutto, Nelson (Allen) 1904- *20*
Hutton, Warwick 1939- *20*
Hyde, Dayton O(gden) *9*
Hyde, Hawk
  See Hyde, Dayton O(gden)
Hyde, Margaret Oldroyd
  1917- *42*
  Earlier sketch in SATA 1
Hyde, Shelley
  See Reed, Kit
Hyde, Wayne F. 1922- *7*
Hylander, Clarence J.
  1897-1964 .... *7*
Hyman, Robin P(hilip) 1931- *12*
Hyman, Trina Schart 1939- *46*
  Earlier sketch in SATA 7
Hymes, Lucia M. 1907- *7*
Hyndman, Jane Andrews
  1912-1978 .... *46*
  Obituary *23*
  Earlier sketch in SATA 1
Hyndman, Robert Utley
  1906(?)-1973 .... *18*

I

Iannone, Jeanne *7*
Ibbotson, Eva 1925- *13*

Ibbotson, M. C(hristine)
  1930- *5*
Ichikawa, Satomi 1949- *47*
  Brief Entry *36*
Ilowite, Sheldon A. 1931- *27*
Ilsley, Dent [Joint pseudonym]
  See Chapman, John Stanton Higham
Ilsley, Velma (Elizabeth)
  1918- *12*
Immel, Mary Blair 1930- *28*
Ingelow, Jean 1820-1897 .... *33*
Ingham, Colonel Frederic
  See Hale, Edward Everett
Ingraham, Leonard W(illiam)
  1913- *4*
Ingrams, Doreen 1906- *20*
Inyart, Gene 1927- *6*
Ionesco, Eugene 1912- *7*
Ipcar, Dahlov (Zorach) 1917- *49*
  Earlier sketch in SATA 1
Irvin, Fred 1914- *15*
Irving, Alexander
  See Hume, Ruth (Fox)
Irving, Robert
  See Adler, Irving
Irving, Washington
  1783-1859 ....*YABC 2*
Irwin, Ann(abelle Bowen)
  1915- *44*
  Brief Entry *38*
Irwin, Constance Frick 1913- *6*
Irwin, Hadley [Joint pseudonym]
  See Hadley, Lee and Irwin, Ann
Irwin, Keith Gordon
  1885-1964 .... *11*
Isaac, Joanne 1934- *21*
Isaacs, Jacob
  See Kranzler, George G(ershon)
Isadora, Rachel 1953(?)-
  Brief Entry *32*
  See also CLR 7
Isham, Charlotte H(ickox)
  1912- *21*
Ish-Kishor, Judith 1892-1972 ..... *11*
Ish-Kishor, Sulamith
  1896-1977 .... *17*
Ishmael, Woodi 1914- *31*
Israel, Elaine 1945- *12*
Israel, Marion Louise 1882-1973
  Obituary *26*
Iwamatsu, Jun Atsushi 1908- *14*

J

Jac, Lee
  See Morton, Lee Jack, Jr.
Jackson, Anne 1896(?)-1984
  Obituary *37*
Jackson, C. Paul 1902- *6*
Jackson, Caary
  See Jackson, C. Paul
Jackson, Jesse 1908-1983 .... *29*
  Obituary *48*
  Earlier sketch in SATA 2
Jackson, O. B.
  See Jackson, C. Paul
Jackson, Robert B(lake) 1926- *8*

Jackson, Sally
  See Kellogg, Jean
Jackson, Shirley 1919-1965 .... *2*
Jacob, Helen Pierce 1927- *21*
Jacobi, Kathy
  Brief Entry *42*
Jacobs, Flora Gill 1918- *5*
Jacobs, Francine 1935- *43*
  Brief Entry *42*
Jacobs, Frank 1929- *30*
Jacobs, Helen Hull 1908- *12*
Jacobs, Joseph 1854-1916 .... *25*
Jacobs, Leland Blair 1907- *20*
Jacobs, Linda C. 1943- *21*
Jacobs, Lou(is), Jr. 1921- *2*
Jacobs, Susan 1940- *30*
Jacobs, William Jay 1933- *28*
Jacobson, Daniel 1923- *12*
Jacobson, Morris K(arl) 1906- *21*
Jacopetti, Alexandra 1939- *14*
Jacques, Robin 1920- *32*
  Brief Entry *30*
  See also SAAS 5
Jaffee, Al(lan) 1921-
  Brief Entry *37*
Jagendorf, Moritz (Adolf)
  1888-1981 .... *2*
  Obituary *24*
Jahn, (Joseph) Michael 1943- *28*
Jahn, Mike
  See Jahn, (Joseph) Michael
Jahsmann, Allan Hart 1916- *28*
James, Andrew
  See Kirkup, James
James, Dynely
  See Mayne, William
James, Edwin
  See Gunn, James E(dwin)
James, Harry Clebourne 1896- *11*
James, Josephine
  See Sterne, Emma Gelders
James, Robin (Irene) 1953- *50*
James, T. F.
  See Fleming, Thomas J(ames)
James, Will(iam Roderick)
  1892-1942 .... *19*
Jance, J. A.
  See Jance, Judith A(nn)
Jance, Judith A(nn) 1944-
  Brief Entry *50*
Jane, Mary Childs 1909- *6*
Janes, Edward C. 1908- *25*
Janes, J(oseph) Robert 1935-
  Brief Entry *50*
Janeway, Elizabeth (Hall)
  1913- *19*
Janice
  See Brustlein, Janice Tworkov
Janosch
  See Eckert, Horst
Jansen, Jared
  See Cebulash, Mel
Janson, Dora Jane 1916- *31*
Janson, H(orst) W(oldemar)
  1913- *9*
Jansson, Tove (Marika) 1914- *41*
  Earlier sketch in SATA 3
  See also CLR 2

Janus, Grete
  See Hertz, Grete Janus
Jaques, Faith 1923- *21*
Jaques, Francis Lee 1887-1969
  Brief Entry *28*
Jaquith, Priscilla 1908- *51*
Jarman, Rosemary Hawley
  1935- *7*
Jarrell, Mary von Schrader
  1914- *35*
Jarrell, Randall 1914-1965 .... *7*
  See also CLR 6
Jarrett, Roxanne
  See Werner, Herma
Jauss, Anne Marie 1907- *10*
Jayne, Lieutenant R. H.
  See Ellis, Edward S(ylvester)
Jaynes, Clare [Joint pseudonym]
  See Mayer, Jane Rothschild
Jeake, Samuel, Jr.
  See Aiken, Conrad
Jefferds, Vincent H(arris) 1916-
  Brief Entry *49*
Jefferies, (John) Richard
  1848-1887 .... *16*
Jeffers, Susan *17*
Jefferson, Sarah
  See Farjeon, Annabel
Jeffries, Roderic 1926- *4*
Jenkins, Marie M. 1909- *7*
Jenkins, William A(twell)
  1922- *9*
Jenkyns, Chris 1924- *51*
Jennings, Gary (Gayne) 1928- *9*
Jennings, Robert
  See Hamilton, Charles H. St. John
Jennings, S. M.
  See Meyer, Jerome Sydney
Jennison, C. S.
  See Starbird, Kaye
Jennison, Keith Warren 1911- *14*
Jensen, Niels 1927- *25*
Jensen, Virginia Allen 1927- *8*
Jeppson, J(anet) O(pal) 1926-
  Brief Entry *46*
Jeschke, Susan *42*
  Brief Entry *27*
Jessel, Camilla (Ruth) 1937- *29*
Jewell, Nancy 1940-
  Brief Entry *41*
Jewett, Eleanore Myers
  1890-1967 .... *5*
Jewett, Sarah Orne 1849-1909 .... *15*
Jezard, Alison 1919-
  Brief Entry *34*
Jiler, John 1946- *42*
  Brief Entry *35*
Jobb, Jamie 1945- *29*
Joerns, Consuelo *44*
  Brief Entry *33*
John, Naomi
  See Flack, Naomi John (White)
Johns, Avery
  See Cousins, Margaret
Johnson, A. E. [Joint pseudonym]
  See Johnson, Annabell and Johnson,
  Edgar
Johnson, Annabell Jones
  1921- *2*

Johnson, Benj. F., of Boone
  See Riley, James Whitcomb
Johnson, Charles R. 1925- *11*
Johnson, Charlotte Buel
  1918-1982 .... *46*
Johnson, Chuck
  See Johnson, Charles R.
Johnson, Crockett
  See Leisk, David (Johnson)
Johnson, D(ana) William
  1945- *23*
Johnson, Dorothy M(arie)
  1905-1984 .... *6*
  Obituary *40*
Johnson, E(ugene) Harper *44*
Johnson, Edgar Raymond
  1912- *2*
Johnson, Elizabeth 1911-1984 ..... *7*
  Obituary *39*
Johnson, Eric W(arner) 1918- *8*
Johnson, Evelyne 1932- *20*
Johnson, Gaylord 1884- *7*
Johnson, Gerald White
  1890-1980 .... *19*
  Obituary *28*
Johnson, Harper
  See Johnson, E(ugene) Harper
Johnson, James Ralph 1922- *1*
Johnson, James Weldon
  See Johnson, James William
Johnson, James William
  1871-1938 .... *31*
Johnson, Jane 1951 .... *48*
Johnson, John E(mil) 1929- *34*
Johnson, LaVerne B(ravo)
  1925- *13*
Johnson, Lois S(mith) *6*
Johnson, Lois W(alfrid) 1936- *22*
Johnson, Margaret S(weet)
  1893-1964 .... *35*
Johnson, Mary Frances K.
  1929(?)-1979
  Obituary *27*
Johnson, Maud Battle 1918(?)-1985
  Obituary *46*
Johnson, Milton 1932- *31*
Johnson, Natalie
  See Robison, Nancy L(ouise)
Johnson, (Walter) Ryerson
  1901- *10*
Johnson, Shirley K(ing) 1927- *10*
Johnson, Siddie Joe 1905-1977
  Obituary *20*
Johnson, Spencer 1938-
  Brief Entry *38*
Johnson, William R. *38*
Johnson, William Weber
  1909- *7*
Johnston, Agnes Christine
  See Dazey, Agnes J.
Johnston, Annie Fellows
  1863-1931 .... *37*
Johnston, H(ugh) A(nthony) S(tephen)
  1913-1967 .... *14*
Johnston, Johanna
  1914(?)-1982 .... *12*
  Obituary *33*
Johnston, Norma *29*

Johnston, Portia
  See Takakjian, Portia
Johnston, Tony 1942- *8*
Jonas, Ann 1932- *50*
  Brief Entry *42*
  See also CLR 12
Jones, Adrienne 1915- *7*
Jones, Diana Wynne 1934- *9*
Jones, Elizabeth Orton 1910- *18*
Jones, Evan 1915- *3*
Jones, Geraldine 1951- *43*
Jones, Gillingham
  See Hamilton, Charles H. St. John
Jones, Harold 1904- *14*
Jones, Helen Hinckley 1903- *26*
Jones, Helen L. 1904(?)-1973
  Obituary *22*
Jones, Hettie 1934- *42*
  Brief Entry *27*
Jones, Hortense P. 1918- *9*
Jones, Jessie Mae Orton 1887(?)-1983
  Obituary *37*
Jones, Margaret Boone
  See Zarif, Margaret Min'imah
Jones, Mary Alice *6*
Jones, McClure *34*
Jones, Penelope 1938- *31*
Jones, Rebecca C(astaldi)
  1947- *33*
Jones, Terry 1942- *51*
Jones, Weyman 1928- *4*
Jonk, Clarence 1906- *10*
Jordan, Don
  See Howard, Vernon (Linwood)
Jordan, E(mil) L(eopold) 1900-
  Brief Entry *31*
Jordan, Hope (Dahle) 1905- *15*
Jordan, Jael (Michal) 1949- *30*
Jordan, June 1936- *4*
  See also CLR 10
Jordan, Mildred 1901- *5*
Jorgensen, Mary Venn *36*
Jorgenson, Ivar
  See Silverberg, Robert
Joseph, Joan 1939- *34*
Joseph, Joseph M(aron)
  1903-1979 .... *22*
Joslin, Sesyle 1929- *2*
Joyce, J(ames) Avery
  1902-1987 .... *11*
  Obituary *50*
Joyce, William 1959(?)-
  Brief Entry *46*
Joyner, Jerry 1938- *34*
Jucker, Sita 1921- *5*
Judd, Denis (O'Nan) 1938- *33*
Judd, Frances K. [Collective
  pseudonym] *1*
Judson, Clara Ingram
  1879-1960 .... *38*
  Brief Entry *27*
Jukes, Mavis
  Brief Entry *43*
Jumpp, Hugo
  See MacPeek, Walter G.
Jupo, Frank J. 1904- *7*
Juster, Norton 1929- *3*
Justus, May 1898- *1*

Juvenilia
    See Taylor, Ann

K

Kabdebo, Tamas
    See Kabdebo, Thomas
Kabdebo, Thomas 1934- *10*
Kabibble, Osh
    See Jobb, Jamie
Kadesch, Robert R(udstone)
    1922- *31*
Kahl, M(arvin) P(hilip) 1934- *37*
Kahl, Virginia (Caroline)
    1919- *48*
    Brief Entry *38*
Kahn, Joan 1914- *48*
Kahn, Roger 1927- *37*
Kakimoto, Kozo 1915- *11*
Kalashnikoff, Nicholas
    1888-1961 .... *16*
Kalb, Jonah 1926- *23*
Kaler, James Otis 1848-1912 ...... *15*
Kalnay, Francis 1899- *7*
Kalow, Gisela 1946- *32*
Kamen, Gloria 1923- *9*
Kamerman, Sylvia E.
    See Burack, Sylvia K.
Kamm, Josephine (Hart)
    1905- *24*
Kandell, Alice S. 1938- *35*
Kane, Henry Bugbee
    1902-1971 .... *14*
Kane, Robert W. 1910- *18*
Kanetzke, Howard W(illiam)
    1932- *38*
Kanzawa, Toshiko
    See Furukawa, Toshi
Kaplan, Anne Bernays 1930- *32*
Kaplan, Bess 1927- *22*
Kaplan, Boche 1926- *24*
Kaplan, Irma 1900- *10*
Kaplan, Jean Caryl Korn
    1926- *10*
Karageorge, Michael
    See Anderson, Poul (William)
Karasz, Ilonka 1896-1981
    Obituary *29*
Karen, Ruth 1922- *9*
Kark, Nina Mary 1925- *4*
Karl, Jean E(dna) 1927- *34*
Karlin, Eugene 1918- *10*
Karp, Naomi J. 1926- *16*
Kashiwagi, Isami 1925- *10*
Kassem, Lou
    Brief Entry *51*
Kästner, Erich 1899-1974 .... *14*
    See also CLR 4
Kasuya, Masahiro 1937- *51*
Katchen, Carole 1944- *9*
Kathryn
    See Searle, Kathryn Adrienne
Katona, Robert 1949- *21*
Katsarakis, Joan Harries
    See Harries, Joan
Katz, Bobbi 1933- *12*
Katz, Fred 1938- *6*
Katz, Jane 1934- *33*

Katz, Marjorie P.
    See Weiscr, Marjorie P(hillis) K(atz)
Katz, William Loren 1927- *13*
Kaufman, Joe 1911- *33*
Kaufman, Mervyn D. 1932- *4*
Kaufmann, Angelika 1935- *15*
Kaufmann, John 1931- *18*
Kaula, Edna Mason 1906- *13*
Kavaler, Lucy 1930- *23*
Kay, Helen
    See Goldfrank, Helen Colodny
Kay, Mara *13*
Kaye, Danny 1913-1987
    Obituary *50*
Kaye, Geraldine 1925- *10*
Keane, Bil 1922- *4*
Keating, Bern
    See Keating, Leo Bernard
Keating, Lawrence A.
    1903-1966 .... *23*
Keating, Leo Bernard 1915- *10*
Keats, Ezra Jack 1916-1983 ...... *14*
    Obituary *34*
    See also CLR 1
Keegan, Marcia 1943- *9*
Keel, Frank
    See Keeler, Ronald F(ranklin)
Keeler, Ronald F(ranklin)
    1913-1983 .... *47*
Keen, Martin L. 1913- *4*
Keene, Carolyn [Collective
    pseudonym]
    See Adams, Harriet S.
Keeping, Charles (William James)
    1924- *9*
Keeshan, Robert J. 1927- *32*
Keir, Christine
    See Pullein-Thompson, Christine
Keith, Carlton
    See Robertson, Keith
Keith, Hal 1934- *36*
Keith, Harold (Verne) 1903- *2*
Keith, Robert
    See Applebaum, Stan
Kelen, Emery 1896-1978 .... *13*
    Obituary *26*
Kelleam, Joseph E(veridge)
    1913-1975 .... *31*
Keller, B(everly) L(ou) *13*
Keller, Charles 1942- *8*
Keller, Dick 1923- *36*
Keller, Gail Faithfull
    See Faithfull, Gail
Keller, Holly
    Brief Entry *42*
Keller, Irene (Barron) 1927- *36*
Keller, Mollie
    Brief Entry *50*
Kelley, Leo P(atrick) 1928- *32*
    Brief Entry *31*
Kelley, True Adelaide 1946- *41*
    Brief Entry *39*
Kellin, Sally Moffet 1932- *9*
Kelling, Furn L. 1914- *37*
Kellogg, Gene
    See Kellogg, Jean
Kellogg, Jean 1916- *10*
Kellogg, Steven 1941- *8*
    See also CLR 6

Kellow, Kathleen
    See Hibbert, Eleanor
Kelly, Eric P(hilbrook)
    1884-1960 ....YABC 1
Kelly, Martha Rose
    1914-1983 .... *37*
Kelly, Marty
    See Kelly, Martha Rose
Kelly, Ralph
    See Geis, Darlene
Kelly, Regina Z. *5*
Kelly, Rosalie (Ruth) *43*
Kelly, Walt(er Crawford)
    1913-1973 .... *18*
Kelsey, Alice Geer 1896- *1*
Kemp, Gene 1926- *25*
Kempner, Mary Jean
    1913-1969 .... *10*
Kempton, Jean Welch 1914- *10*
Kendall, Carol (Seeger) 1917- *11*
Kendall, Lace
    See Stoutenburg, Adrien
Kenealy, James P. 1927-
    Brief Entry *29*
Kenealy, Jim
    See Kenealy, James P.
Kennedy, John Fitzgerald
    1917-1963 .... *11*
Kennedy, Joseph 1929- *14*
Kennedy, Paul E(dward)
    1929- *33*
Kennedy, (Jerome) Richard
    1932- *22*
Kennedy, T(eresa) A. 1953- *42*
    Brief Entry *35*
Kennedy, X. J.
    See Kennedy, Joseph
Kennell, Ruth E(pperson)
    1893-1977 .... *6*
    Obituary *25*
Kenny, Ellsworth Newcomb
    1909-1971
    Obituary *26*
Kenny, Herbert A(ndrew)
    1912- *13*
Kenny, Kathryn
    See Bowden, Joan Chase
    See Krull, Kathleen
Kenny, Kevin
    See Krull, Kathleen
Kent, Alexander
    See Reeman, Douglas Edward
Kent, David
    See Lambert, David (Compton)
Kent, Deborah Ann 1948- *47*
    Brief Entry *41*
Kent, Jack
    See Kent, John Wellington
Kent, John Wellington
    1920-1985 .... *24*
    Obituary *45*
Kent, Margaret 1894- *2*
Kent, Rockwell 1882-1971 .... *6*
Kent, Sherman 1903-1986 .... *20*
    Obituary *47*
Kenward, Jean 1920- *42*
Kenworthy, Leonard S. 1912- *6*
Kenyon, Ley 1913- *6*
Kepes, Juliet A(ppleby) 1919- *13*

Kerigan, Florence 1896- *12*
Kerman, Gertrude Lerner
  1909- *21*
Kerr, Jessica 1901- *13*
Kerr, (Anne) Judith 1923- *24*
Kerr, M. E.
  See Meaker, Marijane
  See also SAAS 1
Kerry, Frances
  See Kerigan, Florence
Kerry, Lois
  See Duncan, Lois S(teinmetz)
Ker Wilson, Barbara 1929- *20*
Kessel, Joyce Karen 1937- *41*
Kessler, Ethel 1922- *44*
  Brief Entry *37*
Kessler, Leonard P. 1921- *14*
Kesteven, G. R.
  See Crosher, G(eoffry) R(obins)
Ketcham, Hank
  See Ketcham, Henry King
Ketcham, Henry King 1920- *28*
  Brief Entry *27*
Kettelkamp, Larry 1933- *2*
  See also SAAS 3
Kevles, Bettyann 1938- *23*
Key, Alexander (Hill)
  1904-1979 .... *8*
  Obituary *23*
Keyes, Daniel 1927- *37*
Keyes, Fenton 1915- *34*
Keyser, Marcia 1933- *42*
Keyser, Sarah
  See McGuire, Leslie (Sarah)
Khanshendel, Chiron
  See Rose, Wendy
Kherdian, David 1931- *16*
Kidd, Ronald 1948- *42*
Kiddell, John 1922- *3*
Kidwell, Carl 1910- *43*
Kiefer, Irene 1926- *21*
Kiesel, Stanley 1925- *35*
Kikukawa, Cecily H. 1919- *44*
  Brief Entry *35*
Kilgore, Kathleen 1946- *42*
Kilian, Crawford 1941- *35*
Killilea, Marie (Lyons) 1913- *2*
Kilreon, Beth
  See Walker, Barbara K.
Kimball, Yeffe 1914-1978 .... *37*
Kimbrough, Emily 1899- *2*
Kimmel, Eric A. 1946- *13*
Kimmel, Margaret Mary
  1938- *43*
  Brief Entry *33*
Kindred, Wendy 1937- *7*
Kines, Pat Decker 1937- *12*
King, Adam
  See Hoare, Robert J(ohn)
King, Arthur
  See Cain, Arthur H.
King, Billie Jean 1943- *12*
King, (David) Clive 1924- *28*
King, Cynthia 1925- *7*
King, Frank O. 1883-1969
  Obituary *22*
King, Marian 1900(?)-1986 .... *23*
  Obituary *47*

King, Martin
  See Marks, Stan(ley)
King, Martin Luther, Jr.
  1929-1968 .... *14*
King, Reefe
  See Barker, Albert W.
King, Stephen 1947- *9*
King, Tony 1947- *39*
Kingman, Dong (Moy Shu)
  1911- *44*
Kingman, (Mary) Lee 1919- *1*
  See also SAAS 3
Kingsland, Leslie William
  1912- *13*
Kingsley, Charles
  1819-1875 .... *YABC 2*
Kingsley, Emily Perl 1940- *33*
King-Smith, Dick 1922- *47*
  Brief Entry *38*
Kinney, C. Cle 1915- *6*
Kinney, Harrison 1921- *13*
Kinney, Jean Stout 1912- *12*
Kinsey, Elizabeth
  See Clymer, Eleanor
Kipling, (Joseph) Rudyard
  1865-1936 .... *YABC 2*
Kirk, Ruth (Kratz) 1925- *5*
Kirkland, Will
  See Hale, Arlene
Kirkup, James 1927- *12*
Kirkus, Virginia
  See Glick, Virginia Kirkus
Kirtland, G. B.
  See Joslin, Sesyle
Kishida, Eriko 1929- *12*
Kisinger, Grace Gelvin
  1913-1965 .... *10*
Kissin, Eva H. 1923- *10*
Kjelgaard, James Arthur
  1910-1959 .... *17*
Kjelgaard, Jim
  See Kjelgaard, James Arthur
Klagsbrun, Francine (Lifton) *36*
Klaperman, Gilbert 1921- *33*
Klaperman, Libby Mindlin
  1921-1982 .... *33*
  Obituary *31*
Klass, Morton 1927- *11*
Klass, Sheila Solomon 1927- *45*
Kleberger, Ilse 1921- *5*
Klein, Aaron E. 1930- *45*
  Brief Entry *28*
Klein, Gerda Weissmann
  1924- *44*
Klein, H. Arthur *8*
Klein, Leonore 1916- *6*
Klein, Mina C(ooper) *8*
Klein, Norma 1938- *7*
  See also CLR 2
  See also SAAS 1
Klein, Robin 1936-
  Brief Entry *45*
Klemm, Edward G., Jr. 1910- *30*
Klemm, Roberta K(ohnhorst)
  1884- *30*
Klevin, Jill Ross 1935- *39*
  Brief Entry *38*
Kliban, B. 1935- *35*
Klimowicz, Barbara 1927- *10*

Kline, Suzy 1943-
  Brief Entry *48*
Klug, Ron(ald) 1939- *31*
Knapp, Ron 1952- *34*
Knebel, Fletcher 1911- *36*
Knickerbocker, Diedrich
  See Irving, Washington
Knifesmith
  See Cutler, Ivor
Knigge, Robert (R.) 1921(?)-1987
  Obituary *50*
Knight, Anne (Katherine)
  1946- *34*
Knight, Damon 1922- *9*
Knight, David C(arpenter) *14*
Knight, Eric (Mowbray)
  1897-1943 .... *18*
Knight, Francis Edgar *14*
Knight, Frank
  See Knight, Francis Edgar
Knight, Hilary 1926- *15*
Knight, Mallory T.
  See Hurwood, Bernhardt J.
Knight, Ruth Adams 1898-1974
  Obituary *20*
Knott, Bill
  See Knott, William Cecil, Jr.
Knott, William Cecil, Jr.
  1927- *3*
Knotts, Howard (Clayton, Jr.)
  1922- *25*
Knowles, Anne 1933- *37*
Knowles, John 1926- *8*
Knox, Calvin
  See Silverberg, Robert
Knox, (Mary) Eleanor Jessie
  1909- *30*
Knox, James
  See Brittain, William
Knudsen, James 1950- *42*
Knudson, Richard L(ewis)
  1930- *34*
Knudson, R. R.
  See Knudson, Rozanne
Knudson, Rozanne 1932- *7*
Koch, Dorothy Clarke 1924- *6*
Kocsis, J. C.
  See Paul, James
Koehn, Ilse
  See Van Zwienen, Ilse (Charlotte
  Koehn)
Koerner, W(illiam) H(enry) D(avid)
  1878-1938 .... *21*
Kogan, Deborah 1940- *50*
Kohl, Herbert 1937- *47*
Kohler, Julilly H(ouse) 1908-1976
  Obituary *20*
Kohn, Bernice (Herstein)
  1920- *4*
Kohner, Frederick 1905-1986 ..... *10*
  Obituary *48*
Koide, Tan 1938-1986 .... *50*
Kolba, Tamara *22*
Komisar, Lucy 1942- *9*
Komoda, Beverly 1939- *25*
Komoda, Kiyo 1937- *9*
Komroff, Manuel 1890-1974 ...... *2*
  Obituary *20*

Konigsburg, E(laine) L(obl) 48
  Earlier sketch in SATA 4
  See also CLR 1
Koning, Hans
  See Koningsberger, Hans
Koningsberger, Hans 1921- 5
Konkle, Janet Everest 1917- 12
Koob, Theodora (Johanna Foth)
  1918- 23
Kooiker, Leonie
  See Kooyker-Romijn, Johanna Maria
Kooyker-Romijn, Johanna Maria
  1927- 48
Kopper, Lisa (Esther) 1950-
  Brief Entry 51
Korach, Mimi 1922- 9
Koren, Edward 1935- 5
Korinetz, Yuri (Iosifovich)
  1923- 9
  See also CLR 4
Korman, Gordon 1963- 49
  Brief Entry 41
Korty, Carol 1937- 15
Kossin, Sandy (Sanford)
  1926- 10
Kotzwinkle, William 1938- 24
  See also CLR 6
Kouhi, Elizabeth 1917-
  Brief Entry 49
Koutoukas, H. M.
  See Rivoli, Mario
Kouts, Anne 1945- 8
Krahn, Fernando 1935- 49
  Brief Entry 31
  See also CLR 3
Kramer, Anthony
  Brief Entry 42
Kramer, George
  See Heuman, William
Kramer, Nora 1896(?)-1984 26
  Obituary 39
Krantz, Hazel (Newman)
  1920- 12
Kranzler, George G(ershon)
  1916- 28
Kranzler, Gershon
  See Kranzler, George G(ershon)
Krasilovsky, Phyllis 1926- 38
  Earlier sketch in SATA 1
  See also SAAS 5
Kraske, Robert
  Brief Entry 36
Kraus, Robert 1925- 4
Krauss, Ruth (Ida) 1911- 30
  Earlier sketch in SATA 1
Krautter, Elisa
  See Bialk, Elisa
Krauze, Andrzej 1947-
  Brief Entry 46
Kredel, Fritz 1900-1973 17
Krementz, Jill 1940- 17
  See also CLR 5
Krensky, Stephen (Alan)
  1953- 47
  Brief Entry 41
Kripke, Dorothy Karp 30
Kristof, Jane 1932- 8
Kroeber, Theodora (Kracaw)
  1897- 1

Kroll, Francis Lynde
  1904-1973 10
Kroll, Steven 1941- 19
Kropp, Paul (Stephen) 1948- 38
  Brief Entry 34
Krull, Kathleen 1952-
  Brief Entry 39
Krumgold, Joseph 1908-1980 48
  Obituary 23
  Earlier sketch in SATA 1
Krush, Beth 1918- 18
Krush, Joe 1918- 18
Krüss, James 1926- 8
  See also CLR 9
Kubie, Nora (Gottheil) Benjamin
  1899- 39
Kubinyi, Laszlo 1937- 17
Kuh, Charlotte 1892(?)-1985
  Obituary 43
Kujoth, Jean Spealman 1935-1975
  Obituary 30
Kullman, Harry 1919-1982 35
Kumin, Maxine (Winokur)
  1925- 12
Kunhardt, Dorothy Meserve
  1901(?)-1979
  Obituary 22
Künstler, Morton 1927- 10
Kupferberg, Herbert 1918- 19
Kuratomi, Chizuko 1939- 12
Kurelek, William 1927-1977 8
  Obituary 27
  See also CLR 2
Kurland, Gerald 1942- 13
Kurland, Michael (Joseph)
  1938- 48
Kuskin, Karla (Seidman)
  1932- 2
  See also CLR 4
  See also SAAS 3
Kuttner, Paul 1931- 18
Kuzma, Kay 1941- 39
Kvale, Velma R(uth) 1898- 8
Kyle, Elisabeth
  See Dunlop, Agnes M. R.
Kyte, Kathy S. 1946- 50
  Brief Entry 44

L

Lacy, Leslie Alexander 1937- 6
Ladd, Veronica
  See Miner, Jane Claypool
Lader, Lawrence 1919- 6
Lady, A
  See Taylor, Ann
Lady Mears
  See Tempest, Margaret Mary
Lady of Quality, A
  See Bagnold, Enid
La Farge, Oliver (Hazard Perry)
  1901-1963 19
La Farge, Phyllis 14
Laffin, John (Alfred Charles)
  1922- 31
La Fontaine, Jean de
  1621-1695 18

Lagercrantz, Rose (Elsa)
  1947- 39
Lagerlöf, Selma (Ottiliana Lovisa)
  1858-1940 15
  See also CLR 7
Laiken, Deirdre S(usan) 1948- 48
  Brief Entry 40
Laimgruber, Monika 1946- 11
Laing, Martha
  See Celestino, Martha Laing
Laird, Jean E(louise) 1930- 38
Laite, Gordon 1925- 31
Lake, Harriet
  See Taylor, Paula (Wright)
Laklan, Carli 1907- 5
la Mare, Walter de
  See de la Mare, Walter
Lamb, Beatrice Pitney 1904- 21
Lamb, Charles 1775-1834 17
Lamb, Elizabeth Searle 1917- 31
Lamb, G(eoffrey) F(rederick) 10
Lamb, Lynton 1907- 10
Lamb, Mary Ann 1764-1847 17
Lamb, Robert (Boyden) 1941- 13
Lambert, David (Compton) 1932-
  Brief Entry 49
Lambert, Janet (Snyder)
  1894-1973 25
Lambert, Saul 1928- 23
Lamburn, Richmal Crompton
  1890-1969 5
Lamorisse, Albert (Emmanuel)
  1922-1970 23
Lampert, Emily 1951-
  Brief Entry 49
Lamplugh, Lois 1921- 17
Lampman, Evelyn Sibley
  1907-1980 4
  Obituary 23
Lamprey, Louise
  1869-1951 .... YABC 2
Lampton, Chris
  See Lampton, Christopher
Lampton, Christopher
  Brief Entry 47
Lancaster, Bruce 1896-1963 9
Lancaster, Matthew 1973(?)-1983
  Obituary 45
Land, Barbara (Neblett) 1923- 16
Land, Jane [Joint pseudonym]
  See Borland, Kathryn Kilby and
    Speicher, Helen Ross (Smith)
Land, Myrick (Ebben) 1922- 15
Land, Ross [Joint pseudonym]
  See Borland, Kathryn Kilby and
    Speicher, Helen Ross (Smith)
Landau, Elaine 1948- 10
Landau, Jacob 1917- 38
Landeck, Beatrice 1904- 15
Landin, Les(lie) 1923- 2
Landon, Lucinda 1950-
  Brief Entry 51
Landon, Margaret (Dorothea
  Mortenson) 1903- 50
Landshoff, Ursula 1908- 13
Lane, Carolyn 1926- 10
Lane, Jerry
  See Martin, Patricia Miles
Lane, John 1932- 15

Lane, Margaret 1907-
  Brief Entry 38
Lane, Rose Wilder 1886-1968 29
  Brief Entry 28
Lanes, Selma G. 1929- 3
Lang, Andrew 1844-1912 16
Lange, John
  See Crichton, (J.) Michael
Lange, Suzanne 1945- 5
Langley, Noel 1911-1980
  Obituary 25
Langner, Nola 1930- 8
Langone, John (Michael)
  1929- 46
  Brief Entry 38
Langstaff, John 1920- 6
  See also CLR 3
Langstaff, Launcelot
  See Irving, Washington
Langton, Jane 1922- 3
  See also SAAS 5
Lanier, Sidney 1842-1881 18
Lansing, Alfred 1921-1975 35
Lantz, Paul 1908- 45
Lantz, Walter 1900- 37
Lappin, Peter 1911- 32
Larom, Henry V. 1903(?)-1975
  Obituary 30
Larrecq, John M(aurice)
  1926-1980 44
  Obituary 25
Larrick, Nancy G. 1910- 4
Larsen, Egon 1904- 14
Larson, Eve
  See St. John, Wylly Folk
Larson, Norita D. 1944- 29
Larson, William H. 1938- 10
Larsson, Carl (Olof)
  1853-1919 35
Lasell, Elinor H. 1929- 19
Lasell, Fen H.
  See Lasell, Elinor H.
Lash, Joseph P. 1909- 43
Lasher, Faith B. 1921- 12
Lasker, David 1950- 38
Lasker, Joe 1919- 9
Lasky, Kathryn 1944- 13
  See also CLR 11
Lassalle, C. E.
  See Ellis, Edward S(ylvester)
Latham, Barbara 1896- 16
Latham, Frank B. 1910- 6
Latham, Jean Lee 1902- 2
Latham, Mavis
  See Clark, Mavis Thorpe
Latham, Philip
  See Richardson, Robert S(hirley)
Lathrop, Dorothy P(ulis)
  1891-1980 14
  Obituary 24
Lathrop, Francis
  See Leiber, Fritz
Lattimore, Eleanor Frances
  1904-1986 7
  Obituary 48
Lauber, Patricia (Grace) 1924- 33
  Earlier sketch in SATA 1
Laugesen, Mary E(akin)
  1906- 5

Laughbaum, Steve 1945- 12
Laughlin, Florence 1910- 3
Lauré, Ettagale
  See Blauer, Ettagale
Lauré, Jason 1940- 50
  Brief Entry 44
Laurence, Ester Hauser 1935- 7
Laurence, (Jean) Margaret (Wemyss)
  1926-1987
  Obituary 50
Laurin, Anne
  See McLaurin, Anne
Lauritzen, Jonreed 1902- 13
Lauscher, Hermann
  See Hesse, Hermann
Laux, Dorothy 1920- 49
Lavine, David 1928- 31
Lavine, Sigmund A. 1908- 3
Laviolette, Emily A. 1923(?)-1975
  Brief Entry 49
Lawrence, Ann (Margaret)
  1942- 41
Lawrence, Isabelle (Wentworth)
  Brief Entry 29
Lawrence, J. T.
  See Rowland-Entwistle, (Arthur)
  Theodore (Henry)
Lawrence, John 1933- 30
Lawrence, Josephine 1890(?)-1978
  Obituary 24
Lawrence, Linda
  See Hunt, Linda Lawrence
Lawrence, Louise 1943- 38
Lawrence, Louise de Kiriline
  1894- 13
Lawrence, Mildred 1907- 3
Lawson, Carol (Antell) 1946- 42
Lawson, Don(ald Elmer)
  1917- 9
Lawson, Marion Tubbs 1896- 22
Lawson, Robert
  1892-1957 .... YABC 2
  See also CLR 2
Laycock, George (Edwin)
  1921- 5
Lazare, Gerald John 1927- 44
Lazare, Jerry
  See Lazare, Gerald John
Lazarevich, Mila 1942- 17
Lazarus, Keo Felker 1913- 21
Lea, Alec 1907- 19
Lea, Richard
  See Lea, Alec
Leach, Maria 1892-1977 39
  Brief Entry 28
Leacroft, Helen 1919- 6
Leacroft, Richard 1914- 6
Leaf, (Wilbur) Munro
  1905-1976 20
Leaf, VaDonna Jean 1929- 26
Leakey, Richard E(rskine Frere)
  1944- 42
Leander, Ed
  See Richelson, Geraldine
Lear, Edward 1812-1888 18
  See also CLR 1
Leavitt, Jerome E(dward)
  1916- 23

LeBar, Mary E(velyn)
  1910-1982 35
LeCain, Errol 1941- 6
Leder, Jane Mersky 1945-
  Brief Entry 51
Lederer, Muriel 1929- 48
Lee, Amanda [Joint pseudonym]
  See Buckholtz, Eileen (Garber)
Lee, Benjamin 1921- 27
Lee, Betsy 1949- 37
Lee, Carol
  See Fletcher, Helen Jill
Lee, Dennis (Beynon) 1939- 14
  See also CLR 3
Lee, Doris (Emrick)
  1905-1983 44
  Obituary 35
Lee, (Nelle) Harper 1926- 11
Lee, John R(obert) 1923-1976 27
Lee, Manning de V(illeneuve)
  1894-1980 37
  Obituary 22
Lee, Marian
  See Clish, (Lee) Marian
Lee, Mary Price 1934- 8
Lee, Mildred 1908- 6
Lee, Robert C. 1931- 20
Lee, Robert J. 1921- 10
Lee, Roy
  See Hopkins, Clark
Lee, Tanith 1947- 8
Leedy, Loreen (Janelle) 1959-
  Brief Entry 50
Leekley, Thomas B(riggs)
  1910- 23
Leeming, Jo Ann
  See Leeming, Joseph
Leeming, Joseph 1897-1968 26
Leeson, R. A.
  See Leeson, Robert (Arthur)
Leeson, Robert (Arthur) 1928- 42
Lefler, Irene (Whitney) 1917- 12
Le Gallienne, Eva 1899- 9
Legg, Sarah Martha Ross Bruggeman
  (?)-1982
  Obituary 40
LeGrand
  See Henderson, LeGrand
Le Guin, Ursula K(roeber)
  1929- 4
  See also CLR 3
Legum, Colin 1919- 10
Lehn, Cornelia 1920- 46
Lehr, Delores 1920- 10
Leiber, Fritz 1910- 45
Leichman, Seymour 1933- 5
Leigh, Tom 1947- 46
Leigh-Pemberton, John 1911- 35
Leighton, Clare (Veronica Hope)
  1900(?)- 37
Leighton, Margaret 1896- 1
Leipold, L. Edmond 1902- 16
Leisk, David (Johnson)
  1906-1975 30
  Obituary 26
  Earlier sketch in SATA 1
Leister, Mary 1917- 29
Leitch, Patricia 1933- 11

LeMair, H(enriette) Willebeek
1889-1966
  Brief Entry *29*
Lemke, Horst 1922- *38*
Lenanton, C.
  See Oman, Carola (Mary Anima)
Lenard, Alexander 1910-1972
  Obituary *21*
L'Engle, Madeleine 1918- *27*
  Earlier sketch in SATA 1
  See also CLR 1
Lengyel, Cornel Adam 1915- *27*
Lengyel, Emil 1895-1985 .... *3*
  Obituary *42*
Lens, Sidney 1912-1986 .... *13*
  Obituary *48*
Lenski, Lois 1893-1974 .... *26*
  Earlier sketch in SATA 1
Lent, Blair 1930- *2*
Lent, Henry Bolles 1901-1973 .... *17*
Leodhas, Sorche Nic
  See Alger, Leclaire (Gowans)
Leokum, Arkady 1916(?)- *45*
Leonard, Constance (Brink)
1923- *42*
  Brief Entry *40*
Leonard, Jonathan N(orton)
1903-1975 .... *36*
Leong Gor Yun
  See Ellison, Virginia Howell
Lerner, Aaron B(unsen) 1920- *35*
Lerner, Carol 1927- *33*
Lerner, Marguerite Rush
1924-1987 .... *11*
  Obituary *51*
Lerner, Sharon (Ruth)
1938-1982 .... *11*
  Obituary *29*
Leroe, Ellen W(hitney) 1949-
  Brief Entry *51*
LeRoy, Gen
  Brief Entry *36*
Lerrigo, Marion Olive 1898-1968
  Obituary *29*
LeShan, Eda J(oan) 1922- *21*
  See also CLR 6
LeSieg, Theo
  See Geisel, Theodor Seuss
Leslie, Robert Franklin 1911- *7*
Leslie, Sarah
  See McGuire, Leslie (Sarah)
Lesser, Margaret 1899(?)-1979
  Obituary *22*
Lester, Alison 1952- *50*
Lester, Helen 1936- *46*
Lester, Julius B. 1939- *12*
  See also CLR 2
Le Sueur, Meridel 1900- *6*
Le Tord, Bijou 1945- *49*
Leutscher, Alfred (George)
1913- *23*
Levai, Blaise 1919- *39*
Levin, Betty 1927- *19*
Levin, Marcia Obrasky 1918- *13*
Levin, Meyer 1905-1981 .... *21*
  Obituary *27*
Levine, David 1926- *43*
  Brief Entry *35*
Levine, Edna S(imon) *35*

Levine, I(srael) E. 1923- *12*
Levine, Joan Goldman *11*
Levine, Joseph 1910- *33*
Levine, Rhoda *14*
Levinson, Nancy Smiler
1938- *33*
Levinson, Riki
  Brief Entry *49*
Levitin, Sonia 1934- *4*
  See also SAAS 2
Levoy, Myron *49*
  Brief Entry *37*
Levy, Elizabeth 1942- *31*
Lewees, John
  See Stockton, Francis Richard
Lewin, Betsy 1937- *32*
Lewin, Hugh (Francis) 1939-
  Brief Entry *40*
  See also CLR 9
Lewin, Ted 1935- *21*
Lewis, Alfred E. 1912-1968
  Brief Entry *32*
Lewis, Alice C. 1936- *46*
Lewis, Alice Hudson 1895(?)-1971
  Obituary *29*
Lewis, (Joseph) Anthony
1927- *27*
Lewis, C(live) S(taples)
1898-1963 .... *13*
  See also CLR 3
Lewis, Claudia (Louise) 1907- *5*
Lewis, E. M. *20*
Lewis, Elizabeth Foreman
1892-1958 ....*YABC 2*
Lewis, Francine
  See Wells, Helen
Lewis, Hilda (Winifred) 1896-1974
  Obituary *20*
Lewis, Lucia Z.
  See Anderson, Lucia (Lewis)
Lewis, Marjorie 1929- *40*
  Brief Entry *35*
Lewis, Paul
  See Gerson, Noel B(ertram)
Lewis, Richard 1935- *3*
Lewis, Roger
  See Zarchy, Harry
Lewis, Shari 1934- *35*
  Brief Entry *30*
Lewis, Thomas P(arker) 1936- *27*
Lewiton, Mina 1904-1970 .... *2*
Lexau, Joan M. *36*
  Earlier sketch in SATA 1
Ley, Willy 1906-1969 .... *2*
Leydon, Rita (Flodén) 1949- *21*
Leyland, Eric (Arthur) 1911- *37*
L'Hommedieu, Dorothy K(easley)
1885-1961
  Obituary *29*
Libby, Bill
  See Libby, William M.
Libby, William M. 1927-1984 .... *5*
  Obituary *39*
Liberty, Gene 1924- *3*
Liebers, Arthur 1913- *12*
Lieblich, Irene 1923- *22*
Liers, Emil E(rnest)
1890-1975 .... *37*
Lietz, Gerald S. 1918- *11*

Lifton, Betty Jean *6*
Lightner, A. M.
  See Hopf, Alice L.
Lignell, Lois 1911- *37*
Lillington, Kenneth (James)
1916- *39*
Lilly, Charles
  Brief Entry *33*
Lilly, Ray
  See Curtis, Richard (Alan)
Lim, John 1932- *43*
Liman, Ellen (Fogelson)
1936- *22*
Limburg, Peter R(ichard)
1929- *13*
Lincoln, C(harles) Eric 1924- *5*
Lindbergh, Anne
  See Sapieyevski, Anne Lindbergh
Lindbergh, Anne Morrow (Spencer)
1906- *33*
Lindbergh, Charles A(ugustus, Jr.)
1902-1974 .... *33*
Lindblom, Steven (Winther)
1946- *42*
  Brief Entry *39*
Linde, Gunnel 1924- *5*
Lindgren, Astrid 1907- *38*
  Earlier sketch in SATA 2
  See also CLR 1
Lindgren, Barbro 1937-
  Brief Entry *46*
Lindman, Maj (Jan)
1886-1972 .... *43*
Lindop, Edmund 1925- *5*
Lindquist, Jennie Dorothea
1899-1977 .... *13*
Lindquist, Willis 1908- *20*
Lindsay, Norman (Alfred William)
1879-1969
  See CLR 8
Lindsay, (Nicholas) Vachel
1879-1931 .... *40*
Line, Les 1935- *27*
Linfield, Esther *40*
Lingard, Joan *8*
  See also SAAS 5
Link, Martin 1934- *28*
Lionni, Leo 1910- *8*
  See also CLR 7
Lipinsky de Orlov, Lino S.
1908- *22*
Lipkind, William 1904-1974 ...... *15*
Lipman, David 1931- *21*
Lipman, Matthew 1923- *14*
Lippincott, Bertram 1898(?)-1985
  Obituary *42*
Lippincott, Joseph Wharton
1887-1976 .... *17*
Lippincott, Sarah Lee 1920- *22*
Lippman, Peter J. 1936- *31*
Lipsyte, Robert 1938- *5*
Lisker, Sonia O. 1933- *44*
Lisle, Janet Taylor
  Brief Entry *47*
Lisle, Seward D.
  See Ellis, Edward S(ylvester)
Lisowski, Gabriel 1946- *47*
  Brief Entry *31*
Liss, Howard 1922- *4*

Lissim, Simon 1900-1981
  Brief Entry 28
List, Ilka Katherine 1935- 6
Liston, Robert A. 1927- 5
Litchfield, Ada B(assett)
  1916- 5
Litowinsky, Olga (Jean) 1936- 26
Littke, Lael J. 1929- 51
Little, A. Edward
  See Klein, Aaron E.
Little, (Flora) Jean 1932- 2
  See also CLR 4
Little, Lessie Jones 1906-1986
  Obituary 50
Little, Mary E. 1912- 28
Littledale, Freya (Lota) 2
Lively, Penelope 1933- 7
  See also CLR 7
Liversidge, (Henry) Douglas
  1913- 8
Livingston, Carole 1941- 42
Livingston, Myra Cohn 1926- 5
  See also CLR 7
  See also SAAS 1
Livingston, Richard R(oland)
  1922- 8
Llerena-Aguirre, Carlos Antonio
  1952- 19
Llewellyn, Richard
  See Llewellyn Lloyd, Richard
  Dafydd Vyvyan
Llewellyn, T. Harcourt
  See Hamilton, Charles H. St. John
Llewellyn Lloyd, Richard Dafydd
  Vyvyan 1906-1983 11
  Obituary 37
Lloyd, Errol 1943- 22
Lloyd, Norman 1909-1980
  Obituary 23
Lloyd, (Mary) Norris 1908- 10
Lobel, Anita 1934- 6
Lobel, Arnold 1933- 6
  See also CLR 5
Lobsenz, Amelia 12
Lobsenz, Norman M. 1919- 6
Lochak, Michèle 1936- 39
Lochlons, Colin
  See Jackson, C. Paul
Locke, Clinton W. [Collective
  pseudonym] 1
Locke, Lucie 1904- 10
Lockwood, Mary
  See Spelman, Mary
Lodge, Bernard 1933- 33
Lodge, Maureen Roffey
  See Roffey, Maureen
Loeb, Robert H., Jr. 1917- 21
Loeper, John J(oseph) 1929- 10
Loescher, Ann Dull 1942- 20
Loescher, Gil(burt Damian)
  1945- 20
Loewenstein, Bernice
  Brief Entry 40
Löfgren, Ulf 1931- 3
Lofting, Hugh 1886-1947 15
Lofts, Norah (Robinson)
  1904-1983 8
  Obituary 36
Logue, Christopher 1926- 23

Loken, Newton (Clayton)
  1919- 26
Lomas, Steve
  See Brennan, Joseph L.
Lomask, Milton 1909- 20
London, Jack 1876-1916 18
London, Jane
  See Geis, Darlene
London, John Griffith
  See London, Jack
Lonergan, (Pauline) Joy (Maclean)
  1909- 10
Lonette, Reisie (Dominee)
  1924- 43
Long, Earlene (Roberta)
  1938- 50
Long, Helen Beecher [Collective
  pseudonym] 1
Long, Judith Elaine 1953- 20
Long, Judy
  See Long, Judith Elaine
Long, Laura Mooney 1892-1967
  Obituary 29
Longfellow, Henry Wadsworth
  1807-1882 19
Longman, Harold S. 1919- 5
Longsworth, Polly 1933- 28
Longtemps, Kenneth 1933- 17
Longway, A. Hugh
  See Lang, Andrew
Loomis, Robert D. 5
Lopshire, Robert 1927- 6
Lord, Athena V. 1932- 39
Lord, Beman 1924- 5
Lord, (Doreen Mildred) Douglas
  1904- 12
Lord, John Vernon 1939- 21
Lord, Nancy
  See Titus, Eve
Lord, Walter 1917- 3
Lorenz, Lee (Sharp) 1932(?)-
  Brief Entry 39
Lorenzini, Carlo 1826-1890 29
Loring, Emilie (Baker)
  1864(?)-1951 51
Lorraine, Walter (Henry)
  1929- 16
Loss, Joan 1933- 11
Lot, Parson
  See Kingsley, Charles
Lothrop, Harriet Mulford Stone
  1844-1924 20
Louie, Ai-Ling 1949- 40
  Brief Entry 34
Louisburgh, Sheila Burnford
  See Burnford, Sheila
Lourie, Helen
  See Storr, Catherine (Cole)
Love, Katherine 1907- 3
Love, Sandra (Weller) 1940- 26
Lovelace, Delos Wheeler
  1894-1967 7
Lovelace, Maud Hart
  1892-1980 2
  Obituary 23
Lovell, Ingraham
  See Bacon, Josephine Dodge
  (Daskam)
Lovett, Margaret (Rose) 1915- 22

Low, Alice 1926- 11
Low, Elizabeth Hammond
  1898- 5
Low, Joseph 1911- 14
Lowe, Jay, Jr.
  See Loper, John J(oseph)
Lowenstein, Dyno 1914- 6
Lowitz, Anson C.
  1901(?)-1978 18
Lowitz, Sadyebeth (Heath)
  1901-1969 17
Lowrey, Janette Sebring
  1892- 43
Lowry, Lois 1937- 23
  See also CLR 6
  See also SAAS 3
Lowry, Peter 1953- 7
Lowther, George F. 1913-1975
  Obituary 30
Lozier, Herbert 1915- 26
Lubell, Cecil 1912- 6
Lubell, Winifred 1914- 6
Lubin, Leonard B. 1943- 45
  Brief Entry 37
Lucas, E(dward) V(errall)
  1868-1938 20
Lucas, Jerry 1940- 33
Luce, Celia (Geneva Larsen)
  1914- 38
Luce, Willard (Ray) 1914- 38
Luckhardt, Mildred Corell
  1898- 5
Ludden, Allen (Ellsworth)
  1918(?)-1981
  Obituary 27
Ludlam, Mabel Cleland
  See Widdemer, Mabel Cleland
Ludwig, Helen 33
Lueders, Edward (George)
  1923- 14
Luenn, Nancy 1954- 51
Lufkin, Raymond H. 1897- 38
Lugard, Flora Louisa Shaw
  1852-1929 21
Luger, Harriett M(andelay)
  1914- 23
Luhrmann, Winifred B(ruce)
  1934- 11
Luis, Earlene W. 1929- 11
Lum, Peter
  See Crowe, Bettina Lum
Lund, Doris (Herold) 1919- 12
Lunn, Janet 1928- 4
Lurie, Alison 1926- 46
Lustig, Loretta 1944- 46
Luther, Frank 1905-1980
  Obituary 25
Luttrell, Guy L. 1938- 22
Luttrell, Ida (Alleene) 1934- 40
  Brief Entry 35
Lutzker, Edythe 1904- 5
Luzzati, Emanuele 1912- 7
Luzzatto, Paola (Caboara)
  1938- 38
Lydon, Michael 1942- 11
Lyfick, Warren
  See Reeves, Lawrence F.
Lyle, Katie Letcher 1938- 8
Lynch, Lorenzo 1932- 7

Lynch, Marietta 1947- 29
Lynch, Patricia (Nora)
  1898-1972 9
Lynds, Dennis 1924- 47
  Brief Entry 37
Lyngseth, Joan
  See Davies, Joan
Lynn, Mary
  See Brokamp, Marilyn
Lynn, Patricia
  See Watts, Mabel Pizzey
Lyon, Elinor 1921- 6
Lyon, Lyman R.
  See De Camp, L(yon) Sprague
Lyons, Dorothy 1907- 3
Lyons, Grant 1941- 30
Lystad, Mary (Hanemann)
  1928- 11
Lyttle, Richard B(ard) 1927- 23
Lytton, Edward G(eorge) E(arle)
  L(ytton) Bulwer-Lytton, Baron
  1803-1873 23

M

Maar, Leonard (F., Jr.) 1927- 30
Maas, Selve 14
Mac
  See MacManus, Seumas
Mac Aodhagáin, Eamon
  See Egan, E(dward) W(elstead)
MacArthur-Onslow, Annette
  (Rosemary) 1933- 26
Macaulay, David (Alexander)
  1946- 46
  Brief Entry 27
  See also CLR 3
MacBeth, George 1932- 4
MacClintock, Dorcas 1932- 8
MacDonald, Anson
  See Heinlein, Robert A(nson)
MacDonald, Betty (Campbell Bard)
  1908-1958 .... YABC 1
Macdonald, Blackie
  See Emrich, Duncan
Macdonald, Dwight
  1906-1982 29
  Obituary 33
MacDonald, George
  1824-1905 33
Mac Donald, Golden
  See Brown, Margaret Wise
Macdonald, Marcia
  See Hill, Grace Livingston
Macdonald, Mary
  See Gifford, Griselda
Macdonald, Shelagh 1937- 25
Macdonald, Zillah K(atherine)
  1885- 11
Mace, Elisabeth 1933- 27
Mace, Varian 1938- 49
MacEwen, Gwendolyn 1941- 50
MacFarlan, Allan A.
  1892-1982 35
MacFarlane, Iris 1922- 11
MacGregor, Ellen 1906-1954 39
  Brief Entry 27
MacGregor-Hastie, Roy 1929- 3

Machetanz, Frederick 1908- 34
Machin Goodall, Daphne
  (Edith) 37
MacInnes, Helen 1907-1985 22
  Obituary 44
MacIntyre, Elisabeth 1916- 17
Mack, Stan(ley) 17
Mackay, Claire 1930- 40
MacKaye, Percy (Wallace)
  1875-1956 32
MacKellar, William 1914- 4
Macken, Walter 1915-1967 36
Mackenzie, Dr. Willard
  See Stratemeyer, Edward L.
MacKenzie, Garry 1921-
  Brief Entry 31
MacKinstry, Elizabeth
  1879-1956 42
MacLachlan, Patricia
  Brief Entry 42
MacLean, Alistair (Stuart)
  1923-1987 23
  Obituary 50
MacLeod, Beatrice (Beach)
  1910- 10
MacLeod, Charlotte (Matilda Hughes)
  1922- 28
MacLeod, Ellen Jane (Anderson)
  1916- 14
MacManus, James
  See MacManus, Seumas
MacManus, Seumas
  1869-1960 25
MacMaster, Eve (Ruth) B(owers)
  1942- 46
MacMillan, Annabelle
  See Quick, Annabelle
MacPeek, Walter G.
  1902-1973 4
  Obituary 25
MacPherson, Margaret 1908- 9
  See also SAAS 4
MacPherson, Thomas George
  1915-1976
  Obituary 30
Macrae, Hawk
  See Barker, Albert W.
MacRae, Travi
  See Feagles, Anita (MacRae)
Macumber, Mari
  See Sandoz, Mari
Madden, Don 1927- 3
Maddison, Angela Mary
  1923- 10
Maddock, Reginald 1912- 15
Madian, Jon 1941- 9
Madison, Arnold 1937- 6
Madison, Winifred 5
Maestro, Betsy 1944-
  Brief Entry 30
Maestro, Giulio 1942- 8
Magorian, James 1942- 32
Maguire, Anne
  See Nearing, Penny
Maguire, Gregory 1954- 28
Maher, Ramona 1934- 13
Mählqvist, (Karl) Stefan
  1943- 30
Mahon, Julia C(unha) 1916- 11

Mahony, Elizabeth Winthrop
  1948- 8
Mahood, Kenneth 1930- 24
Mahy, Margaret 1936- 14
  See also CLR 7
Maidoff, Ilka List
  See List, Ilka Katherine
Maik, Henri
  See Hecht, Henri Joseph
Maiorano, Robert 1946- 43
Maitland, Antony (Jasper)
  1935- 25
Major, Kevin 1949- 32
  See also CLR 11
Makie, Pam 1943- 37
Malcolmson, Anne
  See Storch, Anne B. von
Malcolmson, David 1899- 6
Mali, Jane Lawrence 1937- 51
  Brief Entry 44
Mallowan, Agatha Christie
  See Christie, Agatha (Mary Clarissa)
Malmberg, Carl 1904- 9
Malo, John 1911- 4
Malory, (Sir) Thomas 1410(?)-1471(?)
  Brief Entry 33
Maltese, Michael 1908(?)-1981
  Obituary 24
Malvern, Corinne 1905-1956 34
Malvern, Gladys (?)-1962 23
Mama G.
  See Davis, Grania
Manchel, Frank 1935- 10
Manes, Stephen 1949- 42
  Brief Entry 40
Manfred, Frederick F(eikema)
  1912- 30
Mangione, Jerre 1909- 6
Mangurian, David 1938- 14
Maniscalco, Joseph 1926- 10
Manley, Deborah 1932- 28
Manley, Seon 15
  See also CLR 3
  See also SAAS 2
Mann, Peggy 6
Mannetti, Lisa 1953-
  Brief Entry 51
Mannheim, Grete (Salomon)
  1909- 10
Manniche, Lise 1943- 31
Manning, Rosemary 1911- 10
Manning-Sanders, Ruth 1895- 15
Manson, Beverlie 1945-
  Brief Entry 44
Manton, Jo
  See Gittings, Jo Manton
Manushkin, Fran 1942- 7
Mapes, Mary A.
  See Ellison, Virginia Howell
Mara, Barney
  See Roth, Arthur J(oseph)
Mara, Jeanette
  See Cebulash, Mel
Marais, Josef 1905-1978
  Obituary 24
Marasmus, Seymour
  See Rivoli, Mario
Marcellino
  See Agnew, Edith J.

Marchant, Bessie
1862-1941 ....*YABC* 2
Marchant, Catherine
See Cookson, Catherine (McMulen)
Marcher, Marion Walden
1890- *10*
Marcus, Rebecca B(rian)
1907- *9*
Margaret, Karla
See Andersdatter, Karla M(argaret)
Margolis, Richard J(ules)
1929- *4*
Margolis, Vivienne 1922- *46*
Mariana
See Foster, Marian Curtis
Marino, Dorothy Bronson
1912- *14*
Maris, Ron
Brief Entry *45*
Mark, Jan 1943- *22*
See also CLR 11
Mark, Pauline (Dahlin) 1913- *14*
Mark, Polly
See Mark, Pauline (Dahlin)
Markins, W. S.
See Jenkins, Marie M.
Markle, Sandra L(ee) 1946-
Brief Entry *41*
Marko, Katherine D(olores) *28*
Marks, Burton 1930- *47*
Brief Entry *43*
Marks, Hannah K.
See Trivelpiece, Laurel
Marks, J
See Highwater, Jamake
Marks, J(ames) M(acdonald)
1921- *13*
Marks, Margaret L. 1911(?)-1980
Obituary *23*
Marks, Mickey Klar *12*
Marks, Peter
See Smith, Robert Kimmel
Marks, Rita 1938- *47*
Marks, Stan(ley) 1929- *14*
Marks-Highwater, J
See Highwater, Jamake
Markun, Patricia M(aloney)
1924- *15*
Marlowe, Amy Bell [Collective
pseudonym] *1*
Marokvia, Artur 1909- *31*
Marokvia, Mireille (Journet)
1918- *5*
Marr, John S(tuart) 1940- *48*
Marrin, Albert 1936-
Brief Entry *43*
Marriott, Alice Lee 1910- *31*
Marriott, Pat(ricia) 1920- *35*
Mars, W. T.
See Mars, Witold Tadeusz J.
Mars, Witold Tadeusz J.
1912- *3*
Marsh, J. E.
See Marshall, Evelyn
Marsh, Jean
See Marshall, Evelyn
Marshall, Anthony D(ryden)
1924- *18*

Marshall, (Sarah) Catherine
1914-1983 ....*2*
Obituary *34*
Marshall, Douglas
See McClintock, Marshall
Marshall, Edward
See Marshall, James (Edward)
Marshall, Evelyn 1897- *11*
Marshall, James (Edward)
1942- *51*
Earlier sketch in SATA 6
Marshall, James Vance
See Payne, Donald Gordon
Marshall, Kim
See Marshall, Michael (Kimbrough)
Marshall, Michael (Kimbrough)
1948- *37*
Marshall, Percy
See Young, Percy M(arshall)
Marshall, S(amuel) L(yman) A(twood)
1900-1977 ....*21*
Marsten, Richard
See Hunter, Evan
Marston, Hope Irvin 1935- *31*
Martchenko, Michael 1942- *50*
Martignoni, Margaret E. 1908(?)-1974
Obituary *27*
Martin, Ann M(atthews)
1955- *44*
Brief Entry *41*
Martin, Bill, Jr.
See Martin, William Ivan
Martin, David Stone 1913- *39*
Martin, Dorothy 1921- *47*
Martin, Eugene [Collective
pseudonym] *1*
Martin, Frances M(cEntee)
1906- *36*
Martin, Fredric
See Christopher, Matt(hew F.)
Martin, J(ohn) P(ercival)
1880(?)-1966 ....*15*
Martin, Jeremy
See Levin, Marcia Obransky
Martin, Lynne 1923- *21*
Martin, Marcia
See Levin, Marcia Obransky
Martin, Nancy
See Salmon, Annie Elizabeth
Martin, Patricia Miles
1899-1986 ....*43*
Obituary *48*
Earlier sketch in SATA 1
Martin, Peter
See Chaundler, Christine
Martin, René 1891-1977 ....*42*
Obituary *20*
Martin, Rupert (Claude) 1905- *31*
Martin, Stefan 1936- *32*
Martin, Vicky
See Storey, Victoria Carolyn
Martin, William Ivan 1916-
Brief Entry *40*
Martineau, Harriet
1802-1876 ....*YABC* 2
Martini, Teri 1930- *3*
Marx, Robert F(rank) 1936- *24*
Marzani, Carl (Aldo) 1912- *12*
Marzollo, Jean 1942- *29*

Masefield, John 1878-1967 ....*19*
Mason, Edwin A. 1905-1979
Obituary *32*
Mason, F. van Wyck
1901-1978 ....*3*
Obituary *26*
Mason, Frank W.
See Mason, F. van Wyck
Mason, George Frederick
1904- *14*
Mason, Miriam (Evangeline)
1900-1973 ....*2*
Obituary *26*
Mason, Tally
See Derleth, August (William)
Mason, Van Wyck
See Mason, F. van Wyck
Masselman, George
1897-1971 ....*19*
Massie, Diane Redfield *16*
Masters, Kelly R. 1897- *3*
Masters, Mildred 1932- *42*
Masters, William
See Cousins, Margaret
Matchette, Katharine E. 1941- *38*
Math, Irwin 1940- *42*
Mathews, Janet 1914- *41*
Mathews, Louise
See Tooke, Louise Mathews
Mathiesen, Egon 1907-1976
Obituary *28*
Mathieu, Joe
See Mathieu, Joseph P.
Mathieu, Joseph P. 1949- *43*
Brief Entry *36*
Mathis, Sharon Bell 1937- *7*
See also CLR 3
See also SAAS 3
Matson, Emerson N(els)
1926- *12*
Matsui, Tadashi 1926- *8*
Matsuno, Masako 1935- *6*
Matte, (Encarnacion) L'Enc
1936- *22*
Matthews, Ann
See Martin, Ann M(atthews)
Matthews, Ellen 1950- *28*
Matthews, Jacklyn Meek
See Meek, Jacklyn O'Hanlon
Matthews, Patricia 1927- *28*
Matthews, William Henry III
1919- *45*
Brief Entry *28*
Matthias, Catherine 1945-
Brief Entry *41*
Matthiessen, Peter 1927- *27*
Mattingley, Christobel (Rosemary)
1931- *37*
Matulay, Laszlo 1912- *43*
Matulka, Jan 1890-1972
Brief Entry *28*
Matus, Greta 1938- *12*
Mauser, Patricia Rhoads
1943- *37*
Maves, Mary Carolyn 1916- *10*
Maves, Paul B(enjamin)
1913- *10*
Mawicke, Tran 1911- *15*
Max, Peter 1939- *45*

Maxon, Anne
  See Best, Allena Champlin
Maxwell, Arthur S.
  1896-1970 11
Maxwell, Edith 1923- 7
May, Charles Paul 1920- 4
May, Julian 1931- 11
May, Robert Lewis 1905-1976
  Obituary 27
May, Robert Stephen 1929- 46
May, Robin
  See May, Robert Stephen
Mayberry, Florence V(irginia
  Wilson) 10
Mayer, Albert Ignatius, Jr. 1906-1960
  Obituary 29
Mayer, Ann M(argaret) 1938- 14
Mayer, Jane Rothschild 1903- 38
Mayer, Marianna 1945- 32
Mayer, Mercer 1943- 32
  Earlier sketch in SATA 16
  See also CLR 11
Mayerson, Charlotte Leon 36
Mayhar, Ardath 1930- 38
Maynard, Chris
  See Maynard, Christopher
Maynard, Christopher 1949-
  Brief Entry 43
Maynard, Olga 1920- 40
Mayne, William 1928- 6
Maynes, Dr. J. O. Rocky
  See Maynes, J. Oscar, Jr.
Maynes, J. O. Rocky, Jr.
  See Maynes, J. Oscar, Jr.
Maynes, J. Oscar, Jr. 1929- 38
Mayo, Margaret (Mary) 1935- 38
Mays, Lucinda L(a Bella)
  1924- 49
Mays, (Lewis) Victor, (Jr.)
  1927- 5
Mazer, Harry 1925- 31
Mazer, Norma Fox 1931- 24
  See also SAAS 1
Mazza, Adriana 1928- 19
McBain, Ed
  See Hunter, Evan
McCaffery, Janet 1936- 38
McCaffrey, Anne 1926- 8
McCaffrey, Mary
  See Szudek, Agnes S(usan)
  P(hilomena)
McCain, Murray (David, Jr.)
  1926-1981 7
  Obituary 29
McCall, Edith S. 1911- 6
McCall, Virginia Nielsen
  1909- 13
McCallum, Phyllis 1911- 10
McCann, Gerald 1916- 41
McCannon, Dindga Fatima
  1947- 41
McCarter, Neely Dixon 1929- 47
McCarthy, Agnes 1933- 4
McCarty, Rega Kramer 1904- 10
McCaslin, Nellie 1914- 12
McCaughrean, Geraldine
  See Jones, Geraldine
McCay, Winsor 1869-1934 41

McClintock, Marshall
  1906-1967 3
McClintock, Mike
  See McClintock, Marshall
McClintock, Theodore
  1902-1971 14
McClinton, Leon 1933- 11
McCloskey, (John) Robert
  1914- 39
  Earlier sketch in SATA 2
  See also CLR 7
McClung, Robert M. 1916- 2
  See also CLR 11
McClure, Gillian Mary 1948- 31
McConnell, James Douglas
  (Rutherford) 1915- 40
McCord, Anne 1942- 41
McCord, David (Thompson Watson)
  1897- 18
  See also CLR 9
McCord, Jean 1924- 34
McCormick, Brooks
  See Adams, William Taylor
McCormick, Dell J.
  1892-1949 19
McCormick, (George) Donald (King)
  1911- 14
McCormick, Edith (Joan)
  1934- 30
McCourt, Edward (Alexander)
  1907-1972
  Obituary 28
McCoy, Iola Fuller 3
McCoy, J(oseph) J(erome)
  1917- 8
McCoy, Lois (Rich) 1941- 38
McCrady, Lady 1951- 16
McCrea, James 1920- 3
McCrea, Ruth 1921- 3
McCullers, (Lula) Carson
  1917-1967 27
McCulloch, Derek (Ivor Breashur)
  1897-1967
  Obituary 29
McCulloch, Sarah
  See Ure, Jean
McCullough, Frances Monson
  1938- 8
McCully, Emily Arnold 1939- 5
  See also Arnold, Emily
McCurdy, Michael 1942- 13
McDearmon, Kay 20
McDermott, Beverly Brodsky
  1941- 11
McDermott, Gerald 1941- 16
  See also CLR 9
McDole, Carol
  See Farley, Carol
McDonald, Gerald D.
  1905-1970 3
McDonald, Jamie
  See Heide, Florence Parry
McDonald, Jill (Masefield)
  1927-1982 13
  Obituary 29
McDonald, Lucile Saunders
  1898- 10
McDonnell, Christine 1949- 34
McDonnell, Lois Eddy 1914- 10

McEntee, Dorothy (Layng)
  1902- 37
McEwen, Robert (Lindley) 1926-1980
  Obituary 23
McFall, Christie 1918- 12
McFarland, Kenton D(ean)
  1920- 11
McFarlane, Leslie 1902-1977 31
McGaw, Jessie Brewer 1913- 10
McGee, Barbara 1943- 6
McGiffin, (Lewis) Lee (Shaffer)
  1908- 1
McGill, Marci
  See Ridlon, Marci
McGinley, Phyllis 1905-1978 44
  Obituary 24
  Earlier sketch in SATA 2
McGinnis, Lila S(prague)
  1924- 44
McGough, Elizabeth (Hemmes)
  1934- 33
McGovern, Ann 8
McGowen, Thomas E. 1927- 2
McGowen, Tom
  See McGowen, Thomas E.
McGrady, Mike 1933- 6
McGrath, Thomas 1916- 41
McGraw, Eloise Jarvis 1915- 1
McGraw, William Corbin
  1916- 3
McGregor, Craig 1933- 8
McGregor, Iona 1929- 25
McGuire, Edna 1899- 13
McGuire, Leslie (Sarah) 1945-
  Brief Entry 45
McGurk, Slater
  See Roth, Arthur J(oseph)
McHargue, Georgess 4
  See also CLR 2
  See also SAAS 5
McHugh, (Berit) Elisabet 1941-
  Brief Entry 44
McIlwraith, Maureen 1922- 2
McInerney, Judith Whitelock
  1945- 49
  Brief Entry 46
McKay, Donald 1895- 45
McKay, Robert W. 1921- 15
McKeever, Marcia
  See Laird, Jean E(louise)
McKenzie, Dorothy Clayton
  1910-1981
  Obituary 28
McKillip, Patricia A(nne)
  1948- 30
McKim, Audrey Margaret
  1909- 47
McKinley, (Jennifer Carolyn)
  Robin 50
  Brief Entry 32
  See also CLR 10
McKissack, Patricia (L'Ann) C(arwell)
  1944-
  Brief Entry 51
McKown, Robin 6
McLaurin, Anne 1953- 27
McLean, Kathryn (Anderson)
  1909-1966 9
McLeish, Kenneth 1940- 35

McLenighan, Valjean 1947- 46
    Brief Entry 40
McLeod, Emilie Warren
    1926-1982 23
    Obituary 31
McLeod, Kirsty
    See Hudson, (Margaret) Kirsty
McLeod, Margaret Vail
    See Holloway, Teresa (Braguiner)
McLoughlin, John C. 1949- 47
McMahan, Ian
    Brief Entry 45
McManus, Patrick (Francis)
    1933- 46
McMeekin, Clark
    See McMeekin, Isabel McLennan
McMeekin, Isabel McLennan
    1895- 3
McMillan, Bruce 1947- 22
McMullan, Kate (Hall) 1947-
    Brief Entry 48
McMullen, Catherine
    See Cookson, Catherine (McMullen)
McMurtrey, Martin A(loysius)
    1921- 21
McNair, Kate 3
McNamara, Margaret C(raig)
    1915-1981
    Obituary 24
McNaught, Harry 32
McNaughton, Colin 1951- 39
McNeely, Jeannette 1918- 25
McNeer, May 1
McNeill, Janet 1907- 1
McNickle, (William) D'Arcy
    1904-1977
    Obituary 22
McNulty, Faith 1918- 12
McPhail, David M(ichael)
    1940- 47
    Brief Entry 32
McPharlin, Paul 1903-1948
    Brief Entry 31
McPhee, Richard B(yron)
    1934- 41
McPherson, James M. 1936- 16
McQueen, Lucinda
    Brief Entry 48
McQueen, Mildred Hark
    1908- 12
McShean, Gordon 1936- 41
McSwigan, Marie 1907-1962 24
McVicker, Charles (Taggart)
    1930- 39
McVicker, Chuck
    See McVicker, Charles (Taggart)
McWhirter, Norris (Dewar)
    1925- 37
McWhirter, (Alan) Ross
    1925-1975 37
    Obituary 31
Mead, Margaret 1901-1978
    Obituary 20
Mead, Russell (M., Jr.) 1935- 10
Mead, Stella (?)-1981
    Obituary 27
Meade, Ellen (Roddick) 1936- 5
Meade, Marion 1934- 23

Meader, Stephen W(arren)
    1892- 1
Meadow, Charles T(roub)
    1929- 23
Meadowcroft, Enid LaMonte
    See Wright, Enid Meadowcroft
Meaker, M. J.
    See Meaker, Marijane
Meaker, Marijane 1927- 20
Means, Florence Crannell
    1891-1980 1
    Obituary 25
Mearian, Judy Frank 1936- 49
Medary, Marjorie 1890- 14
Meddaugh, Susan 1944- 29
Medearis, Mary 1915- 5
Mee, Charles L., Jr. 1938- 8
Meek, Jacklyn O'Hanlon
    1933- 51
    Brief Entry 34
Meek, S(terner St.) P(aul) 1894-1972
    Obituary 28
Meeker, Oden 1918(?)-1976 14
Meeks, Esther MacBain 1
Meggendorfer, Lothar 1847-1925
    Brief Entry 36
Mehdevi, Alexander 1947- 7
Mehdevi, Anne (Marie)
    Sinclair 8
Meighan, Donald Charles
    1929- 30
Meigs, Cornelia Lynde
    1884-1973 6
Meilach, Dona Z(weigoron)
    1926- 34
Melady, John 1938-
    Brief Entry 49
Melcher, Daniel 1912-1985
    Obituary 43
Melcher, Frederic Gershom 1879-1963
    Obituary 22
Melcher, Marguerite Fellows
    1879-1969 10
Melin, Grace Hathaway
    1892-1973 10
Mellersh, H(arold) E(dward) L(eslie)
    1897- 10
Meltzer, Milton 1915- 50
    Earlier sketch in SATA 1
    See also SAAS 1
    See also CLR 13
Melville, Anne
    See Potter, Margaret (Newman)
Melwood, Mary
    See Lewis, E. M.
Melzack, Ronald 1929- 5
Memling, Carl 1918-1969 6
Mendel, Jo [House pseudonym]
    See Bond, Gladys Baker
Mendonca, Susan
    Brief Entry 49
    See also Smith, Susan Vernon
Mendoza, George 1934- 41
    Brief Entry 39
Meng, Heinz (Karl) 1924- 13
Menotti, Gian Carlo 1911- 29
Menuhin, Yehudi 1916- 40
Mercer, Charles (Edward)
    1917- 16

Meredith, David William
    See Miers, Earl Schenck
Meriwether, Louise 1923-
    Brief Entry 31
Merriam, Eve 1916- 40
    Earlier sketch in SATA 3
Merrill, Jane 1946- 42
Merrill, Jean (Fairbanks)
    1923- 1
Merrill, Phil
    See Merrill, Jane
Mertz, Barbara (Gross) 1927- 49
Merwin, Decie 1894-1961
    Brief Entry 32
Messick, Dale 1906-
    Brief Entry 48
Messmer, Otto 1892(?)-1983 37
Metcalf, Suzanne
    See Baum, L(yman) Frank
Metos, Thomas H(arry) 1932- 37
Meyer, Carolyn 1935- 9
Meyer, Edith Patterson 1895- 5
Meyer, F(ranklyn) E(dward)
    1932- 9
Meyer, Jean Shepherd 1929- 11
Meyer, Jerome Sydney
    1895-1975 3
    Obituary 25
Meyer, June
    See Jordan, June
Meyer, Kathleen Allan 1918- 51
    Brief Entry 46
Meyer, Louis A(lbert) 1942- 12
Meyer, Renate 1930- 6
Meyers, Susan 1942- 19
Meynier, Yvonne (Pollet)
    1908- 14
Mezey, Robert 1935- 33
Mian, Mary (Lawrence Shipman)
    1902-
    Brief Entry 47
Micale, Albert 1913- 22
Michaels, Barbara
    See Mertz, Barbara (Gross)
Michaels, Ski
    See Pellowski, Michael J(oseph)
Michel, Anna 1943- 49
    Brief Entry 40
Micklish, Rita 1931- 12
Miers, Earl Schenck
    1910-1972 1
    Obituary 26
Miklowitz, Gloria D. 1927- 4
Mikolaycak, Charles 1937- 9
    See also SAAS 4
Mild, Warren (Paul) 1922- 41
Miles, Betty 1928- 8
Miles, Miska
    See Martin, Patricia Miles
Miles, (Mary) Patricia 1930- 29
Miles, Patricia A.
    See Martin, Patricia Miles
Milgrom, Harry 1912- 25
Milhous, Katherine 1894-1977 15
Militant
    See Sandburg, Carl (August)
Millar, Barbara F. 1924- 12

Miller, Albert G(riffith)
1905-1982 .... *12*
Obituary *31*
Miller, Alice P(atricia
McCarthy) *22*
Miller, Don 1923- *15*
Miller, Doris R.
See Mosesson, Gloria R(ubin)
Miller, Eddie
See Miller, Edward
Miller, Edna (Anita) 1920- *29*
Miller, Edward 1905-1974 .... *8*
Miller, Elizabeth 1933- *41*
Miller, Eugene 1925- *33*
Miller, Frances A. 1937-
Brief Entry *46*
Miller, Helen M(arkley) *5*
Miller, Helen Topping 1884-1960
Obituary *29*
Miller, Jane (Judith) 1925- *15*
Miller, John
See Samachson, Joseph
Miller, Margaret J.
See Dale, Margaret J(essy) Miller
Miller, Marilyn (Jean) 1925- *33*
Miller, Mary Beth 1942- *9*
Miller, Natalie 1917-1976 .... *35*
Miller, Ruth White
See White, Ruth C.
Miller, Sandy (Peden) 1948- *41*
Brief Entry *35*
Milligan, Spike
See Milligan, Terence Alan
Milligan, Terence Alan 1918- *29*
Mills, Claudia 1954- *44*
Brief Entry *41*
Mills, Yaroslava Surmach
1925- *35*
Millstead, Thomas Edward *30*
Milne, A(lan) A(lexander)
1882-1956 .... *YABC 1*
See also CLR 1
Milne, Lorus J. *5*
Milne, Margery *5*
Milonas, Rolf
See Myller, Rolf
Milotte, Alfred G(eorge)
1904- *11*
Milton, Hilary (Herbert)
1920- *23*
Milton, John R(onald) 1924- *24*
Milton, Joyce 1946-
Brief Entry *41*
Milverton, Charles A.
See Penzler, Otto
Minarik, Else Holmelund
1920- *15*
Miner, Jane Claypool 1933- *38*
Brief Entry *37*
Miner, Lewis S. 1909- *11*
Minier, Nelson
See Stoutenburg, Adrien
Mintonye, Grace *4*
Mirsky, Jeannette 1903-1987 ...... *8*
Obituary *51*
Mirsky, Reba Paeff
1902-1966 .... *1*
Miskovits, Christine 1939- *10*

Miss Francis
See Horwich, Frances R.
Miss Read
See Saint, Dora Jessie
Mister Rogers
See Rogers, Fred (McFeely)
Mitchell, Cynthia 1922- *29*
Mitchell, (Sibyl) Elyne (Keith)
1913- *10*
Mitchell, Gladys (Maude Winifred)
1901-1983 .... *46*
Obituary *35*
Mitchell, Joyce Slayton 1933- *46*
Brief Entry *43*
Mitchell, Yvonne 1925-1979
Obituary *24*
Mitchison, Naomi Margaret (Haldane)
1897- *24*
Mitchnik, Helen 1901- *41*
Brief Entry *35*
Mitsuhashi, Yoko *45*
Brief Entry *33*
Mizner, Elizabeth Howard
1907- *27*
Mizumura, Kazue *18*
Moché, Dinah (Rachel) L(evine)
1936- *44*
Brief Entry *40*
Mochi, Ugo (A.) 1889-1977 ...... *38*
Modell, Frank B. 1917- *39*
Brief Entry *36*
Moe, Barbara 1937- *20*
Moeri, Louise 1924- *24*
Moffett, Martha (Leatherwood)
1934- *8*
Mofsie, Louis B. 1936-
Brief Entry *33*
Mohn, Peter B(urnet) 1934- *28*
Mohn, Viola Kohl 1914- *8*
Mohr, Nicholasa 1935- *8*
Molarsky, Osmond 1909- *16*
Moldon, Peter L(eonard)
1937- *49*
Mole, John 1941- *36*
Molloy, Anne Baker 1907- *32*
Molloy, Paul 1920- *5*
Momaday, N(avarre) Scott
1934- *48*
Brief Entry *30*
Moncure, Jane Belk *23*
Monjo, F(erdinand) N.
1924-1978 .... *16*
See also CLR 2
Monroe, Lyle
See Heinlein, Robert A(nson)
Monroe, Marion 1898-1983
Obituary *34*
Monsell, Helen (Albee)
1895-1971 .... *24*
Montana, Bob 1920-1975
Obituary *21*
Montgomerie, Norah Mary
1913- *26*
Montgomery, Constance
See Cappell, Constance
Montgomery, Elizabeth Rider
1902-1985 .... *34*
Obituary *41*
Earlier sketch in SATA 3

Montgomery, L(ucy) M(aud)
1874-1942 .... *YABC 1*
See also CLR 8
Montgomery, R(aymond) A., (Jr.)
1936- *39*
Montgomery, Rutherford George
1894- *3*
Montgomery, Vivian *36*
Montresor, Beni 1926- *38*
Earlier sketch in SATA 3
See also SAAS 4
Moody, Ralph Owen 1898- *1*
Moon, Carl 1879-1948 .... *25*
Moon, Grace 1877(?)-1947 .... *25*
Moon, Sheila (Elizabeth)
1910- *5*
Mooney, Elizabeth C(omstock)
1918-1986
Obituary *48*
Moor, Emily
See Deming, Richard
Moore, Anne Carroll
1871-1961 .... *13*
Moore, Clement Clarke
1779-1863 .... *18*
Moore, Don W. 1905(?)-1986
Obituary *48*
Moore, Eva 1942- *20*
Moore, Fenworth
See Stratemeyer, Edward L.
Moore, Jack (William) 1941- *46*
Brief Entry *32*
Moore, Janet Gaylord 1905- *18*
Moore, Jim 1946- *42*
Moore, John Travers 1908- *12*
Moore, Lamont 1909-
Brief Entry *29*
Moore, Margaret Rumberger
1903- *12*
Moore, Marianne (Craig)
1887-1972 .... *20*
Moore, Patrick (Alfred) 1923- *49*
Brief Entry *39*
Moore, Ray (S.) 1905(?)-1984
Obituary *37*
Moore, Regina
See Dunne, Mary Collins
Moore, Rosalie
See Brown, Rosalie (Gertrude)
Moore
Moore, Ruth *23*
Moore, Ruth Nulton 1923- *38*
Moore, S. E. *23*
Moores, Dick
See Moores, Richard (Arnold)
Moores, Richard (Arnold) 1909-1986
Obituary *48*
Mooser, Stephen 1941- *28*
Mordvinoff, Nicolas
1911-1973 .... *17*
More, Caroline [Joint pseudonym]
See Cone, Molly Lamken and
Strachan, Margaret Pitcairn
Morey, Charles
See Fletcher, Helen Jill
Morey, Walt 1907- *51*
Earlier sketch in SATA 3
Morgan, Alfred P(owell)
1889-1972 .... *33*

Morgan, Alison Mary 1930- *30*
Morgan, Geoffrey 1916- *46*
Morgan, Helen (Gertrude Louise)
  1921- *29*
Morgan, Helen Tudor
  See Morgan, Helen (Gertrude
  Louise)
Morgan, Jane
  See Cooper, James Fenimore
Morgan, Lenore 1908- *8*
Morgan, Louise
  See Morgan, Helen (Gertrude
  Louise)
Morgan, Shirley 1933- *10*
Morgan, Tom 1942- *42*
Morgenroth, Barbara
  Brief Entry *36*
Morrah, Dave
  See Morrah, David Wardlaw, Jr.
Morrah, David Wardlaw, Jr.
  1914- *10*
Morressy, John 1930- *23*
Morrill, Leslie H(olt) 1934- *48*
  Brief Entry *33*
Morris, Desmond (John)
  1928- *14*
Morris, Robert A. 1933- *7*
Morris, William 1913- *29*
Morrison, Bill 1935-
  Brief Entry *37*
Morrison, Dorothy Nafus *29*
Morrison, Gert W.
  See Stratemeyer, Edward L.
Morrison, Lillian 1917- *3*
Morrison, Lucile Phillips
  1896- *17*
Morrison, Roberta
  See Webb, Jean Francis (III)
Morrison, Velma Ford 1909- *21*
Morrison, William
  See Samachson, Joseph
Morriss, James E(dward)
  1932- *8*
Morrow, Betty
  See Bacon, Elizabeth
Morse, Carol
  See Yeakley, Marjory Hall
Morse, Dorothy B(ayley) 1906-1979
  Obituary *24*
Morse, Flo 1921- *30*
Mort, Vivian
  See Cromie, Alice Hamilton
Mortimer, Mary H.
  See Coury, Louise Andree
Morton, (Eva) Jane 1931- *50*
Morton, Lee Jack, Jr. 1928- *32*
Morton, Miriam 1918(?)-1985 ..... *9*
  Obituary *46*
Moscow, Alvin 1925- *3*
Mosel, Arlene 1921- *7*
Moser, Don
  See Moser, Donald Bruce
Moser, Donald Bruce 1932- *31*
Mosesson, Gloria R(ubin) *24*
Moskin, Marietta D(unston)
  1928- *23*
Moskof, Martin Stephen
  1930- *27*
Moss, Don(ald) 1920- *11*

Moss, Elaine Dora 1924-
  Brief Entry *31*
Most, Bernard 1937- *48*
  Brief Entry *40*
Motz, Lloyd *20*
Mountain, Robert
  See Montgomery, R(aymond) A.,
  (Jr.)
Mountfield, David
  See Grant, Neil
Moussard, Jacqueline 1924- *24*
Mowat, Farley 1921- *3*
Moyler, Alan (Frank Powell)
  1926- *36*
Mozley, Charles 1915- *43*
  Brief Entry *32*
Mrs. Fairstar
  See Horne, Richard Henry
Mueller, Virginia 1924- *28*
Muir, Frank 1920- *30*
Mukerji, Dhan Gopal
  1890-1936 .... *40*
  See also CLR 10
Mulcahy, Lucille Burnett *12*
Mulford, Philippa Greene
  1948- *43*
Mulgan, Catherine
  See Gough, Catherine
Muller, Billex
  See Ellis, Edward S(ylvester)
Mullins, Edward S(wift)
  1922- *10*
Mulock, Dinah Maria
  See Craik, Dinah Maria (Mulock)
Mulvihill, William Patrick
  1923- *8*
Mun
  See Leaf, (Wilbur) Munro
Munari, Bruno 1907- *15*
  See also CLR 9
Munce, Ruth Hill 1898- *12*
Munowitz, Ken 1935-1977 .... *14*
Muñoz, William 1949- *42*
Munro, Alice 1931- *29*
Munro, Eleanor 1928- *37*
Munsch, Robert N. 1945- *50*
  Brief Entry *48*
Munsinger, Lynn 1951- *33*
Munson(-Benson), Tunie
  1946- *15*
Munves, James (Albert) 1922- *30*
Munzer, Martha E. 1899- *4*
Murch, Mel and Starr, Ward [Joint
  double pseudonym]
  See Manes, Stephen
Murphy, Barbara Beasley
  1933- *5*
Murphy, E(mmett) Jefferson
  1926- *4*
Murphy, Jill 1949- *37*
Murphy, Jim 1947- *37*
  Brief Entry *32*
Murphy, Pat
  See Murphy, E(mmett) Jefferson
Murphy, Robert (William)
  1902-1971 .... *10*
Murphy, Shirley Rousseau
  1928- *36*
Murray, John 1923- *39*

Murray, Marian *5*
Murray, Michele 1933-1974 .... *7*
Murray, Ossie 1938- *43*
Musgrave, Florence 1902- *3*
Musgrove, Margaret W(ynkoop)
  1943- *26*
Mussey, Virginia T. H.
  See Ellison, Virginia Howell
Mutz
  See Kunstler, Morton
Myers, Arthur 1917- *35*
Myers, Bernice *9*
Myers, Caroline Elizabeth (Clark)
  1887-1980 .... *28*
Myers, Elisabeth P(erkins)
  1918- *36*
Myers, Hortense (Powner)
  1913- *10*
Myers, Walter Dean 1937- *41*
  Brief Entry *27*
  See also CLR 4
  See also SAAS 2
Myller, Rolf 1926- *27*
Myra, Harold L(awrence)
  1939- *46*
  Brief Entry *42*
Myrus, Donald (Richard)
  1927- *23*

N

Nakatani, Chiyoko 1930-
  Brief Entry *40*
Namioka, Lensey 1929- *27*
Napier, Mark
  See Laffin, John (Alfred Charles)
Nash, Bruce M(itchell) 1947- *34*
Nash, Linell
  See Smith, Linell Nash
Nash, Mary (Hughes) 1925- *41*
Nash, (Frederic) Ogden
  1902-1971 .... *46*
  Earlier sketch in SATA 2
Nast, Elsa Ruth
  See Watson, Jane Werner
Nast, Thomas 1840-1902 .... *51*
  Brief Entry *33*
Nastick, Sharon 1954- *41*
Nathan, Adele (Gutman) 1900(?)-1986
  Obituary *48*
Nathan, Dorothy (Goldeen)
  (?)-1966 .... *15*
Nathan, Robert (Gruntal)
  1894-1985 .... *6*
  Obituary *43*
Natti, Susanna 1948- *32*
Navarra, John Gabriel 1927- *8*
Naylor, Penelope 1941- *10*
Naylor, Phyllis Reynolds
  1933- *12*
Nazaroff, Alexander I. 1898- *4*
Neal, Harry Edward 1906- *5*
Nearing, Penny 1916- *47*
  Brief Entry *42*
Nebel, Gustave E. *45*
  Brief Entry *33*
Nebel, Mimouca
  See Nebel, Gustave E.

Nee, Kay Bonner 10
Needle, Jan 1943- 30
Needleman, Jacob 1934- 6
Negri, Rocco 1932- 12
Neigoff, Anne 13
Neigoff, Mike 1920- 13
Neilson, Frances Fullerton (Jones)
  1910- 14
Neimark, Anne E. 1935- 4
Neimark, Paul G. 1934-
  Brief Entry 37
Nelson, Cordner (Bruce) 1918-
  Brief Entry 29
Nelson, Esther L. 1928- 13
Nelson, Lawrence E(rnest) 1928-1977
  Obituary 28
Nelson, Mary Carroll 1929- 23
Nerlove, Miriam 1959-
  Brief Entry 49
Nesbit, E(dith)
  1858-1924 .... YABC 1
  See also CLR 3
Nesbit, Troy
  See Folsom, Franklin
Nespojohn, Katherine V.
  1912- 7
Ness, Evaline (Michelow)
  1911-1986 26
  Obituary 49
  Earlier sketch in SATA 1
  See also CLR 6
  See also SAAS 1
Nestor, William P(rodromos)
  1947- 49
Neufeld, John 1938- 6
  See also SAAS 3
Neumeyer, Peter F(lorian)
  1929- 13
Neurath, Marie (Reidemeister)
  1898- 1
Neusner, Jacob 1932- 38
Neville, Emily Cheney 1919- 1
  See also SAAS 2
Neville, Mary
  See Woodrich, Mary Neville
Nevins, Albert J. 1915- 20
Newberry, Clare Turlay
  1903-1970 1
  Obituary 26
Newbery, John 1713-1767 20
Newcomb, Ellsworth
  See Kenny, Ellsworth Newcomb
Newcombe, Jack 45
  Brief Entry 33
Newell, Crosby
  See Bonsall, Crosby (Barbara
  Newell)
Newell, Edythe W. 1910- 11
Newell, Hope (Hockenberry)
  1896-1965 24
Newfeld, Frank 1928- 26
Newlon, (Frank) Clarke
  1905(?)-1982 6
  Obituary 33
Newman, Daisy 1904- 27
Newman, Gerald 1939- 46
  Brief Entry 42
Newman, Robert (Howard)
  1909- 4

Newman, Shirlee Petkin
  1924- 10
Newsom, Carol 1948- 40
Newton, James R(obert)
  1935- 23
Newton, Suzanne 1936- 5
Ney, John 1923- 43
  Brief Entry 33
Nic Leodhas, Sorche
  See Alger, Leclaire (Gowans)
Nichols, Cecilia Fawn 1906- 12
Nichols, Peter
  See Youd, (Christopher) Samuel
Nichols, (Joanna) Ruth 1948- 15
Nicholson, Joyce Thorpe
  1919- 35
Nickelsburg, Janet 1893- 11
Nickerson, Betty
  See Nickerson, Elizabeth
Nickerson, Elizabeth 1922- 14
Nicklaus, Carol
  Brief Entry 33
Nicol, Ann
  See Turnbull, Ann (Christine)
Nicolas
  See Mordvinoff, Nicolas
Nicolay, Helen
  1866-1954 .... YABC 1
Nicole, Christopher Robin
  1930- 5
Nielsen, Kay (Rasmus)
  1886-1957 16
Nielsen, Virginia
  See McCall, Virginia Nielsen
Niland, Deborah 1951- 27
Nixon, Hershell Howard
  1923- 42
Nixon, Joan Lowery 1927- 44
  Earlier sketch in SATA 8
Nixon, K.
  See Nixon, Kathleen Irene (Blundell)
Nixon, Kathleen Irene
  (Blundell) 14
Noble, Iris 1922-1986 5
  Obituary 49
Noble, Trinka Hakes
  Brief Entry 37
Nodset, Joan L.
  See Lexau, Joan M.
Noguere, Suzanne 1947- 34
Nolan, Dennis 1945- 42
  Brief Entry 34
Nolan, Jeannette Covert
  1897-1974 2
  Obituary 27
Nolan, Paul T(homas) 1919- 48
Nolan, William F(rancis) 1928-
  Brief Entry 28
Noonan, Julia 1946- 4
Norcross, John
  See Conroy, Jack (Wesley)
Nordhoff, Charles (Bernard)
  1887-1947 23
Nordlicht, Lillian 29
Nordstrom, Ursula 3
Norman, Charles 1904- 38
Norman, James
  See Schmidt, James Norman
Norman, Mary 1931- 36

Norman, Steve
  See Pashko, Stanley
Norris, Gunilla B(rodde)
  1939- 20
North, Andrew
  See Norton, Alice Mary
North, Captain George
  See Stevenson, Robert Louis
North, Joan 1920- 16
North, Robert
  See Withers, Carl A.
North, Sterling 1906-1974 45
  Obituary 26
  Earlier sketch in SATA 1
Norton, Alice Mary 1912- 43
  Earlier sketch in SATA 1
Norton, André
  See Norton, Alice Mary
Norton, Browning
  See Norton, Frank R(owland)
  B(rowning)
Norton, Frank R(owland) B(rowning)
  1909- 10
Norton, Mary 1903- 18
  See also CLR 6
Nöstlinger, Christine 1936-
  Brief Entry 37
  See also CLR 12
Nourse, Alan E(dward) 1928- 48
Nowell, Elizabeth Cameron 12
Numeroff, Laura Joffe 1953- 28
Nurenberg, Thelma
  See Greenhaus, Thelma Nurenberg
Nurnberg, Maxwell
  1897-1984 27
  Obituary 41
Nussbaumer, Paul (Edmond)
  1934- 16
Nyce, (Nellie) Helene von Strecker
  1885-1969 19
Nyce, Vera 1862-1925 19
Nye, Harold G.
  See Harding, Lee
Nye, Robert 1939- 6

O

Oakes, Vanya 1909-1983 6
  Obituary 37
Oakley, Don(ald G.) 1927- 8
Oakley, Graham 1929- 30
  See also CLR 7
Oakley, Helen 1906- 10
Oana, Katherine D. 1929-
  Brief Entry 37
Oana, Kay D.
  See Oana, Katherine D.
Obligado, Lilian (Isabel) 1931-
  Brief Entry 45
Obrant, Susan 1946- 11
O'Brien, Anne Sibley 1952-
  Brief Entry 48
O'Brien, Esse Forrester 1895(?)-1975
  Obituary 30
O'Brien, Robert C.
  See Conly, Robert Leslie
  See also CLR 2

O'Brien, Thomas C(lement)
1938- 29
O'Carroll, Ryan
See Markun, Patricia M(aloney)
O'Connell, Margaret F(orster)
1935-1977 49
Obituary 30
O'Connell, Peg
See Ahern, Margaret McCrohan
O'Connor, Jane 1947-
Brief Entry 47
O'Connor, Karen 1938- 34
O'Connor, Patrick
See Wibberley, Leonard (Patrick
O'Connor)
O'Connor, Richard 1915-1975
Obituary 21
O'Daniel, Janet 1921- 24
O'Dell, Scott 1903- 12
See also CLR 1
Odenwald, Robert P(aul)
1899-1965 11
Odor, Ruth Shannon 1926-
Brief Entry 44
Oechsli, Kelly 1918- 5
Ofek, Uriel 1926- 36
Offit, Sidney 1928- 10
Ofosu-Appiah, L(awrence) H(enry)
1920- 13
Ogan, George F. 1912- 13
Ogan, M. G. [Joint pseudonym]
See Ogan, George F. and Ogan,
Margaret E. (Nettles)
Ogan, Margaret E. (Nettles)
1923- 13
Ogburn, Charlton, Jr. 1911- 3
Ogilvie, Elisabeth May 1917- 40
Brief Entry 29
O'Hagan, Caroline 1946- 38
O'Hanlon, Jacklyn
See Meek, Jacklyn O'Hanlon
O'Hara, Mary
See Alsop, Mary O'Hara
Ohlsson, Ib 1935- 7
Ohtomo, Yasuo 1946- 37
O'Kelley, Mattie Lou 1908- 36
Okimoto, Jean Davies 1942- 34
Olcott, Frances Jenkins
1872(?)-1963 19
Old Boy
See Hughes, Thomas
Old Fag
See Bell, Robert S(tanley) W(arren)
Oldenburg, E(gbert) William
1936-1974 35
Olds, Elizabeth 1896- 3
Olds, Helen Diehl 1895-1981 9
Obituary 25
Oldstyle, Jonathan
See Irving, Washington
O'Leary, Brian 1940- 6
Oleksy, Walter 1930- 33
Olesky, Walter
See Oleksy, Walter
Oliver, John Edward 1933- 21
Olmstead, Lorena Ann 1890- 13
Olney, Ross R. 1929- 13
Olschewski, Alfred 1920- 7
Olsen, Ib Spang 1921- 6

Olson, Gene 1922- 32
Olson, Helen Kronberg 48
Olugebefola, Ademole 1941- 15
Oman, Carola (Mary Anima)
1897-1978 35
Ommanney, F(rancis) D(ownes)
1903-1980 23
O Mude
See Gorey, Edward St. John
Oneal, Elizabeth 1934- 30
Oneal, Zibby
See Oneal, Elizabeth
See also CLR 13
O'Neill, Judith (Beatrice)
1930- 34
O'Neill, Mary L(e Duc) 1908- 2
Onslow, John 1906-1985
Obituary 47
Opgenoorth, Winfried 1939-
Brief Entry 50
Opie, Iona 1923- 3
Opie, Peter (Mason)
1918-1982 3
Obituary 28
Oppenheim, Joanne 1934- 5
Oppenheimer, Joan L(etson)
1925- 28
Optic, Oliver
See Adams, William Taylor
Orbach, Ruth Gary 1941- 21
Orczy, Emmuska, Baroness
1865-1947 40
O'Reilly, Sean
See Deegan, Paul Joseph
Orgel, Doris 1929- 7
Oriolo, Joe
See Oriolo, Joseph
Oriolo, Joseph 1913-1985
Obituary 46
Orleans, Ilo 1897-1962 10
Ormai, Stella
Brief Entry 48
Ormerod, Jan(ette Louise) 1946-
Brief Entry 44
Ormes, Jackie
See Ormes, Zelda J.
Ormes, Zelda J. 1914-1986
Obituary 47
Ormondroyd, Edward 1925- 14
Ormsby, Virginia H(aire) 11
Orris
See Ingelow, Jean
Orth, Richard
See Gardner, Richard
Orwell, George
See Blair, Eric Arthur
Osborne, Chester G. 1915- 11
Osborne, David
See Silverberg, Robert
Osborne, Leone Neal 1914- 2
Osborne, Mary Pope 1949-
Brief Entry 41
Osceola
See Blixen, Karen (Christentze
Dinesen)
Osgood, William E(dward)
1926- 37
Osmond, Edward 1900- 10

Ossoli, Sarah Margaret (Fuller)
marchesa d' 1810-1850 25
Otis, James
See Kaler, James Otis
O'Trigger, Sir Lucius
See Horne, Richard Henry
Ottley, Reginald (Leslie) 26
Otto, Margaret Glover 1909-1976
Obituary 30
Ouida
See De La Ramée, (Marie) Louise
Ousley, Odille 1896- 10
Overton, Jenny (Margaret Mary) 1942-
Brief Entry 36
Owen, Caroline Dale
See Snedecker, Caroline Dale
(Parke)
Owen, Clifford
See Hamilton, Charles H. St. John
Owen, Dilys
See Gater, Dilys
Owen, (Benjamin) Evan
1918-1984 38
Oxenbury, Helen 1938- 3

P

Pace, Mildred Mastin 1907- 46
Brief Entry 29
Packard, Edward 1931- 47
Packer, Vin
See Meaker, Marijane
Page, Eileen
See Heal, Edith
Page, Eleanor
See Coerr, Eleanor
Page, Lou Williams 1912- 38
Paget-Fredericks, Joseph E. P. Rous-
Marten 1903-1963
Brief Entry 30
Pahz, (Anne) Cheryl Suzanne
1949- 11
Pahz, James Alon 1943- 11
Paice, Margaret 1920- 10
Paige, Harry W. 1922- 41
Brief Entry 35
Paine, Roberta M. 1925- 13
Paisley, Tom
See Bethancourt, T. Ernesto
Palazzo, Anthony D.
1905-1970 3
Palazzo, Tony
See Palazzo, Anthony D.
Palder, Edward L. 1922- 5
Palladini, David (Mario)
1946- 40
Brief Entry 32
Pallas, Norvin 1918- 23
Pallister, John C(lare) 1891-1980
Obituary 26
Palmer, Bernard 1914- 26
Palmer, C(yril) Everard 1930- 14
Palmer, (Ruth) Candida 1926- 11
Palmer, Heidi 1948- 15
Palmer, Helen Marion
See Geisel, Helen
Palmer, Juliette 1930- 15
Palmer, Robin 1911- 43

Paltrowitz, Donna (Milman) 1950-
    Brief Entry 50
Paltrowitz, Stuart 1946-
    Brief Entry 50
Panetta, George 1915-1969 15
Panowski, Eileen Thompson
    1920- 49
Pansy
    See Alden, Isabella (Macdonald)
Pantell, Dora (Fuchs) 1915- 39
Panter, Carol 1936- 9
Papas, William 1927- 50
Papashvily, George
    1898-1978 17
Papashvily, Helen (Waite)
    1906- 17
Pape, D(onna) L(ugg) 1930- 2
Paperny, Myra (Green) 1932- 51
    Brief Entry 33
Paradis, Adrian A(lexis)
    1912- 1
Paradis, Marjorie (Bartholomew)
    1886(?)-1970 17
Parenteau, Shirley (Laurolyn)
    1935- 47
    Brief Entry 40
Parish, Peggy 1927- 17
Park, Barbara 1947- 40
    Brief Entry 35
Park, Bill
    See Park, W(illiam) B(ryan)
Park, Ruth 25
Park, W(illiam) B(ryan) 1936- 22
Parker, Elinor 1906- 3
Parker, Lois M(ay) 1912- 30
Parker, Nancy Winslow 1930- 10
Parker, Richard 1915- 14
Parker, Robert
    See Boyd, Waldo T.
Parkinson, Ethelyn M(inerva)
    1906- 11
Parks, Edd Winfield
    1906-1968 10
Parks, Gordon (Alexander Buchanan)
    1912- 8
Parley, Peter
    See Goodrich, Samuel Griswold
Parlin, John
    See Graves, Charles Parlin
Parnall, Peter 1936- 16
Parr, Letitia (Evelyn) 1906- 37
Parr, Lucy 1924- 10
Parrish, Anne 1888-1957 27
Parrish, Mary
    See Cousins, Margaret
Parrish, (Frederick) Maxfield
    1870-1966 14
Parry, Marian 1924- 13
Parsons, Tom
    See MacPherson, Thomas George
Partch, Virgil Franklin II
    1916-1984 45
    Obituary 39
Partridge, Benjamin W(aring), Jr.
    1915- 28
Partridge, Jenny (Lilian) 1947-
    Brief Entry 37
Pascal, David 1918- 14

Pascal, Francine 1938- 51
    Brief Entry 37
Paschal, Nancy
    See Trotter, Grace V(iolet)
Pashko, Stanley 1913- 29
Patent, Dorothy Hinshaw
    1940- 22
Paterson, Diane (R. Cole) 1946-
    Brief Entry 33
Paterson, Katherine (Womeldorf)
    1932- 13
    See also CLR 7
Paton, Alan (Stewart) 1903- 11
Paton, Jane (Elizabeth) 1934- 35
Paton Walsh, Gillian 1939- 4
    See also SAAS 3
Patten, Brian 1946- 29
Patterson, Geoffrey 1943-
    Brief Entry 44
Patterson, Lillie G. 14
Paul, Aileen 1917- 12
Paul, Elizabeth
    See Crow, Donna Fletcher
Paul, James 1936- 23
Paul, Robert
    See Roberts, John G(aither)
Pauli, Hertha (Ernestine)
    1909-1973 3
    Obituary 26
Paull, Grace A. 1898- 24
Paulsen, Gary 1939- 50
    Earlier sketch in SATA 22
Paulson, Jack
    See Jackson, C. Paul
Pavel, Frances 1907- 10
Payne, Donald Gordon 1924- 37
Payne, Emmy
    See West, Emily G(ovan)
Payson, Dale 1943- 9
Payzant, Charles 18
Payzant, Jessie Mercer Knechtel
    See Shannon, Terry
Paz, A.
    See Pahz, James Alon
Paz, Zan
    See Pahz, Cheryl Suzanne
Peake, Mervyn 1911-1968 23
Peale, Norman Vincent 1898- 20
Pearce, (Ann) Philippa 1920- 1
    See also CLR 9
Peare, Catherine Owens 1911- 9
Pears, Charles 1873-1958
    Brief Entry 30
Pearson, Susan 1946- 39
    Brief Entry 27
Pease, Howard 1894-1974 2
    Obituary 25
Peck, Anne Merriman 1884- 18
Peck, Richard 1934- 18
    See also SAAS 2
Peck, Robert Newton III
    1928- 21
    See also SAAS 1
Peek, Merle 1938- 39
Peel, Norman Lemon
    See Hirsch, Phil
Peeples, Edwin A. 1915- 6

Peet, Bill
    See Peet, William Bartlett
    See also CLR 12
Peet, Creighton B. 1899-1977 30
Peet, William Bartlett 1915- 41
    Earlier sketch in SATA 2
Peirce, Waldo 1884-1970
    Brief Entry 28
Pelaez, Jill 1924- 12
Pellowski, Anne 1933- 20
Pellowski, Michael J(oseph) 1949-
    Brief Entry 48
Pelta, Kathy 1928- 18
Peltier, Leslie C(opus) 1900- 13
Pembury, Bill
    See Gronon, Arthur William
Pemsteen, Hans
    See Manes, Stephen
Pendennis, Arthur, Esquire
    See Thackeray, William Makepeace
Pender, Lydia 1907- 3
Pendery, Rosemary 7
Pendle, Alexy 1943- 29
Pendle, George 1906-1977
    Obituary 28
Penn, Ruth Bonn
    See Rosenberg, Ethel
Pennage, E. M.
    See Finkel, George (Irvine)
Penney, Grace Jackson 1904- 35
Pennington, Eunice 1923- 27
Pennington, Lillian Boyer
    1904- 45
Penrose, Margaret
    See Stratemeyer, Edward L.
Penzler, Otto 1942- 38
Pepe, Phil(ip) 1935- 20
Peppe, Rodney 1934- 4
Percy, Charles Henry
    See Smith, Dodie
Perera, Thomas Biddle 1938- 13
Perkins, Al(bert Rogers)
    1904-1975 30
Perkins, Marlin 1905-1986 21
    Obituary 48
Perl, Lila 6
Perl, Susan 1922-1983 22
    Obituary 34
Perlmutter, O(scar) William
    1920-1975 8
Perrault, Charles 1628-1703 25
Perreard, Suzanne Louise Butler 1919-
    Brief Entry 29
Perrine, Mary 1913- 2
Perry, Barbara Fisher
    See Fisher, Barbara
Perry, Patricia 1949- 30
Perry, Roger 1933- 27
Pershing, Marie
    See Schultz, Pearle Henriksen
Peters, Caroline
    See Betz, Eva Kelly
Peters, Elizabeth
    See Mertz, Barbara (Gross)
Peters, S. H.
    See Porter, William Sydney
Petersen, P(eter) J(ames)
    1941- 48
    Brief Entry 43

Petersham, Maud (Fuller)
1890-1971 .... *17*
Petersham, Miska 1888-1960 ...... *17*
Peterson, Esther (Allen) 1934- *35*
Peterson, Hans 1922- *8*
Peterson, Harold L(eslie)
1922- *8*
Peterson, Helen Stone 1910- *8*
Peterson, Jeanne Whitehouse
See Whitehouse, Jeanne
Peterson, Lorraine 1940-
Brief Entry *44*
Petie, Haris 1915- *10*
Petrides, Heidrun 1944- *19*
Petrie, Catherine 1947-
Brief Entry *41*
Petroski, Catherine (Ann Groom)
1939- *48*
Petrovich, Michael B(oro)
1922- *40*
Petrovskaya, Kyra
See Wayne, Kyra Petrovskaya
Petry, Ann (Lane) 1908- *5*
See also CLR 12
Pevsner, Stella *8*
Peyo
See Culliford, Pierre
Peyton, K. M.
See Peyton, Kathleen (Wendy)
See also CLR 3
Peyton, Kathleen (Wendy)
1929- *15*
Pfeffer, Susan Beth 1948- *4*
See also CLR 11
Phelan, Josephine 1905-
Brief Entry *30*
Phelan, Mary Kay 1914- *3*
Phelps, Ethel Johnston 1914- *35*
Philbrook, Clem(ent E.) 1917- *24*
Phillips, Betty Lou
See Phillips, Elizabeth Louise
Phillips, Elizabeth Louise
Brief Entry *48*
Phillips, Irv
See Phillips, Irving W.
Phillips, Irving W. 1908- *11*
Phillips, Jack
See Sandburg, Carl (August)
Phillips, Leon
See Gerson, Noel B(ertram)
Phillips, Loretta (Hosey)
1893- *10*
Phillips, Louis 1942- *8*
Phillips, Mary Geisler
1881-1964 .... *10*
Phillips, Prentice 1894- *10*
Phillpotts, Eden 1862-1960 .... *24*
Phipson, Joan
See Fitzhardinge, Joan M.
See also CLR 5
See also SAAS 3
Phiz
See Browne, Hablot Knight
Phleger, Fred B. 1909- *34*
Phleger, Marjorie Temple
1908(?)-1986 .... *1*
Obituary *47*
Phypps, Hyacinthe
See Gorey, Edward St. John

Piaget, Jean 1896-1980
Obituary *23*
Piatti, Celestino 1922- *16*
Picard, Barbara Leonie 1917- *2*
Pickard, Charles 1932- *36*
Pickering, James Sayre
1897-1969 .... *36*
Obituary *28*
Pienkowski, Jan 1936- *6*
See also CLR 6
Pierce, Edith Gray 1893-1977 ..... *45*
Pierce, Katherine
See St. John, Wylly Folk
Pierce, Meredith Ann 1958-
Brief Entry *48*
Pierce, Ruth (Ireland) 1936- *5*
Pierce, Tamora 1954- *51*
Brief Entry *49*
Pierik, Robert 1921- *13*
Pig, Edward
See Gorey, Edward St. John
Pike, E(dgar) Royston 1896- *22*
Pilarski, Laura 1926- *13*
Pilgrim, Anne
See Allan, Mabel Esther
Pilkington, Francis Meredyth
1907- *4*
Pilkington, Roger (Windle)
1915- *10*
Pinchot, David 1914(?)-1983
Obituary *34*
Pincus, Harriet 1938- *27*
Pine, Tillie S(chloss) 1897- *13*
Pinkerton, Kathrene Sutherland
(Gedney) 1887-1967
Obituary *26*
Pinkney, Jerry 1939- *41*
Brief Entry *32*
Pinkwater, Daniel Manus
1941- *46*
Earlier sketch in SATA 8
See also CLR 4
See also SAAS 3
Pinner, Joma
See Werner, Herma
Pioneer
See Yates, Raymond F(rancis)
Piowaty, Kim Kennelly 1957- *49*
Piper, Roger
See Fisher, John (Oswald Hamilton)
Piper, Watty
See Bragg, Mabel Caroline
Piro, Richard 1934- *7*
Pirsig, Robert M(aynard)
1928- *39*
Pitman, (Isaac) James 1901-1985
Obituary *46*
Pitrone, Jean Maddern 1920- *4*
Pitz, Henry C(larence)
1895-1976 .... *4*
Obituary *24*
Pizer, Vernon 1918- *21*
Place, Marian T. 1910- *3*
Plaidy, Jean
See Hibbert, Eleanor
Plaine, Alfred R. 1898(?)-1981
Obituary *29*
Platt, Kin 1911- *21*

Plimpton, George (Ames)
1927- *10*
Plomer, William (Charles Franklin)
1903-1973 .... *24*
Plotz, Helen (Ratnoff) 1913- *38*
Plowhead, Ruth Gipson
1877-1967 .... *43*
Plowman, Stephanie 1922- *6*
Pluckrose, Henry (Arthur)
1931- *13*
Plum, J.
See Wodehouse, P(elham)
G(renville)
Plum, Jennifer
See Kurland, Michael (Joseph)
Plumb, Charles P. 1900(?)-1982
Obituary *29*
Plume, Ilse
Brief Entry *43*
Plummer, Margaret 1911- *2*
Podendorf, Illa E.
1903(?)-1983 .... *18*
Obituary *35*
Poe, Edgar Allan 1809-1849 ...... *23*
Pogány, William Andrew
1882-1955 .... *44*
Pogány, Willy
Brief Entry *30*
See Pogány, William Andrew
Pohl, Frederik 1919- *24*
Pohlmann, Lillian (Grenfell)
1902- *11*
Pointon, Robert
See Rooke, Daphne (Marie)
Pola
See Watson, Pauline
Polatnick, Florence T. 1923- *5*
Polder, Markus
See Krüss, James
Polette, Nancy (Jane) 1930- *42*
Polhamus, Jean Burt 1928- *21*
Politi, Leo 1908- *47*
Earlier sketch in SATA 1
Polking, Kirk 1925- *5*
Polland, Barbara K(ay) 1939- *44*
Polland, Madeleine A. 1918- *6*
Pollock, Bruce 1945- *46*
Pollock, Mary
See Blyton, Enid (Mary)
Pollock, Penny 1935- *44*
Brief Entry *42*
Pollowitz, Melinda (Kilborn)
1944- *26*
Polonsky, Arthur 1925- *34*
Polseno, Jo *17*
Pomerantz, Charlotte *20*
Pomeroy, Pete
See Roth, Arthur J(oseph)
Pond, Alonzo W(illiam) 1894- *5*
Pontiflet, Ted 1932- *32*
Poole, Gray Johnson 1906- *1*
Poole, Josephine 1933- *5*
See also SAAS 2
Poole, Lynn 1910-1969 .... *1*
Poole, Peggy 1925- *39*
Poortvliet, Marien
See Poortvliet, Rien
Poortvliet, Rien 1933(?)-
Brief Entry *37*

Pope, Elizabeth Marie 1917- 38
Brief Entry 36
Portal, Colette 1936- 6
Porte, Barbara Ann
Brief Entry 45
Porter, Katherine Anne
1890-1980 39
Obituary 23
Porter, Sheena 1935- 24
Porter, William Sydney
1862-1910 .... YABC 2
Portteus, Eleanora Marie Manthei
(?)-1983
Obituary 36
Posell, Elsa Z. 3
Posten, Margaret L(ois) 1915- 10
Potok, Chaim 1929- 33
Potter, (Helen) Beatrix
1866-1943 .... YABC 1
See also CLR 1
Potter, Margaret (Newman)
1926- 21
Potter, Marian 1915- 9
Potter, Miriam Clark
1886-1965 3
Pournelle, Jerry (Eugene)
1933- 26
Powell, A. M.
See Morgan, Alfred P(owell)
Powell, Ann 1951-
Brief Entry 51
Powell, Richard Stillman
See Barbour, Ralph Henry
Powers, Anne
See Schwartz, Anne Powers
Powers, Bill 1931-
Brief Entry 31
Powers, Margaret
See Heal, Edith
Powledge, Fred 1935- 37
Poynter, Margaret 1927- 27
Prager, Arthur 44
Preiss, Byron (Cary) 47
Brief Entry 42
Prelutsky, Jack 22
See also CLR 13
Presberg, Miriam Goldstein 1919-1978
Brief Entry 38
Preston, Edna Mitchell 40
Preston, Lillian Elvira 1918- 47
Preussler, Otfried 1923- 24
Prevert, Jacques (Henri Marie)
1900-1977
Obituary 30
Price, Christine 1928-1980 3
Obituary 23
Price, Garrett 1896-1979
Obituary 22
Price, Jennifer
See Hoover, Helen (Drusilla Blackburn)
Price, Jonathan (Reeve) 1941- 46
Price, Lucie Locke
See Locke, Lucie
Price, Margaret (Evans) 1888-1973
Brief Entry 28
Price, Olive 1903- 8
Price, Susan 1955- 25

Price, Willard 1887-1983 48
Brief Entry 38
Prideaux, Tom 1908- 37
Priestley, Lee (Shore) 1904- 27
Prieto, Mariana B(eeching)
1912- 8
Primavera, Elise 1954-
Brief Entry 48
Prime, Derek (James) 1931- 34
Prince, Alison 1931- 28
Prince, J(ack) H(arvey) 1908- 17
Pringle, Laurence 1935- 4
See also CLR 4
Pritchett, Elaine H(illyer)
1920- 36
Proctor, Everitt
See Montgomery, Rutherford
Professor Zingara
See Leeming, Joseph
Provensen, Alice 1918- 9
See also CLR 11
Provensen, Martin 1916-1987 9
Obituary 51
See also CLR 11
Pryor, Helen Brenton
1897-1972 4
Pucci, Albert John 1920- 44
Pudney, John (Sleigh)
1909-1977 24
Pugh, Ellen T. 1920- 7
Pullein-Thompson, Christine
1930- 3
Pullein-Thompson, Diana 3
Pullein-Thompson, Josephine 3
Puner, Helen W(alker) 1915- 37
Purdy, Susan Gold 1939- 8
Purscell, Phyllis 1934- 7
Putnam, Arthur Lee
See Alger, Horatio, Jr.
Putnam, Peter B(rock) 1920- 30
Pyle, Howard 1853-1911 16
Pyne, Mable Mandeville
1903-1969 9
Python, Monty
See Jones, Terry

Q

Quackenbush, Robert M.
1929- 7
Quammen, David 1948- 7
Quarles, Benjamin 1904- 12
Queen, Ellery, Jr.
See Holding, James
Quennell, Marjorie (Courtney)
1884-1972 29
Quick, Annabelle 1922- 2
Quigg, Jane (Hulda) (?)-1986
Obituary 49
Quin-Harkin, Janet 1941- 18
Quinn, Elisabeth 1881-1962 22
Quinn, Susan
See Jacobs, Susan
Quinn, Vernon
See Quinn, Elisabeth

R

Rabe, Berniece 1928- 7
Rabe, Olive H(anson)
1887-1968 13
Rabinowich, Ellen 1946- 29
Rabinowitz, Sandy 1954-
Brief Entry 39
Raboff, Ernest Lloyd
Brief Entry 37
Rachlin, Harvey (Brant) 1951- ... 47
Rachlis, Eugene (Jacob) 1920-1986
Obituary 50
Rackham, Arthur 1867-1939 15
Radford, Ruby L(orraine)
1891-1971 6
Radlauer, David 1952- 28
Radlauer, Edward 1921- 15
Radlauer, Ruth (Shaw) 1926- 15
Radley, Gail 1951- 25
Rae, Gwynedd 1892-1977 37
Raebeck, Lois 1921- 5
Raftery, Gerald (Bransfield)
1905- 11
Rahn, Joan Elma 1929- 27
Raible, Alton (Robert) 1918- 35
Raiff, Stan 1930- 11
Rainey, W. B.
See Blassingame, Wyatt Rainey
Ralston, Jan
See Dunlop, Agnes M. R.
Ramal, Walter
See de la Mare, Walter
Rana, J.
See Forrester, Helen
Ranadive, Gail 1944- 10
Rand, Ann (Binkley) 30
Rand, Paul 1914- 6
Randall, Florence Engel 1917- 5
Randall, Janet [Joint pseudonym]
See Young, Janet Randall and
Young, Robert W.
Randall, Robert
See Silverberg, Robert
Randall, Ruth Painter
1892-1971 3
Randolph, Lieutenant J. H.
See Ellis, Edward S(ylvester)
Rands, William Brighty
1823-1882 17
Ranney, Agnes V. 1916- 6
Ransom, Candice F. 1952-
Brief Entry 49
Ransome, Arthur (Michell)
1884-1967 22
See also CLR 8
Rapaport, Stella F(read) 10
Raphael, Elaine (Chionchio)
1933- 23
Rappaport, Eva 1924- 6
Rarick, Carrie 1911- 41
Raskin, Edith (Lefkowitz)
1908- 9
Raskin, Ellen 1928-1984 38
Earlier sketch in SATA 2
See also CLR 1, 12
Raskin, Joseph 1897-1982 12
Obituary 29

Rasmussen, Knud Johan Victor
 1879-1933
  Brief Entry *34*
Rathjen, Carl H(enry) 1909- *11*
Rattray, Simon
 See Trevor, Elleston
Rau, Margaret 1913- *9*
 See also CLR 8
Rauch, Mabel Thompson 1888-1972
  Obituary *26*
Raucher, Herman 1928- *8*
Ravielli, Anthony 1916- *3*
Rawlings, Marjorie Kinnan
 1896-1953 ....*YABC 1*
Rawls, (Woodrow) Wilson
 1913- *22*
Ray, Deborah
 See Kogan, Deborah
Ray, Deborah Kogan
 See Kogan, Deborah
Ray, Irene
 See Sutton, Margaret Beebe
Ray, JoAnne 1935- *9*
Ray, Mary (Eva Pedder)
 1932- *2*
Raymond, James Crossley 1917-1981
  Obituary *29*
Raymond, Robert
 See Alter, Robert Edmond
Rayner, Mary 1933- *22*
Rayner, William 1929-
  Brief Entry *36*
Raynor, Dorka *28*
Rayson, Steven 1932- *30*
Razzell, Arthur (George)
 1925- *11*
Razzi, James 1931- *10*
Read, Elfreida 1920- *2*
Read, Piers Paul 1941- *21*
Ready, Kirk L. 1943- *39*
Reaney, James 1926- *43*
Reck, Franklin Mering 1896-1965
  Brief Entry *30*
Redding, Robert Hull 1919- *2*
Redway, Ralph
 See Hamilton, Charles H. St. John
Redway, Ridley
 See Hamilton, Charles H. St. John
Reed, Betty Jane 1921- *4*
Reed, Gwendolyn E(lizabeth)
 1932- *21*
Reed, Kit 1932- *34*
Reed, Philip G. 1908-
  Brief Entry *29*
Reed, Thomas (James) 1947- *34*
Reed, William Maxwell
 1871-1962 .... *15*
Reeder, Colonel Red
 See Reeder, Russell P., Jr.
Reeder, Russell P., Jr. 1902- *4*
Reeman, Douglas Edward 1924-
  Brief Entry *28*
Rees, David Bartlett 1936- *36*
 See also SAAS 5
Rees, Ennis 1925- *3*
Reeve, Joel
 See Cox, William R(obert)
Reeves, James 1909- *15*
Reeves, Joyce 1911- *17*

Reeves, Lawrence F. 1926- *29*
Reeves, Ruth Ellen
 See Ranney, Agnes V.
Regehr, Lydia 1903- *37*
Reggiani, Renée *18*
Reid, Alastair 1926- *46*
Reid, Barbara 1922- *21*
Reid, Dorothy M(arion) (?)-1974
  Brief Entry *29*
Reid, Eugenie Chazal 1924- *12*
Reid, John Calvin *21*
Reid, (Thomas) Mayne
 1818-1883 .... *24*
Reid, Meta Mayne 1905-
  Brief Entry *36*
Reid Banks, Lynne 1929- *22*
Reiff, Stephanie Ann 1948- *47*
  Brief Entry *28*
Reig, June 1933- *30*
Reigot, Betty Polisar 1924-
  Brief Entry *41*
Reinach, Jacquelyn (Krasne)
 1930- *28*
Reiner, William B(uck)
 1910-1976 .... *46*
  Obituary *30*
Reinfeld, Fred 1910-1964 .... *3*
Reiniger, Lotte 1899-1981 .... *40*
  Obituary *33*
Reiss, Johanna de Leeuw
 1932- *18*
Reiss, John J. *23*
Reit, Seymour *21*
Reit, Sy
 See Reit, Seymour
Rémi, Georges 1907-1983 .... *13*
  Obituary *32*
Remington, Frederic (Sackrider)
 1861-1909 .... *41*
Renault, Mary
 See Challans, Mary
Rendell, Joan *28*
Rendina, Laura Cooper 1902- *10*
Renick, Marion (Lewis) 1905- *1*
Renken, Aleda 1907- *27*
Renlie, Frank H. 1936- *11*
Rensie, Willis
 See Eisner, Will(iam Erwin)
Renvoize, Jean 1930- *5*
Resnick, Michael D(iamond)
 1942- *38*
Resnick, Mike
 See Resnick, Michael D(iamond)
Resnick, Seymour 1920- *23*
Retla, Robert
 See Alter, Robert Edmond
Reuter, Carol (Joan) 1931- *2*
Revena
 See Wright, Betty Ren
Rey, H(ans) A(ugusto)
 1898-1977 .... *26*
  Earlier sketch in SATA 1
  See also CLR 5
Rey, Margret (Elizabeth)
 1906- *26*
  See also CLR 5
Reyher, Becky
 See Reyher, Rebecca Hourwich

Reyher, Rebecca Hourwich
 1897-1987 .... *18*
  Obituary *50*
Reynolds, Dickson
 See Reynolds, Helen Mary
  Greenwood Campbell
Reynolds, Helen Mary Greenwood
 Campbell 1884-1969
  Obituary *26*
Reynolds, John
 See Whitlock, Ralph
Reynolds, Madge
 See Whitlock, Ralph
Reynolds, Malvina 1900-1978 ..... *44*
  Obituary *24*
Reynolds, Pamela 1923- *34*
Rhodes, Bennie (Loran) 1927- *35*
Rhodes, Frank H(arold Trevor)
 1926- *37*
Rhue, Morton
 See Strasser, Todd
Rhys, Megan
 See Williams, Jeanne
Ribbons, Ian 1924- *37*
  Brief Entry *30*
  See also SAAS 3
Ricciuti, Edward R(aphael)
 1938- *10*
Rice, Charles D(uane) 1910-1971
  Obituary *27*
Rice, Dale R(ichard) 1948- *42*
Rice, Edward 1918- *47*
  Brief Entry *42*
Rice, Elizabeth 1913- *2*
Rice, Eve (Hart) 1951- *34*
Rice, Inez 1907- *13*
Rice, James 1934- *22*
Rich, Elaine Sommers 1926- *6*
Rich, Josephine 1912- *10*
Richard, Adrienne 1921- *5*
Richards, Curtis
 See Curtis, Richard (Alan)
Richards, Frank
 See Hamilton, Charles H. St. John
Richards, Hilda
 See Hamilton, Charles H. St. John
Richards, Kay
 See Baker, Susan (Catherine)
Richards, Laura E(lizabeth Howe)
 1850-1943 ....*YABC 1*
Richards, Norman 1932- *48*
Richards, R(onald) C(harles) W(illiam)
 1923-
  Brief Entry *43*
Richardson, Frank Howard 1882-1970
  Obituary *27*
Richardson, Grace Lee
 See Dickson, Naida
Richardson, Robert S(hirley)
 1902- *8*
Richelson, Geraldine 1922- *29*
Richler, Mordecai 1931- *44*
  Brief Entry *27*
Richoux, Pat 1927- *7*
Richter, Alice 1941- *30*
Richter, Conrad 1890-1968 .... *3*
Richter, Hans Peter 1925- *6*
Rico, Don(ato) 1917-1985
  Obituary *43*

Ridge, Antonia (Florence)
(?)-1981 7
  Obituary 27
Ridge, Martin 1923- 43
Ridley, Nat, Jr.
  See Stratemeyer, Edward L.
Ridlon, Marci 1942- 22
Riedman, Sarah R(egal) 1902- 1
Riesenberg, Felix, Jr.
1913-1962 23
Rieu, E(mile) V(ictor)
1887-1972 46
  Obituary 26
Riggs, Sidney Noyes 1892-1975
  Obituary 28
Rikhoff, Jean 1928- 9
Riley, James Whitcomb
1849-1916 17
Riley, Jocelyn (Carol) 1949-
  Brief Entry 50
Rinaldi, Ann 1934- 51
  Brief Entry 50
Rinard, Judith E(llen) 1947- 44
Ringi, Kjell Arne Sörensen
1939- 12
Rinkoff, Barbara (Jean)
1923-1975 4
  Obituary 27
Riordan, James 1936- 28
Rios, Tere
  See Versace, Marie Teresa
Ripley, Elizabeth Blake
1906-1969 5
Ripper, Charles L. 1929- 3
Rissman, Art
  See Sussman, Susan
Rissman, Susan
  See Sussman, Susan
Ritchie, Barbara (Gibbons) 14
Ritts, Paul 1920(?)-1980
  Obituary 25
Rivera, Geraldo 1943-
  Brief Entry 28
Riverside, John
  See Heinlein, Robert A(nson)
Rivkin, Ann 1920- 41
Rivoli, Mario 1943- 10
Roach, Marilynne K(athleen)
1946- 9
Roach, Portia
  See Takakjian, Portia
Robbins, Frank 1917- 42
  Brief Entry 32
Robbins, Raleigh
  See Hamilton, Charles H. St. John
Robbins, Ruth 1917(?)- 14
Robbins, Tony
  See Pashko, Stanley
Roberts, Bruce (Stuart) 1930- 47
  Brief Entry 39
Roberts, Charles G(eorge) D(ouglas)
1860-1943
  Brief Entry 29
Roberts, David
  See Cox, John Roberts
Roberts, Elizabeth Madox
1886-1941 33
  Brief Entry 27

Roberts, Jim
  See Bates, Barbara S(nedeker)
Roberts, John G(aither) 1913- 27
Roberts, Nancy Correll 1924-
  Brief Entry 28
Roberts, Terence
  See Sanderson, Ivan T.
Roberts, Willo Davis 1928- 21
Robertson, Barbara (Anne)
1931- 12
Robertson, Don 1929- 8
Robertson, Dorothy Lewis
1912- 12
Robertson, Jennifer (Sinclair)
1942- 12
Robertson, Keith 1914- 1
Robinet, Harriette Gillem
1931- 27
Robins, Seelin
  See Ellis, Edward S(ylvester)
Robinson, Adjai 1932- 8
Robinson, Barbara (Webb)
1927- 8
Robinson, C(harles) A(lexander), Jr.
1900-1965 36
Robinson, Charles 1870-1937 17
Robinson, Charles 1931- 6
Robinson, Jan M. 1933- 6
Robinson, Jean O. 1934- 7
Robinson, Jerry 1922-
  Brief Entry 34
Robinson, Joan (Mary) G(ale Thomas)
1910- 7
Robinson, Marileta 1942- 32
Robinson, Maudie (Millian Oller)
1914- 11
Robinson, Maurice R. 1895-1982
  Obituary 29
Robinson, Nancy K(onheim)
1942- 32
  Brief Entry 31
Robinson, Ray(mond Kenneth)
1920- 23
Robinson, Shari
  See McGuire, Leslie (Sarah)
Robinson, T(homas) H(eath)
1869-1950 17
Robinson, (Wanda) Veronica
1926- 30
Robinson, W(illiam) Heath
1872-1944 17
Robison, Bonnie 1924- 12
Robison, Nancy L(ouise)
1934- 32
Robottom, John 1934- 7
Roche, A. K. [Joint pseudonym]
  See Abisch, Roslyn Kroop and
  Kaplan, Boche
Roche, P(atricia) K.
  Brief Entry 34
Roche, Terry
  See Poole, Peggy
Rock, Gail
  Brief Entry 32
Rocker, Fermin 1907- 40
Rockwell, Anne F. 1934- 33
Rockwell, Gail
  Brief Entry 36
Rockwell, Harlow 33

Rockwell, Norman (Percevel)
1894-1978 23
Rockwell, Thomas 1933- 7
  See also CLR 6
Rockwood, Joyce 1947- 39
Rockwood, Roy [Collective
pseudonym] 1
  See also McFarlane, Leslie;
  Stratemeyer, Edward L.
Roddenberry, Eugene Wesley
1921- 45
Roddenberry, Gene
  See Roddenberry, Eugene Wesley
Rodgers, Mary 1931- 8
Rodman, Emerson
  See Ellis, Edward S(ylvester)
Rodman, Maia
  See Wojciechowska, Maia
Rodman, Selden 1909- 9
Rodowsky, Colby 1932- 21
Roe, Harry Mason
  See Stratemeyer, Edward L.
Roever, J(oan) M(arilyn)
1935- 26
Roffey, Maureen 1936- 33
Rogers, (Thomas) Alan (Stinchcombe)
1937- 2
Rogers, Frances 1888-1974 10
Rogers, Fred (McFeely) 1928- 33
Rogers, Jean 1919-
  Brief Entry 47
Rogers, Matilda 1894-1976 5
  Obituary 34
Rogers, Pamela 1927- 9
Rogers, Robert
  See Hamilton, Charles H. St. John
Rogers, W(illiam) G(arland)
1896-1978 23
Rojan
  See Rojankovsky, Feodor
  (Stepanovich)
Rojankovsky, Feodor (Stepanovich)
1891-1970 21
Rokeby-Thomas, Anna E(lma)
1911- 15
Roland, Albert 1925- 11
Rolerson, Darrell A(llen)
1946- 8
Roll, Winifred 1909- 6
Rollins, Charlemae Hill
1897-1979 3
  Obituary 26
Romano, Clare
  See Ross, Clare (Romano)
Romano, Louis 1921- 35
Rongen, Björn 1906- 10
Rood, Ronald (N.) 1920- 12
Rooke, Daphne (Marie) 1914- 12
Roop, Constance Betzer 1951-
  Brief Entry 49
Roop, Peter 1951-
  Brief Entry 49
Roos, Stephen (Kelley) 1945- 47
  Brief Entry 41
Roosevelt, (Anna) Eleanor
1884-1962 50
Root, Phyllis
  Brief Entry 48

Root, Shelton L., Jr. 1923-1986
  Obituary *51*
Roote, Mike
  See Fleischer, Leonore
Roper, Laura Wood 1911- *34*
Roscoe, D(onald) T(homas)
  1934- *42*
Rose, Anna Perrot
  See Wright, Anna (Maria Louisa
    Perrot) Rose
Rose, Anne *8*
Rose, Carl 1903-1971
  Brief Entry *31*
Rose, Elizabeth Jane (Pretty) 1933-
  Brief Entry *28*
Rose, Florella
  See Carlson, Vada F.
Rose, Gerald (Hembdon Seymour)
  1935-
  Brief Entry *30*
Rose, Nancy A.
  See Sweetland, Nancy A(nn)
Rose, Wendy 1948- *12*
Rosen, Michael (Wayne)
  1946- *48*
  Brief Entry *40*
Rosen, Sidney 1916- *1*
Rosen, Winifred 1943- *8*
Rosenbaum, Maurice 1907- *6*
Rosenberg, Dorothy 1906- *40*
Rosenberg, Ethel *3*
Rosenberg, Maxine B(erta) 1939-
  Brief Entry *47*
Rosenberg, Nancy Sherman
  1931- *4*
Rosenberg, Sharon 1942- *8*
Rosenblatt, Arthur S. 1938-
  Brief Entry *45*
Rosenbloom, Joseph 1928- *21*
Rosenblum, Richard 1928- *11*
Rosenburg, John M. 1918- *6*
Rosenthal, Harold 1914- *35*
Ross, Alan
  See Warwick, Alan R(oss)
Ross, Alex(ander) 1909-
  Brief Entry *29*
Ross, Clare (Romano) 1922- *48*
Ross, Dave 1949- *32*
Ross, David 1896-1975 .... *49*
  Obituary *20*
Ross, Diana
  See Denney, Diana
Ross, Frank (Xavier), Jr.
  1914- *28*
Ross, John 1921- *45*
Ross, Pat 1943-
  Brief Entry *48*
Ross, Tony 1938- *17*
Ross, Wilda 1915- *51*
  Brief Entry *39*
Rossel, Seymour 1945- *28*
Rössel-Waugh, C. C. [Joint
    pseudonym]
  See Waugh, Carol-Lynn Rössel
Rossetti, Christiana (Georgina)
  1830-1894 .... *20*
Roth, Arnold 1929- *21*
Roth, Arthur J(oseph) 1925- *43*
  Brief Entry *28*

Roth, David 1940- *36*
Roth, Harold
  Brief Entry *49*
Rothkopf, Carol Z. 1929- *4*
Rothman, Joel 1938- *7*
Roueché, Berton 1911- *28*
Roughsey, Dick 1921(?)- *35*
Rounds, Glen (Harold) 1906- *8*
Rourke, Constance (Mayfield)
  1885-1941 .... *YABC 1*
Rowe, Viola Carson 1903-1969
  Obituary *26*
Rowland, Florence Wightman
  1900- *8*
Rowland-Entwistle, (Arthur) Theodore
  (Henry) 1925- *31*
Rowsome, Frank (Howard), Jr.
  1914-1983 .... *36*
Roy, Jessie Hailstalk 1895-1986
  Obituary *51*
Roy, Liam
  See Scarry, Patricia
Roy, Ron(ald) 1940- *40*
  Brief Entry *35*
Rubel, Nicole 1953- *18*
Rubin, Eva Johanna 1925- *38*
Rubinstein, Robert E(dward)
  1943- *49*
Ruby, Lois 1942- *35*
  Brief Entry *34*
Ruchlis, Hy 1913- *3*
Ruckman, Ivy 1931- *37*
Ruck-Pauquèt, Gina 1931- *40*
  Brief Entry *37*
Rudeen, Kenneth
  Brief Entry *36*
Rudley, Stephen 1946- *30*
Rudolph, Marguerita 1908- *21*
Rudomin, Esther
  See Hautzig, Esther
Rue, Leonard Lee III 1926- *37*
Ruedi, Norma Paul
  See Ainsworth, Norma
Ruffell, Ann 1941- *30*
Ruffins, Reynold 1930- *41*
Rugoff, Milton 1913- *30*
Ruhen, Olaf 1911- *17*
Rukeyser, Muriel 1913-1980
  Obituary *22*
Rumsey, Marian (Barritt)
  1928- *16*
Runyan, John
  See Palmer, Bernard
Rush, Alison 1951- *41*
Rush, Peter 1937- *32*
Rushmore, Helen 1898- *3*
Rushmore, Robert (William)
  1926-1986 .... *8*
  Obituary *49*
Ruskin, Ariane
  See Batterberry, Ariane Ruskin
Ruskin, John 1819-1900 .... *24*
Russell, Charlotte
  See Rathjen, Carl H(enry)
Russell, Don(ald Bert) 1899-1986
  Obituary *47*
Russell, Franklin 1926- *11*
Russell, Helen Ross 1915- *8*

Russell, Patrick
  See Sammis, John
Russell, Solveig Paulson
  1904- *3*
Russo, Susan 1947- *30*
Rutgers van der Loeff, An(na) Basenau
  1910- *22*
Ruth, Rod 1912- *9*
Rutherford, Douglas
  See McConnell, James Douglas
    (Rutherford)
Rutherford, Meg 1932- *34*
Ruthin, Margaret *4*
Rutz, Viola Larkin 1932- *12*
Ruzicka, Rudolph 1883-1978
  Obituary *24*
Ryan, Betsy
  See Ryan, Elizabeth (Anne)
Ryan, Cheli Durán *20*
Ryan, Elizabeth (Anne) 1943- *30*
Ryan, John (Gerald Christopher)
  1921- *22*
Ryan, Peter (Charles) 1939- *15*
Rydberg, Ernest E(mil) 1901- *21*
Rydberg, Lou(isa Hampton)
  1908- *27*
Rydell, Wendell
  See Rydell, Wendy
Rydell, Wendy *4*
Ryden, Hope *8*
Ryder, Joanne
  Brief Entry *34*
Rye, Anthony
  See Youd, (Christopher) Samuel
Rylant, Cynthia 1954- *50*
  Brief Entry *44*
Rymer, Alta May 1925- *34*

S

Saal, Jocelyn
  See Sachs, Judith
Saberhagen, Fred (Thomas)
  1930- *37*
Sabin, Edwin Legrand
  1870-1952 .... *YABC 2*
Sabin, Francene *27*
Sabin, Louis 1930- *27*
Sabre, Dirk
  See Laffin, John (Alfred Charles)
Sabuso
  See Phillips, Irving W.
Sachar, Louis 1954-
  Brief Entry *50*
Sachs, Elizabeth-Ann 1946- *48*
Sachs, Judith 1947-
  Brief Entry *51*
Sachs, Marilyn 1927- *3*
  See also CLR 2
  See also SAAS 2
Sackett, S(amuel) J(ohn)
  1928- *12*
Sackson, Sid 1920- *16*
Saddler, Allen
  See Richards, R(onald) C(harles)
    W(illiam)

Saddler, K. Allen
  See Richards, R(onald) C(harles)
  W(illiam)
Sadie, Stanley (John) 1930- *14*
Sadler, Catherine Edwards
  Brief Entry *45*
Sadler, Mark
  See Lynds, Dennis
Sage, Juniper [Joint pseudonym]
  See Brown, Margaret Wise and
  Hurd, Edith
Sagsoorian, Paul 1923- *12*
Saida
  See LeMair, H(enriette) Willebeek
Saint, Dora Jessie 1913- *10*
St. Briavels, James
  See Wood, James Playsted
St. Clair, Byrd Hooper 1905-1976
  Obituary *28*
Saint Exupéry, Antoine de
  1900-1944 .... *20*
  See also CLR 10
St. George, Judith 1931- *13*
St. John, Nicole
  See Johnston, Norma
St. John, Philip
  See Del Rey, Lester
St. John, Wylly Folk
  1908-1985 .... *10*
  Obituary *45*
St. Meyer, Ned
  See Stratemeyer, Edward L.
St. Tamara
  See Kolba, Tamara
Saito, Michiko
  See Fujiwara, Michiko
Salassi, Otto R(ussell) 1939- *38*
Saldutti, Denise 1953- *39*
Salkey, (Felix) Andrew (Alexander)
  1928- *35*
Salmon, Annie Elizabeth
  1899- *13*
Salten, Felix
  See Salzmann, Siegmund
Salter, Cedric
  See Knight, Francis Edgar
Salvadori, Mario (George)
  1907- *40*
Salzer, L. E.
  See Wilson, Lionel
Salzman, Yuri
  Brief Entry *42*
Salzmann, Siegmund
  1869-1945 .... *25*
Samachson, Dorothy 1914- *3*
Samachson, Joseph 1906- *3*
Sammis, John 1942- *4*
Sampson, Fay (Elizabeth)
  1935- *42*
  Brief Entry *40*
Samson, Anne S(tringer)
  1933- *2*
Samson, Joan 1937-1976 .... *13*
Samuels, Charles 1902- *12*
Samuels, Gertrude *17*
Sanborn, Duane 1914- *38*
Sancha, Sheila 1924- *38*
Sanchez, Sonia 1934- *22*

Sánchez-Silva, José María
  1911- *16*
  See also CLR 12
Sand, George X. *45*
Sandak, Cass R(obert) 1950- *51*
  Brief Entry *37*
Sandberg, (Karin) Inger 1930- *15*
Sandberg, Karl C. 1931- *35*
Sandberg, Lasse (E. M.)
  1924- *15*
Sandburg, Carl (August)
  1878-1967 .... *8*
Sandburg, Charles A.
  See Sandburg, Carl (August)
Sandburg, Helga 1918- *3*
Sanderlin, George 1915- *4*
Sanderlin, Owenita (Harrah)
  1916- *11*
Sanders, Winston P.
  See Anderson, Poul (William)
Sanderson, Ivan T. 1911-1973 .... *6*
Sanderson, Ruth (L.) 1951- *41*
Sandin, Joan 1942- *12*
Sandison, Janet
  See Cameron, Elizabeth Jane
Sandoz, Mari (Susette)
  1901-1966 .... *5*
Sanger, Marjory Bartlett
  1920- *8*
Sankey, Alice (Ann-Susan)
  1910- *27*
San Souci, Robert D. 1946- *40*
Santesson, Hans Stefan 1914(?)-1975
  Obituary *30*
Sapieyevski, Anne Lindbergh
  1940- *35*
Sarac, Roger
  See Caras, Roger A(ndrew)
Sarasin, Jennifer
  See Sachs, Judith
Sarg, Anthony Fredrick
  See Sarg, Tony
Sarg, Tony 1880-1942 .... *YABC 1*
Sargent, Pamela *29*
Sargent, Robert 1933- *2*
Sargent, Sarah 1937- *44*
  Brief Entry *41*
Sargent, Shirley 1927- *11*
Sari
  See Fleur, Anne
Sarnoff, Jane 1937- *10*
Saroyan, William 1908-1981 ...... *23*
  Obituary *24*
Sarton, Eleanore Marie
  See Sarton, (Eleanor) May
Sarton, (Eleanor) May 1912- *36*
Sasek, Miroslav 1916-1980 .... *16*
  Obituary *23*
  See also CLR 4
Satchwell, John
  Brief Entry *49*
Sattler, Helen Roney 1921- *4*
Sauer, Julia (Lina) 1891-1983 ..... *32*
  Obituary *36*
Saul, (E.) Wendy 1946- *42*
Saunders, Caleb
  See Heinlein, Robert A(nson)
Saunders, Keith 1910- *12*

Saunders, Rubie (Agnes)
  1929- *21*
Saunders, Susan 1945- *46*
  Brief Entry *41*
Savage, Blake
  See Goodwin, Harold Leland
Savery, Constance (Winifred)
  1897- *1*
Saville, (Leonard) Malcolm
  1901-1982 .... *23*
  Obituary *31*
Saviozzi, Adriana
  See Mazza, Adriana
Savitt, Sam *8*
Savitz, Harriet May 1933- *5*
Sawyer, Ruth 1880-1970 .... *17*
Saxon, Antonia
  See Sachs, Judith
Say, Allen 1937- *28*
Sayers, Frances Clarke 1897- *3*
Sazer, Nina 1949- *13*
Scabrini, Janet 1953- *13*
Scagnetti, Jack 1924- *7*
Scanlon, Marion Stephany *11*
Scarf, Maggi
  See Scarf, Maggie
Scarf, Maggie 1932- *5*
Scarlett, Susan
  See Streatfeild, (Mary) Noel
Scarry, Huck
  See Scarry, Richard, Jr.
Scarry, Patricia (Murphy)
  1924- *2*
Scarry, Patsy
  See Scarry, Patricia
Scarry, Richard (McClure)
  1919- *35*
  Earlier sketch in SATA 2
  See also CLR 3
Scarry, Richard, Jr. 1953- *35*
Schachtel, Roger (Bernard)
  1949- *38*
Schaefer, Jack 1907- *3*
Schaeffer, Mead 1898- *21*
Schaller, George B(eals)
  1933- *30*
Schatell, Brian
  Brief Entry *47*
Schatzki, Walter 1899-
  Brief Entry *31*
Schechter, Betty (Goodstein)
  1921- *5*
Scheer, Julian (Weisel) 1926- *8*
Scheffer, Victor B. 1906- *6*
Scheier, Michael 1943- *40*
  Brief Entry *36*
Schell, Mildred 1922- *41*
Schell, Orville H. 1940- *10*
Schellie, Don 1932- *29*
Schemm, Mildred Walker
  1905- *21*
Scher, Paula 1948- *47*
Scherf, Margaret 1908- *10*
Schermer, Judith (Denise)
  1941- *30*
Schertle, Alice 1941- *36*
Schick, Alice 1946- *27*
Schick, Eleanor 1942- *9*

Schick, Joel 1945- *31*
  Brief Entry *30*
Schiff, Ken 1942- *7*
Schiller, Andrew 1919- *21*
Schiller, Barbara (Heyman)
  1928- *21*
Schiller, Justin G. 1943-
  Brief Entry *31*
Schindelman, Joseph 1923-
  Brief Entry *32*
Schindler, S(tephen) D.
  Brief Entry *50*
Schisgall, Oscar 1901-1984 .... *12*
  Obituary *38*
Schlee, Ann 1934- *44*
  Brief Entry *36*
Schlein, Miriam 1926- *2*
Schloat, G. Warren, Jr. 1914- *4*
Schmid, Eleonore 1939- *12*
Schmiderer, Dorothy 1940- *19*
Schmidt, Elizabeth 1915- *15*
Schmidt, James Norman
  1912- *21*
Schneider, Herman 1905- *7*
Schneider, Laurie
  See Adams, Laurie
Schneider, Nina 1913- *2*
Schneider, Rex 1937- *44*
Schnirel, James R(einhold)
  1931- *14*
Schock, Pauline 1928- *45*
Schoen, Barbara 1924- *13*
Schoenherr, John (Carl) 1935- *37*
Scholastica, Sister Mary
  See Jenkins, Marie M.
Scholefield, Edmund O.
  See Butterworth, W. E.
Scholey, Arthur 1932- *28*
Scholz, Jackson (Volney) 1897-1986
  Obituary *49*
Schone, Virginia *22*
Schongut, Emanuel
  Brief Entry *36*
Schoonover, Frank (Earle)
  1877-1972 .... *24*
Schoor, Gene 1921- *3*
Schraff, Anne E(laine) 1939- *27*
Schrank, Joseph 1900-1984
  Obituary *38*
Schreiber, Elizabeth Anne (Ferguson)
  1947- *13*
Schreiber, Georges 1904-1977
  Brief Entry *29*
Schreiber, Ralph W(alter)
  1942- *13*
Schroeder, Ted 1931(?)-1973
  Obituary *20*
Schulman, Janet 1933- *22*
Schulman, L(ester) M(artin)
  1934- *13*
Schulte, Elaine L(ouise) 1934- *36*
Schultz, Gwendolyn *21*
Schultz, James Willard
  1859-1947 .... *YABC 1*
Schultz, Pearle Henriksen
  1918- *21*
Schulz, Charles M(onroe)
  1922- *10*

Schur, Maxine 1948-
  Brief Entry *49*
Schurfranz, Vivian 1925- *13*
Schutzer, A. I. 1922- *13*
Schuyler, Pamela R(icka)
  1948- *30*
Schwark, Mary Beth 1954- *51*
Schwartz, Alvin 1927- *4*
  See also CLR 3
Schwartz, Amy 1954- *47*
  Brief Entry *41*
Schwartz, Ann Powers 1913- *10*
Schwartz, Charles W(alsh)
  1914- *8*
Schwartz, Daniel (Bennet) 1929-
  Brief Entry *29*
Schwartz, Elizabeth Reeder
  1912- *8*
Schwartz, Joel L. 1940-
  Brief Entry *51*
Schwartz, Julius 1907- *45*
Schwartz, Sheila (Ruth) 1929- *27*
Schwartz, Stephen (Lawrence)
  1948- *19*
Schweitzer, Iris
  Brief Entry *36*
Schweninger, Ann 1951- *29*
Scoggin, Margaret C.
  1905-1968 .... *47*
  Brief Entry *28*
Scoppettone, Sandra 1936- *9*
Scott, Ann Herbert 1926-
  Brief Entry *29*
Scott, Bill 1902(?)-1985
  Obituary *46*
Scott, Cora Annett (Pipitone)
  1931- *11*
Scott, Dan [House pseudonym]
  See Barker, S. Omar; Stratemeyer,
  Edward L.
Scott, Elaine 1940- *36*
Scott, Jack Denton 1915- *31*
Scott, John 1912-1976 .... *14*
Scott, John Anthony 1916- *23*
Scott, John M(artin) 1913- *12*
Scott, Sally (Elisabeth) 1948- *44*
Scott, Sally Fisher 1909-1978 ..... *43*
Scott, Tony
  See Scott, John Anthony
Scott, Sir Walter
  1771-1832 .... *YABC 2*
Scott, Warwick
  See Trevor, Elleston
Scribner, Charles, Jr. 1921- *13*
Scribner, Joanne L. 1949- *33*
Scrimsher, Lila Gravatt 1897-1974
  Obituary *28*
Scuro, Vincent 1951- *21*
Seabrooke, Brenda 1941- *30*
Seaman, Augusta Huiell
  1879-1950 .... *31*
Seamands, Ruth (Childers)
  1916- *9*
Searcy, Margaret Zehmer 1926-
  Brief Entry *39*
Searight, Mary W(illiams)
  1918- *17*
Searle, Kathryn Adrienne
  1942- *10*

Searle, Ronald (William Fordham)
  1920- *42*
Sears, Stephen W. 1932- *4*
Sebastian, Lee
  See Silverberg, Robert
Sebestyen, Igen
  See Sebestyen, Ouida
Sebestyen, Ouida 1924- *39*
Sechrist, Elizabeth Hough
  1903- *2*
Sedges, John
  See Buck, Pearl S.
Seed, Jenny 1930- *8*
Seed, Sheila Turner 1937(?)-1979
  Obituary *23*
Seeger, Elizabeth 1889-1973
  Obituary *20*
Seeger, Pete(r) 1919- *13*
Seever, R.
  See Reeves, Lawrence F.
Sefton, Catherine
  See Waddell, Martin
Segal, Joyce 1940- *35*
Segal, Lore 1928- *4*
Seidelman, James Edward
  1926- *6*
Seiden, Art(hur)
  Brief Entry *42*
Seidler, Tor 1952-
  Brief Entry *46*
Seidman, Laurence (Ivan)
  1925- *15*
Seigel, Kalman 1917- *12*
Seignobosc, Francoise
  1897-1961 .... *21*
Seitz, Jacqueline 1931- *50*
Seixas, Judith S. 1922- *17*
Sejima, Yoshimasa 1913- *8*
Selden, George
  See Thompson, George Selden
  See also CLR 8
Self, Margaret Cabell 1902- *24*
Selig, Sylvie 1942- *13*
Selkirk, Jane [Joint pseudonym]
  See Chapman, John Stanton
  Higham
Sellers, Naomi John
  See Flack, Naomi John (White)
Selsam, Millicent E(llis)
  1912- *29*
  Earlier sketch in SATA 1
  See also CLR 1
Seltzer, Meyer 1932- *17*
Seltzer, Richard (Warren, Jr.)
  1946- *41*
Sendak, Jack *28*
Sendak, Maurice (Bernard)
  1928- *27*
  Earlier sketch in SATA 1
  See also CLR 1
Sengler, Johanna 1924- *18*
Senn, Steve 1950-
  Brief Entry *48*
Serage, Nancy 1924- *10*
Seredy, Kate 1899-1975 .... *1*
  Obituary *24*
  See also CLR 10

Seroff, Victor I(lyitch)
1902-1979 .... *12*
Obituary *26*
Serraillier, Ian (Lucien) 1912- *1*
See also CLR 2
See also SAAS 3
Servello, Joe 1932- *10*
Service, Robert W(illiam)
1874(?)-1958 .... *20*
Serwadda, William Moses
1931- *27*
Serwer, Blanche L. 1910- *10*
Seth, Marie
See Lexau, Joan M.
Seton, Anya *3*
Seton, Ernest Thompson
1860-1946 .... *18*
Seuling, Barbara 1937- *10*
Seuss, Dr.
See Geisel, Theodor Seuss
See also CLR 9
Severn, Bill
See Severn, William Irving
Severn, David
See Unwin, David S(torr)
Severn, William Irving 1914- *1*
Sewall, Marcia 1935- *37*
Seward, Prudence 1926- *16*
Sewell, Anna 1820-1878 .... *24*
Sewell, Helen (Moore)
1896-1957 .... *38*
Sexton, Anne (Harvey)
1928-1974 .... *10*
Seymour, Alta Halverson *10*
Shachtman, Tom 1942- *49*
Shackleton, C. C.
See Aldiss, Brian W(ilson)
Shafer, Robert E(ugene)
1925- *9*
Shahn, Ben(jamin) 1898-1969
Obituary *21*
Shahn, Bernarda Bryson
See Bryson, Bernarda
Shane, Harold Gray 1914- *36*
Shanks, Ann Zane (Kushner) *10*
Shannon, George (William Bones)
1952- *35*
Shannon, Monica (?)-1965 .... *28*
Shannon, Terry *21*
Shapiro, Irwin 1911-1981 .... *32*
Shapiro, Milton J. 1926- *32*
Shapp, Martha 1910- *3*
Sharfman, Amalie *14*
Sharma, Partap 1939- *15*
Sharmat, Marjorie Weinman
1928- *33*
Earlier sketch in SATA 4
Sharmat, Mitchell 1927- *33*
Sharp, Margery 1905- *29*
Earlier sketch in SATA 1
Sharp, Zerna A. 1889-1981
Obituary *27*
Sharpe, Mitchell R(aymond)
1924- *12*
Shaw, Arnold 1909- *4*
Shaw, Charles (Green)
1892-1974 .... *13*
Shaw, Evelyn 1927- *28*

Shaw, Flora Louisa
See Lugard, Flora Louisa Shaw
Shaw, Ray *7*
Shaw, Richard 1923- *12*
Shay, Arthur 1922- *4*
Shay, Lacey
See Shebar, Sharon Sigmond
Shea, George 1940-
Brief Entry *42*
Shearer, John 1947- *43*
Brief Entry *27*
Shearer, Ted 1919- *43*
Shebar, Sharon Sigmond
1945- *36*
Shecter, Ben 1935- *16*
Sheedy, Alexandra (Elizabeth)
1962- *39*
Earlier sketch in SATA 19
Sheedy, Ally
See Sheedy, Alexandra (Elizabeth)
Sheehan, Ethna 1908- *9*
Sheffer, H. R.
See Abels, Harriette S(heffer)
Sheffield, Janet N. 1926- *26*
Shefts, Joelle
Brief Entry *49*
Shekerjian, Regina Tor *16*
Sheldon, Ann [Collective
pseudonym] *1*
Sheldon, Aure 1917-1976 .... *12*
Sheldon, Muriel 1926- *45*
Brief Entry *39*
Shelley, Mary Wollstonecraft
(Godwin) 1797-1851 .... *29*
Shelton, William Roy 1919- *5*
Shemin, Margaretha 1928- *4*
Shenton, Edward 1895-1977 ...... *45*
Shepard, Ernest Howard
1879-1976 .... *33*
Obituary *24*
Earlier sketch in SATA 3
Shepard, Mary
See Knox, (Mary) Eleanor Jessie
Shephard, Esther 1891-1975 ...... *5*
Obituary *26*
Shepherd, Elizabeth *4*
Sherburne, Zoa 1912- *3*
Sherman, D(enis) R(onald)
1934- *48*
Brief Entry *29*
Sherman, Diane (Finn) 1928- *12*
Sherman, Elizabeth
See Friskey, Margaret Richards
Sherman, Harold (Morrow)
1898- *37*
Sherman, Nancy
See Rosenberg, Nancy Sherman
Sherrod, Jane
See Singer, Jane Sherrod
Sherry, (Dulcie) Sylvia 1932- *8*
Sherwan, Earl 1917- *3*
Shiefman, Vicky *22*
Shields, Brenda Desmond (Armstrong)
1914- *37*
Shields, Charles 1944- *10*
Shimin, Symeon 1902- *13*
Shinn, Everett 1876-1953 .... *21*

Shippen, Katherine B(inney)
1892-1980 .... *1*
Obituary *23*
Shipton, Eric 1907- *10*
Shirer, William L(awrence)
1904- *45*
Shirreffs, Gordon D(onald)
1914- *11*
Sholokhov, Mikhail A. 1905-1984
Obituary *36*
Shore, June Lewis *30*
Shore, Robert 1924- *39*
Shortall, Leonard W. *19*
Shotwell, Louisa R. 1902- *3*
Showalter, Jean B(reckinridge) *12*
Showell, Ellen Harvey 1934- *33*
Showers, Paul C. 1910- *21*
See also CLR 6
Shreve, Susan Richards 1939- *46*
Brief Entry *41*
Shtainmets, Leon *32*
Shub, Elizabeth *5*
Shulevitz, Uri 1935- *50*
Earlier sketch in SATA 3
See also CLR 5
Shulman, Alix Kates 1932- *7*
Shulman, Irving 1913- *13*
Shumsky, Zena
See Collier, Zena
Shura, Mary Francis
See Craig, Mary Francis
Shuttlesworth, Dorothy *3*
Shyer, Marlene Fanta *13*
Siberell, Anne *29*
Sibley, Don 1922- *12*
Siculan, Daniel 1922- *12*
Sidjakov, Nicolas 1924- *18*
Sidney, Frank [Joint pseudonym]
See Warwick, Alan R(oss)
Sidney, Margaret
See Lothrop, Harriet Mulford Stone
Siebel, Fritz (Frederick) 1913-
Brief Entry *44*
Siegal, Aranka 1930-
Brief Entry *37*
Siegel, Beatrice *36*
Siegel, Helen
See Siegl, Helen
Siegel, Robert (Harold) 1939- *39*
Siegl, Helen 1924- *34*
Silas
See McCay, Winsor
Silcock, Sara Lesley 1947- *12*
Silver, Ruth
See Chew, Ruth
Silverberg, Robert *13*
Silverman, Mel(vin Frank)
1931-1966 .... *9*
Silverstein, Alvin 1933- *8*
Silverstein, Shel(by) 1932- *33*
Brief Entry *27*
See also CLR 5
Silverstein, Virginia B(arbara
Opshelor) 1937- *8*
Silverthorne, Elizabeth 1930- *35*
Simon, Charlie May
See Fletcher, Charlie May
Simon, Hilda (Rita) 1921- *28*

Simon, Howard 1903-1979 .... *32*
  Obituary *21*
Simon, Joe
  See Simon, Joseph H.
Simon, Joseph H. 1913- *7*
Simon, Martin P(aul William)
  1903-1969 .... *12*
Simon, Mina Lewiton
  See Lewiton, Mina
Simon, Norma 1927- *3*
Simon, Seymour 1931- *4*
  See also CLR 9
Simon, Shirley (Schwartz)
  1921- *11*
Simon, Solomon 1895-1970 .... *40*
Simonetta, Linda 1948- *14*
Simonetta, Sam 1936- *14*
Simons, Barbara B(rooks)
  1934- *41*
Simont, Marc 1915- *9*
Simpson, Colin 1908- *14*
Simpson, Harriette
  See Arnow, Harriette (Louisa)
  Simpson
Simpson, Myrtle L(illias)
  1931- *14*
Sinclair, Clover
  See Gater, Dilys
Sinclair, Emil
  See Hesse, Hermann
Sinclair, Upton (Beall)
  1878-1968 .... *9*
Singer, Isaac Bashevis 1904- *27*
  Earlier sketch in SATA 3
  See also CLR 1
Singer, Jane Sherrod
  1917-1985 .... *4*
  Obituary *42*
Singer, Julia 1917- *28*
Singer, Kurt D(eutsch) 1911- *38*
Singer, Marilyn 1948- *48*
  Brief Entry *38*
Singer, Susan (Mahler) 1941- *9*
Sirof, Harriet 1930- *37*
Sisson, Rosemary Anne 1923- *11*
Sitomer, Harry 1903- *31*
Sitomer, Mindel 1903- *31*
Sive, Helen R. 1951- *30*
Sivulich, Sandra (Jeanne) Stroner
  1941- *9*
Skelly, James R(ichard) 1927- *17*
Skinner, Constance Lindsay
  1882-1939 ....*YABC 1*
Skinner, Cornelia Otis 1901- *2*
Skipper, G. C. 1939- *46*
  Brief Entry *38*
Skofield, James
  Brief Entry *44*
Skold, Betty Westrom 1923- *41*
Skorpen, Liesel Moak 1935- *3*
Skurzynski, Gloria (Joan)
  1930- *8*
Slackman, Charles B. 1934- *12*
Slade, Richard 1910-1971 .... *9*
Slate, Joseph (Frank) 1928- *38*
Slater, Jim 1929-
  Brief Entry *34*
Slaughter, Jean
  See Doty, Jean Slaughter

Sleator, William 1945- *3*
Sleigh, Barbara 1906-1982 .... *3*
  Obituary *30*
Slepian, Jan(ice B.) 1921- *51*
  Brief Entry *45*
Slicer, Margaret O. 1920- *4*
Sloane, Eric 1910(?)-1985
  Obituary *42*
Slobodkin, Florence (Gersh)
  1905- *5*
Slobodkin, Louis 1903-1975 ...... *26*
  Earlier sketch in SATA 1
Slobodkina, Esphyr 1909- *1*
Sloggett, Nellie 1851-1923 .... *44*
Slote, Alfred 1926- *8*
  See also CLR 4
Small, David 1945- *50*
  Brief Entry *46*
Small, Ernest
  See Lent, Blair
Smallwood, Norah (Evelyn)
  1910(?)-1984
  Obituary *41*
Smaridge, Norah 1903- *6*
Smiley, Virginia Kester 1923- *2*
Smith, Anne Warren 1938- *41*
  Brief Entry *34*
Smith, Beatrice S(chillinger) *12*
Smith, Betsy Covington 1937-
  Brief Entry *43*
Smith, Betty 1896-1972 .... *6*
Smith, Bradford 1909-1964 .... *5*
Smith, Caesar
  See Trevor, Elleston
Smith, Datus C(lifford), Jr.
  1907- *13*
Smith, Dodie *4*
Smith, Doris Buchanan 1934- *28*
Smith, Dorothy Stafford
  1905- *6*
Smith, E(lmer) Boyd
  1860-1943 ....*YABC 1*
Smith, E(dric) Brooks 1917- *40*
Smith, Elva S(ophronia) 1871-1965
  Brief Entry *31*
Smith, Emma 1923-
  Brief Entry *36*
Smith, Eunice Young 1902- *5*
Smith, Frances C. 1904- *3*
Smith, Fredrika Shumway 1877-1968
  Brief Entry *30*
Smith, Gary R(ichard) 1932- *14*
Smith, George Harmon 1920- *5*
Smith, H(arry) Allen 1907-1976
  Obituary *20*
Smith, Howard Everett, Jr.
  1927- *12*
Smith, Hugh L(etcher)
  1921-1968 .... *5*
Smith, Imogene Henderson
  1922- *12*
Smith, Jacqueline B. 1937- *39*
Smith, Jean
  See Smith, Frances C.
Smith, Jean Pajot 1945- *10*
Smith, Jessie Willcox
  1863-1935 .... *21*
Smith, Jim 1920-
  Brief Entry *36*

Smith, Joan 1933-
  Brief Entry *46*
Smith, Johnston
  See Crane, Stephen (Townley)
Smith, Lafayette
  See Higdon, Hal
Smith, Lee
  See Albion, Lee Smith
Smith, Lillian H(elena) 1887-1983
  Obituary *32*
Smith, Linell Nash 1932- *2*
Smith, Lucia B. 1943- *30*
Smith, Marion Hagens 1913- *12*
Smith, Marion Jaques 1899- *13*
Smith, Mary Ellen *10*
Smith, Mike
  See Smith, Mary Ellen
Smith, Nancy Covert 1935- *12*
Smith, Norman F. 1920- *5*
Smith, Pauline C(oggeshall)
  1908- *27*
Smith, Philip Warren 1936- *46*
Smith, Robert Kimmel 1930- *12*
Smith, Robert Paul 1915-1977
  Obituary *30*
Smith, Ruth Leslie 1902- *2*
Smith, Samantha 1972-1985
  Obituary *45*
Smith, Sarah Stafford
  See Smith, Dorothy Stafford
Smith, Susan Carlton 1923- *12*
Smith, Susan Mathias 1950- *43*
  Brief Entry *35*
Smith, Susan Vernon 1950- *48*
Smith, Vian (Crocker)
  1919-1969 .... *11*
Smith, Ward
  See Goldsmith, Howard
Smith, William A. *10*
Smith, William Jay 1918- *2*
Smith, Winsome 1935- *45*
Smith, Z. Z.
  See Westheimer, David
Smits, Teo
  See Smits, Theodore R(ichard)
Smits, Theodore R(ichard)
  1905- *45*
  Brief Entry *28*
Smucker, Barbara (Claassen)
  1915- *29*
  See also CLR 10
Snedeker, Caroline Dale (Parke)
  1871-1956 ....*YABC 2*
Snell, Nigel (Edward Creagh) 1936-
  Brief Entry *40*
Sneve, Virginia Driving Hawk
  1933- *8*
  See also CLR 2
Sniff, Mr.
  See Abisch, Roslyn Kroop
Snodgrass, Thomas Jefferson
  See Clemens, Samuel Langhorne
Snook, Barbara (Lillian)
  1913-1976 .... *34*
Snow, Donald Clifford 1917- *16*
Snow, Dorothea J(ohnston)
  1909- *9*
Snow, Richard F(olger) 1947-
  Brief Entry *37*

Snyder, Anne 1922- *4*
Snyder, Carol 1941- *35*
Snyder, Gerald S(eymour)
1933- *48*
Brief Entry *34*
Snyder, Jerome 1916-1976
Obituary *20*
Snyder, Zilpha Keatley 1927- *28*
Earlier sketch in SATA 1
See also SAAS 2
Snyderman, Reuven K. 1922- *5*
Soble, Jennie
See Cavin, Ruth (Brodie)
Sobol, Donald J. 1924- *31*
Earlier sketch in SATA 1
See also CLR 4
Sobol, Harriet Langsam 1936- *47*
Brief Entry *34*
Soderlind, Arthur E(dwin)
1920- *14*
Softly, Barbara (Frewin)
1924- *12*
Soglow, Otto 1900-1975
Obituary *30*
Sohl, Frederic J(ohn) 1916- *10*
Sokol, Bill
See Sokol, William
Sokol, William 1923- *37*
Sokolov, Kirill 1930- *34*
Solbert, Romaine G. 1925- *2*
Solbert, Ronni
See Solbert, Romaine G.
Solomon, Joan 1930(?)- *51*
Brief Entry *40*
Solomons, Ikey, Esquire, Jr.
See Thackeray, William Makepeace
Solonevich, George 1915- *15*
Solot, Mary Lynn 1939- *12*
Sommer, Elyse 1929- *7*
Sommer, Robert 1929- *12*
Sommerfelt, Aimee 1892- *5*
Sonneborn, Ruth (Cantor) A.
1899-1974 .... *4*
Obituary *27*
Sorche, Nic Leodhas
See Alger, Leclaire (Gowans)
Sorel, Edward 1929-
Brief Entry *37*
Sorensen, Virginia 1912- *2*
Sorley Walker, Kathrine *41*
Sorrentino, Joseph N. *6*
Sortor, June Elizabeth 1939- *12*
Sortor, Toni
See Sortor, June Elizabeth
Soskin, V. H.
See Ellison, Virginia Howell
Sotomayor, Antonio 1902- *11*
Soudley, Henry
See Wood, James Playsted
Soule, Gardner (Bosworth)
1913- *14*
Soule, Jean Conder 1919- *10*
Southall, Ivan 1921- *3*
See also CLR 2
See also SAAS 3
Spanfeller, James J(ohn)
1930- *19*
Spangenberg, Judith Dunn
1942- *5*

Spar, Jerome 1918- *10*
Sparks, Beatrice Mathews
1918- *44*
Brief Entry *28*
Sparks, Mary W. 1920- *15*
Spaulding, Leonard
See Bradbury, Ray
Speare, Elizabeth George
1908- *5*
See also CLR 8
Spearing, Judith (Mary Harlow)
1922- *9*
Specking, Inez 1890-196(?) *11*
Speicher, Helen Ross (Smith)
1915- *8*
Spellman, John W(illard)
1934- *14*
Spelman, Mary 1934- *28*
Spence, Eleanor (Rachel)
1927- *21*
Spence, Geraldine 1931- *47*
Spencer, Ann 1918- *10*
Spencer, Cornelia
See Yaukey, Grace S.
Spencer, Donald D(ean) 1931- *41*
Spencer, Elizabeth 1921- *14*
Spencer, William 1922- *9*
Spencer, Zane A(nn) 1935- *35*
Sperry, Armstrong W.
1897-1976 .... *1*
Obituary *27*
Sperry, Raymond, Jr. [Collective
pseudonym] *1*
Spicer, Dorothy (Gladys)
(?)-1975 .... *32*
Spiegelman, Judith M. *5*
Spielberg, Steven 1947- *32*
Spier, Peter (Edward) 1927- *4*
See also CLR 5
Spilhaus, Athelstan 1911- *13*
Spilka, Arnold 1917- *6*
Spinelli, Eileen 1942- *38*
Spinelli, Jerry 1941- *39*
Spink, Reginald (William)
1905- *11*
Spinner, Stephanie 1943- *38*
Spinossimus
See White, William
Splaver, Sarah 1921-
Brief Entry *28*
Spollen, Christopher 1952- *12*
Sprague, Gretchen (Burnham)
1926- *27*
Sprigge, Elizabeth 1900-1974 ..... *10*
Spring, (Robert) Howard
1889-1965 .... *28*
Springer, Marilyn Harris
1931- *47*
Springstubb, Tricia 1950- *46*
Brief Entry *40*
Spykman, E(lizabeth) C.
19(?)-1965 .... *10*
Spyri, Johanna (Heusser)
1827-1901 .... *19*
See also CLR 13
Squire, Miriam
See Sprigge, Elizabeth
Squires, Phil
See Barker, S. Omar

S-Ringi, Kjell
See Ringi, Kjell
Srivastava, Jane Jonas
Brief Entry *37*
Stadtler, Bea 1921- *17*
Stafford, Jean 1915-1979
Obituary *22*
Stahl, Ben(jamin) 1910- *5*
Stahl, Hilda 1938- *48*
Stair, Gobin (John) 1912- *35*
Stalder, Valerie *27*
Stamaty, Mark Alan 1947- *12*
Stambler, Irwin 1924- *5*
Stanek, Muriel (Novella) 1915-
Brief Entry *34*
Stang, Judit 1921-1977 .... *29*
Stang, Judy
See Stang, Judit
Stanhope, Eric
See Hamilton, Charles H. St. John
Stankevich, Boris 1928- *2*
Stanley, Diana 1909-
Brief Entry *30*
Stanley, Diane 1943- *37*
Brief Entry *32*
Stanley, Robert
See Hamilton, Charles H. St. John
Stanli, Sue
See Meilach, Dona Z(weigoron)
Stanovich, Betty Jo 1954-
Brief Entry *51*
Stanstead, John
See Groom, Arthur William
Stapleton, Marjorie (Winifred)
1932- *28*
Stapp, Arthur D(onald)
1906-1972 .... *4*
Starbird, Kaye 1916- *6*
Stark, James
See Goldston, Robert
Starkey, Marion L. 1901- *13*
Starr, Ward and Murch, Mel [Joint
double pseudonym]
See Manes, Stephen
Starret, William
See McClintock, Marshall
Stasiak, Krystyna *49*
Stauffer, Don
See Berkebile, Fred D(onovan)
Staunton, Schuyler
See Baum, L(yman) Frank
Steadman, Ralph (Idris) 1936- *32*
Stearns, Monroe (Mather)
1913- *5*
Steele, Chester K.
See Stratemeyer, Edward L.
Steele, Mary Q(uintard Govan)
1922- *51*
Earlier sketch in SATA 3
Steele, (Henry) Max(well)
1922- *10*
Steele, William O(wen)
1917-1979 .... *51*
Obituary *27*
Earlier sketch in SATA 1
Stegeman, Janet Allais 1923-
Brief Entry *49*
Steig, William 1907- *18*
See also CLR 2

Stein, Harvé 1904-
  Brief Entry 30
Stein, M(eyer) L(ewis) 6
Stein, Mini 2
Stein, R(ichard) Conrad 1937- 31
Stein, Sara Bonnett
  Brief Entry 34
Steinbeck, John (Ernst)
  1902-1968 9
Steinberg, Alfred 1917- 9
Steinberg, Fannie 1899- 43
Steinberg, Fred J. 1933- 4
Steinberg, Phillip Orso 1921- 34
Steinberg, Rafael (Mark)
  1927- 45
Steiner, Barbara A(nnette)
  1934- 13
Steiner, Charlotte 1900-1981 45
Steiner, Jörg 1930- 35
Steiner, Stan(ley) 1925-1987 14
  Obituary 50
Steiner-Prag, Hugo 1880-1945
  Brief Entry 32
Stephens, Mary Jo 1935- 8
Stephens, William M(cLain)
  1925- 21
Stephensen, A. M.
  See Manes, Stephen
Stepp, Ann 1935- 29
Steptoe, John (Lewis) 1950- 8
  See also CLR 2, 12
Sterling, Dorothy 1913- 1
  See also CLR 1
  See also SAAS 2
Sterling, Helen
  See Hoke, Helen (L.)
Sterling, Philip 1907- 8
Stern, Ellen N(orman) 1927- 26
Stern, Madeleine B(ettina)
  1912- 14
Stern, Philip Van Doren
  1900-1984 13
  Obituary 39
Stern, Simon 1943- 15
Sterne, Emma Gelders
  1894-1971 6
Steurt, Marjorie Rankin 1888- 10
Stevens, Carla M(cBride)
  1928- 13
Stevens, Franklin 1933- 6
Stevens, Gwendolyn 1944- 33
Stevens, Kathleen 1936- 49
Stevens, Patricia Bunning
  1931- 27
Stevens, Peter
  See Geis, Darlene
Stevenson, Anna (M.) 1905- 12
Stevenson, Augusta
  1869(?)-1976 2
  Obituary 26
Stevenson, Burton E(gbert)
  1872-1962 25
Stevenson, James 1929- 42
  Brief Entry 34
Stevenson, Janet 1913- 8
Stevenson, Robert Louis
  1850-1894 ....YABC 2
  See also CLR 10, 11
Stewart, A(gnes) C(harlotte) 15

Stewart, Charles
  See Zurhorst, Charles (Stewart, Jr.)
Stewart, Elizabeth Laing
  1907- 6
Stewart, George Rippey
  1895-1980 3
  Obituary 23
Stewart, John (William) 1920- 14
Stewart, Mary (Florence Elinor)
  1916- 12
Stewart, Robert Neil
  1891-1972 7
Stewart, Scott
  See Zaffo, George J.
Stewig, John Warren 1937- 26
Stiles, Martha Bennett 6
Stiles, Norman B. 1942-
  Brief Entry 36
Still, James 1906- 29
Stillerman, Robbie 1947- 12
Stilley, Frank 1918- 29
Stine, G(eorge) Harry 1928- 10
Stine, Jovial Bob
  See Stine, Robert Lawrence
Stine, Robert Lawrence 1943- 31
Stinetorf, Louise 1900- 10
Stirling, Arthur
  See Sinclair, Upton (Beall)
Stirling, Nora B. 3
Stirnweis, Shannon 1931- 10
Stobbs, William 1914- 17
Stockton, Francis Richard
  1834-1902 44
Stockton, Frank R(ichard)
  Brief Entry 32
  See Stockton, Francis Richard
Stoddard, Edward G. 1923- 10
Stoddard, Hope 1900- 6
Stoddard, Sandol
  See Warburg, Sandol Stoddard
Stoiko, Michael 1919- 14
Stoker, Abraham 1847-1912 29
Stoker, Bram
  See Stoker, Abraham
Stokes, Cedric
  See Beardmore, George
Stokes, Jack (Tilden) 1923- 13
Stokes, Olivia Pearl 1916- 32
Stolz, Mary (Slattery) 1920- 10
  See also SAAS 3
Stone, Alan [Collective
  pseudonym] 1
  See also Svenson, Andrew E.
Stone, D(avid) K(arl) 1922- 9
Stone, Eugenia 1879-1971 7
Stone, Gene
  See Stone, Eugenia
Stone, Helen V. 6
Stone, Irving 1903- 3
Stone, Jon 1931- 39
Stone, Josephine Rector
  See Dixon, Jeanne
Stone, Raymond [Collective
  pseudonym] 1
Stone, Richard A.
  See Stratemeyer, Edward L.
Stonehouse, Bernard 1926- 13
Stong, Phil(ip Duffield)
  1899-1957 32

Storch, Anne B. von
  See von Storch, Anne B.
Storey, (Elizabeth) Margaret (Carlton)
  1926- 9
Storey, Victoria Carolyn
  1945- 16
Storme, Peter
  See Stern, Philip Van Doren
Storr, Catherine (Cole) 1913- 9
Story, Josephine
  See Loring, Emilie (Baker)
Stoutenburg, Adrien 1916- 3
Stover, Allan C(arl) 1938- 14
Stover, Marjorie Filley 1914- 9
Stowe, Harriet (Elizabeth) Beecher
  1811-1896 ....YABC 1
Strachan, Margaret Pitcairn
  1908- 14
Strait, Treva Adams 1909- 35
Strand, Mark 1934- 41
Strange, Philippa
  See Coury, Louise Andree
Stranger, Joyce
  See Wilson, Joyce M(uriel Judson)
Strasser, Todd 1950- 45
  Brief Entry 41
  See also CLR 11
Stratemeyer, Edward L.
  1862-1930 1
Stratford, Philip 1927- 47
Stratton, Thomas [Joint pseudonym]
  See DeWeese, Thomas Eugene
Stratton-Porter, Gene
  1863-1924 15
Strayer, E. Ward
  See Stratemeyer, Edward L.
Streano, Vince(nt Catello)
  1945- 20
Streatfeild, Noel 1897-1985 20
  Obituary 48
Street, Julia Montgomery
  1898- 11
Stren, Patti 1949-
  Brief Entry 41
  See also CLR 5
Strete, Craig Kee 1950- 44
Stretton, Barbara (Humphrey)
  1936- 43
  Brief Entry 35
Strong, Charles [Joint pseudonym]
  See Epstein, Beryl and Epstein,
  Samuel
Strong, David
  See McGuire, Leslie (Sarah)
Strong, J. J.
  See Strong, Jeremy
Strong, Jeremy 1949- 36
Ströyer, Poul 1923- 13
Stuart, David
  See Hoyt, Edwin P(almer), Jr.
Stuart, Forbes 1924- 13
Stuart, Ian
  See MacLean, Alistair (Stuart)
Stuart, (Hilton) Jesse
  1907-1984 2
  Obituary 36
Stuart, Sheila
  See Baker, Mary Gladys Steel

Stuart-Clark, Christopher
1940- *32*
Stubis, Talivaldis 1926- *5*
Stubley, Trevor (Hugh) 1932- *22*
Stultifer, Morton
See Curtis, Richard (Alan)
Sture-Vasa, Mary
See Alsop, Mary O'Hara
Sturton, Hugh
See Johnston, H(ugh) A(nthony)
S(tephen)
Sturtzel, Howard A(llison)
1894- *1*
Sturtzel, Jane Levington
1903- *1*
Styles, Frank Showell 1908- *10*
Suba, Susanne *4*
Subond, Valerie
See Grayland, Valerie
Sudbery, Rodie 1943- *42*
Sugarman, Tracy 1921- *37*
Sugita, Yutaka 1930- *36*
Suhl, Yuri 1908-1986 .... *8*
Obituary *50*
See also CLR 2
See also SAAS 1
Suid, Murray 1942- *27*
Sullivan, George E(dward)
1927- *4*
Sullivan, Mary W(ilson)
1907- *13*
Sullivan, Thomas Joseph, Jr.
1947- *16*
Sullivan, Tom
See Sullivan, Thomas Joseph, Jr.
Sumichrast, Jözef 1948- *29*
Sumiko
See Davies, Sumiko
Summers, James L(evingston) 1910-
Brief Entry *28*
Sunderlin, Sylvia 1911- *28*
Sung, Betty Lee *26*
Supraner, Robyn 1930- *20*
Surge, Frank 1931- *13*
Susac, Andrew 1929- *5*
Sussman, Susan 1942- *48*
Sutcliff, Rosemary 1920- *44*
Earlier sketch in SATA 6
See also CLR 1
Sutherland, Efua (Theodora Morgue)
1924- *25*
Sutherland, Margaret 1941- *15*
Sutherland, Zena B(ailey)
1915- *37*
Suttles, Shirley (Smith) 1922- *21*
Sutton, Ann (Livesay) 1923- *31*
Sutton, Eve(lyn Mary) 1906- *26*
Sutton, Felix 1910(?)- *31*
Sutton, Jane 1950-
Brief Entry *43*
Sutton, Larry M(atthew)
1931- *29*
Sutton, Margaret (Beebe)
1903- *1*
Sutton, Myron Daniel 1925- *31*
Svenson, Andrew E.
1910-1975 .... *2*
Obituary *26*

Swain, Su Zan (Noguchi)
1916- *21*
Swan, Susan 1944- *22*
Swarthout, Glendon (Fred)
1918- *26*
Swarthout, Kathryn 1919- *7*
Sweeney, James B(artholomew)
1910- *21*
Sweeney, Karen O'Connor
See O'Connor, Karen
Sweetland, Nancy A(nn)
1934- *48*
Swenson, Allan A(rmstrong)
1933- *21*
Swenson, May 1919- *15*
Swift, David
See Kaufmann, John
Swift, Hildegarde Hoyt 1890(?)-1977
Obituary *20*
Swift, Jonathan 1667-1745 .... *19*
Swift, Merlin
See Leeming, Joseph
Swiger, Elinor Porter 1927- *8*
Swinburne, Laurence 1924- *9*
Swindells, Robert E(dward)
1939- *50*
Brief Entry *34*
Switzer, Ellen 1923- *48*
Sydney, Frank [Joint pseudonym]
See Warwick, Alan R(oss)
Sylvester, Natalie G(abry)
1922- *22*
Syme, (Neville) Ronald 1913- *2*
Symons, (Dorothy) Geraldine
1909- *33*
Synge, (Phyllis) Ursula 1930- *9*
Sypher, Lucy Johnston 1907- *7*
Szasz, Suzanne Shorr 1919- *13*
Szekeres, Cyndy 1933- *5*
Szudek, Agnes S(usan) P(hilomena)
Brief Entry *49*
Szulc, Tad 1926- *26*

T

Taback, Simms 1932- *40*
Brief Entry *36*
Taber, Gladys (Bagg) 1899-1980
Obituary *22*
Tabrah, Ruth Milander 1921- *14*
Tafuri, Nancy 1946- *39*
Tait, Douglas 1944- *12*
Takakjian, Portia 1930- *15*
Takashima, Shizuye 1928- *13*
Talbot, Charlene Joy 1928- *10*
Talbot, Toby 1928- *14*
Talker, T.
See Rands, William Brighty
Tallcott, Emogene *10*
Tallon, Robert 1939- *43*
Brief Entry *28*
Talmadge, Marian *14*
Tamarin, Alfred *13*
Tamburine, Jean 1930- *12*
Tannen, Mary 1943- *37*
Tannenbaum, Beulah 1916- *3*
Tannenbaum, D(onald) Leb
1948- *42*

Tanner, Louise S(tickney)
1922- *9*
Tanobe, Miyuki 1937- *23*
Tapio, Pat Decker
See Kines, Pat Decker
Tapp, Kathy Kennedy 1949-
Brief Entry *50*
Tarkington, (Newton) Booth
1869-1946 .... *17*
Tarry, Ellen 1906- *16*
Tarshis, Jerome 1936- *9*
Tarsky, Sue 1946- *41*
Tashjian, Virginia A. 1921- *3*
Tasker, James *9*
Tate, Eleanora E(laine) 1948- *38*
Tate, Ellalice
See Hibbert, Eleanor
Tate, Joan 1922- *9*
Tate, Mary Anne
See Hale, Arlene
Tatham, Campbell
See Elting, Mary
Taves, Isabella 1915- *27*
Taylor, Ann 1782-1866 .... *41*
Brief Entry *35*
Taylor, Barbara J. 1927- *10*
Taylor, Carl 1937- *14*
Taylor, David 1900-1965 .... *10*
Taylor, Elizabeth 1912-1975 ...... *13*
Taylor, Florence Walton *9*
Taylor, Florence M(arion Tompkins)
1892- *9*
Taylor, Herb(ert Norman, Jr.)
1942- *22*
Taylor, Jane 1783-1824 .... *41*
Brief Entry *35*
Taylor, Jerry Duncan 1938- *47*
Taylor, Judy
See Hough, Judy Taylor
Taylor, Kenneth N(athaniel)
1917- *26*
Taylor, L(ester) B(arbour), Jr.
1932- *27*
Taylor, Louise Todd 1939- *47*
Taylor, Mark 1927- *32*
Brief Entry *28*
Taylor, Mildred D. *15*
See also CLR 9
See also SAAS 5
Taylor, Paula (Wright) 1942- *48*
Brief Entry *33*
Taylor, Robert Lewis 1912- *10*
Taylor, Sydney (Brenner)
1904(?)-1978 .... *28*
Obituary *26*
Earlier sketch in SATA 1
Taylor, Theodore 1924- *5*
See also SAAS 4
Teague, Bob
See Teague, Robert
Teague, Robert 1929- *32*
Brief Entry *31*
Teal, Val 1903- *10*
Teale, Edwin Way 1899-1980 ..... *7*
Obituary *25*
Teasdale, Sara 1884-1933 .... *32*
Tebbel, John (William) 1912- *26*

Tee-Van, Helen Damrosch
  1893-1976 .... *10*
  Obituary *27*
Teleki, Geza 1943- *45*
Telemaque, Eleanor Wong
  1934- *43*
Telescope, Tom
  See Newbery, John
Temkin, Sara Anne (Schlossberg)
  1913- *26*
Temko, Florence *13*
Tempest, Margaret Mary 1892-1982
  Obituary *33*
Templar, Maurice
  See Groom, Arthur William
Temple, Herbert 1919- *45*
Temple, Paul [Joint pseudonym]
  See McConnell, James Douglas
  (Rutherford)
Tenggren, Gustaf 1896-1970 ...... *18*
  Obituary *26*
Tennant, Kylie 1912- *6*
Tennant, Veronica 1946- *36*
Tenniel, Sir John 1820-1914
  Brief Entry *27*
Terban, Marvin
  Brief Entry *45*
ter Haar, Jaap 1922- *6*
Terhune, Albert Payson
  1872-1942 .... *15*
Terlouw, Jan (Cornelis) 1931- *30*
Terris, Susan 1937- *3*
Terry, Luther L(eonidas)
  1911-1985 .... *11*
  Obituary *42*
Terry, Walter 1913- *14*
Terzian, James P. 1915- *14*
Tester, Sylvia Root 1939-
  Brief Entry *37*
Tether, (Cynthia) Graham
  1950- *46*
  Brief Entry *36*
Thacher, Mary McGrath
  1933- *9*
Thackeray, William Makepeace
  1811-1863 .... *23*
Thaler, Michael C. 1936-
  Brief Entry *47*
Thaler, Mike
  See Thaler, Michael C.
Thamer, Katie 1955- *42*
Thane, Elswyth 1900- *32*
Tharp, Louise Hall 1898- *3*
Thayer, Jane
  See Woolley, Catherine
Thayer, Marjorie
  Brief Entry *37*
Thayer, Peter
  See Wyler, Rose
Thelwell, Norman 1923- *14*
Theroux, Paul 1941- *44*
Thieda, Shirley Ann 1943- *13*
Thiele, Colin (Milton) 1920- *14*
  See also SAAS 2
Thiry, Joan (Marie) 1926- *45*
Thistlethwaite, Miles 1945- *12*
Thollander, Earl 1922- *22*
Thomas, Allison
  See Fleischer, Leonore

Thomas, Andrea
  See Hill, Margaret (Ohler)
Thomas, Art(hur Lawrence)
  1952- *48*
  Brief Entry *38*
Thomas, Estelle Webb 1899- *26*
Thomas, H. C.
  See Keating, Lawrence A.
Thomas, Ianthe 1951-
  Brief Entry *42*
  See also CLR 8
Thomas, J. F.
  See Fleming, Thomas J(ames)
Thomas, Jane Resh 1936- *38*
Thomas, Joan Gale
  See Robinson, Joan G.
Thomas, Joyce Carol 1938- *40*
Thomas, Lowell (Jackson), Jr.
  1923- *15*
Thomas, Patricia J. 1934- *51*
Thomas, Victoria [Joint pseudonym]
  See DeWeese, Thomas Eugene
Thompson, Brenda 1935- *34*
Thompson, Christine Pullein
  See Pullein-Thompson, Christine
Thompson, David H(ugh)
  1941- *17*
Thompson, Diana Pullein
  See Pullein-Thompson, Diana
Thompson, Eileen
  See Panowski, Eileen Thompson
Thompson, George Selden
  1929- *4*
Thompson, Harlan H. 1894- *10*
Thompson, Hilary 1943-
  Brief Entry *49*
Thompson, Josephine
  See Pullein-Thompson, Josephine
Thompson, Julian F(rancis) 1927-
  Brief Entry *40*
Thompson, Kay 1912- *16*
Thompson, Stith 1885-1976
  Obituary *20*
Thompson, Vivian L. 1911- *3*
Thomson, David (Robert Alexander)
  1914- *40*
Thomson, Peggy 1922- *31*
Thorndyke, Helen Louise
  [Collective pseudonym] *1*
Thorne, Ian
  See May, Julian
Thornton, W. B.
  See Burgess, Thornton Waldo
Thorpe, E(ustace) G(eorge)
  1916- *21*
Thorvall, Kerstin 1925- *13*
Thrasher, Crystal (Faye)
  1921- *27*
Thum, Gladys 1920- *26*
Thum, Marcella *28*
  Earlier sketch in SATA 3
Thundercloud, Katherine
  See Witt, Shirley Hill
Thurber, James (Grover)
  1894-1961 .... *13*
Thurman, Judith 1946- *33*
Thwaite, Ann (Barbara Harrop)
  1932- *14*

Ticheburn, Cheviot
  See Ainsworth, William Harrison
Tichenor, Tom 1923- *14*
Tichy, William 1924- *31*
Tiegreen, Alan F. 1935-
  Brief Entry *36*
Tilton, Madonna Elaine 1929- *41*
Tilton, Rafael
  See Tilton, Madonna Elaine
Timmins, William F. *10*
Tiner, John Hudson 1944- *32*
Tinkelman, Murray 1933- *12*
Tinkle, (Julien) Lon
  1906-1980 .... *36*
Titler, Dale M(ilton) 1926- *35*
  Brief Entry *28*
Titmarsh, Michael Angelo
  See Thackeray, William Makepeace
Titus, Eve 1922- *2*
Tobias, Tobi 1938- *5*
  See also CLR 4
Todd, Anne Ophelia
  See Dowden, Anne Ophelia
Todd, Barbara K. 1917- *10*
Todd, H(erbert) E(atton)
  1908- *11*
Todd, Loreto 1942- *30*
Tolan, Stephanie S. 1942- *38*
Toland, John (Willard) 1912- *38*
Tolkien, J(ohn) R(onald) R(euel)
  1892-1973 .... *32*
  Obituary *24*
  Earlier sketch in SATA 2
Tolles, Martha 1921- *8*
Tolliver, Ruby C(hangos) 1922-
  Brief Entry *41*
Tolmie, Ken(neth Donald)
  1941- *15*
Tolstoi, Leo (Nikolaevich)
  1828-1910 .... *26*
Tomalin, Ruth *29*
Tomes, Margot (Ladd) 1917- *36*
  Brief Entry *27*
Tomfool
  See Farjeon, Eleanor
Tomkins, Jasper
  See Batey, Tom
Tomline, F. Latour
  See Gilbert, W(illiam) S(chwenk)
Tomlinson, Jill 1931-1976 .... *3*
  Obituary *24*
Tomlinson, Reginald R(obert)
  1885-1979(?)
  Obituary *27*
Tompert, Ann 1918- *14*
Toner, Raymond John 1908- *10*
Took, Belladonna
  See Chapman, Vera
Tooke, Louise Mathews 1950- *38*
Toonder, Martin
  See Groom, Arthur William
Toothaker, Roy Eugene 1928- *18*
Tooze, Ruth 1892-1972 .... *4*
Topping, Audrey R(onning)
  1928- *14*
Tor, Regina
  See Shekerjian, Regina Tor
Torbert, Floyd James 1922- *22*

Torgersen, Don Arthur 1934-
    Brief Entry *41*
Torrie, Malcolm
    See Mitchell, Gladys (Maude
    Winifred)
Totham, Mary
    See Breinburg, Petronella
Tournier, Michel 1924- *23*
Towne, Mary
    See Spelman, Mary
Townsend, John Rowe 1922- *4*
    See also CLR 2
    See also SAAS 2
Townsend, Sue 1946-
    Brief Entry *48*
Toye, Clive 1933(?)-
    Brief Entry *30*
Toye, William E(ldred) 1926- *8*
Traherne, Michael
    See Watkins-Pitchford, D. J.
Trahey, Jane 1923- *36*
Trapp, Maria (Augusta) von
    1905- *16*
Travers, P(amela) L(yndon)
    1906- *4*
    See also CLR 2
    See also SAAS 2
Treadgold, Mary 1910- *49*
Trease, (Robert) Geoffrey
    1909- *2*
Tredez, Alain 1926- *17*
Tredez, Denise (Laugier)
    1930- *50*
Treece, Henry 1911-1966 .... *2*
    See also CLR 2
Tregarthen, Enys
    See Sloggett, Nellie
Tregaskis, Richard 1916-1973 ..... *3*
    Obituary *26*
Trell, Max 1900- *14*
Tremain, Ruthven 1922- *17*
Trent, Robbie 1894- *26*
Trent, Timothy
    See Malmberg, Carl
Tresilian, (Cecil) Stuart
    1891-19(?) *40*
Tresselt, Alvin 1916- *7*
Treviño, Elizabeth B(orton) de
    1904- *29*
    Earlier sketch in SATA 1
    See also SAAS 5
Trevor, Elleston 1920- *28*
Trevor, Glen
    See Hilton, James
Trevor, (Lucy) Meriol 1919- *10*
Trez, Alain
    See Tredez, Alain
Trez, Denise
    See Tredez, Denise (Laugier)
Trimby, Elisa 1948- *47*
    Brief Entry *40*
Tripp, Eleanor B. 1936- *4*
Tripp, Paul *8*
Tripp, Wallace (Whitney)
    1940- *31*
Trivelpiece, Laurel 1926-
    Brief Entry *46*
Trivett, Daphne (Harwood)
    1940- *22*

Trnka, Jiri 1912-1969 .... *43*
    Brief Entry *32*
Trollope, Anthony 1815-1882 ..... *22*
Trost, Lucille Wood 1938- *12*
Trotter, Grace V(iolet) 1900- *10*
Troughton, Joanna (Margaret)
    1947- *37*
Troyer, Johannes 1902-1969
    Brief Entry *40*
Trudeau, G(arretson) B(eekman)
    1948- *35*
Trudeau, Garry B.
    See Trudeau, G(arretson) B(eekman)
Truesdell, Sue
    See Truesdell, Susan G.
Truesdell, Susan G.
    Brief Entry *45*
Truss, Jan 1925- *35*
Tucker, Caroline
    See Nolan, Jeannette
Tudor, Tasha *20*
    See also CLR 13
Tully, John (Kimberley)
    1923- *14*
Tunis, Edwin (Burdett)
    1897-1973 .... *28*
    Obituary *24*
    Earlier sketch in SATA 1
    See also CLR 2
Tunis, John R(oberts)
    1889-1975 .... *37*
    Brief Entry *30*
Turkle, Brinton 1915- *2*
Turlington, Bayly 1919- *5*
Turnbull, Agnes Sligh *14*
Turnbull, Ann (Christine)
    1943- *18*
Turner, Alice K. 1940- *10*
Turner, Ann W(arren) 1945- *14*
Turner, Elizabeth
    1774-1846 .... *YABC 2*
Turner, Josie
    See Crawford, Phyllis
Turner, Philip 1925- *11*
Turner, Sheila R.
    See Seed, Sheila Turner
Turngren, Annette 1902(?)-1980
    Obituary *23*
Turngren, Ellen (?)-1964 .... *3*
Turska, Krystyna Zofia 1933- *31*
    Brief Entry *27*
Tusan, Stan 1936- *22*
Tusiani, Joseph 1924- *45*
Twain, Mark
    See Clemens, Samuel Langhorne
Tweedsmuir, Baron
    See Buchan, John
Tweton, D. Jerome 1933- *48*
Tworkov, Jack 1900-1982 .... *47*
    Obituary *31*
Tyler, Anne 1941- *7*

U

Ubell, Earl 1926- *4*
Uchida, Yoshiko 1921- *1*
    See also CLR 6
    See also SAAS 1

Udall, Jan Beaney 1938- *10*
Uden, (Bernard Gilbert) Grant
    1910- *26*
Udry, Janice May 1928- *4*
Ulam, S(tanislaw) M(arcin)
    1909-1984 .... *51*
Ullman, James Ramsey
    1907-1971 .... *7*
Ulm, Robert 1934-1977 .... *17*
Ulyatt, Kenneth 1920- *14*
Unada
    See Gliewe, Unada
Uncle Gus
    See Rey, H. A.
Uncle Mac
    See McCulloch, Derek (Ivor
    Breashur)
Uncle Ray
    See Coffman, Ramon Peyton
Uncle Shelby
    See Silverstein, Shel(by)
Underhill, Alice Mertie 1900-1971
Underhill, Liz 1936-
    Brief Entry *49*
Ungerer, (Jean) Thomas 1931- *33*
    Earlier sketch in SATA 5
Ungerer, Tomi
    See Ungerer, (Jean) Thomas
    See also CLR 3
Unkelbach, Kurt 1913- *4*
Unnerstad, Edith 1900- *3*
Unrau, Ruth 1922- *9*
Unstead, R(obert) J(ohn)
    1915- *12*
Unsworth, Walt 1928- *4*
Untermeyer, Louis 1885-1977 ..... *37*
    Obituary *26*
    Earlier sketch in SATA 2
Unwin, David S(torr) 1918- *14*
Unwin, Nora S. 1907-1982 .... *3*
    Obituary *49*
Ure, Jean *48*
Uris, Leon (Marcus) 1924- *49*
Usher, Margo Scegge
    See McHargue, Georgess
Uttley, Alice Jane (Taylor)
    1884-1976 .... *3*
    Obituary *26*
Uttley, Alison
    See Uttley, Alice Jane (Taylor)
Utz, Lois 1932-1986 .... *5*
    Obituary *50*
Uzair, Salem ben
    See Horne, Richard Henry

V

Vaeth, J(oseph) Gordon 1921- *17*
Valen, Nanine 1950- *21*
Valencak, Hannelore 1929- *42*
Valens, Evans G., Jr. 1920- *1*
Valleau, Emily 1925- *51*
Van Abbé, Salaman
    1883-1955 .... *18*
Van Allsburg, Chris 1949- *37*
    See also CLR 5
    See also CLR 13
Van Anrooy, Francine 1924- *2*

Van Anrooy, Frans
  See Van Anrooy, Francine
Vance, Eleanor Graham 1908- *11*
Vance, Marguerite 1889-1965 ..... *29*
Vandenburg, Mary Lou 1943- *17*
Vander Boom, Mae M. *14*
Van der Veer, Judy
  1912-1982 .... *4*
  Obituary *33*
Vandivert, Rita (Andre) 1905- *21*
Van Duyn, Janet 1910- *18*
Van Dyne, Edith
  See Baum, L(yman) Frank
Van Horn, William 1939- *43*
Van Iterson, S(iny) R(ose) *26*
Van Leeuwen, Jean 1937- *6*
Van Lhin, Erik
  See Del Rey, Lester
Van Loon, Hendrik Willem
  1882-1944 .... *18*
Van Orden, M(erton) D(ick)
  1921- *4*
Van Rensselaer, Alexander (Taylor
  Mason) 1892-1962 .... *14*
Van Riper, Guernsey, Jr.
  1909- *3*
Van Steenwyk, Elizabeth Ann
  1928- *34*
Van Stockum, Hilda 1908- *5*
Van Tuyl, Barbara 1940- *11*
Van Vogt, A(lfred) E(lton)
  1912- *14*
Van Woerkom, Dorothy (O'Brien)
  1924- *21*
Van Wormer, Joe
  See Van Wormer, Joseph Edward
Van Wormer, Joseph Edward
  1913- *35*
Van-Wyck Mason, F.
  See Mason, F. van Wyck
Van Zwienen, Ilse (Charlotte Koehn)
  1929- *34*
  Brief Entry *28*
Varga, Judy
  See Stang, Judit
Varley, Dimitry V. 1906- *10*
Vasiliu, Mircea 1920- *2*
Vass, George 1927-
  Brief Entry *31*
Vaughan, Carter A.
  See Gerson, Noel B(ertram)
Vaughan, Harold Cecil 1923- *14*
Vaughan, Sam(uel) S. 1928- *14*
Vaughn, Ruth 1935- *14*
Vavra, Robert James 1944- *8*
Vecsey, George 1939- *9*
Veglahn, Nancy (Crary) 1937- *5*
Venable, Alan (Hudson)
  1944- *8*
Venn, Mary Eleanor
  See Jorgensen, Mary Venn
Ventura, Piero (Luigi) 1937-
  Brief Entry *43*
Vequin, Capini
  See Quinn, Elisabeth
Verne, Jules 1828-1905 .... *21*
Verner, Gerald 1897(?)-1980
  Obituary *25*
Verney, John 1913- *14*

Vernon, (Elda) Louise A(nderson)
  1914- *14*
Vernon, Rosemary
  See Smith, Susan Vernon
Vernor, D.
  See Casewit, Curtis
Verral, Charles Spain 1904- *11*
Verrone, Robert J. 1935(?)-1984
  Obituary *39*
Versace, Marie Teresa Rios
  1917- *2*
Vesey, Paul
  See Allen, Samuel (Washington)
Vestly, Anne-Cath(arina)
  1920- *14*
Vevers, (Henry) Gwynne
  1916- *45*
Viator, Vacuus
  See Hughes, Thomas
Vicarion, Count Palmiro
  See Logue, Christopher
Vicker, Angus
  See Felsen, Henry Gregor
Vickery, Kate
  See Kennedy, T(eresa) A.
Victor, Edward 1914- *3*
Victor, Joan Berg 1937- *30*
Viereck, Ellen K. 1928- *14*
Viereck, Phillip 1925- *3*
Viertel, Janet 1915- *10*
Vigna, Judith 1936- *15*
Viguers, Ruth Hill 1903-1971 ..... *6*
Villiard, Paul 1910-1974 .... *51*
  Obituary *20*
Villiers, Alan (John) 1903- *10*
Vincent, Eric Douglas 1953- *40*
Vincent, Félix 1946- *41*
Vincent, Gabrielle
  See CLR 13
Vincent, Mary Keith
  See St. John, Wylly Folk
Vinge, Joan D(ennison) 1948- *36*
Vining, Elizabeth Gray
  See Gray, Elizabeth Janet
Vinson, Kathryn 1911- *21*
Vinton, Iris *24*
Viorst, Judith *7*
  See also CLR 3
Vip
  See Partch, Virgil Franklin II
Visser, W(illiam) F(rederick)
  H(endrik) 1900-1968 .... *10*
Vlahos, Olivia 1924- *31*
Vlasic, Bob
  See Hirsch, Phil
Vo-Dinh, Mai 1933- *16*
Vogel, Ilse-Margret 1914- *14*
Vogel, John H(ollister), Jr.
  1950- *18*
Vogt, Esther Loewen 1915- *14*
Vogt, Gregory
  Brief Entry *45*
Vogt, Marie Bollinger 1921- *45*
Voight, Virginia Frances
  1909- *8*
Voigt, Cynthia 1942- *48*
  Brief Entry *33*
  See also CLR 13
Voigt, Erna 1925- *35*

Voigt-Rother, Erna
  See Voigt, Erna
Vojtech, Anna 1946- *42*
von Almedingen, Martha Edith
  See Almedingen, E. M.
Von Hagen, Victor Wolfgang
  1908- *29*
von Klopp, Vahrah
  See Malvern, Gladys
von Schmidt, Eric 1931- *50*
  Brief Entry *36*
von Storch, Anne B. 1910- *1*
Vosburgh, Leonard (W.)
  1912- *15*
Voyle, Mary
  See Manning, Rosemary

W

Waber, Bernard 1924- *47*
  Brief Entry *40*
Wachter, Oralee Roberts 1935-
  Brief Entry *51*
Waddell, Evelyn Margaret
  1918- *10*
Waddell, Martin 1941- *43*
Wade, Theodore E., Jr. 1936- *37*
Wagenheim, Kal 1935- *21*
Wagner, Jane *33*
Wagner, Sharon B. 1936- *4*
Wagoner, David (Russell)
  1926- *14*
Wahl, Jan 1933- *34*
  Earlier sketch in SATA 2
  See also SAAS 3
Waide, Jan 1952- *29*
Waitley, Douglas 1927- *30*
Wakefield, Jean L.
  See Laird, Jean E(louise)
Wakin, Edward 1927- *37*
Walck, Henry Z(eigler) 1908-1984
  Obituary *40*
Walden, Amelia Elizabeth *3*
Waldman, Bruce 1949- *15*
Waldman, Neil 1947- *51*
Waldron, Ann Wood 1924- *16*
Walker, Alice 1944- *31*
Walker, Barbara K. 1921- *4*
Walker, (James) Braz(elton)
  1934-1983 .... *45*
Walker, David Harry 1911- *8*
Walker, Diana 1925- *9*
Walker, Frank 1930- *36*
Walker, Holly Beth
  See Bond, Gladys Baker
Walker, Louise Jean 1891-1976
  Obituary *35*
Walker, Mildred
  See Schemm, Mildred Walker
Walker, (Addison) Mort
  1923- *8*
Walker, Pamela 1948- *24*
Walker, Stephen J. 1951- *12*
Wallace, Barbara Brooks *4*
Wallace, Beverly Dobrin
  1921- *19*
Wallace, Bill 1947-
  Brief Entry *47*

Wallace, Daisy
 See Cuyler, Margery Stuyvesant
Wallace, John A. 1915- 3
Wallace, Nigel
 See Hamilton, Charles H. St. John
Wallace, Robert 1932- 47
 Brief Entry 37
Wallace-Brodeur, Ruth 1941- 51
 Brief Entry 41
Waller, Leslie 1923- 20
Wallis, G. McDonald
 See Campbell, Hope
Wallner, Alexandra 1946- 51
 Brief Entry 41
Wallner, John C. 1945- 51
 Earlier sketch in SATA 10
Wallower, Lucille 11
Walsh, Ellen Stoll 1942- 49
Walsh, Jill Paton
 See Paton Walsh, Gillian
 See also CLR 2
Walter, Mildred Pitts
 Brief Entry 45
Walter, Villiam Christian
 See Andersen, Hans Christian
Walters, Audrey 1929- 18
Walters, Helen B. (?)-1987
 Obituary 50
Walters, Hugh
 See Hughes, Walter (Llewellyn)
Walther, Thomas A. 1950- 31
Walther, Tom
 See Walther, Thomas A.
Waltner, Elma 1912- 40
Waltner, Willard H. 1909- 40
Walton, Richard J. 1928- 4
Waltrip, Lela (Kingston)
 1904- 9
Waltrip, Mildred 1911- 37
Waltrip, Rufus (Charles)
 1898- 9
Walworth, Nancy Zinsser
 1917- 14
Wangerin, Walter, Jr. 1944- 45
 Brief Entry 37
Wannamaker, Bruce
 See Moncure, Jane Belk
Warbler, J. M.
 See Cocagnac, A. M.
Warburg, Sandol Stoddard
 1927- 14
Ward, John (Stanton) 1917- 42
Ward, Lynd (Kendall)
 1905-1985 36
 Obituary 42
 Earlier sketch in SATA 2
Ward, Martha (Eads) 1921- 5
Ward, Melanie
 See Curtis, Richard (Alan)
Wardell, Dean
 See Prince, J(ack) H(arvey)
Ware, Leon (Vernon) 1909- 4
Warner, Frank A. [Collective
 pseudonym] 1
Warner, Gertrude Chandler
 1890- 9
Warner, Lucille Schulberg 30
Warner, Oliver 1903-1976 29

Warren, Betsy
 See Warren, Elizabeth Avery
Warren, Billy
 See Warren, William Stephen
Warren, Cathy
 Brief Entry 46
Warren, Elizabeth
 See Supraner, Robyn
Warren, Elizabeth Avery
 1916- 46
 Brief Entry 38
Warren, Joyce W(illiams)
 1935- 18
Warren, Mary Phraner 1929- 10
Warren, Robert Penn 1905- 46
Warren, William Stephen
 1882-1968 9
Warrick, Patricia Scott 1925- 35
Warsh
 See Warshaw, Jerry
Warshaw, Jerry 1929- 30
Warshofsky, Fred 1931- 24
Warshofsky, Isaac
 See Singer, Isaac Bashevis
Wartski, Maureen (Ann Crane)
 1940- 50
 Brief Entry 37
Warwick, Alan R(oss)
 1900-1973 42
Wa-sha-quon-asin
 See Belaney, Archibald Stansfeld
Washburn, (Henry) Bradford (Jr.)
 1910- 38
Washburne, Heluiz Chandler
 1892-1970 10
 Obituary 26
Washington, Booker T(aliaferro)
 1858(?)-1915 28
Watanabe, Shigeo 1928- 39
 Brief Entry 32
 See also CLR 8
Waters, John F(rederick)
 1930- 4
Waterton, Betty (Marie) 1923- 37
 Brief Entry 34
Watkins-Pitchford, D. J.
 1905- 6
 See also SAAS 4
Watson, Aldren A(uld) 1917- 42
 Brief Entry 36
Watson, Clyde 1947- 5
 See also CLR 3
Watson, Helen Orr 1892-1978
 Obituary 24
Watson, James 1936- 10
Watson, Jane Werner 1915- 3
Watson, Nancy Dingman 32
Watson, Pauline 1925- 14
Watson, Sally 1924- 3
Watson, Wendy (McLeod)
 1942- 5
Watson Taylor, Elizabeth
 1915- 41
Watt, Thomas 1935- 4
Watts, Bernadette 1942- 4
Watts, Ephraim
 See Horne, Richard Henry

Watts, Franklin (Mowry)
 1904-1978 46
 Obituary 21
Watts, Mabel Pizzey 1906- 11
Waugh, Carol-Lynn Rössel
 1947- 41
Waugh, Dorothy 11
Wayland, Patrick
 See O'Connor, Richard
Wayne, (Anne) Jenifer
 1917-1982 32
Wayne, Kyra Petrovskaya
 1918- 8
Wayne, Richard
 See Decker, Duane
Waystaff, Simon
 See Swift, Jonathan
Weales, Gerald (Clifford)
 1925- 11
Weary, Ogdred
 See Gorey, Edward St. John
Weaver, John L. 1949- 42
Weaver, Ward
 See Mason, F. van Wyck
Webb, Christopher
 See Wibberley, Leonard (Patrick
 O'Connor)
Webb, Jean Francis (III)
 1910- 35
Webb, Sharon 1936- 41
Webber, Irma E(leanor Schmidt)
 1904- 14
Weber, Alfons 1921- 8
Weber, Lenora Mattingly
 1895-1971 2
 Obituary 26
Weber, William John 1927- 14
Webster, Alice (Jane Chandler)
 1876-1916 17
Webster, David 1930- 11
Webster, Frank V. [Collective
 pseudonym] 1
Webster, Gary
 See Garrison, Webb B(lack)
Webster, James 1925-1981 17
 Obituary 27
Webster, Jean
 See Webster, Alice (Jane Chandler)
Wechsler, Herman 1904-1976
 Obituary 20
Weddle, Ethel H(arshbarger)
 1897- 11
Wegen, Ron(ald)
 Brief Entry 44
Wegner, Fritz 1924- 20
Weihs, Erika 1917- 15
Weik, Mary Hays
 1898(?)-1979 3
 Obituary 23
Weil, Ann Yezner 1908-1969 9
Weil, Lisl 7
Weilerstein, Sadie Rose 1894- 3
Weinberg, Larry
 See Weinberg, Lawrence (E.)
Weinberg, Lawrence (E.)
 Brief Entry 48
Weiner, Sandra 1922- 14

Weingarten, Violet (Brown)
    1915-1976 3
    Obituary 27
Weingartner, Charles 1922- 5
Weir, LaVada 2
Weir, Rosemary (Green)
    1905- 21
Weis, Margaret (Edith) 1948- 38
Weisberger, Bernard A(llen)
    1922- 21
Weiser, Marjorie P(hillis) K(atz)
    1934- 33
Weisgard, Leonard (Joseph)
    1916- 30
    Earlier sketch in SATA 2
Weiss, Adelle 1920- 18
Weiss, Ann E(dwards) 1943- 30
Weiss, Ellen 1953- 44
Weiss, Harvey 1922- 27
    Earlier sketch in SATA 1
    See also CLR 4
Weiss, Leatie 1928-
    Brief Entry 50
Weiss, Malcolm E. 1928- 3
Weiss, Miriam
    See Schlein, Miriam
Weiss, Nicki 1954- 33
Weiss, Renee Karol 1923- 5
Weissenborn, Hellmuth 1898-1982
    Obituary 31
Welber, Robert 26
Welch, D'Alte Aldridge 1907-1970
    Obituary 27
Welch, Jean-Louise
    See Kempton, Jean Welch
Welch, Martha McKeen 1914-
    Brief Entry 45
Welch, Pauline
    See Bodenham, Hilda Esther
Welch, Ronald
    See Felton, Ronald Oliver
Weller, George (Anthony)
    1907- 31
Welles, Winifred 1893-1939
    Brief Entry 27
Wellman, Alice 1900-1984 51
    Brief Entry 36
Wellman, Manly Wade
    1903-1986 6
    Obituary 47
Wellman, Paul I. 1898-1966 3
Wells, H(erbert) G(eorge)
    1866-1946 20
Wells, Helen 1910-1986 49
    Earlier sketch in SATA 2
Wells, J. Wellington
    See DeCamp, L(yon) Sprague
Wells, Rosemary 18
    See also SAAS 1
Wels, Byron G(erald) 1924- 9
Welsh, Mary Flynn 1910(?)-1984
    Obituary 38
Weltner, Linda R(iverly)
    1938- 38
Welty, S. F.
    See Welty, Susan F.
Welty, Susan F. 1905- 9
Wendelin, Rudolph 1910- 23

Werner, Herma 1926- 47
    Brief Entry 41
Werner, Jane
    See Watson, Jane Werner
Werner, K.
    See Casewit, Curtis
Wersba, Barbara 1932- 1
    See also CLR 3
    See also SAAS 2
Werstein, Irving 1914-1971 14
Werth, Kurt 1896- 20
West, Anna 1938- 40
West, Barbara
    See Price, Olive
West, Betty 1921- 11
West, C. P.
    See Wodehouse, P(elham)
    G(renville)
West, Emily G(ovan) 1919- 38
West, Emmy
    See West, Emily G(ovan)
West, James
    See Withers, Carl A.
West, Jerry
    See Stratemeyer, Edward L.
West, Jerry
    See Svenson, Andrew E.
West, (Mary) Jessamyn 1902(?)-1984
    Obituary 37
West, Ward
    See Borland, Hal
Westall, Robert (Atkinson)
    1929- 23
    See also SAAS 2
    See also CLR 13
Westerberg, Christine 1950- 29
Westervelt, Virginia (Veeder)
    1914- 10
Westheimer, David 1917- 14
Westmacott, Mary
    See Christie, Agatha (Mary Clarissa)
Westman, Paul (Wendell)
    1956- 39
Weston, Allen [Joint pseudonym]
    See Norton, Alice Mary
Weston, John (Harrison)
    1932- 21
Westwood, Jennifer 1940- 10
Wexler, Jerome (LeRoy)
    1923- 14
Wharf, Michael
    See Weller, George (Anthony)
Wheatley, Arabelle 1921- 16
Wheeler, Captain
    See Ellis, Edward S(ylvester)
Wheeler, Cindy 1955- 49
    Brief Entry 40
Wheeler, Janet D. [Collective
    pseudonym] 1
Wheeler, Opal 1898- 23
Whelan, Elizabeth M(urphy)
    1943- 14
Whistler, Reginald John
    1905-1944 30
Whistler, Rex
    See Whistler, Reginald John
Whitcomb, Jon 1906- 10
White, Anne Hitchcock 1902-1970
    Brief Entry 33

White, Anne Terry 1896- 2
White, Bessie (Felstiner) 1892(?)-1986
    Obituary 50
White, Dale
    See Place, Marian T.
White, Dori 1919- 10
White, E(lwyn) B(rooks)
    1899-1985 29
    Obituary 44
    Earlier sketch in SATA 2
    See also CLR 1
White, Eliza Orne
    1856-1947 .... YABC 2
White, Florence M(eiman)
    1910- 14
White, Laurence B., Jr. 1935- 10
White, Martin 1943- 51
White, Ramy Allison [Collective
    pseudonym] 1
White, Robb 1909- 1
    See also CLR 3
    See also SAAS 1
White, Ruth C. 1942- 39
White, T(erence) H(anbury)
    1906-1964 12
White, William, Jr. 1934- 16
Whitehead, Don(ald) F. 1908- 4
Whitehouse, Arch
    See Whitehouse, Arthur George
Whitehouse, Arthur George
    1895-1979 14
    Obituary 23
Whitehouse, Elizabeth S(cott)
    1893-1968 35
Whitehouse, Jeanne 1939- 29
Whitinger, R. D.
    See Place, Marian T.
Whitlock, Pamela 1921(?)-1982
    Obituary 31
Whitlock, Ralph 1914- 35
Whitman, Walt(er) 1819-1892 20
Whitney, Alex(andra) 1922- 14
Whitney, David C(harles)
    1921- 48
    Brief Entry 29
Whitney, Phyllis A(yame)
    1903- 30
    Earlier sketch in SATA 1
Whitney, Thomas P(orter)
    1917- 25
Wibberley, Leonard (Patrick
    O'Connor) 1915-1983 45
    Obituary 36
    Earlier sketch in SATA 2
    See also CLR 3
Wiberg, Harald (Albin) 1908-
    Brief Entry 40
Widdemer, Mabel Cleland
    1902-1964 5
Widenberg, Siv 1931- 10
Wier, Ester 1910- 3
Wiese, Kurt 1887-1974 36
    Obituary 24
    Earlier sketch in SATA 3
Wiesner, Portia
    See Takakjian, Portia
Wiesner, William 1899- 5
Wiggin, Kate Douglas (Smith)
    1856-1923 .... YABC 1

Wight, James Alfred 1916-
  Brief Entry 44
Wikland, Ilon 1930-
  Brief Entry 32
Wilber, Donald N(ewton)
  1907- 35
Wilbur, C. Keith 1923- 27
Wilbur, Richard (Purdy)
  1921- 9
Wilcox, R(uth) Turner
  1888-1970 36
Wild, Jocelyn 1941- 46
Wild, Robin (Evans) 1936- 46
Wilde, D. Gunther
  See Hurwood, Bernhardt J.
Wilde, Oscar (Fingal O'Flahertie
  Wills) 1854-1900 24
Wilder, Cherry
  See Grimm, Cherry Barbara Lockett
Wilder, Laura Ingalls
  1867-1957 29
  See also CLR 2
Wildsmith, Brian 1930- 16
  See also CLR 2
  See also SAAS 5
Wilkie, Katharine E(lliott)
  1904-1980 31
Wilkin, Eloise (Burns) 1904- 49
Wilkins, Frances 1923- 14
Wilkins, Marilyn (Ruth)
  1926- 30
Wilkins, Marne
  See Wilkins, Marilyn (Ruth)
Wilkinson, (Thomas) Barry
  1923- 50
  Brief Entry 32
Wilkinson, Brenda 1946- 14
Wilkinson, Burke 1913- 4
Wilkinson, Sylvia (J.) 1940-
  Brief Entry 39
Wilkoń, Józef 1930- 31
Wilks, Michael Thomas 1947- 44
Wilks, Mike
  See Wilks, Michael Thomas
Will
  See Lipkind, William
Willard, Barbara (Mary)
  1909- 17
  See also CLR 2
  See also SAAS 5
Willard, Mildred Wilds 1911- 14
Willard, Nancy 1936- 37
  Brief Entry 30
  See also CLR 5
Willcox, Isobel 1907- 42
Willey, Robert
  See Ley, Willy
Williams, Barbara 1925- 11
Williams, Beryl
  See Epstein, Beryl
Williams, Charles
  See Collier, James Lincoln
Williams, Clyde C.
  1881-1974 8
  Obituary 27
Williams, Coe
  See Harrison, C. William

Williams, Eric (Ernest)
  1911-1983 14
  Obituary 38
Williams, Ferelith Eccles
  1920- 22
Williams, Frances B.
  See Browin, Frances Williams
Williams, Garth (Montgomery)
  1912- 18
Williams, Guy R. 1920- 11
Williams, Hawley
  See Heyliger, William
Williams, J. R.
  See Williams, Jeanne
Williams, J. Walker
  See Wodehouse, P(elham)
  G(renville)
Williams, Jay 1914-1978 41
  Obituary 24
  Earlier sketch in SATA 3
  See also CLR 8
Williams, Jeanne 1930- 5
Williams, Kit 1946(?)- 44
  See also CLR 4
Williams, Leslie 1941- 42
Williams, Louise Bonino 1904(?)-1984
  Obituary 39
Williams, Lynn
  See Hale, Arlene
Williams, Maureen 1951- 12
Williams, Michael
  See St. John, Wylly Folk
Williams, Patrick J.
  See Butterworth, W. E.
Williams, Selma R(uth) 1925- 14
Williams, Slim
  See Williams, Clyde C.
Williams, Ursula Moray
  1911- 3
Williams, Vera B. 1927-
  Brief Entry 33
  See also CLR 9
Williams-Ellis, (Mary) Amabel
  (Nassau) 1894-1984 29
  Obituary 41
Williamson, Henry 1895-1977 37
  Obituary 30
Williamson, Joanne Small
  1926- 3
Willson, Robina Beckles (Ballard)
  1930- 27
Wilma, Dana
  See Faralla, Dana
Wilson, Beth P(ierre) 8
Wilson, Budge,
  See Wilson, Marjorie
Wilson, Carter 1941- 6
Wilson, Charles Morrow
  1905-1977 30
Wilson, Christopher B. 1910(?)-1985
  Obituary 46
Wilson, Dagmar 1916-
  Brief Entry 31
Wilson, Dorothy Clarke 1904- 16
Wilson, Edward A(rthur)
  1886-1970 38
Wilson, Ellen (Janet Cameron)
  (?)-1976 9
  Obituary 26

Wilson, Eric H. 1940- 34
  Brief Entry 32
Wilson, Erica 51
Wilson, Forrest 1918- 27
Wilson, Gahan 1930- 35
  Brief Entry 27
Wilson, Gina 1943- 36
  Brief Entry 34
Wilson, (Leslie) Granville
  1912- 14
Wilson, Hazel 1898- 3
Wilson, John 1922- 22
Wilson, Joyce M(uriel Judson) 21
Wilson, Lionel 1924- 33
  Brief Entry 31
Wilson, Marjorie 1927-
  Brief Entry 51
Wilson, Maurice (Charles John)
  1914- 46
Wilson, Ron(ald William) 38
Wilson, Sarah 1934- 50
Wilson, Tom 1931- 33
  Brief Entry 30
Wilson, Walt(er N.) 1939- 14
Wilton, Elizabeth 1937- 14
Wilwerding, Walter Joseph
  1891-1966 9
Winchester, James H(ugh)
  1917-1985 30
  Obituary 45
Winders, Gertrude Hecker 3
Windham, Basil
  See Wodehouse, P(elham)
  G(renville)
Windham, Kathryn T(ucker)
  1918- 14
Windsor, Claire
  See Hamerstrom, Frances
Windsor, Patricia 1938- 30
Winfield, Arthur M.
  See Stratemeyer, Edward L.
Winfield, Edna
  See Stratemeyer, Edward L.
Winn, Chris 1952- 42
Winn, Janet Bruce 1928- 43
Winn, Marie 1936- 38
Winnick, Karen B(eth) B(inkoff)
  1946- 51
Winston, Clara 1921-1983
  Obituary 39
Winter, Milo (Kendall)
  1888-1956 21
Winter, Paula Cecelia 1929- 48
Winter, R. R.
  See Winterbotham, R(ussell)
  R(obert)
Winterbotham, R(ussell) R(obert)
  1904-1971 10
Winters, Jon
  See Cross, Gilbert B.
Winterton, Gayle
  See Adams, William Taylor
Winthrop, Elizabeth
  See Mahony, Elizabeth Winthrop
Wirtenberg, Patricia Z. 1932- 10
Wise, William 1923- 4
Wise, Winifred E. 2
Wiseman, Ann (Sayre) 1926- 31
Wiseman, B(ernard) 1922- 4

Wiseman, David 1916- *43*
  Brief Entry *40*
Wisler, G(ary) Clifton 1950-
  Brief Entry *46*
Wisner, Bill
  See Wisner, William L.
Wisner, William L.
  1914(?)-1983 .... *42*
Witham, (Phillip) Ross 1917- *37*
Withers, Carl A. 1900-1970 .... *14*
Witt, Shirley Hill 1934- *17*
Wittels, Harriet Joan 1938- *31*
Wittman, Sally (Anne Christensen)
  1941- *30*
Witty, Paul A(ndrew)
  1898-1976 .... *50*
  Obituary *30*
Wizard, Mr.
  See Herbert, Don
Wodehouse, P(elham) G(renville)
  1881-1975 .... *22*
Wodge, Dreary
  See Gorey, Edward St. John
Wohlberg, Meg 1905- *41*
Wohlrabe, Raymond A. 1900- *4*
Wojciechowska, Maia 1927- *28*
  Earlier sketch in SATA 1
  See also CLR 1
  See also SAAS 1
Wolcott, Patty 1929- *14*
Wold, Jo Anne 1938- *30*
Woldin, Beth Weiner 1955- *34*
Wolf, Bernard 1930-
  Brief Entry *37*
Wolfe, Burton H. 1932- *5*
Wolfe, Louis 1905- *8*
Wolfe, Rinna (Evelyn) 1925- *38*
Wolfenden, George
  See Beardmore, George
Wolff, (Jenifer) Ashley 1956- *50*
Wolff, Diane 1945- *27*
Wolff, Robert Jay 1905- *10*
Wolitzer, Hilma 1930- *31*
Wolkoff, Judie (Edwards)
  Brief Entry *37*
Wolkstein, Diane 1942- *7*
Wolters, Richard A. 1920- *35*
Wondriska, William 1931- *6*
Wood, Audrey *50*
  Brief Entry *44*
Wood, Catherine
  See Etchison, Birdie L(ee)
Wood, Don 1945- *50*
  Brief Entry *44*
Wood, Edgar A(llardyce)
  1907- *14*
Wood, Esther
  See Brady, Esther Wood
Wood, Frances Elizabeth *34*
Wood, James Playsted 1905- *1*
Wood, Kerry
  See Wood, Edgar A(llardyce)
Wood, Laura N.
  See Roper, Laura Wood
Wood, Nancy 1936- *6*
Wood, Phyllis Anderson
  1923- *33*
  Brief Entry *30*

Wood, Wallace 1927-1981
  Obituary *33*
Woodard, Carol 1929- *14*
Woodburn, John Henry 1914- *11*
Woodford, Peggy 1937- *25*
Woodrich, Mary Neville
  1915- *2*
Woods, George A(llan) 1926- ... *30*
Woods, Geraldine 1948-
  Brief Entry *42*
Woods, Harold 1945-
  Brief Entry *42*
Woods, Margaret 1921- *2*
Woods, Nat
  See Stratemeyer, Edward L.
Woodson, Jack
  See Woodson, John Waddie, Jr.
Woodson, John Waddie, Jr. *10*
Woodward, Cleveland
  1900-1986 .... *10*
  Obituary *48*
Woody, Regina Jones 1894- *3*
Wooldridge, Rhoda 1906- *22*
Woolley, Catherine 1904- *3*
Woolsey, Janette 1904- *3*
Worcester, Donald Emmet
  1915- *18*
Work, Virginia 1946-
  Brief Entry *45*
Worline, Bonnie Bess 1914- *14*
Wormser, Sophie 1896- *22*
Worth, Richard
  Brief Entry *46*
Worth, Valerie 1933- *8*
Wortis, Avi 1937- *14*
Wosmek, Frances 1917- *29*
Wriggins, Sally Hovey 1922 ...... *17*
Wright, Anna (Maria Louisa Perrot)
  Rose 1890-1968
  Brief Entry *35*
Wright, Betty Ren
  Brief Entry *48*
Wright, Dare 1926(?)- *21*
Wright, Enid Meadowcroft
  1898-1966 .... *3*
Wright, Esmond 1915- *10*
Wright, Frances Fitzpatrick
  1897- *10*
Wright, Judith 1915- *14*
Wright, Katrina
  See Gater, Dilys
Wright, Kenneth
  See Del Rey, Lester
Wright, Nancy Means *38*
Wright, R(obert) H. 1906- *6*
Wrightson, Patricia 1921- *8*
  See also CLR 4
  See also SAAS 4
Wronker, Lili Cassel 1924- *10*
Wulffson, Don L. 1943- *32*
Wuorio, Eva-Lis 1918- *34*
  Brief Entry *28*
Wyeth, Betsy James 1921- *41*
Wyeth, N(ewell) C(onvers)
  1882-1945 .... *17*
Wyler, Rose 1909- *18*
Wylie, Betty Jane *48*
Wylie, Laura
  See Matthews, Patricia

Wymer, Norman George
  1911- *25*
Wynants, Miche 1934-
  Brief Entry *31*
Wyndham, Lee
  See Hyndman, Jane Andrews
Wyndham, Robert
  See Hyndman, Robert Utley
Wynter, Edward (John) 1914- *14*
Wynyard, Talbot
  See Hamilton, Charles H. St. John
Wyss, Johann David Von
  1743-1818 .... *29*
  Brief Entry *27*
Wyss, Thelma Hatch 1934- *10*

Y

Yaffe, Alan
  See Yorinks, Arthur
Yamaguchi, Marianne 1936- *7*
Yang, Jay 1941- *12*
Yarbrough, Ira 1910(?)-1983
  Obituary *35*
Yaroslava
  See Mills, Yaroslava Surmach
Yashima, Taro
  See Iwamatsu, Jun Atsushi
  See also CLR 4
Yates, Elizabeth 1905- *4*
Yates, Raymond F(rancis)
  1895-1966 .... *31*
Yaukey, Grace S(ydenstricker)
  1899- *5*
Yeakley, Marjory Hall 1908- *21*
Yeatman, Linda 1938- *42*
Yensid, Retlaw
  See Disney, Walt(er Elias)
Yeo, Wilma (Lethem) 1918- *24*
Yeoman, John (Brian) 1934- *28*
Yep, Laurence M. 1948- *7*
  See also CLR 3
Yerian, Cameron John *21*
Yerian, Margaret A. *21*
Yolen, Jane H. 1939- *40*
  Earlier sketch in SATA 4
  See also CLR 4
  See also SAAS 1
Yonge, Charlotte Mary
  1823-1901 .... *17*
Yorinks, Arthur 1953- *49*
  Earlier sketch in SATA 33
York, Andrew
  See Nicole, Christopher Robin
York, Carol Beach 1928- *6*
York, Rebecca [Joint pseudonym]
  See Buckholtz, Eileen (Garber)
Yost, Edna 1889-1971
  Obituary *26*
Youd, (Christopher) Samuel
  1922- *47*
  Brief Entry *30*
Young, Bob
  See Young, Robert W.
Young, Clarence [Collective
  pseudonym] *1*

Young, Dorothea Bennett
  1924- *31*
Young, Ed 1931- *10*
Young, Edward
  See Reinfeld, Fred
Young, Elaine L.
  See Schulte, Elaine L(ouise)
Young, Jan
  See Young, Janet Randall
Young, Janet Randall 1919- *3*
Young, Lois Horton
  1911-1981 .... *26*
Young, Margaret B(uckner)
  1922- *2*
Young, Miriam 1913-1934 .... *7*
Young, (Rodney Lee) Patrick (Jr.)
  1937- *22*
Young, Percy M(arshall)
  1912- *31*
Young, Robert W. 1916-1969 ..... *3*
Young, Scott A(lexander)
  1918- *5*
Young, Vivien
  See Gater, Dilys
Youngs, Betty 1934-1985
  Obituary *42*

Z

Zach, Cheryl (Byrd) 1947-
  Brief Entry *51*

Zaffo, George J. (?)-1984 .... *42*
Zaid, Barry 1938- *51*
Zaidenberg, Arthur 1908(?)- *34*
Zalben, Jane Breskin 1950- *7*
Zallinger, Jean (Day) 1918- *14*
Zallinger, Peter Franz 1943- *49*
Zappler, Lisbeth 1930- *10*
Zarchy, Harry 1912- *34*
Zarif, Margaret Min'imah
  (?)-1983 .... *33*
Zaring, Jane (Thomas) 1936- *51*
  Brief Entry *40*
Zaslavsky, Claudia 1917- *36*
Zeck, Gerald Anthony 1939- *40*
Zeck, Gerry
  See Zeck, Gerald Anthony
Zei, Alki *24*
  See also CLR 6
Zelazny, Roger (Joseph Christopher)
  1937-
  Brief Entry *39*
Zelinsky, Paul O. 1953- *49*
  Brief Entry *33*
Zellan, Audrey Penn 1950- *22*
Zemach, Harve 1933- *3*
Zemach, Kaethe 1958- *49*
  Brief Entry *39*
Zemach, Margot 1931- *21*
Zens, Patricia Martin 1926-1972
  Brief Entry *50*
Zerman, Melvyn Bernard
  1930- *46*
Ziemienski, Dennis 1947- *10*
Zillah
  See Macdonald, Zillah K.

Zim, Herbert S(pencer) 1909- *30*
  Earlier sketch in SATA 1
  See also CLR 2
  See also SAAS 2
Zim, Sonia Bleeker
  See Bleeker, Sonia
Zimelman, Nathan
  Brief Entry *37*
Zimmerman, Naoma 1914- *10*
Zimnik, Reiner 1930- *36*
  See also CLR 3
Zindel, Bonnie 1943- *34*
Zindel, Paul 1936- *16*
  See also CLR 3
Ziner, (Florence) Feenie
  1921- *5*
Zion, (Eu)Gene 1913-1975 .... *18*
Zollinger, Gulielma 1856-1917
  Brief Entry *27*
Zolotow, Charlotte S. 1915- *35*
  Earlier sketch in SATA 1
  See also CLR 2
Zonia, Dhimitri 1921- *20*
Zubrowski, Bernard 1939- *35*
Zupa, G. Anthony
  See Zeck, Gerald Anthony
Zurhorst, Charles (Stewart, Jr.)
  1913- *12*
Zuromskis, Diane
  See Stanley, Diane
Zweifel, Frances 1931- *14*
Zwinger, Ann 1925- *46*